Saab 9-3
Owners Workshop Manual

A K Legg AAE MIMI

(4614 - 336)

Models covered

Coupe, Hatchback & Convertible, including special/limited editions

Petrol: 2.0 litre (1985cc) & 2.3 litre (2290cc), inc. turbo
Turbo-Diesel: 2.2 litre (2171cc)

Also covers Convertible models to August 2003
Does NOT cover new Saab 9-3 range introduced September 2002 (Convertible September 2003)

© Haynes Group Limited 2007

ABCDE
FGH

A book in the **Haynes Owners Workshop Manual Series**

ISBN **978 1 78521 277 2**

British Library Cataloguing in Publication Data
A catalogue record for this book is available from the British Library.

Printed in India

Haynes Group Limited
Sparkford, Yeovil, Somerset BA22 7JJ, England

Haynes North America, Inc
2801 Townsgate Road, Suite 340, Thousand Oaks, CA 91361

Disclaimer

There are risks associated with automotive repairs. The ability to make repairs depends on the individual's skill, experience and proper tools. Individuals should act with due care and acknowledge and assume the risk of performing automotive repairs.

The purpose of this manual is to provide comprehensive, useful and accessible automotive repair information, to help you get the best value from your vehicle. However, this manual is not a substitute for a professional certified technician or mechanic.

This repair manual is produced by a third party and is not associated with an individual vehicle manufacturer. If there is any doubt or discrepancy between this manual and the owner's manual or the factory service manual, please refer to the factory service manual or seek assistance from a professional certified technician or mechanic.

Even though we have prepared this manual with extreme care and every attempt is made to ensure that the information in this manual is correct, neither the publisher nor the author can accept responsibility for loss, damage or injury caused by any errors in, or omissions from, the information given.

Contents

LIVING WITH YOUR SAAB 9-3

Roadside Repairs

Weekly Checks

Lubricants and fluids

Tyre pressures

MAINTENANCE

Routine maintenance and servicing

Contents

REPAIRS & OVERHAUL

Advanced driving

Many people see the words 'advanced driving' and believe that it won't interest them or that it is a style of driving beyond their own abilities. Nothing could be further from the truth. Advanced driving is straightforward safe, sensible driving - the sort of driving we should all do every time we get behind the wheel.

An average of 10 people are killed every day on UK roads and 870 more are injured, some seriously. Lives are ruined daily, usually because somebody did something stupid. Something like 95% of all accidents are due to human error, mostly driver failure. Sometimes we make genuine mistakes - everyone does. Sometimes we have lapses of concentration. Sometimes we deliberately take risks.

For many people, the process of 'learning to drive' doesn't go much further than learning how to pass the driving test because of a common belief that good drivers are made by 'experience'.

Learning to drive by 'experience' teaches three driving skills:

- ☐ Quick reactions. (Whoops, that was close!)
- ☐ Good handling skills. (Horn, swerve, brake, horn).
- ☐ Reliance on vehicle technology. (Great stuff this ABS, stop in no distance even in the wet...)

Drivers whose skills are 'experience based' generally have a lot of near misses and the odd accident. The results can be seen every day in our courts and our hospital casualty departments.

Advanced drivers have learnt to control the risks by controlling the position and speed of their vehicle. They avoid accidents and near misses, even if the drivers around them make mistakes.

The key skills of advanced driving are **concentration,** effective all-round **observation, anticipation** and **planning.** When **good vehicle handling** is added to these skills, all driving situations can be approached and negotiated in a safe, methodical way, leaving nothing to chance.

Concentration means applying your mind to safe driving, completely excluding anything that's not relevant. Driving is usually the most dangerous activity that most of us undertake in our daily routines. It deserves our full attention.

Observation means not just looking, but seeing and seeking out the information found in the driving environment.

Anticipation means asking yourself what is happening, what you can reasonably expect to happen and what could happen unexpectedly. (One of the commonest words used in compiling accident reports is 'suddenly'.)

Planning is the link between seeing something and taking the appropriate action. For many drivers, planning is the missing link.

If you want to become a safer and more skilful driver and you want to enjoy your driving more, contact the Institute of Advanced Motorists at www.iam.org.uk, phone 0208 996 9600, or write to IAM House, 510 Chiswick High Road, London W4 5RG for an information pack.

Working on your car can be dangerous. This page shows just some of the potential risks and hazards, with the aim of creating a safety-conscious attitude.

General hazards

Scalding

• Don't remove the radiator or expansion tank cap while the engine is hot.
• Engine oil, automatic transmission fluid or power steering fluid may also be dangerously hot if the engine has recently been running.

Burning

• Beware of burns from the exhaust system and from any part of the engine. Brake discs and drums can also be extremely hot immediately after use.

Crushing

• When working under or near a raised vehicle, always supplement the jack with axle stands, or use drive-on ramps. *Never venture under a car which is only supported by a jack.*
• Take care if loosening or tightening high-torque nuts when the vehicle is on stands. Initial loosening and final tightening should be done with the wheels on the ground.

Fire

• Fuel is highly flammable; fuel vapour is explosive.
• Don't let fuel spill onto a hot engine.
• Do not smoke or allow naked lights (including pilot lights) anywhere near a vehicle being worked on. Also beware of creating sparks (electrically or by use of tools).
• Fuel vapour is heavier than air, so don't work on the fuel system with the vehicle over an inspection pit.
• Another cause of fire is an electrical overload or short-circuit. Take care when repairing or modifying the vehicle wiring.
• Keep a fire extinguisher handy, of a type suitable for use on fuel and electrical fires.

Electric shock

• Ignition HT voltage can be dangerous, especially to people with heart problems or a pacemaker. Don't work on or near the ignition system with the engine running or the ignition switched on.

• Mains voltage is also dangerous. Make sure that any mains-operated equipment is correctly earthed. Mains power points should be protected by a residual current device (RCD) circuit breaker.

Fume or gas intoxication

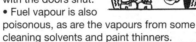

• Exhaust fumes are poisonous; they often contain carbon monoxide, which is rapidly fatal if inhaled. Never run the engine in a confined space such as a garage with the doors shut.
• Fuel vapour is also poisonous, as are the vapours from some cleaning solvents and paint thinners.

Poisonous or irritant substances

• Avoid skin contact with battery acid and with any fuel, fluid or lubricant, especially antifreeze, brake hydraulic fluid and Diesel fuel. Don't syphon them by mouth. If such a substance is swallowed or gets into the eyes, seek medical advice.
• Prolonged contact with used engine oil can cause skin cancer. Wear gloves or use a barrier cream if necessary. Change out of oil-soaked clothes and do not keep oily rags in your pocket.
• Air conditioning refrigerant forms a poisonous gas if exposed to a naked flame (including a cigarette). It can also cause skin burns on contact.

Asbestos

• Asbestos dust can cause cancer if inhaled or swallowed. Asbestos may be found in gaskets and in brake and clutch linings. When dealing with such components it is safest to assume that they contain asbestos.

Special hazards

Hydrofluoric acid

• This extremely corrosive acid is formed when certain types of synthetic rubber, found in some O-rings, oil seals, fuel hoses etc, are exposed to temperatures above 400°C. The rubber changes into a charred or sticky substance containing the acid. *Once formed, the acid remains dangerous for years. If it gets onto the skin, it may be necessary to amputate the limb concerned.*
• When dealing with a vehicle which has suffered a fire, or with components salvaged from such a vehicle, wear protective gloves and discard them after use.

The battery

• Batteries contain sulphuric acid, which attacks clothing, eyes and skin. Take care when topping-up or carrying the battery.
• The hydrogen gas given off by the battery is highly explosive. Never cause a spark or allow a naked light nearby. Be careful when connecting and disconnecting battery chargers or jump leads.

Air bags

• Air bags can cause injury if they go off accidentally. Take care when removing the steering wheel and/or facia. Special storage instructions may apply.

Diesel injection equipment

• Diesel injection pumps supply fuel at very high pressure. Take care when working on the fuel injectors and fuel pipes.

⚠ *Warning: Never expose the hands, face or any other part of the body to injector spray; the fuel can penetrate the skin with potentially fatal results.*

Remember...

DO

• Do use eye protection when using power tools, and when working under the vehicle.

• Do wear gloves or use barrier cream to protect your hands when necessary.

• Do get someone to check periodically that all is well when working alone on the vehicle.

• Do keep loose clothing and long hair well out of the way of moving mechanical parts.

• Do remove rings, wristwatch etc, before working on the vehicle – especially the electrical system.

• Do ensure that any lifting or jacking equipment has a safe working load rating adequate for the job.

DON'T

• Don't attempt to lift a heavy component which may be beyond your capability – get assistance.

• Don't rush to finish a job, or take unverified short cuts.

• Don't use ill-fitting tools which may slip and cause injury.

• Don't leave tools or parts lying around where someone can trip over them. Mop up oil and fuel spills at once.

• Don't allow children or pets to play in or near a vehicle being worked on.

Saab 9-3 Convertible

The Saab 9-3 was introduced in the UK in March 1998, as a replacement for the 900. It is based on the Vauxhall Vectra chassis, and is available as a 2-door Convertible, 3-door Coupe, or 5-door Hatchback. Petrol engines available are 2.0 litre and 2.3 litre, both turbo and non-turbo, and the diesel engine is a 2.2 litre turbo. The petrol engine has two chain-driven overhead camshafts (DOHC) with 16 valves acting on hydraulic tappets, and a balancer shaft. The diesel engine has a chain-driven, single overhead camshaft (SOHC) with 16 valves acting on hydraulic tappets.

Standard equipment includes power-assisted steering, anti-lock brakes, remote deadlock central locking, twin front and side airbags, electric windows and mirrors, and air conditioning. Optional extras include electric sunroof, electric front seats, leather upholstery and CD autochanger.

Models may be fitted with a five-speed manual transmission or four-speed automatic transmission mounted on the left-hand side of the engine.

All models have front-wheel-drive with fully-independent front and rear suspension, incorporating struts, gas-filled shock absorbers, and coil springs.

For the home mechanic, the Saab 9-3 is a relatively straightforward vehicle to maintain and repair, since design features have been incorporated to reduce the actual cost of ownership to a minimum, and most of the items requiring frequent attention are easily accessible.

Your Saab 9-3 manual

The aim of this manual is to help you get the best value from your vehicle. It can do so in several ways. It can help you decide what work must be done (even should you choose to get it done by a garage), provide information on routine maintenance and servicing, and give a logical course of action and diagnosis when random faults occur. However, it is hoped that you will use the manual by tackling the work yourself. On simpler jobs, it may even be quicker than booking the car into a garage and going there twice, to leave and collect it. Perhaps most important, a lot of money can be saved by avoiding the costs a garage must charge to cover its labour and overheads.

The manual has drawings and descriptions to show the function of the various components, so that their layout can be understood. Then the tasks are described and photographed in a clear step-by-step sequence.

References to the 'left' or 'right' are in the sense of a person in the driver's seat, facing forward.

Acknowledgements

Thanks are also due to Draper Tools Limited, who provided some of the workshop tools, and to all those people at Sparkford who helped in the production of this manual.

We take great pride in the accuracy of information given in this manual, but vehicle manufacturers make alterations and design changes during the production run of a particular vehicle of which they do not inform us. No liability can be accepted by the authors or publishers for loss, damage or injury caused by any errors in, or omissions from, the information given.

Project vehicle

The main vehicle used in the preparation of this manual, and which appears in many of the photographic sequences, was a 2001 Saab SE Convertible fitted with the 2.0 litre turbocharged petrol engine and automatic transmission.

Saab 9-3 Hatchback

The following pages are intended to help in dealing with common roadside emergencies and breakdowns. You will find more detailed fault finding information at the back of the manual, and repair information in the main chapters.

If your car won't start and the starter motor doesn't turn

☐ Open the bonnet and make sure that the battery terminals are clean and tight.
☐ Switch on the headlights and try to start the engine. If the headlights go very dim when you're trying to start, the battery is probably flat. Get out of trouble by jump starting (see next page) using a friend's car.

If your car won't start even though the starter motor turns as normal

☐ Is there fuel in the tank?
☐ Is there any moisture on electrical components under the bonnet? Switch off the ignition, then wipe off any obvious dampness with a dry cloth. Spray a water-repellent aerosol product (WD-40 or equivalent) on ignition and fuel system electrical connectors.

A Check that the battery cables are securely connected.

B Check that the ignition discharge module wiring is securely connected.

C Check that the mass airflow meter wiring is securely connected.

Check that electrical connections are secure (with the ignition switched off) and spray them with a water-dispersant spray like WD-40 if you suspect a problem due to damp

D Check the engine wiring loom multiplugs for security.

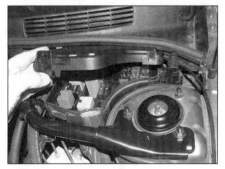

E Check that none of the engine compartment fuses have blown.

Jump starting

When jump-starting a car using a booster battery, observe the following precautions:

✔ Before connecting the booster battery, make sure that the ignition is switched off.

✔ Ensure that all electrical equipment (lights, heater, wipers, etc) is switched off.

✔ Take note of any special precautions printed on the battery case.

✔ Make sure that the booster battery is the same voltage as the discharged one in the vehicle.

✔ If the battery is being jump-started from the battery in another vehicle, the two vehicles MUST NOT TOUCH each other.

✔ Make sure that the transmission is in neutral (or PARK, in the case of automatic transmission).

HAYNES HiNT

Jump starting will get you out of trouble, but you must correct whatever made the battery go flat in the first place. There are three possibilities:

1 *The battery has been drained by repeated attempts to start, or by leaving the lights on.*

2 *The charging system is not working properly (alternator drivebelt slack or broken, alternator wiring fault or alternator itself faulty).*

3 *The battery itself is at fault (electrolyte low, or battery worn out).*

1 Connect one end of the red jump lead to the positive (+) terminal of the flat battery

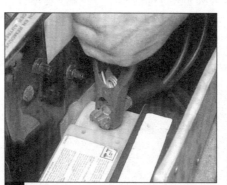

2 Connect the other end of the red lead to the positive (+) terminal of the booster battery.

3 Connect one end of the black jump lead to the negative (-) terminal of the booster battery

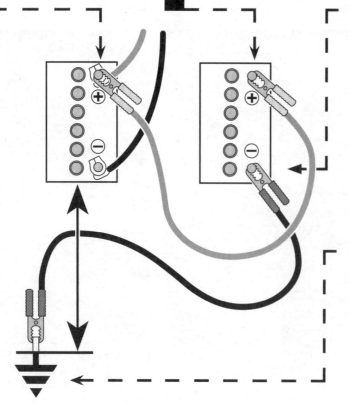

4 Connect the other end of the black jump lead to a suitable metal part of the engine on the car to be started

5 Make sure that the jump leads will not come into contact with the fan, drive-belts or other moving parts of the engine.

6 Start the engine using the booster battery and run it at idle speed. Switch on the lights, rear window demister and heater blower motor, then disconnect the jump leads in the reverse order of connection. Turn off the lights etc.

Wheel changing

⚠ **Warning: Do not change a wheel in a situation where you risk being hit by another vehicle. On busy roads, try to stop in a lay-by or a gateway. Be wary of passing traffic while changing the wheel – it is easy to become distracted by the job in hand.**

Preparation

- ☐ When a puncture occurs, stop as soon as it is safe to do so.
- ☐ Park on firm level ground, if possible, and well out of the way of other traffic.
- ☐ Use hazard warning lights if necessary.
- ☐ If you have one, use a warning triangle to alert other drivers of your presence.
- ☐ Apply the handbrake and engage first or reverse gear (or Park on models with automatic transmission).
- ☐ Chock the wheel diagonally opposite the one being removed – a couple of large stones will do for this.
- ☐ If the ground is soft, use a flat piece of wood to spread the load under the jack.

Changing the wheel

1 The spare wheel, jack and wheel removal tools are stored beneath a cover in the luggage compartment.

2 Unscrew the retaining nut and lift out the spare wheel. Place it beneath the sill as a precaution against the jack failing. Note that the spare wheel is of the 'space saver' type.

3 Where fitted, pull the wheel trim from the wheel. On models with alloy wheels, use the plastic tool provided to prise the cap from the locking wheel bolt, then fit the special adapter.

4 Before you raise the car, loosen each wheel bolt by half a turn only.

5 Locate the jack head below the reinforced jacking points (indicated by the cut-outs in the sill), nearest the wheel to be changed. Turn the handle until the base of the jack touches the ground then make sure that the base is located directly below the sill. Raise the vehicle until the wheel is clear of the ground.

6 If the tyre is flat make sure that the vehicle is raised sufficiently to allow the spare wheel to be fitted. Remove the bolts and lift the wheel from the vehicle. Place it beneath the sill in place of the spare as a precaution against the jack failing.

7 Fit the spare wheel, then insert each of the wheel bolts and tighten them moderately using the wheel brace.

8 Lower the vehicle to the ground, then finally tighten the wheel bolts in a diagonal sequence. Note that the wheel bolts should be tightened to the specified torque at the earliest opportunity.

Finally . . .

- ☐ Remove the wheel chocks.
- ☐ Stow the jack and tools in the correct locations in the car.
- ☐ Check the tyre pressure on the wheel just fitted. If it is low, or if you don't have a pressure gauge with you, drive slowly to the nearest garage and inflate the tyre to the right pressure.
- ☐ Have the damaged tyre or wheel repaired as soon as possible.

⚠ *Warning: You should not exceed 50 mph when driving the vehicle with a space saver spare wheel fitted – consult your vehicle handbook for further information.*

Identifying leaks

Puddles on the garage floor or drive, or obvious wetness under the bonnet or underneath the car, suggest a leak that needs investigating. It can sometimes be difficult to decide where the leak is coming from, especially if the engine bay is very dirty already. Leaking oil or fluid can also be blown rearwards by the passage of air under the car, giving a false impression of where the problem lies.

 Warning: Most automotive oils and fluids are poisonous. Wash them off skin, and change out of contaminated clothing, without delay.

 The smell of a fluid leaking from the car may provide a clue to what's leaking. Some fluids are distinctively coloured. It may help to clean the car carefully and to park it over some clean paper overnight as an aid to locating the source of the leak. Remember that some leaks may only occur while the engine is running.

Sump oil

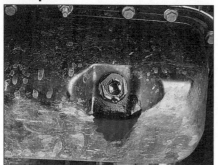

Engine oil may leak from the drain plug...

Oil from filter

...or from the base of the oil filter.

Gearbox oil

Gearbox oil can leak from the seals at the inboard ends of the driveshafts.

Antifreeze

Leaking antifreeze often leaves a crystalline deposit like this.

Brake fluid

A leak occurring at a wheel is almost certainly brake fluid.

Power steering fluid

Power steering fluid may leak from the pipe connectors on the steering rack.

Towing

When all else fails, you may find yourself having to get a tow home – or of course you may be helping somebody else. Long-distance recovery should only be done by a garage or breakdown service. For shorter distances, DIY towing using another car is easy enough, but observe the following points:

• The front towing eye is behind the vent grille on the right-hand side of the front bumper. Squeeze together the horizontal bars to remove the grille (see illustration).

• The rear towing eye is provided beneath the rear of the vehicle (see illustration).

• Use a proper tow-rope – they are not expensive. The vehicle being towed must display an ON TOW sign in its rear window.

• Always turn the ignition key to the 'on' position when the vehicle is being towed, so that the steering lock is released, and that the direction indicator and brake lights will work.

• Only attach the tow-rope to the towing eyes provided. The front towing eye is in the vehicle tool kit, and screws into the hole in the subframe; use the wheel brace to fully tighten the eye. The rear towing eye is located beneath the centre of the rear bumper and is permanently fitted.

• Before being towed, release the handbrake and select neutral on the transmission. On models with automatic transmission, special precautions apply, as follows (if in doubt, do not tow, or transmission damage may result):

  a) The car may only be towed in the forward direction.

  b) The gear selector lever must be in the N position.

  c) The vehicle must not be towed at a speed exceeding 30 mph, nor for a distance of more than 30 miles.

• Note that greater-than-usual pedal pressure will be required to operate the brakes, since the vacuum servo unit is only operational with the engine running.

• Since the power steering will not be functional, greater-than-usual steering effort will also be required.

• The driver of the car being towed must keep the tow-rope taut at all times to avoid snatching.

• Make sure that both drivers know the route before setting off.

• Only drive at moderate speeds and keep the distance towed to a minimum. Drive smoothly and allow plenty of time for slowing down at junctions.

• The driver of the towing vehicle must accelerate very gently from a standstill and must bear in mind the extra length of the vehicle being towed when pulling out at junctions, roundabouts, etc.

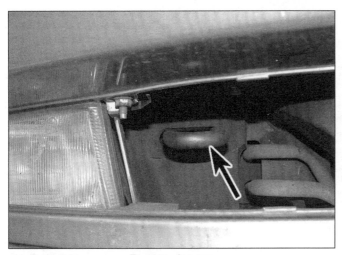

Front towing eye

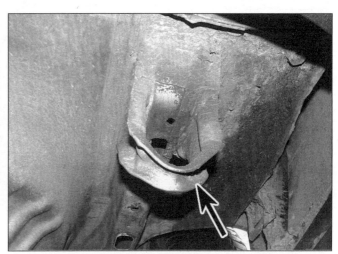

Rear towing eye

Introduction

There are some very simple checks which need only take a few minutes to carry out, but which could save you much inconvenience and expense.

These *Weekly Checks* require no great skill or special tools, and the small amount of time they take to perform could well prove to be very well spent, for example:

☐ Keeping an eye on tyre condition and pressures, will not only help to stop them wearing out prematurely, but could also save your life.

☐ Many breakdowns are caused by electrical problems. Battery-related faults are particularly common, and a quick check on a regular basis will often prevent the majority of these.

☐ If your car develops a brake fluid leak, the first time you might know about it is when your brakes don't work properly. Checking the level regularly will give advance warning of this kind of problem.

☐ If the oil or coolant levels run low, the cost of repairing any engine damage will be far greater than fixing the leak.

Underbonnet check points

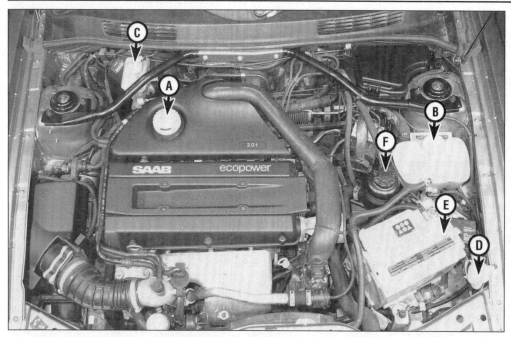

◀ Petrol engines

A Engine oil level filler cap and dipstick

B Coolant reservoir (expansion tank)

C Brake fluid reservoir

D Washer fluid reservoir

E Battery

F Power steering fluid reservoir

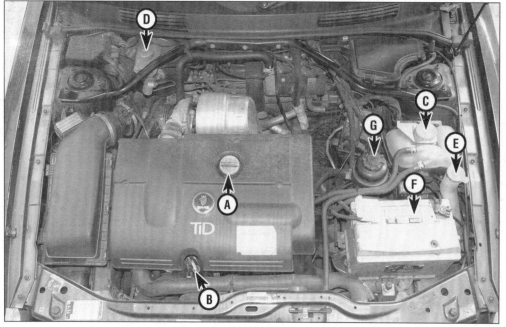

◀ Diesel engines

A Engine oil level filler cap

B Dipstick

C Coolant reservoir (expansion tank)

D Brake fluid reservoir

E Washer fluid reservoir

F Battery

G Power steering fluid reservoir

Engine oil level

Before you start

✔ Make sure that your car is on level ground.
✔ Check the oil level with the engine at operating temperature, and between 2 and 5 minutes after the engine has been switched off.

 If the oil is checked immediately after driving the vehicle, some of the oil will remain in the upper engine components, resulting in an inaccurate reading on the dipstick.

The correct oil

Modern engines place great demands on their oil. It is very important that the correct oil for your car is used (see *Lubricants and fluids*).

Car care

● If you have to add oil frequently, you should check whether you have any oil leaks. Place some clean paper under the car overnight, and check for stains in the morning. If there are no leaks, the engine may be burning oil.
● Always maintain the level between the upper and lower dipstick marks (see photo 4). If the level is too low severe engine damage may occur. Oil seal failure may result if the engine is overfilled by adding too much oil.

1 On petrol models, the dipstick is integral with the oil filler cap, located on the right-hand rear of the engine (see *Underbonnet Check Points* on page 0•12 for exact location). Unscrew the cap and withdraw the integral dipstick.

2 On diesel models, the dipstick is located on the front of the engine, and the oil filler cap is on the top of the engine (see *Underbonnet Check Points* on page 0•12 for exact location). Withdraw the dipstick.

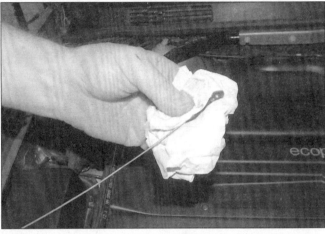

3 Using a clean rag or paper towel remove all oil from the dipstick. Insert the clean dipstick into the tube and, on petrol models, tighten the filler cap, then withdraw it again.

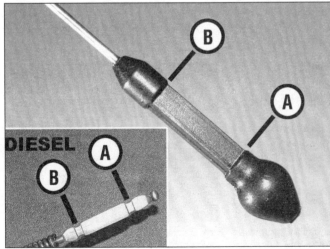

4 Note the oil level on the end of the dipstick, which should be between the upper mark (B) and lower mark (A). Approximately 1.0 litre of oil will raise the level from the lower mark to the upper mark.

5 Oil is added through the filler cap hole. Unscrew the cap and withdraw it. Top-up the level. A funnel may help to reduce spillage. Add the oil slowly, checking the level on the dipstick often. Do not overfill. Refit the cap on completion.

Coolant level

 Warning: DO NOT attempt to remove the expansion tank pressure cap when the engine is hot, as there is a very great risk of scalding. Do not leave open containers of coolant about, as it is poisonous.

Car Care

● With a sealed-type cooling system, adding coolant should not be necessary on a regular basis. If frequent topping-up is required, it is likely there is a leak. Check the radiator, all hoses and joint faces for signs of staining or wetness, and rectify as necessary.

● It is important that antifreeze is used in the cooling system all year round, not just during the winter months. Don't top-up with water alone, as the antifreeze will become too diluted.

1 The coolant level varies with the temperature of the engine. When the engine is cold, the coolant level should be on or slightly above the KALT/COLD mark on the side of the tank. When the engine is hot, the level will rise.

2 If topping-up is necessary, **wait until the engine is cold**. Slowly unscrew the expansion tank cap, to release any pressure present in the cooling system, and remove it.

3 Top-up the level by adding a mixture of water and antifreeze to the expansion tank. A funnel may help to reduce spillage. Refit the cap and tighten it securely.

Brake (and clutch) fluid level

Note: *On manual transmission models, the fluid reservoir also supplies the clutch master cylinder with fluid.*

Before you start

✔ Make sure that the car is on level ground.
✔ Cleanliness is of great importance when dealing with the braking system, so take care to clean around the reservoir cap before topping-up. Use only clean brake fluid.

Safety first!

● If the reservoir requires repeated topping-up, this is an indication of a fluid leak somewhere in the system, which should be investigated immediately. Note that the level will drop naturally as the brake pad linings wear, but must never be allowed to fall below the MIN mark.

● If a leak is suspected, the car should not be driven until the braking system has been checked. Never take any risks where brakes are concerned.

 Warning: Brake fluid can harm your eyes and damage painted surfaces, so use extreme caution when handling and pouring it. Do not use fluid which has been standing open for some time, as it absorbs moisture from the air, which can cause a dangerous loss of braking effectiveness.

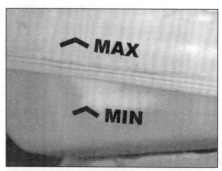

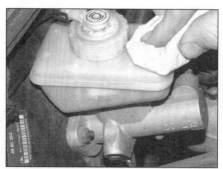

1 The MIN and MAX marks are indicated on the front of the reservoir located in the right-hand rear corner of the engine compartment. The fluid level must always be kept between the marks.

2 If topping-up is necessary, first wipe clean the area around the filler cap to prevent dirt entering the hydraulic system. Unscrew the cap and place it on an absorbent rag.

3 Carefully add fluid, taking care not to spill it onto the surrounding components. Use only the specified fluid; mixing different types can cause damage to the system. After topping-up to the correct level, securely refit the cap and wipe off any spilt fluid.

Tyre condition and pressure

It is very important that tyres are in good condition, and at the correct pressure - having a tyre failure at any speed is highly dangerous. Tyre wear is influenced by driving style - harsh braking and acceleration, or fast cornering, will all produce more rapid tyre wear. As a general rule, the front tyres wear out faster than the rears. Interchanging the tyres from front to rear ("rotating" the tyres) may result in more even wear. However, if this is completely effective, you may have the expense of replacing all four tyres at once! Remove any nails or stones embedded in the tread before they penetrate the tyre to cause deflation. If removal of a nail does reveal that the tyre has been punctured, refit the nail so that its point of penetration is marked. Then immediately change the wheel, and have the tyre repaired by a tyre dealer.

Regularly check the tyres for damage in the form of cuts or bulges, especially in the sidewalls. Periodically remove the wheels, and clean any dirt or mud from the inside and outside surfaces. Examine the wheel rims for signs of rusting, corrosion or other damage. Light alloy wheels are easily damaged by "kerbing" whilst parking; steel wheels may also become dented or buckled. A new wheel is very often the only way to overcome severe damage.

New tyres should be balanced when they are fitted, but it may become necessary to re-balance them as they wear, or if the balance weights fitted to the wheel rim should fall off. Unbalanced tyres will wear more quickly, as will the steering and suspension components. Wheel imbalance is normally signified by vibration, particularly at a certain speed (typically around 50 mph). If this vibration is felt only through the steering, then it is likely that just the front wheels need balancing. If, however, the vibration is felt through the whole car, the rear wheels could be out of balance. Wheel balancing should be carried out by a tyre dealer or garage.

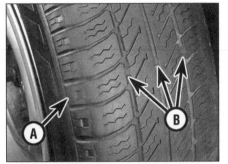

1 Tread Depth - visual check
The original tyres have tread wear safety bands (B), which will appear when the tread depth reaches approximately 1.6 mm. The band positions are indicated by a triangular mark on the tyre sidewall (A).

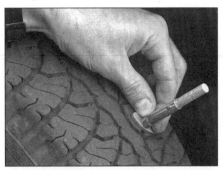

2 Tread Depth - manual check
Alternatively, tread wear can be monitored with a simple, inexpensive device known as a tread depth indicator gauge.

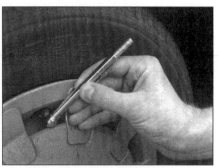

3 Tyre Pressure Check
Check the tyre pressures regularly with the tyres cold. Do not adjust the tyre pressures immediately after the vehicle has been used, or an inaccurate setting will result.

Tyre tread wear patterns

Shoulder Wear

Underinflation (wear on both sides)
Under-inflation will cause overheating of the tyre, because the tyre will flex too much, and the tread will not sit correctly on the road surface. This will cause a loss of grip and excessive wear, not to mention the danger of sudden tyre failure due to heat build-up.
Check and adjust pressures
Incorrect wheel camber (wear on one side)
Repair or renew suspension parts
Hard cornering
Reduce speed!

Centre Wear

Overinflation
Over-inflation will cause rapid wear of the centre part of the tyre tread, coupled with reduced grip, harsher ride, and the danger of shock damage occurring in the tyre casing.
Check and adjust pressures

If you sometimes have to inflate your car's tyres to the higher pressures specified for maximum load or sustained high speed, don't forget to reduce the pressures to normal afterwards.

Uneven Wear

Front tyres may wear unevenly as a result of wheel misalignment. Most tyre dealers and garages can check and adjust the wheel alignment (or "tracking") for a modest charge.
Incorrect camber or castor
Repair or renew suspension parts
Malfunctioning suspension
Repair or renew suspension parts
Unbalanced wheel
Balance tyres
Incorrect toe setting
Adjust front wheel alignment
Note: *The feathered edge of the tread which typifies toe wear is best checked by feel.*

Washer fluid level

● Screenwash additives not only keep the windscreen clean, they also prevent the washer system freezing in cold weather – which is when you are likely to need it most. Don't top-up using plain water as the screenwash will become too diluted, and will freeze during cold weather.
● Check the operation of the windscreen and rear window washers. Adjust the nozzles using a pin if necessary, aiming the spray to a point slightly above the centre of the swept area.

 Warning: On no account use coolant antifreeze in the washer system – this could discolour or damage paintwork.

1 The reservoir for the windscreen and rear window (where applicable) washer systems is located on the front left-hand corner of the engine compartment. If topping-up is necessary, open the cap.

2 When topping-up the reservoir a screenwash additive should be added in the quantities recommended on the bottle.

Electrical systems

✔ Check all external lights and the horn. Refer to the appropriate Sections of Chapter 12 for details if any of the circuits are found to be inoperative.

✔ Visually check all accessible wiring connectors, harnesses and retaining clips for security, and for signs of chafing or damage.

HAYNES HiNT *If you need to check your brake lights and indicators unaided, back up to a wall or garage door and operate the lights. The reflected light should show if they are working properly.*

1 If a single indicator light, stop-light or headlight has failed, it is likely that a bulb has blown and will need to be renewed. Refer to Chapter 12 for details. If both stop-lights have failed, it is possible that the switch has failed (see Chapter 9).

2 If more than one indicator light or headlight has failed, it is likely that either a fuse has blown or that there is a fault in the circuit (see Chapter 12). The main fuses are accessed by removing a cover on the driver's end of the facia. Additional fuses and relays are located in the left-hand side of the engine compartment.

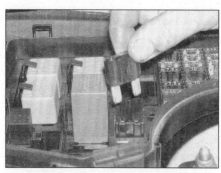

3 To renew a blown fuse, remove it using the plastic tool provided. Fit a new fuse of the same rating, available from car accessory shops. If the fuse blows repeatedly, refer to Chapter 12 to locate the fault.

Battery

Caution: Before carrying out any work on the vehicle battery, read the precautions given in 'Safety first!' at the start of this manual.

● Make sure that the battery tray is in good condition, and that the clamp is tight. Corrosion on the tray, retaining clamp and the battery itself can be removed with a solution of water and baking soda. Thoroughly rinse all cleaned areas with water. Any metal parts damaged by corrosion should be covered with a zinc-based primer, then painted.
● Periodically (approximately every three months), check the charge condition of the battery as described in Chapter 5A.
● If the battery is flat, and you need to jump start your vehicle, see *Roadside Repairs*.

 HAYNES HiNT *Battery corrosion can be kept to a minimum by applying a layer of petroleum jelly to the clamps and terminals after they are reconnected.*

1 The battery is located at the front, left-hand side of the engine compartment. The exterior of the battery should be inspected periodically for damage such as a cracked case or cover.

2 Check the tightness of battery clamps to ensure good electrical connections. You should not be able to move them. Also check each cable for cracks and frayed conductors.

3 If corrosion (white, fluffy deposits) is evident, remove the cables from the battery terminals, clean them with a small wire brush, then refit them. Automotive stores sell a tool for cleaning the battery post . . .

4 . . . as well as the battery cable clamps.

Wiper blades

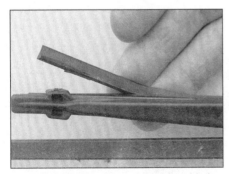

1 Check the condition of the wiper blades; if they are cracked or show any signs of deterioration, or if the glass swept area is smeared, renew them. For maximum clarity of vision, wiper blades should be renewed annually.

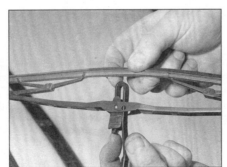

2 To remove a windscreen wiper blade, pull the arm fully away from the glass until it locks. Swivel the blade through 90°, then squeeze the locking clip, and detach the blade from the arm. When fitting the new blade, make sure that the blade locks securely into the arm, and that the blade is orientated correctly.

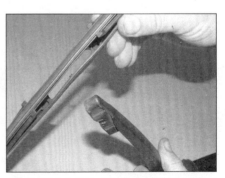

3 Don't forget to check the tailgate wiper blade as well on Hatchback models. The blade is clipped onto the arm.

Lubricants and fluids

Engine:

Petrol . . . . Saab Turbo Engine Oil or engine oil with viscosity 5W-30, 0W-30 or 5W-40 to specification API SG/SH/SJ and ACEA A2-96/A3-96, including CCMC G4/G5

Diesel . . . . Saab Turbo Engine Oil or engine oil with viscosity 0W-40 or 5W-40 to specification ACEA B2-96/B3-96, API at least CD, including CCMC PD2

Cooling system . . . . Saab original coolant/antifreeze only

Manual gearbox . . . . Saab synthetic manual gearbox oil 400 108 247

Automatic transmission . . . . Saab automatic transmission fluid (mineral oil based) or Dexron III ATF

Power steering reservoir . . . . Saab Power Steering Fluid CHF 11S

Brake fluid reservoir . . . . Hydraulic fluid to DOT 4

Tyre pressures (cold)

Note: *Pressures apply to original-equipment tyres, and may vary if any other make or type of tyre is fitted; check with the tyre manufacturer or supplier for correct pressures if necessary.*

Tyre size	Front	Rear
185/65 R15	30 psi (2.1 bar)	30 psi (2.1 bar)
195/60 R15	32 psi (2.2 bar)	32 psi (2.2 bar)
205/50 R16	33 psi (2.3 bar)	33 psi (2.3 bar)
215/45 ZR17	32 psi (2.2 bar)	29 psi (2.0 bar)

Chapter 1 Part A:
Routine maintenance and servicing – petrol models

Contents

Degrees of difficulty

| **Easy,** suitable for novice with little experience | | **Fairly easy,** suitable for beginner with some experience | | **Fairly difficult,** suitable for competent DIY mechanic | | **Difficult,** suitable for experienced DIY mechanic | | **Very difficult,** suitable for expert DIY or professional | |

Lubricants and fluids

See end of *Weekly checks*

Capacities

Engine oil

Drain and refill, with filter change............................	4.0 litres
Total from dry, including engine oil cooler	5.4 litres
Between dipstick MAX and MIN markings......................	1.0 litres

Cooling system......................................	8.5 litres

Transmission

Manual (drain and refill)	1.9 litres
Automatic:	
Drain and refill...............................	3.3 litres
Total from dry (including torque converter and cooler)...........	7.2 litres

Braking system

System capacity:	
Except Viggen models	0.58 litres
Viggen models	1.08 litres

Fuel tank

All models....................................	64.0 litres

Power assisted steering

System capacity....................................	1.0 litres

Cooling system

Antifreeze mixture*:	
50% antifreeze	Protection down to -37°C
55% antifreeze	Protection down to -45°C

* Note: *Refer to antifreeze manufacturer for latest recommendations.*

Ignition system

Firing order..	1 – 3 – 4 – 2	
Spark plugs:	**Type**	**Electrode gap**
B204i	NGK BCP 5EV	0.6 to 0.7 mm
B204E	NGK BCPR 7ES-11	1.0 to 1.1 mm
B204L	NGK BCPR 7ES-11	1.0 to 1.1 mm
B204R	NGK BCPR 7ES-11	1.0 to 1.1 mm
B205E	NGK BCPR 6ES-11	1.0 to 1.1 mm
B205L:		
MY 2000....................................	NGK PFR 7H-10	0.9 to 1.0 mm
MY 2000 1/2-on	NGK PFR 6H-10	0.9 to 1.0 mm
B205R:		
MY 2000....................................	NGK PFR 7H-10	0.9 to 1.0 mm
MY 2000 1/2-on	NGK PFR 6H-10	0.9 to 1.0 mm
B234i	NGK BCP 6EV	0.6 to 0.7 mm
B235R:		
Up to MY 1999 1/2................................	NGK PFR 7H-10	1.0 to 1.1 mm
MY 1999 1/2-on	NGK PFR 6H-10	0.9 to 1.0 mm

Brakes

Front brake pad friction material minimum thickness	5.0 mm at time of service (acoustic warning at 3.0 mm)
Rear brake pad friction material minimum thickness...............	5.0 mm

Tyre pressures

Refer to the end of *Weekly checks*

Torque wrench settings

	Nm	lbf ft
Automatic transmission drain plug...........................	40	30
Engine oil sump drain plug................................	25	18
Manual transmission drain, level and filler plugs	50	37
Spark plugs	27	20
Wheel bolts..	110	80

The maintenance intervals in this manual are provided with the assumption that you will be carrying out the work yourself. These are the minimum maintenance intervals recommended by the manufacturer for vehicles driven daily. If you wish to keep your vehicle in peak condition at all times, you may wish to perform some of these procedures more often. We encourage frequent maintenance, because it enhances the efficiency, performance and resale value of your vehicle.

If the vehicle is driven in dusty areas, used to tow a trailer, or driven frequently at slow speeds (idling in traffic) or on short journeys, more frequent maintenance intervals are recommended.

When the vehicle is new, it should be serviced by a dealer service department (or other workshop recognised by the vehicle manufacturer as providing the same standard of service) in order to preserve the warranty. The vehicle manufacturer may reject warranty claims if you are unable to prove that servicing has been carried out as and when specified, using only original equipment parts or parts certified to be of equivalent quality.

All Saab models are equipped with a service interval display (or Saab Information Display – SID) on the facia, which will indicate TIME FOR SERVICE when a service is due. However, Saab point out that, 'due to the relationship between time and mileage, some operating conditions will make annual service more suitable'.

Every 250 miles or weekly
☐ Refer to *Weekly checks*

Every 6000 miles or 6 months
☐ Engine oil and filter – renewal (Section 3)

After first 6000 miles and thereafter every 12 000 miles or 12 months
Note: *The 12 000 mile intervals start at 18 000 miles, ie, at 18 000 miles, 30 000 miles, 42 000 miles, 54 000 miles, etc.*
☐ Service indicator – resetting (Section 4)
☐ Hoses and fluids – leak check (Section 5)
☐ Steering and suspension components – check (Section 6)
☐ Front wheel toe-in – check and adjust (Section 7)
☐ Rear brake pad wear – check (Section 8)
☐ Handbrake – check and adjustment (Section 9)
☐ Seat belt condition – check (Section 10)
☐ Airbag system – check (Section 11)
☐ Headlight beam alignment – check (Section 12)
☐ Power steering fluid level – check (Section 13)
☐ Road test (Section 14)

Every 18 000 miles or 18 months
Note: *The 18 000 mile intervals start at 24 000 miles, ie, at 24 000 miles, 42 000 miles, 60 000 miles, 78 000 miles, etc.*
☐ Coolant antifreeze concentration – check (Section 15)
☐ Transmission lubricant level – check (Section 16)
☐ Driveshaft joints and gaiters – check (Section 17)
☐ Exhaust system – check (Section 18)
☐ Front brake pad wear – check (Section 19)
☐ Hinges and locks – lubrication (Section 20)
☐ Plenum chamber drain hose – clean (Section 21)
☐ Pollen air filter – renew (Section 22)
☐ Auxiliary drivebelt condition – check (Section 23)

Every 24 000 miles or 2 years
Note: *The interval for this service item is based on time <u>and</u> mileage. It must be carried out every 24 000 miles, **or** every 2 years, whichever comes sooner.*
☐ Brake fluid – renewal (Section 24)

Every 30 000 miles
Note: *The 30 000 mile intervals start at 36 000 miles, ie, at 36 000 miles, 66 000 miles, 96 000 miles, etc.*
☐ Spark plugs – renewal (Section 25)
☐ Air filter element – renewal (Section 26)

Every 48 000 miles
Note: *The 48 000 mile intervals start at 54 000 miles, ie, at 54 000 miles, 102 000 miles, etc.*
☐ Automatic transmission fluid – renewal (Section 27)

Every 66 000 miles
Note: *The 66 000 mile intervals start at 72 000 miles, ie, at 72 000 miles, 144 000 miles, etc.*
☐ Auxiliary drivebelt – renew (Section 28)
☐ Fuel filter – renewal (Section 29)

Every 3 years
☐ Coolant – renewal (Section 30)

Underbonnet view of a 2.0 litre turbocharged model

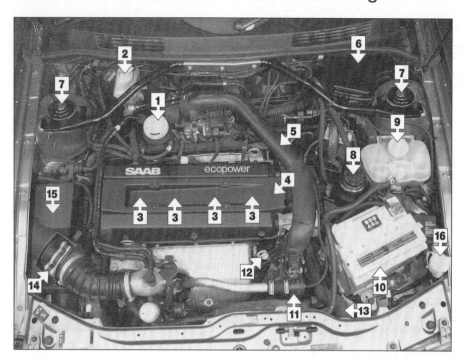

1 Engine oil filler cap and dipstick
2 Hydraulic brake fluid reservoir
3 Spark plugs (hidden)
4 Ignition coil module
5 Turbocharger-to-engine air inlet pipe
6 Engine compartment fusebox
7 Front suspension strut top mountings
8 Power steering fluid reservoir
9 Coolant expansion tank
10 Battery
11 Turbocharger control by-pass valve
12 Automatic transmission fluid level dipstick
13 Radiator top hose
14 Fuel injection system air mass meter
15 Air filter
16 Windscreen washer fluid reservoir filler
     cap

Front underbody view of a 2.0 litre turbocharged model

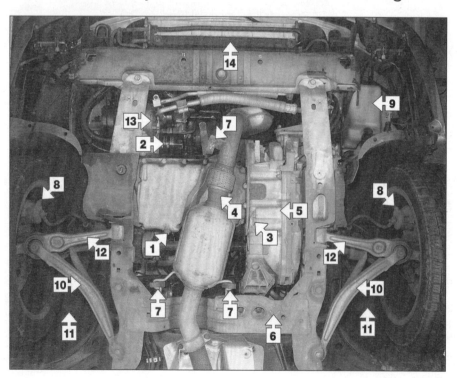

1 Engine oil drain plug
2 Oil filter
3 Transmission drain plug
4 Front exhaust pipe and silencers
5 Manual transmission
6 Front suspension/engine subframe
7 Exhaust mountings
8 Front brake calipers
9 Screen washer fluid reservoir
10 Front suspension radius arm
11 Steering track rod ends
12 Front suspension lower control arm
13 Air conditioning compressor
14 Radiator

Rear underbody view of a 2.0 litre turbocharged model

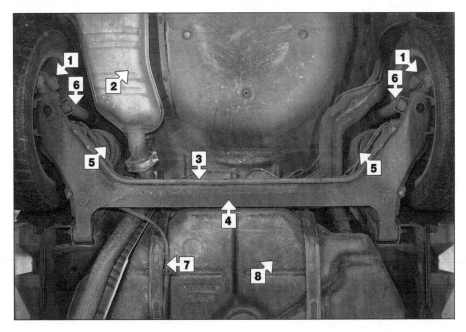

1 Rear brake caliper
2 Exhaust system tail box
3 Rear suspension anti-roll bar
4 Rear suspension beam axle
5 Rear suspension coil spring
6 Rear suspension shock absorber lower
   mounting
7 Handbrake cable
8 Fuel tank

1 General information

This Chapter is designed to help the home mechanic maintain his/her vehicle for safety, economy, long life and peak performance.

The Chapter contains a master maintenance schedule, followed by Sections dealing specifically with each task in the schedule. Visual checks, adjustments, component renewal and other helpful items are included. Refer to the accompanying illustrations of the engine compartment and the underside of the vehicle for the locations of the various components.

Servicing your vehicle in accordance with the mileage/time maintenance schedule and the following Sections will provide a planned maintenance programme, which should result in a long and reliable service life. This is a comprehensive plan, so maintaining some items, but not others, at the specified service intervals will not produce the same results.

As you service your vehicle, you will discover that many of the procedures can – and should – be grouped together, because of the particular procedure being performed, or because of the close proximity of two otherwise-unrelated components to one another. For example, if the vehicle is raised for any reason, the exhaust system could be inspected at the same time as the suspension and steering components.

The first step in this maintenance programme is to prepare yourself before the actual work begins. Read through all the Sections relevant to the work to be carried out, then make a list and gather together all the parts and tools required. If a problem is encountered, seek advice from a parts specialist, or a dealer service department.

2 Regular maintenance

If, from the time the vehicle is new, the routine maintenance schedule is followed closely, and frequent checks are made of fluid levels and high-wear items, as suggested throughout this manual, the engine will be kept in relatively good running condition, and the need for additional work will be minimised.

It is possible that there will be times when the engine is running poorly due to the lack of regular maintenance. This is even more likely if a used vehicle, which has not received regular and frequent maintenance checks, is purchased. In such cases, additional work may need to be carried out, outside of the regular maintenance intervals.

If engine wear is suspected, a compression test (refer to Chapter 2A) will provide valuable information regarding the overall performance of the main internal components. Such a test can be used as a basis to decide on the extent of the work to be carried out. If, for example, a compression test indicates serious internal engine wear, conventional maintenance as described in this Chapter will not greatly improve the performance of the engine, and may prove a waste of time and money, unless extensive overhaul work (Chapter 2C) is carried out first.

The following series of operations are those most often required to improve the performance of a generally poor-running engine:

Primary operations

a) Clean, inspect and test the battery ('Weekly checks' and Chapter 5A)
b) Check all the engine-related fluids ('Weekly checks').
c) Check the condition and tension of the auxiliary drivebelt (Section 23).
d) Renew the spark plugs (Section 24).
e) Inspect the distributor cap, rotor arm and HT leads – as applicable (Chapter 5B).
f) Check the condition of the air filter element, and renew if necessary (Section 26).
g) Renew the fuel filter (Section 29).
h) Check the condition of all hoses, and check for fluid leaks (Section 5).

If the above operations do not prove fully effective, carry out the following secondary operations:

Secondary operations

a) Check the charging system (Chapter 5A).
b) Check the ignition system (Chapter 5B).
c) Check the fuel system (Chapter 4A).
d) Renew the distributor cap and rotor arm – as applicable (Chapter 5B).
e) Renew the ignition HT leads – as applicable (Chapter 5B).

3.4 Unscrew and remove the sump oil drain plug

3.5a Allow some time for the old oil to drain . . .

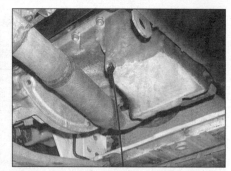

3.5b . . . noting that it may be necessary to reposition the container as the oil flow slows to a trickle

Every 6000 miles or 6 months

3 Engine oil and filter – renewal

1 Frequent oil changes are the most important preventative maintenance the DIY home mechanic can give the engine, because ageing oil becomes diluted and contaminated, which leads to premature engine wear.

2 Before starting this procedure, gather together all the necessary tools and materials. Also make sure that you have plenty of clean rags and newspapers handy, to mop-up any spills. Ideally, the engine oil should be warm, as it will drain better, and more built-up sludge will be removed with it. Take care, however, not to touch the exhaust or any other hot parts of the engine when working under the vehicle. To avoid any possibility of scalding, and to protect yourself from possible skin irritants and other harmful contaminants in used engine oils, it is advisable to wear gloves when carrying out this work.

3 Apply the handbrake, then jack up the front of the vehicle and support it on axle stands (see *Jacking and vehicle support*).

4 The engine oil drain plug is located on the front of the sump; slacken the plug about half a turn. Position the draining container under the drain plug, then remove the plug completely – recover the sealing washer **(see illustration)**.

5 Allow some time for the old oil to drain,

HAYNES HINT *Keep the plug pressed into the sump while unscrewing it by hand the last couple of turns. As the plug releases from the threads, move it away sharply so the stream of oil issuing from the sump runs into the container, not up your sleeve.*

noting that it may be necessary to reposition the container as the oil flow slows to a trickle **(see illustrations)**.

6 After all the oil has drained, wipe off the drain plug with a clean rag. Check the sealing washer for condition, and renew it if necessary **(see illustration)**. Clean the area around the drain plug opening, and refit the plug. Tighten the plug to the specified torque.

3.6 Renew the sump oil drain plug washer if necessary

7 Move the container into position under the oil filter which is located on the rear of the cylinder block and accessed from under the vehicle.

8 Using an oil filter removal tool or strap, slacken the filter initially, then unscrew it by hand the rest of the way **(see illustrations)**. Empty the oil from the old filter into the container, and discard the filter.

9 Use a clean rag to remove all oil, dirt and sludge from the filter sealing area on the mounting bracket.

10 Apply a light coating of clean engine oil to the sealing ring on the new filter, then screw it into position on the engine **(see illustrations)**. Tighten the filter firmly by hand only – **do not** use any tools. Wipe clean the filter and sump drain plug.

3.8a Loosen the oil filter using a removal tool . . .

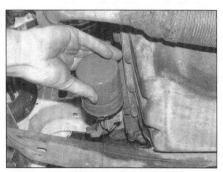

3.8b . . . and remove it from the engine

3.10a Apply a light coating of clean engine oil to the sealing ring on the new filter . . .

3.10b . . . then screw it into position on the engine

3.12a Remove the oil filler cap and withdraw the dipstick from the top of the filler tube

3.12b Fill the engine, using the correct oil

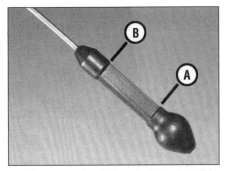

3.12c Lower mark(A) and upper mark(B) on the engine oil dipstick

11 Remove the old oil and all tools, then lower the vehicle to the ground.

12 Remove the oil filler cap and withdraw the dipstick from the top of the filler tube. Fill the engine, using the correct oil (see *Lubricants and fluids*). An oil can spout or funnel may help to reduce spillage. Pour in half the specified quantity of oil first, then wait a few minutes for the oil to fall to the sump. Continue adding oil a small quantity at a time until the level is

up to the lower mark on the dipstick. Adding a further 1.0 litre will bring the level up to the upper mark on the dipstick. Insert the dipstick, and refit the filler cap **(see illustrations)**.

13 Start the engine and run it for a few minutes; check for leaks around the oil filter seal and the sump drain plug. Note that there may be a delay of a few seconds before the oil pressure warning light goes out when the engine is first started, as the oil circulates

through the engine oil galleries and the new oil filter, before the pressure builds-up.

14 Switch off the engine, and wait a few minutes for the oil to settle in the sump once more. With the new oil circulated and the filter completely full, recheck the level on the dipstick, and add more oil as necessary.

15 Dispose of the used engine oil safely, in accordance with the guidance given in *General repair procedures*.

Every 12 000 miles or 12 months

Note: *The 12 000 mile intervals start at 18 000 miles, ie, at 18 000 miles, 30 000 miles, 42 000 miles, 54 000 miles, etc.*

4 Service indicator – resetting

1 The facia-mounted SID (Saab Information Display) system incorporates a service interval indicator. When the distance covered between services approaches the next service, a visual message is displayed. The service indicator is manually reset to zero after the vehicle has been serviced. **Note:** *The indicator is automatically reset after the message has been displayed for 20 times.* The indicator can be reset at any time using the Saab diagnostic tool.

2 On the SID panel, press and hold the CLEAR button (furthermost left) for 8 seconds,

then release it **(see illustration)**. During this period, the display should read CLEARED for the first four seconds, followed by SERVICE for the remaining 4 seconds. An audible signal will also be sounded during this time. The service indicator will then be reset.

5 Hoses and fluids – leak check

Cooling system

⚠ **Warning: Refer to the safety information given in 'Safety first!' and Chapter 3 before disturbing any of the cooling system components.**

1 Carefully check the radiator and heater coolant hoses along their entire length. Renew any hose which is cracked, swollen or which shows signs of deterioration. Cracks will show

up better if the hose is squeezed. Pay close attention to the clips that secure the hoses to the cooling system components. Hose clips that have been over-tightened can pinch and puncture hoses, resulting in cooling system leaks **(see illustration)**.

2 Inspect all the cooling system components (hoses, joint faces, etc) for leaks. Where any problems of this nature are found on system components, renew the component or gasket with reference to Chapter 3 **(see Haynes Hint)**.

Fuel system

⚠ **Warning: Refer to the safety information given in 'Safety first!' and Chapter 4A before disturbing any of the fuel system components.**

HAYNES HINT

A leak in the cooling system will usually show up as white- or antifreeze-coloured, crusty deposits around the area of the leak.

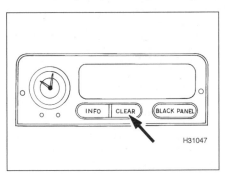

H31047

4.2 On the SID panel, press and hold the CLEAR button for 8 seconds, then release it

5.1 Check all cooling system hoses for signs of leakage

5.7a Inspect the area around the camshaft cover joint face for signs of engine oil leakage

5.7b Where applicable, check the area around the ignition distributor mounting flange

3 Petrol leaks can be difficult to pinpoint, unless the leakage is significant and hence easily visible. Fuel tends to evaporate quickly once it comes into contact with air, especially in a hot engine bay. Small drips can disappear before you get a chance to identify the point of leakage. If you suspect that there is a fuel leak from the area of the engine bay, leave the vehicle overnight then start the engine from cold, with the bonnet open. Metal components tend to shrink when they are cold, and rubber seals and hoses tend to harden, so any leaks will be more apparent whilst the engine is warming-up from a cold start.

4 Check all fuel lines at their connections to the fuel rail, fuel pressure regulator and fuel filter. Examine each rubber fuel hose along its length for splits or cracks. Check for leakage from the crimped joints between rubber and metal fuel lines. Examine the unions between the metal fuel lines and the fuel filter housing. Also check the area around the fuel injectors for signs of O-ring leakage.

5 To identify fuel leaks between the fuel tank and the engine bay, the vehicle should be raised and securely supported on axle stands (see *Jacking and vehicle support*). Inspect the petrol tank and filler neck for punctures, cracks and other damage. The connection between the filler neck and tank is especially critical. Sometimes a rubber filler neck or connecting hose will leak due to loose retaining clamps or deteriorated rubber.

6 Carefully check all rubber hoses and metal fuel lines leading away from the petrol tank. Check for loose connections, deteriorated

hoses, kinked lines, and other damage. Pay particular attention to the vent pipes and hoses, which often loop up around the filler neck and can become blocked or kinked, making tank filling difficult. Follow the fuel supply and return lines to the front of the vehicle, carefully inspecting them all the way for signs of damage or corrosion. Renew damaged sections as necessary.

Engine oil

7 Inspect the area around the camshaft cover, cylinder head, oil filter and sump joint faces. Where applicable, check the area around the ignition distributor mounting flange **(see illustrations)**. Bear in mind that, over a period of time, some very slight seepage from these areas is to be expected – what you are really looking for is any indication of a serious leak caused by gasket failure. Engine oil seeping from the base of the timing chain cover or the transmission bellhousing may be an indication of crankshaft or transmission input shaft oil seal failure. Should a leak be found, renew the failed gasket or oil seal by referring to the appropriate Chapters in this manual.

Automatic transmission fluid

8 Where applicable, check the hoses leading to the transmission fluid cooler at the front of the engine bay for leakage. Look for deterioration caused by corrosion and damage from grounding, or debris thrown up from the road surface. Automatic transmission fluid is a thin oil and is usually red in colour.

5.9 Examine the power steering fluid supply and return hoses and pipes for signs of leakage

5.15 Check the area around the base of brake fluid reservoir, for signs of leakage

Power-assisted steering fluid

9 Examine the hose running between the fluid reservoir and the power steering pump, and the return hose running from the steering rack to the fluid reservoir. Also examine the high pressure supply hose between the pump and the steering rack **(see illustration)**.

10 Check the condition of each hose carefully. Look for deterioration caused by corrosion and damage from grounding, or debris thrown up from the road surface.

11 Pay particular attention to crimped unions, and the area surrounding the hoses that are secured with adjustable worm-drive clips. Like automatic transmission fluid, PAS fluid is a thin oil, and is usually red in colour.

Air conditioning refrigerant

⚠️ **Warning: Refer to the safety information given in 'Safety first!' and Chapter 3 regarding the dangers of disturbing any of the air conditioning system components.**

12 The air conditioning system is filled with a liquid refrigerant, which is retained under high pressure. If the air conditioning system is opened and depressurised without the aid of specialised equipment, the refrigerant will immediately turn into gas and escape into the atmosphere. If the liquid comes into contact with your skin, it can cause severe frostbite. In addition, the refrigerant contains substances which are environmentally damaging; for this reason, it should not be allowed to escape into the atmosphere in an uncontrolled fashion.

13 Any suspected air conditioning system leaks should be immediately referred to a Saab dealer or air conditioning specialist. Leakage will be shown up as a steady drop in the level of refrigerant in the system.

14 Note that water may drip from the condenser drain pipe, underneath the car, immediately after the air conditioning system has been in use. This is normal, and should not be cause for concern.

Brake fluid

⚠️ **Warning: Refer to the safety information given in 'Safety first!' and Chapter 9 regarding the dangers of handling brake fluid.**

15 With reference to Chapter 9, examine the area surrounding the brake pipe unions at the master cylinder for signs of leakage. Check the area around the base of fluid reservoir, for signs of leakage caused by seal failure **(see illustration)**. Also examine the brake pipe unions at the ABS hydraulic unit.

16 If fluid loss is evident, but the leak cannot be pinpointed in the engine bay, the brake calipers and underbody brake lines should be carefully checked with the vehicle raised and supported on axle stands (see *Jacking and vehicle support*). Leakage of fluid from the braking system is a serious fault that must be rectified immediately.

17 Brake/clutch hydraulic fluid is a toxic substance with a watery consistency. New fluid is almost colourless, but it becomes darker with age and use.

Unidentified fluid leaks

18 If there are signs that a fluid of some description is leaking from the vehicle, but you cannot identify the type of fluid or its exact origin, park the vehicle overnight and slide a large piece of card underneath it. Providing that the card is positioned in roughly the right location, even the smallest leak will show up on the card. Not only will this help you to pinpoint the exact location of the leak, it should be easier to identify the fluid from its colour. Bear in mind, though, that the leak may only be occurring when the engine is running!

Vacuum hoses

19 Although the braking system is hydraulically-operated, the brake servo unit amplifies the effort applied at the brake pedal by making use of the vacuum in the inlet manifold generated by the engine. Vacuum is ported to the servo by means of a large-bore hose. Any leaks that develop in this hose will reduce the effectiveness of the braking system, and may affect the running of the engine.

20 In addition, a number of the underbonnet components, particularly the emission control components, are driven by vacuum supplied from the inlet manifold via narrow-bore hoses. A leak in a vacuum hose means that air is being drawn into the hose (rather than escaping from it) and this makes leakage very difficult to detect. One method is to use an old length of vacuum hose as a kind of stethoscope – hold one end close to (but not in!) your ear and use the other end to probe the area around the suspected leak. When the end of the hose is directly over a vacuum leak, a hissing sound will be heard clearly through the hose. Care must be taken to avoid contacting hot or moving components, as the engine must be running, when testing in this manner. Renew any vacuum hoses that are found to be defective.

6 Steering and suspension components – check

Front suspension and steering

1 Raise the front of the vehicle, and securely support it on axle stands (see *Jacking and vehicle support*).

2 Visually inspect the balljoint dust covers and the steering rack-and-pinion gaiters for splits, chafing or deterioration. Any wear of these components will cause loss of lubricant, together with dirt and water entry, resulting in rapid deterioration of the balljoints or steering gear.

3 Check the power steering fluid hoses for chafing or deterioration, and the pipe and

6.4 Check for wear in the hub bearings by grasping the wheel and trying to rock it

hose unions for fluid leaks. Also check for signs of fluid leakage under pressure from the steering gear rubber gaiters, which would indicate failed fluid seals within the steering gear.

4 Grasp the roadwheel at the 12 o'clock and 6 o'clock positions, and try to rock it **(see illustration)**. Very slight free play may be felt, but if the movement is appreciable, further investigation is necessary to determine the source. Continue rocking the wheel while an assistant depresses the footbrake. If the movement is now eliminated or significantly reduced, it is likely that the hub bearings are at fault. If the free play is still evident with the footbrake depressed, then there is wear in the suspension joints or mountings.

5 Now grasp the wheel at the 9 o'clock and 3 o'clock positions, and try to rock it as before. Any movement felt now may again be caused by wear in the hub bearings or the steering track rod balljoints. If the outer balljoint is worn, the visual movement will be obvious. If the inner joint is suspect, it can be felt by placing a hand over the rack-and-pinion rubber gaiter and gripping the track rod. If the wheel is now rocked, movement will be felt at the inner joint if wear has taken place.

6 Using a large screwdriver or flat bar, check for wear in the suspension mounting bushes by levering between the relevant suspension component and its attachment point. Some movement is to be expected, as the mountings are made of rubber, but excessive wear should be obvious. Also check the condition of any visible rubber bushes, looking for splits, cracks or contamination of the rubber.

7 With the car standing on its wheels, have an assistant turn the steering wheel back-and-forth, about an eighth of a turn each way. There should be very little, if any, lost movement between the steering wheel and roadwheels. If this is not the case, closely observe the joints and mountings previously described. In addition, check the steering column universal joints for wear, and also check the rack-and-pinion steering gear itself.

8 The front suspension mountings should be checked for tightness.

Rear suspension

9 Chock the front wheels, then jack up the

rear of the vehicle and support securely on axle stands (see *Jacking and vehicle support*).

10 Working as described previously for the front suspension, check the rear hub bearings, the suspension bushes and the strut or shock absorber mountings (as applicable) for wear.

11 The rear suspension mountings should be checked for tightness.

Shock absorber

12 Check for any signs of fluid leakage around the shock absorber bodies, or from the rubber gaiters around the piston rods. Should any fluid be noticed, the shock absorber is defective internally, and should be renewed. **Note:** *Shock absorbers should always be renewed in pairs on the same axle.*

13 The efficiency of the shock absorber may be checked by bouncing the vehicle at each corner. Generally speaking, the body will return to its normal position and stop after being depressed. If it rises and returns on a rebound, the shock absorber is probably suspect. Also examine the shock absorber upper and lower mountings for any signs of wear.

Removable towbar attachment

14 Where applicable, clean the coupling pin then apply a little grease to the socket. Make sure that the removable towbar attachment fits easily to its mounting and locks correctly in position.

7 Front wheel toe-in – check and adjust

Refer to Chapter 10, Section 20, for details.

8 Rear brake pad wear – check

1 To check the rear brake pads, firmly apply the handbrake, then jack up the rear of the vehicle and support it securely on axle stands (see *Jacking and vehicle support*). Remove the rear roadwheels.

2 For a quick check, the pad thickness can be carried out via the inspection hole on the rear of the caliper. Using a steel rule, measure the thickness of the pad lining including the backing plate. This must not be less than that indicated in the Specifications.

3 The view through the caliper inspection hole gives a rough indication of the state of the brake pads. For a comprehensive check, the brake pads should be removed and cleaned. The operation of the caliper can then also be checked, and the condition of the brake disc itself can be fully examined on both sides.

4 If any pad's friction material is worn to the specified thickness or less, *all four pads must be renewed as a set*. Refer to Chapter 9 for details.

5 On completion, refit the roadwheels and lower the vehicle to the ground.

9 Handbrake – check and adjustment

1 Chock the front wheels, then jack up the rear of the vehicle and support on axle stands (see *Jacking and vehicle support*).
2 Fully release the handbrake lever.
3 Apply the lever to the 4th notch position, and check that both rear wheels are locked when attempting to turn them by hand.
4 If adjustment is necessary, refer to Chapter 9.
5 Lower the vehicle to the ground.

10 Seat belt condition – check

1 Working on each seat belt in turn, carefully examine the seat belt webbing for cuts, or for any signs of serious fraying or deterioration. Pull the belt all the way out, and examine the full extent of the webbing.
2 Fasten and unfasten the belt, ensuring that the locking mechanism holds securely, and releases properly when intended. Check also that the retracting mechanism operates correctly when the belt is released.
3 Check the security of all seat belt mountings and attachments which are accessible, without removing any trim or other components, from inside the vehicle.
4 Check the function of the seat belt reminder lamp.

13.1 Power steering fluid reservoir location

13.2 Unscrewing the filler cap

11 Airbag system – check

1 The following work can be carried out by the home mechanic, however, if an electronic fault is apparent, it will be necessary to take the car to a Saab dealer, who will have the necessary diagnostic equipment to extract fault codes from the system.
2 Turn the ignition switch to the drive position (ignition warning lights on), and check that the SRS (Supplementary Restraint System) warning light is illuminated for 3 to 4 seconds. After this period the light should go out, indicating that the system has been checked and is functioning correctly.
3 If the warning light remains on or refuses to light, have the system checked by a Saab dealer.
4 Visually examine the steering wheel centre pad and the passenger airbag module for external damage. Also check the exterior of the front seats around the side airbag locations. If damage is evident, consult a Saab dealer.
5 In the interests of safety, make sure that there are no loose items inside the car which could be thrown onto the airbag modules in the event of an accident.

12 Headlight beam alignment – check

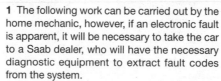

Refer to Chapter 12 for details

13 Power steering fluid level – check

1 The power steering fluid reservoir is located on the left-hand side of the engine compartment behind the battery **(see illustration)**. The fluid level should be checked with the engine stopped.
2 Unscrew the filler cap from the top of the reservoir, and wipe all fluid from the cap dipstick with a clean rag. Refit the filler cap, then remove it again. Note the fluid level on the dipstick **(see illustration)**.
3 When the engine is cold, the fluid level

13.3 MIN and MAX marks on the filler cap

should be between the upper MAX and lower MIN marks on the dipstick. Where only one mark is provided, the level should be between the bottom of the dipstick and the mark **(see illustration)**.
4 Top-up the fluid level using the specified type of fluid (do not overfill the reservoir), then refit and tighten the filler cap **(see illustration)**.

14 Road test

Instruments and electrical equipment

1 Check the operation of all instruments and electrical equipment.
2 Make sure that all instruments read correctly, and switch on all electrical equipment in turn to check that it functions properly. Check the function of the heating, air conditioning and automatic climate control systems.

Steering and suspension

3 Check for any abnormalities in the steering, suspension, handling or road 'feel'.
4 Drive the vehicle, and check that there are no unusual vibrations or noises.
5 Check that the steering feels positive, with no excessive 'sloppiness', or roughness, and check for any suspension noises when cornering, or when driving over bumps. Check that the power steering system operates correctly.

Drivetrain

6 Check the performance of the engine, clutch (manual transmission), transmission and driveshafts. Check that the turbo boost pressure needle moves up to the upper limit during sharp acceleration. The needle may occasionally enter the red zone for an instant, but if this happens frequently, or for extended periods, a problem may exist within the turbo boost control mechanism (see Chapter 4A).
7 Listen for any unusual noises from the engine, clutch (manual transmission) and transmission.
8 Make sure that the engine runs smoothly when idling, and that there is no hesitation when accelerating.
9 On manual transmission models, check that the clutch action is smooth and progressive,

13.4 Topping-up the fluid level

that the drive is taken up smoothly, and that the pedal travel is correct. Also listen for any noises when the clutch pedal is depressed. Check that all gears can be engaged smoothly, without noise, and that the gear lever action is smooth and not abnormally vague or 'notchy'.

10 On automatic transmission models, make sure that all gearchanges occur smoothly without snatching, and without an increase in engine speed between changes. Check that all the gear positions can be selected with the vehicle at rest. If any problems are found, they should be referred to a Saab dealer.

11 Listen for a metallic clicking sound from the front of the vehicle, as the vehicle is driven slowly in a circle with the steering on full lock. Carry out this check in both directions. If a clicking noise is heard, this indicates wear in a driveshaft joint, in which case, refer to Chapter 8.

Braking system

12 Make sure that the vehicle does not pull to one side when braking, and that the wheels do not lock when braking hard.

13 Check that there is no vibration through the steering when braking.

14 Check that the handbrake operates correctly, without excessive movement of the lever, and that it holds the vehicle stationary on a slope.

15 Test the operation of the brake servo unit as follows. With the engine off, depress the footbrake four or five times to exhaust the vacuum, then start the engine while holding the brake pedal depressed. As the engine starts, there should be a noticeable 'give' in the brake pedal as vacuum builds-up. Allow the engine to run for at least two minutes, and then switch it off. If the brake pedal is now depressed again, it should be possible to detect a 'hiss' from the servo as the pedal is depressed. After about four or five applications, no further sound should be heard, and the pedal should feel considerably harder.

Every 18 000 miles or 18 months

Note: *The 18 000 mile intervals start at 24 000 miles, ie, at 24 000 miles, 42 000 miles, 60 000 miles, 78 000 miles, etc.*

15 Coolant antifreeze concentration – check
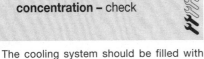

1 The cooling system should be filled with the recommended antifreeze and corrosion protection fluid. Over a period of time, the concentration of fluid may be reduced due to topping-up (this can be avoided by topping-up with the correct antifreeze mixture) or fluid loss. If loss of coolant has been evident, it is important to make the necessary repair before adding fresh fluid. The exact mixture of antifreeze-to-water which you should use depends on the relative weather conditions. The mixture should contain at least 40% antifreeze, but not more than 70%. Consult the mixture ratio chart on the antifreeze container before adding coolant. Hydrometers are available at most automotive accessory shops to test the coolant. Use antifreeze which meets the vehicle manufacturer's specifications.

2 With the engine **cold**, carefully remove the cap from the expansion tank. If the engine is not completely cold, place a cloth rag over the cap before removing it, and remove it slowly to allow any pressure to escape.

3 Antifreeze checkers are available from car accessory shops. Draw some coolant from the expansion tank and observe how many plastic balls are floating in the checker **(see illustration)**. Usually, 2 or 3 balls must be floating for the correct concentration of antifreeze, but follow the manufacturer's instructions.

4 If the concentration is incorrect, it will be necessary to either withdraw some coolant and add antifreeze, or alternatively drain the old coolant and add fresh coolant of the correct concentration.

16 Transmission lubricant level – check

Manual transmission

Note: *Saab do not specify an interval for checking the oil level on manual transmission models, however, we recommend making the check every 18 000 miles or 18 months.*

1 Make sure that the car is parked on a level surface. Wipe clean the area around the level plug, which is located on the left hand side of the differential casing at the rear of the transmission, behind the left-hand driveshaft. Access to the plug can be gained from the engine compartment or, alternatively, chock the rear wheels and firmly apply the handbrake, then jack up the front of the vehicle and support it on axle stands (*see Jacking and vehicle support*), but note that the vehicle must be level when making the check.

2 Unscrew the level plug, using a suitable Allen key or hex bit and wipe it clean **(see illustration)**. The oil level should reach the lower edge of the level hole. A certain amount of oil will have gathered behind the level plug, and will trickle out when it is removed; this does **not** necessarily indicate that the level is correct. To ensure that a true level is established, wait until the initial trickle has stopped, then use a length of clean wire, bent into a right angle, as a dipstick.

3 If the oil level requires topping-up, wipe clean the area around the filler plug, which is located on top of the transmission. Unscrew the plug, and wipe it clean **(see illustrations)**.

15.3 Using a proprietary tester, draw out some of the coolant and check the concentration of the antifreeze

16.2 Unscrew the transmission oil level plug, using a suitable Allen key (arrowed)

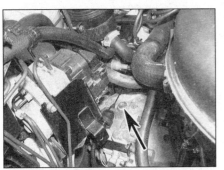

16.3a The transmission oil filler plug (arrowed) is located at the top of the transmission casing

16.3b Unscrew the plug using a suitable Allen key

16.4 Topping-up the transmission

4 Add oil as necessary until a steady trickle of oil can be seen emerging from the level hole **(see illustration)**. Use **only** good-quality synthetic oil of the specified grade. A funnel will be helpful when adding oil to the transmission through the filler plug aperture.

5 When the level is correct, refit and tighten the filler plug (and, where necessary, the level plug) to the specified torque wrench setting. Wipe off any spilt oil.

Automatic transmission

6 The fluid level is checked using the dipstick located on the front of the transmission, on the left-hand side of the engine compartment, beneath the battery location.

7 With the engine idling, select D for approximately 15 seconds, then engage R and wait a further 15 seconds. Do this again in position P, and leave the engine idling.

16.8c Removing the dipstick on later models

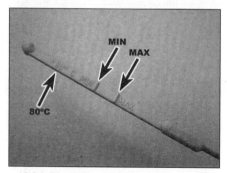

16.8d Dipstick marking on later models

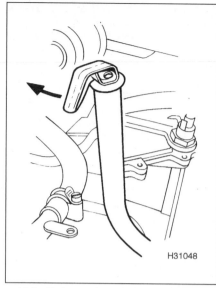

16.8a Release the locking catch (early models only) and withdraw the dipstick from the tube

8 Release the locking catch (early models only) and withdraw the dipstick from the tube. Wipe all the fluid from its end with a clean rag or paper towel. Insert the clean dipstick back into the tube as far as it will go, then withdraw it once more. Note the fluid level on the end of the dipstick – there are two sets of level marks, the lower ones are for a fluid temperature of 20°C, and the upper ones are for a temperature of 80°C **(see illustrations)**. If the engine is at normal operating temperature, use the upper level marks.

9 If topping-up is necessary, add fluid as necessary via the dipstick tube until the level is on the upper mark on the dipstick. **Note:** *Never overfill the transmission so that the fluid level is above the upper mark.* Use a funnel with a fine mesh gauze, to avoid spillage and to ensure that no foreign matter enters the transmission **(see illustration)**. Note that the quantity of oil between the MIN and MAX marks is 0.4 litres.

10 After topping-up, take the car on a short run to distribute the fresh fluid, then recheck the level again, topping-up if necessary.

11 Always maintain the level between the

16.9 Topping-up the automatic transmission fluid level

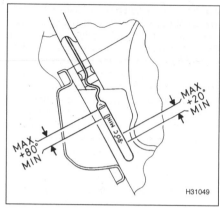

16.8b Note the two sets of level marks on the end of the dipstick (see text for details)

two dipstick marks. If the level is allowed to fall below the lower mark, fluid starvation may result, which could lead to severe transmission damage.

17 Driveshaft joints and gaiters – check

1 With the front of the vehicle raised and securely supported on stands, turn the steering onto full lock then slowly rotate the roadwheel. Inspect the condition of the outer constant velocity (CV) joint rubber gaiters while squeezing the gaiters to open out the folds **(see illustration)**. Check for signs of cracking, splits or deterioration of the rubber which may allow the grease to escape and lead to water and grit entry into the joint. Also check the security and condition of the retaining clips. Repeat these checks on the inner CV joints. If any damage or deterioration is found, the gaiters should be renewed as described in Chapter 8.

2 At the same time check the general condition of the CV joints themselves by first holding the driveshaft and attempting to rotate the wheel. Repeat this check by holding the inner joint and attempting to rotate the driveshaft. Any appreciable movement indicates wear in the joints, wear in the driveshaft splines or a loose driveshaft retaining nut.

17.1 Checking the condition of the driveshaft gaiters

19.0 Acoustic wear warning device fitted to the outer front brake pad

19.2 The brake pad wear can be measured through the aperture in the front brake caliper

18 Exhaust system – check

1 With the engine cold, check the complete exhaust system, from its starting point at the engine to the end of the tailpipe. If necessary, raise the front and rear of the vehicle and support it on axle stands (see *Jacking and vehicle support*). Remove any engine undershields as necessary for full access to the exhaust system.

2 Check the exhaust pipes and connections for evidence of leaks, severe corrosion, and damage. Make sure that all brackets and mountings are in good condition and that all relevant nuts and bolts are tight. Leakage at any of the joints or in other parts of the system will usually show up as a black sooty stain in the vicinity of the leak.

3 Rattles and other noises can often be traced to the exhaust system, especially the brackets and rubber mountings. Try to move the pipes and silencers. If the components are able to come into contact with the body or suspension parts, secure the system with new mountings. Otherwise separate the joints (if possible) and twist the pipes as necessary to provide additional clearance.

19 Front brake pad wear – check

Note: *An acoustic wear warning device is fitted to the outer pad, consisting of a metal strip which contacts the brake disc when the thickness of the friction material is less than 3.0 mm. This device causes a scraping noise which warns the driver that the pads are worn excessively (see illustration).*

1 To check the front brake pads, firmly apply the handbrake, then jack up the front of the vehicle and support it securely on axle stands (see *Jacking and vehicle support*). Remove the front roadwheels.

2 For a quick check, the pad thickness can be checked via the inspection hole on the front of the caliper **(see illustration)**. Using a steel rule, measure the thickness of the pad lining excluding the backing plate. This must not be less than that indicated in the Specifications.

3 The view through the caliper inspection hole gives an indication of the **inner** brake pad wear only. For a comprehensive check, the brake pads should be removed and cleaned. The operation of the caliper can then also be checked, and the condition of the brake disc itself can be fully examined on both sides.

4 If any pad's friction material is worn to the specified thickness or less, *all four pads must be renewed as a set*. Refer to Chapter 9 for details.

5 On completion, refit the roadwheels and lower the vehicle to the ground.

20 Hinges and locks – lubrication

1 Work around the vehicle and lubricate the hinges of the bonnet, doors and tailgate with a light machine oil.

22.2 Unclip and remove the pollen air filter element

2 Lightly lubricate the two bonnet release locks with a smear of grease.

3 Check carefully the security and operation of all hinges, latches and locks. Check that the central locking system operates correctly.

4 Check the condition and operation of the bonnet and tailgate struts, renewing them if either is leaking or no longer able to support the bonnet/tailgate.

21 Plenum chamber drain hose – clean

1 At the rear of the engine compartment, remove the plenum chamber drain hose and clean away any accumulated debris.

2 Refit the drain hose, making sure that it is secure.

22 Pollen air filter – renew

1 Remove the windscreen wiper motor and linkage as described in Chapter 12.

2 Unclip and remove the pollen air filter element **(see illustration)**.

3 With the element removed, clean the plenum chamber drain hoses and the air conditioning drain hoses.

4 Fit the new element using a reversal of the removal procedure.

23 Auxiliary drivebelt condition – check

1 On all engines, a single, multi-grooved auxiliary drivebelt is used to transmit drive from the crankshaft pulley to the coolant pump, alternator, power steering pump and, on models equipped with air conditioning, the refrigerant compressor.

23.2a Remove the lower section of the plastic liner from under the right-hand wheel arch to expose the crankshaft pulley

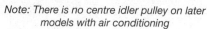
23.2b Remove the air cleaner and its ducting to expose the auxiliary drivebelt.
Note: There is no centre idler pulley on later models with air conditioning

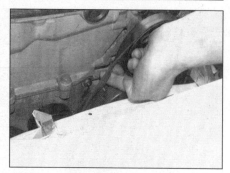
23.3 Examining the auxiliary drivebelt for signs of wear or damage

The drivebelt is guided by one or two idler pulleys and is tensioned automatically by a spring-loaded tensioner pulley.
2 For better access to the drivebelt, apply the handbrake then jack up the front of the car and support it on axle stands (see *Jacking and vehicle support*). Remove the right-hand front roadwheel, then remove the lower section of the plastic liner from under the right-hand wheel arch to expose the crankshaft pulley. Remove the air cleaner and its associated intake air ducting with reference to Chapter 4A **(see illustrations)**.
3 Using a suitable socket and extension bar fitted to the crankshaft pulley bolt, rotate the crankshaft so that the entire length of the drivebelt(s) can be examined. Examine the drivebelt for cracks, splitting, fraying, or other damage **(see illustration)**. Check also for signs of glazing (shiny patches) and for separation of the belt plies. Renew the belt if worn or damaged.

Every 24 000 miles or 2 years

24 Brake fluid – renewal

> ⚠️ **Warning: Brake hydraulic fluid can harm your eyes and damage painted surfaces, so use extreme caution when handling and pouring it. Do not use fluid that has been standing open for some time, as it absorbs moisture from the air. Excess moisture can cause a dangerous loss of braking effectiveness.**

1 The procedure is similar to that for the bleeding of the hydraulic system as described in Chapter 9.
2 Working as described in Chapter 9, open the first bleed screw in the sequence, and pump the brake pedal gently until nearly all the old fluid has been emptied from the master cylinder reservoir. Top-up to the MAX level with new fluid, and continue pumping until only the new fluid remains in the reservoir, and new fluid can be seen emerging from the bleed screw. Tighten the screw, and top the reservoir level up to the MAX level line.
3 Work through all the remaining bleed screws in the sequence until new fluid can be seen at all of them. Be careful to keep the master cylinder reservoir topped-up to above the MIN level at all times, or air may enter the system and greatly increase the length of the task.
4 When the operation is complete, check that all bleed screws are securely tightened, and that their dust caps are refitted. Wash off all traces of spilt fluid, and recheck the master cylinder reservoir fluid level.
5 Check the operation of the brakes before taking the car on the road.

> **HAYNES HiNT** *Old hydraulic fluid is invariably much darker in colour than the new, making it easy to distinguish the two.*

Every 30 000 miles

Note: *The 30 000 mile intervals start at 36 000 miles, ie, at 36 000 miles, 66 000 miles, 96 000 miles, etc.*

25 Spark plugs – renewal

1 The correct functioning of the spark plugs is vital for the correct running and efficiency of the engine. It is essential that the plugs fitted are appropriate for the engine. If this type is used and the engine is in good condition, the spark plugs should not need attention between scheduled renewal intervals.

Models without Direct Ignition

2 Remove the screws, and lift the inspection cover from the centre of the camshaft cover **(see illustrations)**.

25.2a Remove the screws . . .

25.2b . . . and lift the inspection cover from the centre of the camshaft cover

25.3 Cylinder number markings cast into the cylinder head

25.4 Pull the HT leads from the spark plugs by gripping the end fitting, not the lead itself

HAYNES
HiNT

It is very often difficult to insert spark plugs into their holes without cross-threading them. To avoid this possibility, fit a short length of 8 mm internal diameter rubber hose over the end of the spark plug. The flexible hose acts as a universal joint to help align the plug with the plug hole. Should the plug begin to cross-thread, the hose will slip on the spark plug, preventing thread damage to the aluminium cylinder head.

3 If the marks on the spark plug (HT) leads cannot be seen, mark the leads 1 to 4, to correspond to the cylinder the lead serves (No 1 cylinder is at the timing chain end of the engine) **(see illustration)**.

4 Pull the leads from the plugs by gripping the end fitting, not the lead, otherwise the lead connection may be fractured **(see illustration)**. With all the leads disconnected, lift the rubber grommet from the distributor end of the cylinder head, and position the leads to one side.

Models with Direct Ignition

5 Carry out the following operations with reference to Chapter 5B:
a) *Disconnect the wiring multiplug from the flywheel end of the ignition cartridge.*
b) *Unscrew the four screws securing the ignition module to the top of the cylinder head. An Allen key or hex bit will be required for this.*
c) *Where applicable, unscrew the bolt and release the cartridge wiring support clip.*
d) *Where applicable, unscrew the bolt and disconnect the earth lead.*
e) *Carefully lift the ignition cartridge, at the same time releasing it from the tops of the spark plugs.*

All models

6 It is advisable to remove the dirt from the spark plug recesses using a clean brush, vacuum cleaner or compressed air before removing the plugs, to prevent dirt dropping into the cylinders.

7 Unscrew the plugs using a spark plug spanner, suitable box spanner or a deep socket and extension bar. Keep the socket aligned with the spark plug – if it is forcibly moved to one side, the ceramic insulator may be broken off. As each plug is removed, examine it as follows.

8 Examination of the spark plugs will give a good indication of the condition of the engine. If the insulator nose of the spark plug is clean and white, with no deposits, this is indicative of a weak mixture or too hot a plug (a hot plug transfers heat away from the electrode slowly, a cold plug transfers heat away quickly).

9 If the tip and insulator nose are covered with hard black-looking deposits, then this is indicative that the mixture is too rich. Should the plug be black and oily, then it is likely that the engine is fairly worn, as well as the mixture being too rich.

10 If the insulator nose is covered with light tan to greyish-brown deposits, then the mixture is correct, and it is likely that the engine is in good condition.

11 The electrode gap is of considerable importance as, if it is too large or too small, the size of the spark and its efficiency will be seriously impaired. The gap should be set to the value given in the Specifications.

12 To set the gap, measure it with a feeler blade or wire gauge and then bend open, or closed, the outer plug electrode until the correct gap is achieved. The centre electrode should never be bent, as this will crack the insulator and cause plug failure, if nothing

worse. If using feeler blades, the gap is correct when the appropriate-size blade is a firm sliding fit. Note that some models may be fitted with multi-electrode spark plugs – no attempt to adjust the electrode gap should be made on this type of spark plug.

13 Special spark plug electrode gap adjusting tools are available from most motor accessory shops, or from some spark plug manufacturers.

14 Before fitting the spark plugs, check that the threaded connector sleeves are tight, and that the plug exterior surfaces and threads are clean. It is very often difficult to insert spark plugs into their holes without cross-threading them. To avoid this possibility, fit a short length of hose over the end of the spark plug **(see Haynes Hint)**.

15 Remove the rubber hose (if used), and tighten the plug to the specified torque (see Specifications) using the spark plug socket and a torque wrench. Refit the remaining plugs in the same way **(see illustration)**.

16 Where applicable, reconnect the HT leads in the correct firing order (see Specifications)

Models with Direct Ignition

17 Refit the ignition module using a reversal of the removal procedure. Tighten the four screws to the specified torque (see Chapter 5B Specifications).

Models without Direct Ignition

18 Connect the HT leads in their correct order, and refit the rubber grommet. Press the HT lead guides into their respective slots in the cylinder head **(see illustration)**.

19 Refit the inspection cover, and tighten the retaining screws.

25.15 Refit the spark plugs and tighten them to the specified torque

25.18 Press the HT lead guides (arrowed) into their respective slots in the cylinder head

26.1 The air cleaner is located on the front right-hand corner of the engine compartment (non-turbo model shown)

26.2a Remove the evaporative purge valve . . .

26.2b . . . and the air duct leading from the air filter to the turbocharger

26.3 Release the clips and screws, and remove the cover with mass airflow meter from the air cleaner housing (turbo model shown)

26.4a Lifting out the air cleaner filter element – on turbo models . . .

26.4b . . . and non-turbo models

26.5 Wipe out the inner surfaces of the cover and main housing

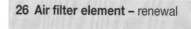

26 Air filter element – renewal

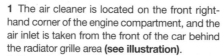

1 The air cleaner is located on the front right-hand corner of the engine compartment, and the air inlet is taken from the front of the car behind the radiator grille area (see illustration).

2 On turbo models, remove the evaporative purge valve from the rear of the air filter cover, then disconnect and remove the air duct leading from the air filter to the turbocharger (see illustrations).

3 Remove the toggle clips and screws, and remove the top cover from the air cleaner filter housing (see illustration).

4 Lift out the air cleaner filter element, noting which way round it is fitted (see illustrations).

5 Wipe clean the inner surfaces of the cover and main housing (see illustration), then locate the new element in the housing, making sure that the sealing lip is correctly engaged with the edge of the housing.

6 Refit the cover, and secure with the toggle clips.

7 Reconnect the air ducting and secure it by tightening the hose clip. Refit the purge valve on turbo models.

Every 48 000 miles

Note: *The 48 000 mile intervals start at 54 000 miles, ie, at 54 000 miles, 102 000 miles, etc.*

27 Automatic transmission fluid – renewal

1 Take the car on a short journey to warm the transmission up to normal operating temperature. Position the car over an inspection pit, or alternatively jack up the front and rear of the car and support on axle stands (see *Jacking and vehicle support*). Whichever method is used, make sure that the car is level for checking the fluid level later.

2 Position a suitable container beneath the transmission, then unscrew the drain plug and allow the fluid to drain. Note that a special adapter key will be required to unscrew the plug.

 Warning: The fluid will be very hot, so take necessary precautions to prevent scalding. The use of thick waterproof gloves is recommended.

3 With all the fluid drained, wipe clean the plug and refit it to the automatic transmission housing. Where applicable fit a new sealing washer. Tighten the plug to the specified torque.

4 Fill the automatic transmission with the specified grade and quantity of fluid. Referring to Section 16, top it up to the correct level. Use the low temperature set of dipstick markings first, then take the car for a run. With the fluid at operating temperature, recheck the fluid level using the high temperature set of dipstick markings.

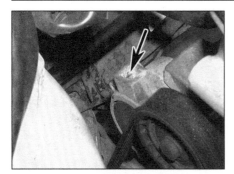

28.3a Insert a 1/2" drive breaker bar or similar into the lug (arrowed) at the top of the front section of the tensioner assembly

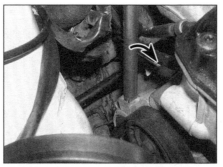

28.3b Rotate the tensioner clockwise, against the spring tension, until the locking lug lines up with the corresponding hole in the rear section of the tensioner assembly

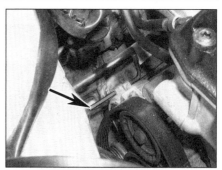

28.4 Use a 6mm drill bit or similar tool to lock the tensioner assembly in position

Every 66 000 miles

Note: *The 66 000 mile intervals start at 72 000 miles, ie, at 72 000 miles, 144 000 miles, etc.*

28 Auxiliary drivebelt – renew

1 On all engines, a single, multi-grooved auxiliary drivebelt is used to transmit drive from the crankshaft pulley to the coolant pump, alternator, power steering pump and, on models equipped with air conditioning, the refrigerant compressor. The drivebelt is guided by one or two idler pulleys and is tensioned automatically by a spring-loaded tensioner pulley.

2 For better access to the drivebelt, apply the handbrake then jack up the front of the car and support it on axle stands (see *Jacking and vehicle support*). Remove the right-hand front roadwheel, then remove the lower section of the plastic liner from under the right-hand wheel arch, to expose the crankshaft pulley. Remove the air cleaner and its associated intake air ducting with reference to Chapter 4A.

3 The tensioner pulley spring must now be compressed and locked in position. Insert a 1/2" drive breaker bar or similar into the lug at the top of the front section of the tensioner assembly. Rotate the tensioner clockwise, against the spring tension, until the locking

28.5 Removing the auxiliary drivebelt from the crankshaft pulley

lug lines up with the corresponding hole in the rear section of the tensioner assembly. Note that the tensioner spring is very strong, and considerable pressure is required to compress it, but **do not** try to force it beyond the limit of its travel **(see illustrations)**.

4 Hold the tensioner in position, then slide a 6mm drill bit (or similar tool) through the tensioner locking lug and engage it with the hole in the rear section of the tensioner assembly **(see illustration)**. Release the effort on the breaker bar slowly, checking that the tensioner remains in the locked position.

5 Slip the drivebelt from the water pump, power steering pump, crankshaft (and, where applicable, the air conditioning compressor) pulleys, then remove it from the engine compartment from the right-hand wheel arch **(see illustration)**.

6 Locate the new drivebelt over all the pulleys, making sure that the multi-grooved side is correctly engaged with the grooves on the pulleys **(see illustration)**.

7 Compress the tensioner spring using a breaker bar as described for the removal procedure. Remove the locking tool and then

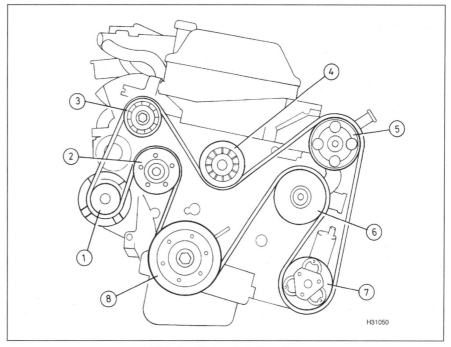

28.6 Auxiliary drivebelt routing

1 Alternator	5 Power steering pump
2 Tensioner	6 Coolant pump
3 Idler pulley	7 Air conditioning refrigerant
4 Idler pulley (not on later models	compressor (where fitted)
with air conditioning)	8 Crankshaft pulley

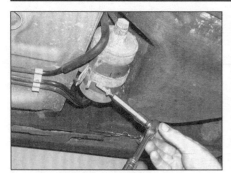

29.6 **Loosen the fuel filter mounting bracket securing screw**

29.7 **Unscrew the banjo coupling bolts from each end of the filter**

29.9 **Make sure that the direction of flow arrow on the filter body is pointing towards the outlet which leads to the engine compartment**

slowly release the tensioner, allowing it to apply pressure to the rear surface of drivebelt.
8 Ensure that the belt is correctly seated on all the pulleys, then start the engine and allow it to idle for a few minutes. This will allow the tensioner to settle in position and distribute the tension evenly throughout the belt. Stop the engine and check once again that the belt is correctly seated on all the pulleys.
9 On completion, refit the plastic wheel arch liner and roadwheel, and then lower the car to the ground.

29 Fuel filter – renewal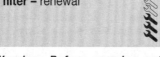

> ⚠ **Warning: Before carrying out the following operation, refer to the precautions given in 'Safety first!' at the beginning of this manual, and follow them implicitly. Petrol is a highly-**

dangerous and volatile liquid, and the precautions necessary when handling it cannot be overstressed.

1 On all models, the fuel filter is mounted adjacent to the fuel tank underneath the rear of the car.
2 Depressurise the fuel system with reference to Chapter 4A.
3 Chock the front wheels, then jack up the rear of the car and support on axle stands (see *Jacking and vehicle support*).
4 Pull off the plastic guard where fitted, then clean the areas around the fuel filter inlet and outlet unions.
5 Position a small container or cloth rags beneath the filter to catch spilt fuel.
6 Loosen the mounting bracket securing screw **(see illustration)**.
7 Unscrew the banjo coupling bolts from each end of the filter, while holding the coupling with a further spanner **(see illustration)**. Recover the sealing washers.
8 Remove the filter from its mounting bracket,

noting the direction of the arrow marked on the filter body, loosen the retaining clip and withdraw the filter from under the car.
9 Locate the new filter in the retaining clip, then fit and tighten the securing screw. Make sure that the direction of flow arrow on the filter body is pointing towards the outlet which leads to the engine compartment **(see illustration)**.
10 Check the condition of the sealing washers, and renew them if necessary.
11 Refit the banjo couplings and hoses to each end of the filter, together with the sealing washers. Tighten the bolts securely, while holding the couplings with a second spanner.
12 Wipe away any excess fuel, refit the plastic cover where fitted, then lower the car to the ground.
13 Start the engine, and check the filter hose connections for leaks.
14 The old filter should be disposed of safely, bearing in mind that it will be highly inflammable.

Every 3 years

30 Coolant – renewal

> ⚠ **Warning: Wait until the engine is cold before starting this procedure. Do not allow antifreeze to come into contact with your skin, or with the painted surfaces of the vehicle. Rinse off spills immediately with plenty of water.**

Cooling system draining

1 With the engine completely cold, remove the expansion tank filler cap. Turn the cap anti-clockwise, wait until any pressure remaining in the system is released, then unscrew it and lift it off.
2 Where applicable, remove the engine undershield, then position a suitable container beneath the left-hand side of the radiator.

3 Loosen the drain plug located on the left-hand lower mounting stub, and allow the coolant to drain into the container **(see illustration)**. If necessary, attach a hose to the drain plug to direct the coolant into the container.
4 When the flow of coolant stops, tighten the drain plug and where necessary refit the undershield.
5 If the coolant has been drained for a reason other than renewal, then provided it is clean and less than two years old, it can be re-used, though this is not recommended.

Cooling system flushing

6 If coolant renewal has been neglected, or if the antifreeze mixture has become diluted, then in time the cooling system may gradually lose efficiency, as the coolant passages become restricted due to rust, scale deposits and other sediment. The cooling system efficiency can be restored by flushing the system clean.

7 The radiator should be flushed independently of the engine, to avoid unnecessary contamination.

Radiator flushing

8 Disconnect the top and bottom hoses and any other relevant hoses from the radiator, with reference to Chapter 3.

30.3 **The drain plug is located on the left-hand side of the radiator**

9 Insert a garden hose into the radiator top inlet. Direct a flow of clean water through the radiator, and continue flushing until clean water emerges from the radiator bottom outlet.

10 If after a reasonable period, the water still does not run clear, the radiator can be flushed with a good proprietary cleaning agent. It is important that the manufacturer's instructions are followed carefully. If the contamination is particularly bad, remove the radiator and insert the hose in the bottom outlet, and reverse-flush the radiator, then refit it.

Engine flushing

11 Remove the thermostat as described in Chapter 3, then temporarily refit the thermostat cover. If the radiator top hose has been disconnected, temporarily reconnect the hose.

12 With the top and bottom hoses disconnected from the radiator, insert a garden hose into the radiator top hose. Direct a clean flow of water through the engine, and continue flushing until clean water emerges from the radiator bottom hose.

13 On completion of flushing, refit the thermostat and reconnect the hoses with reference to Chapter 3.

Cooling system filling

14 Before attempting to fill the cooling system, make sure that all hoses and clips are in good condition, and that the clips are tight. Note that an antifreeze mixture must be used all year round, to prevent corrosion of the engine components.

15 Make sure that the air conditioning (A/C) or automatic climate control (ACC) is switched off. This is to prevent the air conditioning system starting the radiator cooling fan before the engine is at normal temperature when refilling the system.

16 Remove the expansion tank filler cap and slowly fill the system until the coolant level reaches the MAX mark on the side of the expansion tank.

17 Refit and tighten the expansion tank filler cap.

18 Start the engine and set the heater to hot, then run the engine until it reaches normal operating temperature (until the cooling fan cuts in and out). Running the engine at varying speeds will allow the engine to warm-up quickly.

19 Stop the engine, and allow it to cool, then recheck the coolant level with reference to *Weekly checks*. Top-up the level if necessary and refit the expansion tank filler cap. Refit the splash cover beneath the radiator.

Antifreeze mixture

19 The antifreeze should always be renewed at the specified intervals. This is necessary not only to maintain the antifreeze properties, but also to prevent corrosion which would otherwise occur as the corrosion inhibitors become progressively less effective.

20 Always use an ethylene-glycol based antifreeze which is suitable for use in mixed-metal cooling systems. The quantity of antifreeze and levels of protection are given in the Specifications.

21 Before adding antifreeze, the cooling system should be completely drained, preferably flushed, and all hoses checked for condition and security.

22 After filling with antifreeze, a label should be attached to the expansion tank, stating the type and concentration of antifreeze used, and the date installed. Any subsequent topping-up should be made with the same type and concentration of antifreeze.

23 Do not use engine antifreeze in the windscreen/tailgate washer system, as it will cause damage to the vehicle paintwork. A screenwash additive should be added to the washer system in the quantities stated on the bottle.

Chapter 1 Part B:
Routine maintenance and servicing – diesel models

Contents

Degrees of difficulty

Easy, suitable for novice with little experience		**Fairly easy,** suitable for beginner with some experience		**Fairly difficult,** suitable for competent DIY mechanic		**Difficult,** suitable for experienced DIY mechanic		**Very difficult,** suitable for expert DIY or professional	

Lubricants and fluids

See end of *Weekly checks*

Capacities

Engine oil

Drain and refill, with filter change	5.5 litres
Total from dry, including engine oil cooler	5.8 litres
Between dipstick MAX and MIN markings	1.0 litres

Cooling system ... 8.3 litres

Manual transmission

Drain and refill ... 1.9 litres

Braking system

System capacity ... 0.58 litres

Fuel tank

All models ... 68.0 litres

Power assisted steering

System capacity ... 1.0 litres

Cooling system

Antifreeze mixture*:

50% antifreeze	Protection down to -37°C
55% antifreeze	Protection down to -45°C

* Note: *Refer to antifreeze manufacturer for latest recommendations.*

Brakes

Front brake pad friction material minimum thickness	5.0 mm at time of service (acoustic warning at 3.0 mm)
Rear brake pad friction material minimum thickness	5.0 mm

Tyre pressures

Refer to the end of *Weekly checks*

Torque wrench settings

	Nm	lbf ft
Engine oil drain plug	18	13
Manual transmission drain, level and filler plugs	50	37
Wheel bolts	110	80

The maintenance intervals in this manual are provided with the assumption that you will be carrying out the work yourself. These are the minimum maintenance intervals recommended by the manufacturer for vehicles driven daily. If you wish to keep your vehicle in peak condition at all times, you may wish to perform some of these procedures more often. We encourage frequent maintenance, because it enhances the efficiency, performance and resale value of your vehicle.

If the vehicle is driven in dusty areas, used to tow a trailer, or driven frequently at slow speeds (idling in traffic) or on short journeys, more frequent maintenance intervals are recommended.

When the vehicle is new, it should be serviced by a dealer service department (or other workshop recognised by the vehicle manufacturer as providing the same standard of service) in order to preserve the warranty. The vehicle manufacturer may reject warranty claims if you are unable to prove that servicing has been carried out as and when specified, using only original equipment parts or parts certified to be of equivalent quality.

All Saab models are equipped with a service interval display (or Saab Information Display – SID) on the facia, which will indicate TIME FOR SERVICE when a service is due. However, Saab point out that, 'due to the relationship between time and mileage, some operating conditions will make annual service more suitable'.

Every 250 miles or weekly
☐ Refer to *Weekly checks*

Every 6000 miles or 6 months
☐ Engine oil and filter – renewal (Section 3)

At first 6000 miles and thereafter every 12 000 miles or 12 months
Note: *The 12 000 mile intervals start at 18 000 miles, ie, at 18 000 miles, 30 000 miles, 42 000 miles, 54 000 miles, etc.*
☐ Service indicator – resetting (Section 4)
☐ Hoses and fluids – leak check (Section 5)
☐ Steering and suspension components – check (Section 6)
☐ Driveshaft joints and gaiters – check (Section 7)
☐ Fuel filter – drain (Section 8)
☐ Front wheel toe-in – check and adjust (Section 9)
☐ Rear brake pad wear – check (Section 10)
☐ Handbrake – check and adjustment (Section 11)
☐ Seat belt condition – check (Section 12)
☐ Airbag system – check (Section 13)
☐ Headlight beam alignment – check (Section 14)
☐ Power steering fluid level – check (Section 15)
☐ Hinges and locks – lubrication (Section 16)
☐ Plenum chamber drain hose – clean (Section 17)
☐ Road test (Section 18)

Every 18 000 miles or 18 months
Note: *The 18 000 mile intervals start at 24 000 miles ie, at 24 000 miles, 42 000 miles, 60 000 miles, 78 000 miles, etc.*
☐ Coolant antifreeze concentration – check (Section 19)
☐ Transmission lubricant level – check (Section 20)
☐ Fuel filter – renewal (Section 21)
☐ Exhaust system – check (Section 22)
☐ Front brake pad wear – check (Section 23)
☐ Pollen air filter – renew (Section 24)
☐ Mass airflow sensor – clean (Section 25)
☐ Auxiliary drivebelt and tensioner – check (Section 26)

Every 24 000 miles or 2 years
Note: *The interval for this service item is based on time and mileage. It must be carried out every 24 000 miles, or every 2 years, whichever comes sooner.*
☐ Brake fluid – renewal (Section 27)

Every 30 000 miles
Note: *The 30 000 mile intervals start at 36 000 miles, ie, at 36 000 miles, 66 000 miles, 96 000 miles, etc.*
☐ Air filter element – renewal (Section 28)

Every 66 000 miles
Note: *The 66 000 mile intervals start at 72 000 miles, ie, at 72 000 miles, 144 000 miles, etc.*
☐ Auxiliary drivebelt – renew (Section 29)

Every 3 years
☐ Coolant – renewal (Section 30)

Underbonnet view of a diesel model

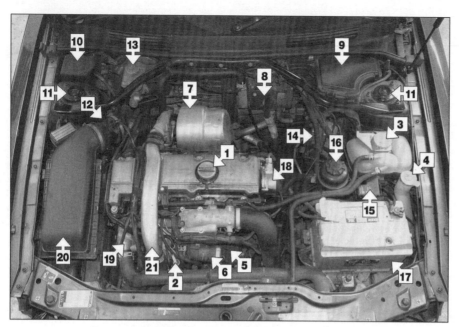

1 Engine oil filler cap
2 Engine oil level dipstick
3 Coolant expansion tank
4 Windscreen washer fluid reservoir
5 Engine oil filter
6 EGR valve
7 Turbocharger
8 Auxiliary heater
9 Engine compartment fusebox
10 Cruise control unit
11 Front suspension strut top mountings
12 Mass airflow meter
13 Hydraulic brake fluid reservoir
14 Brake ABS hydraulic unit
15 Fusible link box
16 Power steering fluid reservoir
17 Battery
18 Brake vacuum pump
19 Thermostat housing
20 Air filter
21 Air duct leading from turbocharger to
   intercooler

Front underbody view of a diesel model

1 Engine oil drain plug
2 Transmission
3 Auxiliary driveshaft
4 Air conditioning compressor
5 Front suspension lower control arm
6 Front suspension radius arm
7 Auxiliary heater exhaust pipe
8 Front suspension anti-roll bar
9 Exhaust front pipe mountings
10 Front exhaust pipe

Rear underbody view

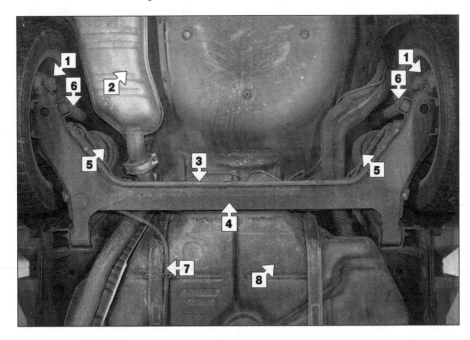

1 Rear brake caliper
2 Exhaust system tail box
3 Rear suspension anti-roll bar
4 Rear suspension beam axle
5 Rear suspension coil spring
6 Rear suspension shock absorber lower mounting
7 Handbrake cable
8 Fuel tank

1 General information

This Chapter is designed to help the home mechanic maintain his/her vehicle for safety, economy, long life and peak performance.

The Chapter contains a master maintenance schedule, followed by Sections dealing specifically with each task in the schedule. Visual checks, adjustments, component renewal and other helpful items are included. Refer to the accompanying illustrations of the engine compartment and the underside of the vehicle for the locations of the various components.

Servicing your vehicle in accordance with the mileage/time maintenance schedule and the following Sections will provide a planned maintenance programme, which should result in a long and reliable service life. This is a comprehensive plan, so maintaining some items, but not others, at the specified service intervals, will not produce the same results.

As you service your vehicle, you will discover that many of the procedures can – and should – be grouped together, because of the particular procedure being performed, or because of the close proximity of two otherwise-unrelated components to one another. For example, if the vehicle is raised for any reason, the exhaust system could be inspected at the same time as the suspension and steering components.

The first step in this maintenance programme is to prepare yourself before the actual work begins. Read through all the Sections relevant to the work to be carried out, then make a list and gather together all the parts and tools required. If a problem is encountered, seek advice from a parts specialist, or a dealer service department.

2 Regular maintenance

If, from the time the vehicle is new, the routine maintenance schedule is followed closely, and frequent checks are made of fluid levels and high-wear items, as suggested throughout this manual, the engine will be kept in relatively good running condition, and the need for additional work will be minimised.

It is possible that there will be times when the engine is running poorly due to the lack of regular maintenance. This is even more likely if a used vehicle, which has not received regular and frequent maintenance checks, is purchased. In such cases, additional work may need to be carried out, outside of the regular maintenance intervals.

If engine wear is suspected, a compression test (refer to Chapter 2B) will provide valuable information regarding the overall performance of the main internal components. Such a test can be used as a basis to decide on the extent of the work to be carried out. If, for example, a compression test indicates serious internal engine wear, conventional maintenance as described in this Chapter will not greatly improve the performance of the engine, and may prove a waste of time and money, unless extensive overhaul work (Chapter 2C) is carried out first.

The following series of operations are those most often required to improve the performance of a generally poor-running engine:

Primary operations

a) Clean, inspect and test the battery ('Weekly checks' and Chapter 5A)
b) Check all the engine-related fluids ('Weekly checks').
c) Check the condition and tension of the auxiliary drivebelt (Section 26).
d) Check the condition of the air filter element, and renew if necessary (Section 28).
e) Renew the fuel filter (Section 21).
f) Check the condition of all hoses, and check for fluid leaks (Section 5).

If the above operations do not prove fully effective, carry out the following secondary operations:

Secondary operations

a) Check the charging system (Chapter 5A).
b) Check the preheating system (Chapter 5C).
c) Check the fuel system (Chapter 4B).

3.4 Removing the oil filler cap

3.5 Engine oil drain plug

As the drain plug releases from the threads, move it away quickly so that the stream of oil running out of the sump goes into the drain pan and not up your sleeve.

Every 6000 miles or 6 months

3 Engine oil and filter – renewal

1 Frequent oil and filter changes are the most important preventative maintenance procedures which can be undertaken by the DIY owner. As engine oil ages, it becomes diluted and contaminated, which leads to premature engine wear.

2 Before starting this procedure, gather together all the necessary tools and materials. Also make sure that you have plenty of clean rags and newspapers handy, to mop-up any spills. Ideally, the engine oil should be warm, as it will drain more easily, and more built-up sludge will be removed with it. Take care not to touch the exhaust or any other hot parts of the engine when working under the vehicle. To avoid any possibility of scalding, and to protect yourself from possible skin irritants and other harmful contaminants in used engine oils, it is advisable to wear gloves when carrying out this work.

3 Firmly apply the handbrake then jack up the front of the vehicle and support it on axle stands (see *Jacking and vehicle support*). Remove the engine undertray where necessary.

4 Remove the oil filler cap **(see illustration)**.

5 Using a spanner, or preferably a suitable socket and bar, slacken the drain plug about half a turn **(see illustration)**. Position the draining container under the drain plug, then remove the plug completely **(see Haynes Hint)**.

6 Allow some time for the oil to drain, noting that it may be necessary to reposition the container as the oil flow slows to a trickle.

7 To gain access to the oil filter housing, first remove the engine top cover.

8 Using a large socket, unscrew the cover and remove it from the top of the oil filter housing **(see illustration)**. Lift out the old filter element.

9 Fit the new filter element to the housing **(see illustration)**.

10 Renew the sealing rings then refit the oil filter cover and tighten it securely **(see illustration)**. Refit the plastic cover to the engine and securely tighten its screws.

11 After all the oil has drained, wipe the drain plug and the sealing washer with a clean rag. Examine the condition of the sealing washer, and renew it if it shows signs of scoring or other damage which may prevent an oil-tight seal. Clean the area around the drain plug opening, and refit the plug complete with the washer and tighten it to the specified torque.

12 Remove the old oil and all tools from under the vehicle then lower the vehicle to the ground.

13 Fill the engine through the filler hole, using the correct oil (refer to *Weekly Checks* for details of topping-up). Pour in half the specified quantity of oil first, then wait a few minutes for the oil to drain into the sump. Continue to add oil, a small quantity at a time, until the level is up to the lower mark on the dipstick. Adding approximately a further 1.0 litre will bring the level up to the upper mark on the dipstick.

14 Start the engine and run it for a few minutes, while checking for leaks around the oil filter seal and the sump drain plug. Note that there may be a delay of a few seconds before the low oil pressure warning light goes out when the engine is first started, as the oil circulates through the new oil filter and the engine oil galleries before the pressure builds-up.

15 Stop the engine, and wait a few minutes for the oil to settle in the sump once more. With the new oil circulated and the filter now completely full, recheck the level on the dipstick, and add more oil as necessary.

16 Dispose of the used engine oil safely with reference to *General repair procedures*.

3.8 Unscrew the oil filter housing cover and lift out the old filter element

3.9 Fit the new filter element to the housing . . .

3.10 . . . then fit the new sealing rings to the cover recesses and refit the cover to the housing

Every 12 000 miles or 12 months

Note: *The 12 000 mile intervals start at 18 000 miles, ie, at 18 000 miles, 30 000 miles, 42 000 miles, 54 000 miles, etc.*

4 Service indicator – resetting

1 The facia-mounted SID (Saab Information Display) system incorporates a service interval indicator. When the distance covered between services approaches the next service, a visual message is displayed. The service indicator is manually reset to zero after the vehicle has been serviced. **Note:** *The indicator is automatically reset after the message has been displayed for 20 times.* The indicator can be reset at any time using the Saab diagnostic tool.

2 On the SID panel, press and hold the CLEAR button (furthermost left) for 8 seconds, then release it **(see illustration)**. During this period, the display should read CLEARED for the first four seconds, followed by SERVICE for the remaining 4 seconds. An audible signal will also be sounded during this time. The service indicator will then be reset.

5 Hoses and fluids – leak check

1 Visually inspect the engine joint faces, gaskets and seals for any signs of water or oil leaks. Pay particular attention to the areas around the cylinder head cover, cylinder head, oil filter and sump joint faces. Bear in mind that, over a period of time, some very slight seepage from these areas is to be expected – what you are really looking for is any indication of a serious leak. Should a leak be found, renew the offending gasket or oil seal by referring to the appropriate Chapters in this manual. Similarly, check for leaks around the transmission casing.

2 Also check the security and condition of all the engine-related pipes and hoses, and

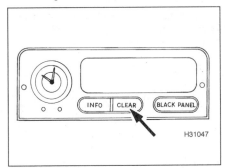

4.2 On the SID panel, press and hold the CLEAR button for 8 seconds, then release it

all braking system pipes and hoses, and fuel lines. Ensure that all cable ties or securing clips are in place, and in good condition. Clips which are broken or missing can lead to chafing of the hoses, pipes or wiring, which could cause more serious problems in the future.

3 Carefully check the radiator hoses and heater hoses along their entire length. Renew any hose which is cracked, swollen or deteriorated. Cracks will show up better if the hose is squeezed. Pay close attention to the hose clips that secure the hoses to the cooling system components. Hose clips can pinch and puncture hoses, resulting in cooling system leaks. If the crimped-type hose clips are used, it may be a good idea to update them with standard worm-drive clips.

4 Inspect all the cooling system components (hoses, joint faces, etc) for leaks **(see Haynes Hint)**.

5 Where any problems are found on system components, renew the component or gasket with reference to Chapter 3.

6 With the vehicle raised, inspect the fuel tank and filler neck for punctures, cracks and other damage. The connection between the filler neck and tank is especially critical. Sometimes a rubber filler neck or connecting hose will leak due to loose retaining clamps or deteriorated rubber.

7 Carefully check all rubber hoses and metal fuel lines leading away from the fuel tank. Check for loose connections, deteriorated hoses, crimped lines, and other damage. Pay particular attention to the vent pipes and hoses, which often loop up around the filler neck and can become blocked or crimped. Follow the lines to the front of the vehicle, carefully inspecting them all the way. Renew damaged sections as necessary. Similarly, whilst the vehicle is raised, take the opportunity to inspect the exhaust system and all underbody brake fluid pipes and hoses.

8 From within the engine compartment, check the security of all fuel, vacuum and brake hose

A leak in the cooling system will usually show up as white- or antifreeze-coloured, crusty deposits around the area of the leak.

attachments and pipe unions, and inspect all hoses for kinks, chafing and deterioration.

9 Check the condition of the power steering fluid pipes and hoses.

6 Steering and suspension components – check

Front suspension and steering

1 Raise the front of the vehicle, and securely support it on axle stands (see *Jacking and vehicle support*).

2 Visually inspect the balljoint dust covers and the steering rack-and-pinion gaiters for splits, chafing or deterioration. Any wear of these components will cause loss of lubricant, together with dirt and water entry, resulting in rapid deterioration of the balljoints or steering gear.

3 Check the power steering fluid hoses for chafing or deterioration, and the pipe and hose unions for fluid leaks. Also check for signs of fluid leakage under pressure from the steering gear rubber gaiters, which would indicate failed fluid seals within the steering gear.

4 Grasp the roadwheel at the 12 o'clock and 6 o'clock positions, and try to rock it **(see illustration)**. Very slight free play may be felt, but if the movement is appreciable, further investigation is necessary to determine the source. Continue rocking the wheel while an assistant depresses the footbrake. If the movement is now eliminated or significantly reduced, it is likely that the hub bearings are at fault. If the free play is still evident with the footbrake depressed, then there is wear in the suspension joints or mountings.

5 Now grasp the wheel at the 9 o'clock and 3 o'clock positions, and try to rock it as before. Any movement felt now may again be caused by wear in the hub bearings or the steering track rod balljoints. If the outer balljoint is worn, the visual movement will be obvious. If the inner joint is suspect, it can be felt by placing a hand over the rack-and-pinion

6.4 Check for wear in the hub bearings by grasping the wheel and trying to rock it

rubber gaiter and gripping the track rod. If the wheel is now rocked, movement will be felt at the inner joint if wear has taken place.

6 Using a large screwdriver or flat bar, check for wear in the suspension mounting bushes by levering between the relevant suspension component and its attachment point. Some movement is to be expected, as the mountings are made of rubber, but excessive wear should be obvious. Also check the condition of any visible rubber bushes, looking for splits, cracks or contamination of the rubber.

7 With the car standing on its wheels, have an assistant turn the steering wheel back-and-forth, about an eighth of a turn each way. There should be very little, if any, lost movement between the steering wheel and roadwheels. If this is not the case, closely observe the joints and mountings previously described. In addition, check the steering column universal joints for wear, and also check the rack-and-pinion steering gear itself.

8 The front suspension mountings should be checked for tightness.

Rear suspension

9 Chock the front wheels, then jack up the rear of the vehicle and support securely on axle stands (see *Jacking and vehicle support*).
10 Working as described previously for the front suspension, check the rear hub bearings, the suspension bushes and the strut or shock absorber mountings (as applicable) for wear.
11 The rear suspension mountings should be checked for tightness.

Shock absorber

12 Check for any signs of fluid leakage around the shock absorber bodies, or from the rubber gaiters around the piston rods. Should any fluid be noticed, the shock absorber is defective internally, and should be renewed. **Note:** *Shock absorbers should always be renewed in pairs on the same axle.*
13 The efficiency of the shock absorber may be checked by bouncing the vehicle at each corner. Generally speaking, the body will return to its normal position and stop after being depressed. If it rises and returns on a rebound, the shock absorber is probably suspect. Also examine the shock absorber upper and lower mountings for any signs of wear.

Removable towbar attachment

14 Where applicable, clean the coupling pin then apply a little grease to the socket. Make sure that the removable towbar attachment fits easily to its mounting and locks correctly in position.

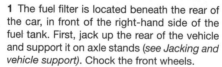

7 Driveshaft joints and gaiters – check

1 With the front of the vehicle raised and securely supported on stands, turn the steering onto full lock then slowly rotate the

7.1 Checking the condition of the driveshaft gaiters

roadwheel. Inspect the condition of the outer constant velocity (CV) joint rubber gaiters while squeezing the gaiters to open out the folds **(see illustration)**. Check for signs of cracking, splits or deterioration of the rubber which may allow the grease to escape and lead to water and grit entry into the joint. Also check the security and condition of the retaining clips. Repeat these checks on the inner CV joints. If any damage or deterioration is found, the gaiters should be renewed as described in Chapter 8.

2 At the same time check the general condition of the CV joints themselves by first holding the driveshaft and attempting to rotate the wheel. Repeat this check by holding the inner joint and attempting to rotate the driveshaft. Any appreciable movement indicates wear in the joints, wear in the driveshaft splines or a loose driveshaft retaining nut.

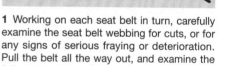

8 Fuel filter – drain

1 The fuel filter is located beneath the rear of the car, in front of the right-hand side of the fuel tank. First, jack up the rear of the vehicle and support it on axle stands (see *Jacking and vehicle support*). Chock the front wheels.
2 Position a suitable container beneath the fuel filter, then unscrew the drain plug and allow the water/condensation to drain.
3 When fuel free of water runs from the filter, refit and tighten the drain plug.
4 Lower the car to the ground.

9 Front wheel toe-in – check and adjust

Refer to Chapter 10, Section 20, for details.

10 Rear brake pad wear – check

1 To check the rear brake pads, firmly apply the handbrake, then jack up the rear of the

vehicle and support it securely on axle stands (see *Jacking and vehicle support*). Remove the rear roadwheels.
2 For a quick check, the pad thickness can be carried out via the inspection hole on the rear of the caliper. Using a steel rule, measure the thickness of the pad lining including the backing plate. This must not be less than that indicated in the Specifications.
3 The view through the caliper inspection hole gives a rough indication of the state of the brake pads. For a comprehensive check, the brake pads should be removed and cleaned. The operation of the caliper can then also be checked, and the condition of the brake disc itself can be fully examined on both sides.
4 If any pad's friction material is worn to the specified thickness or less, *all four pads must be renewed as a set*. Refer to Chapter 9 for details.
5 On completion, refit the roadwheels and lower the vehicle to the ground.

11 Handbrake – check and adjustment

1 Chock the front wheels, then jack up the rear of the vehicle and support on axle stands (see *Jacking and vehicle support*).
2 Fully release the handbrake lever.
3 Apply the lever to the 4th notch position, and check that both rear wheels are locked when attempting to turn them by hand.
4 If adjustment is necessary, refer to Chapter 9.
5 Lower the vehicle to the ground.

12 Seat belt condition – check

1 Working on each seat belt in turn, carefully examine the seat belt webbing for cuts, or for any signs of serious fraying or deterioration. Pull the belt all the way out, and examine the full extent of the webbing.
2 Fasten and unfasten the belt, ensuring that the locking mechanism holds securely, and releases properly when intended. Check also that the retracting mechanism operates correctly when the belt is released.
3 Check the security of all seat belt mountings and attachments which are accessible, without removing any trim or other components, from inside the vehicle.
4 Check the function of the seat belt reminder lamp.

13 Airbag system – check

1 The following work can be carried out by the home mechanic, however, if an electronic fault is apparent, it will be necessary to take the car to a Saab dealer, who will have the necessary diagnostic equipment to extract fault codes from the system.

2 Turn the ignition switch to the drive position (ignition warning lights on), and check that the SRS (Supplementary Restraint System) warning light is illuminated for 3 to 4 seconds. After this period the light should go out, indicating that the system has been checked and is functioning correctly.

3 If the warning light remains on or refuses to light, have the system checked by a Saab dealer.

4 Visually examine the steering wheel centre pad and the passenger airbag module for external damage. Also check the exterior of the front seats around the side airbag locations. If damage is evident, consult a Saab dealer.

5 In the interests of safety, make sure that there are no loose items inside the car which could be thrown onto the airbag modules in the event of an accident.

14 Headlight beam alignment – check

Refer to Chapter 12 for details

15 Power steering fluid level – check
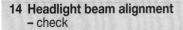

1 The power steering fluid reservoir is located on the left-hand side of the engine compartment behind the battery **(see illustration)**. The fluid level should be checked with the engine stopped.

2 Unscrew the filler cap from the top of the reservoir, and wipe all fluid from the cap dipstick with a clean rag. Refit the filler cap, then remove it again. Note the fluid level on the dipstick **(see illustration)**.

3 When the engine is cold, the fluid level should be between the upper MAX and lower MIN marks on the dipstick. Where only one mark is provided, the level should be between the bottom of the dipstick and the mark **(see illustration)**.

4 Top-up the fluid level using the specified type of fluid (do not overfill the reservoir), then refit and tighten the filler cap **(see illustration)**.

16 Hinges and locks – lubrication

1 Work around the vehicle and lubricate the hinges of the bonnet, doors and tailgate with a light machine oil.

2 Lightly lubricate the two bonnet release locks with a smear of grease.

3 Check carefully the security and operation of all hinges, latches and locks. Check that the central locking system operates correctly.

4 Check the condition and operation of the

15.1 Power steering fluid reservoir location

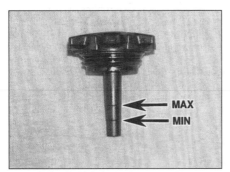

15.3 MIN and MAX marks on the filler cap

bonnet and tailgate struts, renewing them if either is leaking or no longer able to support the bonnet/tailgate.

17 Plenum chamber drain hose – clean

1 At the rear of the engine compartment, remove the plenum chamber drain hose and clean away any accumulated debris.

2 Refit the drain hose, making sure that it is secure.

18 Road test

Instruments and electrical equipment

1 Check the operation of all instruments and electrical equipment.

2 Make sure that all instruments read correctly, and switch on all electrical equipment in turn to check that it functions properly. Check the function of the heating, air conditioning and automatic climate control systems.

Steering and suspension

3 Check for any abnormalities in the steering, suspension, handling or road 'feel'.

4 Drive the vehicle, and check that there are no unusual vibrations or noises.

5 Check that the steering feels positive, with no excessive 'sloppiness', or roughness,

15.2 Unscrewing the filler cap

15.4 Topping-up the fluid level

and check for any suspension noises when cornering, or when driving over bumps. Check that the power steering system operates correctly.

Drivetrain

6 Check the performance of the engine, clutch (manual transmission), transmission and driveshafts. Check that the turbo boost pressure needle moves up to the upper limit during sharp acceleration. The needle may occasionally enter the red zone for an instant, but if this happens frequently, or for extended periods, a problem may exist within the turbo boost control mechanism (see Chapter 4B).

7 Listen for any unusual noises from the engine, clutch (manual transmission) and transmission.

8 Make sure that the engine runs smoothly when idling, and that there is no hesitation when accelerating.

9 On manual transmission models, check that the clutch action is smooth and progressive, that the drive is taken up smoothly, and that the pedal travel is correct. Also listen for any noises when the clutch pedal is depressed. Check that all gears can be engaged smoothly, without noise, and that the gear lever action is smooth and not abnormally vague or 'notchy'.

10 Listen for a metallic clicking sound from the front of the vehicle, as the vehicle is driven slowly in a circle with the steering on full lock. Carry out this check in both directions. If a clicking noise is heard, this indicates wear in a driveshaft joint, in which case, refer to Chapter 8.

Braking system

11 Make sure that the vehicle does not pull to one side when braking, and that the wheels do not lock when braking hard.
12 Check that there is no vibration through the steering when braking.
13 Check that the handbrake operates correctly, without excessive movement of the lever, and that it holds the vehicle stationary on a slope.
14 Test the operation of the brake servo unit as follows. With the engine off, depress the footbrake four or five times to exhaust the vacuum, then start the engine while holding the brake pedal depressed. As the engine starts, there should be a noticeable 'give' in the brake pedal as vacuum builds-up. Allow the engine to run for at least two minutes, and then switch it off. If the brake pedal is now depressed again, it should be possible to detect a 'hiss' from the servo as the pedal is depressed. After about four or five applications, no further sound should be heard, and the pedal should feel considerably harder.

Every 18 000 miles or 18 months

Note: *The 18 000 mile intervals start at 24 000 miles ie, at 24 000 miles, 42 000 miles, 60 000 miles, 78 000 miles, etc.*

19 Coolant antifreeze concentration – check

1 The cooling system should be filled with the recommended antifreeze and corrosion protection fluid. Over a period of time, the concentration of fluid may be reduced due to topping-up (this can be avoided by topping-up with the correct antifreeze mixture) or fluid loss. If loss of coolant has been evident, it is important to make the necessary repair before adding fresh fluid. The exact mixture of antifreeze-to-water which you should use depends on the relative weather conditions. The mixture should contain at least 40% antifreeze, but not more than 70%. Consult the mixture ratio chart on the antifreeze container before adding coolant. Hydrometers are available at most automotive accessory shops to test the coolant. Use antifreeze which meets the vehicle manufacturer's specifications.
2 With the engine **cold**, carefully remove the cap from the expansion tank. If the engine is not completely cold, place a cloth rag over the cap before removing it, and remove it slowly to allow any pressure to escape.
3 Antifreeze checkers are available from car accessory shops. Draw some coolant from the expansion tank and observe how many plastic balls are floating in the checker **(see illustration)**. Usually, 2 or 3 balls must be floating for the correct concentration of antifreeze, but follow the manufacturer's instructions.
4 If the concentration is incorrect, it will be necessary to either withdraw some coolant and add antifreeze, or alternatively drain the old coolant and add fresh coolant of the correct concentration.

19.3 Using a proprietary tester, draw out some of the coolant and check the concentration of the antifreeze

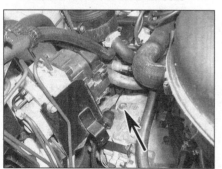

20.3a The transmission oil filler plug (arrowed) is located at the top of the transmission casing

20.2 Unscrew the transmission oil level plug, using a suitable Allen key (arrowed)

20.3b Unscrew the plug using a suitable Allen key

20 Transmission lubricant level – check

Note: *Saab do not specify an interval for checking the oil level on manual transmission models, however, we recommend making the check every 18 000 miles or 18 months.*
1 Make sure that the car is parked on a level surface. Wipe clean the area around the level plug, which is located on the left hand side of the differential casing at the rear of the transmission, behind the left-hand driveshaft. Access to the plug can be gained from the engine compartment or, alternatively, chock the rear wheels and firmly apply the handbrake, then jack up the front of the vehicle and support it on axle stands (*see Jacking and vehicle support),* but note that the vehicle must be level when making the check.
2 Unscrew the level plug, using a suitable Allen key or hex bit, and wipe it clean **(see illustration)**. The oil level should reach the lower edge of the level hole. A certain amount of oil will have gathered behind the level plug, and will trickle out when it is removed; this does **not** necessarily indicate that the level is correct. To ensure that a true level is established, wait until the initial trickle has stopped, then use a length of clean wire, bent into a right angle, as a dipstick.
3 If the oil level requires topping-up, wipe clean the area around the filler plug, which is located on top of the transmission. Unscrew the plug, and wipe it clean **(see illustrations)**.
4 Add oil as necessary until a steady trickle of oil can be seen emerging from the level hole **(see illustration)**. Use **only** good-

20.4 Topping-up the transmission

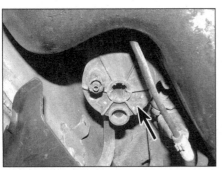

21.1 The fuel filter is located beneath the rear of the car

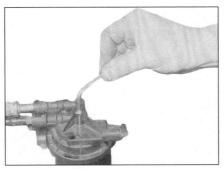

21.5a Unscrew the through-bolt . . .

21.5b . . . and remove the filter cover . . .

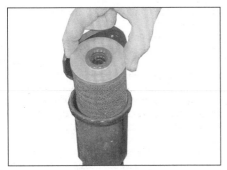

21.5c . . . and canister

21.6a Check the cover sealing ring for signs of damage

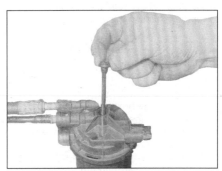

21.6b Refit the through-bolt, ensuring the sealing ring is in position

quality synthetic oil of the specified grade. A funnel will be helpful when adding oil to the transmission through the filler plug aperture.

5 When the level is correct, refit and tighten the filler plug (and, where necessary, the level plug) to the specified torque wrench setting. Wipe off any spilt oil.

21 Fuel filter – renewal

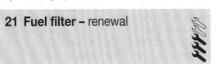

1 The fuel filter is located beneath the rear of the car, in front of the right-hand side of the fuel tank **(see illustration)**. First, jack up the rear of the vehicle and support it on axle stands (*see Jacking and vehicle support*). Chock the front wheels.

2 Remove the plastic cover, then use a small drift to remove the holder from the bracket. Take care not to strain the filter heating wiring.

3 Fit hose clamps to the filter inlet and outlet hoses.

4 Position a container beneath the filter, then unscrew the lower drain plug and drain the fuel – loosening the upper through-bolt will speed up the draining. Discard the seals as new ones must be fitted. Tighten the lower drain plug.

5 Unscrew the upper through-bolt and remove the filter cover and canister **(see illustrations)**.

6 Clean the filter bowl and spring, then fit the new filter and seals using a reversal of the removal procedure **(see illustrations)**.

7 Start the engine and check for leaks. The fuel lines will purge themselves of air.

8 Lower the car to the ground.

22 Exhaust system – check

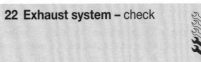

1 With the engine cold, check the complete exhaust system, from its starting point at the engine to the end of the tailpipe. If necessary, raise the front and rear of the vehicle and support it on axle stands (see *Jacking and vehicle support*). Remove any engine undershields as necessary for full access to the exhaust system.

2 Check the exhaust pipes and connections for evidence of leaks, severe corrosion, and damage. Make sure that all brackets and mountings are in good condition and that all relevant nuts and bolts are tight. Leakage at any of the joints or in other parts of the system will usually show up as a black sooty stain in the vicinity of the leak.

3 Rattles and other noises can often be traced to the exhaust system, especially the brackets and rubber mountings. Try to move the pipes and silencers. If the components are able to come into contact with the body or suspension parts, secure the system with new mountings. Otherwise separate the joints (if possible) and twist the pipes as necessary to provide additional clearance.

23 Front brake pad wear – check

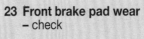

Note: *An acoustic wear warning device is fitted to the outer pad, consisting of a metal strip which contacts the brake disc when the thickness of the friction material is less than 3.0 mm. This device causes a scraping noise which warns the driver that the pads are worn excessively* **(see illustration)**.

1 To check the front brake pads, firmly apply the handbrake, then jack up the front of the vehicle and support it securely on axle stands (see *Jacking and vehicle support*). Remove the front roadwheels.

2 For a quick check, the pad thickness can be checked via the inspection hole on the front

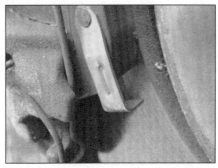

23.0 Acoustic wear warning device fitted to the outer front brake pad

of the caliper **(see illustration)**. Using a steel rule, measure the thickness of the pad lining excluding the backing plate. This must not be less than that indicated in the Specifications.

3 The view through the caliper inspection hole gives an indication of the **inner** brake pad wear only. For a comprehensive check, the brake pads should be removed and cleaned. The operation of the caliper can then also be checked, and the condition of the brake disc itself can be fully examined on both sides.

4 If any pad's friction material is worn to the specified thickness or less, *all four pads must be renewed as a set.* Refer to Chapter 9 for details.

5 On completion, refit the roadwheels and lower the vehicle to the ground.

24 Pollen air filter – renew

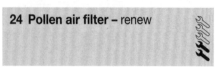

1 Remove the windscreen wiper motor and linkage as described in Chapter 12.

2 Unclip and remove the pollen air filter element **(see illustration)**.

3 With the element removed, clean the plenum chamber drain hoses and the air conditioning drain hoses.

4 Fit the new element using a reversal of the removal procedure.

25 Mass airflow sensor – clean

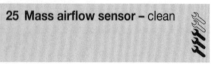

Note: *Saab recommend that electronics cleaner 30 04 223 be used for this procedure.*

1 The mass airflow sensor is located in a housing at the air cleaner outlet. First make sure that the ignition is switched off.

2 Mark the sensor and housing in relation to each other to ensure correct refitting, then

23.2 The brake pad wear can be measured through the aperture in the front brake caliper

disconnect the wiring. **Note**: *The sensor is calibrated in this position and must therefore be refitted in the identical place.*

3 Using a 'safety' Torx key (ie, with centre hole), unscrew the sensor mounting screws, and withdraw the sensor.

4 Clean the sensor thoroughly, then dry using air pressure preferably from an airline. The sensor is delicate, and the air pressure should not be directed closer than 30 cm.

5 Repeat the cleaning 2 or 3 times, then lubricate the sensor seal with petroleum jelly, and refit it to the housing, making sure that the previously-made marks are aligned. Tighten the screws securely.

6 Reconnect the wiring.

26 Auxiliary drivebelt and tensioner – check

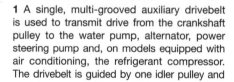

1 A single, multi-grooved auxiliary drivebelt is used to transmit drive from the crankshaft pulley to the water pump, alternator, power steering pump and, on models equipped with air conditioning, the refrigerant compressor. The drivebelt is guided by one idler pulley and

24.2 Unclip and remove the pollen air filter element

is tensioned automatically by a spring-loaded tensioner pulley.

2 For better access to the drivebelt, apply the handbrake then jack up the front of the car and support it on axle stands (see *Jacking and vehicle support*). Remove the right-hand front roadwheel, then remove the lower section of the plastic liner from under the right-hand wheel arch to expose the crankshaft pulley. Remove the air cleaner and its associated intake air ducting with reference to Chapter 4B.

3 Using a suitable socket and extension bar fitted to the crankshaft pulley bolt, rotate the crankshaft so that the entire length of the drivebelt can be examined. Examine the drivebelt for cracks, splitting, fraying, or other damage. Check also for signs of glazing (shiny patches) and for separation of the belt plies.

4 Check the drivebelt pulleys for nicks, cracks, distortion and corrosion.

5 If the belt shows signs of wear or damage, it must be renewed.

6 To check the drivebelt tensioner, turn the tensioner anti-clockwise as far as possible using a socket on the special hexagon, then release it and check that it returns to its original position, making sure that the belt is correctly located in the multi-grooves. It the tensioner has any tight spots or fails to return fully, it must be renewed.

Every 24 000 miles or 2 years

27 Brake fluid – renewal

> ⚠ **Warning: Brake hydraulic fluid can harm your eyes and damage painted surfaces, so use extreme caution when handling and pouring it. Do not use fluid that has been standing open for some time, as it absorbs moisture from the air. Excess moisture can cause a dangerous loss of braking effectiveness.**

1 The procedure is similar to that for the

bleeding of the hydraulic system as described in Chapter 9.

2 Working as described in Chapter 9, open the first bleed screw in the sequence, and pump the brake pedal gently until nearly all the old fluid has been emptied from the master cylinder reservoir. Top-up to the MAX level with new fluid, and continue pumping until only the new fluid remains in the reservoir, and new fluid can be seen emerging from the

HAYNES HINT *Old hydraulic fluid is invariably much darker in colour than the new, making it easy to distinguish the two.*

bleed screw. Tighten the screw, and top the reservoir level up to the MAX level line.

3 Work through all the remaining bleed screws in the sequence until new fluid can be seen at all of them. Be careful to keep the master cylinder reservoir topped-up to above the MIN level at all times, or air may enter the system and greatly increase the length of the task.

4 When the operation is complete, check that all bleed screws are securely tightened, and that their dust caps are refitted. Wash off all traces of spilt fluid, and recheck the master cylinder reservoir fluid level.

5 Check the operation of the brakes before taking the car on the road.

Every 30 000 miles

Note: *The 30 000 mile intervals start at 36 000 miles, ie, at 36 000 miles, 66 000 miles, 96 000 miles, etc.*

28 Air filter element – renewal

1 The air cleaner is located on the front right-hand corner of the engine compartment, and the air inlet is taken from the front of the car behind the radiator grille area.
2 Release the toggle clips **(see illustration)**, and remove the top cover from the air cleaner filter housing.
3 Lift out the air cleaner filter element,

28.2 Release the toggle clips . . .

noting which way round it is fitted **(see illustration)**.
4 Wipe clean the inner surfaces of the cover and main housing, then locate the new element in the housing, making sure that the

28.3 . . . then remove the top cover and lift out the air cleaner filter element

sealing lip is correctly engaged with the edge of the housing.
5 Refit the cover, and secure with the toggle clips.
6 Reconnect the air ducting and secure it by tightening the hose clip.

Every 66 000 miles

Note: *The 66 000 mile intervals start at 72 000 miles, ie, at 72 000 miles, 144 000 miles, etc.*

29 Auxiliary drivebelt – renew

1 Remove the air cleaner housing as described in Chapter 4B.
2 Firmly apply the handbrake then jack up the front of the vehicle and support it on axle stands (see *Jacking and vehicle support*). Remove the engine undertray. To improve access, remove the right-hand front roadwheel and inner wheel arch liner.
3 Prior to removal make a note of the correct routing of the belt around the various pulleys **(see illustrations)**. If the belt is to be re-used, also mark the direction of rotation on the belt to ensure the belt is refitted the same way around.

4 Using a suitable spanner or socket fitted to the special hexagonal section on the tensioner pulley backplate, lever the tensioner anti-clockwise away from the belt until there is sufficient slack to enable the belt to be slipped off the pulleys **(see illustration)**. Carefully release the tensioner pulley until it is against its stop then remove the belt from the vehicle.
5 If the tensioner is being renewed, unbolt the bracket and damper from the timing cover.
6 Manoeuvre the belt into position, routing it correctly around the pulleys; if the original belt is being fitted, use the marks made prior to removal to ensure it is fitted the correct way around.
7 Lever the tensioner roller back against its spring, and seat the belt on the pulleys. Ensure the belt is centrally located on all pulleys then slowly release the tensioner pulley until the belt is correctly tensioned.
8 Refit the wheel arch cover, roadwheel and

engine undertray, then lower the vehicle to the ground and tighten the wheel bolts to the specified torque
9 Refit the air cleaner housing as described in Chapter 4B.

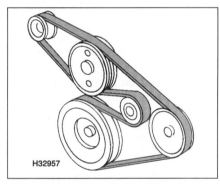

29.3a Auxiliary drivebelt configuration on models without air conditioning

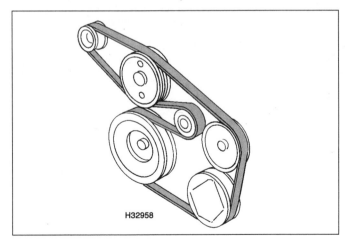

29.3b Auxiliary drivebelt configuration on models with air conditioning

29.4 Release the drivebelt tension and slip the belt off the pulleys

Every 3 years

30 Coolant – renewal

⚠ **Warning: Wait until the engine is cold before starting this procedure. Do not allow antifreeze to come into contact with your skin, or with the painted surfaces of the vehicle. Rinse off spills immediately with plenty of water.**

Cooling system draining

1 With the engine completely cold, remove the expansion tank filler cap. Turn the cap anti-clockwise, wait until any pressure remaining in the system is released, then unscrew it and lift it off.

2 Where applicable, remove the engine undershield, then position a suitable container beneath the left-hand side of the radiator.

3 Loosen the drain plug located on the left-hand lower mounting stub, and allow the coolant to drain into the container **(see illustration)**. If necessary, attach a hose to the drain plug to direct the coolant into the container.

4 When the flow of coolant stops, tighten the drain plug and where necessary refit the undershield.

5 If the coolant has been drained for a reason other than renewal, then provided it is clean and less than two years old, it can be re-used, though this is not recommended.

Cooling system flushing

6 If coolant renewal has been neglected, or

30.3 The drain plug is located on the left-hand side of the radiator

if the antifreeze mixture has become diluted, then in time the cooling system may gradually lose efficiency, as the coolant passages become restricted due to rust, scale deposits and other sediment. The cooling system efficiency can be restored by flushing the system clean.

7 The radiator should be flushed independently of the engine, to avoid unnecessary contamination.

Radiator flushing

8 Disconnect the top and bottom hoses and any other relevant hoses from the radiator, with reference to Chapter 3.

9 Insert a garden hose into the radiator top inlet. Direct a flow of clean water through the radiator, and continue flushing until clean water emerges from the radiator bottom outlet.

10 If after a reasonable period, the water still does not run clear, the radiator can be flushed with a good proprietary cleaning agent. It is important that the manufacturer's instructions are followed carefully. If the contamination is particularly bad, remove the radiator and insert the hose in the bottom outlet, and reverse-flush the radiator, then refit it.

Engine flushing

11 Remove the thermostat as described in Chapter 3, then temporarily refit the thermostat cover. If the radiator top hose has been disconnected, temporarily reconnect the hose.

12 With the top and bottom hoses disconnected from the radiator, insert a garden hose into the radiator top hose. Direct a clean flow of water through the engine, and continue flushing until clean water emerges from the radiator bottom hose.

13 On completion of flushing, refit the thermostat and reconnect the hoses with reference to Chapter 3.

Cooling system filling

14 Before attempting to fill the cooling system, make sure that all hoses and clips are in good condition, and that the clips are tight. Note that an antifreeze mixture must be used all year round, to prevent corrosion of the engine components.

15 Make sure that the air conditioning (A/C) or automatic climate control (ACC) is switched off. This is to prevent the air conditioning system starting the radiator cooling fan before the engine is at normal temperature when refilling the system.

16 Remove the expansion tank filler cap and slowly fill the system until the coolant level reaches the MAX mark on the side of the expansion tank.

17 Refit and tighten the expansion tank filler cap.

18 Start the engine and set the heater to hot, then run the engine until it reaches normal operating temperature (until the cooling fan cuts in and out). Running the engine at varying speeds will allow the engine to warm-up quickly.

19 Stop the engine, and allow it to cool, then recheck the coolant level with reference to *Weekly checks*. Top-up the level if necessary and refit the expansion tank filler cap. Refit the splash cover beneath the radiator.

Antifreeze mixture

20 The antifreeze should always be renewed at the specified intervals. This is necessary not only to maintain the antifreeze properties, but also to prevent corrosion which would otherwise occur as the corrosion inhibitors become progressively less effective.

21 Always use an ethylene-glycol based antifreeze which is suitable for use in mixed-metal cooling systems. The quantity of antifreeze and levels of protection are given in the Specifications.

22 Before adding antifreeze, the cooling system should be completely drained, preferably flushed, and all hoses checked for condition and security.

23 After filling with antifreeze, a label should be attached to the expansion tank, stating the type and concentration of antifreeze used, and the date installed. Any subsequent topping-up should be made with the same type and concentration of antifreeze.

24 Do not use engine antifreeze in the windscreen/tailgate washer system, as it will cause damage to the vehicle paintwork. A screenwash additive should be added to the washer system in the quantities stated on the bottle.

Chapter 2 Part A:
Petrol engine in-car repair procedures

Contents

Degrees of difficulty

| Easy, suitable for novice with little experience | 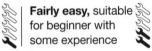 | Fairly easy, suitable for beginner with some experience | | Fairly difficult, suitable for competent DIY mechanic | | Difficult, suitable for experienced DIY mechanic | | Very difficult, suitable for expert DIY or professional | |

Specifications

General

Engine type.	Four-cylinder, in-line, water-cooled. Chain-driven, 16 valve, DOHC (double overhead camshaft), acting on hydraulic tappets
Designation:	
1985 cc non-turbo engine	B204i
1985 cc low-pressure turbo engine	B204E or B205E
1985 cc Stage 1 turbo engine	B204L or B205L
1985 cc Stage 2 turbo engine	B204R or B205R
2290 cc non-turbo engine	B234i
2290 cc Stage 2 turbo engine	B235R
Bore	90.00 mm
Stroke:	
1985 cc engine.	78.00 mm
2290 cc engine.	90.00 mm
Direction of crankshaft rotation	Clockwise (viewed from right-hand side of vehicle)
No 1 cylinder location.	At timing chain end of engine
Compression ratio:	
B205E/L/R	8.8 : 1
B235R	9.3 : 1
Maximum power/torque:	
B204i	96 kW (130 bhp) @ 6100 rpm/177 Nm @ 4300 rpm
B204E/L	114 kW (155 bhp) @ 5500 rpm/219 Nm @ 3600 rpm
B205E	110 kW (150 bhp) @ 5500 rpm/240 Nm @ 1800-3500 rpm
B205L:	
Manual transmission.	136 kW (185 bhp) @ 5500 rpm/263 Nm @ 2100 rpm
Automatic transmission.	136 kW (185 bhp) @ 5500 rpm/250 Nm @ 1900 rpm
B204R and B205R:	
Manual transmission.	151 kW (205 bhp) @ 5500 rpm/280 Nm @ 2200 rpm
Automatic transmission	151 kW (205 bhp) @ 5750 rpm/250 Nm @ 1900 rpm
B234i	110 kW (150 bhp) @ 5700 rpm/210 Nm @ 4300 rpm
B235R	171 kW (230 bhp) @ 5500 rpm/350 Nm @ 4000 rpm

Engine codes

Note: *The engine code is situated on the front of the engine at the transmission end, stamped directly onto the cylinder block.*

Character 1:

B . . . . Petrol engine

Characters 2 & 3:

20 . . . . 1985 cc

23 . . . . 2290 cc

Character 4:

4 . . . . 4 cylinders, in-line block with 2 balancer shafts, double overhead camshafts with 4 valves per cylinder

5 . . . . 4 cylinders, in-line block with 2 balancer shafts, double overhead camshafts with 4 valves per cylinder, low-friction engine

Character 5:

i . . . . Fuel injection engine, non-turbo

E . . . . Low-pressure turbocharged engine with intercooler

L . . . . Turbocharged engine with intercooler – Stage 1

R . . . . Turbocharged engine with intercooler – Stage 2

Character 6:

1 . . . . Saab 9-3 with exhaust emission control ECE-R15/04

3, 5 and 7 . . . . Saab 9-3 with exhaust emission control to European, Swedish and US standards

Character 7:

A . . . . Automatic transmission

M . . . . Manual transmission

Characters 8 & 9:

00 . . . . Basic engine

18 . . . . Engine adapted for automatic

19 . . . . Engine with oil cooler

20 . . . . Engine with OBD II

Character 10:

W 1998

X 1999

Y 2000

1 2001

2 2002

Characters 11 to 16 . . . . Serial numbers

Camshafts

Drive . . . . Chain from crankshaft

Number of bearings . . . . 5 per camshaft

Camshaft bearing journal diameter (outside diameter) . . . . 28.922 to 28.935 mm

Endfloat . . . . 0.08 to 0.35 mm

Lubrication system

Oil pump type. . . . . Bi-rotor type in timing cover, driven off the crankshaft

Minimum oil pressure at 80°C . . . . 2.5 bars at 2000 rpm, using 10W30 engine oil

Oil pressure warning switch operating pressure . . . . 0.3 to 0.5 bar

Clearance between pump outer rotor and timing cover housing. . . . . . 0.03 to 0.08 mm

Pressure release valve opens at. . . . . 3.8 bar

Oil cooler thermostat opens at. . . . . 105°C approximately

Torque wrench settings

	Nm	lbf ft
Balancer shaft chain idler sprocket	25	18
Balancer shaft chain tensioner	10	7
Balancer shaft housing to block	10	7
Big-end bearing cap nuts:		
Stage 1	20	15
Stage 2	Angle-tighten a further 70°	
Camshaft bearing cap	15	11
Camshaft sprockets	63	46
Coolant pipe	25	18
Crankshaft pulley bolt	175	129
Cylinder head bolts:		
Stage 1	40	30
Stage 2	60	44
Stage 3	Angle-tighten a further 90°	
Cylinder head cover	15	11

Torque wrench settings (continued)

	Nm	lbf ft
Engine mountings:		
RH mounting centre bolt to bracket	39	29
RH mounting to body	73	54
LH mounting to bracket	39	29
LH mounting to body	73	54
Rear mounting to bracket/subframe	85	63
Rear mounting centre nut	45	33
Engine oil drain plug	25	18
Engine subframe:		
Front	115	85
Centre	190	140
Rear:		
Stage 1	110	81
Stage 2	Angle-tighten a further 75°	
Engine-to-transmission bolts	70	52
Flywheel/driveplate:		
Stage 1	20	15
Stage 2	Angle-tighten a further 50°	
Main bearing cap bolts:		
Stage 1	20	15
Stage 2	Angle-tighten a further 70°	
Oil cooler hose unions	8	6
Oil cooler thermostat plug	60	44
Piston cooling jet	18	13
Plug for oil pressure reducing valve	30	22
Subframe:		
Front	115	85
Centre	190	140
Rear:		
Stage 1	110	81
Stage 2	Angle-tighten a further 75°	
Sump bolts	22	16
Timing chain guide	10	7
Timing chain tensioner body	63	46
Timing chain tensioner spring plug	23	17
Timing cover:		
To cylinder block	22	16
To cylinder head	24	18

1 General information

How to use this Chapter

Chapter 2 is divided into three Parts: A, B and C. Repair operations that can be carried out with the engine in the vehicle are described in Part A (petrol engines), and Part B (diesel engines). Part C covers the removal of the engine/transmission as a unit, and describes the engine dismantling and overhaul procedures.

In Parts A and B, the assumption is made that the engine is installed in the vehicle, with all ancillaries connected. If the engine has been removed for overhaul, the preliminary dismantling information which precedes each operation may be ignored.

Note that, while it may be possible to overhaul items such as the piston/connecting rod assemblies while the engine is in the car, such tasks are not normally carried out as separate operations. Usually, several additional procedures (including the cleaning of components and of oilways) have to be carried out, and these are more easily carried out with the engine removed from the vehicle. For this reason, all such tasks are classed as major overhaul procedures, and are described in Part C of this Chapter.

Engine description

The engine is of in-line four-cylinder, double-overhead camshaft (DOHC), 16-valve type, mounted transversely at the front of the car with the transmission attached to its left-hand end. The Saab 9-3 is fitted with 1985 cc or 2290 cc engine versions which have balancer shafts, located on each side of the cylinder block, to smooth out vibrations. All engines are controlled by full engine management systems; a variant of the Bosch Motronic system is fitted to normally-aspirated models, and the Saab-manufactured Trionic engine management system is fitted to turbo models; see Chapter 4A for further details.

The crankshaft runs in five main bearings. Thrustwashers are fitted to the centre main bearing (upper half only) to control crankshaft endfloat.

The connecting rods rotate on horizontally-split bearing shells at their big-ends. The pistons are attached to the connecting rods by fully-floating gudgeon pins, which are retained in the pistons by circlips. The aluminium-alloy pistons are fitted with three piston rings – two compression rings and an oil control ring.

The cylinder block is of cast-iron, and the cylinder bores are an integral part of the cylinder block. The inlet and exhaust valves are closed by coil springs, and operate in guides pressed into the cylinder head; the valve seat inserts are also pressed into the cylinder head, and can be renewed separately if worn. There are four valves per cylinder.

The camshafts are driven by a single-row timing chain, and they operate the 16 valves via hydraulic cam followers. The hydraulic cam followers maintain a predetermined clearance between the cam lobe and the end of the valve stem, using hydraulic chambers and a tension spring. The followers are fed with oil from the main engine lubrication circuit.

The balancer shafts are driven in counter-rotation by a small single-row chain from a sprocket on the front of the crankshaft.

The balancer shaft chain run is controlled by two fixed guide rails and an idler sprocket. The chain is located on the outside of the main camshaft timing chain, with its tension being controlled by a dedicated oil pressure-driven tensioner.

The engine/transmission assembly is supported on three hydraulic-type rubber mountings, one on the right-hand side, one on the left-hand side, and the third at the rear of the engine.

Lubrication is by means of a bi-rotor oil pump, driven from the front of the crankshaft and located in the timing cover. A relief valve in the timing cover limits the oil pressure at high engine speeds by returning excess oil to the sump. Oil is drawn from the sump through a strainer and, after passing through the oil pump, is forced through an externally-mounted filter and oil cooler (on certain models) into galleries in the cylinder block/crankcase. From there, the oil is distributed to the crankshaft (main bearings), balancer shafts, camshaft bearings and hydraulic cam followers. It also lubricates the water-cooled turbocharger and the crankcase-mounted piston cooling jets. The big-end bearings are supplied with oil via internal drillings in the crankshaft, while the camshaft lobes and valves are lubricated by splash, as are all other engine components.

Repairs with engine in car

The following work can be carried out with the engine in the car:

a) Compression pressure – testing.
b) Cylinder head cover – removal and refitting.
c) Camshaft oil seals – renewal.
d) Camshafts – removal, inspection and refitting.
e) Cylinder head – removal and refitting.
f) Cylinder head and pistons – decarbonising (refer to Part C of this Chapter).
g) Sump – removal and refitting.
h) Oil pump – removal, overhaul and refitting.
i) Crankshaft oil seals – renewal.
j) Flywheel/driveplate – removal, inspection and refitting.
k) Engine/transmission mountings – inspection and renewal.

2 Compression test – description and interpretation

1 When engine performance is down, or if misfiring occurs which cannot be attributed to the ignition or fuel systems, a compression test can provide diagnostic clues as to the engine's condition. If the test is performed regularly, it can give warning of trouble before any other symptoms become apparent.
2 The engine must be fully warmed-up to normal operating temperature, the battery must be fully-charged, and all the spark plugs

must be removed (Chapter 1A). The aid of an assistant will also be required.
3 Disable the ignition system by disconnecting the wiring plug from the ignition coil or Direct Ignition module (as applicable).
4 To prevent unburnt fuel from being supplied to the catalytic converter, the fuel pump must also be disabled by removing the relevant fuse and/or relay; see Chapter 4A for further details.
5 Fit a compression tester to the No 1 cylinder spark plug hole – the type of tester which screws into the plug thread must be used to obtain accurate readings.
6 Have the assistant depress the accelerator pedal fully, and crank the engine on the starter motor; after one or two revolutions, the compression pressure should build-up to a maximum figure, and then stabilise. Record the highest reading obtained.
7 Repeat the test on the remaining cylinders, recording the pressure in each.
8 All cylinders should produce very similar pressures; a difference of more than 2 bars between any two cylinders indicates a fault. Note that the compression should build-up quickly in a healthy engine; low compression on the first stroke, followed by gradually-increasing pressure on successive strokes, indicates worn piston rings. A low compression reading on the first stroke, which does not build-up during successive strokes, indicates leaking valves or a blown head gasket (a cracked cylinder head could also be the cause). Deposits on the undersides of the valve heads can also cause low compression.
9 Saab do not state specific compression pressures, but as a guide, any cylinder pressure of below 10 bars can be considered as less than healthy. Refer to a Saab dealer or other specialist if in doubt as to whether a particular pressure reading is acceptable.
10 If the pressure in any cylinder is low, carry out the following test to isolate the cause. Introduce a teaspoonful of clean oil into that cylinder through its spark plug hole, and repeat the test.
11 If the addition of oil temporarily improves the compression pressure, this indicates that bore or piston wear is responsible for the pressure loss. No improvement suggests that leaking or burnt valves, or a blown head

gasket, may be to blame.
12 A low reading only from two adjacent cylinders is almost certainly due to the head gasket having blown between them; the presence of coolant in the engine oil will confirm this.
13 On completion of the test, refit the spark plugs and reconnect the ignition system and fuel pump as necessary.

3 Top dead centre (TDC) for No 1 piston – locating

1 TDC timing marks are provided in the form of a slot machined into the crankshaft pulley and a corresponding bar cast into the timing chain cover. In addition, TDC marks are provided on the flywheel and oil seal housing – these are useful if the engine is being dismantled on the bench **(see illustration)**. Note: *With the timing marks correctly aligned, piston Nos 1 (at the timing chain end of the engine) and 4 (at the flywheel end of the engine) will be at top dead centre (TDC), with piston No 1 on its compression stroke.*
2 For access to the crankshaft pulley bolt, jack up the front of the car and support on axle stands (see Jacking and vehicle support). Remove the right-hand front wheel, then remove the screws and detach the inspection cover from the right-hand wheel arch liner.
3 Using a socket on the crankshaft pulley, turn the engine until the TDC slot in the crankshaft pulley is aligned with the slot on the timing cover **(see illustration)**. No 1 piston (at the timing chain end of the engine) will be at the top of its compression stroke. The compression stroke can be confirmed by removing the No 1 spark plug, and checking for compression with the wooden handle of a screwdriver over the plug hole as the piston approaches the top of its stroke. No compression indicates that the cylinder is on its exhaust stroke and is therefore one crankshaft revolution out of alignment.
4 Remove the cylinder head cover with reference to Section 4.
5 Check that the TDC marks at the sprocket ends of the camshafts are aligned with the corresponding TDC marks on the camshaft

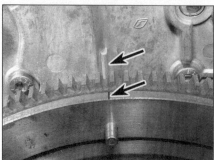

3.1 TDC timing marks on the flywheel and engine backplate

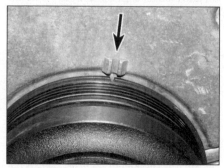

3.3 TDC timing marks on the timing chain cover and crankshaft pulley

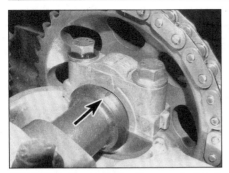

3.5 TDC timing marks on the camshaft and bearing cap

bearing caps **(see illustration)**. If necessary, turn the crankshaft to bring the marks into alignment.

4 Cylinder head cover – removal and refitting

Removal

1 Open the bonnet and remove the engine top cover, then unclip the inlet manifold cover from the inlet manifold. Undo the retaining screw (where applicable) and disconnect the wiring and crankcase breather pipe bracket from the right-hand end of the cylinder head cover **(see illustration)**.
2 Disconnect the crankcase breather hose (and, where applicable, the vacuum hose), and position them to one side **(see illustration)**.

4.2 Disconnect the breather hose from the cover

4.5a Refitting the cylinder head cover inner gasket . . .

4.1 Where applicable, undo the retaining bolt to disconnect breather pipe

Note: *On later models, release the securing clip to disconnect the hose.*
3 On models not fitted with DI ignition, disconnect the HT leads from the spark plugs. On models with DI ignition, disconnect the wiring connector, then undo the screws and remove the ignition module from the centre of the cylinder head cover; refer to Chapter 5B, if necessary **(see illustrations)**.
4 Unbolt and remove the cylinder head cover, and remove the gasket. If the cover is stuck, tap it gently with the palm of your hand to free it.

Refitting

5 Clean the contact surfaces of the cylinder head cover and cylinder head. Locate the gasket securely in the groove in the cylinder head cover. **Note:** *The gasket is in two parts: the inner and outer gaskets (see illustrations).*

4.3a Disconnect the wiring connector . . .

4.5b . . . and outer gasket securely in the groove

6 Refit the cylinder head cover, and insert the securing bolts. Tighten the bolts progressively and in sequence **(see illustration)** until all the bolts are tightened to the specified torque.
7 Reconnect the crankcase breather hose (and where applicable, the vacuum hose) to the cylinder head cover.
8 Reconnect the HT leads, or fit the direct ignition module to the centre of the cylinder head cover, and tighten the screws; refer to Chapter 5B if necessary.
9 Reconnect the breather pipe and wiring to the cylinder head cover.
10 Refit the inlet manifold cover and engine top cover.

5 Camshafts and hydraulic cam followers – removal, inspection and refitting

Note: *The following procedure describes removal and refitting of the camshafts and hydraulic cam followers with the cylinder head in position in the car. If necessary, the work can be carried out on the bench, with the cylinder head removed from the engine. In this case, start the procedure at paragraph 8, after removing the cylinder head.*

Removal

1 Open the bonnet, and clean the engine around the cylinder head.
2 Apply the handbrake, then jack up the front of the car and support on axle stands (see *Jacking and vehicle support*). Remove the right-hand front wheel.

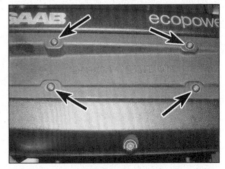

4.3b . . . then remove the ignition module retaining screws

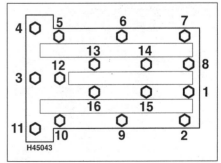

4.6 Tightening sequence for the cylinder head cover bolts

5.9 The camshaft bearing caps are marked for position (No 10 bearing cap arrowed)

3 Remove the screws, and withdraw the front wing moulding and wheel arch liner from under the right-hand front wing.
4 Remove the battery cover then disconnect the battery negative lead, and position the lead away from the battery terminal.
5 Unbolt and remove the cylinder head cover as described in Section 4.
6 Using a socket on the crankshaft pulley, turn the engine until the TDC slot in the crankshaft pulley is aligned with the timing bar on the timing cover. If necessary, refer to Section 3 for more information. Check also that the TDC marks on the sprocket ends of the camshafts are aligned with the corresponding TDC marks on the camshaft bearing caps.
7 Unscrew the bolt on the idler sprocket and remove the timing chain tensioner, use a 27 mm socket after removing the plug with spring and pushrod.
8 While holding each camshaft stationary with a spanner on the special flats at the transmission end of the camshaft, unscrew the bolts, then withdraw the sprockets and allow them to rest on the timing chain guides. Note that the sprockets have projections which engage with cut-outs in the ends of the camshafts. The timing chain cannot come off the crankshaft sprocket, since there is a guide located below the sprocket.
9 Check that the camshaft bearing caps and the camshafts are identified for position. They have stamped markings on the caps – do not mix up these when refitting, 1 to 5 for the inlet side and 6 to 10 for the exhaust side (see illustration).
10 Progressively unscrew the bearing cap

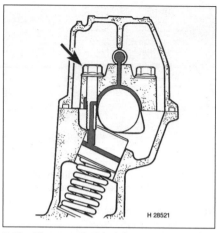

5.10a The camshaft bearing cap inner bolts are hollow for the oil supply to the hydraulic cam followers

bolts, so that the caps are not stressed unduly by the valve springs. Ensure that the bearing caps closest to the open valves are removed last, to avoid stressing the camshaft unduly. Fully remove the bolts and lift off the caps, then lift the camshafts from the cylinder head. Note that the bearing cap inner bolts (except at the timing chain end) have black heads, and incorporate drillings for the oil supply to the hydraulic cam followers; always make sure that the correct bolts are fitted (see illustrations). Keep the camshafts carefully identified for location.
11 Obtain sixteen small, clean plastic containers, and number them 1i to 8i (inlet) and 1e to 8e (exhaust). Alternatively, divide a larger container into sixteen compartments, similarly marked for the inlet and exhaust camshafts. Using a rubber sucker or a magnet, withdraw each hydraulic cam follower in turn, and place it in its respective container (see illustrations). **Do not** interchange the cam followers. To prevent the oil draining from the hydraulic cam followers, pour fresh oil into the containers until it covers them.
Caution: Take great care to avoid scratching the cylinder head bores as the followers are withdrawn.

Inspection

12 Examine the camshaft bearing surfaces and cam lobes for signs of wear ridges

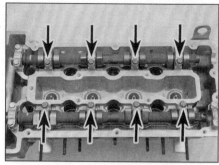

5.10b Locations of the black-headed inner bearing cap bolts incorporating oil drillings

and scoring. Renew the camshaft if any of these conditions are apparent. Examine the condition of the bearing surfaces on the camshaft journals, in the camshaft bearing caps, and in the cylinder head. If the head or cap bearing surfaces are worn excessively, the cylinder head will need to be renewed. If the necessary measuring equipment is available, camshaft bearing journal wear can be checked by direct measurement and comparison with the specifications given.
13 Camshaft endfloat can be measured by locating each camshaft in the cylinder head, refitting the sprockets, and using feeler blades between the shoulder on the front of the camshaft and the front bearing surface on the cylinder head.
14 Check the hydraulic cam followers where they contact the bores in the cylinder head for wear, scoring and pitting. Occasionally, a hydraulic cam follower may be noisy and require renewal, and this will have been noticed when the engine was running. It is not easy to check a cam follower for internal damage or wear once it has been removed; if there is any doubt, the complete set of cam followers should be renewed.
15 Clean the internal drillings of the hollow camshaft bearing cap bolts, to ensure oil supply to the hydraulic cam followers.

Refitting

16 Lubricate the bores for the hydraulic cam followers in the cylinder head, and the followers themselves, then insert them in their original positions (see illustration).

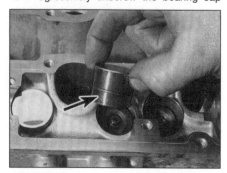

5.11a Removing a hydraulic cam follower

5.11b Hydraulic cam follower removed from the cylinder head. Store cam followers in an oil bath while removed

5.16 Oiling a hydraulic cam follower prior to fitting

17 Lubricate the bearing surfaces of the camshafts in the cylinder head.

18 Locate the camshafts in their correct positions in the cylinder head, so that the valves of No 1 cylinder (timing chain end) are closed, and the valves of No 4 cylinder are 'rocking'.

19 The timing marks on the sprocket ends of the camshafts should be aligned **(see illustration 3.5)**.

20 Lubricate the bearing surfaces in the bearing caps, then locate them in their correct positions and insert the retaining bolts. Progressively tighten the bolts to the specified torque. **Note:** *Ensure that the black-coloured oil supply bolts are in their correct positions (see illustration 5.10b).*

21 Check that each camshaft is at its TDC position – the timing marks are located on the front of the camshafts, and must be aligned with the mark on the bearing caps – see Section 3.

22 Check that the TDC slot in the crankshaft pulley is aligned with the timing bar on the timing cover **(see illustration 3.3)**.

23 Locate the sprockets on the camshafts, fitting the exhaust one first, followed by the inlet one. Do not fully tighten the bolts at this stage. Check that the timing chain is correctly located on the guides and sprockets.

24 Refit the timing chain tensioner, with reference to Chapter 2C.

25 Using a socket on the crankshaft pulley, rotate the engine two complete turns clockwise, then check that the TDC timing marks are still correctly aligned.

5.26 Tighten the camshaft sprocket retaining bolts, using a spanner on the camshaft flats to hold it stationary

26 Fully tighten the camshaft sprocket retaining bolts to the specified torque, while holding them stationary with a spanner on the special flats provided **(see illustration)**.

27 Clean the contact surfaces of the cylinder head cover and cylinder head. Refit the cylinder head cover with reference to Section 4.

28 Refit the inspection cover or DI ignition module to the centre of the cylinder head cover, and tighten the securing screws.

29 Reconnect the crankcase breather hose.

30 Refit the front wing moulding and wheel arch liner under the right-hand front wing, and tighten the screws.

31 Refit the right-hand front wheel, and lower the car to the ground.

32 Reconnect the battery negative lead and refit the covers to the battery and the engine.

6 Cylinder head – removal and refitting

Removal

1 Open the bonnet, and clean the engine around the cylinder head. Run the engine at idling speed and remove the fuel pump fuse (fuse number 32 – see Chapter 12). Turn the ignition off after the engine has stopped, there will then be no fuel pressure in the fuel lines. Refit the fuse.

2 Apply the handbrake, then jack up the front of the car and support on axle stands (see *Jacking and vehicle support*). Remove the right-hand front wheel and remove the lower engine cover.

3 Remove the battery cover and disconnect the battery negative lead, and position the lead away from the battery terminal.

4 Remove the retaining screws, and withdraw the wheel arch liner from under the right-hand front wing.

5 Drain the cooling system, with reference to Chapter 1A.

6 Unbolt and remove the turbocharger stay.

7 Where applicable, loosen the clip between the air hose and turbo inlet pipe, and remove the evaporative purge valve from the air collection box.

8 Disconnect the wiring from the mass airflow sensor, and the vacuum pipe, then remove the air filter element (Chapter 1A), unscrew the nuts and remove the air filter assembly from the engine compartment. Also, disconnect the wiring from the charge air control valve **(see illustrations)**.

9 Remove the rear engine cover and the heat shield from the exhaust manifold.

10 At the front of the engine, remove the turbocharger air duct and bypass pipe, and disconnect the vacuum hose from the bypass valve, and the hose from the pressure/temperature sensor. Also, disconnect the hose from the charge air pipe.

11 Disconnect the vacuum hose from the turbocharger wastegate, then disconnect the delivery air duct from the turbocharger after releasing the wiring cable ties. Cover the turbocharger ports to prevent entry of dust and dirt.

12 Remove the auxiliary drivebelt as described in Chapter 1A.

13 On the front of the engine, unscrew the union bolt and detach the crankcase ventilation pipe **(see illustration)**, then disconnect the carbon canister hose above the turbocharger.

14 Unbolt the lifting eye and bracket **(see illustration)** and, where applicable, the turbo inlet pipe support, then disconnect the inlet pipe.

15 Refer to Chapter 10, and unbolt the power steering pump and bracket from the engine, leaving the hydraulic lines still connected **(see**

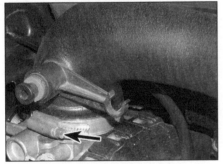

6.8a Slacken the retaining clip . . .

6.8b . . . then disconnect the sensor wiring connector and vacuum pipe

6.8c Disconnecting the wiring plug from the charge air control valve

6.13 Slackening the banjo bolt for the crankcase breather pipe

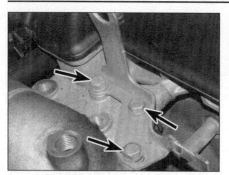

6.14 Undo the retaining bolts to remove the engine lifting eye

6.15 Remove the lower retaining bolt from the power steering pump bracket

6.22 Remove the cover to access the throttle linkage/cable

illustration). Support or tie the pump to one side.

16 Undo the screws securing the vacuum unit to the turbocharger, then unscrew the nuts securing the turbocharger to the exhaust manifold.

17 As applicable, disconnect the wiring from the ignition discharge module, turbo pressure sensor and coolant temperature sensor.

18 Disconnect the coolant hoses from the cylinder head and thermostat housing. Unscrew the bolt securing the coolant pipe to the turbo-to-pressure sensor mounting, and remove the banjo connection. Unbolt the coolant pipe from the coolant pump and cylinder block.

19 Disconnect the throttle body air ducts.

20 Remove the oil dipstick tube and plug the hole.

21 Disconnect the crankcase ventilation hose and vacuum hose from the cylinder head cover, and release the support cable ties.

22 Disconnect the accelerator cable from the throttle body **(see illustration)**.

23 Unbolt the wiring conduit and earthing points.

24 Disconnect the fuel line quick-release couplings.

25 Disconnect the vacuum hoses from the throttle body, inlet manifold and brake servo.

26 Disconnect the wiring from the following:
a) *Oxygen sensor.*
b) *Crankshaft TDC sensor.*
c) *Limp-home solenoid.*

d) *Throttle body.*
e) *MAP sensor.*
f) *Fuel injectors.*

27 Release the cable ties securing the starter motor solenoid conduit, and move to one side.

28 Unbolt and remove the inlet manifold stay **(see illustration)**.

29 On models with DI ignition, refer to Chapter 5B and remove the ignition discharge module from the top of the cylinder head.

30 Remove the spark plugs as described in Chapter 1A.

31 Unbolt and remove the cylinder head cover, and remove the gasket with reference to Section 4. If the cover is stuck, tap it gently with the palm of your hand to free it.

32 Using a socket on the crankshaft pulley, turn the engine until the TDC mark on the crankshaft pulley is aligned with the timing mark on the timing cover, and No 1 piston (at the timing chain end of the engine) is at the top of its compression stroke. If necessary, refer to Section 3 for more information. Check also that the TDC marks on the sprocket ends of the camshafts are aligned with the corresponding TDC marks on the camshaft bearing caps.

33 While holding each camshaft stationary with a spanner on the special flats at the flywheel/driveplate end of the camshaft, slacken the bolts **(see illustration 5.26)**. Do not remove at this stage.

34 Unscrew the bolt on the idler roller and remove the timing chain tensioner **(see**

illustration), use a 27 mm socket after removing the plug with spring and pushrod.

35 Unscrew the camshaft sprocket retaining bolts, then disengage the sprockets from the chain and remove from the engine. Fit a rubber band/cable tie around the chain guides, to prevent the chain from dropping down.

36 Unscrew and remove the two bolts securing the timing cover to the cylinder head **(see illustration)**.

37 Working in the **reverse** sequence **(see illustration 6.53)**, progressively slacken the ten cylinder head bolts by half a turn at a time, until all bolts can be unscrewed by hand. The bolts require the use of a Torx socket to unscrew them, as they have six external splines.

38 With all the cylinder head bolts removed, check that the timing chain is positioned so that the pivoting chain guide will not obstruct removal of the head. Lift the cylinder head directly from the top of the cylinder block and place it on a clean workbench, without damaging the mating surface. If necessary, enlist the help of an assistant, since the cylinder head is quite heavy. If the cylinder head is stuck, try rocking it slightly to free it from the gasket – **do not** insert a screwdriver or similar tool between the gasket joint, otherwise the gasket mating faces will be damaged. The head is located on dowels, so do not try to free it by tapping it sideways.

39 Remove the gasket from the top of the block, noting the two locating dowels. If the locating dowels are a loose fit, remove them

6.28 Unbolt and remove the intake manifold stay

6.34 Remove the idler roller, then slacken and remove the timing chain tensioner

6.36 Slacken and remove the two bolts securing the timing cover to the cylinder head

6.39 Removing a cylinder head locating dowel

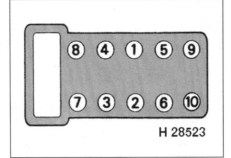

6.53 Cylinder head bolt tightening sequence

6.55 Using an angle-measuring gauge to tighten the cylinder head bolts through their Stage 3 angle

and store them with the head for safe-keeping **(see illustration)**. Do not discard the gasket – it may be needed for identification purposes.

40 If the cylinder head is to be dismantled for overhaul, remove the inlet and exhaust manifolds as described in Chapter 4A, and the camshafts as described in Section 5 of this Chapter.

Preparation for refitting

41 The mating faces of the cylinder head and cylinder block must be perfectly clean before refitting the head. Use a hard plastic or wood scraper to remove all traces of gasket and carbon; also clean the piston crowns. Take particular care during the cleaning operations, as the soft aluminium alloy is damaged easily. Also, make sure that the carbon is not allowed to enter the oil and water passages – this is particularly important for the lubrication system, as carbon could block the oil supply to the engine's components. Using adhesive tape and paper, seal the water, oil and bolt holes in the cylinder block. After cleaning each piston, use a small brush to remove all traces of grease and carbon from the gap, then wipe away the remainder with a clean rag. Clean all the pistons in the same way.

HAYNES HiNT *To prevent carbon entering the gap between the pistons and bores, smear a little grease in the gap.*

42 Check the mating surfaces of the cylinder block and the cylinder head for nicks, deep scratches and other damage. If slight, they may be removed carefully with a file, but if excessive, machining may be the only alternative to renewal.

43 If warpage of the cylinder head gasket surface is suspected, use a straight-edge to check it for distortion. Refer to Part C of this Chapter if necessary.

44 Check the condition of the cylinder head bolts, and particularly their threads. Wash the bolts in suitable solvent, and wipe them dry. Check each for any sign of visible wear or damage, renewing any bolt if necessary.

Measure the length of each bolt, and compare with the length of a new bolt. Although Saab do not specify that the bolts must be renewed, it is strongly recommended that the bolts are renewed as a complete set if the engine has completed a high mileage.

Refitting

45 Where removed, refit the camshafts with reference to Section 5, and the inlet and exhaust manifolds with new gaskets as described in Chapter 4A.

46 Wipe clean the mating surfaces of the cylinder head and cylinder block/crankcase. Clean away all oil from the bolt holes in the cylinder block. Check that the two locating dowels are in position on the cylinder block.

47 Position a new gasket on the cylinder block surface, making sure that it is fitted the correct way round.

48 Check that each camshaft is at its TDC position – the timing marks are located on the front of the camshaft, and must be aligned with the marks on the bearing caps – see Section 3.

49 Rotate the crankshaft one quarter of a turn away from TDC; this will position all four pistons part-way down their bores, keeping them out of way during cylinder head refitting.

50 Prior to refitting the cylinder head, apply a 2.0 mm thick bead of sealant (Locktite 518), 10.0 to 20.0 mm long, to the inner part of the upper contact surface of the timing cover which is against the cylinder head.

51 Check that the timing chain is located correctly on the chain guides, then carefully lower the cylinder head onto the block, aligning it with the locating dowels.

52 Lightly oil the threads and head undersides of the cylinder head bolts, then insert them and screw them in finger-tight.

53 Working progressively and in sequence, tighten the cylinder head bolts to their Stage 1 torque setting, using a torque wrench **(see illustration)**.

54 Using the same sequence, tighten the cylinder head bolts to their Stage 2 torque setting.

55 With all the cylinder head bolts tightened

to their Stage 2 setting, working again in the given sequence, angle-tighten the bolts further through the specified Stage 3 angle, using a socket and extension bar. It is recommended that an angle-measuring gauge is used during this stage of the tightening, to ensure accuracy **(see illustration)**.

HAYNES HiNT *If a gauge is not available, use white paint to make alignment marks between the bolt head and cylinder head prior to tightening; the marks can then be used to check that the bolt has been rotated through the correct angle during tightening.*

56 Rotate the crankshaft through one quarter of a turn back to its TDC position (see Section 3).

57 Insert and tighten to the specified torque, the two bolts securing the timing cover to the cylinder head.

58 With reference to Section 3, check that the camshafts are both aligned at their respective TDC positions. Engage the camshaft sprockets with the timing chain (with reference to Chapter 2C if necessary) and then locate the sprockets on the camshafts, fitting the exhaust one first, followed by the inlet one. Do not fully tighten the bolts at this stage. Check that the timing chain is correctly located on the guides and sprockets.

59 Refit the timing chain tensioner with reference to Chapter 2C, Section 10, if necessary.

60 Using a socket on the crankshaft pulley, rotate the engine two complete turns clockwise, then check that the TDC timing marks are still correctly aligned.

61 Fully tighten the camshaft sprocket retaining bolts to the specified torque, while holding each camshaft stationary, using a spanner on the special flats machined into the transmission end of each shaft.

62 Refit the cylinder head cover as described in Section 4, then refit the spark plugs with reference to Chapter 1A.

63 On models with DI ignition, refit the ignition discharge module with reference to Chapter 5B.

64 Refit and tighten the top bolt of the inlet manifold stay.

65 Refit the starter motor solenoid conduit and secure with new cable ties.
66 Reconnect the wiring to the following:
 a) *Oxygen sensor.*
 b) *Crankshaft TDC sensor.*
 c) *Limp-home solenoid.*
 d) *Throttle body.*
 e) *MAP sensor.*
 f) *Fuel injectors.*
67 Reconnect the vacuum hoses to the throttle body, inlet manifold and brake servo.
68 Reconnect the fuel lines, then refit the wiring conduit and earthing points.
69 Reconnect the accelerator cable.
70 Reconnect the crankcase ventilation hose and vacuum hose to the cylinder head cover, and fit new cable support ties.
71 Refit the oil dipstick tube, and reconnect the throttle body air ducts.
72 Refit the coolant pipe to the cylinder block, and tighten the mounting bolts.
73 Reconnect the coolant hoses and tighten the clips where applicable.
74 As applicable, reconnect the wiring to the ignition discharge module, turbo pressure sensor and coolant temperature sensor.
75 Refit and tighten the bolts securing the turbocharger to the exhaust manifold.
76 Refer to Chapter 10 and refit the power steering pump and bracket to the engine.
77 Refit the turbo inlet pipe and support, where applicable.
78 Refit the lifting eye and bracket and tighten the bolt.
79 Reconnect the crankcase ventilation pipe and carbon canister hose.

7.4 Oxygen sensor wiring connectors – model with two oxygen sensors fitted

7.13 Remove the retaining bolts to remove the oil pump pick-up and strainer

80 Refit the auxiliary drivebelt with reference to Chapter 1A.
81 Reconnect the turbocharger vacuum pipes and air ducts.
82 Refit the rear engine cover and heat shield.
83 Refit the air filter assembly and reconnect the wiring to the mass airflow sensor.
84 Refit the EVAP purge valve and turbocharger stay.
85 Refit the wheel arch liner, then reconnect the battery negative lead and refit the battery cover.
86 Refit the engine lower cover and right-hand wheel, then lower the car to the ground.
87 Refill the cooling system (see Chapter 1A).
88 Start the engine, observing the precautions given in Chapter 2C.

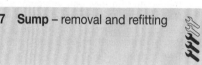

7 Sump – removal and refitting

Removal

1 Firmly apply the handbrake, then jack up the front of the car and support it on axle stands (see *Jacking and vehicle support*). Remove the battery cover and disconnect the negative lead.
2 Remove both front roadwheels, then undo the securing screws and lower the undertray from under the vehicle. Remove the resonator and wheel arch liner on the right-hand side.
3 Remove the engine top cover then drain the engine oil, clean and refit the engine oil drain plug, and tighten it to the specified torque.

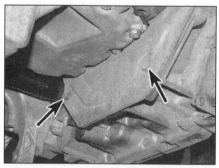

7.9 Remove the retaining bolts and remove the cover plate

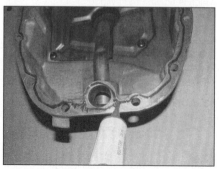

7.16 Apply a bead of sealant to the sump flange

Remove the dipstick from its tube and place clean rag over the engine oil filler neck to prevent the ingress of debris. If the engine is nearing its service interval when the oil and filter are due for renewal, it is recommended that the filter is also removed, and a new one fitted. After reassembly, the engine can then be refilled with fresh oil. Refer to Chapter 1A for further information.
4 Unplug the oxygen sensor wiring connectors, located on a bracket at the left-hand end of the cylinder head **(see illustration)**.
5 With reference to Chapter 4A, unbolt the exhaust system front pipe and catalytic converter from the turbocharger. Unbolt the front pipe from its support bracket and withdraw it from the underside of the engine compartment.
Note: *The flexible section of the exhaust pipe MUST NOT be put under excessive strain, as it may cause it to leak and eventually break.*
6 Unbolt the oil filter adapter housing from the front of the cylinder block, and tie it to one side, away from the engine. Be prepared for spilt oil. Discard the O-ring seals.
7 Support the right-hand end of the engine with a hoist or lifting beam. Raise the engine slightly, then unbolt the right-hand engine mounting. Raise the engine to allow sufficient room to remove the sump.
8 Unscrew the bolts securing the right-hand side of the front subframe to the underbody. Use blocks of wood to wedge the subframe away from the body.
9 Undo the retaining bolts and remove the flywheel cover plate from the transmission end of the sump **(see illustration)**.
10 Where applicable, disconnect the crankcase breather hose from the rear of the sump.
11 Progressively unscrew and remove the bolts securing the sump to the cylinder block, leaving one or two bolts in position to prevent the sump falling.
12 Remove the remaining bolts, and lower the sump to the ground. Break the joint between the sump and crankcase by striking the sump with the palm of your hand.
13 While the sump is removed, take the opportunity to check the oil pump pick-up/strainer for signs of clogging or damage. Unbolt the cover then unbolt the pick-up/strainer from inside the sump **(see illustration)**.

Refitting

14 Clean all traces of sealant from the mating surfaces of the cylinder block/crankcase and sump, then use a clean rag to wipe out the sump and the engine's interior.
15 Where removed, refit the pick-up/strainer to the sump and tighten the bolts. Make sure the pipe to the oil filter adapter is positioned correctly.
16 Ensure that the sump and cylinder block/crankcase mating surfaces are clean and dry, then apply a bead of suitable sealant approximately 1mm thick to the sump flange **(see illustration)**.

17 Offer up the sump and refit the retaining bolts, tightening them progressively to the specified torque. When lifting the sump, turn it at a slightly anti-clockwise angle before finally positioning it on the crankcase, and make sure that the sealant is not disturbed.

18 Where applicable, reconnect the crankcase breather hose.

19 Refit the flywheel cover plate and tighten the bolts.

20 Remove the wooden blocks then refit and tighten the right-hand subframe bolts.

21 Position the engine as necessary, and refit the right-hand engine mounting. Tighten the bolts to the specified torques. Remove the hoist or lifting beam.

22 Apply suitable sealant to the flange of the oil filter adapter housing. Lubricate a new O-ring with engine oil, then fit it to the adapter oil pipe, and locate the housing on the front of the cylinder block. Tighten the bolts. Check that the turbocharger and oil cooler lines are securely connected to the housing, as applicable. Fit a new oil filter with reference to Chapter 1A.

23 Refit the exhaust system front pipe and catalytic converter with reference to Chapter 4A.

24 Reconnect the oxygen sensor wiring.

25 Refit the resonator and wheel arch liner, then refit the roadwheels and lower the car to the ground.

26 Refill the engine with the correct oil as described in Chapter 1A, then clean and refit the dipstick/filler cap.

27 Start the engine and allow it to warm-up. Check around the sump mating surface for signs of leakage.

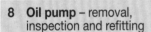

8 Oil pump – removal, inspection and refitting

Removal

1 Apply the handbrake, then jack up the front of the car and support on axle stands (see *Jacking and vehicle support*). Remove the right-hand front wheel.

2 Undo the securing screws and withdraw the wheel arch liner from under the wing, then unclip the power steering pipe from the subframe.

8.6 Remove the crankshaft pulley bolt and withdraw the crankshaft pulley

3 Support the engine under the right-hand side, then undo the retaining bolts and remove the right-hand upper engine mounting assembly from the vehicle.

4 Remove the auxiliary drivebelt with reference to Chapter 1A.

5 Slacken the centre bolt from the crankshaft pulley. To do this, the crankshaft must be held stationary using one of the following methods. On manual transmission models, have an assistant depress the brake pedal and engage 4th gear. Alternatively, remove the flywheel cover or starter motor as described in Chapter 5A, then insert a stout flat-bladed screwdriver through the transmission bellhousing and engage it with the starter ring gear to prevent the crankshaft turning. On automatic transmission models, use the latter method only.

6 Remove the crankshaft pulley bolt, then withdraw the crankshaft pulley and hub from

8.7b Withdrawing the oil pump cover from the timing cover

8.8 Removing the O-ring seal from the groove in the oil pump cover

8.9a Using a vernier gauge to check the depth of the oil seal in the cover . . .

8.7a Using circlip pliers to remove the oil pump cover circlip

the end of the crankshaft. If it is tight, careful use of two levers may be required **(see illustration)**.

7 Extract the large circlip, then withdraw the oil pump cover from the timing cover. Note that the circlip has a high tension, and a large pair of circlip pliers will be required to compress it. Also note the alignment arrows on the oil pump cover and timing cover **(see illustrations)**.

8 Remove the O-ring seal from the groove in the cover **(see illustration)**.

9 Note the position of the crankshaft oil seal in the oil pump cover, then prise it out with a screwdriver **(see illustrations)**.

Inspection

10 Wipe clean the inner faces of the pump rotors, and identify them for position with a marker pen. It is important that the rotors remain in their correct original positions

8.7c Alignment arrows on the oil pump cover

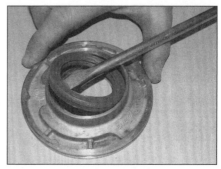

8.9b . . . then prise out the crankshaft oil seal from the oil pump cover

8.11a Removing the inner rotor . . .

8.11b . . . and outer rotor from the timing cover. Note that the position mark is facing outwards

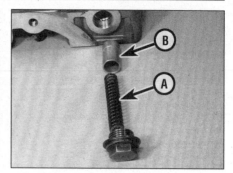

8.12 Unscrew the plug and remove the relief valve spring (A) and plunger (B)

on reassembly. Note that the outer rotor position is identified by the punch hole facing outwards.

11 Remove the rotors from the timing cover (oil pump body), keeping them identified for position **(see illustrations)**.

12 Unscrew the plug, and remove the relief valve spring and plunger, noting which way round they are fitted **(see illustration)**. Recover the plug washer.

13 Clean all components, and examine them for wear and damage. Examine the pump rotors and body for signs of wear ridges and scoring. Using a feeler blade check the clearance between the outer rotor and the timing cover, with reference to the Specifications **(see illustration)**. If worn excessively, the complete pump assembly must be renewed.

14 Examine the relief valve plunger for signs of wear or damage, and renew if necessary. The condition of the relief valve spring can only be measured by comparing it with a new one; if there is any doubt about its condition, it should also be renewed.

15 If there are any signs of dirt or sediment in the oil pump, it will be necessary to remove the sump (see Section 7), and clean the pick-up/strainer.

16 Insert the relief valve plunger and spring, then refit the plug together with a new washer, and tighten the plug.

17 Lubricate the rotors with fresh engine oil, then insert them in the oil pump body in their original positions. The rotors must be

positioned with the identification mark facing outwards, see paragraph 11.

Refitting

18 Wipe clean the oil seal seating in the oil pump casing, then drive a new oil seal into the casing **(see illustration)**, making sure that it enters squarely and is fitted in the previously-noted position.

19 Fit a new O-ring seal, then insert the oil pump in the timing cover, making sure that the alignment arrows point to each other. Refit the large circlip in the groove with its chamfer facing outwards, and the opening facing downwards.

20 Locate the crankshaft pulley and hub on the end of the crankshaft. Insert the centre bolt and tighten it to the specified torque, holding the crankshaft stationary using one of the methods described in paragraph 5.

21 Refit the auxiliary drivebelt with reference to Chapter 1A.

22 Refit the wing liner and moulding, and tighten the screws.

23 Refit the right-hand front wheel, and lower the car to the ground.

24 Before running the engine, disable the ignition system by disconnecting the wiring from the ignition coil or DI ignition module, as applicable (see Chapter 5B), then remove the fuel pump fuse (see Chapter 12). Crank the engine on the starter motor until oil pressure is restored and the oil pressure warning light is extinguished. Restore the ignition and fuel systems, and run the engine to check for oil leaks.

9 Oil cooler, adapter and thermostat – removal and refitting

Oil cooler

Removal

1 An engine oil cooler is fitted to automatic transmission models only. It is located beneath the radiator and connected to ports on an adapter fitted to the oil filter **(see illustration)**. To remove the oil cooler, first drain the engine oil as described in Chapter 1A, then refit and tighten the drain plug.

2 Jack up the front of the car and support it securely on axle stands (see *Jacking and vehicle support*). Slacken and withdraw the securing screws, and remove the front lower spoiler.

3 Position a suitable container beneath the oil cooler on the right-hand side of the engine compartment. Unscrew the unions from the top and bottom of the oil cooler, and disconnect the oil supply and return hoses. Allow any oil to drain into the container.

4 Unscrew the mounting bolts and remove the oil cooler.

Refitting

5 Refitting is a reversal of removal, but tighten the unions to the specified torque. Fill the engine with oil with reference to Chapter 1A. On completion, start the engine and run it at a

8.13 Checking the clearance between the oil pump outer rotor and the timing cover

8.18 Fitting a new oil seal to the oil pump cover

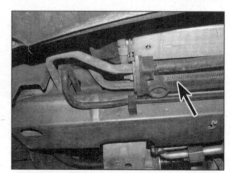

9.1 Engine oil cooler and connecting pipes

9.9a Undo the oil pipe retaining bolt . . .

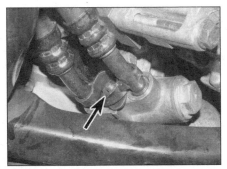

9.9b . . . and the oil pipe retaining bracket and nut from the oil filter adapter

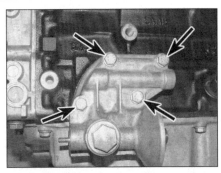

9.10 Slacken and remove the mounting bolts to remove the adapter

fast idle speed for several minutes, to allow the oil to fill the oil cooler. Check and if necessary top-up the engine oil level with reference to *Weekly checks*.

Adapter

Removal

6 An adapter is fitted between the oil filter and cylinder block; the oil cooler is incorporated into the bottom of the radiator. If the engine is nearing its service interval when the oil and filter are due for renewal, it is recommended that the filter is removed, and a new one fitted. After reassembly, the engine can then be refilled with fresh oil. Refer to Chapter 1A for further information.
7 Drain the engine oil as described in Chapter 1A, then refit and tighten the drain plug.
8 Jack up the front of the car and support it securely on axle stands (see *Jacking and vehicle support*). Slacken and withdraw the securing screws, and remove the front lower cover/spoiler as applicable.
9 Position a suitable container beneath the oil filter adapter on the right-hand side front of the engine compartment. Unscrew the unions from the top and bottom of the adapter **(see illustrations)**. Allow any oil to drain into the container.
10 Unscrew the mounting bolts and remove the oil filter adapter from the engine compartment **(see illustration)**.

Refitting

11 Refitting is a reversal of removal, but tighten the unions to the specified torque. Fill

9.14 Slacken and remove the plug to access the thermostat

the engine with oil with reference to Chapter 1A. On completion, start the engine and run it at a fast idle speed for several minutes, to allow the oil to fill the oil cooler. Check and if necessary top-up the engine oil level with reference to *Weekly checks*.

Thermostat

Removal

12 The oil temperature thermostat is mounted on the right-hand side front of the oil filter cooler/adapter.
13 Drain the engine oil as described in Chapter 1A, then refit and tighten the drain plug.
14 Position a suitable container beneath the thermostat, then unscrew the plug, recover the seal/washer and allow the surplus oil to run into the container **(see illustration)**.

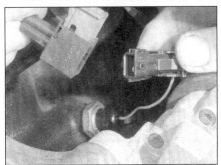

10.2 Disconnecting the wiring from the oil pressure switch

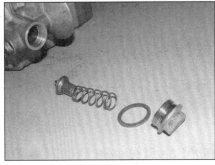

9.15 Thermostat, spring, sealing washer and securing bolt/plug

15 Withdraw the thermostat and spring from the filter adapter **(see illustration)**.

Refitting

16 Fit the new thermostat into the filter adapter, ensuring that the flange rests on the machined recess in the housing.
17 Slide the spring into position, then fit the seal/washer to the plug and screw the plug into the filter housing, tightening it to the correct torque.
18 Fill the engine with oil with reference to Chapter 1A. On completion, start the engine and run it at a fast idle speed for several minutes, then check around the thermostat plug for signs of leakage. Check the engine oil level and top-up if necessary (see *Weekly checks*).

---

10 Oil pressure warning light switch – removal and refitting

Removal

1 The oil pressure switch is screwed into the rear of the cylinder block, beneath the inlet manifold and behind the starter motor **(see illustration)**. First jack up the front of the car, and support on axle stands (see *Jacking and vehicle support*).
2 Trace the wiring back from the switch and disconnect the wiring block connector **(see illustration)**.
3 Unscrew the switch from the cylinder

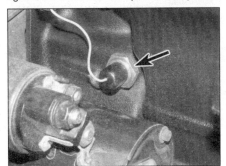

10.1 The oil pressure switch is screwed into the rear of the cylinder block

block; be prepared for slight loss of oil **(see illustration)**. If the switch is to be left removed for any length of time, plug the hole, to prevent the entry of debris.

Refitting

4 Wipe clean the threads of the switch and the location aperture. Do not insert tools or wire into the hole at the tip of the switch, in an attempt to clean it out; as this may damage the internal components.

5 Insert the switch into the cylinder block and tighten it securely.

6 Reconnect the switch wiring block connector.

7 Start the engine and check for leakage, then lower the car to the ground. Check the engine oil level and top-up if necessary (see *Weekly checks*).

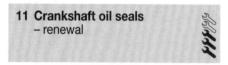

11 Crankshaft oil seals – renewal

Right-hand oil seal

Note: *This procedure explains the fitting of the seal in situ. See Section 8 for the removal of the oil pump cover and renewing the seal off the engine.*

1 Apply the handbrake, then jack up the front of the car and support on axle stands (see *Jacking and vehicle support*). Remove the right-hand front wheel, undo the securing screws and withdraw the wheel arch liner. Where applicable, unclip the power steering pipe from the subframe.

2 Support the engine under the right-hand side, then undo the retaining bolts and remove the right-hand upper engine mounting assembly from the vehicle (with reference to Section 13).

3 Remove the auxiliary drivebelt with reference to Chapter 1A.

4 Unscrew and remove the centre bolt from the crankshaft pulley. To do this, the crankshaft must be held stationary using one of the following methods. On manual transmission models, have an assistant depress the brake pedal and engage 4th gear. Alternatively, remove the flywheel cover plate or starter motor as described in Chapter 5A, then insert a flat-bladed screwdriver through the bellhousing and jam the starter ring gear to prevent the crankshaft turning. On automatic transmission models, use the latter method only.

5 Pull the crankshaft pulley and hub from the end of the crankshaft. If it is tight, careful use of two levers may be required.

6 Note the fitted depth of the oil seal in its housing, then using a screwdriver, carefully prise the oil seal from the oil pump casing. Alternatively, punch or drill two small holes opposite each other in the seal. Thread a self-

10.3 Using a ring spanner to remove the oil pressure switch

tapping screw into each hole, and pull on the screw heads with pliers to extract the seal. Another method is to remove the oil pump cover as described in Section 8, and remove the oil seal on the bench **(see illustrations in Section 8)**.

7 Clean the seating in the oil pump casing, then lubricate the lips of the new oil seal with clean engine oil, and locate it squarely on the oil pump casing. Make sure that the closed side is facing outwards. Using a suitable tubular drift (such as a socket) which bears only on the hard outer edge of the seal, tap the seal into position to the same depth in the casing as the original was prior to removal.

8 Locate the crankshaft pulley and hub on the end of the crankshaft. Insert the centre bolt and tighten it to the specified torque, holding the crankshaft stationary using one of the methods described in paragraph 4.

9 Refit the auxiliary drivebelt with reference to Chapter 1A, then refit the engine mounting assembly.

10 Refit the wheel arch liner front section and moulding, and tighten the screws.

11 Refit the right-hand front wheel, and lower the car to the ground.

Left-hand oil seal

12 Remove the flywheel/driveplate as described in Section 12.

13 Make a note of the fitted depth of the seal in its housing. Punch or drill two small holes opposite each other in the seal. Thread a self-tapping screw into each hole, and pull on the screw heads with pliers to extract the seal. Alternatively, use a screwdriver to prise out the oil seal.

14 Clean the seal housing, then lubricate the lips of the new seal with clean engine oil, and carefully locate the seal on the end of the crankshaft.

15 Using a suitable tubular drift, which bears only on the hard outer edge of the seal, drive the seal into position, to the same depth in the housing as the original was prior to removal.

16 Wipe clean the oil seal, then refit the flywheel/driveplate as described in Section 12.

12 Flywheel/driveplate – removal, inspection and refitting

Removal

1 Remove the transmission as described in Chapter 7A or 7B.

2 On manual transmission models, remove the clutch assembly as described in Chapter 6.

3 Prevent the flywheel/driveplate from turning by jamming the ring gear teeth with a wide-bladed screwdriver or similar tool. Alternatively, bolt a metal link between the flywheel/driveplate (using the clutch or torque converter bolt holes) and the cylinder block/crankcase.

4 Unscrew and remove the retaining bolts, remove the locking tool, then remove the flywheel/driveplate from the crankshaft flange. Note that the unit is located by a dowel pin, and must be fitted correctly.

Inspection

5 On manual transmission models, if the flywheel's clutch mating surface is deeply scored, cracked or otherwise damaged, the flywheel must be renewed. However, it may be possible to have it surface-ground; seek the advice of a Saab dealer or engine reconditioning specialist.

6 Similarly check the condition of the driveplate on automatic transmission models.

7 If the ring gear is badly worn or has missing teeth, it may be possible to renew it. This job is best left to a Saab dealer or engine reconditioning specialist. The temperature to which the new ring gear must be heated for installation is critical and, if not done accurately, the hardness of the teeth will be destroyed.

Refitting

8 Clean the mating surfaces of the flywheel/driveplate and crankshaft. Clean the threads of the retaining bolts and the crankshaft holes.

> **HAYNES HiNT**
> *If a suitable tap is not available, cut two slots into the threads of an old flywheel bolt, and use the bolt to clean the threads.*

9 Ensure that the locating dowel is in position, then offer up the flywheel and locate it on the dowel.

10 Apply locking fluid to the threads of the retaining bolts. Insert and tighten them to the specified torque, holding the flywheel/driveplate stationary using one of the methods described in paragraph 3 **(see illustration)**.

12.10 Apply locking fluid to the bolt threads, and tighten to the specified torque

13.10 Right-hand engine mounting, viewed from below

11 On manual transmission models, refit the clutch assembly as described in Chapter 6.
12 Refit the transmission with reference to Chapter 7A or 7B.

13 Engine/transmission mountings – inspection and renewal

Inspection

1 For improved access, raise the front of the car and support it securely on axle stands (see *Jacking and vehicle support*).
2 The engine mountings are located at the front right-hand side, beneath the left-hand side of the transmission, and at the rear of the engine. With the exception of the upper right-hand mounting, all mountings are of hydraulic type, incorporating an inner chamber filled with oil. Vibration damping is progressive depending on the load applied, and works for both horizontal and vertical movement.
3 Check the mounting rubbers to see if they are cracked, hardened or separated from the metal at any point; renew the mounting if any such damage or deterioration is evident.
4 Check that all the mounting's fasteners are securely tightened.
5 Using a large screwdriver or a crowbar, check for wear in the mounting by carefully levering against it to check for freeplay. Where this is not possible, enlist the aid of an assistant to move the engine/transmission back-and-forth, or from side-to-side, while you watch the mounting. While some freeplay is to be expected even from new components, excessive wear should be obvious. If excessive freeplay is found, check first that the fasteners are securely tightened, then if necessary renew any worn components as described below.

Renewal

Right-hand engine mounting

6 Apply the handbrake, then jack up the front of the car and support on axle stands (see *Jacking and vehicle support*). Remove the right-hand front wheel.
7 Remove the screws, and withdraw the right-hand front wing plastic moulding and front wheel arch liner.
8 Remove the securing screws and detach the plastic undertray from the front spoiler.
9 Position a trolley jack underneath the engine and raise the jack head until it is just taking the weight of the engine. Ensure that the jack head does not bear on the underside of the sump. Alternatively, position a lifting beam across the engine bay and support the engine by the lifting eyelet located at the rear right hand side of the cylinder head.
10 Unscrew the bolts securing the engine mounting bracket to the bodywork **(see illustration)**. Lower the jack slightly, until the engine mounting bracket is clear of the bodywork. Take care to avoid straining the rear and left-hand engine mountings as you do this.
11 Unscrew and remove the centre bolt and remove the engine mounting from its bracket. Note the location pin to ensure correct refitting. If necessary, unbolt the bracket from the front of the cylinder block.
12 Fit the new mountings using a reversal of the removal procedure, making sure that the nuts are tightened to the correct torque.

Left-hand engine/transmission mounting

13 Apply the handbrake, then jack up the front of the car and support on axle stands (see *Jacking and vehicle support*). Remove the left-hand front wheel.
14 Remove the screws, and withdraw the left-hand front wing plastic moulding and front wheel arch liner.

15 Remove the securing screws and detach the plastic undertray from the front spoiler.
16 Position a trolley jack underneath the transmission and raise the jack head until it is just taking the combined weight of the engine and transmission. On models with automatic transmission, ensure that the jack head does not bear on the underside of the transmission sump. Alternatively, position a lifting beam across the engine bay and support the engine by the lifting eyelet located at the rear left hand side of the cylinder head.
17 Unscrew the bolts securing the engine/transmission mounting bracket to the bodywork. Lower the jack slightly, until the engine mounting bracket is clear of the bodywork. Take care to avoid straining the rear and right-hand engine mountings as you do this.
18 Unscrew and remove the bolts and remove the engine/transmission mounting, together with its mounting bracket, from the transmission casing. Unbolt the mounting from the bracket.
19 Fit the new mounting using a reversal of the removal procedure, making sure that the bolts are tightened to the correct torque.

Rear engine mounting

20 Mount a lifting beam across the engine compartment, in-line with the front suspension turrets. Attach the jib to the engine lifting eyelet at the left hand end of the cylinder head. Raise the jib until the beam just starts to take the weight of the engine.
21 Unplug the oxygen sensor wiring at the connector, located on a bracket at the left hand end of the cylinder head.
22 Raise the front of the vehicle and support it securely on axle stands (see *Jacking and vehicle support*). Remove both front roadwheels.
23 With reference to Chapter 4A, unbolt the exhaust system intermediate pipe from the front pipe, then unbolt the front pipe from the turbocharger or exhaust manifold, as applicable. Unbolt the front pipe from its support bracket and withdraw it from the underside of the engine compartment.
24 Ensure that the lifting beam is supporting the engine and transmission adequately, then unscrew and remove the rear engine mounting stud nuts from the bracket and subframe.
25 Unbolt the engine mounting bracket from the rear of the transmission casing and remove it from the engine compartment.
26 Fit the new mounting using a reversal of the removal procedure, making sure that the nuts/bolts are tightened to the correct torque.

Notes

Chapter 2 Part B:
Diesel engine in-car repair procedures

Contents

Degrees of difficulty

Easy, suitable for novice with little experience	Fairly easy, suitable for beginner with some experience	Fairly difficult, suitable for competent DIY mechanic	Difficult, suitable for experienced DIY mechanic	Very difficult, suitable for expert DIY or professional

Specifications

General

Engine type	Four-cylinder, in-line, water-cooled. Chain-driven, 16 valve, SOHC (single overhead camshaft), acting on hydraulic tappets
Designation	D223L
Bore	84 mm
Stroke	98 mm
Capacity	2171 cc
Compression ratio	18.5:1
Maximum power:	
To October 2000	85 kW (115 bhp) at 4300 rpm
October 2000-on	92 kW (125 bhp) at 4000 rpm
Maximum torque:	
To October 2000	260 Nm at 2000 rpm
October 2000-on	280 Nm at 1500 to 2750 rpm
Injection sequence	1-3-4-2 (No 1 cylinder at timing chain end of engine)
Direction of crankshaft rotation	Clockwise (viewed from timing chain end of engine)

Compression pressures

Standard	32 to 36 bar
Maximum difference between any two cylinders	1 bar (14.5 psi) or 10%
Pressure loss	Not more than 25% max per cylinder

Camshaft

Endfloat	0.04 to 0.14 mm
Maximum permissible radial run-out	0.06 mm
Cam lift (inlet and exhaust)	8.0 mm

Lubrication system

Oil pump type	Rotor-type, driven directly from crankshaft
Minimum permissible oil pressure at idle speed, with engine at operating temperature (oil temperature of at least 80°C)	1.5 bar (22 psi)

Torque wrench settings

	Nm	lbf ft
Auxiliary drivebelt tensioner assembly bolts:		
Pulley backplate pivot bolt	42	31
Strut mounting bolts	23	17
Balancer shaft chain tensioner bolt	9	7
Balancer shaft sprocket bolt*:		
Stage 1	90	66
Stage 2	Angle-tighten a further 30°	
Balancer shaft to cylinder block*	20	15
Camshaft bearing cap bolts	20	15
Camshaft cover bolts	8	6
Camshaft sprocket bolt*:		
Stage 1	90	66
Stage 2	Angle-tighten a further 60°	
Connecting rod big-end bearing cap bolt*:		
Stage 1	35	26
Stage 2	Angle-tighten a further 45°	
Crankshaft position sensor	8	6
Crankshaft pulley bolt*:		
Stage 1	150	111
Stage 2	Angle-tighten a further 45°	
Cylinder head bolts*:		
Stage 1	25	18
Stage 2	Angle-tighten a further 65°	
Stage 3	Angle-tighten a further 65°	
Stage 4	Angle-tighten a further 65°	
Stage 5	Angle-tighten a further 65°	
Cylinder head-to-timing chain cover	20	15
Engine oil drain plug	18	13
Engine/transmission mounting bolts:		
Rear engine mounting:		
To transmission	84	62
To subframe	50	37
To bracket	47	35
Right-hand engine mounting:		
To timing cover	47	35
To body	47	35
To bracket:		
Stage 1	47	35
Stage 2	Angle-tighten a further 45°	
Left-hand engine mounting:		
Bracket to transmission	47	35
To body	62	46
To bracket	47	35
Exhaust front pipe to turbocharger	25	18
Exhaust manifold stay	25	18
Flywheel bolts*:		
Stage 1	45	33
Stage 2	Angle-tighten a further 30°	
Injection pump bracket	20	15
Injection pump sprocket	20	15
Injection pump sprocket cover bolts	6	4
Main bearing cap bolts*:		
Stage 1	90	66
Stage 2	Angle-tighten a further 60°	
Oil cooler-to-oil filter housing bolts	20	15
Oil delivery pipe to block	20	15
Oil filter cap	26	19
Oil filter housing	20	15
Oil pressure sensor	30	22
Oil return pipe to block	30	22
Oil delivery pipe to turbocharger	12	9
Oil pump:		
Oil pressure relief valve bolt	45	33
Pump cover screws	8	6
Pump pick-up/strainer bolts	8	6
Oil pressure reducing valve	60	44
Oil return pipe to turbocharger	8	6

Torque wrench settings (continued)

	Nm	lbf ft
Piston cooling jet	22	16
Roadwheel bolts	110	81
Sump bolts:		
Sump-to-cylinder block/timing chain cover bolts	20	15
Sump flange-to-transmission bolts:		
M8 bolts	20	15
M10 bolts	40	30
Timing chain cover bolts	20	15
Timing chain guide*:		
Fixed	8	6
Movable	22	16
Timing chain tensioner blade pivot bolt	20	15
Timing chain tensioner cap	60	44
Upper timing chain sprocket to fuel injection pump	20	15
Water pump	20	15
Water pump pulley	20	15

* Use new fasteners

1 General information

How to use this Chapter

1 This Part of Chapter 2 describes those repair procedures that can reasonably be carried out on the 2.2 litre diesel engine while it remains in the car. If the engine has been removed from the car and is being dismantled as described in Part C, any preliminary dismantling procedures can be ignored.

2 Note that, while it may be possible physically to overhaul items such as the piston/connecting rod assemblies while the engine is in the car, such tasks are not normally carried out as separate operations. Usually, several additional procedures (not to mention the cleaning of components and of oilways) have to be carried out. For this reason, all such tasks are classed as major overhaul procedures, and are described in Part C of this Chapter.

3 Part C describes the removal of the engine/transmission unit from the vehicle, and the full overhaul procedures that can then be carried out.

Engine description

4 The engine is of sixteen-valve, in-line four-cylinder, single overhead camshaft (SOHC) type, mounted transversely at the front of the car with the transmission attached to its left-hand end.

5 The crankshaft runs in five main bearings. Thrustwashers are fitted to No 3 main bearing to control crankshaft endfloat.

6 The connecting rods rotate on horizontally-split bearing shells at their big-ends. The pistons are attached to the connecting rods by gudgeon pins, which are a sliding fit in the connecting rod small-end eyes and retained by circlips. The aluminium-alloy pistons are fitted with three piston rings – two compression rings and an oil control ring.

7 The cylinder block is made of cast iron and the cylinder bores are an integral part of the block. On this type of engine the cylinder bores are sometimes referred to as having dry liners.

8 The inlet and exhaust valves are each closed by coil springs, and operate in guides pressed into the cylinder head.

9 The camshaft is driven by the crankshaft by a double timing chain arrangement; the lower timing chain links the crankshaft to the fuel injection pump and the upper chain links the injection pump to the camshaft. The camshaft rotates directly in the head and operates the sixteen valves by followers and hydraulic tappets. The followers are situated directly below the camshaft, each one operating two valves. Valve clearances are automatically adjusted by the hydraulic tappets.

10 Lubrication is by means of an oil pump, which is driven off the right-hand end of the crankshaft. It draws oil through a strainer located in the sump, and then forces it through an externally-mounted filter into galleries in the cylinder block/crankcase. From there, the oil is distributed to the crankshaft (main bearings) and camshaft. The big-end bearings are supplied with oil through internal drillings in the crankshaft, while the camshaft bearings also receive a pressurised supply. The camshaft lobes and valves are lubricated by splash, as are all other engine components. An oil cooler is fitted between the oil filter adapter and cylinder block, to keep the oil temperature stable under arduous operating conditions. Coolant from the engine cooling system is circulated through the cooler.

11 An intercooler is fitted in front of the radiator.

12 A balancer unit is fitted to the bottom of the engine, consisting of two balancer shafts which are driven by chain from the crankshaft. The balancer shafts rotate in opposite directions at double the crankshaft speed. This unit is to help reduce the natural vibrations of the engine.

Operations with engine in car

13 The following work can be carried out with the engine in the car:
  a) *Compression pressure – testing.*
  b) *Camshaft cover – removal and refitting.*
  c) *Timing chain cover – removal and refitting.*
  d) *Timing chains – removal and refitting.*
  e) *Timing chain tensioners, guides and sprockets – removal and refitting.*
  f) *Camshaft and followers – removal, inspection and refitting.*
  g) *Cylinder head – removal and refitting.*
  h) *Connecting rods and pistons – removal and refitting*.*
  i) *Sump – removal and refitting.*
  j) *Oil pump – removal, overhaul and refitting.*
  k) *Oil cooler – removal and refitting.*
  l) *Crankshaft oil seals – renewal.*
  m) *Engine/transmission mountings – inspection and renewal.*
  n) *Flywheel – removal, inspection and refitting.*
* Although the operation marked with an asterisk can be carried out with the engine in the car after removal of the sump, it is better for the engine to be removed, in the interests of cleanliness and improved access. For this reason, the procedure is described in Chapter 2C.

2 Compression and leakdown tests – description and interpretation

Compression test

Note: *A compression tester specifically intended for diesel engines must be used, because of the higher pressures involved.*

1 When engine performance is down, or if misfiring occurs which cannot be attributed to the fuel system, a compression test can provide diagnostic clues as to the engine's condition. If the test is performed regularly, it can give warning of trouble before any other symptoms become apparent.

2 The tester is connected to an adapter which screws into the glow plug or injector hole. On these models, an adapter suitable for use in the glow plug holes will be required, due to the design of the injectors. It is unlikely to be worthwhile buying such a tester for occasional use, but it may be possible to borrow or hire one – if not, have the test performed by a garage.

3 Unless specific instructions to the contrary are supplied with the tester, observe the following points:

a) *The battery must be in a good state of charge, the air filter must be clean, and the engine should be at normal operating temperature.*

b) *All the glow plugs should be removed before starting the test (see Chapter 5C).*

c) *Refer to Chapter 12 and remove the fuel pump fuse (No 32) from the fusebox. Release the retaining clip and disconnect the wiring connector from the fuel injection pump (see Chapter 4B) to prevent the engine from running or fuel from being discharged.*

4 There is no need to hold the accelerator pedal down during the test, because the diesel engine air inlet is not throttled.

5 Crank the engine on the starter motor; after one or two revolutions, the compression pressure should build-up to a maximum figure, and then stabilise. Record the highest reading obtained.

6 Repeat the test on the remaining cylinders, recording the pressure in each.

7 All cylinders should produce very similar pressures; any difference greater than that specified indicates the existence of a fault. Note that the compression should build-up

quickly in a healthy engine; low compression on the first stroke, followed by gradually-increasing pressure on successive strokes, indicates worn piston rings. A low compression reading on the first stroke, which does not build-up during successive strokes, indicates leaking valves or a blown head gasket (a cracked head could also be the cause). **Note:** *The cause of poor compression is less easy to establish on a diesel engine than on a petrol one. The effect of introducing oil into the cylinders ('wet' testing) is not conclusive, because there is a risk that the oil will sit in the swirl chamber or in the recess on the piston crown instead of passing to the rings.*

8 On completion of the test, refit the fuel pump fuse, reconnect the injection pump wiring then refit the glow plugs as described in Chapter 5C.

Leakdown test

9 A leakdown test measures the rate at which compressed air fed into the cylinder is lost. It is an alternative to a compression test, and in many ways it is better, since the escaping air provides easy identification of where pressure loss is occurring (piston rings, valves or head gasket).

10 The equipment needed for leakdown testing is unlikely to be available to the home mechanic. If poor compression is suspected, have the test performed by a suitably-equipped garage.

3 Top dead centre (TDC) for No 1 piston – locating

1 Top Dead Centre (TDC) is the precise highest point that each piston reaches as the crankshaft rotates. While each piston reaches TDC both at the top of the compression stroke and again at the top of the exhaust stroke, for the purpose of timing the engine, TDC refers to the piston position (usually number 1) at the top of its compression stroke.

2 Number 1 piston (and cylinder) is at the right-hand (timing chain) end of the engine, and its TDC position is located as follows. Note that the crankshaft rotates clockwise when viewed from the right-hand side of the car.

3 To improve access to the crankshaft pulley, apply the handbrake, then jack up the front of the vehicle and support it on axle stands. Remove the retaining screws/clips and remove the engine undertray.

4 To check the position of the camshaft either remove the camshaft cover (Section 5), so that the position of the cam lobes can be seen, or remove the braking system vacuum pump (Chapter 9) so the timing hole on the camshaft end can be seen.

5 Using a socket and extension bar on the crankshaft pulley bolt, rotate the crankshaft until the notch on the crankshaft pulley rim is aligned with the mark on the timing chain cover. Once the mark is correctly aligned, No 1 and 4 pistons are at TDC.

6 To determine which piston is at TDC on its compression stroke, check the position of the camshaft lobes/timing hole (as applicable). When No 1 piston is at TDC on its compression stroke, No 1 cylinder camshaft lobes will be pointing upwards and the timing hole on the left-hand of the camshaft will be at the top (12 o'clock position) with the camshaft slot parallel with the head surface (see illustrations). If No 1 cylinder camshaft lobes are pointing downwards and the camshaft end timing mark is at the bottom (6 o'clock position) then No 4 cylinder is at TDC on its compression stroke; rotate the crankshaft through a further complete turn (360°) to bring No 1 cylinder to TDC on its compression stroke.

7 With No 1 piston at TDC on its compression stroke, if necessary, the crankshaft can be locked in position by inserting a pin in through the crankshaft sensor bore on the front of the cylinder block. If access to the special Saab tool (86 12 871) cannot be gained, a home-made alternative will have to be manufactured (see Section 4). Remove the crankshaft sensor (see Chapter 4B, Section 9) and insert the pin, making sure it is correctly located in the crankshaft web slot (see illustrations).

8 Note that checking the TDC position of the injection pump sprocket is covered in Section 4.

3.6a When No 1 cylinder is at TDC on its compression stroke, its camshaft lobes (arrowed) will be pointing upwards . . .

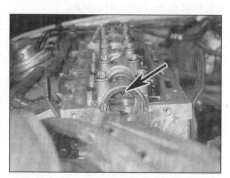

3.6b . . . and the timing hole (arrowed) on the left-hand end of the camshaft will be at the top

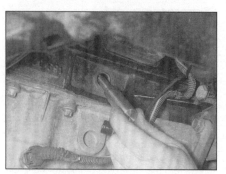

3.7a Remove the crankshaft sensor from the cylinder block and insert the locking pin . . .

3.7b . . . making sure it is correctly engaged with the crankshaft cut-out (arrowed – shown with sump removed)

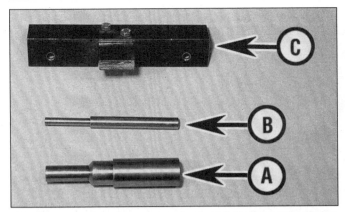

4.0a Home-made tools necessary to check/adjust the valve timing

A *Crankshaft locking pin*
B *Injection pump flange locking pin*
C *Camshaft locking tool*

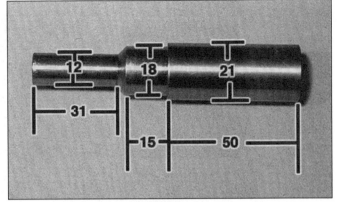

4.0b Crankshaft locking pin dimensions (in mm)

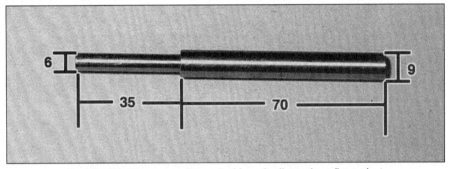

4.0c Injection pump flange locking pin dimensions (in mm)

4 Valve timing – checking and adjustment

Note: *To check the valve (and fuel injection pump) timing, it will be necessary to use the following Saab special tools (or suitable equivalents): the camshaft locking tool (83 95 386), the injection pump flange locking pin (83 95 337), and the crankshaft locking pin (83 95 352). If access to these tools cannot be gained, this task must be entrusted to a Saab dealer. If the necessary facilities are available to manufacture home-made tools, the dimensions of the locking pins are given in the accompanying illustrations (see illustrations). The camshaft locking tool (also pictured) ensures that the camshaft remains correctly positioned by keeping the camshaft slot parallel to the cylinder head surface.*

1 Remove the auxiliary drivebelt as described in Chapter 1B. Undo the auxiliary drivebelt tensioner pulley strut lower mounting bolt and the pulley backplate pivot bolt and remove the tensioner assembly from the engine. **Note:** *Store the assembly so the tensioner strut is the correct way up; if the strut is not stored properly it will have to be primed once it is refitted.*

2 Remove the braking system vacuum pump as described in Chapter 9.

3 To improve access to the injection pump sprocket cover and the pump, carry out the following:

a) *Remove the air cleaner housing and exhaust system front pipe (see Chapter 4B).*

b) *Mark the position of the right-hand engine mounting bracket in relation to the cylinder head bracket. Undo the three bolts securing the right-hand engine mounting to the cylinder head bracket, and the three bolts securing the right-hand engine mounting to the inner wing, then raise the right-hand end of the engine using a jack/engine support bar*

(see Section 17). Raise the engine as high as possible without placing any excess strain on the remaining mountings or any pipes/hoses or wiring.

4 Remove the camshaft cover and position No 1 cylinder at TDC on it compression stroke as described in Section 3.

5 Remove the crankshaft sensor as described in Chapter 4B, Section 9.

6 Undo the retaining screws and remove the injection pump sprocket cover from the timing chain cover.

7 Ensure the crankshaft pulley notch is correctly aligned with the timing chain cover mark then insert the crankshaft locking pin into the crankshaft sensor aperture and engage it with the slot in the crankshaft web **(see illustrations 3.7a and 3.7b)**.

8 With the crankshaft locked in position, insert the injection pump flange locking pin into the hole in the flange and engage it with hole in the pump body, then slide the camshaft locking tool into position on the left-hand end of the camshaft **(see illustrations)**.

9 If all the locking tools can be correctly fitted, the valve timing is correctly set and no adjustment is necessary; proceed as described in paragraphs 21 to 26. If either of the tools can not be inserted, adjust the timing as follows, noting that a new camshaft sprocket bolt and tensioner bolt sealing ring will be required.

10 Remove the camshaft/injection pump sprocket locking tool (as applicable) then unbolt the right-hand mounting bracket assembly from the cylinder head.

4.8a Insert the locking pin in through the flange cut-out and engage it in the pump body hole

4.8b Engage the camshaft locking tool with the camshaft cut-out (arrowed)

4.14 Ensure the pump sprocket timing mark (arrowed) is correctly positioned then tighten the sprocket bolts

4.18 Adjust the upper timing chain tension as described then tighten the camshaft sprocket bolt to the Stage 1 torque setting

4.21 Apply a bead of sealant to the mating surface of the injection pump sprocket cover mating surface

11 Unscrew the upper timing chain tensioner cap from the rear of the cylinder head and remove the plunger, noting which way around it is fitted. Remove the sealing ring from the cap and discard it, a new one should be used on refitting.

12 Hold the camshaft, using an open-ended spanner on the flats provided, then slacken and remove the camshaft sprocket retaining bolt. Fit the new bolt, tightening it finger-tight only at this stage.

13 Slacken the bolts securing the injection pump sprocket to the pump flange.

14 With the crankshaft locked in position, ensure the timing mark on the injection pump upper timing chain sprocket is correctly aligned with the pump flange timing hole. Insert the flange locking pin, making sure it is correctly seated, then tighten the sprocket retaining bolts to the specified torque **(see illustration)**.

15 Slide the camshaft locking tool into position making sure its pin engages centrally in the camshaft bore.

16 With all locking tools in position, fit the sprocket wrench to the camshaft sprocket; in the absence of the special wrench, pass two bolts through the sprocket holes and use a screwdriver to lever on the bolts. Have an assistant keep the timing chain taut on its guide (upper) side by applying **slight** pressure to the sprocket; this will ensure all slack in the chain is on the tensioner side of chain.

17 With the upper timing chain tensioned as described, check that the injection pump locking pin slides in and out of position with only a slight amount of drag. If excessive force is needed to move the pin, have your assistant decrease the pressure on the sprocket or, if the pin moves easily, increase the pressure.

18 Once the upper timing chain is correctly tensioned, retain the camshaft with an open-ended spanner and tighten the camshaft sprocket retaining bolt to the specified Stage 1 torque setting **(see illustration)**. Check the injection pump pin action then tighten the bolt through the specified Stage 2 angle. It is recommended that an angle-measuring gauge is used during the final stage of the tightening, to ensure accuracy. If a gauge is not available, use white paint to make alignment marks

between the bolt head and pulley prior to tightening; the marks can then be used to check that the bolt has been rotated through the correct angle.

19 Remove all the locking tools and fit a new sealing ring to the upper timing chain tensioner cap. Insert the plunger into the cylinder head, ensuring its closed end is facing the timing chain, then install the cap and tighten it to the specified torque. **Note:** *If a new tensioner is being fitted, release it by pushing the cap centre pin fully in until it is heard to 'click', the tensioner pin should then be able to be easily depressed and return smoothly.*

20 Rotate the crankshaft through two complete rotations (720°) in the correct direction of rotation (to bring number 1 piston back to TDC on its compression stroke) and check that all the locking tools can be inserted correctly.

21 Ensure the mating surfaces of the pump sprocket cover and timing chain cover are clean and dry. Where the cover was originally fitted with a gasket, fit the cover with a new gasket and tighten the retaining bolts to the specified torque. If no gasket was fitted, apply a bead of sealant (approximately 2 mm thick) to the cover mating surface then refit the cover and tighten its retaining bolts to the specified torque **(see illustration)**.

22 Refit the auxiliary drivebelt tensioner assembly to the engine unit, tightening the strut and backplate pivot bolts to their specified torque settings. If a new tensioner strut is being fitted, or the original was not stored properly, prime the strut by repeatedly compressing it using a socket on the backplate hexagonal section. Once the strut is functioning correctly, refit the auxiliary drivebelt as described in Chapter 1B.

23 Refit the right-hand mounting bracket assembly to the cylinder head (where removed) then lower the engine/transmission unit back down. Refit the right-hand engine mounting to the inner wing and align the mounting with the previously made marks on the cylinder head bracket, fit and tighten the bolts to the specified torque. Refit the camshaft cover (see Section 5).

24 Refit the exhaust front pipe and air cleaner housing as described in the Chapter 4B.

25 Refit the vacuum pump to the cylinder head (see Chapter 9).

26 Fit the crankshaft sensor to the cylinder block (see Chapter 4B, Section 9) and reconnect the battery.

5 Camshaft cover – removal and refitting

Removal

1 Undo the retaining screws and remove the plastic cover from the top of the camshaft cover.

2 Slacken the retaining clip and disconnect the breather hose from the rear of the cover.

3 Release the retaining clips and bracket bolts, and remove the charge air pipe from the turbocharger to the intercooler.

4 Carefully unclip and release the glow plug wiring guide from the rear of the cover. Undo the bolt securing the inlet manifold wiring harness tray to the cover. Where applicable, unclip the vacuum pipe and fuel hoses from the right-hand end of the cover.

5 Unscrew and remove the camshaft cover retaining bolts along with their sealing washers then lift the camshaft cover and seal away from the cylinder head **(see illustration)**. Examine the cover seal and retaining bolt sealing washers for signs of damage or deterioration and renew if necessary.

5.5 Slacken and remove the camshaft cover retaining bolts noting the sealing washer (arrowed) which is fitted to each bolt

5.6 Fit the seal to the camshaft cover groove

5.8a Apply a smear of sealant to the semi-circular cut-out on the right-hand end of the cylinder head . . .

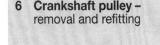

5.8b . . . and to the areas of the cylinder head surface on each side of the left-hand end camshaft cap (arrowed)

Refitting

6 Ensure the cover and cylinder head surfaces are clean and dry then fit the seal to the cover groove **(see illustration)**.

7 Fit the sealing washers to the retaining bolts, ensuring they are fitted the correct way up. Fit the retaining bolts to the cover making sure the cover seal is held firmly in position by the lower shoulder on each bolt.

8 Apply a smear of sealant to the circular cut-out on the right-hand end of the cylinder head mating surface and the areas of the cylinder head mating surface on either side of the left-hand end of the camshaft **(see illustrations)**.

9 Carefully lower the cover into position and screw in the retaining bolts. Once all bolts are hand-tight, go around and tighten them all to the specified torque setting.

10 Clip the vacuum pipe and wiring back into position and reconnect the breather hose to the rear of the cover. Where applicable, reposition the fuel hoses into their retaining clips on the right-hand end of the cover.

11 Refit the wiring harness tray and the glow plug wiring guide.

12 Refit the turbocharger-to-intercooler hose then tighten the mounting bracket bolt and retaining clips securely.

13 Reconnect the breather hose and tighten the clip.

14 Refit the plastic cover and securely tighten its retaining bolts.

6 Crankshaft pulley – removal and refitting

Note: *A new pulley retaining bolt will be required on refitting.*

Removal

1 Apply the handbrake, then jack up the front of the car and support it on axle stands. Remove the right-hand roadwheel and wheel arch liner (Chapter 11, Section 23).

2 Remove the auxiliary drivebelt as described in Chapter 1B. Prior to removal, mark the direction of rotation on the belt to ensure the belt is refitted the same way around.

3 Slacken the crankshaft pulley retaining bolt. To prevent crankshaft rotation whilst the retaining bolt is slackened, have an assistant select top gear and apply the brakes firmly, however, temporarily refit the right-hand roadwheel bolts to prevent damage to the brake disc retaining screw. If the engine is removed from the vehicle it will be necessary to lock the flywheel (see Section 16).

4 Unscrew the retaining bolt and washer and remove the crankshaft pulley from the end of the crankshaft. Whilst the pulley is removed check the oil seal for signs of wear or damage and, if necessary, renew as described in Section 15.

Refitting

5 Carefully locate the crankshaft pulley on the crankshaft end, aligning the pulley slot with the crankshaft key. Slide the pulley fully into position, taking great care not to damage the oil seal, then fit the washer and new retaining bolt **(see illustrations)**.

6 Lock the crankshaft by the method used on removal, and tighten the pulley retaining bolt to the specified Stage 1 torque setting then angle-tighten the bolt through the specified Stage 2 angle, using a socket and extension bar. It is recommended that an angle-measuring gauge is used during the final stage of the tightening, to ensure accuracy **(see illustration)**. If a gauge is not available, use white paint to make alignment marks between the bolt head and pulley prior to tightening; the marks can then be used to check that the bolt has been rotated through the correct angle.

7 Refit the auxiliary drivebelt as described in Chapter 1B using the mark made prior to removal to ensure the belt is fitted the correct way around.

8 Refit the wheel arch liner and roadwheel, then lower the car to the ground and tighten the wheel bolts to the specified torque.

7 Timing chain cover – removal and refitting

Note: *In theory it is possible to remove the timing chain cover without disturbing the cylinder head. However, this procedure carries*

6.5a Slide the crankshaft pulley carefully into position engaging its slot (arrowed) with the Woodruff key . . .

6.5b . . . then fit the retaining bolt and washer

6.6 Lock the crankshaft then tighten the pulley retaining bolt

7.9 Timing chain cover retaining bolt locations (arrowed)

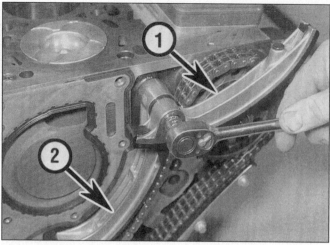

7.11 Unscrew the pivot bolt and remove the upper (1) and lower (2) timing chain tensioner blades

a high risk of damaging the head gasket, resulting in oil/coolant leakage once the cover is refitted. If you wish to attempt this, leave the cylinder head in position and just undo the retaining bolts securing the head to the top of the timing chain cover. Be warned though that, after refitting, you may find the head gasket will need renewing, meaning that the cylinder head will have to be removed after all. The decision is yours as to whether this is a chance worth taking.

Removal

1 Remove the upper timing chain and sprockets as described in Section 9.
2 Remove the cylinder head as described in Section 11.
3 Remove the water pump as described in Chapter 3.
4 Remove the crankshaft pulley as described in Section 6. Prior to slackening the pulley bolt, temporarily remove the locking pin from the crankshaft to prevent damage. Refit the pin once the bolt is loose.
5 Remove the sump as described in Section 12.
6 Remove the alternator as described in Chapter 5A.

7 Remove the power steering pump as described in Chapter 10.
8 Unscrew the lower timing chain tensioner cap from the rear of the timing chain cover and remove the tensioner plunger, noting which way around it is fitted. Remove the sealing ring from the cap and discard it, a new one should be used on refitting.
9 Noting each bolt's correct fitted location (the bolts are not all the same length), slacken and remove all the bolts securing the timing chain cover to the cylinder block **(see illustration)**.
10 Carefully ease the timing cover squarely away from the cylinder block and manoeuvre it out of position, noting the correct fitted positions of its locating dowels. If the locating dowels are a loose fit, remove them and store with the cover for safe-keeping.
11 Undo the pivot bolt and remove the upper and lower timing chain tensioner blades from the cylinder block **(see illustration)**.
12 Undo the retaining bolts and remove the lower timing chain guide from the cylinder block, noting which way around the guide is fitted **(see illustration)**.
13 Temporarily free the lower timing chain sprocket from the injection pump and manoeuvre the timing chain cover gasket

away from the cylinder block. Once the gasket has been removed, seat the sprocket back on the injection pump flange **(see illustration)**.

Refitting

14 Prior to refitting the cover, it is recommended that the crankshaft oil seal should be renewed. Carefully lever the old seal out of the cover using a large flat-bladed screwdriver. Fit the new seal to the cover, making sure its sealing lip is facing inwards. Press/tap the seal into position until it is flush with the cover, using a suitable tubular drift, such as a socket, which bears only on the hard outer edge of the seal.
15 Ensure the mating surfaces of the cover and cylinder block are clean and dry and the locating dowels are in position.
16 Temporarily free the sprocket from the injection pump flange then manoeuvre the gasket into position and locate it on the dowels. Locate the sprocket back on the injection pump flange.
17 Refit the lower timing chain guide to the cylinder block and tighten its new retaining bolts to the specified torque. Ensure the guide is fitted the correct way around with its stepped face on the inside **(see illustration)**.

7.12 Undo the retaining bolts (arrowed) and remove the lower timing chain guide

7.13 Free the sprocket from the injection pump and remove the timing chain cover gasket

7.17 Refit the lower timing chain guide and tighten its retaining bolts to the specified torque

7.18 Refit the pivot bolt to the tensioner blades and tighten to the specified torque

8.6a Unscrew the tensioner cap from the rear of the cylinder head . . .

8.6b . . . and withdraw the plunger, noting which way round it is fitted

18 Manoeuvre the timing chain tensioner blades into position and refit the pivot bolt, tightening it to the specified torque **(see illustration)**.

19 Manoeuvre the timing cover into position. Align the oil pump drivegear with the crankshaft sprocket and slide the cover into position, locating it on the dowels.

20 Refit the timing chain cover retaining bolts, ensuring each one is fitted in its original location, and tighten them evenly and progressively to the specified torque.

21 Fit a new sealing ring to the lower timing chain tensioner cap. Insert the plunger, ensuring its closed end is facing the timing chain, then fit the cap to the timing chain cover and tighten to the specified torque. **Note:** *If a new tensioner is being fitted, release it by pushing the cap centre pin fully in until it is heard to 'click', the tensioner pin should then be able to be easily depressed and return smoothly.*

22 Refit the crankshaft pulley as described in Section 6.

23 Refit the cylinder head as described in Section 11.

24 Refit the upper timing chain and sprockets as described in Section 9.

25 Refit the sump as described in Section 12.

26 Refit the water pump, alternator and power steering pump (see Chapter 3, 5A and 10) and refit the auxiliary drivebelt (see Chapter 1B).

27 On completion refill the engine with oil and coolant as described in Chapter 1A. Start the engine and check for signs of oil leaks.

8 Timing chain tensioners – removal and refitting

Upper chain tensioner

Removal

1 Remove the air cleaner housing together with the mass airflow meter as described in Chapter 4B.

2 Apply the handbrake, then jack up the front of the vehicle and support it on axle stands (see *Jacking and vehicle support*). Remove the right-hand front roadwheel and wheel arch liner, and the engine undertray.

3 Unscrew the nuts securing the exhaust front pipe to the turbocharger.

4 Remove the auxiliary drivebelt as described in Chapter 1B, then unbolt and remove the auxiliary drivebelt tensioner.

5 Referring to Section 17 support the engine/

transmission unit and unbolt the right-hand mounting assembly from the cylinder head.

6 Unscrew the tensioner cap from the rear of the cylinder head and remove the plunger, noting which way round it is fitted **(see illustrations)**. Remove the sealing ring from the cap and discard it, a new one should be used on refitting.

Caution: Do not rotate the engine whilst the tensioner is removed.

7 Inspect the tensioner plunger for signs of wear or damage and renew if necessary.

Refitting

8 Lubricate the tensioner plunger with clean engine oil and insert it into the cylinder head. Ensure the plunger is fitted the correct way around with its closed end facing the timing chain.

9 Fit a new sealing ring to the tensioner cap then fit the cap to the cylinder head, tightening it to the specified torque. **Note:** *If a new tensioner is being fitted, release it by pushing the cap centre pin fully in until it is heard to 'click', the tensioner pin should then be able to be easily depressed and return smoothly (see illustrations).*

10 Refit the engine/transmission right-hand mounting assembly (see Section 17).

11 Refit the auxiliary drivebelt tensioner and tighten the bolts to the specified torque.

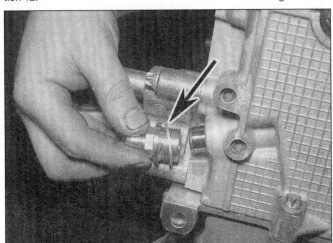

8.9a Insert the plunger, making sure its closed end facing the timing chain, then fit tensioner cap and sealing washer (arrowed)

8.9b If a new tensioner is being fitted, release it by depressing the cap centre pin until it is heard to click

8.17a Slacken and remove the lower timing chain tensioner cap and sealing washer from the rear of the timing chain cover . . .

8.17b . . . then withdraw the tensioner plunger

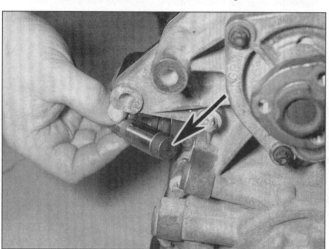

8.19 Ensure the plunger is fitted the correct way around with its closed end (arrowed) facing the timing chain

8.20 If a new tensioner is being fitted, release it by depressing the centre pin until it is heard to click

12 Refit the auxiliary drivebelt with reference to Chapter 1B.

13 Refit the exhaust front pipe to the turbocharger and tighten the nuts to the specified torque.

14 Refit the engine undertray, wheel arch liner and front roadwheel, then lower the vehicle to the ground.

15 Refit the air cleaner housing as described in Chapter 4B.

Lower chain tensioner

Removal

16 Apply the handbrake, then jack up the front of the vehicle and support it on axle stands (see *Jacking and vehicle support*). Remove the right-hand front roadwheel and the wheel arch liner, and if necessary the engine undertray.

17 Unscrew the tensioner cap from the rear of the timing chain cover and remove the plunger, noting which way round it is fitted. Remove the sealing ring from the cap and discard it, a new one should be used on refitting **(see illustrations)**.

Caution: Do not rotate the engine whilst the tensioner is removed.

18 Inspect the tensioner plunger for signs of wear or damage and renew if necessary.

Refitting

19 Lubricate the tensioner plunger with clean engine oil and insert it into the timing chain cover. Ensure the plunger is fitted the correct way around with its closed end facing the timing chain **(see illustration)**.

20 Fit a new sealing ring to the tensioner cap then fit the cap to the cover, tightening it to the specified torque. **Note:** *If a new tensioner is being fitted, release it by pushing the cap centre pin fully in until it is heard to 'click', the tensioner pin should then be able to be easily depressed and return smoothly (see illustration)*.

21 Refit the engine undertray, wheel arch liner and roadwheel, and lower the vehicle to the ground.

Tensioner blades

22 Tensioner blade removal and refitting is part of the timing chain cover removal and refitting procedure (see Section 7). The blades must be renewed if they show signs of wear or damage on their chain surfaces.

9 Timing chains and sprockets – removal, inspection and refitting

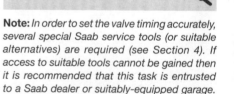

Note: *In order to set the valve timing accurately, several special Saab service tools (or suitable alternatives) are required (see Section 4). If access to suitable tools cannot be gained then it is recommended that this task is entrusted to a Saab dealer or suitably-equipped garage. If the task is to be carried out without the tools then accurate alignment marks must be made between the sprocket(s), chain(s) and the shaft(s) prior to removal to ensure the valve timing is correctly set on refitting.*

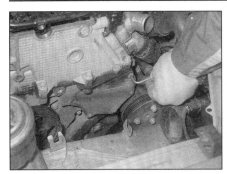

9.7a Undo the retaining screws . . .

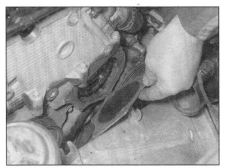

9.7b . . . and remove the injection pump sprocket cover from the engine

9.9a To ease removal, heat the upper timing chain guide bolts with a hot air gun prior to removal

Removal

Upper chain and sprockets

Note: *A new camshaft sprocket bolt and new timing chain guide retaining bolts will be required on refitting.*

1 Disconnect the battery negative lead then remove the camshaft cover (see Section 5).

2 Position No 1 cylinder at TDC on its compression stroke as described in Section 3 and lock the crankshaft in position.

3 To allow access to the injection pump sprocket cover, carry out the following.

  a) *Remove the air cleaner housing together with the mass airflow meter and hoses, and the exhaust system front pipe (see Chapter 4B).*

  b) *Remove the auxiliary drivebelt (Chapter 1B).*

  c) *Remove the right-hand engine mounting as described in Section 17, then raise the engine as high as possible without placing any excess strain on the remaining mountings or any pipes/hoses or wiring.*

4 Refer to Chapter 4B and detach the fuel lines from the injection pump by unscrewing the union bolts. Tape over or plug the fuel lines and apertures to prevent entry of dust and dirt.

5 Remove the upper and lower timing chain tensioners (Section 8).

6 Undo the auxiliary drivebelt tensioner pulley strut lower mounting bolt and the pulley backplate pivot bolt and remove the tensioner assembly from the engine. **Note:** *Store the assembly so the tensioner strut is the correct way up; if the strut is not stored properly it will have to be primed once it is refitted.*

7 Undo the retaining bolts and remove the injection pump sprocket cover from the timing chain cover **(see illustrations)**.

8 If the special locking tools are available, lock the injection pump sprockets and camshaft in position (see Section 4). If the tools are not being used, make accurate alignment marks between the chain and sprockets, and the sprockets and the camshaft/pump flange.

9 Undo the retaining bolts then lift the upper

9.9b Unscrew both retaining bolts . . .

chain guide out from the top of the cylinder head. **Note:** *The upper timing chain guide bolts should be heated with a hot air gun prior to removal; this loosens the locking compound on the bolt head and significantly eases removal of the bolts* **(see illustrations)**.

10 Hold the camshaft using an open-ended spanner on the flats provided, then slacken and remove the camshaft sprocket retaining bolt **(see illustration)**. To ensure the camshaft sprocket and chain remain correctly mated, cable tie the chain to the sprocket. **Note:** *If the locking tools are being used, remove them prior to slackening the sprocket bolt and refit them once the bolt is loose.*

11 Remove the injection pump locking tool (where fitted) then slacken and remove the

9.10 Retain the camshaft with an open-ended spanner and unscrew the sprocket retaining bolt

9.9c . . . and lift the upper guide out from the top of the cylinder head

bolts securing the injection pump sprockets to the pump flange. Manoeuvre the injection pump upper chain sprocket out of position then free the camshaft sprocket from the camshaft end and lift the sprocket and upper timing chain out from the top of the cylinder head **(see illustration)**.

Lower chain and sprockets

12 Remove the upper timing chain and sprockets as described in paragraphs 1 to 11.

13 Remove the timing chain cover as described in Section 7.

14 Make alignment marks between the chain and sprockets and the injection pump sprocket and pump flange.

15 Free the pump sprocket from its flange and remove the sprocket and timing chain

9.11 Unbolt the sprocket from the injection pump then free it from the chain and remove it through the cover aperture

9.15 Free the sprocket from the injection pump flange and remove it, complete with the lower timing chain

9.16a Slide the sprocket off from the end of the crankshaft . . .

9.16b . . . and remove the Woodruff key

from the engine, noting which way around the sprocket is fitted (see illustration).

16 Slide the crankshaft sprocket off from the crankshaft end and recover the Woodruff key from the crankshaft groove (see illustrations).

Inspection

17 Examine the teeth on the sprockets for any sign of wear or damage such as chipped, hooked or missing teeth. If there is any sign of wear or damage on either sprocket, both sprockets and the relevant chain should be renewed as a set.

18 Inspect the links of each timing chain for signs of wear or damage on the rollers. The extent of wear can be judged by checking the amount by which the chain can be bent sideways; a new chain will have very little sideways movement. If there is an excessive amount of side play in a timing chain, it must be renewed.

19 Note that it is a sensible precaution to renew the timing chains, regardless of their apparent condition, if the engine has covered a high mileage, or if it has been noted that the chain(s) have sounded noisy when the engine is running. Although not strictly necessary, it is always worth renewing the chains and sprockets as a matched set, since it is false economy to run a new chain on worn sprockets and vice-versa. If there is any doubt about the condition of the timing chains and sprockets, seek the advice of a Saab dealer

service department, who will be able to advise you as to the best course of action, based on their previous knowledge of the engine.

20 Examine the chain guide(s) and tensioner blade(s) for signs of wear or damage to their chain contact faces, renewing any which are badly marked.

Refitting

Upper chain and sprockets

21 If any new components are being fitted, transfer the alignment marks from the original components to aid refitting. Ensure the crankshaft is still locked in the TDC position.

22 Engage the camshaft sprocket with the chain and lower the assembly into position, then manoeuvre the injection pump sprocket into position and engage it with the timing chain.

23 Ensure the marks made prior to removal are all correctly aligned then engage the sprockets with the camshaft and injection pump flange. Where necessary, remove the cable tie from the camshaft sprocket.

24 Align the injection pump sprocket timing mark with the hole in the pump flange then refit the retaining bolts, tightening them by hand only at this stage (see illustration).

25 Fit the new sprocket retaining bolt to the camshaft end, tightening by hand only at this stage (see illustration).

26 Refit the lower timing chain tensioner as described in Section 8.

27 Slide the upper timing chain guide

into position, ensuring its locating lug is uppermost, then fit the new retaining bolts and tighten them to the specified torque (see illustration).

28 If the special tools are available, fit all the tools to ensure the pump, camshaft and crankshaft are correctly positioned. If the tools are not being used, ensure the marks made prior to removal are realigned.

29 If the special tools are available, adjust the valve timing as described in Section 4, paragraphs 14 to 18. Remove all the locking tools.

30 If the tools are not available, align the marks made prior to removal then tighten the injection pump sprocket bolts to the specified torque. Tighten the camshaft sprocket bolt to the specified Stage 1 torque setting, whilst preventing the camshaft from rotating. Ensure the marks remain in alignment then tighten the bolt through the specified Stage 2 angle. It is recommended that an angle-measuring gauge is used during the final stage of the tightening, to ensure accuracy. If a gauge is not available, use white paint to make alignment marks prior to tightening; the marks can then be used to check that the bolt has been rotated through the correct angle.

31 Refit the upper timing chain tensioner as described in Section 8.

32 Ensure the mating surfaces of the pump sprocket cover and timing chain cover are clean and dry. Where the cover was originally fitted with a gasket, fit the cover with a new

9.24 Align the injection pump sprocket timing mark (arrowed) with the pump flange hole and refit the retaining bolts

9.25 Fit the new camshaft sprocket retaining bolt and tighten it by hand only

9.27 Refit the upper timing chain guide to the cylinder head making sure its locating lug (arrowed) is uppermost

gasket and tighten the retaining bolts to the specified torque. If no gasket was fitted, apply a bead of sealant (approximately 2 mm thick) to the cover groove then refit the cover and tighten its retaining bolts to the specified torque.

33 Refit the camshaft cover with reference to Section 5.

34 Refit the auxiliary drivebelt tensioner assembly to the engine unit, tightening the strut and backplate pivot bolts to their specified torque settings. If a new tensioner strut is being fitted, or the original was not stored properly, prime the strut by repeatedly compressing it using a socket on the backplate hexagonal section. Once the strut is functioning correctly, refit the auxiliary drivebelt as described in Chapter 1B.

35 Refit the right-hand mounting with reference to Section 17.

36 Check and if necessary renew the sealing washers, then refit the fuel lines to the injection pump and tighten the union bolts with reference to Chapter 4B.

37 Refit the exhaust front pipe and air cleaner housing with reference to Chapter 4B. Where the TDC timing tools have been used, refit the crankshaft sensor and brake vacuum pump.

Lower chain and sprockets

38 If any new components are being fitted, transfer the alignment marks from the original components to aid refitting.

39 Refit the Woodruff key to the crankshaft then slide on the crankshaft sprocket, aligning the sprocket groove with the key.

40 Ensure the injection pump flange is still correctly positioned with the flange timing cut-out aligned with the hole in the pump body and the crankshaft is still locked at TDC.

41 Aligning the marks made prior to removal, engage the pump sprocket with the chain and manoeuvre the assembly into position. Engage the chain with the crankshaft sprocket and seat the pump sprocket on the flange, ensuring the sprocket is fitted the correct way around. Check that all the marks made prior to removal are correctly aligned and that the injection pump flange timing cut-out is correctly position in the oblong slot in the sprocket.

42 Refit the timing cover as described in Section 7 then refit the upper timing chain as described earlier in this Section.

10 Camshaft and followers – removal, inspection and refitting

Note: *A new camshaft sprocket retaining bolt and new upper timing chain guide retaining bolts will be required on refitting.*

Removal

1 Disconnect the battery negative lead (see *Disconnecting the battery*) then remove the camshaft cover as described in Section 5.

2 Apply the handbrake, then jack up the front of the vehicle and support it on axle stands (see *Jacking and vehicle support*). Remove the right-hand front roadwheel, wheel arch liner and engine undertray.

3 Remove the braking system vacuum pump as described in Chapter 9.

4 Remove the exhaust manifold heat shield, then unbolt and remove the engine lifting eye and bracket.

5 Position No 1 cylinder at TDC on its compression stroke as described in Section 3 and lock the crankshaft in position.

6 To improve access to the injection pump sprocket cover, carry out the following.

a) *Remove the air cleaner housing together with the mass airflow meter and hoses, and the exhaust system front pipe (see Chapter 4B).*

b) *Remove the auxiliary drivebelt (see Chapter 1B).*

c) *Remove the right-hand engine mounting assembly with reference to Section 17. Unscrew and remove the rear engine mounting upper nut. Raise the engine as high as possible without placing any excess strain on the remaining mountings or any pipes/hoses or wiring.*

7 Remove the upper timing chain tensioner as described in Section 8.

8 Undo the auxiliary drivebelt tensioner pulley strut lower mounting bolt and the pulley backplate pivot bolt and remove the tensioner assembly from the engine. **Note:** *Store the assembly so the tensioner strut is the correct*

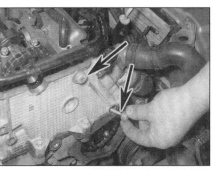

10.11 Remove the retaining bolts (arrowed) and lift out the upper timing chain guide

way up; if the strut is not stored properly it will have to be primed once it is refitted.

9 Undo the retaining bolts and remove the injection pump sprocket cover from the timing chain cover.

10 Make accurate alignment marks between the upper timing chain and sprockets, and the camshaft sprocket and camshaft.

11 Undo the retaining bolts then lift the upper chain guide out from the top of the cylinder head **(see illustration)**. **Note:** *The upper timing chain guide bolts should be heated with a hot air gun prior to removal; this loosens the locking compound on the bolt head and significantly eases removal of the bolts.*

12 Hold the camshaft, using an open-ended spanner on the flats provided, then slacken and remove the camshaft sprocket retaining bolt. Remove the crankshaft locking tool prior to slackening the sprocket bolt and refit it once the bolt is loose.

13 Disengage the camshaft sprocket from the upper timing chain and remove it from the engine. Pass a screwdriver or extension bar through the upper chain, to prevent it falling down into the cylinder head, and rest it on the head upper surface **(see illustrations)**.

14 Note the identification markings on the camshaft bearing caps. The caps are numbered 1 to 5 with all numbers being the right way up when viewed from the front of the engine; number 1 cap being at the timing chain end of the engine and number 5 at the flywheel end **(see illustration)**. If the markings are not

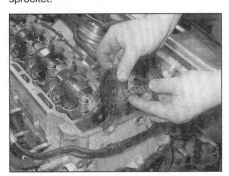

10.13a Free the camshaft sprocket from the timing chain . . .

10.13b . . . then pass a screwdriver or extension bar through the chain to prevent it falling down into the engine

10.14 Each camshaft bearing cap should be stamped with an identification number (arrowed)

10.16 Removing a camshaft follower

clearly visible, make identification marks to ensure each cap is fitted correctly on refitting.

15 Working in a spiral pattern from the outside inwards, slacken the camshaft bearing cap retaining bolts by one turn at a time, to relieve the pressure of the valve springs on the bearing caps gradually and evenly. Once the valve spring pressure has been relieved, the bolts can be fully unscrewed and removed, along with the caps. Take care not to lose the locating dowels which are fitted to left-hand end (No 5) bearing cap and lift the camshaft out from the head.

Caution: If the bearing cap bolts are carelessly slackened, the bearing caps might break. If any bearing cap breaks then the complete cylinder head assembly must be renewed; the bearing caps are matched to the head and are not available separately.

16 Obtain eight (twenty-four if the hydraulic tappets are also to be removed) small, clean plastic containers, and label them for identification. Alternatively, divide a larger container into compartments. Lift the followers out from the top of the cylinder head and store each one in its respective fitted position **(see illustration)**.

17 If the hydraulic tappets are also to be removed, remove the injector crossover pipes as described in Chapter 4B, Section 12. Using a rubber sucker or magnet, withdraw each hydraulic tappet and place it in its container.

Inspection

18 Examine the camshaft bearing surfaces and cam lobes for signs of wear ridges and scoring. Renew the camshaft if any of these conditions are apparent. Examine the condition of the bearing surfaces both on the camshaft journals and in the cylinder head. If the head bearing surfaces are worn excessively, the cylinder head will need to be renewed.

19 Support the camshaft end journals on V-blocks, and measure the run-out at the centre journal using a dial gauge. If the run-out exceeds the specified limit, the camshaft should be renewed.

20 Examine the follower bearing surfaces which contact the camshaft lobes for wear ridges and scoring. Renew any followers on which these conditions are apparent.

21 Check the hydraulic tappets (where removed) and their bores in the cylinder head

for signs of wear or damage. If any tappet is thought to be faulty it should be renewed.

Refitting

22 Where removed, lubricate the hydraulic tappets with clean engine oil and carefully insert each one into its original location in the cylinder head **(see illustration)**. Refit the injector crossover pipes as described in Chapter 4B.

23 Refit the camshaft followers to the cylinder head. Ensure each follower is fitted in its original location and the punch marks on the follower upper surface are facing the injector crossover pipe **(see illustration)**.

24 Lubricate the camshaft followers with clean engine oil then lay the camshaft in position. Ensure the crankshaft is still locked in position and position the camshaft so that the lobes of No 1 cylinder are pointing upwards and the slot on the left-hand end of the camshaft is parallel with the cylinder head surface (timing hole at the top) **(see illustrations)**.

25 Ensure the mating surfaces of the bearing caps and cylinder head are clean and dry and lubricate the camshaft journals and lobes with clean engine oil.

26 Apply a smear of sealant to the cylinder head mating surface of the left-hand (No 5) bearing cap and fit the cap locating dowels to the cylinder head **(see illustration)**.

27 Refit the camshaft bearing caps and the retaining bolts in their original locations on the cylinder head **(see illustration)**. The caps are

10.22 Lubricate the hydraulic tappets with clean engine oil and install them in the cylinder head

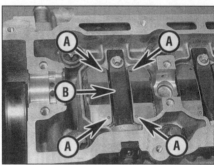

10.23 On refitting ensure that all followers are correctly positioned and that the punch marks (A) are facing towards the injector crosspipe (B)

10.24a Refit the camshaft, positioning it so that No 1 cylinder lobes are pointing upwards (arrowed) . . .

10.24b . . . and the slot in its left-hand end is parallel to the cylinder head with the timing hole (arrowed) at the top

10.26 Apply sealant to the areas shown on the left-hand end of the cylinder head (arrowed)

10.27 Refit the camshaft bearing caps using the identification markings to ensure each one is correctly positioned

10.28 Working as described in text, tighten the bearing cap bolts to the specified torque

10.29 Refit the camshaft sprocket and install the new retaining bolt

10.32a If the timing tools are not available, align the marks made prior to removal then tighten the sprocket bolt to the Stage 1 torque setting . . .

10.32b . . . and then through the specified Stage 2 angle

numbered 1 to 5 from timing chain end of the cylinder head and all numbers should be the right way up when viewed from the front of the engine.

28 Tighten all bolts by hand only, then, working in a spiral pattern from the centre outwards, tighten the bolts by one turn at a time to gradually impose the pressure of the valve springs on the bearing caps. Repeat this sequence until all bearing caps are in contact with the cylinder head then go around and tighten the camshaft bearing cap bolts to the specified torque **(see illustration)**.

Caution: If the bearing cap bolts are carelessly tightened, the bearing caps might break. If any bearing cap breaks then the complete cylinder head assembly must be renewed; the bearing caps are matched to the head and are not available separately.

29 Using the marks made on removal, ensure that the upper timing chain is still correctly engaged with the injection pump sprocket then refit the camshaft sprocket to the chain. Seat the sprocket on the end of the camshaft and fit the new retaining bolt **(see illustration)**.

30 Slide the upper timing chain guide into position, ensuring its locating lug is uppermost, then fit the new retaining bolts and tighten them to the specified torque.

31 If the special tools are available, adjust the valve timing as described in Section 4. Remove all the locking tools.

32 If the tools are not available, align the marks made prior to removal on the camshaft and sprocket. Hold the camshaft with an open-ended spanner and tighten the sprocket bolt to the specified Stage 1 torque setting. Ensure the marks have remained in alignment then tighten the bolt through the specified Stage 2 angle. It is recommended that an angle-measuring gauge is used during the final stage of the tightening, to ensure accuracy **(see illustrations)**. If a gauge is not available, use white paint to make alignment marks prior to tightening; the marks can then be used to check that the bolt has been rotated through the correct angle.

33 Refit the upper timing chain tensioner as described in Section 8.

34 Ensure the mating surfaces of the pump

sprocket cover and timing chain cover are clean and dry. Where the cover was originally fitted with a gasket, fit the cover with a new gasket and tighten the retaining bolts to the specified torque. If no gasket was fitted, apply a bead of sealant (approximately 2 mm thick) to the cover groove then refit the cover and tighten its retaining bolts to the specified torque.

35 Refit the auxiliary drivebelt tensioner assembly to the engine unit, tightening the strut and backplate pivot bolts to their specified torque settings. If a new tensioner strut is being fitted, or the original was not stored properly, prime the strut by repeatedly compressing it using a socket on the backplate hexagonal section. Once the strut is functioning correctly, refit the auxiliary drivebelt as described in Chapter 1B.

36 Refit the right-hand engine mounting assembly with reference to Section 17 and tighten the bolts to the specified torque. Also, tighten the rear engine mounting upper nut to the specified torque.

37 Refit the camshaft cover as described in Section 5.

38 Refit the exhaust front pipe, air cleaner housing and crankshaft sensor (see Chapter 4B).

39 Refit the engine lifting eye and bracket, and tighten the bolts. Also, refit the exhaust manifold heat shield.

40 Refit the braking system vacuum pump as described in Chapter 9.

41 Refit the engine undertray, wheel arch liner and roadwheel, and lower the vehicle to the ground.

42 Reconnect the battery negative lead.

11 Cylinder head – removal and refitting

Caution: Be careful not to allow dirt into the fuel injection pump or injector pipes during this procedure.

Note: *New cylinder head bolts, upper timing chain guide bolts and a camshaft sprocket retaining bolt will be required on refitting.*

Removal

1 Remove the engine top cover, then drain the cooling system as described in Chapter 1B.

2 Carry out the operations described in paragraphs 1 to 13 of Section 10, noting that it will be necessary to raise the engine on a jack. Support the engine by inserting a stout block of wood between the right-hand end of the sump and the subframe. **Note:** *If the sump needs to be removed at the same time as the head, it will be necessary to fabricate a supporting cradle while the right-hand engine mounting is removed.*

3 Disconnect the wiring from the oil level sensor and oil temperature sensor on the sump, then release the wiring from the cable tie.

4 On the rear right-hand corner of the engine compartment, disconnect the two fuel lines and tape over or plug them to prevent entry of dust and dirt.

5 Unscrew the bolts and remove the charge air hose leading from the turbocharger to the inlet manifold.

6 Disconnect the wiring from the following, and release the wiring from the cable tie:
 a) *Atmospheric pressure sensor.*
 b) *Coolant temperature sensor.*
 c) *Engine management ECU.*
 d) *EGR valve.*
 e) *TDC sensor.*
 f) *Pressure/temperature sensor.*

7 Remove the wiring harness conduit from the cylinder head.

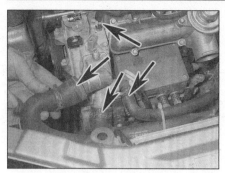

11.11 Disconnect the coolant hoses (arrowed) from the thermostat housing

11.13a Unscrew the union bolts (arrowed) then disconnect the fuel feed and return hose unions from the injection pump . . .

11.13b . . . and disconnect the return pipe

8 Disconnect the wiring from the glow plugs, then remove the wiring harness and bracket from the engine mounting.

9 Release the vent hose from the thermostat housing, then remove the EGR valve with reference to Chapter 4C.

10 Disconnect the fuel leak-off hoses from the injectors.

11 Release the clips and disconnect the two coolant hoses from the thermostat housing **(see illustration)**.

12 Note the position of the fuel lines from the fuel injection pump to the injectors, then unscrew the union nuts and remove the lines. Tape over or plug the ports to prevent entry of dust and dirt.

13 Wipe clean the area around the fuel hose unions on the injection pump then slacken and remove the union bolts and sealing washers. Disconnect the return pipe from the pump union then release the hoses from their retaining clips, and position them clear of the cylinder head **(see illustrations)**.

14 Disconnect the vacuum hose from the swirl throttle control valve on the left-hand end of the cylinder head.

15 Unbolt the coolant hose support hook from the rear engine lifting eye.

16 Remove the heat shields from the turbocharger, exhaust manifold and starter motor.

17 Disconnect the vacuum hose from the turbocharger wastegate.

18 Refer to Chapter 4B, and remove the front

exhaust pipe from the turbocharger.

19 Release the clip and disconnect the coolant hose located above the alternator on the rear of the cylinder block **(see illustration)**. Take care to prevent coolant entering the alternator.

20 Unscrew the upper bolt securing the stay to the exhaust manifold, then loosen the lower bolt and turn the stay to one side.

21 Unscrew the union nuts and disconnect the turbocharger oil pipes from the cylinder block.

22 Remove the pulley and water pump with reference to Chapter 3, in order to provide additional working room.

23 Unscrew the alternator upper mounting bolt, then loosen the lower mounting bolt and swivel the alternator downwards, away from the cylinder head **(see illustration)**.

24 At this stage, the inlet and exhaust manifolds may be removed with reference to Chapter 4B, in order to lessen the weight of the cylinder head. Alternatively, if no work is to be carried out on the cylinder head, the head can be removed complete with manifolds.

25 Unscrew and remove the bolts securing the right-hand end of the cylinder head to the top of the timing chain cover and block **(see illustration)**.

26 Working in the **reverse** of the sequence shown in illustration 11.44, progressively slacken the ten main cylinder head bolts by half a turn at a time, until all bolts can be unscrewed by hand.

27 Lift out the cylinder head bolts and recover the washers.

28 Lift the cylinder head away, at the same time feeding the upper timing chain down through the hole in the head. Seek assistance if possible, as it is a heavy assembly (especially if complete with manifolds). Remove the gasket, noting the two locating dowels fitted to the top of the cylinder block. If they are a loose fit, remove the locating dowels and store them with the head for safe-keeping. Keep the head gasket for identification purposes (see paragraph 35).

Caution: Do not lay the head on its lower mating surface; support the head on wooden blocks, ensuring each block only contacts the head mating surface not the glow plugs or injector nozzles. The glow plugs and injector nozzles protrude out of the bottom of the head and they will be damaged if the head is placed directly onto a bench.

29 If the cylinder head is to be dismantled for overhaul, then refer to Part C of this Chapter.

Preparation for refitting

30 The mating faces of the cylinder head and cylinder block/crankcase must be perfectly clean before refitting the head. Use a hard plastic or wood scraper to remove all traces of gasket and carbon; also clean the piston crowns. Take particular care, as the surfaces are damaged easily. Also, make sure that the carbon is not allowed to enter the oil and

11.19 Disconnect the coolant hose from the rear of the engine

11.23 Remove the upper mounting bolt and pivot the alternator away from the cylinder head

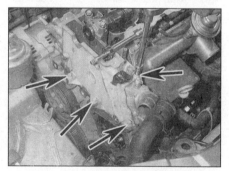

11.25 Unscrew the bolts (arrowed) securing the right-hand end of the cylinder head to the timing chain cover/block

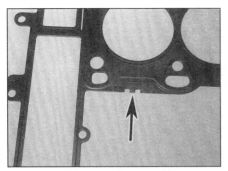

11.35 Cylinder head gasket thickness identification cut-outs (arrowed)

11.36 Measuring piston protrusion using a dial gauge

11.40 Ensure the locating dowels are in position (arrowed) and fit the new gasket

water passages – this is particularly important for the lubrication system, as carbon could block the oil supply to any of the engine's components. Using adhesive tape and paper, seal the water, oil and bolt holes in the cylinder block/crankcase. To prevent carbon entering the gap between the pistons and bores, smear a little grease in the gap. After cleaning each piston, use a small brush to remove all traces of grease and carbon from the gap, then wipe away the remainder with a clean rag. Clean all the pistons in the same way.

31 Check the mating surfaces of the cylinder block/crankcase and the cylinder head for nicks, deep scratches and other damage. If slight, they may be removed carefully with a file, but if excessive, machining may be the only alternative to renewal.

32 Ensure that the cylinder head bolt holes in the crankcase are clean and free of oil. Syringe or soak up any oil left in the bolt holes. This is most important in order that the correct bolt tightening torque can be applied and to prevent the possibility of the block being cracked by hydraulic pressure when the bolts are tightened.

33 The cylinder head bolts must be discarded and renewed, regardless of their apparent condition.

34 If warpage of the cylinder head gasket surface is suspected, use a straight-edge to check it for distortion. Refer to Part C of this Chapter if necessary.

35 On this engine, the cylinder head-to-piston clearance is controlled by fitting different thickness head gaskets. The gasket thickness can be determined by looking at the tab situated directly in front of No 1 cylinder **(see illustration)**.

Notches on tab	Gasket thickness
No notches	1.2 mm
One notch	1.3 mm
Two notches	1.4 mm

The correct thickness of gasket required is selected by measuring the piston protrusions as follows.

36 Ensure that the crankshaft is still locked in the TDC position. Mount a dial test indicator securely on the block so that its pointer can be easily pivoted between the piston crown and block mating surface. Zero the dial test indicator on the gasket surface of the cylinder block then

carefully move the indicator over No 1 piston and measure its protrusion **(see illustration)**. Repeat this procedure on No 4 piston.

37 Remove the crankshaft locking tool and rotate the crankshaft half a turn (180°) clockwise to bring No 2 and 3 pistons to TDC. As the upper timing chain is still engaged with the sprocket on the injection pump, it will be necessary to have an assistant hold the chain in a raised position while the engine is turned. Ensure the crankshaft is accurately positioned then measure the protrusions of No 2 and 3 pistons. Once both pistons have been measured, turn the crankshaft half a turn (180°) anti-clockwise to bring No 1 and 4 pistons back to TDC and lock the crankshaft in position again. Check also that the TDC mark on the injection pump sprocket is aligned correctly.

Caution: When rotating the crankshaft, keep the upper timing chain taut to prevent the chain jamming around the injection pump sprocket.

38 Using the largest protrusion measurement of the four pistons, select the correct thickness of head gasket required using the following table.

Piston protrusion measurement	Gasket thickness required
0.40 to 0.50 mm	1.2 mm
0.51 to 0.60 mm	1.3 mm
0.61 to 0.70 mm	1.4 mm

Refitting

39 Wipe clean the mating surfaces of the cylinder head and cylinder block/crankcase. Apply a little sealant to the timing end of the cylinder block, at the two points where the timing cover joins the block.

40 Check that the two locating dowels are in position then fit a new gasket to the cylinder block **(see illustration)**.

41 Ensure the crankshaft is locked in the TDC position and the camshaft is correctly positioned with the lobes of No 1 cylinder pointing upwards and the slot on the left-hand end of the camshaft parallel with the cylinder head surface (timing hole at the top). Note that the injection pump sprocket TDC holes will also be aligned.

42 With the aid of an assistant, carefully refit the cylinder head assembly to the block, aligning it

with the locating dowels. As the head is fitted, pass the upper timing chain up through the hole in the cylinder head, holding it in position by passing a screwdriver through the upper chain and resting it on the head upper surface.

43 Apply a smear of oil to the threads and the underside of the heads of the new cylinder head bolts and carefully enter each bolt into its relevant hole (*do not drop them in*). Screw all bolts in, by hand only, until finger-tight.

44 Working progressively and in sequence, tighten the cylinder head bolts to their Stage 1 torque setting, using a torque wrench and suitable socket **(see illustration)**.

45 Once all bolts have been tightened to the Stage 1 torque, working again in sequence, go around and tighten all bolts through the specified Stage 2 angle. It is recommended that an angle-measuring gauge is used to ensure accuracy. If a gauge is not available, use white paint to make alignment marks prior to tightening; the marks can then be used to check that the bolt has been rotated through the correct angle.

46 Go around again in sequence and angle tighten the bolts through the specified Stage 3 angle.

47 Working again in sequence, go around and tighten all bolts through the specified Stage 4 angle.

48 Finally go around in sequence and angle tighten the bolts through the specified Stage 5 angle.

49 Refit the bolts securing the right-hand end of

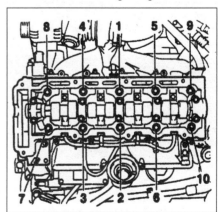

11.44 Cylinder head bolt tightening sequence

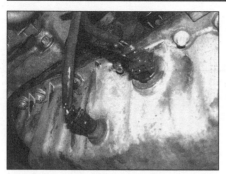

12.4 Disconnect the wiring from the oil temperature and oil level sensors

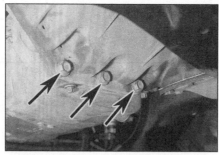

12.5 Slacken and remove the bolts securing the sump flange to the transmission housing (lower bolts arrowed)

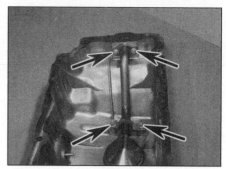

12.7 Oil pump pick-up/strainer retaining bolts (arrowed)

the cylinder head to the block/timing cover and tighten them to the specified torque setting.

50 If removed, refit the inlet and exhaust manifolds together with associated components with reference to Chapter 4B.

51 Swivel the alternator back into position and tighten the mounting bolts to the specified torque (see Chapter 5A).

52 Refit the water pump together with a new O-ring with reference to Chapter 3.

53 Reconnect the turbocharger oil pipes and tighten the union nuts to the specified torques.

54 Refit the exhaust manifold stay and tighten the bolts.

55 Reconnect the coolant hose to the rear of the cylinder block.

56 Refit the front exhaust pipe (Chapter 4B).

57 Reconnect the vacuum hose to the turbocharger wastegate.

58 Refit the heat shields to the turbocharger, exhaust manifold and starter motor.

59 Refit the coolant hose support hook to the rear engine lifting eye, and tighten the bolts.

60 Reconnect the swirl throttle control valve vacuum hose.

61 Position a new sealing washer on each side of the injection pump fuel hose unions then refit both union bolts and tighten them to the specified torque (see Chapter 4B).

62 Refit the fuel lines between the injectors and injection pump, and tighten the union nuts to the specified torque (see Chapter 4B).

63 Reconnect the two coolant hoses to the thermostat housing.

64 Reconnect the fuel leak-off hoses to the injectors.

65 Refit the EGR valve with reference to Chapter 4B, then attach the vent hose to the thermostat housing.

66 Refit the wiring harness and bracket, and reconnect the wiring to the glow plugs. Refit the wiring harness conduit.

67 Reconnect all wiring disconnected in paragraph 6, then refit the turbocharger charge air hose.

68 Reconnect the two fuel lines, and reconnect the wiring to the oil level and temperature sensors.

69 Refit the camshaft sprocket and camshaft cover with reference to Sections 10 and 5.

70 On completion refill the cooling system as described in Chapter 1B, and prime the fuel system with reference to Chapter 4B.

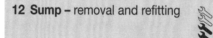

12 Sump – removal and refitting

Removal

1 Disconnect the battery negative terminal (see *Disconnecting the battery*).

2 Firmly apply the handbrake then jack up the front of the car and support it on axle stands. Where necessary, undo the retaining screws and remove the engine undertray.

3 Drain the engine oil as described in Chapter 1B, then fit a new sealing washer and refit the drain plug, tightening it to the specified torque.

4 Disconnect the wiring connector(s) from the

oil temperature sensor and (where fitted) the oil level sensor **(see illustration)**.

5 Unscrew and remove the bolts securing the sump flange to the transmission housing **(see illustration)**.

6 Progressively slacken and remove the bolts securing the sump to the base of the cylinder block/oil pump. Break the sump joint by striking the sump with the palm of the hand, then lower the sump away from the engine and withdraw it. Remove the gasket and discard it.

7 While the sump is removed, take the opportunity to check the oil pump pick-up/strainer for signs of clogging or splitting. If necessary, unbolt the pick-up/strainer and remove it from the sump along with its sealing ring **(see illustration)**. The strainer can then be cleaned easily in solvent or renewed.

Refitting

8 Remove all traces of dirt and oil from the mating surfaces of the sump and cylinder block and (where removed) the pick-up/strainer.

9 Where necessary, position a new sealing ring on the oil pump pick-up/strainer flange and fit the strainer to the sump, tightening its retaining bolts to the specified torque.

10 Apply a smear of suitable sealant to the areas of the cylinder block mating surface around the oil pump housing and rear main bearing cap joints **(see illustrations)**.

11 Fit a new gasket to the sump then offer up the sump to the cylinder block and loosely refit all the retaining bolts **(see illustration)**.

12.10a Apply a smear of sealant to the areas of the cylinder block/timing chain cover joints . . .

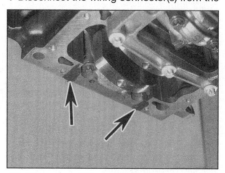

12.10b . . . and the rear main bearing cap/ cylinder block joints

12.11 Fit a new gasket to the sump and manoeuvre it up into position

13.2 Remove the oil pump cover from the rear of the timing chain cover . . .

12 Working out from the centre in a diagonal sequence, progressively tighten the bolts securing the sump to the cylinder block/oil pump to their specified torque setting.

13 Tighten the bolts securing the sump flange to the transmission housing to their specified torque settings.

14 Reconnect the oil temperature/level sensor wiring connector(s) (as applicable). Where necessary refit the engine undertray.

15 Lower the vehicle to the ground then fill the engine with fresh oil (see Chapter 1B).

16 Reconnect the battery negative terminal.

13 Oil pump – removal, inspection and refitting

Note: *The oil pump safety valve can be removed with the timing chain cover in position on the engine and the pressure relief valve can be removed once the sump has been removed.*

Removal

1 The oil pump assembly is built into the timing chain cover. Removal and refitting is as described in Section 7.

Inspection

2 Undo the retaining screws and lift off the pump cover from the inside of the timing chain cover **(see illustration)**.

13.4a . . . then lift out the pump inner . . .

13.5a Unscrew the oil pressure relief valve bolt and sealing washer . . .

3 Using a suitable marker pen, mark the surface of both the pump inner and outer rotors; the marks can then be used to ensure the rotors are refitted the correct way around.

4 Lift out the inner and outer rotors from the cover **(see illustrations)**.

5 Unscrew the oil pressure relief valve bolt from the base of the timing chain cover and withdraw the spring, spring sleeve and plunger, noting which way around the plunger is fitted. Remove the sealing ring from the valve bolt **(see illustrations)**.

6 Unscrew the safety valve bolt from the rear of the timing chain cover, the safety valve is the uppermost of the three bolts on the rear of the cover. Withdraw the spring and plunger from the cover, noting which way round the plunger is fitted **(see illustrations)**. Remove the sealing ring from the valve bolt.

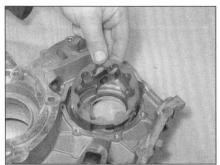

13.4b . . . and outer rotors

13.5b . . . and withdraw the spring, spring sleeve (arrowed) . . .

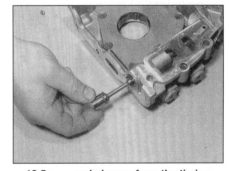

13.5c . . . and plunger from the timing chain cover

7 Clean the components, and carefully examine the rotors, pump body and valve plungers for any signs of scoring or wear.

13.6a Unscrew the safety valve bolt and washer . . .

13.6b . . . then remove the spring and valve plunger from the timing chain cover

13.8 On refitting tighten the pump cover screws to the specified torque

Renew any component which shows signs of wear or damage; if the rotors or pump housing are marked then the complete pump assembly should be renewed.

8 If the pump is satisfactory, reassemble the components in the reverse order of removal, noting the following.

a) *Ensure both rotors and the valve plungers are fitted the correct way around.*

b) *Fit new sealing rings to the pressure relief valve and safety valve bolts and tighten both bolts to their specified torque settings.*

c) *Refit the pump cover tightening the cover screws to the specified torque (see illustration).*

d) *On completion prime the oil pump by filling it with clean engine oil whilst rotating the inner rotor.*

Refitting

9 Refit the timing chain cover as described in Section 7.

14 Oil cooler –
removal and refitting

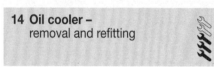

Removal

1 The oil cooler/filter assembly is mounted onto the front, left-hand end of cylinder block and the cooler is bolted onto the front of the oil filter housing. To improve access, firmly apply the handbrake then jack up the front of the car and support it on axle stands. Where necessary, undo the retaining clips/screws and

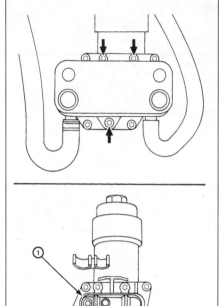

14.4 Undo the three retaining screws (arrowed) and remove the oil cooler from the oil filter housing

1 *Cooler-to-oil filter housing oil seal*

remove the engine/transmission undertray. Also remove the engine top cover.

2 To minimise coolant loss, clamp the coolant hoses on either side of the oil cooler then release the retaining clips and detach both hoses. Be prepared for some coolant loss and mop-up any spilt coolant.

3 Although the oil cooler can be removed from the oil filter housing *in situ*, it is better to remove the housing first, then separate the cooler on the bench. Unscrew the upper and lower bolts and remove the housing with the cooler from the front of the engine. Remove and discard the sealing ring, and obtain a new one.

4 Unscrew the bolts and remove the cooler from the oil filter housing **(see illustration)**.

Remove and discard the sealing ring, and obtain a new one.

Refitting

5 Refitting is the reverse of removal, but clean the mating surfaces and use new sealing rings. Tighten the mounting bolts to the specified torque. Check and top-up the coolant as described in *Weekly checks*.

15 Crankshaft oil seals
– renewal

Right-hand (timing chain end)

1 Remove the crankshaft pulley as described in Section 6.

2 Using a large flat-bladed screwdriver, carefully lever the seal out from the timing chain cover **(see illustration)**.

3 Clean the seal housing and polish off any burrs or raised edges which may have caused the seal to fail in the first place.

4 Lubricate the lips of the new seal with clean engine oil and press/tap it squarely into position until it is flush with the cover **(see illustration)**. If necessary, a suitable tubular drift, such as a socket, which bears only on the hard outer edge of the seal can be used to tap the seal into position. Take great care not to damage the seal lips during fitting and ensure that the seal lips face inwards.

5 Wash off any traces of oil, then refit the crankshaft pulley as described in Section 6.

Left-hand (flywheel end)

6 Remove the flywheel as described in Section 16.

7 Carefully punch or drill two small holes opposite each other in the oil seal. Screw a self-tapping screw into each and pull on the screws with pliers to extract the seal **(see illustration)**.

8 Clean the seal housing and polish off any burrs or raised edges which may have caused the seal to fail in the first place.

9 Lubricate the lips of the new seal with clean engine oil and ease it into position on the end of the crankshaft. Press the seal squarely into position until it is flush with the bearing cap.

15.2 Lever the right-hand crankshaft oil seal out from the timing chain cover

15.4 Press/tap the new seal squarely into position until it is flush with the cover

15.7 Removing the crankshaft left-hand oil seal

15.9 Carefully ease the new seal over the end of the crankshaft and tap/press it squarely into position

16.2 Lock the flywheel ring gear . . .

16.3 . . . then unscrew the retaining bolts and remove the flywheel

If necessary, a suitable tubular drift, such as a socket, which bears only on the hard outer edge of the seal can be used to tap the seal into position. Take great care not to damage the seal lips during fitting and ensure that the seal lips face inwards **(see illustration)**.

10 Refit the flywheel as described in Section 16.

16 Flywheel – removal, inspection and refitting

Note: *New flywheel retaining bolts will be required on refitting.*

Removal

1 Remove the transmission as described in Chapter 7A then remove the clutch assembly as described in Chapter 6.

2 Prevent the flywheel from turning by locking the ring gear teeth with a similar arrangement to that shown **(see illustration)**. Alternatively, bolt a strap between the flywheel and the cylinder block/crankcase. Make alignment marks between the flywheel and crankshaft using paint or a suitable marker pen.

3 Slacken and remove the retaining bolts and remove the flywheel **(see illustration)**. **Note:** *The flywheel is very heavy, take care not to drop it when removing.*

Inspection

4 Examine the flywheel for wear or chipping of the ring gear teeth. On some models, renewal of the ring gear is possible but it is not a task for the home mechanic; renewal requires the new ring gear to be heated (up to 180° to 230°C) to allow it to be fitted.

5 Examine the flywheel for scoring of the clutch face. If the clutch face is scored, the flywheel may be surface-ground, but renewal is preferable.

6 If there is any doubt about the condition of the flywheel, seek the advice of a Saab dealer or engine reconditioning specialist. They will be able to advise if it is possible to recondition it or whether renewal is necessary.

Refitting

7 Clean the mating surfaces of the flywheel and crankshaft.

8 Offer up the flywheel and fit the new retaining bolts. If the original is being refitted align the marks made prior to removal.

9 Lock the flywheel using the method employed on dismantling then, working in a diagonal sequence, evenly and progressively tighten the retaining bolts to the specified Stage 1 torque setting.

10 Once all bolts have been tightened to the Stage 1 torque, go around and tighten all bolts through the specified Stage 2 angle. It is recommended that an angle-measuring gauge is used during the final stage of the tightening, to ensure accuracy. If a gauge is not available, use white paint to make alignment marks prior to tightening; the marks can then be used to check that the bolt has been rotated through the correct angle.

11 Refit the clutch as described in Chapter 6 then remove the locking tool and refit the transmission as described in Chapter 7A.

17 Engine/transmission mountings – inspection and renewal

Note: *Saab recommend that both the right-hand and left-hand mountings should be renewed if either one is damaged.*

Inspection

1 If improved access is required, raise the front of the car and support it securely on axle stands. Where necessary, undo the retaining bolts and remove the undercover from beneath the engine/transmission unit.

2 Check the mounting rubber to see if it is cracked, hardened or separated from the metal at any point; renew the mounting if any such damage or deterioration is evident.

3 Check that all the mounting fasteners are securely tightened; use a torque wrench to check if possible.

4 Using a large screwdriver or lever, check for wear in the mounting by carefully levering against it to check for free play; where this is not possible, enlist the aid of an assistant to move the engine/transmission unit back-and-forth, or from side-to-side, while you watch the mounting. While some free play is to be expected, even from new components, excessive wear should be obvious.

5 If excessive free play is found, check first that the fasteners are correctly secured, then renew any worn components as described below.

Renewal

Note: *Before slackening any of the engine mounting bolts/nuts, the relative positions of the mountings to their various brackets should be marked to ensure correct alignment upon refitting.*

Right-hand mounting

6 Apply the handbrake, then jack up the front of the vehicle and support it on axle stands (see *Jacking and vehicle support*). Remove the engine undertray.

7 Refer to Chapter 4B and remove the air cleaner together with the mass airflow meter and air ducts from the turbocharger and camshaft cover.

8 Release the fuel hoses and wiring conduit from the support bracket and position to one side.

9 Support the weight of the engine/transmission beneath the sump, using a trolley jack and block of wood. **Note:** *Take care not to place any excess stress on the exhaust system when raising the engine. If necessary, disconnect the front pipe from the manifold (see Chapter 4B).*

10 Unscrew the four bolts securing the mounting brackets to the engine and body, and manoeuvre out from the engine compartment. If necessary, the mounting bracket can be unbolted from the right-hand end of the cylinder block.

11 Refitting is a reversal of removal but tighten the bolts to the specified torque.

Left-hand mounting

12 Apply the handbrake, then jack up the front of the vehicle and support it on axle stands (see *Jacking and vehicle support*).

Remove the engine undertray and left-hand air shield.

13 Support the weight of the engine/transmission beneath the transmission, using a trolley jack and block of wood. **Note:** *Take care not to place any excess stress on the exhaust system when raising the engine. If necessary, disconnect the front pipe from the manifold (see Chapter 4B).*

14 Unscrew and remove the centre bolt from the mounting, then unscrew the bolts securing the mounting to the body. Remove the mounting from the engine compartment. If necessary, the mounting bracket can be unbolted from the transmission, noting that an earth cable is attached to the outer stud of one of the bolts.

15 Refitting is a reversal of removal but tighten the bolts to the specified torque.

Rear mounting

16 Apply the handbrake, then jack up the front of the vehicle and support it on axle stands (see *Jacking and vehicle support*). Remove the engine undertray.

17 Support the weight of the engine/transmission with a trolley jack and block of wood. Position the jack underneath the transmission and raise the transmission slightly to remove all load from the rear mounting.

18 Unscrew the nut from the top of the rear mounting.

19 Unscrew the bolts securing the gear selector link bracket to the transmission, and lift the bracket from the top of the mounting.

20 Unscrew the lower mounting nut and remove the rear mounting from the subframe.

21 Refitting is a reversal of removal but make sure that the location pins on the mounting align correctly with the holes in the bracket and subframe. Tighten the nuts and bolts to the specified torque.

---

18 Balancer unit – general information, removal and refitting

---

General information

1 A balancer unit is fitted to the engine to reduce vibrations and noise. It consists of two balancer shafts which are driven by chain from the crankshaft, and the chain is kept under tension by a hydraulic chain tensioner located on the front of the balancer unit housing **(see illustration)**. The balancer shafts rotate in opposite directions at double the crankshaft speed.

2 The balancer unit is mounted on the 2nd and 3rd crankshaft main bearings, and the oil supply to the balancer unit is through these two main bearings.

Removal

3 Remove the sump as described in Section 12, noting the length of the bolts as they are different.

4 Set the engine to TDC for No 1 cylinder as described in Section 3, and insert the timing pin.

5 The balancer shafts must now be locked in their TDC position. Saab technicians insert tool 83 95 469 through the hole at the rear of the unit, however, welding (or similar) rod of suitable diameter may be used instead. Also, remove the chain cover.

6 Press back and lock the chain tensioner then unscrew the bolt and remove the sprocket from the unit.

7 Unscrew the 7 outer bolts only, and lower the balancer shaft unit from the bottom of the engine.

8 With the unit on the bench, unbolt the chain tensioner and bracket.

9 Remove the locking tool, then unscrew the remaining bolts, and lift off the cover. Identify the balancer shafts for position, then remove them from the unit.

10 Clean all the components and inspect them for excessive wear and damage. Where evident, renew the unit complete.

Refitting

11 Locate the balancer shafts in their original positions in the unit, then refit the cover and tighten the bolts securely.

12 Turn the shafts so that the weights are up, and insert the locking tool to lock them.

13 Refit the chain tensioner and bracket and tighten the bolts to the specified torque.

14 Locate the balancer shaft on the engine crankcase, insert the bolts, and tighten to the specified torque.

15 Refit the sprocket, insert the bolt, and tighten to the specified torque and angle.

16 With the chain engaged with the sprocket, release the chain tensioner, and refit the chain cover.

17 Remove the locking tool, then refit the sump with reference to Section 12.

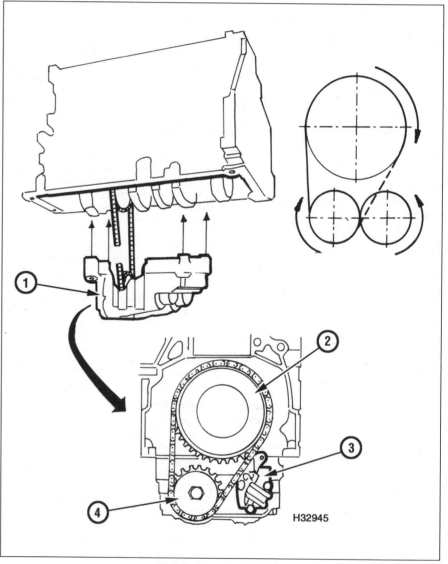

18.1 Balancer unit layout

1 Balancer unit   2 Crankshaft sprocket   3 Chain tensioner   4 Drive sprocket for balancer shaft

Chapter 2 Part C:
Engine removal and overhaul procedures

Contents

Degrees of difficulty

Easy, suitable for novice with little experience	**Fairly easy,** suitable for beginner with some experience	**Fairly difficult,** suitable for competent DIY mechanic	**Difficult,** suitable for experienced DIY mechanic	**Very difficult,** suitable for expert DIY or professional

Specifications

Petrol engines

Valves

Valve head diameter:
    Inlet . . . . 33.0 mm
    Exhaust. . . . . 29.0 mm
Valve stem diameter:
    Inlet . . . . 4.970 to 4.985 mm
    Exhaust:
        Except B235R, B205R and B205L . . . . 4.950 to 4.965 mm
        B235R, B205R and B205L . . . . 4.965 to 7.980 mm
Valve spring:
    Free length . . . . 57.1 to 60.1 mm
    Fitted length . . . . 37.5 mm
Valve length:
    Inlet . . . . 107.30 mm
    Exhaust. . . . . 107.84 mm

Cylinder head

Height (new)	139.4 to 139.6 mm
Height (minimum)	139.0 mm
Valve guide-to-valve stem clearance (max):	
Inlet	0.17 mm
Exhaust	0.22 mm

Cylinder block

Cylinder bore diameter:	
Standard (A)	90.000 to 90.020 mm
Standard (B)	90.020 to 90.040 mm
First oversize	90.500 to 90.520 mm
Second oversize	91.000 to 91.020 mm

Balancer shafts

Endfloat	0.060 to 0.460 mm
Diameter of journal:	
Larger, inner	39.892 to 39.908 mm
Smaller, outer	19.947 to 19.960 mm
Diameter of bearing:	
Larger, inner	39.988 to 40.043 mm
Smaller, outer	20.000 to 20.021 mm
Bearing running clearance:	
Standard	0.080 to 0.151 mm
Maximum	0.18 mm

Pistons

Note: *Piston diameter is measured at right-angles to the gudgeon pin holes, 11mm from the bottom of the piston skirt. The piston classification is stamped on the crown.*

Piston diameter:	
AB (for standard bore A or B)	89.966 to 89.975 mm
B (for standard bore B)	89.975 to 89.982 mm
First oversize (+0.5 mm)	90.457 to 90.475 mm
Second oversize (+1.0 mm)	90.957 to 90.975 mm
Nominal piston clearance (new)	0.025 to 0.056 mm

Connecting rods

Length (centre to centre):	
B204 and B205	159 mm
B234 and B235	153 mm

Crankshaft

Endfloat	0.08 to 0.34 mm
Maximum bearing journal out-of-round	0.005 mm
Main bearing journal diameter:	
Standard	57.981 to 58.000 mm
First undersize	57.731 to 57.750 mm
Second undersize	57.481 to 57.500 mm
Main bearing running clearance	0.014 to 0.062 mm
Big-end bearing journal diameter:	
Standard	51.981 to 52.000 mm
First undersize	51.731 to 51.750 mm
Second undersize	51.481 to 51.500 mm
Big-end bearing running clearance	0.020 to 0.068 mm

Piston rings

End gaps in cylinder:	
Upper compression ring	0.30 to 0.50 mm
Lower compression ring	0.30 to 0.50 mm
Scraper ring	0.75 to 1.00 mm
Side clearance in groove:	
Top compression ring	0.035 to 0.080 mm
Second compression ring	0.040 to 0.075 mm
Oil control ring	Not applicable

Torque wrench settings

Refer to Chapter 2A Specifications.

Diesel engine

Cylinder head
Maximum gasket face distortion . . . . N/A
Cam lift . . . . 8.0 mm
Cylinder head height . . . . 140 mm
Valve seat angle in cylinder head . . . . 90°
Valve seat width . . . . 1.4 to 1.8 mm

Valves and guides
Valve guide height in cylinder head . . . . 11.20 to 11.50 mm
Valve seat angle in at the valve head . . . . 90° 40'

Valve stem diameter:	Inlet	Exhaust
Standard (K)	5.955 to 5.970 mm	5.945 to 5.960 mm
1st oversize – 0.075 mm (K1)	6.030 to 6.045 mm	6.020 to 6.035 mm
2nd oversize – 0.150 mm (K2)	6.105 to 6.120 mm	6.095 to 6.110 mm

Valve stem run-out . . . . Less than 0.03 mm
Valve guide bore diameter:
    Standard (K) . . . . 6.000 to 6.012 mm
    1st oversize – 0.075 mm (K1) . . . . 6.075 to 6.090 mm
    2nd oversize – 0.150 mm (K2) . . . . 6.150 to 6.165 mm
Valve guide length:
    Inlet . . . . 44.75 to 45.25 mm
    Exhaust . . . . 34.75 to 35.25 mm
Stem-to-guide clearance:
    Inlet . . . . 0.030 to 0.057 mm
    Exhaust . . . . 0.040 to 0.067 mm
Valve length:
    Inlet:
        Standard . . . . 97.10 mm
        Oversize . . . . 97.20 mm
    Exhaust:
        Standard . . . . 96.90 mm
        Oversize . . . . 97.00 mm
Valve head diameter:
    Inlet . . . . 28.9 to 29.1 mm
    Exhaust . . . . 25.9 to 26.1 mm

Cylinder block
Maximum gasket face distortion . . . . N/A
Cylinder bore diameter:
    Standard:
        Size group 8 . . . . 83.975 to 83.985 mm
        Size group 99 . . . . 83.985 to 83.995 mm
        Size group 00 . . . . 83.995 to 84.005 mm
        Size group 01 . . . . 84.005 to 84.015 mm
        Size group 02 . . . . 84.015 to 84.025 mm
    Oversize – 0.5 mm . . . . 84.475 to 84.485 mm
Maximum cylinder bore ovality . . . . N/A
Maximum cylinder bore taper . . . . N/A

Pistons and rings
Piston diameter:
    Standard:
        Size group 8 . . . . 83.905 to 83.915 mm
        Size group 99 . . . . 83.915 to 83.925 mm
        Size group 00 . . . . 83.925 to 83.935 mm
        Size group 01 . . . . 83.935 to 83.945 mm
        Size group 02 . . . . 83.945 to 83.955 mm
    Oversize – 0.5 mm . . . . 84.385 to 84.395 mm
Piston-to-bore clearance . . . . 0.08 to 0.10 mm
Piston ring end gaps (fitted in bore):
    Top and second compression rings . . . . 0.3 to 0.5 mm
    Oil control ring . . . . 0.4 to 1.4 mm
Piston ring-to-groove clearance:
    Top and second compression rings . . . . 0.02 to 0.04 mm
    Oil control ring . . . . 0.01 to 0.03 mm
Piston ring thickness:
    Top compression ring . . . . 2.00 mm
    Second compression ring . . . . 1.75 mm
    Oil control ring . . . . 3.00 mm
Piston ring gap arrangement in cylinder . . . . 120°

Gudgeon pins

Diameter . . . . 29 mm
Length . . . . 68 mm

Connecting rod

Big-end side clearance. . . . . 0.07 to 0.28 mm

Crankshaft

Endfloat . . . . 0.050 to 0.152 mm
Main bearing journal diameter:
  Standard:
    Green . . . . 67.966 to 67.974 mm
    Brown . . . . 67.974 to 67.982 mm
  1st undersize – 0.25 mm:
    Green/blue . . . . 67.716 to 67.724 mm
    Brown/blue . . . . 67.724 to 67.732 mm
  2nd undersize – 0.50 mm:
    Green/violet . . . . 67.466 to 67.474 mm
    Brown/violet . . . . 67.474 to 67.482 mm
Big-end bearing journal (crankpin) diameter:
  Standard. . . . . 48.971 to 48.990 mm
  1st undersize – 0.25 mm . . . . 48.721 to 48.740 mm
  2nd undersize – 0.50 mm . . . . 48.471 to 48.490 mm
Journal out-of round. 0.03
Journal taper . . . . N/A
Crankshaft run-out. . . . . Less than 0.03 mm
Main bearing running clearance. . . . . 0.016 to 0.069 mm
Big-end bearing (crankpin) running clearance . . . . 0.010 to 0.061 mm

Torque wrench settings

Refer to Chapter 2B Specifications.

1 General information

Included in this Part of Chapter 2 are details of removing the engine/transmission from the vehicle, and general overhaul procedures for the cylinder head, cylinder block/crankcase, and all engine internal components. Note that timing chain and balancer shaft removal on petrol engines is included in this Chapter as it is considered more practical with the engine removed.

The information given ranges from advice concerning preparation for an overhaul and the purchase of new parts, to detailed step-by-step procedures covering removal, inspection, renovation and refitting of engine internal components.

After Section 5, all instructions are based on the assumption that the engine has been removed from the vehicle. For information concerning in-car engine repair, as well as the removal and refitting of those external components necessary for full overhaul, refer to Part A or B of this Chapter; ignore any preliminary dismantling operations described that are no longer relevant once the engine has been removed from the vehicle.

Apart from torque wrench settings, which are given at the beginning of the relevant in-car repair procedures in Chapters 2A and 2B, all specifications relating to engine overhaul are at the beginning of this Part of Chapter 2.

2 Engine overhaul – general information

It is not always easy to determine when, or if, an engine should be completely overhauled, as a number of factors must be considered.

High mileage is not necessarily an indication that an overhaul is needed, while low mileage does not preclude the need for an overhaul. Frequency of servicing is probably the most important consideration. An engine which has had regular and frequent oil and filter changes, as well as other required maintenance, should give many thousands of miles of reliable service. Conversely, a neglected engine may require an overhaul very early in its life.

Excessive oil consumption is an indication that piston rings, valve seals and/or valve guides are in need of attention. Make sure that oil leaks are not responsible before deciding that the rings and/or guides are worn. Perform a compression test, as described in Part A or B of this Chapter, to determine the likely cause of the problem.

Check the oil pressure with a gauge fitted in place of the oil pressure switch, and compare it with that specified. If it is extremely low, the main and big-end bearings, and/or the oil pump, are probably worn out.

Loss of power, rough running, knocking or metallic engine noises, excessive valve gear noise, and high fuel consumption may also point to the need for an overhaul, especially if they are all present at the same time. If a complete service does not remedy the situation, major mechanical work is the only solution.

An engine overhaul involves restoring all internal parts to the specification of a new engine. During an overhaul, the cylinders are rebored (where necessary) and the pistons and the piston rings are renewed. New main and big-end bearings are generally fitted; if necessary, the crankshaft may be renewed or reground, to restore the journals. The valves are also serviced as well, since they are usually in less-than-perfect condition at this point. While the engine is being overhauled, other components, such as the distributor (where applicable), starter and alternator, can be overhauled as well. The end result should be an as-new engine that will give many trouble-free miles.

Note: *Critical cooling system components such as the hoses, thermostat and water pump should be renewed when an engine is overhauled. The radiator should be checked carefully, to ensure that it is not clogged or leaking. Also, it is a good idea to renew the oil pump whenever the engine is overhauled.*

Before beginning the engine overhaul, read through the entire procedure, to familiarise yourself with the scope and requirements of the job. Overhauling an engine is not difficult if you follow carefully all of the instructions, have the necessary tools and equipment, and pay close attention to all specifications. It can, however, be time-consuming. Plan on the car being off the road for a minimum of two weeks, especially if parts must be taken to an engineering works for repair or reconditioning. Check on the availability of parts, and make sure that any necessary special tools and equipment are obtained in advance. Most work can be done with typical hand tools, although a number of precision measuring tools are required for inspecting parts to determine if they must be renewed. Often the engineering works will handle the inspection of parts, and will offer advice concerning reconditioning and renewal.

Note: *Always wait until the engine has been completely dismantled, and until all components (especially the cylinder block/ crankcase and the crankshaft) have been inspected, before deciding what service and repair operations must be performed by an engineering works. The condition of these components will be the major factor to consider when determining whether to overhaul the original engine, or to buy a reconditioned unit. Do not, therefore, purchase parts or have overhaul work done on other components until they have been thoroughly inspected. As a general rule, time is the primary cost of an overhaul, so it does not pay to fit worn or sub-standard parts.*

As a final note, to ensure maximum life and minimum trouble from a reconditioned engine, everything must be assembled with care, in a spotlessly-clean environment.

3 Engine removal – methods and precautions

If you have decided that the engine must be removed for overhaul or major repair work, several preliminary steps should be taken.

Locating a suitable place to work is extremely important. Adequate workspace, along with storage space for the vehicle, will be needed. If a workshop or garage is not available, at the very least, a flat, level, clean work surface is required.

Cleaning the engine compartment and engine/transmission before beginning the removal procedure will help keep tools clean and organised.

An engine hoist or A-frame will also be necessary. Make sure the equipment is rated in excess of the combined weight of the engine and transmission. Safety is of primary importance, considering the potential hazards involved in lifting the engine/transmission out of the vehicle.

If this is the first time you have removed an engine, an assistant should ideally be available. Advice and aid from someone more experienced would also be helpful. There are many instances when one person cannot simultaneously perform all of the operations required when lifting the engine out of the vehicle.

Plan the operation ahead of time. Before starting work, arrange for the hire of, or obtain,

all of the tools and equipment you will need. Some of the equipment necessary to perform engine/transmission removal and installation safely and with relative ease (in addition to an engine hoist) is as follows: a heavy-duty trolley jack, complete sets of spanners and sockets as described in the back of this manual, wooden blocks, and plenty of rags and cleaning solvent for mopping-up spilled oil, coolant and fuel. If the hoist must be hired, make sure that you arrange for it in advance, and perform all of the operations possible without it beforehand. This will save you money and time.

Plan for the vehicle to be out of use for quite a while. An engineering works will be required to perform some of the work which the do-it-yourselfer cannot accomplish without special equipment. These places often have a busy schedule, so it would be a good idea to consult them before removing the engine, in order to accurately estimate the amount of time required to rebuild or repair components that may need work.

Always be extremely careful when removing and refitting the engine/transmission. Serious injury can result from careless actions. Plan ahead and take your time, and a job of this nature, although major, can be accomplished successfully.

The engine/transmission is removed by lowering it from the underside of the engine compartment.

4 Engine and transmission – removal, separation and refitting

Note: *The engine is removed together with the transmission by lowering from the engine compartment. Note, however, that it is possible to remove the transmission, leaving the engine in situ – refer to Chapter 7A or 7B (as applicable) for details.*

Removal

1 Park the vehicle on firm, level ground. Apply the handbrake, then jack up the front of the vehicle and support it on axle stands (see *Jacking and vehicle support*). Allow sufficient room to withdraw the engine/transmission under the front of the vehicle.

2 Remove both front wheels, and remove the engine undertray and both front wheel arch liners for access to either side of the engine bay.

3 Drain the coolant with reference to Chapter 1A or 1B. Save the coolant in a clean container if it is fit for re-use. Tighten the drain plug on the left-hand bottom of the radiator.

 Warning: The engine must be cold before draining the coolant.

4 If the engine is to be dismantled, drain the oil and remove the oil filter as described in Chapter 1A or 1B.

5 Disconnect the support struts from the bonnet, and support it in the fully-open

position. Alternatively, remove the bonnet as described in Chapter 11.

6 Remove the covers from the top of the engine, inlet manifold and battery, then remove the battery with reference to Chapter 5A. Also, remove the battery tray.

7 At the rear of the engine compartment, loosen the clips and disconnect the coolant hoses from the heater. Identify each hose for position.

8 Refer to Chapter 4A or 4B and remove the air cleaner assembly together with the air mass meter and adjacent air ducts.

Petrol engine models

9 Disconnect the accelerator cable from the throttle housing (see Chapter 4A).

10 Disconnect the crankcase ventilation hose from the cylinder head cover.

11 Disconnect the quick-release fuel supply and return lines, then disconnect the carbon canister hose from the throttle housing. Plug both sides of the open fuel lines to minimise leakage and to prevent the ingress of foreign material.

12 Loosen the clips, disconnect the wiring from the pressure/temperature sensor, and where necessary disconnect the venturi hose, then unbolt the turbocharger air pipe from the left-hand side of the engine compartment.

13 Remove the heat shield from the exhaust manifold.

14 Remove the lower facia panel (RHD) or glovebox (LHD), then fold back the carpet and remove the air duct. Disconnect the wiring from the heater and facia, pull it through into the engine compartment, and position it on the engine.

15 Disconnect the brake servo vacuum hose from the inlet manifold **(see illustration)**.

16 Disconnect the air ducts from the turbocharger and intercooler where applicable.

17 Disconnect the wiring from the carbon canister purge valve, then remove the bypass valve from the bulkhead and position it on the engine. Also, remove the earthing wire between the transmission and body.

18 Disconnect the wiring for the oxygen sensor, then unbolt the front exhaust pipe from the turbocharger and support it to one side.

4.15 Disconnect the vacuum hose (arrowed) from the rear of the intake manifold

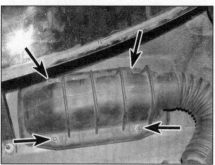

4.19a Remove the four retaining nuts (arrowed) . . .

4.19b . . . and release the multiplug wiring connector from the control module

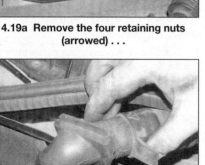
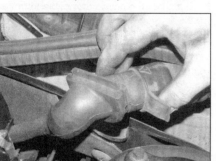

4.19c Withdraw the rubber wiring grommet from the bulkhead panel

4.19d Unclip the cover from the wiring block connector on the bulkhead

Diesel engine models

19 On early models with the EDC15 system, remove the lower facia panel (RHD) or glovebox (LHD), then fold back the carpet and remove the air duct. Disconnect the wiring from the heater, then refer to Chapter 4B and remove the engine management ECU. Disconnect the wiring from the ECU and earth point **(see illustrations)**.

20 Refer to Chapter 4B, Section 9, and remove the accelerator pedal position sensor from the bulkhead.

21 Disconnect the quick-release fuel supply and return lines. Saab technicians use a special tool to do this, however, a small screwdriver can be used instead by depressing the tabs on each side. Plug both sides of the open fuel lines to minimise leakage and to prevent the ingress of foreign material.

22 Disconnect the wiring at the bulkhead, release it from the cable ties, and pull it through into the engine compartment. Release the fuel lines, then remove the wiring harness and bracket and position it on the engine.

23 Disconnect the vacuum hose from the brake vacuum pump.

24 Unbolt and remove the turbocharger delivery pipe.

25 Disconnect the air hoses from the intercooler and inlet manifold.

26 Disconnect the vacuum hoses from the EGR and swirl throttle valves.

27 Unbolt the front exhaust pipe from the turbocharger and support it to one side. Also, disconnect the vacuum hose from the turbocharger wastegate.

All models

28 Remove the auxiliary drivebelt as described in Chapter 1A or 1B.

29 Refer to Chapter 10 and unbolt the power steering pump from the engine, leaving the hydraulic fluid hoses still attached. Tie the pump to one side.

30 Loosen the clips and disconnect the coolant hoses from the radiator, water pump, expansion tank, cylinder head and bypass valve.

31 Disconnect the wiring from the air conditioning compressor, then unbolt it from the engine with reference to Chapter 3, without disconnecting the refrigerant lines. Tie the compressor to one side.

32 Remove the lid from the fusebox next to the battery location, then disconnect the positive and negative cables from their terminals. Position the wiring on the engine.

33 On automatic transmission models, carry out the following:
a) Unscrew the nut and remove the selector lever from the transmission.
b) Disconnect all wiring from the transmission **(see illustration)**.
c) Remove the oil cooler pipes and tape over the holes to prevent entry of dust and dirt.

34 On manual models, carry out the following:
a) Unplug the wiring from the reversing lamp switch at the connector on the top of the transmission casing.
b) Refer to Chapter 7A, Section 3, and lock the transmission and gear lever inside the car.
c) Release the securing clip and disconnect the connection for the clutch fluid delivery at the top of the transmission. Refit the securing clip to the connector after it has been disconnected for safe-keeping. Plug both sides of the open clutch fluid lines to minimise leakage and to prevent the ingress of foreign material.

35 Place a container beneath the engine oil cooler pipes, if applicable. Undo the nut and disconnect the oil cooler pipes from the oil filter housing, then undo the retaining bolts and remove the engine oil cooler, complete with cooler pipes from the vehicle **(see illustrations)**.

36 Attach a suitable hoist to the engine lifting eyes at either end of the cylinder head. It may be necessary to attach an extra lifting eye to the transmission to allow the engine/transmission to be kept level for removal.

4.33 Unplug the automatic transmission control system wiring harness

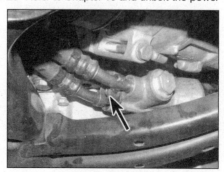

4.35a Undo the oil cooler pipe retaining nut (arrowed) . . .

4.35b . . . and the retaining bolts securing the oil cooler (arrowed)

4.38 Slowly lower the subframe away from the underside of the engine compartment using the trolley jacks

Raise the hoist until it is just taking the weight of the engine/transmission.

37 Referring to Chapter 8, unbolt and remove both driveshafts.

38 Remove the front subframe **(see illustration)** using the following procedure:

a) *Support the engine assembly using a suitable hoist or engine support bar which straddles the engine compartment. Slightly lift the engine assembly so that its weight is supported.*

b) *Remove the exhaust front pipe as described in Chapter 4A or 4B.*

c) *Disconnect the front suspension lower arms from the hub carriers, and remove the front anti-roll bar as described in Chapter 10.*

d) *Support the subframe using a trolley jack.*

e) *Unscrew and remove the subframe front and rear mounting bolts, and also the two mounting nuts, then lower the subframe to the ground.*

39 Unbolt and remove the right- and left-hand engine/transmission mountings, with reference to Chapter 2A or 2B.

40 Make a final check that any components which would prevent the removal of the engine/transmission from the car have been removed or disconnected. Ensure that components such as the gearchange selector rod, clutch cable and accelerator cable are secured so that they cannot be damaged on removal.

41 Slowly lower the engine/transmission assembly from the engine compartment, making sure that it clears the components on the surrounding panels **(see illustration)**. In particular, make sure that it clears the ABS unit and the radiator. Enlist the help of an assistant during this procedure, as it may be necessary to tilt and twist the assembly slightly to clear the body panels. Lower the assembly to the ground and remove it from under the engine compartment.

Separation from transmission

42 Support the engine/transmission assembly on suitable blocks of wood, on a workbench (or failing that, on a clean area of the workshop floor).

43 Remove the starter motor with reference to Chapter 5A.

Manual transmission models

44 Where applicable, unscrew the bolt securing the turbo oil pipe bracket to the transmission.

45 Unbolt and remove the flywheel protection plate from the underside of the transmission bellhousing.

46 Ensure that both engine and transmission are adequately supported then, with reference to Chapter 7A, unscrew the bolts securing the transmission housing to the engine. Note the correct fitted positions of each bolt as they are removed, to use as a reference on refitting. Withdraw the transmission directly from the engine **(see illustration)**. Take care not to allow the weight of the transmission to bear on the input shaft and clutch friction plate.

Automatic transmission models

47 Working through the aperture exposed by the removal of the starter motor, unscrew the bolts securing the driveplate to the torque converter **(see illustration)**. To bring each bolt into view, turn the engine using a socket on the crankshaft pulley bolt.

48 Saab technicians use a special tool to hold the torque converter inside the transmission while the transmission is separated from the engine. The tool is quite basic, and consists of a plate which engages the torque converter through the timing hole in the top of the transmission.

49 Support the weight of the transmission, preferably using a hoist.

50 Ensure that both engine and transmission are adequately supported, then unscrew the bolts securing the transmission housing to the engine. Note the correct fitted positions of each bolt as they are removed, to use as a reference on refitting. Withdraw the transmission directly from the engine (see Chapter 7B for details). Make sure that the torque converter stays inside the transmission bellhousing, otherwise it may fall out and be damaged.

Reconnection to transmission

Automatic transmission models

51 Carefully offer the transmission to the engine. Make sure that the torque converter is held fully engaged with the transmission, using the special tool described earlier in this procedure (refer to Chapter 7B for settings and further details).

52 Insert and tighten to the specified torque the bolts securing the transmission to the engine.

53 Remove the special tool, then insert and tighten to the specified torque the bolts securing the driveplate to the torque converter. Turn the engine by means of a socket on the crankshaft pulley.

Manual transmission models

Caution: If a new clutch slave cylinder has been fitted, or if any hydraulic fluid has been allowed to drain from the existing slave cylinder, the cylinder must be primed and bled BEFORE the transmission is refitted; see Chapter 6 for details.

54 Apply a smear of high-melting-point grease to the splines of the transmission input shaft. Do not apply too much, otherwise there is a possibility of the grease contaminating the clutch friction plate.

55 Carefully offer the transmission to the engine. Ensure that the weight of the transmission is not allowed to hang on the input shaft as it is engaged with the clutch friction plate. Insert and tighten the bolts securing the transmission to the engine to the specified torque.

56 Where applicable, insert and tighten the bolts securing the turbo oil pipe bracket to the transmission.

All models

57 Refit the lower cover plate to the transmission bellhousing, and tighten the bolts.

58 Refit the starter motor with reference to Chapter 5A.

4.41 Slowly lower the engine/transmission assembly from the engine compartment

4.46 Separating the transmission from the engine (manual transmission shown)

4.47 Undo the bolts (one shown) securing the torque converter to the driveplate

Refitting

59 Refit the engine and transmission by following the removal procedure in reverse, noting the following additional points:

a) *Tighten all nuts and bolts to the specified torque, where given.*

b) *Renew all copper sealing washers on unions, as applicable.*

c) *With reference to Chapter 6, reconnect the fluid supply pipe to the slave cylinder, then bleed the clutch hydraulic system.*

d) *Ensure that all wiring has been securely reconnected, and all nuts and bolts have been tightened.*

e) *Refill the engine and transmission with the correct quantity and grade of oil/fluid, with reference to Chapter 1A or 1B.*

f) *Refill the cooling system with reference to Chapter 1A or 1B.*

g) *Check and if necessary top-up the power steering fluid, with reference to Chapter 1A or 1B.*

5 Engine overhaul – dismantling sequence

1 It is much easier to dismantle and work on the engine if it is mounted on a portable engine stand. These stands can often be hired from a tool hire shop. Before the engine is mounted on a stand, the flywheel/driveplate should be removed, so that the stand bolts can be tightened into the end of the cylinder block/crankcase.

2 If a stand is not available, it is possible to

6.4a Using a compressor to compress the valve springs in order to remove the split collets

dismantle the engine with it blocked up on a sturdy workbench, or on the floor. Be extra careful not to tip or drop the engine when working without a stand.

3 If you are going to obtain a reconditioned engine, all the external components must be removed first, to be transferred to the new engine (just as they will if you are doing a complete engine overhaul yourself). These components normally include the following, but check with your engine supplier first:

a) *Inlet and exhaust manifolds (Chapter 4A or 4B).*

b) *Alternator/power steering pump/air conditioning compressor brackets (as applicable).*

c) *Water pump (Chapter 3).*

d) *Fuel system components (Chapter 4A, 4B or 4C).*

e) *Wiring harness and all electrical switches and sensors.*

f) *Oil filter (Chapter 1A or 1B).*

g) *Flywheel/driveplate (Chapter 2A or 2B).*

h) *Engine mounting brackets (Chapter 2A or 2B).*

> **HAYNES HiNT** *When removing the external components from the engine, pay close attention to details that may be helpful or important during refitting. Note the fitted position of gaskets, seals, spacers, pins, washers, bolts and other small items.*

4 If you are obtaining a 'short' engine (which consists of the engine cylinder block/crankcase, crankshaft, pistons and connecting rods all assembled), then the cylinder head and sump will have to be removed also.

5 If you are planning a complete overhaul, the engine can be dismantled, and the internal components removed, in the order given below:

a) *Inlet and exhaust manifolds (Chapter 4A or 4B).*

b) *Cylinder head (Chapter 2A or 2B).*

c) *Timing chain and balancer shaft chain, sprockets and tensioner (Sections 10 and 11 for petrol models, Chapter 2B for diesel models).*

d) *Flywheel/driveplate (Chapter 2A or 2B).*

e) *Balancer shafts (Section 12 for petrol models, Chapter 2B for diesel models).*

f) *Sump (Chapter 2A or 2B).*

g) *Piston/connecting rod assemblies (Section 13).*

h) *Crankshaft (Section 14).*

6 Before beginning the dismantling and overhaul procedures, make sure that you have all of the correct tools necessary. Refer to *Tools and working facilities* for further information.

6 Cylinder head – dismantling

Note: *New/reconditioned cylinder heads are obtainable from Saab, or from engine overhaul specialists. Be aware that some specialist tools are required for the dismantling and inspection procedures, and new components may not be readily available. It may therefore be more practical and economical for the home mechanic to purchase a reconditioned head, rather than dismantle, inspect and recondition the original head.*

1 Remove the cylinder head as described in Part A or B, then unbolt the external components – these include the right-hand engine mounting bracket and the engine lifting eyes, etc, depending on model.

2 Remove the camshaft(s) and hydraulic cam followers, with reference to Chapter 2A or 2B.

3 Before removing the valves, consider obtaining plastic protectors for the hydraulic cam follower bores. When using certain valve spring compressors, the bores can easily be damaged should the compressor slip off the end of the valve.

> **HAYNES HiNT** *The cam follower bore protectors can be obtained from a Saab dealer; alternatively, a protector may be made out of plastic cut from a washing-up liquid container or similar.*

4 Position the protector in the cam follower bore then, using a valve spring compressor, compress the valve spring until the split collets can be removed. Release the compressor, and lift off the spring retainer, spring and seat. Using a pair of pliers, carefully extract the valve stem seal from the top of the guide **(see illustrations)**.

6.4b Removing the spring retainer . . .

6.4c . . . valve spring . . .

6.4d . . . and seat

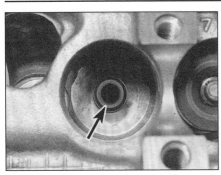

6.4e Valve stem seal location

6.4f Removing a valve stem seal

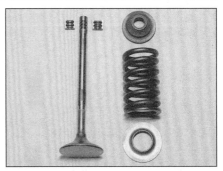

6.7a The valve spring components

5 If, when the valve spring compressor is screwed down, the spring retainer refuses to free and expose the split collets, gently tap the top of the tool, directly over the retainer, with a light hammer. This will free the retainer.

6 Withdraw the valve through the combustion chamber.

7 It is essential that each valve is stored together with its collets, retainer, spring, and spring seat. The valves should also be kept in their correct sequence, unless they are so badly worn that they are to be renewed. If they are going to be kept and used again, place each valve assembly in a labelled polythene bag or similar small container **(see illustrations)**. Note that No 1 cylinder is nearest to the timing chain end of the engine.

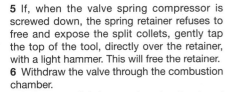

---

7 Cylinder head and valves – cleaning and inspection

1 Thorough cleaning of the cylinder head and valve components, followed by a detailed inspection, will enable you to decide how much valve service work must be carried out during the engine overhaul. **Note:** *If the engine has been severely overheated, it is best to assume that the cylinder head is warped – check carefully for signs of this.*

Cleaning

2 Scrape away all traces of old gasket material from the cylinder head.

3 Scrape away the carbon from the combustion chambers and ports, then wash the cylinder head thoroughly with paraffin or a suitable solvent.

4 Scrape off any heavy carbon deposits that may have formed on the valves, then use a power-operated wire brush to remove deposits from the valve heads and stems.

Inspection

Note: *Be sure to perform all the following inspection procedures before concluding that the services of a machine shop or engine overhaul specialist are required. Make a list of all items that require attention.*

Cylinder head

5 Inspect the head very carefully for cracks, evidence of coolant leakage, and other

damage. If cracks are found, a new cylinder head should be obtained.

6 Use a straight-edge and feeler blade to check that the cylinder head surface is not distorted **(see illustration)**. If it is, it may be possible to have it machined, provided that the cylinder head is not reduced to less than the specified height (where given).

7 Examine the valve seats in each of the combustion chambers. If they are severely pitted, cracked, or burned, they will need to be renewed or recut by an engine overhaul specialist. If they are only slightly pitted, this can be removed by grinding-in the valve heads and seats with fine valve-grinding compound, as described below. Note that on petrol engines the exhaust valves have a hardened coating and, although they may be ground-in with paste, they must not be machined.

8 Check the valve guides for wear by inserting the relevant valve, and checking for side-to-side motion of the valve. A very small amount of movement is acceptable. If the movement seems excessive, remove the valve. Measure the valve stem diameter (see below), and renew the valve if it is worn. If the valve stem is not worn, the wear must be in the valve guide, and the guide must be renewed. The renewal of valve guides is best carried out by a Saab dealer or engine overhaul specialist, who will have the necessary tools available.

Valves

9 Examine the head of each valve for pitting, burning, cracks, and general wear. Check the valve stem for scoring and wear ridges. Rotate the valve, and check for any obvious

6.7b Place each valve and its associated components in a labelled polythene bag

indication that it is bent. Look for pits and excessive wear on the tip of each valve stem. Renew any valve that shows any such signs of wear or damage.

10 If the valve appears satisfactory at this stage, measure the valve stem diameter at several points using a micrometer **(see illustration)**. Any significant difference in the readings obtained indicates wear of the valve stem. Should any of these conditions be apparent, the valve(s) must be renewed.

11 If the valves are in satisfactory condition, they should be ground (lapped) into their respective seats, to ensure a smooth, gas-tight seal. If the seat is only lightly pitted, or if it has been recut, fine grinding compound should be used to produce the required finish. Coarse valve-grinding compound should *not* be used, unless a seat is badly burned or deeply pitted. If this is the case, the cylinder head and valves should be inspected by an

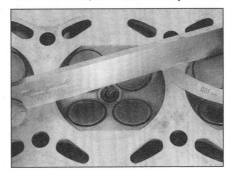

7.6 Checking the cylinder head gasket face for distortion

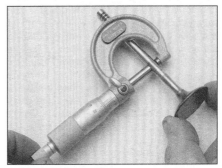

7.10 Measuring a valve stem diameter

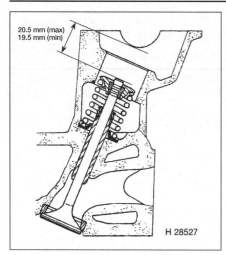

7.16 Check the depth of the valve stems below the camshaft bearing surface

expert, to decide whether seat recutting, or even the renewal of the valve or seat insert (where possible) is required.

12 Valve grinding is carried out as follows. Place the cylinder head upside-down on a bench.

13 Smear a trace of (the appropriate grade of) valve-grinding compound on the seat face, and press a suction grinding tool onto the valve head. With a semi-rotary action, grind the valve head to its seat, lifting the valve occasionally to redistribute the grinding compound. A light spring placed under the valve head will greatly ease this operation.

14 If coarse grinding compound is being used, work only until a dull, matt even surface is produced on both the valve seat and the valve, then wipe off the used compound, and repeat the process with fine compound. When a smooth unbroken ring of light grey matt finish is produced on both the valve and seat, the grinding operation is complete. *Do not* grind-in the valves any further than absolutely necessary, or the seat will be prematurely sunk into the cylinder head.

15 When all the valves have been ground-in, carefully wash off *all* traces of grinding compound using paraffin or a suitable solvent, before reassembling the cylinder head.

16 On petrol engines, make the following check to ensure that the hydraulic cam followers operate correctly. The depth of the valve stems below the camshaft bearing surface must be within certain limits. It may be possible to obtain a Saab checking tool from a dealer, but if not, the check may be made using a steel rule and straight-edge. Check that the dimension is within the limits given in the illustration by inserting each valve it its guide in turn, and measuring the dimension between the end of the valve stem and the camshaft bearing surface **(see illustration)**. If the dimension is not within the specified limits, adjustment must be made either to the end of the valve stem or to the valve seat height. If

7.17 Checking the valve spring free length

lower than the minimum amount, the length of the valve stem must be reduced, and if more than the maximum amount, the valve seat must be milled. Seek the advice of a Saab dealer or engine reconditioning specialist.

Valve components

17 Examine the valve springs for signs of damage and discoloration, and measure their free length **(see illustration)**.

18 Stand each spring on a flat surface, and check it for squareness **(see illustration)**. If any of the springs are less than the minimum free length (where given), or are damaged, distorted or have lost their tension, obtain a complete new set of springs.

19 Obtain new valve stem oil seals, regardless of their apparent condition.

8 Cylinder head – reassembly

1 Lubricate the stems of the valves, and insert the valves into their original locations **(see illustration)**. If new valves are being fitted, insert them into the locations to which they have been ground.

2 Working on the first valve, dip the new valve stem seal in fresh engine oil. Carefully locate it over the valve and onto the guide. Take care not to damage the seal as it is passed over the valve stem. Use a suitable socket or metal tube to press the seal firmly onto the guide **(see illustration)**.

3 Refit the valve seat and spring followed

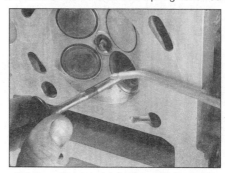

8.1 Inserting a valve in the cylinder head

7.18 Checking the valve springs for squareness

by the spring retainer, then locate the plastic protector in the hydraulic cam follower bore.

4 Compress the valve spring, and locate the split collets in the recess in the valve stem. Release the compressor and remove the protector on the remaining valves.

> **HAYNES HINT** *Use a little dab of grease to locate the collets on the valve stems, and to hold them in place while the spring compressor is released.*

5 With all the valves installed, place the cylinder head flat on the bench and, using a hammer and interposed block of wood, tap the end of each valve stem to settle the components.

6 Refit the hydraulic cam followers and camshafts with reference to Chapter 2A or 2B.

7 Refit the external components removed in Section 6.

8 The cylinder head may now be refitted as described in Chapter 2A or 2B.

9 Timing cover (petrol engines) – removal and refitting

Note: *This procedure describes removal of the timing cover, leaving the cylinder head in position. The alternative method (which is less likely to damage the cylinder head gasket) is to remove the cylinder head first, as described in Chapter 2A.*

8.2 Using a socket to fit the valve stem seals

9.1a Unscrewing the tensioner retaining bolt . . .

9.1b . . . and idler pulley retaining bolt

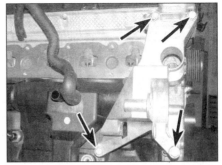

9.2 Unscrew the mounting bracket retaining bolts (arrowed)

Removal

1 Unbolt and remove the auxiliary drivebelt tensioner unit and idler pulley **(see illustrations)**.

2 Remove the alternator as described in Chapter 5A, then undo the retaining bolts and remove the mounting bracket from the rear of the cylinder block **(see illustration)**.

3 Undo the retaining bolts and remove the power steering pump mounting bracket including the lifting eye from the front of the cylinder head.

4 Remove the water pump as described in Chapter 3.

5 Have an assistant hold the crankshaft/ flywheel by inserting a flat-bladed screwdriver through the bellhousing and locking the starter ring gear to prevent the crankshaft turning. Loosen the crankshaft pulley bolt using a long socket bar. Note that the bolt is tightened to a very high torque.

6 Fully unscrew the crankshaft pulley bolt, and slide the pulley off the end of the crankshaft **(see illustrations)**.

7 Remove the sump as described in Chapter 2A.

8 Remove the two locating dowels (one in the left-hand bottom corner and one in the top right-hand corner) in the timing cover by cutting an internal thread in them using a 3/8 in UNC thread tap and withdraw them with sliding hammer. A bolt can be threaded into the locating dowels, then attached to the end of the slide hammer **(see illustrations)**.

9 Unscrew and remove the bolts securing the timing cover to the cylinder block and cylinder head. Note the fitted position of the bolts, the two upper bolts on the cylinder head and the two lower bolts in the sump are different **(see illustrations)**.

10 Taking care not to damage the cylinder head gasket, withdraw the timing cover complete with the oil pump from the end of the crankshaft. Carefully move the timing cover down and outwards, away from the cylinder block.

9.6a Remove the crankshaft pulley bolt . . .

9.6b . . . and slide the pulley off the crankshaft

9.8a Cutting an internal thread in the dowel using a thread tap

9.8b A bolt fitted to the end of a slide hammer

9.8c Using the slide hammer to withdraw the dowels from the timing cover

9.9a Note two upper bolts securing the timing cover to the cylinder head

9.9b Removing the timing cover from the engine

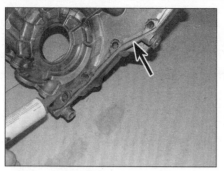

9.14 Applying sealant (arrowed) on the timing cover flanges

9.15 Tap the dowels back into the timing cover

10.2 Removing the oil pump drive dog from the crankshaft

11 Thoroughly clean all traces of sealant from the contact faces of the timing cover, sump, cylinder head and block. **Note:** *Check the condition of the cylinder head gasket, if there is any damage to the gasket, then the cylinder head will need to be removed to renew the gasket.*

12 If required, remove the oil pump from the timing cover, with reference to Chapter 2A.

Refitting

13 Where applicable, refit the oil pump with reference to Chapter 2A.

14 Apply a bead of sealant (Loctite 518 or similar) about 1 mm thick to the timing cover flanges, then carefully locate the timing cover on the cylinder block **(see illustration)**.

15 Insert the timing cover retaining bolts including the two upper cylinder head bolts but do not tighten them at this stage. Tap the locating dowels back into place **(see**

illustration), then tighten the cover retaining bolts to the specified torque, including the two upper cylinder head bolts.

16 Refit the sump as described in Chapter 2A.

17 Slide the crankshaft pulley onto the crankshaft, then insert the pulley bolt. Tighten the bolt to the specified torque, while an assistant holds the crankshaft stationary using a wide-bladed screwdriver inserted in the starter ring gear.

18 Refit the water pump, with reference to Chapter 3.

19 Refit the alternator and power steering pump mounting brackets, and tighten the retaining bolts.

20 Refit the alternator with reference to Chapter 5A.

21 Refit the drivebelt tensioner assembly and idler pulley, and tighten the bolts.

10 Timing chain and sprockets (petrol engines) – removal, inspection and refitting

Removal

1 Position the crankshaft at TDC compression for No 1 piston (timing chain end of the engine) as described in Chapter 2A.

2 Remove the timing cover as described in Section 9. Also remove the oil pump drive dog from the crankshaft **(see illustration)**.

3 The balancer shafts are 'timed' at TDC, but since they rotate at twice the speed of the crankshaft, they may also be correctly 'timed' at BDC. Check that the timing marks on the shafts are correctly aligned with the marks on the front of the cylinder block/bearing housing. Note that the balancer shaft sprockets are marked 'inlet' and 'exhaust' for their positions, but both front bearings are marked identically. However, as the bearings are located with single bolts, the 'inlet' and 'exhaust' marks will always be correctly located at the top of the bearings **(see illustrations)**.

> **HAYNES HiNT** *Apply alignment markings (small dabs of paint are ideal) to the chain and sprockets, to ensure correct refitting.*

4 Unbolt the balancer shaft chain upper guide, then remove the tensioner and side guide **(see illustrations)**.

10.3a INL mark on the inlet balancer shaft front bearing

10.3b EXH mark on the exhaust balancer shaft front bearing

10.4a Unscrew the bolts (arrowed) and remove the balancer shaft chain upper guide

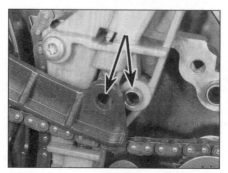

10.4b Note how the upper guide locates on the dowel

10.4c Removing the balancer shaft chain tensioner . . .

10.4d . . . and side guide

10.5a Unscrew . . .

10.5b . . . and remove the idler retaining bolt (note alignment marks between idler and chain) . . .

5 Unbolt the idler from the block, then release the chain from the balancer shaft sprockets and crankshaft sprocket. Note that the idler is in two parts **(see illustrations)**.

6 Slide the balancer shaft chain sprocket from the front of the crankshaft **(see illustration)**. Note that the word 'Saab' is facing outwards.

7 Unscrew the retaining bolts, and remove the sprockets from the ends of the balancer shafts. To do this, hold the sprockets stationary with a chain-type oil filter removal tool or similar. Keep the sprockets identified for position.

8 Remove the cylinder head cover as described in Chapter 2A.

9 Unscrew and remove the timing chain tensioner from the rear of the cylinder head. To do this, first unscrew the centre bolt and remove the spring, then unscrew and remove

10.5c . . . then withdraw the idler and remove the balancer shaft chain

10.5d The idler is in two parts

the tensioner from the cylinder head **(see illustrations)**.

10 While holding each camshaft stationary with

a spanner on the flats at the flywheel/driveplate end of the camshaft, loosen (but do not remove) the camshaft sprocket securing bolts.

10.6 Removing the balancer shaft chain sprocket from the front of the crankshaft

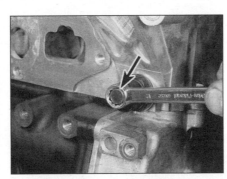

10.9a Unscrew the centre bolt . . .

10.9b . . . and remove the spring . . .

10.9c . . . then unscrew the tensioner . . .

10.9d . . . and remove it from the cylinder head

10.9e The timing chain tensioner components

10.11 Removing the sprocket from the end of the inlet camshaft

10.13a Remove the retaining bolt . . .

10.13b . . . then disengage the sprocket from the chain

11 Unscrew and remove the bolt, and withdraw the sprocket from the end of the inlet camshaft **(see illustration)**. Hold the timing chain with one hand, and release the sprocket from it with the other hand.

12 Identify each sprocket for position. Note that each sprocket has a projection which engages with a cut-out in the end of the camshaft.

13 Unscrew the bolt and withdraw the sprocket from the end of the exhaust camshaft, then disengage it from the chain **(see illustrations)**.

14 Unscrew the bolts, and remove the timing chain fixed guide from the cylinder block **(see illustrations)**.

15 Unbolt the chain retainer from the cylinder block, then disengage the timing chain and remove the sprocket from the end of the crankshaft **(see illustrations)**. If necessary, remove the Woodruff key from the groove in the crankshaft using a screwdriver.

Inspection

16 The timing chain **(see illustration)** (and where applicable, the balancer shaft chain)

should be renewed if the sprockets are worn, or if the chain is loose and noisy in operation. It's a good idea to renew the chain as a matter of course if the engine is stripped down for overhaul. The rollers on a very badly worn chain may be slightly grooved. To avoid future problems, if there's any doubt at all about the chain's condition, renew it. The chain tensioner and guides should be examined and if necessary renewed at the same time (refer to Section 11).

17 Examine the teeth on the crankshaft sprocket, camshaft sprockets and the

10.14a Unscrew the bolts . . .

10.14b . . . and remove the timing chain fixed guide

10.15a Removing the timing chain retainer (arrowed) from the cylinder block

10.15b Removing the crankshaft sprocket from the end of the crankshaft

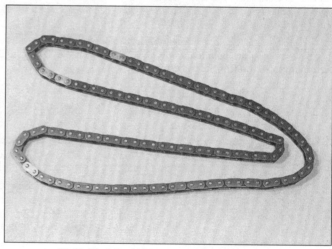

10.16 Timing chain removed from the engine

10.19a Where timing chain has bright links, these must be aligned with the slot in the sprocket (arrowed)

10.19b Tightening the timing chain retainer bolts

10.25 Setting the timing chain tensioner

balancer shaft sprockets for wear. Each tooth forms an inverted V. If worn, the side of each tooth under tension will be slightly concave (hooked) in shape, when compared with the other side of the tooth (ie, one side of the inverted V will be concave when compared with the other). If the teeth appear to be worn, the sprockets must be renewed.

Refitting

18 Locate the Woodruff key in the groove in the crankshaft. Tap it fully into the groove, making sure that its plane surface is parallel to the crankshaft.

19 Engage the timing chain with the crankshaft sprocket, then locate the crankshaft sprocket on the end of the crankshaft, making sure that it locates correctly on the Woodruff key. Where the timing chain has bright links, locate the single bright link at the bottom of the sprocket, aligned with the slot in the sprocket. Refit the chain retainer and tighten the bolts **(see illustrations)**.

20 Locate the timing chain in the fixed guide, then refit the guide and tighten the bolts.

21 Refit the sprocket to the end of the exhaust camshaft, insert the bolt and finger-tighten it at this stage. **Do not** apply thread-locking fluid to the threads of the bolt.

22 Check that the crankshaft and camshafts are still aligned at their TDC positions.

23 Feed the timing chain up through the cylinder head aperture, and locate it on the

exhaust camshaft sprocket, making sure that it is taut between the two sprockets. Check that it is correctly located on the guides. Where the chain has a bright link, make sure that it is aligned with the timing mark.

24 Engage the inlet sprocket with the timing chain so that the engagement cut-out and projection are in alignment, then locate the sprocket on the inlet camshaft, and insert the bolt. Finger-tighten the bolt at this stage. **Do not** apply thread-locking fluid to the threads of the bolt. Where the chain has a bright link, make sure that it is aligned with the timing mark.

25 Set the timing chain tensioner by pressing down on the ratchet with a screwdriver, then push the plunger fully into the tensioner, and release the ratchet **(see illustration)**. Check the tensioner washer for condition and renew it if necessary.

26 Insert the tensioner body in the cylinder head, and tighten to the specified torque.

27 Insert the spring and plastic guide pin in the tensioner, then fit the plug together with a new O-ring, and tighten it to the specified torque. **Note:** *New tensioners are supplied with the tensioner spring held pretensioned with a pin. **Do not** remove this pin until after the tensioner has been tightened into the cylinder head. When the engine is started, hydraulic pressure will take up any remaining slack.*

28 Temporarily refit the crankshaft pulley

bolt, and rotate the engine two complete turns clockwise. Check that the timing marks still align correctly. Remove the pulley bolt. Where the chain has bright links, note that these will not now be aligned with the timing marks.

29 Fully tighten the camshaft sprocket bolts to the specified torque, while holding the camshafts with a spanner on the flats.

30 Refit the cylinder head cover with reference to Chapter 2A.

31 Refit the sprockets to the ends of the balancer shafts, and tighten the retaining bolts.

32 Locate the balancer shaft chain sprocket on the front of the crankshaft, with the word 'Saab' facing outwards.

33 Fit the chain to the sprockets, making sure that the timing marks are aligned correctly **(see illustration)**.

34 Refit the idler to the front of the block, and tighten the retaining bolt.

35 Refit the side guide, tensioner and upper guide to the balancer shaft chain **(see illustration and Tool tip)**.

36 Rotate the crankshaft one turn, and check that the balancer shaft timing marks are still correctly aligned.

37 Refit the timing cover with reference to Section 5.

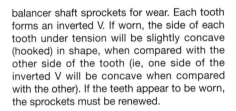

10.33 The balancer shaft timing marks must be correctly aligned before refitting the chain

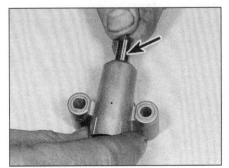

10.35 Depress the balancer shaft chain tensioner plunger (arrowed) and retain with a plastic cable-tie

TOOL TiP

Before refitting the tensioner, hold its plunger depressed by fitting a plastic cable-tie around it. Cut the tie after refitting.

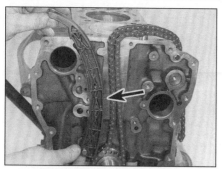

11.2 Removing the pivoting guide from the pin on the cylinder block

11 Timing chain guides and tensioner (petrol engines) – removal, inspection and refitting

Removal

1 Remove the timing chain as described in Section 10; note that this procedure includes removal of the fixed guide and balancer shaft chain guides. The timing chain need not be removed from the crankshaft sprocket.
2 Unbolt and remove the fixed timing chain guide and release the pivoting guide from the pin on the cylinder block (**see illustration**).

Inspection

3 Inspect the chain guides for damage and excessive wear, and renew them if necessary.
4 Clean the tensioner plunger and body, and examine them for damage and wear (**see**

12.7a Unscrew the bearing retaining bolts . . .

12.7b . . . and withdraw the exhaust balancer shaft from the cylinder block

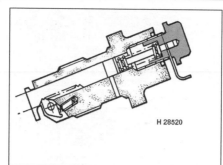

11.4 Cross-section of the timing chain tensioner

illustration). The plunger may be removed by depressing the ratchet against the spring. If the plunger or body is excessively scored, the complete tensioner should be renewed.

Refitting

5 Locate the pivoting guide on the pin on the cylinder block, then refit the fixed guide and tighten the retaining bolts.
6 Refit the timing chain with reference to Section 10.

12 Balancer shafts (petrol engines) – removal, inspection and refitting

Removal

1 Position the crankshaft at TDC compression for No 1 piston (timing chain end of the engine) as described in Chapter 2A.
2 Remove the timing cover as described in Section 9.
3 The balancer shafts are 'timed' at TDC, but since they rotate at twice the speed of the crankshaft, they may also be correctly 'timed' at BDC. Check that the timing marks on the shafts are correctly aligned with the marks on the bearing brackets. As an extra precaution, apply dabs of paint to the chain and sprockets, to ensure correct refitting. Note that the balancer shaft sprockets are marked 'inlet' and 'exhaust' for position, but the front bearings are marked identically. However, as the bearings are located with single bolts, the 'inlet' and 'exhaust' marks will always be correctly located at the top of the bearings

12.7c Removing the inlet balancer shaft from the cylinder block

– refer to Section 10 for further information.
4 Unbolt the balancer shaft chain upper guide, then remove the tensioner and side guide (see illustrations in Section 10 of this Chapter).
5 Unscrew the retaining bolt and remove the idler from the block.
6 Release the chain from the balancer shaft sprockets and crankshaft sprocket.
7 Unscrew the bearing retaining bolts, and withdraw the balancer shafts from the cylinder block (**see illustrations**). Keep the shafts identified for position.
8 Unscrew the retaining bolts, and remove the sprockets from the ends of the balancer shafts, while holding each shaft in a soft-jawed vice.

Inspection

9 Clean the balancer shafts and examine the bearing journals for wear and damage. The bearings inside the cylinder block should also be examined. If these are excessively worn or damaged, get advice from a Saab dealer or engine reconditioner.

Refitting

10 Fit the sprockets to the ends of the balancer shafts, and tighten the retaining bolts.
11 Lubricate the bearing journals with clean engine oil, then insert the balancer shafts in the cylinder block in their correct positions.
12 Locate the balancer shaft chain sprocket on the front of the crankshaft, with the word 'Saab' facing outwards.
13 Fit the chain to the sprockets, and refit the idler to the front of the block, making sure that the timing marks remain aligned correctly.
14 Refit the side guide, tensioner and upper guide to the balancer shaft chain.
15 Rotate the crankshaft one turn, and check that the balancer shaft sprockets are still correctly aligned.
16 Refit the timing cover with reference to Section 9.

13 Piston/connecting rod assembly – removal

1 Remove the cylinder head, sump and oil pump pick-up/strainer as described in Part A or B of this Chapter.

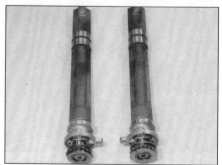

12.7d The two balancer shafts removed from the engine

2 If there is a pronounced wear ridge at the top of any bore, it may be necessary to remove it with a scraper or ridge reamer, to avoid piston damage during removal. Such a ridge indicates excessive wear of the cylinder bore.

3 Using a hammer and centre-punch, paint or similar, mark each connecting rod big-end bearing cap with its respective cylinder number on the flat machined surface provided; if the engine has been dismantled before, note carefully any identifying marks made previously. Note that No 1 cylinder is at the timing chain end of the engine.

4 Turn the crankshaft to bring pistons 1 and 4 to BDC (bottom dead centre).

5 Unscrew the nuts (petrol engines) or bolts (diesel engines) from No 1 piston big-end bearing cap. Take off the cap, and recover the bottom half bearing shell. If the bearing shells are to be re-used, tape the cap and the shell together **(see illustrations)**.

6 To prevent the possibility of damage to the crankshaft bearing journals, tape over the connecting rod stud threads.

7 Using a hammer handle, push the piston up through the bore, and remove it from the top of the cylinder block. Recover the bearing shell, and tape it to the connecting rod for safe-keeping.

8 Loosely refit the big-end cap to the connecting rod, and secure with the nuts/bolts – this will help to keep the components in their correct order.

9 Remove No 4 piston assembly in the same way.

13.5a Removing a big-end bearing cap

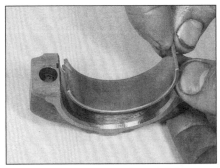

13.5b Removing a bearing shell from a big-end bearing cap

10 Turn the crankshaft through 180° to bring pistons 2 and 3 to BDC (bottom dead centre), and remove them in the same way.

14 Crankshaft – removal

1 Remove the timing chain and sprocket, the sump and oil pump pick-up/strainer/transfer tube, and the flywheel/driveplate. On diesel engines, also remove the balancer shaft unit as described in Chapter 2B.

2 Remove the pistons and connecting rods, as described in Section 13. **Note:** *If no work is to be done on the pistons and connecting rods, there is no need to remove the cylinder head, or to push the pistons out of the cylinder bores. The pistons should just be pushed far*

enough up the bores that they are positioned clear of the crankshaft journals.

3 Check the crankshaft endfloat with reference to Section 17, then proceed as follows.

4 Unbolt and remove the crankshaft oil seal housing from the left-hand end of the cylinder block, noting the correct fitted locations of the locating dowels. If the locating dowels are a loose fit, remove them and store them with the housing for safe-keeping. Remove the gasket.

5 Identification numbers should already be cast onto the base of each main bearing cap **(see illustration)**. If not, number the cap and crankcase using a centre-punch, as was done for the connecting rods and caps.

6 Unscrew and remove the main bearing cap retaining bolts, and withdraw the caps, complete with bearing shells **(see illustrations)**. Tap the caps with a wooden or copper mallet if they are stuck.

7 Remove the bearing shells from the caps, but keep them with their relevant caps and identified for position to ensure correct refitting **(see illustration)**.

8 Carefully lift the crankshaft from the crankcase **(see illustration)**. On diesel engines, unhook and remove the balancer shaft drive chain from the crankshaft gear.

9 Remove the upper bearing shells from the crankcase, keeping them identified for position. Also remove the thrustwashers at each side of the centre main bearing, and

14.5 The main bearing caps are numbered from the timing chain end of the engine

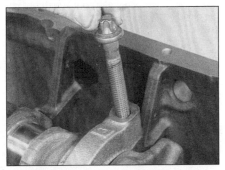

14.6a Unscrew and remove the main bearing cap bolts . . .

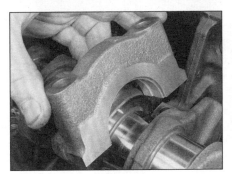

14.6b . . . and remove the main bearing caps

14.7 Removing a main bearing shell from its cap

14.8 Lifting the crankshaft from the crankcase

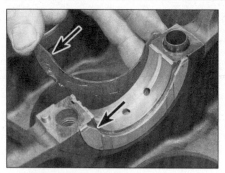

14.9a Removing the thrustwashers (arrowed) . . .

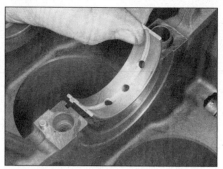

14.9b . . . and main bearing shells

14.10 Location of the screws securing the crankshaft position sensor reluctor

store them with the bearing cap **(see illustrations)**.

10 On petrol engines, with the crankshaft removed, the crankshaft position sensor reluctor may be removed if necessary, by unscrewing the screws and withdrawing the reluctor over the end of the crankshaft **(see illustration)**. Note that the screws are arranged so that it is only possible to refit the reluctor in one position.

15 Cylinder block/crankcase – cleaning and inspection

Cleaning

1 Remove all external components and electrical switches/sensors from the block. For complete cleaning, the core plugs should ideally be removed, as follows. Drill a small hole in the plugs, then insert a self-tapping screw into the hole. Pull out the plugs by pulling on the screw with a pair of grips, or by using a slide hammer. Also unbolt the four oil jets (where fitted) from the lower part of the crankcase **(see illustration)**.

2 Scrape all traces of sealant from the cylinder block/crankcase, taking care not to damage the gasket/sealing surfaces.

3 Remove all oil gallery plugs (where fitted). The plugs are usually very tight – they may have to be drilled out, and the holes retapped. Use new plugs when the engine is reassembled.

4 If the cylinder block/crankcase is extremely dirty, it should be steam-cleaned.

5 Clean all oil holes and oil galleries, and flush all internal passages with warm water until the water runs clear. Dry thoroughly, and apply a light film of oil to all mating surfaces, to prevent rusting. Also oil the cylinder bores. If you have access to compressed air, use it to speed up the drying process, and to blow out all the oil holes and galleries.

 Warning: Wear eye protection when using compressed air.

6 If the cylinder block is not very dirty, you can do an adequate cleaning job with hot (as hot as you can stand!), soapy water and a stiff brush. Take plenty of time, and do a thorough job. Regardless of the cleaning method used, be sure to clean all oil holes and galleries very thoroughly, and to dry all components well. On completion, protect the cylinder bores as described above, to prevent rusting.

7 All threaded holes must be clean, to ensure accurate torque readings during reassembly. To clean the threads, run the correct-size tap into each of the holes to remove rust, corrosion, thread sealant or sludge, and to restore damaged threads **(see illustration)**. If possible, use compressed air to clear the holes of debris produced by this operation.

 HAYNES HiNT *A good alternative to compressed air is to inject aerosol-applied water-dispersant lubricant into each hole, using the long tube usually supplied.*

 Warning: Wear eye protection when cleaning out these holes in this way.

8 Apply suitable sealant to the new oil gallery plugs, and insert them into the holes in the block. Tighten them securely. Apply suitable sealant to new core plugs and tap them into place with a socket or tube. Refit and tighten the oil jets to the bottom of the crankcase where applicable.

9 If the engine is not going to be reassembled right away, cover it with a large plastic bag to keep it clean; protect all mating surfaces and the cylinder bores as described above, to prevent rusting.

15.1 Removing an oil jet from the crankcase

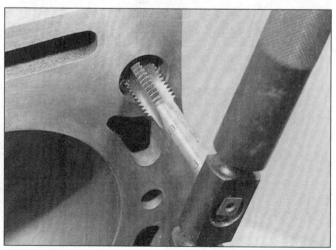

15.7 Cleaning a cylinder head bolt hole in the cylinder block using a tap

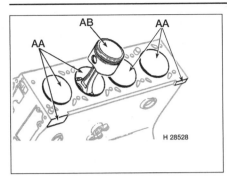

15.12a Piston and cylinder bore classification code locations

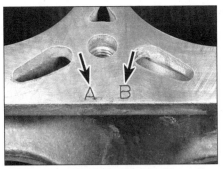

15.12b Cylinder bore classification on the front of the block

15.12c Piston classification on the piston crown

Inspection

10 Visually check the cylinder block for cracks and corrosion. Look for stripped threads in the threaded holes. If there has been any history of internal water leakage, it may be worthwhile having an engine overhaul specialist check the cylinder block/crankcase with special equipment. If defects are found, have them repaired if possible; otherwise, a new block will be needed.

11 Check each cylinder bore for scuffing and scoring. Check for signs of a wear ridge at the top of the cylinder, indicating that the bore is excessively worn.

12 The cylinder bores and pistons are matched, and classified with codes stamped on the piston crowns and on the front of the cylinder block **(see illustrations)**. Note that different classifications may occur in the same cylinder block.

13 Wear of the cylinder bores and pistons can be measured by inserting the relevant piston (without piston rings) in its bore and using a feeler blade. Make the check with the piston near the top of its bore. If the clearance is more than the amount given in the Specifications, a rebore should be considered, and the opinion of an engine reconditioner sought.

16 Piston/connecting rod assembly – inspection

1 Before the inspection process can begin, the piston/connecting rod assemblies must be cleaned, and the original piston rings removed from the pistons **(see illustration)**.

2 Carefully expand the old rings over the top of the pistons. The use of two or three old feeler blades will be helpful in preventing the rings dropping into empty grooves **(see illustrations)**. Be careful not to scratch the piston with the ends of the ring. The rings are brittle, and will snap if they are spread too far. They're also very sharp – protect your hands and fingers. Note that the third ring incorporates an expander. Always remove the rings from the top of the piston. Keep each set of rings with its piston, if the old rings are to be re-used.

3 Scrape away all traces of carbon from the top of the piston. A hand-held wire brush (or a piece of fine emery cloth) can be used, once the majority of the deposits have been scraped away.

4 Remove the carbon from the ring grooves in the piston, using an old ring. Break the ring in half to do this (be careful not to cut your fingers – piston rings are sharp). Be careful to remove only the carbon deposits – do not remove any metal, and do not nick or scratch the sides of the ring grooves.

5 Once the deposits have been removed, clean the piston/connecting rod assembly

with paraffin or a suitable solvent, and dry thoroughly. Make sure that the oil return holes in the ring grooves are clear.

6 If the pistons and cylinder bores are not damaged or worn excessively, and if the cylinder block does not need to be rebored, the original pistons can be refitted. Normal piston wear shows up as even vertical wear on the piston thrust surfaces, and slight looseness of the top ring in its groove.

7 Carefully inspect each piston for cracks around the skirt, around the gudgeon pin holes, and at the piston ring 'lands' (between the ring grooves).

8 Look for scoring and scuffing on the piston skirt, holes in the piston crown, and burned areas at the edge of the crown. If the skirt is scored or scuffed, the engine may have been suffering from overheating, and/or abnormal combustion which caused excessively high operating temperatures. The cooling and lubrication systems should be checked thoroughly. Scorch marks on the sides of the pistons show that blow-by has occurred. A hole in the piston crown, or burned areas at the edge of the piston crown, indicates that abnormal combustion (pre-ignition, knocking, or detonation) has been occurring. If any of the above problems exist, the causes must be investigated and corrected, or the damage will occur again. The causes may include incorrect ignition timing and/or fuel/air mixture.

9 Corrosion of the piston, in the form of pitting, indicates that coolant has been leaking into the combustion chamber and/or the crankcase. Again, the cause must be

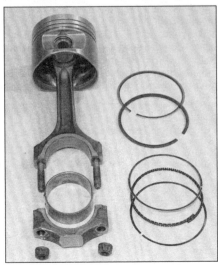

16.1 Piston/connecting rod assembly components

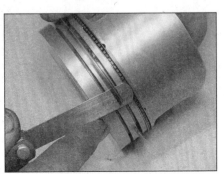

16.2a Removing a piston compression ring with the aid of a feeler blade

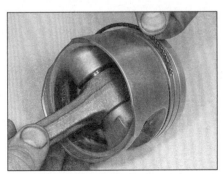

16.2b Removing the oil control ring

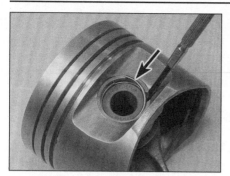

16.13a Prise out the gudgeon pin circlip . . .

16.13b . . . then withdraw the gudgeon pin, and separate the piston from the connecting rod

corrected, or the problem may persist in the rebuilt engine.

10 Where needed, pistons can be purchased from a Saab dealer.

11 Examine each connecting rod carefully for signs of damage, such as cracks around the big-end and small-end bearings. Check that the rod is not bent or distorted. Damage is highly unlikely, unless the engine has been seized or badly overheated. Detailed checking of the connecting rod assembly can only be carried out by a Saab dealer or engine repair specialist with the necessary equipment.

12 The gudgeon pins are of the floating type, secured in position by two circlips, and the pistons and connecting rods can be separated and reassembled as follows.

13 Using a small flat-bladed screwdriver, prise out the circlips, and push out the gudgeon pin (see illustrations). Hand pressure should be sufficient to remove the pin. Identify the piston, gudgeon pin and rod to ensure correct reassembly.

14 Examine the gudgeon pin and connecting rod small-end bearing for signs of wear or damage. Wear can be cured by renewing both the pin and bush. Bush renewal, however, is a specialist job – press facilities are required, and the new bush must be reamed accurately.

15 The connecting rods themselves should not be in need of renewal, unless seizure or some other major mechanical failure has occurred. Check the alignment of the

connecting rods visually, and if the rods are not straight, take them to an engine overhaul specialist for a more detailed check.

16 Examine all components, and obtain any new parts from your Saab dealer. If new pistons are purchased, they will be supplied complete with gudgeon pins and circlips. Circlips can also be purchased individually.

17 On petrol engines, position the piston so that the notch on the edge of the crown faces the timing end of the engine, and the numbers on the connecting rod and big-end cap face the exhaust side of the cylinder block; with the piston held in your hand and the notch facing the left, the connecting rod numbering should face towards you (see illustration). On diesel engines, the assembly mark cast onto

one side of the connecting rod (on the top of the big-end bore), must face the opposite way to the arrow on the top of the piston (see illustration).

18 Apply a smear of clean engine oil to the gudgeon pin. Slide it into the piston and through the connecting rod small-end. Check that the piston pivots freely on the rod, then secure the gudgeon pin in position with the circlips. Ensure that each circlip is correctly located in its groove in the piston, with their end gaps at the top (Saab state this position is critical).

19 Measure the piston diameters, and check that they are within limits for the corresponding bore diameters. If the piston-to-bore clearance is excessive, the block will have to be rebored, and new pistons and rings fitted.

20 Examine the mating surfaces of the big-end caps and connecting rods, to see if they have ever been filed in a mistaken attempt to take up bearing wear. This is extremely unlikely, but if evident, the offending connecting rods and caps must be renewed.

17 Crankshaft – inspection

Checking endfloat

1 If the crankshaft endfloat is to be checked, this must be done when the crankshaft is still installed in the cylinder block/crankcase, but is free to move (see Section 14).

2 Check the endfloat using a dial gauge in contact with the end of the crankshaft. Push the crankshaft fully one way, and then zero the gauge. Push the crankshaft fully the other way, and check the endfloat (see illustration). The result can be compared with the specified amount, and will give an indication as to whether new thrustwashers are required.

3 If a dial gauge is not available, feeler blades can be used. First push the crankshaft fully towards the flywheel end of the engine, then use feeler blades to measure the gap between the No 3 crankpin web and

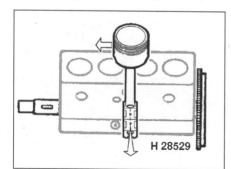

16.17a Relationship of the piston and connecting rod – petrol engines

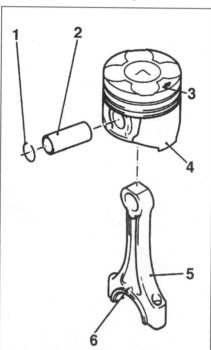

16.17b Piston/connecting rod assembly components – diesel engines

1 Circlip	4 Piston
2 Gudgeon pin	5 Connecting rod
3 Arrow on piston crown	6 Connecting rod assembly mark

17.2 Using a dial gauge to check the crankshaft endfloat

17.3 Using feeler blades to check the crankshaft endfloat

the centre main bearing thrustwasher **(see illustration)**.

Inspection

4 Clean the crankshaft using paraffin or a suitable solvent, and dry it, preferably with compressed air if available. Be sure to clean the oil holes with a pipe cleaner or similar probe, to ensure that they are not obstructed. *Warning: Wear eye protection when using compressed air.*

5 Check the main and big-end bearing journals for uneven wear, scoring, pitting and cracking.

6 Big-end bearing wear is accompanied by distinct metallic knocking when the engine is running (particularly noticeable when the engine is pulling from low speed), and some loss of oil pressure.

7 Main bearing wear is accompanied by severe engine vibration and rumble – getting progressively worse as engine speed increases – and again by loss of oil pressure.

8 If there are any signs of wear, take the crankshaft to your local engine reconditioning specialist, where they will check the bearing journals. Any roughness (which will be accompanied by obvious bearing wear) indicates that the crankshaft requires regrinding (where possible) or renewal.

9 If the crankshaft has been reground, check for burrs around the crankshaft oil holes (the holes are usually chamfered, so burrs should not be a problem, unless regrinding has been carried out carelessly). Remove any burrs with a fine file or scraper, and thoroughly clean the oil holes as described previously.

10 Using a micrometer, measure the diameter of the main and big-end bearing journals, and compare the results with the Specifications **(see illustration)**. By measuring the diameter at a number of points around each journal's circumference, you will be able to determine whether or not the journal is out-of-round. Take the measurement at each end of the journal, near the webs, to determine if the journal is tapered. Compare the results obtained with those given in the Specifications.

11 Check the oil seal contact surfaces at each end of the crankshaft for wear and damage. If the seal has worn a deep groove in the surface of the crankshaft, consult an

17.10 Measuring a crankshaft big-end bearing journal diameter

engine overhaul specialist; repair may be possible, but otherwise a new crankshaft will be required.

18 Main and big-end bearings – inspection

1 Even though the main and big-end bearings are renewed during the engine overhaul, the old bearings should be retained for close examination, as they may reveal valuable information about the condition of the engine. The bearing shells are graded by thickness, the grade of each shell being indicated by the colour code marked on it – they may also have markings on their backing faces **(see illustration)**.

Petrol engines
The thinnest shells are red –
   0.005mm thinner than yellow.
The standard shells are yellow
   (only size stocked as spare part).
The first undersize shells are blue –
   0.005mm thicker than yellow.

Diesel engines
See Specifications

2 Bearing failure can occur due to lack of lubrication, the presence of dirt or other foreign particles, overloading the engine, or corrosion **(see illustration)**. Regardless of the cause of bearing failure, the cause must be corrected (where applicable) before the engine is reassembled, to prevent it from happening again.

3 When examining the bearing shells, remove

18.1 STD marking on the backing of a big-end bearing shell

them from the cylinder block/crankcase, the main bearing caps, the connecting rods and the connecting rod big-end bearing caps. Lay them out on a clean surface in the same general position as their location in the engine. This will enable you to match any bearing problems with the corresponding crankshaft journal. *Do not* touch any shell's bearing surface with your fingers while checking it, or the delicate surface may be scratched.

4 Dirt and other foreign matter gets into the engine in a variety of ways. It may be left in the engine during assembly, or it may pass through filters or the crankcase ventilation system. It may get into the oil, and from there into the bearings. Metal chips from machining operations and normal engine wear are often present. Abrasives are sometimes left in engine components after reconditioning, especially when parts are not thoroughly cleaned using the proper cleaning methods. Whatever the source, these foreign objects often end up embedded in the soft bearing material, and are easily recognised. Large particles will not embed in the bearing, and will score or gouge the bearing and journal. The best prevention for this cause of bearing failure is to clean all parts thoroughly, and keep everything spotlessly-clean during engine assembly. Frequent and regular engine oil and filter changes are also recommended.

5 Lack of lubrication (or lubrication breakdown) has a number of interrelated causes. Excessive heat (which thins the oil), overloading (which squeezes the oil from the bearing face) and oil leakage (from excessive bearing clearances, worn oil pump or high engine speeds) all contribute to lubrication breakdown. Blocked oil passages, which usually are the result of misaligned oil holes in a bearing shell, will also oil-starve a bearing, and destroy it. When lack of lubrication is the

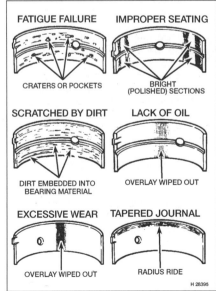

18.2 Typical bearing failures

cause of bearing failure, the bearing material is wiped or extruded from the steel backing of the bearing. Temperatures may increase to the point where the steel backing turns blue from overheating.

6 Driving habits can have a definite effect on bearing life. Full-throttle, low-speed operation (labouring the engine) puts very high loads on bearings, tending to squeeze out the oil film. These loads cause the bearings to flex, which produces fine cracks in the bearing face (fatigue failure). Eventually, the bearing material will loosen in pieces, and tear away from the steel backing.

7 Short-distance driving leads to corrosion of bearings, because insufficient engine heat is produced to drive off the condensed water and corrosive gases. These products collect in the engine oil, forming acid and sludge. As the oil is carried to the engine bearings, the acid attacks and corrodes the bearing material.

8 Incorrect bearing installation during engine assembly will lead to bearing failure as well. Tight-fitting bearings leave insufficient bearing running clearance, and will result in oil starvation. Dirt or foreign particles trapped behind a bearing shell result in high spots on the bearing, which lead to failure.

9 *Do not* touch any shell's bearing surface with your fingers during reassembly; there is a risk of scratching the delicate surface, or of depositing particles of dirt on it. **Note:** *Bearing shells should be renewed as a matter of course during engine overhaul; to do otherwise is false economy.*

19 Engine overhaul – reassembly sequence

1 Before reassembly begins, ensure that all new parts have been obtained, and that all necessary tools are available. Read through the entire procedure, to familiarise yourself with the work involved, and to ensure that all items necessary for reassembly of the engine are at hand. In addition to all normal tools and materials, thread-locking compound will be needed. A suitable tube of sealant will also be required for the joint faces that are fitted without gaskets.

2 In order to save time and avoid problems, engine reassembly can be carried out in the following order:
 a) *Crankshaft (Section 21).*
 b) *Piston/connecting rod assemblies (Section 22).*
 c) *Sump (Chapter 2A or 2B).*
 d) *Balancer shafts (Section 12 for petrol models, Chapter 2B for diesel models).*
 e) *Flywheel/driveplate (Chapter 2A or 2B).*
 f) *Timing chain and balancer shaft chain, sprockets and tensioner (Sections 10 and 11 for petrol models, Chapter 2B for diesel models)*
 g) *Cylinder head (Chapter 2A or 2B).*
 h) *Inlet and exhaust manifolds (Chapter 4A or 4B).*

20.3 Using the top of a piston to push a piston ring into the bore

3 At this stage, all engine components should be absolutely clean and dry, with all faults repaired. The components should be laid out (or in individual containers) on a completely clean work surface.

20 Piston rings – refitting

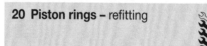

1 Before fitting new piston rings, the ring end gaps must be checked as follows.
2 Lay out the piston/connecting rod assemblies and the new piston ring sets, so that the ring sets will be matched with the same piston and cylinder during the end gap measurement and subsequent engine reassembly.
3 Insert the top ring into the first cylinder, and push it down the bore using the top of the piston **(see illustration)**. This will ensure that the ring remains square with the cylinder walls. Position the ring near the bottom of the cylinder bore, at the lower limit of ring travel. Note that the top and second compression rings are different.
4 Measure the end gap using feeler blades, and compare the measurements with the figures given in the Specifications **(see illustration)**.
5 If the gap is too small (unlikely if genuine Saab parts are used), it must be enlarged, or the ring ends may contact each other during engine operation, causing serious damage. Ideally, new piston rings providing the correct end gap should be fitted. As a last resort, the end gap can be increased by filing the ring

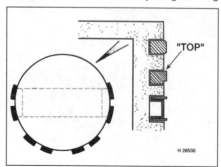

20.9a Piston ring cross-section and gap positioning – petrol engines

20.4 Measuring a piston ring end gap

ends very carefully with a fine file. Mount the file in a vice with soft jaws, slip the ring over the file with the ends contacting the file face, and slowly move the ring to remove material from the ends. Take care, as piston rings are sharp, and are easily broken.
6 With new piston rings, it is unlikely that the end gap will be too large. If the gaps are too large, check that you have the correct rings for your particular engine.
7 Repeat the checking procedure for each ring in the first cylinder, and then for the rings in the remaining cylinders. Remember to keep rings, pistons and cylinders matched up.
8 Once the ring end gaps have been checked and if necessary corrected, the rings can be fitted to the pistons.
9 Fit the piston rings using the same technique as for removal. Fit the bottom (oil control) ring first, and work up. When fitting the oil control ring, first insert the expander, then fit the lower and upper rings with the ring gaps both on the non-thrust side of the piston, with approximately 60° between them. Ensure that the second compression ring is fitted the correct way up, with the word TOP uppermost. On petrol engines, arrange the gaps of the top and second compression rings on opposite sides of the piston, above the ends of the gudgeon pin. On diesel engines, arrange the gaps at 120° intervals **(see illustrations)**. **Note:** *Always follow any instructions supplied with the new piston ring sets – different manufacturers may specify*

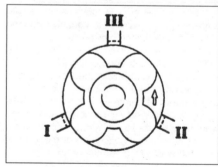

20.9b Piston ring end gap positions – diesel engines

I Top compression ring
II Second compression ring
III Oil control ring

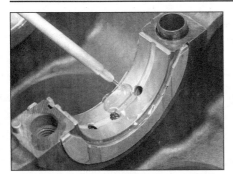

21.3 Lubricating the main bearing shells

21.10a Driving the crankshaft oil seal into the housing

21.10b Fitting the crankshaft oil seal using a block of wood in a vice

different procedures. Do not mix up the top and second compression rings, as they have different cross-sections.

21 Crankshaft – refitting

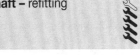

1 On petrol engines, refit the crankshaft position sensor reluctor if removed and tighten the screws. On diesel engines, locate the balancer shaft drive chain on the crankshaft gear.
2 Using a little grease, stick the upper thrustwashers to each side of the centre main bearing upper location; ensure that the oilway grooves on each thrustwasher face outwards (away from the cylinder block).
3 Place the bearing shells in their locations in the caps, ensuring that the tab on each shell engages in the notch in the cylinder block or main bearing cap location. Take care not to touch any shell's bearing surface with your fingers. If new shells are being fitted, ensure that all traces of protective grease are cleaned off, using paraffin. Wipe dry the shells and connecting rods with a lint-free cloth. Liberally lubricate each bearing shell in the cylinder block/crankcase with clean engine oil **(see illustration)**.
4 Lower the crankshaft into position so that Nos 2 and 3 cylinder crankpins are at TDC. In this position, Nos 1 and 4 cylinder crankpins will be at BDC, ready for fitting No 1 piston. Check the crankshaft endfloat as described

in Section 17. **Note:** *On diesel engines, the balancer shaft unit drive chain must be kept taut to prevent it snagging on the piston oil cooling jet located within the crankcase.*
5 Lubricate the lower bearing shells in the main bearing caps with clean engine oil. Make sure that the locating lugs on the shells engage with the corresponding recesses in the caps.
6 Fit the main bearing caps to their correct locations, ensuring that they are fitted the correct way round (the bearing shell lug recesses in the block and caps must be on the same side). Insert the bolts loosely.
7 Progressively tighten the main bearing cap bolts to the specified torque wrench setting.
8 Check that the crankshaft rotates freely.
9 Refit the piston/connecting rod assemblies to the crankshaft, as described in Section 22.
10 Before refitting the crankshaft oil seal housing to the left-hand end of the cylinder block, fit a new oil seal in the housing with reference to Chapter 2A or 2B. Use a mallet and block of wood to drive it into the housing, or alternatively, use the block of wood in a vice **(see illustrations)**.
11 Apply suitable sealant to the contact faces of the oil seal housing, then smear a little oil on the oil seal lips, and refit the locating dowels where necessary. Locate the housing on the cylinder block. To prevent damage to the oil seal as it locates over the crankshaft, make up a guide out of a plastic container, or alternatively use adhesive tape. Once the housing is in position, remove the guide or

tape, then insert the bolts and tighten them securely **(see illustrations)**.
12 On diesel engines, refit the balancer shaft unit with reference to Chapter 2B.
13 Refit the flywheel/driveplate, oil pick-up/strainer/transfer tube and sump, with reference to Chapter 2A or 2B.
14 Where removed, refit the cylinder head as described in Chapter 2A or 2B.
15 Refit the timing chain and sprocket.

22 Piston/connecting rod assembly – refitting and big-end bearing clearance check

Running clearance check

1 One method of checking the clearance is to refit the big-end bearing cap to the connecting rod before refitting the pistons to the cylinder block, ensuring that they are fitted the correct way round, with the bearing shells in place. With the cap retaining nuts correctly tightened, use an internal micrometer or vernier caliper to measure the internal diameter of each assembled pair of bearing shells. If the diameter of each corresponding crankshaft journal is measured and then subtracted from the bearing internal diameter, the result will be the big-end bearing running clearance.
2 The alternative is to take the components to your local engine reconditioning specialist, where they will be able to do a more comprehensive check.

21.11a Adhesive tape over the end of the crankshaft will prevent damage to the oil seal when refitting

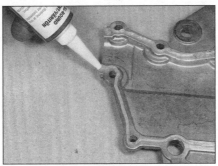

21.11b Applying sealant to the oil seal housing

21.11c Refitting the oil seal housing (engine backplate)

22.5 Piston ring compressor fitted over the piston rings

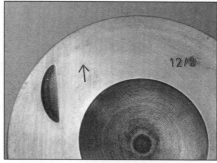

22.6a The arrow on the piston crown must point towards the timing chain end of the engine

22.6b Using a hammer handle to tap the piston down the cylinder bore

Refitting

3 Lubricate the cylinder bores, pistons, piston rings and bearing shells with clean engine oil, then lay out each piston/connecting rod assembly in its respective position on a clean dust free surface.

4 Press the bearing shells into their locations, ensuring that the tab on each shell engages in the notch in the connecting rod and cap. Take care not to touch any shell's bearing surface with your fingers. If the original bearing shells are being used for the check, ensure that they are refitted in their original locations.

5 Start with assembly No 1. Position No 1 crankpin at the bottom of its stroke. Make sure that the piston rings are still spaced as described in Section 20, then clamp them in position with a piston ring compressor **(see illustration)**.

6 Insert the piston/connecting rod assembly into the top of cylinder No 1, taking care not to mark the cylinder bores. Ensure that the

22.8 Tightening the big-end bearing cap nuts

notch or arrow on the piston crown is pointing towards the timing chain end of the engine. Using a block of wood or hammer handle against the piston crown, tap the assembly into the cylinder bore until the piston crown is flush with the top of the cylinder **(see illustrations)**.

7 With the No 1 crankpin at the bottom of its stroke, guide the connecting rod onto it while tapping the top of the piston with the hammer handle.

8 Refit the big-end bearing cap, using the marks made or noted on removal to ensure that they are fitted the correct way round. Tighten the bearing cap nuts to the specified torque **(see illustration)**.

9 Rotate the crankshaft. Check that it turns freely; some stiffness is to be expected if new components have been fitted, but there should be no signs of binding or tight spots.

10 Refit the remaining three piston/connecting rod assemblies to their crankpins in the same way.

11 Refit the oil pump pick-up/strainer, sump and cylinder head with reference to Chapter 2A or 2B.

23 Engine –
initial start-up after overhaul

1 With the engine refitted in the vehicle, double-check the engine oil and coolant levels. Make a final check that everything has been reconnected, and that there are no tools or rags left in the engine compartment.

2 On petrol engine models, disable the

ignition system by disconnecting wiring from the ignition coil or disconnecting the wiring plug from the ignition discharge module as applicable (see Chapter 5B). To prevent unburnt fuel from being supplied to the catalytic converter, the fuel pump must also be disabled by removing the relevant fuse and/or relay.

3 On diesel engine models, remove all the glow plugs (see Chapter 5C), then remove the fuel pump fuse from the fusebox (see Chapter 12).

4 Turn the engine on the starter until the oil pressure warning light goes out, then stop and reconnect the wiring/components/fuse removed in paragraphs 2 and 3.

5 On all models, start the engine as normal noting that this may take a little longer than usual, due to the fuel system components having been disturbed.

6 While the engine is idling, check for fuel, water and oil leaks. Don't be alarmed if there are some odd smells and smoke from parts getting hot and burning off oil deposits.

7 Assuming all is well, keep the engine idling until hot water is felt circulating through the top hose, then switch off the engine.

8 Allow the engine to cool then recheck the oil and coolant levels as described in *Weekly Checks*, and top-up as necessary.

9 If new pistons, rings or crankshaft bearings have been fitted, the engine must be treated as new, and run-in for the first 500 miles. *Do not* operate the engine at full-throttle, or allow it to labour at low engine speeds in any gear. It is recommended that the oil and filter be changed at the end of this period.

Chapter 3
Cooling, heating and air conditioning systems

Contents

Degrees of difficulty

Easy, suitable for novice with little experience	Fairly easy, suitable for beginner with some experience	Fairly difficult, suitable for competent DIY mechanic	Difficult, suitable for experienced DIY mechanic	Very difficult, suitable for expert DIY or professional

Specifications

General
Expansion tank cap opening pressure......................... 1.4 to 1.5 bars

Thermostat
Opening temperature:
  Petrol models .... 89°C ± 2°C
  Diesel models .... 92°C ± 2°C

Electric cooling fan
Cut-in temperature:
  Petrol models:
    Stage 1 .... 100° ± 2°C
    Stage 2 .... 113° ± 2°C
  Diesel models:
    Stage 1 .... 100° ± 2°C
    Stage 2 .... 108° ± 2°C
Cut-out temperature:
  Petrol models:
    Stage 1 .... 96° ± 1°C
    Stage 2 .... 109° ± 1°C
  Diesel models:
    Stage 1 .... 96° ± 1°C
    Stage 2 .... 104° ± 1°C

Coolant temperature sensor

	Resistance
At 0°C	5.7 kohms
At 20°C	2.4 kohms
At 30°C	1.6 kohms
At 50°C	800 ohms
At 85°C	300 ohms
At 110°C	140 ohms
At 130°C	100 ohms

Torque wrench settings

	Nm	lbf ft
Coolant temperature sensor:		
Petrol engines	13	10
Diesel engines	18	13
Electric cooling fan unit	8	6
Rigid heater pipe (petrol engines):		
To turbocharger	25	18
To water pump	20	15
To cylinder block	10	7
Thermostat housing	8	6
Water pump:		
Petrol engines (to block)	22	16
Diesel engines	20	15
Water pump pulley (diesel engines)	20	15

1 General information and precautions

General information

The cooling system is of pressurised type, comprising a water pump driven by the auxiliary drivebelt, a crossflow radiator, electric cooling fan, a thermostat, heater matrix and all associated hoses. The expansion tank is located on the left-hand side of the engine compartment. The water pump is bolted to the cylinder block. On petrol engines, the pump outlet is sealed to the block by a sleeve and O-rings, whereas on diesel engines the water pump body is inserted into the block and sealed with a single large O-ring.

The system functions as follows. Cold coolant in the bottom of the radiator passes through the bottom hose to the water pump, where it is pumped around the cylinder block and head passages. After cooling the cylinder bores, combustion surfaces and valve seats, the coolant reaches the underside of the thermostat, which is initially closed. The coolant passes through the heater, and is returned to the water pump. On petrol models, a small proportion of coolant is channelled from the cylinder head through the throttle body, and a further amount is channelled through the turbocharger.

When the engine is cold, the coolant circulates only through the cylinder block, cylinder head, throttle body, heater and turbocharger, as applicable. When the coolant reaches a predetermined temperature, the thermostat opens, and the coolant passes through the top hose to the radiator. As the coolant circulates through the radiator, it is cooled by the inrush of air when the car is in forward motion, and also by the action of the electric cooling fan when necessary. Upon reaching the bottom of the radiator, the coolant has now cooled, and the cycle is repeated.

When the engine is at normal operating temperature, the coolant expands, and some of it is displaced into the expansion tank. Coolant collects in the tank, and is returned to the radiator when the system cools.

A double-speed electric cooling fan is mounted on the rear of the radiator, and is controlled by a thermostatic switch. At a predetermined coolant temperature, the switch/sensor actuates the fan. On models with air conditioning, two double-speed fans are fitted.

Precautions

 Warning: Do not attempt to remove the expansion tank filler cap, or to disturb any part of the cooling system, while the engine is hot, as there is a high risk of scalding. If the expansion tank filler cap must be removed before the engine and radiator have fully cooled (even though this is not recommended), the pressure in the cooling system must first be relieved. Cover the cap with a thick layer of cloth, to avoid scalding, and slowly unscrew the filler cap until a hissing sound is heard. When the hissing has stopped, indicating that the pressure has reduced, slowly unscrew the filler cap until it can be removed; if more hissing sounds are heard, wait until they have stopped before unscrewing the cap completely. At all times, keep well away from the filler cap opening, and protect your hands.

Warning: Do not allow antifreeze to come into contact with your skin, or with the painted surfaces of the vehicle. Rinse off spills immediately, with plenty of water. Never leave antifreeze lying around in an open container, or in a puddle in the driveway or on the garage floor. Children and pets are attracted by its sweet smell, but antifreeze can be fatal if ingested.

Warning: If the engine is hot, the electric cooling fan may start rotating even if the engine is not running. Be careful to keep your hands, hair and any loose clothing well clear when working in the engine compartment.

Warning: Refer to Section 10 for precautions to be observed when working on models with air conditioning.

2 Cooling system hoses – disconnection and renewal

1 The number, routing and pattern of the hoses will vary according to the model, but the same basic procedure applies. Before commencing work, make sure that the new hoses are to hand, along with new hose clips if needed. It is good practice to renew the hose clips at the same time as the hoses.

2 Drain the cooling system, as described in Chapter 1A or 1B, saving the coolant if it is fit for re-use. Squirt a little penetrating oil onto the hose clips if they are corroded.

3 Loosen and release the hose clips from the hose concerned.

4 Unclip any wires, cables or other hoses which may be attached to the hose being removed. Make notes for reference when reassembling if necessary. The hoses can be removed with relative ease when new, however on an older vehicle they may be stuck to the outlet.

5 If a hose proves stubborn, try to release it by rotating it before attempting to work it off. Take care not to damage the pipe stubs or hoses. Note in particular that the radiator hose stubs are fragile; do not use excessive force when attempting to remove the hoses.

6 Before fitting the new hose, smear the stubs with washing-up liquid or a suitable rubber lubricant to aid fitting. Do not use oil or grease, which may attack the rubber.

7 Fit the hose clips over the ends of the hose, then fit the hose to the stub. Work the hose into position. When satisfied, locate and tighten the hose clips.

8 Refill the cooling system as described in Chapter 1A or 1B. Run the engine, and check that there are no leaks.

9 Top-up the coolant level if necessary (see *Weekly checks*).

3 Radiator – removal, inspection and refitting

Note: *If the reason for removing the radiator is to cure a leak, bear in mind that minor leaks can often be cured using a radiator sealant added to the coolant.*

Removal

1 Apply the handbrake, then jack up the front of the vehicle and support it on axle stands (see *Jacking and vehicle support*). Remove the engine and radiator undertrays.

2 Drain the cooling system as described in Chapter 1A or 1B. If the coolant is relatively new or in good condition, drain it into a clean container for re-use.

3 On turbo models, remove the intercooler as described in Chapter 4A or 4B.

4 Remove the radiator grille as described in Chapter 11. On 2001-on petrol models and all diesel models, remove both headlights (see Chapter 12, Section 6), then unclip the two radiator air shields.

5 Where fitted to petrol engine models, unbolt the engine oil cooler from the bottom of the radiator and suspend it to one side, leaving the hoses attached.

6 Unbolt and unclip the air conditioning condenser from the front of the radiator and suspend to one side.

7 Remove the battery as described in Chapter 5A. Also, remove the engine top cover where applicable.

8 On 2001-on petrol models and all diesel models, position the power steering fluid reservoir to one side, then remove the bracket from the battery tray and bend to one side. Also remove the horn.

9 Loosen the clips and remove the air intake hoses from the turbocharger, intercooler and the air cleaner.

10 On 2001-on petrol models, remove the exhaust manifold heat shield.

11 On diesel models, unbolt the EGR valve (see Chapter 4C) and move it to one side.

12 Loosen the clips and disconnect the top hose and purge hose from the radiator **(see illustrations)**.

13 Remove the electric cooling fan(s) and cowling as described in Section 5.

3.12a Disconnecting the top hose from the radiator

14 Unscrew the bolt and detach the power steering hydraulic hose from the top of the radiator. Also, unclip the radiator purge hose.

15 On automatic transmission models the fluid oil cooler is incorporated in the radiator. Position suitable containers beneath the radiator and transmission, then disconnect the oil cooler-to-transmission hoses or pipes (as applicable) and allow the hydraulic fluid to drain. Tape over or plug the ends of the hoses/pipes, and discard the O-rings/seals as applicable.

16 Loosen the clip and disconnect the bottom hose from the lower right-hand side of the radiator **(see illustration)**. Alternatively, if the radiator clip is not accessible, disconnect the hose from the water pump on the right-hand end of the engine.

17 Release the top mountings and lift the radiator from the lower mounting rubbers so that the wiring can be disconnected from the air conditioning compressor. Withdraw the radiator from the engine compartment, taking care not to damage the radiator cooling fins **(see illustrations)**.

Inspection

18 If the radiator has been removed due to suspected blockage, reverse-flush it as described in Chapter 1A or 1B. Clean dirt and debris from the radiator fins, using an air line or a soft brush.

19 If necessary, a radiator specialist can perform a flow test on the radiator, to establish whether an internal blockage exists. A leaking radiator must be referred to a specialist for

3.12b Disconnecting the expansion tank purge hose from the top of the radiator

permanent repair. Do not attempt to weld or solder a leaking radiator. If the radiator is to be sent for repair, or is to be renewed, remove the cooling fan thermostatic switch.

20 Inspect the condition of the upper and lower radiator mounting rubbers, and renew them if necessary.

Refitting

21 Refitting is a reversal of removal, but note the following additional points.

a) Before positioning the radiator in the car, fit the bottom hose making sure that the retaining clip will be accessible when in situ.

b) Tighten all nuts and bolts to the specified torque where given.

c) Check and if necessary top-up the fluid level in the automatic transmission with reference to Chapter 1A.

d) Finally, check the cooling system for leaks.

4 Thermostat – removal, testing and refitting

Petrol models

Removal

1 The thermostat is located on the left-hand end of the cylinder head. First, drain the cooling system as described in Chapter 1A. If the coolant is relatively new or in good condition, drain it into a clean container for re-use.

3.16 Disconnecting the bottom hose from the radiator

3.17a Remove the upper clamps . . .

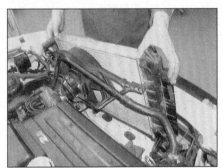

3.17b . . . then lift the radiator from the engine compartment

4.4a Disconnect the preheating coolant hose from the rigid pipe . . .

2 On turbo models, remove the engine top cover.

3 At the left-hand end of the cylinder head, loosen the clip and disconnect the top hose from the thermostat housing. Move the hose to one side. Alternatively, if preferred, leave the hose connected to the thermostat cover, however, this will make it more difficult to clean the cover later.

4 On 1998 to 2000 models, carry out the following:

a) *Remove the intercooler bypass hose and the inlet hose from the throttle body.*

b) *Unscrew the bolt and disconnect the rigid coolant pipe from the water pump, then unscrew the bolt which secures the pipe to the front left-hand corner of the engine. Remove the O-ring from the water pump.*

c) *Loosen the clip and disconnect the preheating coolant hose from the throttle body or from the rigid pipe, then unbolt*

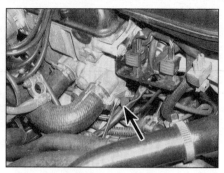

4.4b . . . then unbolt the rigid pipe from the thermostat cover

the pipe from the thermostat cover (see illustrations).

5 On 2001-on models, carry out the following:

a) *Unbolt the hose support bracket from the thermostat housing.*

6 Unscrew the bolts and remove the thermostat cover, then remove the thermostat from the cylinder head **(see illustrations)**. Recover the sealing ring.

Testing

7 A rough test of the thermostat may be made by suspending it with a piece of string in a container full of water. Heat the water to boiling point and check that the thermostat opens. If not, renew it.

8 If a thermometer is available, the precise opening temperature of the thermostat may be determined and compared with the figures given in the Specifications. The opening temperature is normally marked on the thermostat.

9 A thermostat which fails to close as the water cools must also be renewed.

Refitting

10 Clean the surfaces of the thermostat housing, cover and cylinder head. Smear a little petroleum jelly on the new sealing ring.

11 Locate the thermostat and sealing ring in the cylinder head, making sure that the vent hole is located at the top. The hole is to allow air to purge from the system.

12 Refit the thermostat housing and tighten the bolts to the specified torque.

13 The remaining refitting procedure is a reversal of removal, but refill and bleed the cooling system with reference to Chapter 1A.

Diesel models

Removal

14 The thermostat is located on the front right-hand end of the cylinder head, and is integral with the housing. First, drain the cooling system as described in Chapter 1B. If the coolant is relatively new or in good condition, drain it into a clean container for re-use.

15 Remove the engine compartment undertray, and also remove the top cover from the engine.

16 Disconnect the wiring from the coolant temperature sensor on the thermostat housing.

17 Loosen the clips and disconnect the hoses from the thermostat housing **(see illustrations)**.

18 Unbolt the thermostat housing from the cylinder head **(see illustrations)**. Clean away all traces of gasket from the housing and cylinder head.

4.6a Remove the thermostat cover . . .

4.6b . . . and remove the thermostat from the cylinder head

4.17a Release the clip . . .

4.17b . . . and disconnect the top hose from the thermostat housing cover

4.18a Unscrew the mounting bolts . . .

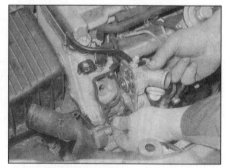

4.18b . . . then remove the thermostat and cover together with the gasket.

5.10a Unscrew the mounting bolt . . .

5.10b . . . and slide the cooling fan assembly from the location slots

19 To remove the oil cooler thermostat located on the left-hand end of the cylinder block, first disconnect the hose then unscrew the bolts and remove the housing which includes the integral thermostat. Recover the gasket.

Testing
20 Refer to paragraphs 7 to 9.

Refitting
21 Refitting is a reversal of removal, but fit a new gasket and tighten the mounting bolts to the specified torque. Refill and bleed the cooling system with reference to Chapter 1B.

---

5 Electric cooling fan – testing, removal and refitting

Testing
1 Current supply to the cooling fan is controlled by the Dashboard Integrated Central Electronics Control Module. The module is supplied with information of the coolant temperature sensor, air conditioning pressure, vehicle speed and outside temperature. Models with air conditioning are fitted with two cooling fans controlled by the DICE Control Module.
2 If the fan does not appear to work, first check that the wiring plug located near the cooling fan is intact. Note that Saab technicians use an electronic tester to check

5.11 Cooling fan motor mounting nuts

the DICE Control Module for fault codes, and if necessary a Saab dealer should carry out a diagnostic check to locate the fault.
3 If the wiring is in good condition, use a voltmeter to check that 12 volts is reaching the motor when the engine temperature dictates. The motor itself can be checked by disconnecting it from the wiring loom, and connecting a 12 volt supply directly to it.

Removal
4 Remove the engine top cover as applicable, then remove the battery as described in Chapter 5A.
5 Remove the power steering fluid reservoir and position it to one side.
6 On diesel models, carry out the following:
  a) *Unbolt and remove the battery tray.*
  b) *Loosen the clips and remove the air intake hoses from the turbocharger, intercooler and the air cleaner.*
  c) *Unbolt the EGR valve (see Chapter 4C) and move it to one side.*
7 Disconnect the wiring for the cooling fan(s).
8 On 2001-on petrol models, carry out the following:
  a) *Remove the bracket from the battery tray and bend it to one side.*
  b) *Remove the exhaust manifold heat shield.*
9 Unscrew the bolt and detach the power steering hydraulic hose from the top of the radiator. Also, unclip the radiator purge hose.
10 Unscrew the mounting bolts and lift the cowling complete with cooling fan from the radiator **(see illustrations)**.

6.2 Disconnecting the wiring from the engine coolant temperature sensor

11 With the assembly on the bench, unscrew the nuts and remove the resistor, then disconnect the wiring and remove the cooling fan from the cowling **(see illustration)**.

Refitting
12 Refitting is a reversal of removal but tighten the mounting bolts securely.

---

6 Coolant temperature sensor – testing, removal and refitting

Testing
1 On petrol engines, the coolant temperature sensor is threaded into the inlet manifold on the front of the engine. On diesel engines, the coolant temperature sensor is located on the thermostat housing on the right-hand end of the cylinder head. The resistance of the sensor varies according to the temperature of the coolant.
2 To test the sensor, disconnect the wiring at the plug then connect an ohmmeter to the sensor **(see illustration)**.
3 Determine the temperature of the coolant, then compare the resistance with the information given in the Specifications. If the reading is incorrect, the sender must be renewed.

Removal and refitting
4 Refer to Chapter 4A or 4B, as applicable.

---

7 Water pump – removal and refitting

Removal
1 Apply the handbrake, then jack up the front of the vehicle and support it on axle stands (see *Jacking and vehicle support*). Remove the engine top cover, engine compartment undertray(s), and the right-hand front roadwheel.
2 Drain the cooling system as described in Chapter 1A or 1B. If the coolant is relatively

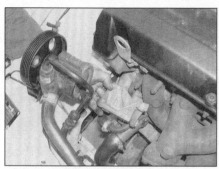

7.14 Removing the power steering pump mounting bracket from the cylinder head

7.15 Disconnecting the bottom hose from the water pump

7.16 Remove the bolt securing the rigid coolant pipe to the front left-hand side of the cylinder head

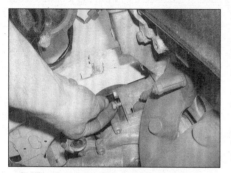

7.17a Unscrew the mounting bolts . . .

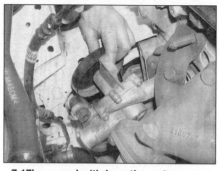

7.17b . . . and withdraw the water pump from the front of the cylinder block

7.17c Water pump removed from the engine

new or in good condition, drain it into a clean container and re-use it.

3 Remove the air cleaner complete with mass airflow meter as described in Chapter 4A or 4B.

Petrol models

4 Where necessary, remove the air inlet duct between the intercooler and throttle body/ turbocharger. Also, unscrew the bolt and detach the coolant pipe from the turbocharger.

5 Remove the auxiliary drivebelt as described in Chapter 1A.

6 Disconnect the crankcase ventilation hose and release it from the turbocharger inlet pipe and camshaft cover.

7 Disconnect the wiring from the turbocharger boost pressure control valve. Where necessary, unbolt the valve and position it to one side.

8 Unbolt the engine lifting eye from the cylinder head.

9 Disconnect the hoses from the turbocharger wastegate valve.

10 Disconnect the turbocharger by-pass pipe and valve, noting that there is an O-ring at the connection to the turbo inlet pipe.

11 Unscrew the nut and unclip the heat shield from the exhaust manifold.

12 Disconnect the crankcase ventilation hose at the quick-release coupling.

13 Remove the turbocharger inlet pipe, and cover the inlet aperture with tape or a plastic bag to prevent entry of dust and dirt.

14 Refer to Chapter 10 and remove the power steering pump and bracket and suspend to one side, however, do not disconnect the fluid hoses **(see illustration)**.

15 Loosen the clips and disconnect the bottom hose and heater hoses from the water pump **(see illustration)**.

16 Unscrew the two bolts from the left-

hand end of the cylinder block, and remove the rigid heater return pipe from the water pump. Recover the O-ring from the water pump. Also, unscrew the bolt from the left-hand side of the cylinder head and remove the rigid heater supply pipe support **(see illustration)**.

17 Unscrew the three water pump mounting bolts and carefully ease the pump from the bracket and connecting adapter on the cylinder block **(see illustrations)**.

18 Remove the adapter from the cylinder block, and examine the O-ring seals for deterioration. It is recommended that new seals are fitted. Note that on later models, the adapter has two location tabs of different widths which locate in the water pump; the adapter can only be fitted one way round; this ensures the correct direction of the internal channel **(see illustrations)**.

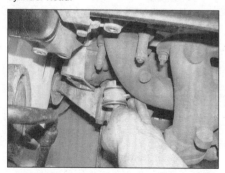

7.18a Removing the adapter sleeve and O-rings from the cylinder block

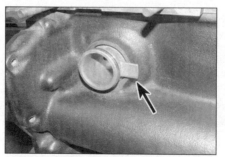

7.18b 'Wide' location tab on the adaptor which locates in the 'wide' cut-out on the water pump

7.18c The adaptor locates in cut-outs in the water pump body

7.18d Removing the O-ring seals from the adapter

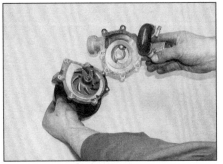

7.19 Separating the two halves of the water pump

7.26 Unscrew the mounting bolts . . .

19 The water pump may be obtained as a complete unit, or alternatively just the impeller/pulley section may be obtained. To separate the two sections, first mark them in relation to each other. Unscrew the bolts and separate the two halves **(see illustration)**.

Diesel models

20 Release the fuel hoses from the supports, then unscrew the nut and position the support bracket and wiring to one side.
21 Remove the auxiliary drivebelt as described in Chapter 1B.
22 Using a trolley jack and block of wood, support the right-hand end of the engine beneath the sump. Alternatively, connect a hoist to the right-hand side of the engine. Raise the engine to take its weight. Make sure the engine is adequately supported.
23 Unbolt the remove the right-hand engine mounting and bracket (refer to Chapter 2B if necessary).
24 Unscrew the nut from the rear engine mounting, then slightly raise the engine for access to the water pump.
25 Hold the water pump pulley stationary using an old auxiliary drivebelt or an oil filter strap wrench, then unscrew and remove the bolts and remove the pulley from the drive flange on the water pump.
26 Unscrew and remove the three water pump securing bolts **(see illustration)**.
27 Withdraw the water pump from the cylinder block, noting that it may be necessary to tap the pump lightly with a soft-faced

mallet to free it from the cylinder block **(see illustration)**.
28 Recover the pump sealing ring, and discard it; a new one must be used on refitting **(see illustration)**.
29 Note that it is not possible to overhaul the pump. If it is faulty, the unit must be renewed complete.

Refitting

30 Refitting is a reversal of removal, but note the following additional points:
  a) Clean the pump and block contact faces.
  b) Fit new O-rings, and apply a little petroleum jelly to them to aid seating.
  c) On petrol engines, fit the pump loosely at first, then tighten the turbocharger coolant pipe, followed by the pump mounting bolts and transverse coolant pipes.
  d) Tighten all nuts/bolts to the specified torque where given.
  e) Refill and bleed the cooling system with reference to Chapter 1A or 1B.

8 Heating and ventilation system – general information

1 Three types of heating/ventilation system are fitted – the Standard Manual Climate Control (MCC) system, the Standard Air Conditioning (A/C) system, and the Automatic Climate Control (ACC) system

which maintains the temperature inside the car at a selected temperature, regardless of the temperature outside the car. The basic heating/ventilation unit is common to all versions, and consists of air ducting from the centrally-located heater assembly to a central vent and two side vents, with an extension leading from the bottom of the heater through the centre console to the rear passenger footwell areas. A four-speed heater blower motor is fitted.
2 The heating and ventilation controls are mounted in the centre of the facia. Cable-controlled flap valves are contained in the air distribution housing, to divert the air to the various ducts and vents.
3 Cold air enters the system through the grille at the bottom of the windscreen. If required, the airflow is boosted by the blower, and then flows through the various ducts, according to the settings of the controls. Stale air is expelled through ducts at the rear of the vehicle. If warm air is required, the cold air is passed over the heater matrix, which is heated by the engine coolant.
4 On models fitted with air conditioning, a recirculation switch enables the outside air supply to be closed off, while the air inside the vehicle is recirculated. This can be useful to prevent unpleasant odours entering from outside the vehicle, but should only be used briefly, as the recirculated air inside the vehicle will soon become stale.
5 A solar sensor located on top of the facia panel detects increased solar radiation, and increases the speed of the blower motor. This is necessary in order to increase the throughput of air in the vehicle.

9 Heating and ventilation system components – removal and refitting

Heater blower motor

Removal

1 Remove the wiper motor and linkage as described in Chapter 12.
2 Unclip the pollen filter from over the heater motor.

7.27 . . . withdraw the water pump from the cylinder block . . .

7.28 . . . and recover the sealing ring

9.3 Disconnecting the heater motor wiring

9.4a Unscrew the bolts . . .

9.4b . . . and remove the pollen filter frame

3 Disconnect the wiring from the heater motor (see illustration).
4 Unscrew the bolts and remove the pollen filter frame (see illustrations).
5 Unclip and remove the cover (see illustrations).
6 Undo the screw securing the wiring socket to the bulkhead (see illustration).
7 Undo the remaining screws and lift the heater motor from the bulkhead. On right-hand drive models, there may be insufficient clearance between the windscreen and engine compartment rear panel, in which case the panel must be temporarily pulled back using a ratchet strap between the panel and front crossmember.

Refitting

8 Refitting is a reversal of removal but make sure that the wiring is clear of the fan before refitting the cover.

Heater matrix

Removal

9 Fit hose clamps to the heater hoses at the bulkhead. Identify the hoses for position, then loosen the clips and disconnect them from the heater matrix. Plug the stubs to prevent coolant spilling onto the floor when the matrix is removed from inside the car. To remove most of the coolant from the matrix, blow through one of the pipes and the coolant will escape from the other.
10 Where fitted, remove the automatic climate control (ACC) module as described later in this Section.
11 Remove the glovebox and centre console as described in Chapter 11.
12 Release the cable ties and remove the air ducts from the rear of the heater housing (see illustration).
13 Unclip the rear cover from the heater housing (see illustration).

14 Using a screwdriver, release the clips securing the two hoses to the heater matrix (see illustration).
15 Place cloth rags beneath the matrix, then release the clips on each side of the heater housing and pull the hoses down from the matrix. Expect some loss of coolant.
16 Carefully slide the heater matrix from the housing.

Refitting

17 Refitting is a reversal of removal, but top-up the cooling system with reference to Weekly checks.

Heater unit

Removal

18 On models with air conditioning, the refrigerant must be evacuated by a qualified engineer.

9.5a Release the clips . . .

9.5b . . . and remove the cover from over the heater blower motor

9.6 Heater blower motor wiring socket

9.12 Removing the air ducts from the rear of the heater housing

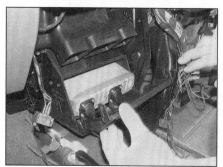

9.13 Unclip the rear cover from the heater housing

9.14 Releasing the heater hose clips from the matrix

Warning: Do not attempt to carry out this work yourself, as it is potentially dangerous.

19 Remove the facia panel (see Chapter 11).
20 On models with air conditioning, unscrew the bolt and disconnect the refrigerant hoses at the bulkhead.
21 Fit hose clamps to the heater hoses at the bulkhead. Identify the hoses for position, then loosen the clips and disconnect them from the heater matrix. Plug the stubs to prevent coolant spilling onto the floor when the matrix is removed from inside the car. To remove most of the coolant from the matrix, blow through one of the pipes and the coolant will escape from the other.
22 Remove the A/C drain hose from the bulkhead.
23 On the driver's side, remove the knee guard.
24 Working inside the car, remove the lower trim panel from the facia with reference to Chapter 11.
25 Release the cable ties, then disconnect and remove the air ducts from the rear of the heater housing.
26 Disconnect the air ducts from the sides of the heater housing.
27 Remove the windscreen wiper motor and linkage with reference to Chapter 12.
28 Inside the car, unscrew the dashboard crossmember mounting nuts and bolts.
29 Unbolt the support bracket from the heater housing.
30 Where a passenger airbag is fitted, remove the knee guard from the bulkhead.
31 Remove the steering column as described in Chapter 10.
32 Unscrew the nuts and fold out the support brackets from the top of the pedal assembly.
33 Unscrew the bolts securing the fusebox to the dashboard crossmember.
34 Note how the wiring cables are located, then remove the dashboard crossmember.
35 Disconnect the wiring from the heater housing.
36 In the engine compartment, remove the heater blower motor as described in paragraphs 1 to 7.
37 Unscrew the bolts and remove the motor mounting frame from the top of the bulkhead.

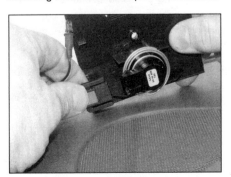

9.53 Disconnect the LED and sensor wiring

9.47 Control cable on the side of the heater housing

38 Inside the engine compartment, unscrew the bolts securing the heater housing to the lower floor.
39 Place polythene sheeting or cloth rags in the passenger compartment, then withdraw the heater housing.

Refitting

40 Refitting is a reversal of removal, but refill the cooling system as described in Chapter 1A or 1B. Have the air conditioning system recharged by a qualified engineer.

MCC module

Removal

41 Remove the glovebox as described in Chapter 11.
42 Unscrew the bolt and remove the centre console side panel for access to the rear of the heater control panel.
43 Carefully press out the panel from the rear, and disconnect the control shaft.
44 Disconnect the wiring. Note the location of the plugs to ensure correct refitting.
45 Release the clip and disconnect the control cable.
46 Withdraw the heater control panel.
47 If necessary, the switch panel can be removed by pulling off the knobs and removing the screws. Also if necessary disconnect the control cables from the heater housing **(see illustration)**.

Refitting

48 Refitting is a reversal of removal.

9.54 Depress and twist the solar sensor to remove it from the cover

9.52 Slide the solar sensor cover forwards and lift from the facia

ACC module

Removal

49 Using a screwdriver, carefully prise out the two switches each side of the ACC module, and disconnect the wiring.
50 Press out the ACC module from behind and disconnect the wiring.

Refitting

51 Refitting is a reversal of removal, but on completion calibrate the ACC system by pressing the AUTO and OFF buttons simultaneously.

Solar sensor

Removal

52 At the centre top of the facia panel, slide the solar sensor cover forwards to release it from the facia **(see illustration)**.
53 Disconnect the wiring and remove the anti-theft LED **(see illustration)**.
54 With the cover on the bench, depress and twist the solar sensor anti-clockwise to remove it from the cover **(see illustration)**.

Refitting

55 Refitting is a reversal of removal, but on completion calibrate the ACC system by pressing the AUTO and OFF buttons simultaneously.

Interior temperature sensor

Removal

56 Remove the control module as described earlier.
57 Depress the covers each side of the temperature sensor, then pull the cover from the sensor.
58 Using a screwdriver, release the catches and press the sensor inwards.
59 Withdraw the sensor and disconnect the wiring.

Refitting

60 Refitting is a reversal of removal, but on completion calibrate the ACC system by pressing the AUTO and OFF buttons simultaneously.

Mixed air sensor

Removal

61 Remove the glovebox as described in Chapter 11.

62 Undo the screw and remove the panel from the side of the centre console.
63 Remove the air duct for the floor ventilation, then unhook the mixed air sensor and disconnect the wiring. Press out the sensor leads from the connector.

Refitting

64 Refitting is a reversal of removal, but on completion calibrate the ACC system by pressing the AUTO and OFF buttons simultaneously.

Air distribution stepping motor

Removal

65 Remove the ACC control module as described earlier.
66 Undo the screws and remove the stepping motor.
67 Disconnect the wiring.

Refitting

68 Refitting is a reversal of removal, but on completion calibrate the ACC system by pressing the AUTO and OFF buttons simultaneously.

Air blending stepping motor

Removal

69 Remove the glovebox, then undo the screws and remove the panel from the side of the centre console.
70 Remove the air duct from the floor.
71 Disconnect the wiring.
72 Undo the screws and withdraw the air blending stepping motor.

Refitting

73 Refitting is a reversal of removal, but on completion calibrate the ACC system by pressing the AUTO and OFF buttons simultaneously.

Many car accessory shops sell one-shot air conditioning recharge aerosols. These generally contain refrigerant, compressor oil, leak sealer and system conditioner. Some also have a dye to help pinpoint leaks.

Warning: These products must only be used as directed by the manufacturer, and do not remove the need for regular maintenance.

Fan control unit

Removal

74 Remove the glovebox as described in Chapter 11.
75 Undo the screw and remove the panel from the side of the centre console.
76 Undo the screws and remove the fan control unit, then disconnect the wiring.

Refitting

77 Before refitting the control unit, smear some silicone paste on the surface which contacts the evaporator. **Do not** fit the spacer supplied with a new control unit. Tighten the screws.
78 Reconnect the wiring and start the ventilation fan. Check that no condensate leaks from the control unit.
79 Refit the panel to the side of the centre console, then refit the glovebox.
80 On completion, calibrate the ACC system by pressing the AUTO and OFF buttons simultaneously.

10 Air conditioning system – general information and precautions

General information

1 Air conditioning is available as an option on all models. It enables the temperature of air inside the car to be lowered, and also dehumidifies the air, which makes for rapid demisting and increased comfort.
2 The cooling side of the system works in the same way as a domestic refrigerator. Refrigerant gas is drawn into a belt-driven compressor, and passes into a condenser mounted in front of the radiator, where it loses heat and becomes liquid. The liquid passes through a receiver and expansion valve to an evaporator, where it changes from liquid under high pressure to gas under low pressure. This change is accompanied by a drop in temperature, which cools the evaporator. The refrigerant returns to the compressor, and the cycle begins again.
3 Air drawn through the evaporator passes to the air distribution unit. The air conditioning system is switched on with the switch located on the heater panel.
4 The heating side of the system works in the same way as on models without air conditioning.
5 The compressor operation is controlled by an electromagnetic clutch on the drive pulley. Any problems with the system should be referred to a Saab dealer **(see Tool tip)**.

Precautions

6 When working on the air conditioning system, it is necessary to observe special precautions. If for any reason the system must be disconnected, entrust this task to your Saab dealer or a refrigeration engineer.

 Warning: The refrigeration circuit contains a liquid refrigerant under pressure, and it is therefore dangerous to disconnect any part of the system without specialised knowledge and equipment. The refrigerant is potentially dangerous, and should only be handled by qualified persons. If it is splashed onto the skin, it can cause frostbite. It is not itself poisonous, but in the presence of a naked flame (including a cigarette) it forms a poisonous gas. Uncontrolled discharging of the refrigerant is dangerous, and potentially damaging to the environment. Do not operate the air conditioning system if it is known to be short of refrigerant, as this may damage the compressor.

11 Air conditioning system components – removal and refitting

 Warning: Do not attempt to open the refrigerant circuit. Refer to the precautions given in Section 10.

1 The only operation which can be carried out easily without discharging the refrigerant is renewal of the compressor drivebelt. This is described in Chapter 1A and 1B. All other operations must be referred to a Saab dealer or an air conditioning specialist.
2 If necessary for access to other components, the compressor can be unbolted and moved aside, **without** disconnecting its flexible hoses, after removing the drivebelt.
3 Access to the condenser is gained by removing the grille and both headlight units.

12 Auxiliary heating system – general description

1 On some models, an optional auxiliary heating system may be fitted which uses fuel from the fuel tank. The heater unit is mounted on the bulkhead at the rear of the engine compartment **(see illustration)**, and heats coolant from the engine, both to heat the interior of the vehicle and to increase the temperature of the engine for improved starting. The unit is functional without the

12.1 Auxiliary heater unit mounted on the bulkhead

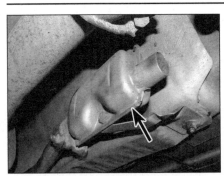

12.2 Auxiliary heater exhaust pipe located beneath the vehicle floor

engine being started, although it may be activated when the engine is running to allow the engine to quickly reach normal operating temperature. For diesel versions the maximum running time for the heater is 60 minutes,

and for petrol versions it is 30 minutes. The auxiliary heater is more commonly fitted to diesel engine models, as compared to petrol engines the diesel engine produces less heat and takes longer to achieve normal operating temperature, particularly in extremely cold conditions.

2 The auxiliary heater uses fuel from the fuel tank to provide a flame inside the heater unit which heats the coolant from the engine. A glow plug is used to ignite the fuel. Air for the heater is drawn through an inlet pipe beneath the unit, and the exhaust gases are taken through an exhaust pipe beneath the vehicle floor **(see illustration)**.

3 The main components of the system are as follows:

a) *Control module.*
b) *Blower fan.*
c) *Glow plug.*
d) *Flame detector.*
e) *Temperature sensor.*
f) *Overheating protection circuit.*
g) *Relay.*
h) *Fuel pump, located in front of the fuel tank beneath the rear of the vehicle.*
i) *Diagnostic socket.*

4 The system is controlled by a module which monitors outside temperature and engine coolant temperature. The heater will only start if the coolant temperature is below a nominal 80°C, and there is a minimum of 10 litres in the fuel tank. The heater operates at two levels: 1500 W and 3000 W, which are automatically selected by the module; the two outputs are achieved by different blower speeds.

5 A diagnostic socket is provided in the engine compartment fusebox, to enable Saab technicians to pinpoint any faults with the auxiliary heating system. If it is not operating correctly, the vehicle should be taken to a Saab dealer who will have the necessary

Chapter 4 Part A:
Fuel and exhaust systems – petrol engine models

Contents

Degrees of difficulty

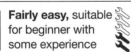

| **Easy,** suitable for novice with little experience | **Fairly easy,** suitable for beginner with some experience | **Fairly difficult,** suitable for competent DIY mechanic | **Difficult,** suitable for experienced DIY mechanic | **Very difficult,** suitable for expert DIY or professional |

Specifications

System type

Non-turbo models (204i and 234i) .... Bosch Motronic 2.10.3 engine management system
Turbo models .... Saab Trionic engine management system
Application:
  1998 models:
    B204i and B234i..................................... Motronic 2.10.3
    Except B204i and B234i.............................. Trionic T5 or T5 OBDII
  1999 models:
    B204i and B234i..................................... Motronic 2.10.3
    Except B204i and B234i.............................. Trionic T5, T5 OBDII or T7
  2000 models:
    B204i.. Motronic 2.10.3
    B204E with 1 oxygen sensor .... Trionic T5
    B204E with 2 oxygen sensors .... Trionic T5 OBD II (USA and Canada)
    B205E/L/R and B235R................................ Trionic T7 LEV
  2001 models.. Trionic T7
  2002 models.. Trionic T7

Bosch 2.10.3 engine management system

Air mass flow meter
Operating temperature	165°C
Output:	
No flow	0.2 V
4 grams/sec	1.0 V
33 grams/sec	2.6 V
133 grams/sec	4.6 V

Electronic Control Unit (ECM)
Power consumption	<2.5 mA

Throttle Position Sensor
Resistance:	
At idle	2.4 to 3.4 V
At full throttle	0.7 to 1.0 V

Idle Air Control Valve (IAC)
No of coils	2
Coil winding resistance	9 to 15 ohms
Operating frequency	100Hz

Coolant temperature sensor
Resistance:	
20°C	2.3 to 2.7 ohms
60°C	565 to 670 ohms
90°C	200 to 240 ohms

Fuel injectors
Type	EV1-3E colour code Blue, 4-hole
Resistance	14.5 ± 0.35 ohms
Flow rating (at 3 bar fuel pressure)	126 ml per 30 secs

Crankshaft position sensor
Resistance	540 ± 55 ohms
Sensor to reluctor disc clearance	0.4 to 1.3 mm

Oxygen sensor
Preheater rating	12 W
Sensor resistance	3.5 ohms
Output signal range	0 to 1.0 V

Fuel pressure regulator
Opening fuel pressure	3.0 bar

Fuel pump/gauge sender unit
Fuel pump capacity	700ml per 30 secs at 3.0 bar
Fuel gauge sender resistance:	
Full tank	390 ohms
Empty tank	60 ohms

Recommended fuel
All models	95 RON unleaded

Idle speed
All models	900 rpm, controlled by ECM (not adjustable)

Exhaust gas CO content
All models	Controlled by ECM (not adjustable)

Saab Trionic engine management system

Manifold absolute pressure (MAP) sensor
Supply voltage	5 volts
Pressure:	**Voltage (approximately)**
-0.75 bar	0.9
-0.50 bar	1.3
0 bar	2.1
0.25 bar	2.5
0.50 bar	2.9
0.75 bar	3.3

Intake air temperature (IAC) sensor

Supply voltage	5 volts
Temperature (°C):	**Voltage (approximately)**
-30	4.5
-10	3.9
20	2.4
40	1.5
60	0.9
80	0.54
90	0.41

Throttle position switch (T5 system)

	Resistance (Ω)	Voltage (V)
Pins 1 and 2	1.6 to 2.4	5 ± 0.1
Pins 2 and 3 – idling	0.8 to 1.2	0.5 ± 0.4
Pins 2 and 3 – wide open	2.0 to 3.0	4.5 ± 0.4

Crankshaft position sensor

Resistance (pins 1 and 2) at 20°C:
- T5 system .... 540 ± 55 ohms
- T7 system .... 860 ± 90 ohms

Fuel pressure regulator

Fuel pressure at manifold pressure of:
- 0 bar .... 3.0 bar
- -0.2 bar .... 2.8 bar
- -0.4 bar .... 2.6 bar
- -0.6 bar .... 2.4 bar
- +0.2 bar .... 3.2 bar
- +0.4 bar .... 3.4 bar
- +0.6 bar .... 3.6 bar

Fuel Injectors

1998 models:
- T5 system .... EV1-3E colour code Red, 4-hole

1999 models:
- T5 system .... EV1-3E colour code Red, 4-hole
- T7 system .... EV6E colour code Red, 4-hole, air-flushed

2000-on models:
- T5 system:
- T7 system:
  - B205L engine .... EV6E colour code Grey, 4-hole
  - B205R and B235R engines .... EV6E colour code Brown, 4-hole

Resistance at 20°C:
- T5 system .... 12.0 ± 0.35 ohms
- T7 system .... 15.95 ± 0.8 ohms

Flow rating (at 3 bar fuel pressure):
- T5 system .... 126 ± 5 ml/30 seconds
- T7 system .... 176 ± 7 ml/30 seconds

Maximum flow difference between injectors:
- T5 system:
  - B204E .... 18 ml
- T7 system:
  - B205L .... 12 ml
  - B235 (up to 2000) .... 14 ml
  - B205E/L/R and B235R (2001-on) .... 20 ml

Idle air control valve

Resistance at 20°C:
- T5 system .... 7.7 ± 1 ohms

Fuel pump/gauge sender unit

Type	Electric immersed in fuel tank
Capacity	700 ml per 30 seconds at 3.0 bar

Resistance:
- Fuel level sensor in full position .... 390 ± 6.0 ohms
- Fuel level sensor in empty position .... 60 ± 2.6 ohms

Turbocharger

Type:
B204L/E/R	Garrett GT17
Pressure	0.40 ± 0.03 bar
B205L/E	Garrett GT17
Pressure	0.40 ± 0.03 bar
B205R (up to 2000)..	Garrett GT17
Pressure	0.40 ± 0.03 bar
B235R and B205R (2001-on)	Mitsubishi TD04HL-15T-5
Pressure	0.45 ± 0.03 bars
Wastegate preload (all types)...............................	2.0 mm
Turbo shaft play (axial)	0.0254 to 0.0840 mm

Fuel system

System pressure...	3.0 bars
Residual pressure (after 20 mins)...........................	2.0 bars (min)

Recommended fuel

B204L/E/R and B205L/E	95 RON unleaded
B205R and B235R	98 RON unleaded

Idle speed

Trionic T5	900 ± 50 rpm – controlled by ECM (not adjustable)
Trionic T7	N/A – controlled by ECM (not adjustable)

Exhaust gas CO content

All models..	Controlled by ECM (not adjustable)

Torque wrench settings

	Nm	lbf ft
Coolant temperature sensor................................	13	10
Crankshaft position sensor (Motronic)	8	6
Exhaust manifold to cylinder head:		
Non-turbo models	18	13
Turbo models	24	18
Exhaust manifold-to-turbocharger nuts	25	18
Exhaust pipe to exhaust manifold (non-turbo models)	40	30
Exhaust pipe to turbocharger...............................	25	19
Exhaust system joint clamp	30	22
Inlet manifold	24	18
Oxygen sensor	55	41
Throttle body to inlet manifold	8	6
Turbocharger to exhaust manifold	24	18

---

1 General information and precautions

The fuel supply system consists of a fuel tank mounted under the rear of the car (with an electric fuel pump immersed in it), a fuel filter, and the fuel feed and return lines. The fuel pump supplies fuel to the fuel rail, which acts as a reservoir for the four fuel injectors which inject fuel into the intake tracts. A fuel filter is incorporated in the feed line from the pump to the fuel rail to ensure that the fuel supplied to the injectors is clean. The filter is mounted adjacent to the fuel tank.

The engine management system is of Bosch Motronic (normally-aspirated models) or Saab Trionic type (turbo models). Refer to the relevant Sections for further information on the operation of the system.

A cruise control system is fitted as standard equipment on most of the later Saab models, and is available as an option on earlier models.

The turbocharger fitted is of a water-cooled type. Boost pressure is controlled by the Saab Trionic engine management.

Precautions

⚠ *Warning:Many of the procedures in this Chapter require the disconnection of fuel lines, which may result in some fuel spillage. Before carrying out any operation on the fuel system, refer to Section 8. See the precautions given in 'Safety first!' at the front of this manual and follow them implicitly. Petrol is a highly-dangerous and volatile liquid, and the precautions necessary when handling it cannot be overstressed.*

2 Air cleaner assembly – removal and refitting

Removal

1 Release the clip and disconnect the air mass flow meter air duct from the ducting leading to the inlet manifold (non-turbo engines) or turbocharger (turbo engines).
2 Ensure that the ignition is switched off, then unplug the wiring from the air mass flow meter, and release the wiring from the retaining straps as necessary.
3 Release the spring clips and, on turbo models, unscrew the 4 screws holding the air cleaner cover to the base.
4 Remove the cover and lift out the air filter element, noting which way up it is fitted. Take care not to damage the air mass flow meter internal components.

3.1a Release the clips . . .

3.1b . . . and lift the resonator assembly (non-turbo model shown) from the top of the throttle body

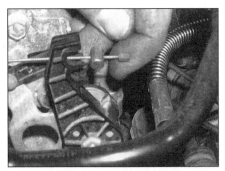

3.2a Unhook the accelerator cable from the throttle disc arm . . .

5 Unscrew the mounting nuts and remove the air cleaner base from the engine compartment. If required, the intake duct can be removed by depressing the locking button and withdrawing the duct from the front of the housing.

⚠ *Warning: Do not run the engine with the air cleaner housing and/ or ducting removed, particularly on turbo models – the depression at the turbocharger intake may increase very suddenly if the engine speed is raised above idle.*

6 Clean away any debris from inside the air cleaner base and cover.

Refitting

7 Refitting is a reversal of removal.

3 Accelerator cable – removal, refitting and adjustment

Removal

1 Working in the engine compartment, undo the screws/release the clips and lift off the cover panel (turbo models – Trionic system) or resonator assembly (normally-aspirated models – Motronic system) from the top of the throttle body **(see illustrations)**.
2 Open the throttle by hand slightly, unhook the accelerator cable from the throttle disc arm and then release the throttle. On the Motronic system, extract the spring clip and withdraw the accelerator cable outer from its mounting bracket **(see illustrations)**. On the Trionic system, pull out the locking/adjustment clip (noting its position in the grooves on the sleeve), and disconnect the accelerator outer cable from the bracket on the throttle body **(see illustration)**.
3 Release the accelerator cable from any securing clips in the engine compartment.
4 Working in the driver's footwell, disconnect the accelerator cable from the top of the accelerator pedal with reference to Section 4 **(see illustration)**.
5 Pull the accelerator cable through the bulkhead into the engine compartment and remove it from the vehicle.

Refitting

6 Pass the accelerator cable through the bulkhead aperture and into the space behind the facia, above the driver's footwell.
7 Lay the cable in position through the engine compartment securing it with the retaining clips, where applicable. Ensure that the cable is not kinked or twisted at any point.
8 Insert the end of the cable outer into its mounting bracket at the throttle body and secure it in position with the metal spring clip.
9 Open the throttle by hand slightly, then hook the end of the cable inner into the recess in the throttle disc arm. Release the throttle and allow it to return to its idle stop.

Adjustment

10 Have an assistant depress the accelerator pedal to the wide-open throttle position. On models with manual transmission, the pedal should be touching its stop. On models with automatic transmission, the pedal should be just touching, but **not** operating, the kickdown switch (see Chapter 7B, Section 8) **Note:** *On automatic transmission models, the accelerator cable incorporates a spring to provide 'kickdown feeling'.* Hold the pedal stationary in this position.

Motronic system

11 Working in the engine compartment, turn the knurled knob at the end of the accelerator cable outer until the throttle disc arm reaches its full-throttle stop.
12 Release the accelerator pedal and allow it to return to its rest position.
13 Working in the driver's footwell, turn the pedal adjustment screw, located on the accelerator pedal arm, just above the pivot shaft, so that any slack in the cable inner is eliminated.
14 At the throttle body, verify that the throttle arm still rests against its idle stop.

Trionic system

15 Check that the locking clip is located in the groove noted on removal. If necessary, locate it in the groove which allows minimal freeplay of the inner cable.

3.2b . . . then extract the spring clip and withdraw the accelerator cable outer from its mounting bracket (Motronic)

3.2c Pull out the locking/adjustment clip (Trionic)

3.4 Disconnect the accelerator cable from the top of the accelerator pedal

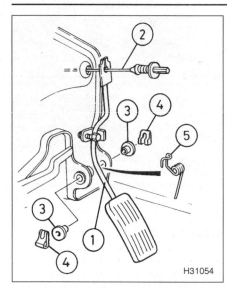

4.6 Accelerator pedal assembly

1	Pedal	3	Bush
2	Accelerator cable	4	Locking clip
		5	Return spring

Both systems

16 Refit the cover panel/resonator assembly over the inlet manifold and throttle body.
17 Refit the lower cover panel to the underside of the facia.

4 Accelerator pedal –
removal and refitting

Removal

1 Disconnect the accelerator cable from the throttle body, with reference to Section 3.
2 Working in the driver's footwell, release the fasteners and detach the lower cover panel from the underside of the facia. On certain models, it may be necessary to first undo the screws and release the diagnostic connector from the underside of the facia.
3 Reach up behind the facia and unhook the accelerator cable from the top of the accelerator pedal.
4 Compress the pedal return spring and release it from the pedal arm.

5.5 The cruise control system ECM/control unit is located behind the right hand front suspension turret

5 Using a pair of pliers, pull the locking clip from the end of the pedal pivot shaft and recover the bush.
6 Withdraw the pedal from its mounting bracket and remove it from the vehicle **(see illustration)**.

Refitting

7 Refitting is a reversal of removal. On completion, adjust the accelerator cable with reference to Section 3.

5 Cruise control system
– description and component renewal

Description

1 The cruise control system allows the driver to preselect the speed of the car and then release the accelerator pedal. The cruise control system then adjusts the throttle automatically to maintain a constant roadspeed. The system is deactivated when either the clutch or brake pedals are depressed, when neutral gear is selected (models with automatic transmission) or when the main cruise control switch is switched off. The system has a memory function which allows a preselected cruising speed to be resumed if the operation of the cruise control has been interrupted by depressing the brake or clutch pedals.
2 When the cruise control system is active, the preselected roadspeed may be increased or decreased in small increments, by means of the multi-function cruise control system switch.
3 In the event of a fault in the cruise control system, first check all relevant wiring for security. Further testing is best left to a Saab dealer, who will have the necessary diagnostic equipment to find the fault quickly.
4 The main components of the system are as follows:

a) *Electronic Control Module (ECM): The module is supplied with the speed of the car by signals sent from the speedometer in the instrument panel. The system is not operative at speeds below 25 mph. When the cruise control system is active,*

the engine management system ECM is informed of this fact by a signal, to ensure smoother control of the car's speed. The ECM determines the vehicle's roadspeed from a signal supplied by the Anti-lock Braking System (ABS) ECM. Note that on pre-MY 2001 models, the ECM is mounted on the cruise control unit, and is separate to the engine management ECM, being located behind the right-hand front suspension turret. On MY 2001-on models, the ECM function is integral with the engine management ECM, however, the cruise control unit is mounted in the same location.

b) *Switches: The main multi-function control switch for the cruise control system is integral with the steering column left-hand stalk switch. Switches mounted behind the facia and operated by the brake and clutch pedals deactivate the system when either pedal is depressed. As a fail-safe, the brake pedal cruise control switch is earthed through the brake stop-light bulbs, via the main stop-light switch – if this circuit develops a fault, the cruise control system will not operate.*

c) *Indicator light: the CRUISE indicator light on the instrument panel is illuminated whenever the cruise control system is operating.*

Component renewal

Electronic Control Module/control unit

5 The cruise control system ECM/control unit is located in the engine compartment, behind the right hand front suspension turret **(see illustration)**. Ensure that the ignition is switched before proceeding.
6 Turn the control cable union to disengage the bayonet fixing. Withdraw the cable outer from the control unit slightly, then unhook the cable inner from the internal control chain. Unplug the wiring from the control unit.
7 Slacken and withdraw the bolt that secures the control unit mounting bracket to the bodywork. Turn the bracket over, then undo the retaining screws and detach the control unit from the mounting bracket **(see illustration)**.
8 Refitting is a reversal of removal.

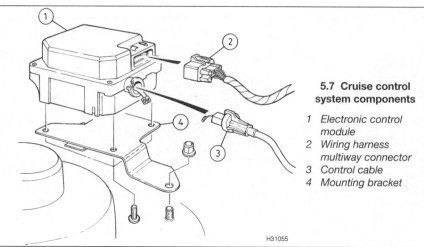

5.7 Cruise control system components

1 *Electronic control module*
2 *Wiring harness multiway connector*
3 *Control cable*
4 *Mounting bracket*

H31055

Control cable

9 Disconnect the control cable from the control unit as described in the previous sub-Section.

10 Undo the securing screws and remove the cover panel/resonator assembly from above the inlet manifold.

11 Disconnect the accelerator cable from the throttle disc arm, as described in Section 3, then unhook the control cable inner from the throttle disc arm.

12 Depress the locking tabs and release the control cable outer from the accelerator cable mounting bracket,

13 Release the control cable from its securing clips, then remove the control cable from the engine compartment.

14 Refitting is a reversal of removal.

Multi-function control switch

15 Refer to the information given in Chapter 12, Section 4, for the removal of the direction indicator/dip beam/main beam steering column stalk switch.

Pedal switches

16 Remove the fasteners and detach the lower cover panel from the driver's side of the facia. On certain models, it may be necessary to first undo the screws and release the diagnostic connector from the underside of the facia.

17 Reach behind the facia and unplug the wiring from the relevant switch.

18 Carefully prise the switch from its mounting bracket.

19 To refit the switch, carefully pull the switch plunger out, then depress the brake/clutch pedal (as applicable). Insert the switch into its mounting bracket, and slowly release the pedal until it contacts the switch plunger. Reconnect the wiring securely.

Stop-light switch

20 Refer to the information given in Chapter 9.

6 Unleaded petrol – general information and usage

Note: *The information given in this Chapter is correct at the time of writing, and applies only to fuels currently available in the UK. If updated information is thought to be required, check with a Saab dealer. If travelling abroad, consult one of the motoring organisations (or a similar authority) for advice on the petrols available, and their suitability for your vehicle.*

1 The fuel recommended by Saab is given in the Specifications at the start of this Chapter.

2 RON and MON are different testing standards; RON stands for Research Octane Number (also written as RM), while MON stands for Motor Octane Number (also written as MM).

3 All models are equipped with a catalytic converter, and must be run on unleaded fuel

only. Under no circumstances should leaded fuel/LRP be used, as this will damage the catalytic converter.

7 Engine management system – general information

Trionic management system

The Saab Trionic engine management system controls three functions of the engine from a single electronic control module (ECM). The three functions comprise the fuel injection system, ignition system, and the turbocharger boost control system. Details of the components related to the ignition function are given in Chapter 5B.

The system is microprocessor-controlled, and the fuel system provides the correct amount of fuel necessary for complete combustion under all engine conditions. Data from various sensors is processed in the ECM, in order to determine the opening period of the fuel injectors for the exact amount of fuel to be injected into the inlet manifold.

The system is of sequential type, where fuel is injected in sequence with the engine's firing order. Conventional sequential fuel injection systems requires a camshaft sensor, which works in conjunction with the crankshaft position sensor to indicate which cylinder at TDC is on its compression stroke and which is on its exhaust stroke. The Trionic system has no camshaft sensor, it determines each cylinder's stroke by applying a small, direct current voltage across each spark plug. When a cylinder on its combustion stroke approaches TDC, this voltage causes an ionisation current to flow across the terminals of the spark plug, thus indicating which cylinder requires fuel injection and ignition next. Sequential control of the ignition timing to control combustion knock is achieved in the same manner (see Chapter 5B).

When the ignition is initially switched on and after the fuel pump is operating, all the injectors operate simultaneously for a short period; this helps to minimise cold start cranking times.

The main components of the system are as follows:

a) **ECM:** *The electronic control module controls the entire operation of the fuel injection system, ignition system, cruise control and turbocharger boost control system.*

b) **Crankshaft position sensor:** *The crankshaft position sensor provides a datum for the ECM to calculate the position of the crankshaft in relation to TDC. The sensor is triggered by a reluctor disc that rotates inside the crankcase.*

c) **Manifold absolute pressure (MAP) sensor:** *The MAP sensor provides a voltage to the ECM, proportional to the pressure in the inlet manifold.*

d) **Charge air (boost) pressure/temperature sensor:** *The air pressure/temperature sensor is integrated into one component and informs the ECM of the pressure and temperature of the air in the hose between the intercooler and the throttle body.*

e) **Engine coolant temperature sensor:** *The engine coolant temperature sensor informs the ECM of the engine temperature.*

f) **Mass airflow sensor:** *is located behind the right-hand headlamp. The engine load is measured by means of a hot-film type air mass flow meter, rather than by measuring inlet manifold depression. The meter houses a heated metal filament which is mounted in the flow of the air intake. The temperature reduction in the wire caused by the flow of air over it causes a change in electrical resistance, which is converted to a variable voltage output signal. Measuring air mass flow, rather than volume flow compensates for the changes in air density encountered when driving on roads at different altitudes above sea level. Note that this method of measurement also precludes the need for a measurement of intake air temperature.*

g) **Throttle position sensor:** *The throttle position sensor informs the ECM of the throttle valve position.*

h) **Charge air (boost) control valve:** *The boost pressure control valve (also referred to as the solenoid valve) is located on a bracket at the front of the cylinder head. It controls the operation of the turbocharger. Under certain conditions (ie, in 1st gear), boost pressure is reduced.*

i) **Charge air (boost) bypass valve:** *The bypass valve is located on the engine wiring harness connector bracket at the rear of the engine compartment on the bulkhead. It is a safety device to prevent any damage to the turbocharger. Under certain conditions, when there is a build-up of pressure the valve is opened by the vacuum from the inlet manifold.*

j) **Fuel pressure regulator:** *The regulator is connected to the end of the fuel rail on the inlet manifold and regulates the fuel pressure to approximately 3.0 bars.*

k) **Fuel pump:** *The fuel pump is housed in the fuel tank. The pump housing incorporates a separate feed pump which supplies the main fuel pump with pressurised fuel, free of air bubbles.*

l) **Injectors:** *Each fuel injector consists of a solenoid-operated needle valve, which opens under the commands from the ECM. Fuel from the fuel rail is then delivered through the injector nozzle into the inlet manifold.*

m) **Oxygen sensor:** *The oxygen sensor provides the ECM with constant feedback on the oxygen content of the exhaust gases (see Chapter 4C).*

n) *EVAP canister-purge valve:* The EVAP canister-purge valve is operated when the engine is started, to purge fuel accumulated in the canister. In order to allow the oxygen sensor to compensate for the additional fuel, the system is operated in short phases (see Chapter 4C).

o) *Ignition discharge module and spark plugs:* The ignition discharge module (or cartridge) contains four HT coils connected directly to the spark plugs (see Chapter 5B).

p) *Limp-home solenoid:* The limp-home solenoid is only fitted to the T7 Trionic system. It is located on the rear of the throttle body. If a safety-related fault occurs in the throttle control, it will go into the limp-home mode. The **Check Engine** lamp will go on immediately and the diagnostic trouble code will have to be cleared with the diagnostic tool.

q) *Idle speed control valve:* The idle speed control valve is only fitted to the T5 Trionic system, and is located on the right-hand rear of the engine, on top of the inlet manifold. The idle air control valve controls the volume of air bypassing the throttle butterfly. The system maintains the engine idle speed under all conditions of load imposed by the alternator, air conditioning compressor, or when a gear other than P or N is selected on automatic transmission models. If there is a break in the idle air control valve circuit, the valve opening is set by an internal spring, to control the engine speed at approximately 1000 rpm. The idle air control valve is also used as an exhaust emission control device; when the engine is on overrun, insufficient air intake can cause poor combustion leading to high emissions of hydrocarbons. During these conditions, the ECM opens the Idle Air Control Valve (IAC) to increase air intake flow and control hydrocarbon emissions.

Motronic management system

The operation of the Bosch Motronic engine management system is very similar to the Saab Trionic system described in the previous sub-Section. Principal differences are detailed below.

a) *Ignition system:* A conventional ignition system is employed, using a separate HT ignition coil and rotary distributor. Combustion knock detection is provided by means of a cylinder block-mounted knock sensor (see Chapter 5B for details).

b) *Camshaft position sensor:* The ignition distributor houses the camshaft position sensor. It informs the ECM when cylinder No 1 is on its combustion stroke, allowing sequential fuel injection and ignition timing (for combustion knock control) to be employed.

'Check Engine' indicator

With either type of engine management system, if the 'Check Engine' warning light comes on, the car should be taken to a Saab dealer at the earliest opportunity. A complete test of the engine management system can then be carried out, using dedicated Saab electronic diagnostic test equipment. The engine management system can be set into a 'self-test' mode, which will cause it to display any stored fault code information by flashing the 'Check Engine' light in a coded sequence. This sequence can then be interpreted to determine what faults have been detected by the engine management system; refer to Section 13 for greater detail.

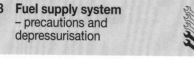

8 Fuel supply system – precautions and depressurisation

Note: *Refer to the Precautions at the end of Section 1 before proceeding.*

⚠ **Warning: The following procedure will merely relieve the pressure in the fuel system – remember that fuel will still be present in the system components, and to take precautions accordingly before disconnecting any of them.**

1 The fuel system referred to in this Section is defined as the tank-mounted fuel pump, the fuel filter, the fuel injectors, the fuel rail and the pressure regulator, and the metal pipes and flexible hoses connected between these components. All these contain fuel, which will be under pressure while the engine is running and/or while the ignition is switched on.

⚠ **Warning: Residual fuel pressure may remain for some time after the ignition has been switched off, and must be relieved before any of these components are disturbed for servicing work.**

2 Open the fusebox, beneath a cover panel on the right-hand side of the facia panel (see *Weekly checks*) and remove the fuel pump fuse (No 32). If necessary, refer to Chapter 12 for more information.

3 Turn the ignition key and crank the engine. If it starts and runs, allow it to idle until it stops through fuel starvation; this should not take more than a few seconds. Try to start it again, to ensure that all pressure has been relieved.

4 Disconnect the battery negative terminal, then refit the fuel pump fuse.

5 Place a suitable container beneath the relevant connection/union to be disconnected, and have a large rag ready to soak up any escaping fuel not being caught by the container.

6 Slowly loosen the connection or union nut (as applicable) to avoid a sudden release of pressure, and position the rag around the connection to catch any fuel spray which may be expelled. Once the pressure is released, disconnect the fuel line.

> **HAYNES HiNT**
> *Cut the fingers from an old pair of rubber gloves and secure them over the open fuel lines or ports with elastic bands to minimise fuel loss and to prevent the entry of dirt into the fuel system.*

9 Fuel pump – removal and refitting

⚠ **Warning: Refer to the precautions given in Section 8, and the information detailed in the 'Safety first!' Section of this manual, before disturbing any component in the fuel supply system.**

Note: *On all models, the fuel pump also incorporates the fuel gauge sender unit.*

Removal

1 Disconnect the battery negative cable and position it away from the terminal.

2 Remove the fuel tank as described in Section 12.

3 The unit is secured by a screwed ring. Saab technicians use a special tool to unscrew the ring, but a large pair of grips (water pump pliers) inserted between the serrations on the inside edge of the ring will achieve the same result. Unscrew and remove the ring **(see illustration)**. Note the location arrows on the top of the pump and tank.

4 Carefully lift the pump flange away from the surface of the fuel tank. Allow the excess fuel to drain back into the tank, then rotate the pump clockwise through about one quarter of a turn and withdraw it from the fuel tank **(see illustration)**. Recover the O-ring seal from the tank aperture.

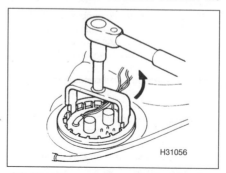

9.3 Unscrew and remove the locking ring from the top of the fuel pump

9.4 Fuel pump removed from the fuel tank

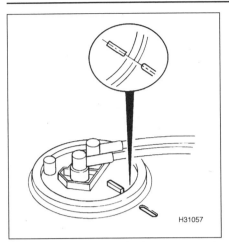

9.6 When refitting the fuel pump, ensure that the markings on the fuel pump and tank are aligned

Refitting

5 Fit a new O-ring seal to the fuel tank aperture, pressing it firmly into its recess.
6 Lower the fuel pump into the fuel tank, rotating it to ensure that the alignment markings on the fuel pump and tank line up **(see illustration)**.
7 Screw the large plastic locking ring into position and tighten it using the method described for its removal.
8 Refit the fuel tank as described in Section 12.
9 Reconnect the battery negative cable.

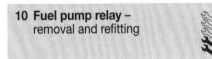

10 Fuel pump relay – removal and refitting

Removal

1 The fuel pump relay is located on the main relay board, behind the facia.
2 Remove the battery cover, then disconnect the battery negative cable and position it away from the terminal.
3 Release the fasteners and detach the lower cover panel from the driver's side of the facia.
4 Remove the securing screw and lower the fuseboard away from the facia.

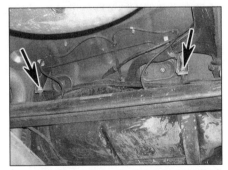

12.7 Progressively undo the nuts (arrowed) securing the fuel tank support straps to their respective mounting brackets

5 The fuel pump relay is in position 1, 3rd row from the top.
6 Grasp the relay and pull it squarely from the relay board.

Refitting

7 Refitting is a reversal of removal. Ensure that the relay is pushed firmly into its base.

11 Fuel gauge sender unit – removal and refitting

On all models, the fuel gauge sender unit is integral with the fuel pump and can only be purchased as a complete assembly; refer to Section 9 for fuel pump removal and refitting.

12 Fuel tank – removal, repair and refitting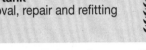

 Warning: Refer to the precautions given in Section 8, and the information detailed in the 'Safety first!' Section of this manual, before disturbing any component in the fuel supply system.

1 Before removing the fuel tank, it is preferable that all the fuel is first syphoned from the tank. Since a fuel tank drain plug is not provided, carry out the removal operation when the tank is almost empty.

Removal

2 Release the pressure in the fuel system as described in Section 8, then disconnect the battery negative cable and position it away from the terminal.
3 Select first gear (manual transmission) or Park (automatic transmission) and chock the front wheels securely. Raise the rear of the car and support it securely on axle stands (see *Jacking and vehicle support*).
4 Loosen the clips and disconnect the filler and breather hoses from the fuel tank. Tape over the ends of the hoses to prevent entry of dust and dirt.
5 Remove the plastic cover from the fuel filter located in front of the tank, then undo the screws and release the clamp holding the filter.
6 Position a trolley jack centrally beneath the fuel tank, with a plank of wood placed on the jack head. Raise the jack until it just starts to take the weight of the fuel tank.
7 Progressively undo the bolts securing the fuel tank support straps to their respective mounting brackets **(see illustration)**. Unhook the ends of each support strap from their brackets, as they become slack.
8 Slowly lower the fuel tank, right-hand side first, until it is possible to disconnect the fuel lines from the top. Also, disconnect the wiring from the fuel pump/gauge.
9 Disconnect any remaining breather hoses or cables that may prevent the removal of the

tank, then, with the help of an assistant, lower the fuel tank to the ground and remove it from under the car.

Repair

10 If the tank is contaminated with sediment or water, remove the fuel pump and wash the tank out with clean fuel. In certain cases, it may be possible to have small leaks or minor damage repaired. Seek the advice of a suitable specialist before attempting to repair the fuel tank.

Refitting

11 Refitting is a reversal of removal, noting the following points:
 a) *Inspect the O-rings at the fuel supply and return quick-release unions, on the top of the fuel pump.*
 b) *Ensure that all fuel lines and breather hoses are correctly routed and are not kinked or twisted.*
 c) *Tighten the fuel tank support straps securely.*

13 Engine management system – testing, checking and adjustment

1 On both Bosch Motronic and Saab Trionic engine management systems, the engine idle speed and air-to-fuel mixture (and hence the exhaust gas CO content) are automatically controlled by the ECM. The *checking* of idle speed and mixture is possible on all models by using a tachometer and exhaust gas analyser, but some difficulty may be experienced connecting a conventional tachometer to the engine on the turbo models which are fitted with Direct Ignition. In addition, as all models are fitted with catalytic converters, the levels of CO, HC and NOx produced may be difficult to measure accurately with anything other than professional test equipment if the system is operating normally. However, it may be possible to at least confirm the existence of a fuelling or ignition fault, by detecting high levels of one or more of these exhaust gas pollutants, using a commercially-available exhaust gas analyser.
2 If a fault appears to be present in the engine management system, first ensure that all the system wiring connectors are securely connected and free of corrosion. Then ensure that the fault is not due to poor maintenance – ie, check that the air cleaner filter element is clean, that the fuel filter has been renewed at the specified interval, and that the spark plugs and associated HT components (including the distributor and ignition coil, where applicable) are in good condition. Also check that the engine breather hoses are clear and undamaged. Finally, check that the cylinder compression pressures are correct, referring to Chapters 1A, 2A and 5B for further information.
3 If these checks fail to reveal the cause of the problem, the car should be taken to a Saab dealer for testing. A diagnostic connector

is incorporated in the engine management system wiring harness, into which a special Saab electronic diagnostic tester can be plugged. The tester will identify any faults detected by the engine management system ECM by interpreting fault codes stored in the ECM's memory. It also allows system sensors and actuators to be tested remotely without disconnecting them or removing them from the vehicle. This alleviates the need to test all the system components individually, using conventional test equipment. The diagnostic connector is located on the underside of the facia, on the driver's side of the vehicle.

4 If the Check Engine warning light comes on, the car should be taken to a Saab dealer at the earliest opportunity. A complete test of the engine management system can then be carried out, using dedicated Saab electronic diagnostic test equipment.

14 Engine management system components (Bosch Motronic) – removal and refitting

⚠️ **Warning: Refer to the precautions given in Section 8, and the information detailed in the 'Safety first!' Section of this manual, before disturbing any component in the fuel supply system.**

Electronic Control Module (ECM)
Removal

1 Ensure that the ignition is switched off. Disconnect the battery negative lead (refer to *Disconnecting the battery* in the *Reference* Chapter at the end of this manual).

2 Working inside the vehicle, in the right-hand footwell, remove the fixings and lower the cover panel away from the underside of the facia and steering column. On LHD models, it will be necessary to remove the glovebox.

3 Peel back the carpet to expose the ECM mounted on the bodywork at the base of the A-pillar.

4 Release the locking lever and unplug the multiplug wiring harness connector from the underside of the ECM. **Note:** *To prevent potential damage to the internal circuitry of the ECM from static electricity, prior to*

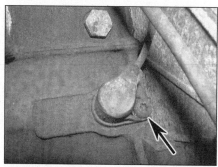
14.9a Crankshaft position sensor securing screw (arrowed)

disconnecting the multiplug, earth yourself by touching part of the vehicle body.

5 Unscrew the mounting bolt and withdraw the ECM from inside the car.

Refitting

6 Refitting is a reversal of removal. Ensure that the wiring harness multiplug connector is secured with the locking lever. Note that if a new ECM has been fitted, it will gradually 'learn' the engines characteristics as the vehicle is driven. Drivability, performance and fuel economy may be slightly reduced during this period. Saab also state that the immobiliser must be reset using their Tech2 diagnostic tool.

Crankshaft position sensor
Removal

7 The crankshaft position sensor is located on the front surface of the cylinder block, adjacent to the transmission bellhousing mating surface. However, the wiring connector is located on the bulkhead behind the engine. First, remove the inlet air resonator above the throttle body.

8 Note the routing of the wiring for the crankshaft position sensor. Disconnect the wiring at the connector, then release the wiring from the retaining clips along its length.

9 Remove the retaining screw and withdraw the sensor from its location on the front left-hand side of the cylinder block **(see illustrations)**. Recover the O-ring, noting how it is fitted. Clean the seating in the cylinder block.

Refitting

10 Refitting is a reversal of removal, ensuring

14.9b Removing the crankshaft position sensor from the cylinder block

that the O-ring is properly seated. Tighten the sensor securing screw to the specified torque. Ensure that the wiring is retained with the clips/cable ties, following its original routing, and that the multiway connector is securely reconnected. Check the condition of the resonator O-rings before refitting.

Coolant temperature sensor
Removal

11 The sensor is threaded into the inlet manifold **(see illustration)**. Ensure that the engine is completely cold, then release the pressure in the cooling system by removing and then refitting the expansion tank filler cap (see *Weekly checks*).

12 Release the clips and remove the intake air resonator assembly from the top of the throttle body.

13 Unplug the wiring connector from the sensor.

14 Unscrew the sensor from the lower inlet manifold. Be prepared for some coolant loss.

Refitting

15 Clean the threads, then insert the sensor into the inlet manifold, and tighten securely.

16 Refit the wiring connector, then refit the intake air resonator, ensuring that the two O-ring seals are properly seated.

17 Top-up the cooling system with reference to *Weekly checks*.

Throttle position sensor
Removal

18 Ensure that the ignition switch is turned to the OFF position.

19 Release the clips and remove the intake air resonator assembly from the top of the throttle body.

20 Release the clips and remove the crankcase breather hose from the cylinder head cover and throttle body.

21 Slide the idle air control valve from its mounting stud and move it to one side.

22 Unplug the wiring connector from the throttle position sensor.

23 Unscrew the securing screws, then withdraw the sensor from the end of the throttle spindle **(see illustration)**. Recover the O-ring seal.

Refitting

24 Refitting is a reversal of removal. Ensure that the throttle position sensor O-ring seal is

14.11 The coolant temperature sensor (arrowed) is threaded into the inlet manifold (fuel rail and injectors removed)

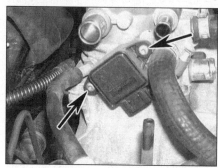
14.23 Throttle position sensor securing screws (arrowed)

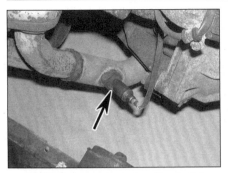

14.26 Oxygen sensor location in the exhaust system front pipe

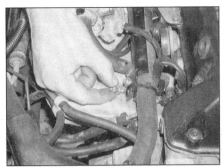

14.36a Undo the screws . . .

14.36b . . . then remove the cable guide

correctly seated. When refitting the intake air resonator to the throttle body, ensure that the two O-ring seals are properly seated.

Oxygen (Lambda) sensor
Removal
25 Ensure that the ignition is switched to the OFF position.
26 Unscrew the sensor from the exhaust system front pipe **(see illustration)**. A slotted socket will be required as the sensor incorporates a flying lead.
27 Release the sensor wiring from the retaining clips in the engine compartment, noting how it is routed.
28 Unplug the sensor wiring from the main harness at the connector situated at the left-hand end of the cylinder head and remove it from the engine compartment.

Refitting
29 Refitting is a reversal of the removal procedure. Coat the threads of the sensor with a suitable high-temperature anti-seize grease, then refit and tighten it to the specified torque.

Injectors, fuel rail and pressure regulator
Note: *Refer to the warning at the end of Section 1 before proceeding.*
Removal
30 Depressurise the fuel system as descried in Section 8. Ensure that the ignition switch is then turned to the OFF position.

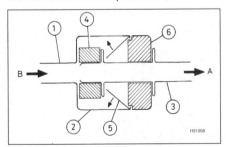

14.38b Sectional view of the quick-release fuel hose fittings

A *To fuel rail*
B *From fuel tank*
1 *Fuel hose*
2 *Quick-release fitting*

3 *Fuel pipe*
4 *Seal*
5 *Spring tab*
6 *Grommet*

14.37 Unplug the wiring connectors from the fuel injectors

31 Release the clips and remove the intake air resonator assembly from the top of the throttle body.
32 Release the clips and remove the crankcase breather hose from the cylinder head cover and throttle body.
33 Slide the idle air control valve from its mounting stud and move it to one side.
34 Unbolt the dipstick cap/neck support bracket from the rear of the cylinder head.
35 Refer to Section 3 and disconnect the accelerator cable from the throttle body. Where applicable, refer to Section 5 and disconnect the cruise control cable from the throttle body.
36 Slacken and withdraw the two screws securing the cable guide to the fuel rail. Release the cable ties and detach the wiring harness from the cable guide. Remove the cable guide from the engine compartment **(see illustrations)**.

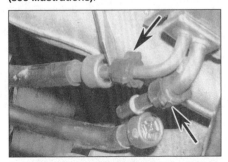

14.38c The rubber grommets must be prised from the fittings, before the hoses can be disconnected

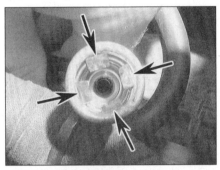

14.38a The quick-release fitting contains four internal tabs (arrowed)

37 Release the locking clips and then unplug the wiring from all four injectors **(see illustration)**. Mark each connector to avoid confusion on refitting.
38 Disconnect the fuel supply and return hoses from the right-hand end of the fuel rail. The hoses incorporate quick-release connectors, which ordinarily require access to a special separation tool. The tool consists of a plastic collar which slides between the fuel hose fitting and the fuel pipe leading to the fuel rail; when pushed into position, the tool splays out the four internal tabs inside the quick-release fitting allowing the hose to be disconnected. The same effect can be achieved with a length of plastic tubing, cut along its length to allow it to be fitted over the fuel pipe. Note that the rubber grommets must be prised from the fittings, before the hoses can be disconnected **(see illustrations)**.
39 Remove the two screws securing the fuel

14.38d Disconnecting the fuel supply and return hoses from the fuel rail

14.39 Remove the screws . . .

14.40a . . . and lift the fuel rail from the inlet manifold

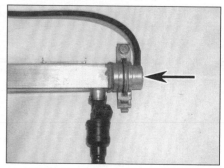

14.40b To remove the fuel pressure regulator (arrowed), undo the screw and release the metal clamp

rail to the cylinder head **(see illustration)**. Place a cloth beneath the fuel rail to soak up fuel which will escape as the fuel rail is removed.

40 Lift the fuel rail from the inlet manifold, complete with the fuel injectors. If required, release the metal clamp and remove the fuel pressure regulator from the left hand end

of the fuel rail. Recover the O-ring seal **(see illustrations)**.
41 Prise out the retaining clips, and pull the injectors from the fuel rail **(see illustrations)**. Recover the rubber O-ring seals.

Refitting

42 Refitting is a reversal of the removal procedure. Fit the injectors to the fuel rail, then press the fuel rail and injectors into the inlet manifold as an assembly. Before locating the rubber O-rings in the inlet manifold, apply a little petroleum jelly to them, to facilitate entry of the injectors. Make sure that the correct wiring plugs are connected to the injectors. When refitting the intake air resonator to the throttle body, ensure that the two large O-ring seals are properly seated.

Idle air control valve

Removal

43 Ensure that the ignition switch is turned to the OFF position.
44 Release the clips and remove the intake air resonator assembly from the top of the throttle body.
45 Unplug the wiring connector from the base of the valve, then slide the valve from its mounting stud **(see illustrations)**.
46 Release the air hoses from the ports on the throttle body and then remove the valve from the engine compartment **(see illustrations)**.

Refitting

47 Refitting is a reversal of removal, but make sure that the arrow on the side of the

14.41a Prise out the retaining clips . . .

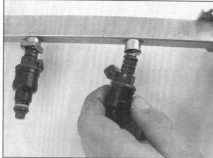

14.41b . . . and pull the injectors from the fuel rail

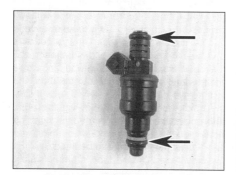

14.41c Renew the O-ring seals

14.45a Unplug the wiring connector from the base of the valve . . .

14.45b . . . then slide the valve from its mounting stud (arrowed)

14.46a Release the air hoses from the ports on the throttle body (arrowed) . . .

14.46b . . . and then remove the valve from the engine compartment

14.54 Unplug the wiring connector from the side of the air mass flow meter

14.55a Slacken the hose clips . . .

14.55b . . . release the clips and detach the meter from the air cleaner and flexible intake air ducting

valve is pointing in the direction of airflow. When refitting the intake air resonator to the throttle body, ensure that the two O-ring seals are properly seated.

Evaporative loss system purge valve

Removal

48 Ensure that the ignition switch is turned to the OFF position.
49 Remove the section of flexible intake air ducting that connects the air mass flow meter to the resonator assembly.
50 Unplug the wiring from the purge valve, then disconnect the vacuum hoses, noting their order of fitment to avoid confusion on refitting.
51 Release the valve from its mounting collar and remove it from the engine compartment.

Refitting

52 Refitting is a reversal of removal, but make sure it is fitted the correct way round.

Air mass flow meter

Removal

53 Ensure that the ignition switch is turned to the OFF position.
54 Unplug the wiring connector from the side of the air mass flow meter **(see illustration)**.
55 Slacken the hose clips, release the spring clips and detach the meter from the air cleaner and flexible intake air ducting **(see illustrations)**.

Refitting

56 Refitting is a reversal of removal.

Camshaft position sensor

57 The camshaft position sensor is integral with the ignition distributor; refer to Chapter 5B for details of its removal and refitting.

Throttle body

Removal

58 Release the clips and remove the intake air resonator assembly from the top of the throttle body.
59 Disconnect the wiring plug from the throttle position sensor.
60 With the engine cold, unscrew the filler cap on the coolant expansion tank, then refit and tighten the cap.
61 Loosen the clips, then disconnect and plug the coolant hoses from the throttle body.
62 Disconnect the crankcase breather hose from the throttle body **(see illustration)**.
63 Disconnect the IAC valve hose from the throttle body.
64 Disconnect the accelerator cable (and, where necessary, the cruise control cable) with reference to Sections 3 and 5.
65 Slacken and remove the mounting screws, then lift the throttle body from the inlet manifold **(see illustration)**. Recover the O-ring.

Refitting

66 Clean the contact surfaces of the throttle body and inlet manifold, then refit the throttle

body together with a new O-ring. Tighten the mounting screws.
67 Reconnect and adjust the accelerator cable (and, where necessary, the cruise control cable) with reference to Section 3.
68 Reconnect the IAC valve hose and the crankcase breather hose.
69 Reconnect the coolant hoses and tighten the clips.
70 Reconnect the wiring plug to the throttle position sensor.
71 Refit the intake air resonator assembly, ensuring that the two O-ring seals are properly seated.
72 Top-up the cooling system with reference to *Weekly checks*.

15 Engine management system components (Saab Trionic) – removal and refitting

⚠️ *Warning: Refer to the precautions given in Section 8, and the information detailed in the 'Safety first!' Section of this manual, before disturbing any component in the fuel supply system.*

Electronic Control Module (ECM)

Removal

1 Ensure that the ignition is switched off. Disconnect the battery negative lead (refer to *Disconnecting the battery* in the *Reference* Chapter at the end of this manual).
2 Working inside the vehicle, in the right-hand footwell, remove the fixings and lower the cover panel away from the underside of the facia and steering column. On LHD models, it will be necessary to remove the glovebox.
3 Peel back the carpet to expose the ECM mounted on the bodywork at the base of the A-pillar.
4 Release the locking lever and unplug the multiplug wiring harness connector from the underside of the ECM. **Note:** *To prevent potential damage to the internal circuitry of the ECM from static electricity, prior to disconnecting the multiplug, earth yourself by touching part of the vehicle body.*
5 Unscrew the mounting bolt and withdraw the ECM from inside the car.

14.62 Disconnect the crankcase breather hose from the throttle housing

14.65 Unscrew the throttle housing mounting screws

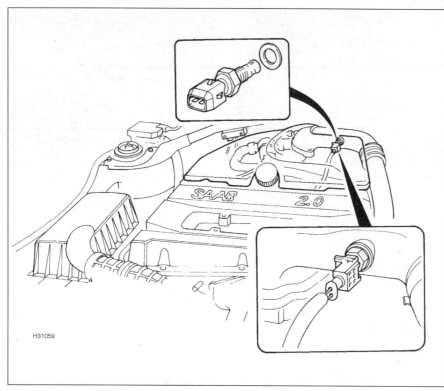

15.8 Inlet air temperature (IAT) sensor

Refitting

6 Refitting is a reversal of removal. Ensure that the wiring harness multiplug connector is secured with the locking lever. Note that if a new ECM has been fitted, it will gradually 'learn' the engines characteristics as the vehicle is driven. Drivability, performance and fuel economy may be slightly reduced during this period. Saab also state that the immobiliser must be reset using their Tech2 diagnostic tool.

Inlet air temperature sensor (Trionic T5)

Removal

7 Release the fixings and remove the cover panel from above the throttle body.
8 Disconnect the wiring from the sensor, which is located in the main air inlet duct to the throttle body. Unscrew the sensor from the air inlet duct, and recover the sealing washer **(see illustration)**.

Refitting

9 Refitting is a reversal of removal, but check and if necessary renew the sealing washer.

Throttle position sensor (Trionic T5)

Removal

10 Ensure that the ignition switch is turned to the OFF position.
11 Release the fixings and remove the cover panel from the top of the throttle body.
12 Release the clips and remove the

crankcase breather hose from the cylinder head cover and throttle body.
13 Slide the idle air control valve from its mounting stud and move it to one side.
14 Unplug the wiring connector from the throttle position sensor.
15 Slacken and remove the securing screws, then withdraw the sensor from the end of the throttle spindle. Recover the O-ring seal.

Refitting

16 Refitting is a reversal of removal. Ensure that the throttle position sensor O-ring seal is correctly seated.

Idle air control valve (Trionic T5)

Removal

17 Ensure that the ignition switch is turned to the OFF position.

15.38 Undo the retaining bolts (arrowed) and remove the cover

18 Release the fixings and remove the cover panel from the top of the throttle body.
19 Unplug the wiring connector from the base of the valve, then slide the valve from its mounting stud. Note the direction of flow arrow on the valve body.
20 Release the air hoses from the ports on the throttle body and then remove the valve from the engine compartment.

Refitting

21 Refitting is a reversal of removal. The direction of flow arrow on the valve body must face away from the throttle body.

Throttle body (Trionic T5)

Removal

22 Loosen the clip, and disconnect the rubber connecting hose from the throttle body.
23 Disconnect the wiring plug from the throttle position sensor.
24 With the engine cold, unscrew the filler cap on the coolant expansion tank, then refit and tighten the cap.
25 Loosen the clips, then disconnect and plug the coolant hoses from the throttle body.
26 Disconnect the crankcase breather hose from the throttle body.
27 Disconnect the IAC valve hose from the throttle body.
28 Disconnect the accelerator cable (and, where necessary, the cruise control cable) with reference to Sections 3 and 5.
29 Unscrew the four mounting bolts, and remove the throttle body from the inlet manifold. Recover the O-ring.

Refitting

30 Clean the contact surfaces of the throttle body and inlet manifold, then refit the throttle body together with a new O-ring. Tighten the mounting bolts.
31 Reconnect and adjust the accelerator cable (and, where necessary, the cruise control cable) with reference to Section 3.
32 Reconnect the IAC valve hose and the crankcase breather hose.
33 Reconnect the coolant hoses and tighten the clips.
34 Reconnect the wiring plug to the throttle position sensor.
35 Reconnect the rubber connecting hose to the throttle body, and tighten the clip.
36 Top-up the cooling system with reference to *Weekly checks*.

Throttle body (Trionic T7)

Removal

37 Ensure that the ignition switch is turned to the OFF position. Making sure the engine is completely cold, release the pressure in the cooling system by removing and then refitting the expansion tank filler cap (see *Weekly checks*).
38 Unclip the engine upper cover panel from the top of the throttle body, then undo the retaining bolts and remove the cover from the throttle linkage **(see illustration)**.

15.39 Disconnect the vacuum pipe (arrowed)

15.40a Clamp the coolant hoses . . .

15.40b . . . then release the securing clips (arrowed) and disconnect the coolant hoses

15.41 Disconnect the hose (arrowed) from the rear of the throttle body

15.42a Undo the retaining bolt (arrowed) . . .

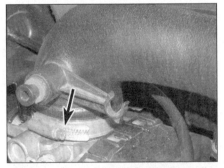

15.42b . . . then slacken the retaining clip on the air intake pipe

39 Remove the lower vacuum hose from the throttle body **(see illustration)**.

40 Clamp the two coolant hoses that are connected to the throttle body, then release the retaining clips and disconnect the hoses **(see illustrations)**.

41 Remove the air bypass hose from the front lower part of the throttle body. Slacken the securing clip and disconnect the hose at the rear of the throttle body, below the limp-home solenoid **(see illustration)**.

42 Undo the retaining bolt for the turbocharger delivery pipe on the front of the cylinder head. Slacken the retaining clip and carefully lift the delivery pipe from the top of the throttle body **(see illustrations)**.

43 Unclip the accelerator inner cable from the throttle linkage, then remove the rubber cover and disconnect the wiring connector from the

limp-home solenoid on the back of the throttle body **(see illustration)**.

44 Disconnect the 10-pin multiplug connector from the side of the throttle body **(see illustration)**.

45 Undo the three mounting bolts and remove the throttle body from the inlet manifold **(see illustration)**.

Refitting

46 Refitting is a reversal of removal. Renew the seal if necessary and ensure that all connections are secure.

Charge air (boost) pressure/temperature sensor

Removal

47 The pressure/temperature sensor is located in the main air intake duct to the throttle body.

48 Disconnect the wiring connector from the sensor, unscrew the sensor from the air intake duct, and recover the sealing washer **(see illustration)**.

15.43 Disconnecting the wiring plug from the limp-home solenoid

15.44 Pull out locking clip (arrowed) to disconnect the wiring plug connector from the throttle body

15.45 Undo the three throttle body retaining bolts (arrowed)

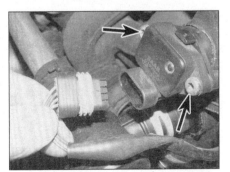

15.48 Disconnect the wiring plug, then undo the two retaining screws (arrowed)

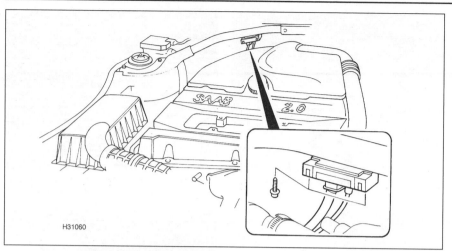

15.50 Manifold absolute pressure (MAP) sensor (T5 system)

15.51a Removing the engine upper cover panel

15.51b Disconnect the wiring plug . . .

15.54a Slacken the hose clip, and withdraw the airflow sensor . . .

Refitting

49 Refitting is a reversal of removal, but check and if necessary renew any sealing washers.

Manifold absolute pressure sensor

Removal

50 On the Trionic T5 system, release the fixings and remove the cover panel from above the throttle body. Disconnect the wiring plug and vacuum hose, then remove the securing screw and detach the sensor from the underside of the engine compartment cross-bracing bar **(see illustration)**.

15.51c . . . then undo the two retaining screws (arrowed)

15.54b . . . note the direction of the arrow

51 On the Trionic T7 system, unclip the engine upper cover panel from above the inlet manifold, then disconnect the wiring plug, and remove the securing screws. Withdraw the sensor from the inlet manifold **(see illustrations)**.

Refitting

52 Refitting is a reversal of removal, but check and if necessary renew any sealing washers.

Mass airflow sensor

Removal

53 The mass airflow sensor is located in the right-hand front corner of the engine bay behind the right-hand headlamp unit. Slacken the two retaining clips and withdraw the rubber intake hose from the vehicle **(see illustration)**.
54 Slacken the hose clip on the intake hose and withdraw the airflow sensor. Note the direction of the arrow on the sensor, this is for the correct direction of the airflow **(see illustrations)**.
55 Disconnect the wiring connector from the bottom of the sensor as it is removed **(see illustration)**.

Refitting

56 Refitting is a reversal of removal, but check that the arrows on the sensor are pointing in the direction of flow and the wiring connector is secure.

Coolant temperature sensor
Removal

57 The coolant temperature sensor is threaded into the inlet manifold on the front of the engine. Ensure that the engine is completely cold, then release the pressure in the cooling system by

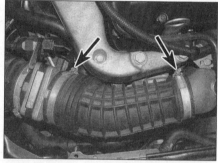

15.53 Slacken the two retaining clips (arrowed)

15.55 Disconnecting the wiring connector as the sensor is withdrawn

15.59 Disconnect the wiring connector (arrowed) . . .

15.60 . . . then remove the sensor (arrowed) from the coolant housing

15.64 Crankshaft sensor is located behind a shield on the front of the cylinder block

removing and then refitting the expansion tank filler cap (see *Weekly checks*).

58 To make access easier, it may be necessary to slacken the hose clips and remove the air intake assembly from the top of the throttle body.

59 Unplug the wiring connector from the sensor **(see illustration)**.

60 Unscrew the sensor from the coolant housing on the left-hand end of the cylinder head. Be prepared for some coolant loss **(see illustration)**.

Refitting

61 Clean the threads, then insert the sensor into the inlet manifold, and tighten securely. Fit new sealing washer if necessary.

62 Ensure that the wiring connector is securely refitted.

63 Top-up the cooling system with reference to *Weekly checks*.

Crankshaft position sensor

Removal

64 The crankshaft position sensor is located on the front surface of the cylinder block, at the transmission end **(see illustration)**.

65 Undo the retaining nut and unclip the heat shield from the exhaust manifold, then undo the securing bolt and remove the shield/cover from the sensor **(see illustrations)**.

 Warning: The exhaust system and turbocharger may be hot.

66 Withdraw the sensor from its location on the front left-hand side of the cylinder block **(see illustration)**. Recover the O-ring, noting how it is fitted. Clean the seating in the cylinder block.

67 Note the routing of the wiring around the left-hand end of the cylinder head, then disconnect the wiring at the connector **(see**

illustrations). Release the wiring from any retaining clips along its length.

Refitting

68 Refitting is a reversal of removal, ensuring that the O-ring is properly seated. Tighten the sensor retaining screw securely. Ensure that the wiring is retained with the clips/cable ties, following its original routing, and that the multiway connector is securely reconnected.

Fuel supply rail, injectors and pressure regulator

Removal

69 Depressurise the fuel system as described in Section 8. Ensure that the ignition switch is then turned to the OFF position.

70 Unclip the engine upper cover panel from the top of the throttle body.

71 Disconnect the crankcase breather hose from the cylinder head cover **(see illustration)**.

15.65a Undo the retaining nut (arrowed) and remove the heat shield

15.65b Undo the retaining screw and remove the sensor shield

15.66 Withdraw the sensor and recover the O-ring

15.67a Wiring plug connector location (arrowed)

15.67b Pull out locking clip (arrowed) to disconnect the wiring plug connector

15.71 Disconnect the breather hose from the cylinder head cover

15.72a Undo the retaining bolt (arrowed) . . .

15.72b . . . and withdraw the oil filler tube

15.73 Using a plastic sleeve to release the securing clips on the fuel lines

Note: *On later models, release the securing clip to disconnect the hose.*

72 Unbolt the dipstick/filler cap support bracket from the rear of the cylinder head and remove **(see illustrations)**. Plug up the pipe to prevent dirt entering the engine.

73 Refer to Section 3 and disconnect the accelerator cable from the throttle body. Disconnect the quick-release fuel lines from the fuel rail, fit caps to the open fuel lines to prevent ingress of dirt **(see illustration)**.

74 Undo the retaining bolt on the front of the cylinder head for the turbocharger delivery pipe. Slacken the retaining clip and carefully lift the delivery pipe from the top of the throttle body.

75 Slacken and withdraw the bolts securing the cable guide bracket to the left-hand end of the cylinder head/inlet manifold **(see illustrations)**. For better access, release the cable ties and detach the wiring harness from the cable guide, then move the cable guide to one side.

76 Release the locking clips and then unplug the wiring from all four injectors **(see illustrations)**, release any cable ties and move wiring loom to one side.

77 Remove the two bolts securing the fuel rail to the cylinder head **(see illustration)**. Place a cloth beneath the fuel rail to soak up fuel which will escape as the fuel rail is removed.

78 Disconnect the vacuum hose from the fuel pressure regulator, then lift the fuel rail from the inlet manifold complete with the fuel injectors **(see illustrations)**. Recover the O-ring seals and discard, new ones should be used on refitting. Plug up the holes in the cylinder head to prevent dirt entering the engine.

79 If required, release the metal clamp and

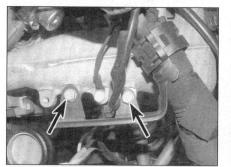

15.75a Undo the two lower retaining bolts (arrowed) . . .

15.75b . . . and the upper retaining bolt (arrowed) from the wiring harness guide

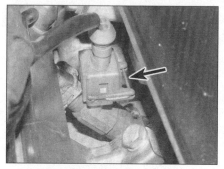

15.76a Press in the securing clip (arrowed) . . .

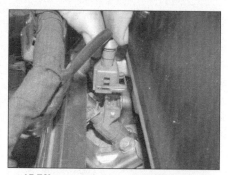

15.76b . . . and disconnect the wiring connector from the injector

15.77 Fuel rail securing bolts (arrowed)

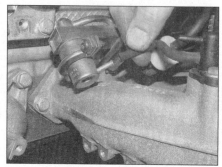

15.78a Disconnect the vacuum hose from the regulator . . .

15.78b . . . then withdraw the fuel rail from the intake manifold

15.79 Undo the retaining screw (arrowed) to release the regulator from the fuel rail

15.80a Prise out the retaining clips . . .

15.80b . . . and pull the injectors from the fuel rail

remove the fuel pressure regulator from the end of the fuel rail **(see illustration)**.

80 To remove the injectors from the fuel rail, release the retaining clips and pull the injectors from the fuel rail. Recover the rubber O-ring seals and discard, new ones should be used on refitting **(see illustrations)**.

Refitting

81 Refitting is a reversal of the removal procedure. Fit the injectors to the fuel rail (using new O-rings), then press the fuel rail and injectors into the inlet manifold as an assembly. Before locating the new rubber O-rings in the inlet manifold, apply a little petroleum jelly to them, to facilitate entry of the injectors. Make sure that all the wiring plugs are connected securely. When refitting the turbocharger air intake to the throttle body, ensure that the O-ring seals are properly seated.

Charge air (boost) control valve

Removal – T5 system

82 The valve is located at the front right hand corner of the engine compartment.

83 Ensure that the ignition is switched off, then unplug the wiring connector from the valve. Mark each of the hoses leading to the valve to identify their fitted positions, then release the clips and detach the hoses from the valve ports **(see illustration)**. Undo the screws and remove the boost control valve from the engine compartment.

Removal – T7 system

84 The valve is located at the front right-hand

corner of the engine, mounted on a bracket on the air intake pipe. Ensure that the ignition is switched off, then unplug the wiring connector from the valve. Mark each of the hoses leading to the valve to identify their fitted positions, then release the clips and detach the hoses from the valve ports **(see illustrations)**.

85 Slide the control valve off the two locating pegs and remove from the engine compartment.

Refitting

86 Refitting is a reversal of removal. It is vitally important that the hoses are refitted to the correct ports on the boost control valve.

Charge air (boost) bypass valve

Removal – T5 system

87 Unplug the vacuum hose from the top of the valve body. Slacken the clips then

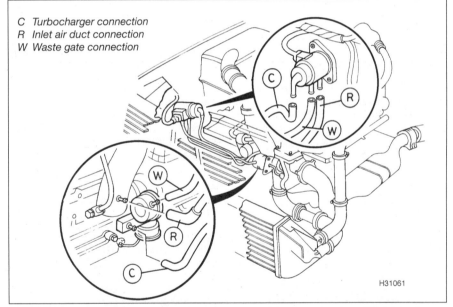

C Turbocharger connection
R Inlet air duct connection
W Waste gate connection

H31061

15.83 Boost pressure control valve location and hose connections (T5 system)

15.84a Charge air (boost) control valve (T7 system)

15.84b Pull back rubber cover and disconnect the wiring connector

15.84c Note the markings on the valve for the hoses

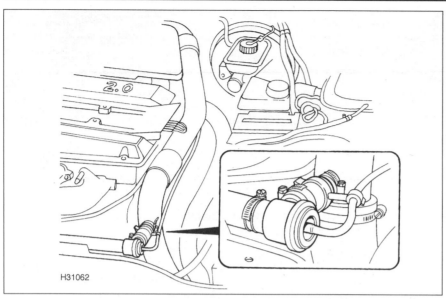

H31062

15.87 Boost pressure bypass valve location (T5 system)

disconnect the air intake ducts from the sides of the bypass valve **(see illustration)**.

Removal – T7 system

88 Unclip the engine upper cover panel from the top of the throttle body, then lift the rubber moulding and unclip the cover from the engine harness bracket on the bulkhead.
89 Undo the two retaining nuts from the mounting bracket, then lift the control valve mounting plate and unhook it from the bulkhead. As the unit is withdrawn, disconnect the lower multiplug connector from the bypass valve.
90 Mark each of the vacuum hoses leading to the valve to identify their fitted positions, then detach the hoses from the valve body.
91 Drill out the two rivets and remove the control valve.

Refitting

92 Refitting is a reversal of removal. Using new pop rivets, fasten the control valve to the mounting plate.

Limp-home solenoid (Trionic T7)

Note: *Removing the limp-home solenoid will cause the throttle body to go into mechanical*

limp-home mode. After refitting, the solenoid must be reset, and all fault codes cleared by a Saab dealer using the Tech2 diagnostic tool.

Removal

93 Unclip the engine upper cover panel from above the inlet manifold.
94 Pull back the rubber cover then disconnect the wiring plug from the limp-home solenoid located on the rear of the throttle body. Remove the Torx securing screws and withdraw the sensor from the throttle body **(see illustrations)**.

Refitting

95 Refitting is a reversal of removal, but check and if necessary renew any sealing washers. Before refitting the engine upper cover, reset the solenoid as follows, although it will also be necessary for a Saab dealer to clear the fault codes from the ECM memory. At the bottom of the accelerator cable sector, carefully push the end of the spring in towards the throttle body. Now, use a screwdriver to turn the black tooth disc anti-clockwise until a click is heard. Rotate the accelerator cable sector clockwise, making sure that the disc does not follow. The cover can now be refitted.

Oxygen (Lambda) sensor

Removal

96 Ensure that the ignition is switched to the OFF position.
97 Remove the engine top cover, followed by the turbocharger delivery pipe, for access to the oxygen sensor cable connection. Disconnect the wiring.
98 Apply the handbrake, then jack up the front of the vehicle and support it on axle stands (see *Jacking and vehicle support*).
99 Unscrew the sensor from the exhaust system front pipe.

Refitting

100 Refitting is a reversal of the removal procedure. Coat the threads of the sensor with a suitable high temperature anti-seize grease, then refit and tighten it to the specified torque.

16 Turbocharger – description and precautions

Description

1 The turbocharger increases engine efficiency and performance by raising the pressure in the inlet manifold above atmospheric pressure. Instead of the intake air being sucked into the combustion chambers, it is forced in under pressure. This leads to a greater charge pressure increase during combustion and improved fuel burning, which raises the thermal efficiency of the engine. Under these conditions, additional fuel is supplied by the fuel injection system, in proportion to the increased airflow.
2 Energy for the operation of the turbocharger comes from the exhaust gas. The gas flows through a specially-shaped housing (the turbine housing) and in so doing spins the turbine wheel. The turbine wheel is attached to a shaft, at the end of which is another vaned wheel known as the compressor wheel. The compressor wheel spins in its own housing, and compresses the intake air on the way to the inlet manifold.
3 Between the turbocharger and the inlet manifold, the compressed air passes through an intercooler. This is an air-to-air heat exchanger, mounted in front of the radiator and supplied with cooling air from the front grille and electric cooling fans. The temperature of the intake air rises due to the compression action of the turbocharger – the purpose of the intercooler is to cool the intake air again, before it enters the engine. Because cool air is denser than hot air, this allows a greater mass of air (occupying the same volume) to be forced into the combustion chambers, resulting in a further increase in the engine's thermal efficiency.
4 Boost pressure (the pressure in the inlet manifold) is limited by a wastegate, which diverts the exhaust gas away from the turbine

15.94a Disconnect the wiring plug from the limp-home solenoid (arrowed) . . .

15.94b . . . then undo the two retaining screws (arrowed)

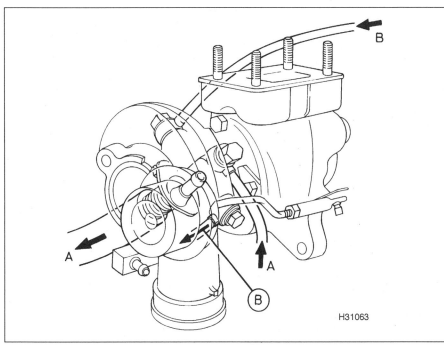

16.6 Turbocharger lubrication and cooling circuit connections

A Lubrication   *B Cooling*

wheel in response to a pressure-sensitive actuator. The wastegate valve is controlled by the engine management system ECM, via an electronic boost control valve. The ECM opens and closes (modulates) the boost valve several times a second, which results in manifold vacuum being applied to the wastegate valve in a series of rapid pulses – the duty ratio of the pulses depends primarily on engine speed and load. The ECM monitors boost pressure via the manifold pressure sensor, and uses the boost control valve to maintain pressure at an optimum level throughout the engine speed range. If the ECM detects that combustion pre-ignition ('pinking' or 'knocking') is taking place, the boost pressure is reduced accordingly to prevent engine damage; see Chapter 5B for greater detail.

5 A boost bypass valve fitted in the airflow between the low-pressure supply and high-pressure delivery sides of the turbocharger compressor allows excess boost to be dumped into the intake air ducting when the throttle is closed at high engine speed (ie, during overrun or deceleration). This improves driveability by preventing compressor stall (and therefore reducing turbo 'lag'), and also by eliminating the surging that would otherwise occur when the throttle is reopened.

6 The turbo shaft is pressure-lubricated by an oil feed pipe from the main oil gallery. The shaft 'floats' on a cushion of oil and has no moving bearings. A drain pipe returns the oil to the sump. The turbine housing is water-cooled and has a dedicated system of coolant supply and return pipes **(see illustration)**.

Precautions

- The turbocharger operates at extremely high speeds and temperatures. Certain precautions must be observed during servicing activities, to avoid injury to the operator, or premature failure of the turbo.
- Do not operate the turbo with any of its parts exposed, or with any of its hoses removed. Foreign objects falling onto the rotating vanes could cause excessive damage, and (if ejected) personal injury.
- Do not race the engine immediately after start-up, especially if it is cold. Give the oil a few seconds to circulate.
- Always allow the engine to return to idle speed before switching it off – do not blip the throttle and switch off, as this will leave the turbo spinning without lubrication.
- Allow the engine to idle for a few minutes before switching off after a high-speed run. This will allow the turbine housing to cool before the coolant stops circulating under pressure.
- Observe the recommended intervals for oil and filter changing, and use a reputable oil of the specified quality. Infrequent oil changes, or use of inferior oil, can cause carbon formation on the turbo shaft, leading to subsequent failure.

17 Turbocharger – removal and refitting

Note 1: The exhaust system and turbocharger may still be hot, make sure the vehicle has cooled down before working on the engine.
Note 2: Saab recommend that the oil and filter should be changed (as described in Chapter 1A) when renewing the turbocharger.

Removal

1 Apply the handbrake, then jack up the front of the car and support on axle stands (see *Jacking and vehicle support*).
2 Remove the shield from beneath the radiator, then drain the cooling system as described in Chapter 1A.
3 Undo the retaining bolts and remove the turbocharger stay bracket **(see illustration)**.
4 Slacken the unions and disconnect the oil supply and return pipes from the turbocharger **(see illustrations)**. Plug the open ports to prevent contamination.
5 Working at the top of the engine, undo the

17.3 Undo the two retaining bolts (arrowed) from the exhaust stay bracket

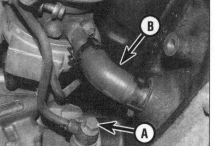

17.4a Disconnect the oil supply pipe (A) and oil return pipe (B)

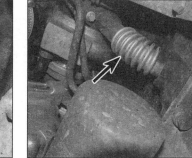

17.4b On some models the return pipe (arrowed) is a metal corrugated pipe

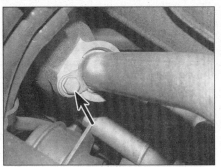

17.6a Undo the retaining bolt (arrowed) . . .

17.6b . . . and release the securing clip (arrowed)

17.7 Remove the rubber cover (arrowed) and disconnect the wiring connector

retaining nut and unclip the heat shield from the exhaust manifold.

6 Undo the retaining bolt/clips and remove the air bypass hose **(see illustrations)**. Note

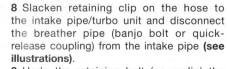
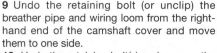

17.8a Slacken the retaining clip (A) and breather pipe banjo bolt (B)

that there is an O-ring seal at the connection to the intake pipe.

7 Disconnect the wiring connectors from the charge air control valve **(see illustration)**.

17.8b On some models the breather pipe has a quick-release coupling (arrowed)

8 Slacken retaining clip on the hose to the intake pipe/turbo unit and disconnect the breather pipe (banjo bolt or quick-release coupling) from the intake pipe **(see illustrations)**.

9 Undo the retaining bolt (or unclip) the breather pipe and wiring loom from the right-hand end of the camshaft cover and move them to one side.

10 Undo the retaining bolt(s) and remove the lifting eye from the front of the cylinder head **(see illustration)**.

11 Disconnect the quick-release coupling on the EVAP hose **(see illustration)**.

12 Undo the retaining bolt and withdraw the intake pipe V-clamp from the turbo, then withdraw the intake pipe **(see illustrations)**. Disconnect the vacuum hose as the intake pipe is removed.

13 From under the vehicle, slacken the securing clip on the hose from the charge air cooler to the turbo and disconnect **(see illustration)**. Plug the open ports to prevent contamination or damage to the turbo.

14 Unbolt and remove the exhaust system front pipe from the turbo, carefully lower the front pipe on to an axle stand (or similar) taking care not to damage it (see Section 21 of this Chapter).

⚠️ *Warning: The flexible section of the exhaust should not be bent out of alignment by anymore than 5° as this can cause damage to the exhaust causing leakage and noise.*

15 Undo the unions and detach the coolant supply pipe from the water pump and the

17.10 Undo the three retaining bolts (arrowed)

17.11 Disconnect the coupling on the EVAP hose

17.12a Slacken the clamp securing bolt (arrowed)

17.12b Disconnect the vacuum pipe as the intake pipe is removed

17.13 Slacken the retaining clip (arrowed) from the hose

17.15a Undo the coolant pipe (arrowed) from the water pump . . .

17.15b . . . and the coolant pipe (arrowed) from the front of the turbocharger

17.16 Undo the coolant pipe (arrowed) from the rear of the turbocharger

turbo housing **(see illustrations)**, retrieve the copper sealing washers. Plug the open ports to prevent contamination.

16 Undo the unions and detach the coolant return pipe from the turbo housing **(see illustration)**. Retrieve the copper sealing washers, then plug the open ports to prevent contamination.

17 Apply some easing oil to the exhaust manifold studs, then slacken the turbocharger securing nuts and remove the turbocharger from the vehicle **(see illustration)**. Check around the turbocharger for any pipes that may still be connected.

Refitting

18 Refitting is a reversal of removal, noting the following points:

a) Fill the turbocharger interchamber with clean engine oil, through the oil supply union on the turbocharger. This is important, as the turbocharger must have oil in it when the engine is started.

b) Thoroughly clean the exhaust manifold mating surface, before refitting the turbocharger.

c) Renew all copper union sealing washers, O-ring seals and gaskets, where applicable.

d) Tighten all nuts, bolts and oil and coolant unions to the correct torque settings, where specified.

e) Apply a suitable high-temperature, anti-seize compound to the threads of the exhaust system-to-turbocharger and exhaust manifold-to-turbocharger studs and nuts.

f) Ensure that the charge air (boost) control valve hoses are refitted correctly to the turbocharger, wastegate actuator and air hose.

19 On completion, check that the radiator drain plug is tight, then refit the shield panel.

20 Lower the car to the ground, then check and if necessary top-up the engine oil level (see Weekly checks). If not already done, it is strongly recommended that the engine oil is changed before starting the engine if a new turbocharger has been fitted, as this will protect the turbo bearings during the 'running-in' period.

21 Refill the cooling system (see Chapter 1A).

22 It is recommended that the boost pressure is checked by a Saab dealer at the earliest opportunity.

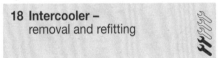

18 Intercooler – removal and refitting

Removal

1 Remove the front grille as described in Chapter 11.

2 Refer to Chapter 12 and remove the horn, both headlights and both direction indicators.

3 Raise the front of the vehicle and support it securely on axle stands (see Jacking and vehicle support). Remove the front bumper, as described in Chapter 11.

4 Release the hose clips and disconnect the air hoses from the left hand end of the intercooler. On some models it will also be necessary to unbolt the heat shield from the exhaust manifold.

5 Unscrew the intercooler securing bolts, and remove them together with the mounting pillars, washers and grommets.

6 Move the intercooler away from the front panel, lift it from its mountings, and withdraw it from the engine compartment.

Refitting

7 Refitting is a reversal of removal. Ensure that the air hose clips are securely tightened.

19 Inlet manifold – removal and refitting

> **Warning: Refer to the precautions given in Section 1, and the information detailed in the 'Safety first!' Section of this manual, before disturbing any component in the fuel supply system.**

Removal

1 Disconnect the battery negative lead (refer to Disconnecting the battery in the Reference Chapter at the end of this manual).

2 Refer to Section 14 or 15, and remove the throttle body from the inlet manifold.

3 Remove the fuel rail and fuel injectors from the inlet manifold as described in Section 14 or 15.

4 Disconnect the brake servo vacuum hose from the inlet manifold **(see illustration)**.

5 Unplug the wiring from the coolant temperature sensor **(see illustration)**.

6 Unscrew the mounting bolts securing

17.17 Slacken the four turbocharger securing bolts (arrowed)

19.4 Press the collar down and release the vacuum pipe

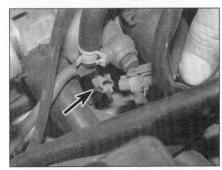

19.5 Disconnecting the wiring connector from the temperature sensor (arrowed)

19.6 Remove the upper and lower retaining bolts (arrowed)

19.7 Removing the intake manifold and gasket

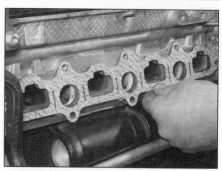

19.8a Fitting an inlet manifold gasket – non-turbo model shown

the inlet manifold to the cylinder head. Also unscrew the lower bolt from the steady bar **(see illustration)**.

7 Withdraw the inlet manifold from the cylinder head **(see illustration)**. Where applicable, carefully withdraw the intake air heating plate, unplugging the wiring at the multiway connector. Recover the gasket from the cylinder head.

Refitting

8 Refitting is a reversal of removal. Fit a new gasket **(see illustrations)** and, where applicable, reconnect the intake air heating plate wiring. Ensure that the manifold retaining bolts are tightened to the specified torque.

20 Exhaust manifold – removal and refitting

Non-turbo models

Removal

1 Apply the handbrake, then jack up the front of the car and support on axle stands (see *Jacking and vehicle support*).

2 Disconnect the oxygen sensor wiring with reference to Section 14.

3 Remove the exhaust system front pipe and catalytic converter with reference to Section 21.

4 Remove the auxiliary drivebelt as described in Chapter 1A. To gain access to the right-hand exhaust manifold nuts, the power steering fluid pump must be unbolted and moved aside; see Chapter 10 for details. Note that there is no need to disconnect the hydraulic fluid pipes.

5 Unscrew and remove the exhaust manifold mounting nuts, then lift the manifold from the cylinder head. Note that the manifold is in two sections; the centre section should be removed first, noting that on the remaining section, sleeves are fitted beneath all the mounting nuts **(see illustrations)**.

H31064

19.8b Inlet manifold and associated components – Turbo model shown

1 Gasket	3 Heating plate wiring	4 Inlet manifold
2 Heating plate	connector	5 Support stay

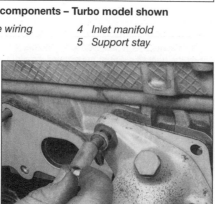

20.5a Removing the centre section of the exhaust manifold (non-turbo models)

20.5b Removing the sleeves from the outer section of the exhaust manifold (non-turbo models)

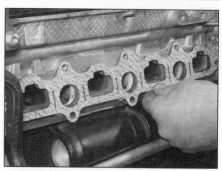

20.5c Removing the outer section of the exhaust manifold (non-turbo models)

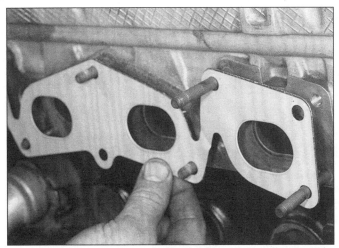

20.6 Removing the exhaust manifold gasket (non-turbo models)

20.8 Tighten the exhaust manifold nuts to the specified torque

6 Remove the gasket from the studs on the cylinder head **(see illustration)**.

Refitting

7 Clean the contact surfaces of the cylinder head and exhaust manifold.

8 Refit the exhaust manifold to the studs on the cylinder head, together with a new gasket, then tighten the mounting nuts to the specified torque **(see illustration)**. Make sure that the sleeves are correctly located, as previously described. Refit the outer section of the manifold first, and tighten the mounting nuts to the specified torque, then refit the centre section and tighten the nuts.

9 Refit the power steering pump with reference to Chapter 10.

10 Refit the auxiliary drivebelt as described in Chapter 1A.

11 Refit the exhaust front pipe with reference to Section 21.

12 Reconnect the oxygen sensor wiring with reference to Section 14.

13 Lower the car to the ground.

Turbo models

Removal

14 Remove the turbocharger as described in Section 17.

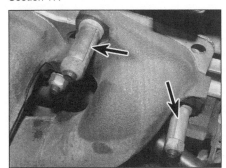

20.16 Note the position of the sleeves fitted beneath some of the stud nuts (turbo models)

15 Remove the auxiliary drivebelt as described in Chapter 1A. To gain access to the right-hand exhaust manifold nuts, the power steering fluid pump must be unbolted and moved aside; see Chapter 10 for details. Note that there is no need to disconnect the hydraulic fluid pipes.

16 Unscrew and remove the exhaust manifold mounting nuts, then lift the manifold from the cylinder head. Note that sleeves are fitted beneath the outer nuts on the longer studs **(see illustration)**.

17 Remove the gasket from the studs on the cylinder head **(see illustration)**.

Refitting

18 Clean the contact surfaces of the cylinder head and exhaust manifold.

19 Refit the exhaust manifold to the studs on the cylinder head together with a new gasket, then tighten the mounting nuts to the specified torque. Make sure that the sleeves are correctly located, as previously noted.

20 Refit the power steering pump with reference to Chapter 10.

21 Refit the auxiliary drivebelt as described in Chapter 1A.

22 Refit the turbocharger with reference to Section 17.

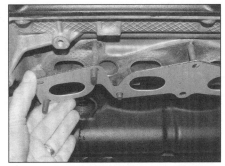

20.17 Renew the manifold gasket (turbo models)

21 Exhaust system – general information and component removal

General information

1 The exhaust system consists of four sections:

  a) *The front pipe (incorporating a three-way catalytic converter).*
  b) *The intermediate pipe.*
  c) *The centre silencer.*
  d) *The rear silencer and tailpipe.*

2 The exhaust system sections are joined by flanges with internal flared tube ends, and no gaskets. The front pipe-to-manifold/turbocharger joint is gasketed, and is secured by studs and nuts. The front pipe and the connector pipes between the silencers are aluminium-plated. The silencers are made of chrome steel plate.

3 A oxygen (lambda) sensor is located in the front pipe, upstream of the catalytic converter, and, on later models there is a second sensor located downstream of the catalytic converter.

4 On non-turbo models, the front pipe is of twin-branch type. On turbo models, the single front pipe incorporates an elbow at its front end which is connected to the turbocharger.

5 On all models, the system is suspended throughout its entire length by rubber mountings.

Removal

6 Each exhaust section can be removed individually. Alternatively, it is possible to remove the complete exhaust system in one piece.

7 To remove a section of the system, first jack up the front or rear of the car and support it on axle stands (see *Jacking and vehicle support*). Alternatively, position the car over an inspection pit, or on car ramps.

21.9 Unscrew the nuts and separate the flange joint between the front pipe and the intermediate pipe

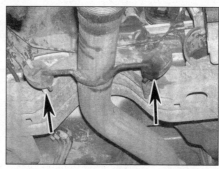

21.10 Unhook the mounting rubbers from the underbody

Intermediate silencer

14 Unscrew the nuts/bolts, and separate the flange joints connecting the intermediate silencer to the intermediate pipe, and to the rear silencer and tailpipe.

15 Unhook the mounting rubbers from the underbody, and lower the intermediate silencer and pipe to the ground.

Rear silencer and tailpipe

16 Unscrew the bolts, and separate the flange joint connecting the rear silencer and tailpipe to the intermediate silencer and pipe.

17 Unhook the mounting rubbers from the underbody, and lower the rear silencer and tailpipe to the ground.

Front pipe and catalytic converter

Note: *The catalytic converter contains a fragile ceramic element, and should be handled with care to prevent internal damage.*

8 Remove the oxygen sensor(s) as described in Section 14 or 15.

9 Unscrew the nuts and separate the flange joint between the front pipe and the intermediate pipe **(see illustration)**.

10 Unhook the mounting rubbers from the underbody **(see illustration)**. Where applicable, remove the bolt securing the catalytic converter to its support bracket.

11 Unscrew the nuts securing the front pipe to the turbocharger or exhaust manifold (as

applicable), then lower the pipe between the engine and the front subframe crossmember **(see illustrations)**. Recover the gaskets.

Intermediate pipe

⚠️ **Warning: The flexible section of the exhaust should not be bent out of alignment by anymore than 5° as this can cause damage causing leakage and noise.**

12 Unscrew the nuts, and separate the flange joints connecting the intermediate pipe to the front pipe, and the intermediate silencer.

13 Unhook the mounting rubbers from the underbody, and lower the front silencer and pipe to the ground.

Heat shields

18 The heat shields are secured to the underbody by bolts. Each shield can be removed once the relevant exhaust section has been removed. If a shield is being removed to gain access to a component located behind it, it may prove sufficient in some cases to remove the retaining nuts and/or bolts, and simply lower the shield, without disturbing the exhaust system.

Refitting

19 Each section is refitted by a reversal of the removal sequence, noting the following points:

a) *Ensure that all traces of corrosion have been removed from the flared tube ends in the flanges, and renew the front pipe-to-exhaust manifold/turbocharger gasket(s).*

b) *Inspect the rubber mountings for signs of damage or deterioration, and renew as necessary.*

c) *Refit the oxygen sensors with reference to Section 14 or 15 as applicable.*

d) *Make sure that all rubber mountings are correctly located, and that there is adequate clearance between the exhaust system and underbody.*

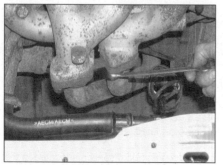

21.11a Unscrew the nuts securing the front pipe to the exhaust manifold (non-turbo model shown) . . .

21.11b . . . then remove the front pipe

Chapter 4 Part B:
Fuel and exhaust systems – diesel engine models

Contents

Degrees of difficulty

Easy, suitable for novice with little experience	**Fairly easy,** suitable for beginner with some experience	**Fairly difficult,** suitable for competent DIY mechanic	**Difficult,** suitable for experienced DIY mechanic	**Very difficult,** suitable for expert DIY or professional

Specifications

Engine identification

Manufacturer's code
D223L ....

Engine type
2.2 litre high-pressure turbo diesel engine

General
System type ....

System designation:
  1998 to 2001 models ....
  2001 to 2002 models ....

Direct injection system incorporating an electronically-controlled VP44 fuel injection pump. Turbocharger and intercooler on all engines

Bosch EDC15
Bosch PSG16

Adjustment data
Idle speed
  Cold engine ....
  Warm engine ....
Maximum speed ....

1150 rpm – controlled by ECU
900 rpm – controlled by ECU
4930 to 5070 rpm – controlled by ECU

Injection pump
Direction of rotation ....
Pump timing (static) ....

Clockwise, viewed from sprocket end
Preset – controlled by ECU

Injectors
Opening pressure ....

220 to 380 bar

Torque wrench settings

	Nm	lbf ft
Camshaft sprocket bolt*:		
Stage 1	90	66
Stage 2	Angle-tighten a further 60°	
Coolant temperature sensor	18	13
Crankshaft position sensor	8	6
Exhaust front pipe:		
To intermediate pipe	20	15
To turbocharger*	20	15
Exhaust manifold:		
Retaining nuts*	22	16
Support bracket bolts	25	18
Fuel injector pipe union nuts	25	18
Fuel supply and return pipe union bolts	25	18
High-pressure fuel lines to injection pump and crossover pipes	25	18
Inlet manifold:		
Lower section-to-cylinder head nuts	20	15
Upper section-to-lower section bolts	10	7
Injection pump:		
Front mounting bolts	25	18
Rear mounting bracket bolts	20	15
MAP sensor	8	6
Timing chain:		
Tensioner cap (upper and lower)	60	44
Upper chain guide bolts*	8	6
Turbocharger	30	22
Turbocharger oil delivery pipe	20	15
Turbocharger oil return pipe	30	22
Vacuum hose to vacuum pump	18	13

* Use new fasteners

---

1 General information and precautions

General information

1 The fuel system consists of a rear-mounted fuel tank, a fuel filter with integral water separator, a fuel injection pump, injectors and associated components.

2 Fuel is drawn from the fuel tank by the fuel injection pump. Before reaching the pump, the fuel passes through a fuel filter, where foreign matter and water are removed. Excess fuel lubricates the moving components of the pump, and is then returned to the tank.

3 The fuel injection pump is driven at half-crankshaft speed by the timing chain. The high pressure required to inject the fuel into the compressed air in the cylinder is achieved by a radial piston pump.

4 The injection pump is electronically-controlled to meet the latest emission standards. The system consists of the engine electronic control unit (ECU) and the following sensors and components. On the EDC15 system, the ECU is mounted remotely on the right-hand side of the bulkhead, whereas on the PSG16 system, the ECU is integral with the injection pump.

a) *ECU – the electronic control unit controls the entire operation of the fuel injection and turbocharger systems.*

b) *Accelerator pedal position sensor – informs the ECU of the accelerator pedal position.*

c) *Coolant temperature sensor – informs the ECU of engine temperature.*

d) *Oil temperature sensor – informs ECU of the temperature of the engine oil.*

e) *Mass airflow meter – informs the ECU of the amount of air passing through the intake duct.*

f) *Crankshaft position sensor – informs the ECU of engine speed and crankshaft position.*

g) *Charge air boost pressure control valve – controls the turbocharger wastegate.*

h) *Manifold absolute pressure sensor (EDC15 system only) – informs ECU of the pressure in the inlet manifold in order to calculate the duration of fuel injection and turbocharger wastegate.*

i) *Intake air temperature sensor – informs the ECU of the temperature of the air passing through the airflow meter. On the EDC15 system, the air temperature sensor is built into the mass airflow meter, and cannot be renewed separately. On the PSG16 system, the sensor is mounted on the inlet manifold – note that as from VIN 12020001-on, the sensor also includes a pressure sensor.*

j) *Swirl throttle control valve and vacuum box (PSG16 system only) – during light loads, diverts all air through the inlet manifold swirl passage in order to improve combustion chamber mixing.*

k) *Atmospheric pressure sensor (PSG16 system only) – informs the ECU of ambient atmospheric pressure*

l) *Oil level sensor (PSG16 system only) – informs the ECU of engine oil level.*

m) *EGR valve and control module – see Chapter 4C.*

n) *Glow plug control module – see Chapter 5C.*

Other sensors which send information to the ECU are as follows:

a) *Cruise control switch – driver input for speed adjustment.*

b) *Brake pedal switch – used by the ECUs for cruise control functions.*

c) *Clutch switch – used by the ECUs for cruise control functions.*

d) *Air conditioning system relay – informs ECU when the air conditioning system is switched on.*

5 All the above information is analysed by the ECU and, based on this, the ECU determines the appropriate injection requirements for the engine. The ECU controls the injection pump timing, to provide the best setting for cranking, starting (with either a hot or cold engine), warm-up, idle, cruising, and acceleration.

6 Basic injection timing is determined when the pump is fitted. When the engine is running, it is varied automatically to suit the prevailing engine speed by the engine management ECU.

7 The ECU also controls the exhaust gas recirculation (EGR) system (see Chapter 4C), however, the glow plug preheating system is controlled by a separate module mounted in the engine compartment (see Chapter 5C).

8 The four fuel injectors produce a spray of fuel directly into the cylinders. The injectors are calibrated to open and close at critical pressures to provide efficient and even combustion. Each injector needle is lubricated by fuel, which accumulates in the spring chamber and is channelled to the injection pump return hose by leak-off pipes.

9 On the PSG16 system, the inlet manifold is fitted with a butterfly valve arrangement to improve efficiency at low engine speeds. Each cylinder has two intake tracts in the manifold, one of which is fitted a valve (swirl control valve); the operation of the valve is controlled by the ECU via a solenoid valve and vacuum diaphragm unit. At low engine speeds (below approximately 1500 rpm) the valves remain closed, meaning that air entering each cylinder is passing through only one of the two manifold tracts. At higher engine speeds, the ECU opens up each of the four valves allowing the air passing through the manifold to pass through both inlet tracts.

10 A turbocharger is fitted to increase engine efficiency by raising the pressure in the inlet manifold above atmospheric pressure. Instead of the air simply being sucked into the cylinders, it is forced in. Additional fuel is supplied by the injection pump in proportion to the increased air intake.

11 Energy for the operation of the turbocharger comes from the exhaust gas. The gas flows through a specially-shaped housing (the turbine housing) and in so doing, spins the turbine wheel. The turbine wheel is attached to a shaft, at the end of which is another vaned wheel known as the compressor wheel. The compressor wheel spins in its own housing, and compresses the inlet air on the way to the inlet manifold.

12 Between the turbocharger and the inlet manifold, the compressed air passes through an intercooler. This air-to-air heat exchanger is mounted next to the radiator, and supplied with cooling air from the front of the vehicle. The purpose of the intercooler is to remove some of the heat gained by the inlet air by being compressed. Because cooler air is denser, removal of this heat further increases engine efficiency.

13 Charge (boost) pressure which is the pressure in the inlet manifold, is limited by a wastegate. This diverts the exhaust gas away from the turbine wheel in response to a pressure-sensitive actuator. A pressure-operated switch operates a warning light on the instrument panel in the event of excessive charge pressure developing.

14 The turbo shaft is pressure-lubricated by an oil feed pipe from the engine main oil so that the shaft 'floats' on a cushion of oil. A drain pipe returns the oil to the sump.

15 The charge (boost) pressure wastegate is controlled by the ECU via a solenoid valve.

16 If there is an abnormality in any of the readings obtained from any sensor, the ECU

enters its back-up mode. In this event, the ECU ignores the abnormal sensor signal, and assumes a preprogrammed value which will allow the engine to continue running (albeit at reduced efficiency). If the ECU enters this back-up mode, the warning light on the instrument panel will come on, and the relevant fault code will be stored in the ECU memory.

17 If the warning light comes on, the vehicle should be taken to a Saab dealer at the earliest opportunity. A complete test of the injection system can then be carried out, using a special electronic diagnostic test unit which is simply plugged into the system's diagnostic connector. The connector is located on the underside of the facia, on the driver's side of the vehicle.

Precautions

⚠️ *Warning: It is necessary to take certain precautions when working on the fuel system components, particularly the fuel injectors. Before carrying out any operations on the fuel system, refer to the precautions given in 'Safety first!' at the beginning of this manual, and to any additional warning notes at the start of the relevant Sections. Caution: Do not operate the engine if any of air intake ducts are disconnected or the filter element is removed. Any debris entering the engine will cause severe damage to the turbocharger.*
Caution: To prevent damage to the turbocharger, do not race the engine immediately after start-up, especially if it is cold. Allow it to idle smoothly to give the oil a few seconds to circulate around the turbocharger bearings. Always allow the engine to return to idle speed before switching it off – do not blip the throttle and switch off, as this will leave the turbo spinning without lubrication.
Caution: Observe the recommended intervals for oil and filter changing, and use a reputable oil of the specified quality. Neglect of oil changing, or use of inferior oil, can cause carbon formation on the turbo shaft, leading to subsequent failure.

---

2 Air cleaner assembly and intake ducts – removal and refitting

Removal

1 Loosen the clip securing the mass airflow meter to the air cleaner cover, and release the airflow meter.

2 Release the clips and lift off the cover from the air cleaner base.

3 Note how the filter element is fitted, then lift it out.

4 Unscrew the mounting nuts (one at the front and one at the rear), then withdraw the base from the engine compartment.

5 The inlet air resonator is located beneath the right-hand front wing. To remove it, apply the handbrake, then jack up the front of the vehicle and support it on axle stands (see *Jacking and vehicle support*). Remove the splash guard, then undo the screws and lower the resonator.

6 Clean away any debris from inside the air cleaner base and cover.

Refitting

7 Refitting is a reversal of removal, ensuring that all intake ducts are properly reconnected and their retaining clips securely tightened.

---

3 Accelerator cable – removal, refitting and adjustment

Removal

1 At the right-hand rear corner of the engine compartment, remove the cover from the pedal position sensor (potentiometer).

2 Release the clip and unhook the accelerator inner cable from the sensor sector. Release the outer cable from the bracket.

3 Release the cable ties securing the cable to the crossbar.

4 Working in the driver's footwell, remove the facia lower trim panel, then disconnect the accelerator cable from the top of the accelerator pedal with reference to Section 4.

5 Pull the accelerator cable through the bulkhead into the engine compartment and remove it from the vehicle. If necessary to facilitate refitting, attach a length of string to the cable as it is being removed, then untie the string and leave it in position through the bulkhead.

Refitting and adjustment

6 Pass the accelerator cable through the bulkhead aperture and into the space behind the facia, above the driver's footwell. Reconnect the inner cable and bushing to the top of the accelerator pedal, and the outer cable to the bracket.

7 In the engine compartment, fit the outer cable to the bracket, then hook the inner cable onto the pedal position sensor sector and fit the clip.

8 To adjust the cable, turn the outer cable adjuster until the sector starts to move, then back it off by one half turn.

9 Refit the cover to the sensor.

10 Refit the facia lower trim panel.

---

4 Accelerator pedal – removal and refitting

Removal

1 Disconnect the accelerator cable from the pedal position sensor with reference to Section 3.

2 Working in the driver's footwell, release the fasteners and detach the lower cover panel from the underside of the facia. On certain models, it may be necessary to first undo the screws and release the diagnostic connector from the underside of the facia.

3 Reach up behind the facia and unhook the accelerator cable from the top of the accelerator pedal.

4 Compress the pedal return spring and release it from the pedal arm.

5 Using a pair of pliers, pull the locking clip from the end of the pedal pivot shaft and recover the bush.

6 Withdraw the pedal from its mounting bracket and remove it from the vehicle.

Refitting

7 Refitting is a reversal of removal. On completion, adjust the accelerator cable with reference to Section 3.

5	**Fuel system –** priming and bleeding

1 It is not essential to manually prime and bleed the fuel system after any operation on the system components, although, the start-up time can be reduced by connecting a suitable vacuum pump to the service outlet on the injection pump and drawing fuel through the system until it is bubble-free. Refit the service outlet cap before starting the engine.

2 Start the engine (this may take longer than usual, especially if the fuel system has been allowed to run dry – operate the starter in ten second bursts with 5 seconds rest in between each operation) and run it at a fast idle speed for a minute or so to purge any trapped air from the fuel lines. After this time the engine should idle smoothly at a constant speed.

3 If the engine idles roughly, then there is still some air trapped in the fuel system. Increase the engine speed again for another minute or so then recheck the idle speed. Repeat this procedure as necessary until the engine is idling smoothly.

6	**Fuel gauge sender unit** – removal and refitting

1 Refer to Chapter 4A, noting that there is no fuel pump in the fuel tank, just a fuel pick-up filter and sender unit.

7	**Fuel tank –** removal and refitting

1 Refer to Chapter 4A, noting that instead of a fuel filter clipped to the tank strap, it will be necessary to remove the fuel filter as described in Chapter 1B. Plug the fuel hose ends to prevent the fuel draining from the system;

this will enable the engine to be started more easily once the fuel tank has been refitted. Note that in some cold territories, an auxiliary heater fuel pump is fitted in front of the fuel tank.

8	**Maximum speed –** checking and adjustment	

Caution: The maximum speed is controlled by the ECU and cannot be adjusted by the home mechanic. The speed can be checked using a tachometer as described below, but if adjustment is needed, it will be necessary to take the vehicle to a Saab dealer who will have access to the necessary diagnostic equipment required to test and adjust the settings.

1 Run the engine to normal operating temperature.

2 Have an assistant fully depress the accelerator pedal, and check that the maximum engine speed is as given in the Specifications. Do not keep the engine at maximum speed for more than two or three seconds.

9	**Injection system electrical components –** removal and refitting	

Electronic control unit (EDC15 system)

Removal

1 Ensure that the ignition is switched off. Disconnect the battery negative lead (refer to *Disconnecting the battery* in the *Reference* Chapter at the end of this manual).

2 Working inside the vehicle, in the right-hand footwell, remove the fixings and lower the cover panel away from the underside of the facia and steering column. On LHD models, it will be necessary to remove the glovebox.

3 Peel back the carpet to expose the ECU mounted on the bodywork at the base of the A-pillar.

4 Release the locking lever and unplug the multiplug wiring harness connector from the underside of the ECU. **Note:** *To prevent potential damage to the internal circuitry of the ECU from static electricity, prior to disconnecting the multiplug, earth yourself by touching part of the vehicle body.*

5 Unscrew the mounting bolt and withdraw the ECU from inside the car.

Refitting

6 Refitting is a reversal of removal. Ensure that the wiring harness multiplug connector is secured with the locking lever. Note that if a new ECU has been fitted, it will gradually 'learn' the engines characteristics as the vehicle is driven. Drivability, performance and fuel economy may be slightly reduced

during this period. Saab also state that the immobiliser must be reset using their Tech2 diagnostic tool.

Electronic control unit (PSG16 system)

7 The control unit is an integral part of the injection pump and should not be disturbed. **Never** attempt to separate the control unit and pump.

Accelerator pedal position sensor

Removal

8 At the right-hand rear corner of the engine compartment, remove the cover from the pedal position sensor (potentiometer) and disconnect the wiring.

9 Release the clip and unhook the accelerator inner cable from the sensor sector.

10 Unbolt and remove the pedal position sensor.

Refitting

11 Refit the sensor and tighten the bolts.

12 Hook the inner cable onto the pedal position sensor sector and fit the clip.

13 To adjust the cable, turn the outer cable adjuster until the sector starts to move, then back it off by one half turn.

14 Refit the cover to the sensor.

Coolant temperature sensor

Removal

15 Drain the cooling system as described in Chapter 1B. Alternatively, the new sensor may be fitted immediately after removing the old one, or a suitable plug may be fitted in the aperture while the sensor is removed. If the latter option is used, carefully loosen the expansion tank filler cap to release any pressure in the cooling system, then retighten the cap.

16 With the wiring disconnected, unscrew the sensor and remove it. If the new sensor is at hand, place a finger over the aperture to prevent loss of coolant from the cylinder head.

Refitting

17 Apply some copper grease to its threads, then insert the sensor, and tighten it to the specified torque.

18 Reconnect the wiring.

9.18 Disconnect the oil temperature sensor wiring connector

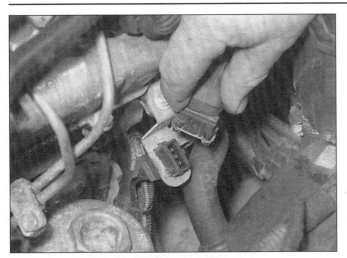

9.24 Disconnect the wiring connector . . .

9.26 . . . then undo the retaining screw and remove the crankshaft sensor from the front of the cylinder block (sealing ring arrowed)

19 Refill the cooling system as described in Chapter 1B. If the system was not completely drained, top it up.

Oil temperature sensor

Removal

20 Firmly apply the handbrake then jack up the front of the vehicle and support it on axle stands. Where necessary, undo the retaining bolts and remove the undercover from beneath the engine/transmission unit.
21 Drain the engine oil as described in Chapter 1B. Once the oil has finished draining, fit a new sealing ring then refit the drain plug and tighten it to the specified torque.
22 Disconnect the wiring connector then unscrew the sensor from the front of the sump (see illustration). Discard the seal.

Refitting

23 Refitting is the reverse of removal, but use a new seal and refill the engine with oil as described in Chapter 1B.

Mass airflow meter

Removal

24 Ensure the ignition is switched off then disconnect the wiring connector from the airflow meter.
25 Unscrew the retaining clips then free the airflow meter from the intake ducts and remove it from the engine compartment.

Refitting

26 Refitting is the reverse of removal, ensuring the intake ducts are correctly seated and their retaining clips are securely tightened.

Crankshaft position sensor

Removal

27 The crankshaft position sensor is located on the front left-hand end of the cylinder block. First, remove the engine top cover.
28 Trace the wiring back from the crankshaft

sensor to its wiring connector then free the connector from its bracket and disconnect it from the main harness (see illustration).
29 Apply the handbrake, then jack up the front of the vehicle and support it on axle stands (see *Jacking and vehicle support*). Remove the lower engine cover.
30 Wipe clean the area around the crankshaft sensor then unscrew and remove the retaining bolt. Remove the sensor from the front of the cylinder block and recover the sealing ring (see illustration).

Refitting

31 Refitting is the reverse of removal, using a new sealing ring. Tighten the sensor retaining bolt to the specified torque.

Charge air boost pressure control valve

Removal

32 At the rear of the engine compartment, lift the sealing moulding from the bulkhead for access to the pressure control valve bracket. Remove the bracket then disconnect the vacuum hoses and wiring, noting their locations.
33 Remove the control valve from the engine compartment.

Refitting

34 Refitting is a reversal of removal.

Manifold absolute pressure (MAP) sensor (EDC15 system)

Removal

35 Remove the engine top cover.
36 Undo the screws securing the wiring harness tray to the top of the inlet manifold and disconnect the wiring connector from the MAP sensor.
37 Unscrew the retaining bolt and remove the sensor from the top of the inlet manifold, noting the sealing ring fitted to the sensor shaft (see illustration).

Refitting

38 Refitting is the reverse of removal, using a new sealing ring and tightening the retaining bolt to the specified torque.

Intake air temperature/ pressure sensor (PSG16 system)

Removal

39 The intake air temperature sensor is located on the rear, left-hand end of the inlet manifold. First, remove the engine top cover.
40 Disconnect the wiring, then unclip the sensor from the bracket.

Refitting

41 Refitting is a reversal of removal.

Swirl throttle control valve

Removal

42 Unbolt the power steering fluid reservoir from behind the battery, and position it to one side.
43 Loosen the bolts from the swirl throttle control valve mounting bracket and lift the bracket. The bolt holes are slotted to enable the bracket to be removed. Note that there are two valves, the EGR system valve and

9.37 Disconnect the wiring connector then undo the retaining bolt (arrowed) and remove the pressure sensor

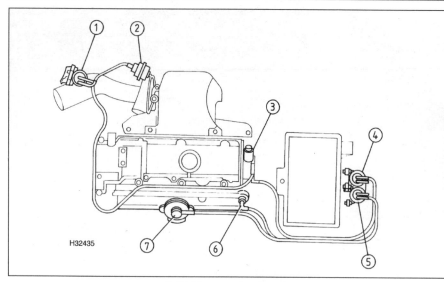

9.45 Vacuum pipe layout

1 *Charge pressure control solenoid valve*
2 *Charge pressure control actuator*
3 *Vacuum pump*
4 *EGR (exhaust gas recirculation) solenoid valve*
5 *Inlet manifold switchover solenoid valve*
6 *Inlet manifold switchover valve*
7 *EGR (exhaust gas recirculation) valve*

the manifold switchover valve; the manifold switchover valve can be identified by its grey wiring connector

44 Note the position of the vacuum hoses, then disconnect them.

45 Disconnect the wiring, then remove the control valve from the bracket **(see illustration)**.

Refitting

46 Refitting is a reversal of removal.

Swirl throttle vacuum box

Removal

47 The swirl throttle vacuum box is located on the left-hand end of the cylinder head. First, remove the engine top cover.

48 Disconnect the vacuum hose.

49 Unscrew the mounting bolts, then turn the vacuum box until the retaining tab and groove are aligned with each other so that the arm can be disconnected.

50 Remove the vacuum box from the bracket.

Refitting

51 Refitting is a reversal of removal, but apply a little grease to the arm bush.

Atmospheric pressure sensor (PSG16 system)

Removal

52 The atmospheric pressure sensor is located on the front right-hand end of the cylinder block.

53 Disconnect the wiring, then unscrew the mounting bolts and remove the sensor.

Refitting

54 Refitting is a reversal of removal.

Oil level sensor (PSG16 system)

Removal

55 Note that the oil level sensor and connector wire are removed from the inside of the sump. Refer to Chapter 2B and remove the sump. Clean all oil from the inside surfaces of the sump.

56 Extract the circlip from the outside of the sump, and withdraw the wiring socket into the sump.

57 Unbolt and remove the sensor from inside the sump.

Refitting

58 Refitting is a reversal of removal, but ensure that the mounting hole is clean before inserting the wiring socket in the sump. Apply a little petroleum jelly to the socket before refitting it.

Turbocharger wastegate solenoid

59 The wastegate (charge pressure) solenoid valve is located in the right-hand rear corner of the engine compartment.

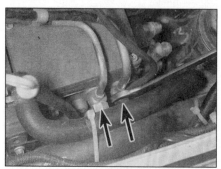

10.2 Undo the union bolts (arrowed) and disconnect the feed and return pipes from the pump

60 To gain access to the valve, remove the intake duct assembly linking the air cleaner housing to the turbocharger (see Section 2).

61 Disconnect the wiring connector and vacuum hoses from the valve then undo the retaining screws and remove the valve from its mounting bracket.

62 Refitting is the reverse of removal.

10 Fuel injection pump – removal and refitting

Caution: Be careful not to allow dirt into the injection pump or injector pipes during this procedure.

Note: Since it is necessary to remove the upper timing chain and sprockets to remove the injection pump, several special Saab service tools (or suitable alternatives) will be required on refitting to enable the valve timing to be accurately adjusted (see Section 4 of Chapter 2B). If access to suitable tools cannot be gained then it is recommended that this task is entrusted to a Saab dealer or suitably-equipped garage. If the task is to be carried out without these tools then accurate alignment marks must be made between the sprockets, camshaft and injection pump flange prior to removal. It is also likely that a special socket will also be needed to unscrew the pump front mounting bolts.

Note: A new camshaft sprocket bolt and upper timing chain guide bolts will be required on refitting.

Removal

1 Remove the inlet manifold as described in Section 15.

2 Remove all traces of dirt from around the injection pump fuel feed and return pipe unions. Unscrew the union bolts and sealing washers then disconnect both pipes and position them clear of the pump **(see illustration)**.

3 Remove the upper timing chain and sprockets as described in Chapter 2B.

4 Working through the holes in the lower timing chain sprocket, unscrew the pump front mounting bolts **(see illustration)**.

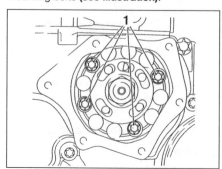

10.4 Unscrew the injection pump front mounting bolts (1) through the holes in the lower timing chain sprocket

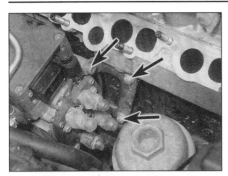

10.5a Unscrew the retaining bolts (arrowed – one hidden) and remove the rear mounting bracket . . .

10.5b . . . then remove the pump from the engine, noting the sealing ring

12.4 Remove the injector crossover pipe from the cylinder head (sealing ring arrowed) . . .

5 Unscrew the retaining bolts and remove the pump rear mounting bracket. Manoeuvre the pump out of position along with its sealing ring. Discard the sealing ring, a new one must be used on refitting **(see illustrations)**.
Caution: Never attempt to dismantle the pump assembly. If there is a problem, take the pump to a Saab dealer/diesel injection specialist for testing/repair.

Refitting

6 Prior to refitting, ensure the timing cut-out in the pump sprocket flange is correctly aligned with the locating hole in the pump body and check that the camshaft and crankshaft are still correctly positioned.
7 Ensure the mating surfaces are clean and dry and fit a new sealing ring to the pump flange.
8 Manoeuvre the pump into position, engaging the lower timing chain sprocket with the pump flange. Refit the pump front mounting bolts and tighten them to the specified torque setting.
9 Refit the mounting bracket to the rear of the injection pump and tighten its retaining bolts to the specified torque.
10 Refit the upper timing chain and sprockets as described in Chapter 2B.
11 Position a new sealing washer on each side of the injection pump feed and return pipe unions then refit the union bolts, tightening them to the specified torque.
12 Refit the inlet manifold as described in Section 15.
13 Reconnect the battery negative lead then

start the engine and bleed the fuel system as described in Section 5.

11 Injection timing – checking methods and adjustment

1 The injection timing is determined by the ECU using the information supplied by the various sensors. Checking of the injection system can only be carried out using specialist diagnostic equipment (see Section 1).

12 Fuel injectors – removal and refitting

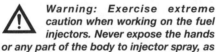

⚠ *Warning: Exercise extreme caution when working on the fuel injectors. Never expose the hands or any part of the body to injector spray, as the high working pressure can cause the fuel to penetrate the skin, with possibly fatal results. You are strongly advised to have any work which involves testing the injectors under pressure carried out by a dealer or fuel injection specialist.*
Caution: Be careful not to allow dirt into the injection pump, injectors or pipes during this procedure.
Caution: Take care not to drop the injectors, or allow the needles at their tips to become damaged. The injectors are precision-made

to fine limits, and must not be handled roughly. In particular, never mount them in a bench vice.
Note: *If the injector nozzle is to be removed from the cylinder head, it is likely that the special Saab puller (87 91 360) and adapter (83 95 378) will be needed. New injector crossover pipe bolts should be used on refitting.*
1 Remove the upper section of the inlet manifold as described in Section 15.
2 Remove the camshaft and followers as described in Chapter 2B.
3 Disconnect the return pipe from the injector crossover pipe.
4 Unscrew the retaining bolt then carefully free the crossover pipe from the top of the injector nozzle and ease it from the cylinder head **(see illustration)**.
5 Remove the sealing rings from the crossover pipe and the top of the injector nozzle and discard, new ones must be used on refitting **(see illustration)**.
6 Fit the adapter and puller to the top of the injector nozzle and carefully pull the nozzle squarely out of the top of the cylinder head. Recover the sealing washer which is fitted to the base of the nozzle and discard it.
7 Fit a new sealing washer to the base of the injector nozzle then carefully ease the nozzle into position in the cylinder head, aligning its locating pin with the cylinder head cut-out **(see illustrations)**.
8 Ensure the injector nozzle is pushed fully into the cylinder head then fit a new sealing ring to its upper end.

12.5 . . . then remove the sealing ring from the top of the injector nozzle

12.7a Fit a new sealing washer to the base of the nozzle . . .

12.7b . . . then refit the nozzle to the cylinder head, aligning its locating pin with the head cut-out (arrowed)

12.9a Tighten the injector crossover pipe bolt as tight as possible by hand . . .

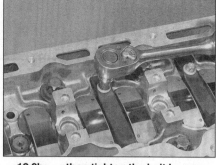

12.9b . . . then tighten the bolt by one complete turn

14.1 The intercooler is located in front of the radiator

9 Fit a new sealing ring to the crossover pipe recess. Ease the crossover pipe into position in the cylinder head, seating it correctly on the top of the injector nozzle, fit the new retaining bolt. Tighten the retaining bolt as tight as possible by hand, then using a socket and extension bar, tighten it through a further complete rotation (360°) **(see illustrations)**.

10 Connect the return pipe to the crossover pipe then refit the inlet manifold section as described in Section 15.

11 Refit the camshaft and followers as described in Chapter 2B.

12 On completion start the engine and bleed the fuel system as described in Section 4.

13 Turbocharger –
removal and refitting

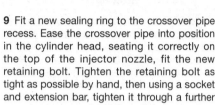

Note: *The turbocharger is of variable geometry design. At low engine speeds the vanes close to give less flow cross-section, then as the speed increases the vanes open to give an increased flow cross-section. This helps improve the efficiency of the turbocharger.*

Removal

1 Remove the exhaust manifold and turbocharger assembly as described in Section 16 and proceed as described under the relevant sub-heading.

2 With the assembly on bench, undo the retaining bolts and remove the exhaust connection flange and gasket from the turbocharger.

3 Unscrew the union bolt and remove the oil feed pipe. Recover the sealing washers fitted on each side of the pipe union.

4 Undo the retaining bolts and remove the oil return pipe and gasket.

5 Unscrew the mounting bolts then remove the turbocharger and gasket from the manifold.

6 Do not attempt to dismantle the turbocharger any further. If the unit is thought to be faulty take it to a turbo specialist or Saab dealer for testing and examination. They will be able to

inform you if the unit can be overhauled or will need renewing.

Refitting

7 Refitting is the reverse of removal, using new gaskets/sealing washers, and tightening the fasteners to their specified torque settings (where given). Refit the manifold and turbocharger assembly as described in Section 16.

14 Intercooler –
removal and refitting

Removal

1 The intercooler is located in front of the radiator. First, remove the front bumper as described in Chapter 11 **(see illustration)**.

2 Note the position of the hoses on the intercooler, then release the clips and disconnect them.

3 Unscrew and remove the intercooler securing bolts, together with the mounting pillars, washers and grommets.

4 Move the intercooler away from the front panel, lift it from its mountings, and withdraw it from the engine compartment.

Refitting

5 Refitting is a reversal of removal. Ensure that the air hose clips are securely tightened.

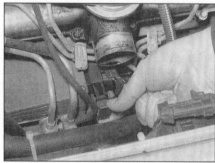

15.4 Disconnect the various wiring connectors and position the wiring harness tray clear of the manifold

15 Inlet manifold –
removal and refitting

Note: *New lower manifold section retaining nuts will be required on refitting.*

Removal

1 Disconnect the battery negative lead (refer to *Disconnecting the battery* in the *Reference* Chapter at the end of this manual). Remove the engine top cover, then remove the air duct linking the turbocharger to the intercooler. Release the cable ties where necessary.

2 Release the clip and disconnect the intercooler air duct from the inlet manifold, positioning it to one side.

3 Undo the retaining screws securing the wiring harness tray to the valve cover and inlet manifold elbow.

4 Disconnect the wiring connectors from the timing sensor, temperature sensor, EGR valve and oil filter housing **(see illustration)**.

5 Disconnect the vacuum pipe from the exhaust gas recirculation (EGR) valve on the manifold.

6 Undo the screws and remove the inlet elbow from the top of the inlet manifold **(see illustration)**. Recover the gasket.

7 Identify their positions, then disconnect the fuel return hoses from the injectors.

8 Wipe clean the pipe unions then unscrew the union nuts securing the injector pipes to the injectors and the four union nuts securing

15.6 Inlet elbow on top of the inlet manifold

15.8a Unscrew the union nuts securing the injector pipes to the injectors . . .

15.8b . . . and injection pump

15.11a Disconnect the vacuum pipe from the manifold switchover (swirl) valve . . .

15.11b . . . then remove the bolt securing the crankshaft sensor wiring to the manifold lower section

15.11c Unscrew the retaining nuts and remove the inlet manifold lower section from the engine

15.13 On refitting, use a new manifold gasket

the pipes to the rear of the injection pump; as each pump union nut is slackened, retain the adapter with a suitable open-ended spanner to prevent it being unscrewed from the pump. With all the union nuts undone, remove the injector pipes from the engine unit and mop-up any spilt fuel **(see illustrations)**. Seal the pipe end fittings to minimise fuel loss and prevent the entry of dirt.

9 Either unbolt the EGR valve unit from the upper inlet manifold or, alternatively, fit hose clamps to the coolant hoses and disconnect them leaving the EGR valve on the inlet manifold.

10 Evenly and progressively unscrew the retaining bolts then lift off the upper part of the manifold. Recover the gasket and discard it.

11 To remove the lower section of the manifold, disconnect the vacuum pipe from the manifold switchover (swirl) valve diaphragm unit and unbolt the wiring connector bracket from the manifold. Evenly and progressively unscrew the retaining nuts then remove the manifold lower section and gasket from the cylinder head **(see illustrations)**.

12 Note that if the upper part of the inlet manifold is to be renewed, the pressure sensor and EGR valve must be transferred. If the lower part of the manifold is to be renewed, the vacuum valve and crankshaft position sensor bracket must be transferred.

Refitting

13 Ensure that all mating surfaces are clean and dry. Fit a new gasket to the cylinder head then refit the lower manifold section **(see illustration)**. Fit the new retaining nuts and, working in a diagonal sequence, evenly and progressively tighten them to the specified torque setting. Reconnect the switchover valve hose and refit the wiring bracket.

14 Fit a new gasket to the top of the manifold lower section then refit the upper section of the manifold, tightening its retaining bolts to the specified torque.

15 Refit the EGR valve unit or reconnect the coolant hoses as applicable.

16 Refit the injector pipes, tightening the union nuts to the specified torque.

17 Reconnect the fuel return hoses to the injectors.

18 Refit the inlet elbow together with a new gasket and tighten the nuts securely.

19 Reconnect the vacuum pipe to the EGR valve.

20 Reconnect all wiring and secure the wiring harness tray.

21 Refit the air ducts and tighten the clips.

22 Refit the engine top cover, then reconnect the battery negative lead. Start the engine and bleed the fuel system as described in Section 4. Top-up the cooling system as necessary.

16 Exhaust manifold – removal and refitting
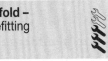

Note: *New manifold retaining nuts and exhaust front pipe nuts will be required on refitting.*

Removal

1 Disconnect the battery negative lead (refer to *Disconnecting the battery* in the *Reference* Chapter at the end of this manual). Remove the engine top cover.

2 Apply the handbrake, then jack up the front of the vehicle and support it on axle stands (see *Jacking and vehicle support*). Remove the engine undertray.

3 Referring to Section 2, remove the air cleaner housing duct assembly and remove the metal air pipe linking the turbocharger to the intercooler. Also, remove the inlet hose from the turbocharger.

4 Disconnect the wiring from the top of each glow plug **(see illustration)**.

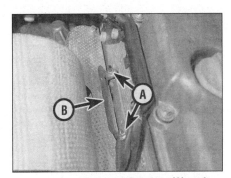

16.4 Undo the retaining nuts (A) and remove the connector strap (B) from the glow plugs (left-hand arrangement shown)

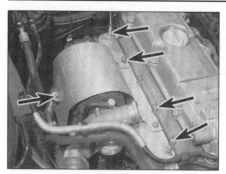

16.5a Undo the retaining screws (arrowed) . . .

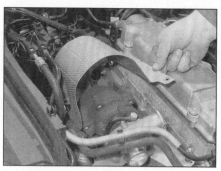

16.5b . . . and remove the heat shields from the manifold assembly

16.7 Separate the exhaust front pipe from the manifold and collect the gasket

16.9 Disconnect the vacuum hose from the turbocharger wastegate

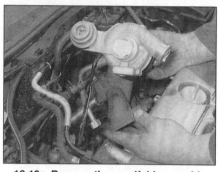

16.10a Remove the manifold assembly from the engine . . .

16.10b . . . and remove the gasket

5 Undo the retaining screws and remove the heat shields from the top of the manifold assembly and from the starter motor **(see illustrations)**. Note that the lower screw on the starter motor only needs to be loosened.
6 Undo the retaining bolts and remove the wiring harness guide from the rear of the cylinder block.
7 Undo the nuts securing the exhaust system front pipe to the turbocharger and free the pipe **(see illustration)**. Loosen the joint between the front and intermediate exhaust pipes, and unhook the front rubber mountings. Support the front pipe, making sure that the flexible section is not strained.
8 Remove all traces of dirt from around the turbocharger oil feed and return pipe unions. Unscrew the union nuts securing the pipes to the cylinder block and allow the oil to drain into a suitable container. Mop-up any spilt oil.
9 Unscrew the retaining bolts and remove the manifold support bracket. Disconnect the vacuum hose from the turbocharger wastegate diaphragm **(see illustration)**.
10 Working in a diagonal sequence, evenly and progressively unscrew and remove the exhaust manifold retaining nuts. Manoeuvre the manifold assembly out of position and recover the gasket **(see illustrations)**. If necessary, separate the turbocharger from the manifold as described in Section 13.

Refitting

11 Refitting is the reverse of removal, noting the following points.

a) *Ensure all mating surfaces are clean and dry and renew all gaskets.*
b) *Fit the new manifold nuts and tighten them evenly and progressively to the specified torque, working in a diagonal sequence. Also tighten the support bracket bolts to the specified torque.*
c) *Before refitting the oil pipes to the turbocharger, pour engine oil into the oil channel to ensure there is sufficient lubrication when the engine is first started.*
d) *Tighten the turbocharger oil pipe union nuts to the specified torque.*
e) *On completion check and, if necessary, top-up the oil and coolant levels as described in 'Weekly checks'.*
f) *On starting the engine for the first time, allow the engine to idle for a few minutes before increasing the engine speed; this will allow oil to be circulated around the turbocharger bearings.*

17 Exhaust system – general information, removal and refitting

General information

1 The exhaust system consists of three sections: the front pipe (which incorporates the catalytic converter), the intermediate pipe

and silencer, and the tailpipe and silencer. The front pipe is fitted with a flexible section to allow for movement in the exhaust system. The intermediate pipe-to-tailpipe joint is also spring-loaded to allow for movement in the system.
2 The system is suspended throughout its entire length by rubber mountings.

Removal

3 Each exhaust section can be removed individually, or the complete system can be removed as an assembly. Even if only one part of the system needs attention, in some cases it can be easier to remove the whole system and separate the sections on the bench.
4 To remove the system or part of the system, first jack up the front or rear of the car, and support it on axle stands. Alternatively, position the car over an inspection pit, or on car ramps. Where necessary, remove the engine undertray.

Front pipe (with catalytic converter)

Note: *New pipe-to-manifold nuts should be used on refitting.*
5 Undo the nuts securing the front pipe to the turbocharger. Unscrew the bolts securing the front pipe to the intermediate pipe.
6 Unhook the rubber mounting rings, then free the front pipe from the turbocharger, recovering the gasket. Free the front pipe from the intermediate pipe, then remove

it from underneath the vehicle **(see illustration)**.

Intermediate pipe

7 Unscrew the bolts securing the intermediate pipe to the front pipe and the bolts and springs securing it to the tailpipe.

8 Bend out the securing clips and release the intermediate pipe from its mounting rubbers **(see illustration)**. Disengage the intermediate pipe from the front pipe and tailpipe and remove it from underneath the vehicle.

Tailpipe

9 Unscrew the bolts securing the tailpipe to the intermediate pipe joint.

10 Bend out the securing clips then release the tailpipe from its mounting rubbers, and free it from the intermediate pipe.

Complete system

Note: *New pipe-to-manifold nuts should be used on refitting.*

11 Unscrew the nuts securing the front pipe flange joint to the turbocharger.

12 Bend out the securing clips then free the system from its mounting rubbers and remove it from underneath the vehicle. Recover the gasket from the front pipe joint.

Heat shield(s)

13 The heat shields are secured to the

17.6 Free the front pipe from the turbocharger

underside of the body by various nuts and bolts. Each shield can be removed once the relevant exhaust section has been removed. If a shield is being removed to gain access to a component located behind it, it may prove sufficient in some cases to remove the retaining nuts and/or bolts, and simply lower the shield, without disturbing the exhaust system.

Refitting

14 Each section is refitted by reversing the removal sequence, noting the following points:

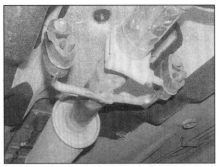

17.8 Release the pipe from the mounting rubbers

a) *Renew the front pipe nuts whenever they are disturbed.*

b) *Ensure that all traces of corrosion have been removed from the flanges, and apply a smear of exhaust system jointing paste to the joint to ensure a gas-tight seal.*

c) *Inspect the rubber mountings for signs of damage or deterioration, and renew as necessary.*

d) *Prior to tightening the exhaust system fasteners, ensure that all rubber mountings are correctly located, and that there is adequate clearance between the exhaust system and vehicle underbody.*

Chapter 4 Part C:
Emission control systems

Contents

Degrees of difficulty

Easy, suitable for novice with little experience	**Fairly easy,** suitable for beginner with some experience	**Fairly difficult,** suitable for competent DIY mechanic	**Difficult,** suitable for experienced DIY mechanic	**Very difficult,** suitable for expert DIY or professional

Specifications

EVAP canister-purge valve
Resistance at 20°C. . . . . 45 ± 5 ohms

EVAP pressure sensor (T7 system)

Pressure	Voltage (approximately)
-0.038 bar.	0.1
0 bar	2.5
0.012 bar	2.0

EVAP shut-off control valve (T7 system)
Resistance at 20°C. . . . . 24.5 ±1.5 ohms

Oxygen (Lambda) sensor
Type:
    Motronic. . . . . Bosch LSH25 (with preheating)
    Trionic T5 . . . . Bosch LSH25P (with preheating)
    Trionic T7 . . . . Bosch LSF4.7 (with preheating)
Resistance at 20°C (pins 1 and 2):
    Motronic. . . . . 3.5 ohms (approximately)
    Trionic T5 . . . . 2.0 ohms (approximately)
    Trionic T7 . . . . 9.0 ohms (approximately)

Torque wrench settings

	Nm	lbf ft
Exhaust gas recirculation (EGR) valve bolts	8	6
Oxygen (Lambda) sensor.	55	41

1 General information

1 All petrol engine models use unleaded petrol and also have various other features built into the fuel system to help minimise harmful emissions. All models are equipped with a crankcase emission control system, a catalytic converter and an evaporative emission control (EVAP) system to keep fuel vapour/exhaust gas emissions down to a minimum.
2 All diesel engine models are also designed to meet strict emission requirements. All models are fitted with a crankcase emission control system, a catalytic converter and an exhaust gas recirculation (EGR) system to keep exhaust emissions down to a minimum.
3 The emission control systems function as follows.

Petrol models

Crankcase emissions control

To reduce emissions of unburned hydrocarbons from the crankcase into the atmosphere, the engine is sealed. The blow-by gases and oil vapour are drawn from inside the crankcase, through an external oil trap which is connected to the crankcase via the camshaft cover and breather hose. The gases are then evacuated to the throttle housing and also via the turbocharger to the inlet manifold.

Under conditions of high manifold depression (idling, deceleration) the gases will be sucked positively out of the crankcase to the throttle housing. Under conditions of low manifold depression (acceleration, full-throttle running) the gases are forced out of the crankcase by the (relatively) higher crankcase pressure; if the engine is worn, the raised crankcase pressure (due to increased blow-by) will cause some of the flow to return under all manifold conditions.

Exhaust emissions control

To minimise the amount of pollutants which escape into the atmosphere all models are fitted with a catalytic converter in the exhaust system. The catalytic converter system is of the 'closed-loop' type, in which an oxygen sensor (two on some models) in the exhaust system provides the fuel injection/ignition system ECU with constant feedback on the oxygen content of the exhaust gases. This enables the ECU to adjust the mixture to provide the best possible conditions for the converter to operate.

The oxygen sensors have a built-in heating element, controlled by the ECU through the sensor relay, to quickly bring the sensor's tip to an efficient operating temperature. The sensor's tip is sensitive to oxygen, and sends the ECU a varying voltage depending on the amount of oxygen in the exhaust gases; if the inlet air/fuel mixture is too rich, the sensor sends a high-voltage signal. The voltage falls as the mixture weakens. Peak conversion efficiency of all major pollutants occurs if

the inlet air/fuel mixture is maintained at the chemically-correct ratio for the complete combustion of petrol – 14.7 parts (by weight) of air to 1 part of fuel (the 'stoichiometric' ratio). The sensor output voltage alters in a large step at this point, the ECU using the signal change as a reference point, and correcting the inlet air/fuel mixture accordingly by altering the fuel injector pulse width (injector opening time).

Evaporative emissions control

To minimise the escape into the atmosphere of unburned hydrocarbons, an evaporative emissions control system is fitted. The system is sometimes referred to as the 'evaporative-loss control device' (ELCD). The fuel tank filler cap is sealed, and a charcoal canister is mounted on the front right-hand side of the car beneath the right-hand wing. The charcoal canister collects the petrol vapours generated in the tank when the car is parked. The vapours are stored until they can be cleared from the canister (under the control of the fuel system ECU via the purge valve, into the inlet tract, to be burned by the engine during normal combustion.

To ensure that the engine runs correctly when it is cold and/or idling, and to protect the catalytic converter from the effects of an over-rich mixture, the purge control valve is not opened by the ECU until the engine has warmed-up, and the engine is under load; the valve solenoid is then modulated on and off, to allow the stored vapour to pass into the inlet tract.

Diesel models

Crankcase emissions control

Refer to the description given for petrol models.

Exhaust emissions control

To minimise the level of exhaust pollutants released into the atmosphere, a three-way catalytic converter is fitted in the exhaust system. The catalytic converter consists of a canister containing a fine mesh impregnated with a catalyst material, over which the hot exhaust gases pass. The catalyst speeds up the oxidation of harmful carbon monoxide, unburned hydrocarbons and soot, effectively reducing the quantity of harmful products released into the atmosphere by the exhaust gases.

2.1a Oil trap mounted on the rear of the cylinder block

Exhaust gas recirculation system

This system is designed to recirculate small quantities of exhaust gas into the inlet tract, and therefore into the combustion process. This process reduces the level of unburnt hydrocarbons present in the exhaust gas before it reaches the catalytic converter. The system is controlled by the injection system ECU and EGR valve on the upper section of the inlet manifold, using the information from various sensors. The EGR valve is vacuum-operated and is switched on and off by an electrical solenoid valve.

2 Petrol engine emission control systems – testing and component renewal

Crankcase emission control

1 The components of this system require no attention other than to check that the hose(s) are clear and undamaged at regular intervals (see illustrations).

Exhaust emission control

Testing

2 The performance of the catalytic converter can be checked only by measuring the exhaust gases using a good-quality exhaust gas analyser.
3 If the CO level at the tailpipe is too high, the vehicle should be taken to a Saab dealer so that the complete fuel injection and ignition systems, including the oxygen sensor(s), can be thoroughly checked using the special diagnostic equipment. Once these have been checked and are known to be free from faults, the fault must be in the catalytic converter, which must be renewed.

Catalytic converter renewal

4 Refer to Chapter 4A.

Oxygen (Lambda) sensor renewal

5 Refer to the information given in Chapter 4A.

Evaporative emission control

Testing

6 If the system is thought to be faulty, disconnect the hoses from the charcoal

2.1b On later models, the hoses have quick-release connections on the oil trap

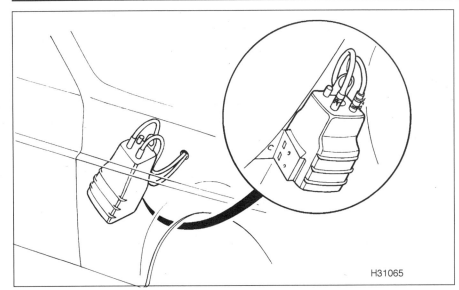

2.9 Disconnect the vapour hoses then slide the charcoal canister from its mounting bracket

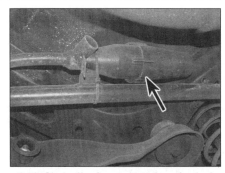

2.16 Shut-off valve mounted on the fuel filler pipe

canister and purge control valve and check that they are clear by blowing through them. Full testing of the system can only be carried out using specialist electronic equipment which is connected to the engine management system diagnostic wiring connector (see Chapter 4A). If the purge control valve or charcoal canister are thought to be faulty, they must be renewed.

Charcoal canister renewal

7 The charcoal canister is located behind the right-hand front wing. To gain access to the canister, firmly apply the handbrake then jack up the front of the vehicle and support it on axle stands (see *Jacking and vehicle support*).
8 Remove the retaining screws and fasteners and remove the wheel arch liner to gain access to the canister.
9 Mark the vapour hoses for identification purposes then disconnect. Slide the canister from its mounting bracket and remove it from the vehicle **(see illustration)**.
10 Refitting is a reverse of the removal procedure, ensuring the hoses are correctly and securely reconnected.

Purge valve renewal

11 Refer to the information given in Chapter 4A.

Pressure sensor renewal (T7 system)

12 The pressure sensor is located on top of the fuel tank, remove the fuel tank as described in Chapter 4A.
13 Clean around the pressure sensor, to make sure no dirt enters the fuel tank when the sensor is removed.
14 Undo the retaining screw and withdraw the sensor and O-ring seal from the fuel tank.
15 Refitting is a reversal of removal procedure. **Note:** *Renew the sensor O-ring*

seal and lubricate with acid-free petroleum jelly or similar.

Shut-off control valve renewal (T7 system)

16 The shut-off valve is clipped to the side of the fuel filler pipe at the right-hand rear of the vehicle **(see illustration)**. Park the vehicle on a firm level surface, then select first gear (manual transmission) or Park (automatic transmission) and chock the front wheels securely. Raise the rear of the car and support it securely on axle stands (see *Jacking and vehicle support*).
17 Cut the cable tie and disconnect the wiring connector to the shut-off valve.
18 Using a screwdriver carefully prise the control valve, to unclip it from the fuel filler pipe.
19 Clean off any dirt from around the control valve, then unclip the cover from the top of the valve. Disconnect the wiring connector from the top of the valve and withdraw the washer.
20 Unclip the cover from the bottom of the valve, then release the securing clip and disconnect the hose from the bottom of the valve. If required, the filter can now be renewed.
21 Refitting is a reversal of the removal procedure, but make sure that the wiring at the top of the valve locates correctly in the recess in the washer.

3 Diesel engine emission control systems – testing and component renewal

Crankcase emission control

1 The components of this system require no attention other than to check that the hose(s) are clear and undamaged at regular intervals.

Exhaust emission control

Testing

2 The performance of the catalytic converter can be checked only by measuring the exhaust gases using a good-quality, carefully-calibrated exhaust gas analyser.
3 If the catalytic converter is thought to be faulty, before assuming the catalytic converter is faulty, it is worth checking the problem is not due to a faulty injector(s). Refer to your Saab dealer for further information.

Catalytic converter renewal

4 The catalytic converter is an integral part of the exhaust system front pipe/manifold. Refer to Chapter 4B for removal and refitting details.

Exhaust gas recirculation (EGR)

Testing

5 Comprehensive testing of the system can only be carried out using specialist electronic equipment which is connected to the injection system diagnostic wiring connector (see Chapter 4B). If the EGR valve or solenoid valve are thought to be faulty, they must be renewed.

EGR valve renewal

6 Remove the engine top cover, then disconnect the vacuum hose from the valve which is located on the upper part of the inlet manifold at the front of the engine.
7 Unscrew the two mounting bolts and remove the valve from the inlet manifold.
8 Refitting is a reversal of removal.

EGR solenoid valve renewal

9 Unbolt the power steering fluid reservoir and position it to one side without disconnecting the fluid lines.
10 Loosen the two main screws securing the control valve bracket, and raise the bracket for access to the solenoid valve.
11 Note the position of the vacuum hoses, then disconnect them. Also disconnect the wiring plug.
12 Unbolt the valve from the bracket. Note that there are two valves, the EGR system valve and the inlet manifold switchover valve; the EGR system valve can be identified by its black wiring connector.
13 Refitting is a reversal of removal.

4 Catalytic converter – general information and precautions

1 The catalytic converter is a reliable and simple device which needs no maintenance in itself, but there are some facts of which an owner should be aware if the converter is to function properly for its full service life.

Petrol models

a) DO NOT use leaded petrol or LRP in a car equipped with a catalytic converter – the lead will coat the precious metals, reducing their converting efficiency and will eventually destroy the converter.

b) Always keep the ignition and fuel systems well-maintained in accordance with the manufacturer's schedule.

c) If the engine develops a misfire, do not drive the car at all (or at least as little as possible) until the fault is cured.

d) DO NOT push- or tow-start the car – this will soak the catalytic converter in unburned fuel, causing it to overheat when the engine does start.

e) DO NOT switch off the ignition at high engine speeds.

f) DO NOT use fuel or engine oil additives – these may contain substances harmful to the catalytic converter.

g) DO NOT continue to use the car if the engine burns oil to the extent of leaving a visible trail of blue smoke.

h) Remember that the catalytic converter operates at very high temperatures. DO NOT, therefore, park the car in dry undergrowth, over long grass or piles of dead leaves after a long run.

i) Remember that the catalytic converter is FRAGILE – do not strike it with tools during servicing work.

j) In some cases a sulphurous smell (like that of rotten eggs) may be noticed from the exhaust. This is common to many catalytic converter-equipped cars and once the car has covered a few thousand miles the problem should disappear. Sometimes this is also caused by the brand of fuel used.

k) The catalytic converter, used on a well-maintained and well-driven car, should last for between 50 000 and 100 000 miles – if the converter is no longer effective it must be renewed.

Diesel models

2 Refer to the information given in parts f, g, h, i and k of the petrol models information given above.

Chapter 5 Part A:
Starting and charging systems

Contents

Degrees of difficulty

Easy, suitable for novice with little experience	Fairly easy, suitable for beginner with some experience	Fairly difficult, suitable for competent DIY mechanic	Difficult, suitable for experienced DIY mechanic	Very difficult, suitable for expert DIY or professional

Specifications

System type .... 12 volt, negative earth

Battery
Type   Lead-acid, low-maintenance or 'maintenance-free' (sealed for life)
Battery capacity .... 60 or 85 amp-hour
Charge condition:
  Poor   .... 12.5 volts
  Normal .... 12.6 volts
  Good   .... 12.7 volts

Alternator
Type   .... Bosch KC–14V 45-90A, NC-14V 70-120A or NC-14V 65-130A
Rated voltage 14V
Slip-ring diameter:
  Minimum... 15.4 mm
  New   .... 14.4 mm
Minimum brush protrusion from holder .... 7.5 mm
Output current:
  Bosch KC-14V 45-90A:
    At 1800 rpm .... 45 amps
    At 6000 rpm .... 90 amps
  Bosch NC-14V 70-120A:
    At 1800 rpm .... 70 amps
    At 6000 rpm .... 120 amps
  Bosch NC-14V 65-130A:
    At 1800 rpm .... 65 amps
    At 6000 rpm .... 130 amps

Starter motor

Type:
  Petrol engines:
    Up to 2001 . . . . Bosch DW 12V 0 001 108 151
    2002-on . . . . Mitsubishi M000T86781
  Diesel engines . . . . Bosch DW 12V 0 001 109 015
Output:
  Petrol engines. . . . . 1.4 kW
  Diesel engines . . . . 2.0 kW
No of teeth on pinion:
  Petrol engines:
    Up to 2001 9
    2002-on 10
  Diesel engines 10
No of teeth on ring gear 135
Ratio – engine/starter motor:
  Petrol engines:
    Up to 2001 . . . . 15:1
    2002-on 13.5:1
  Diesel engines 13.5:1

Torque wrench settings

	Nm	lbf ft
Alternator bracket.	20	15
Alternator mounting bolt.	35	26
Starter motor:		
To bracket.	7	5
Bracket to block.	25	18
Starter to block.	45	33

---

1 General information and precautions

General information

Because of their engine-related functions, the components of the starting and charging systems are covered separately from the body electrical devices such as the lights, instruments, etc (which are covered in Chapter 12). Refer to Part B or C of this Chapter for information on the ignition system.

The electrical system is of the 12 volt negative earth type. The battery fitted as original equipment is of low-maintenance or 'maintenance-free' (sealed for life) type. The battery is charged by the alternator, which is belt-driven from the crankshaft pulley. During the life of the car, the original battery may have been renewed with a standard type battery.

The starter motor is of the pre-engaged type, incorporating an integral solenoid. On starting, the solenoid moves the drive pinion into engagement with the flywheel/driveplate ring gear before the starter motor is energised. Once the engine has started, a one-way clutch prevents the motor armature being driven by the engine until the pinion disengages from the ring gear. Unlike some modern starter motors, it incorporates epicyclic reduction gears between the armature and the pinion.

Precautions

• Further details of the various systems are given in the relevant Sections of this Chapter.

While some repair procedures are given, the usual course of action is to renew the component concerned. The owner whose interest extends beyond mere component renewal should obtain a copy of the *Automotive Electrical & Electronic Systems Manual*, available from the publishers of this manual.

• It is necessary to take extra care when working on the electrical system, to avoid damage to semi-conductor devices (diodes and transistors), and to avoid the risk of personal injury. In addition to the precautions given in *Safety first!* observe the following when working on the system:

• *Always remove rings, watches, etc, before working on the electrical system.* Even with the battery disconnected, capacitive discharge could occur if a component's live terminal is earthed through a metal object. This could cause a shock or nasty burn.

• *Do not reverse the battery connections.* Components such as the alternator, electronic control units, or any other components having semi-conductor circuitry, could be irreparably damaged.

• If the engine is being started using jump leads and a slave battery, connect the batteries *positive-to-positive* and *negative-to-negative* (see *Jump starting*). This also applies when connecting a battery charger.

Caution: Never disconnect the battery terminals, the alternator, any electrical wiring, or any test instruments, when the engine is running.

• Do not allow the engine to turn the alternator when the alternator is not connected.

• Never 'test' for alternator output by 'flashing' the output lead to earth.

• Never use an ohmmeter of the type incorporating a hand-cranked generator for circuit or continuity testing.

• Always ensure that the battery negative lead is disconnected when working on the electrical system.

• Before using electric-arc welding equipment on the car, disconnect the battery, alternator, and components such as the fuel injection/ignition electronic control unit, to protect them from the risk of damage.

2 Electrical fault finding – general information

Refer to Chapter 12.

3 Battery – testing and charging

Testing

Standard and low-maintenance battery

1 If the vehicle covers a small annual mileage, it is worthwhile checking the specific gravity of the electrolyte every three months, to determine the state of charge of the battery. Use a hydrometer to make the check, and

compare the results with the following table. Note that the specific gravity readings assume an electrolyte temperature of 15°C; for every 10°C below 15°C, subtract 0.007. For every 10°C above 15°C, add 0.007. However, for convenience, the temperatures quoted in the following table are **ambient** (outdoor air) temperatures, above or below 25°C:

	Ambient temperature	
	Above	**Below**
	25°C	**25°C**
Fully-charged	1.210 to 1.230	1.270 to 1.290
70% charged	1.170 to 1.190	1.230 to 1.250
Discharged	1.050 to 1.070	1.110 to 1.130

2 If the battery condition is suspect, first check the specific gravity of electrolyte in each cell. A variation of 0.040 or more between any cells indicates loss of electrolyte or deterioration of the internal plates.

3 If the specific gravity variation is 0.040 or more, the battery should be renewed. If the cell variation is satisfactory but the battery is discharged, it should be charged as described later in this Section.

Maintenance-free battery

4 In cases where a 'sealed for life' maintenance-free battery is fitted, topping-up and testing of the electrolyte in each cell is not possible. The condition of the battery can therefore only be tested using a battery condition indicator or a voltmeter.

5 A battery with a built-in charge condition indicator may be fitted. The indicator is located in the top of the battery casing, and indicates the condition of the battery from its colour. If the indicator shows green, then the battery is in a good state of charge. If the indicator turns darker, eventually to black, then the battery requires charging, as described later in this Section. If the indicator shows clear/yellow, then the electrolyte level in the battery is too low to allow further use, and the battery should be renewed. **Do not** attempt to charge, load or jump start a battery when the indicator shows clear/yellow.

All battery types

6 If testing the battery using a voltmeter, connect the voltmeter across the battery, and compare the result with those given in the Specifications under 'charge condition'. The test is only accurate if the battery has not been subjected to any kind of charge for the previous six hours, including charging by the alternator. If this is not the case, switch on the headlights for 30 seconds, then wait four to five minutes after switching off the headlights before testing the battery. All other electrical circuits must be switched off, so check (for instance) that the doors and tailgate or boot lid are fully shut when making the test.

7 If the voltage reading is less than 12.2 volts, then the battery is discharged. A reading of 12.2 to 12.4 volts indicates a partially-discharged condition.

8 If the battery is to be charged, remove it from the vehicle (Section 4) and charge it as described in the following paragraphs.

Charging

Note: *The following is intended as a guide only. Always refer to the manufacturer's recommendations (often printed on a label attached to the battery) before charging a battery.*

Standard and low-maintenance battery

9 Charge the battery at a rate of 3.5 to 4 amps, and continue to charge the battery at this rate until no further rise in specific gravity is noted over a four hour period.

10 Alternatively, a trickle charger charging at the rate of 1.5 amps can safely be used overnight.

11 Specially rapid 'boost' charges which are claimed to restore the power of the battery in 1 to 2 hours are not recommended, as they can cause serious damage to the battery plates through overheating.

12 While charging the battery, note that the temperature of the electrolyte should never exceed 38°C.

Maintenance-free battery

13 This battery type requires a longer period to fully recharge than the standard type, the time taken being dependent on the extent of discharge, but it can take anything up to three days.

14 A constant-voltage type charger is required, to be set, where possible, to 13.9 to 14.9 volts with a charger current below 25 amps. Using this method, the battery should be usable within three hours, giving a voltage reading of 12.5 volts, but this is for a partially-discharged battery and, as mentioned, full charging can take considerably longer.

15 Use of a normal trickle charger should not be detrimental to the battery, provided excessive gassing is not allowed to occur, and the battery is not allowed to become hot.

---

4 Battery – removal and refitting

Removal

1 The battery is located at the front left-hand side of the engine compartment. Unclip the cover from the battery.

2 Loosen the clamp nut and disconnect the lead at the negative (earth) terminal. Disconnect the lead at the positive terminal in the same way.

3 Unscrew the battery mounting clamp bolt located at the front of the battery, and remove the clamp.

4 Lift the battery out of the engine compartment (take care not to tilt it excessively).

Refitting

5 Refitting is a reversal of removal. Smear petroleum jelly on the terminals after

reconnecting the leads, and always reconnect the positive lead first, and the negative lead last.

---

5 Charging system – testing

Note: *Refer to the warnings given in 'Safety first!' and in Section 1 of this Chapter before starting work.*

1 If the ignition/no-charge warning light does not come on when the ignition is switched on, first check the alternator wiring connections for security. If satisfactory, check that the warning light bulb has not blown, and that the bulbholder is secure in its location in the instrument panel. If the light still fails to illuminate, check the continuity of the warning light feed wire from the alternator to the bulbholder. If all is satisfactory, the alternator is at fault, and should be taken to an auto-electrician for testing and repair, or else renewed.

2 If the ignition warning light comes on when the engine is running, stop the engine. Check that the drivebelt is intact and correctly tensioned (see Chapter 1A or 1B), and that the alternator connections are secure. If all is satisfactory, check the alternator brushes and slip-rings as described in Section 8. If the fault persists, the alternator should be taken to an auto-electrician for testing and repair, or else renewed.

3 If the alternator output is suspect even though the warning light functions correctly, the regulated voltage may be checked as follows.

4 Connect a voltmeter across the battery terminals, and start the engine.

5 Increase the engine speed until the voltmeter reading remains steady; the reading should be approximately 12 to 13 volts, and no more than 14 volts.

6 Switch on as many electrical accessories (eg, the headlights, heated rear window and heater blower) as possible, and check that the alternator maintains the regulated voltage at around 13 to 14 volts.

7 If the regulated voltage is not as stated, the fault may be due to worn brushes, weak brush springs, a faulty voltage regulator, a faulty diode, a severed phase winding, or worn or damaged slip-rings. The brushes and slip-rings may be checked (see Section 8), but if the fault persists, the alternator should be taken to an auto-electrician for testing and repair, or else renewed.

---

6 Alternator drivebelt – removal, refitting and tensioning

Refer to the procedure given for the auxiliary drivebelt in Chapter 1A or 1B.

7.4 Removing the auxiliary drivebelt tensioner

7.5 Unscrew the terminal nuts and disconnect the wiring from the rear of the alternator

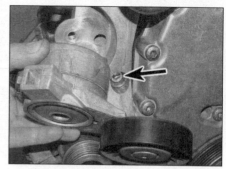

7.8a Remove the alternator upper mounting bolt ...

7.8b ... and lower mounting bolt

7.8c Metal sleeve in the mounting bracket ...

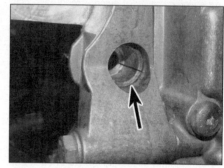

7.8d ... this sleeve will need to be tapped outwards to release the alternator

7 Alternator – removal and refitting

Removal

1 Remove the engine top cover. Disconnect the battery negative lead (refer to *Disconnecting the battery* in the *Reference* Chapter at the end of this manual).

2 Apply the handbrake, then jack up the front of the vehicle and support it on axle stands (see *Jacking and vehicle support*). Remove the right-hand front roadwheel, and the engine undertray.

3 Remove the right-hand front wing inner plastic moulding/wheel arch liner for access to the rear of the engine.

4 Remove the auxiliary drivebelt as described in Chapter 1A or 1B, then unbolt the drivebelt tensioner and remove it from the engine **(see illustration)**.

5 Unscrew the nuts and disconnect the two wires from the alternator terminals **(see illustration)**.

Petrol models

6 Refer to Chapter 4A and remove the air cleaner and the hose leading to the throttle body.

7 Refer to Chapter 4A and detach the exhaust front pipe from the exhaust manifold. Release the rubber mountings and support the front pipe.

8 Unscrew and remove the mounting bolts, then push the exhaust front pipe to one side and withdraw the alternator downwards. Note

the alternator will be a tight in fit the mounting bracket, and the metal sleeves in the mounting bolt holes will need to be carefully moved outwards to release the alternator **(see illustrations)**.

Diesel models

9 Remove the air cleaner assembly and mass airflow meter from the right-hand side of the engine compartment with reference to Chapter 4B.

10 Release the fuel hoses from the support bracket, and cut the supporting cable ties.

11 At the rear of the engine, disconnect the vacuum hose leading to the turbocharger wastegate, then unbolt the wastegate.

12 Unscrew and remove the mounting bolts, and lift the alternator from the rear of the engine. On RHD models, extra working room can be gained by unscrewing the engine right-hand mounting bolts and pushing the engine slightly forwards.

Refitting

13 Refitting is a reversal of removal, however, clean the alternator mounting points, and coat them with petroleum jelly to ensure a good electrical connection to the engine. Ensure that the alternator mountings are securely tightened, and refit the components referring to the relevant Chapters. On RHD diesel models, tighten the right-hand engine mounting bolts to the specified torque given in Chapter 2B, if necessary.

8 Alternator brushes and regulator – inspection and renewal

1 Remove the alternator as described in Section 7.

2 Unscrew the large terminal nut and the screws securing the cover to the rear of the alternator **(see illustrations)**.

8.2a Unscrew the large terminal nut ...

8.2b ... and the screws securing the cover to the rear of the alternator

8.3a Lever off the cover . . .

8.3b . . . and remove it from the alternator

8.4a Remove the screws . . .

3 Using a screwdriver, lever off the cover, and remove it from the rear of the alternator **(see illustrations)**.

4 Unscrew and remove the two retaining screws, and remove the regulator/brush holder from the rear of the alternator **(see illustrations)**.

5 Measure the protrusion of each brush from its holder, using a steel rule or vernier calipers **(see illustration)**. If less than 7.5 mm, a new regulator/brush assembly should be obtained.

6 If the brushes are in good condition, clean them and check that they move freely in their holders.

7 Wipe clean the alternator slip-rings, and check them for signs of scoring or burning. It may be possible to have the slip-rings renovated by an electrical specialist.

8 Refit the regulator/brush holder assembly, and securely tighten the retaining screws.

9 Refit the cover, then insert and tighten the retaining screws and refit the large terminal nut.

10 Refit the alternator with reference to Section 7.

8.4b . . . and withdraw the regulator/brush holder from the rear of the alternator

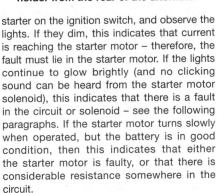

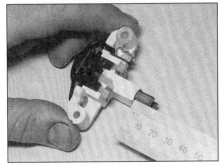

8.5 Measuring the brush protrusion from the holder

---

9 Starting system – testing

Note: *Refer to the precautions given in 'Safety first!' and in Section 1 of this Chapter before starting work.*

1 If the starter motor fails to operate when the ignition key is turned to the appropriate position, the following possible causes may apply:

a) *The battery is faulty.*
b) *The electrical connections between the switch, solenoid, battery and starter motor are somewhere failing to pass the necessary current from the battery through the starter to earth.*
c) *The solenoid is faulty.*
d) *The starter motor is mechanically or electrically defective.*

2 To check the battery, switch on the headlights. If they dim after a few seconds, this indicates that the battery is discharged – recharge (see Section 3) or renew the battery. If the headlights glow brightly, operate the starter on the ignition switch, and observe the lights. If they dim, this indicates that current is reaching the starter motor – therefore, the fault must lie in the starter motor. If the lights continue to glow brightly (and no clicking sound can be heard from the starter motor solenoid), this indicates that there is a fault in the circuit or solenoid – see the following paragraphs. If the starter motor turns slowly when operated, but the battery is in good condition, then this indicates that either the starter motor is faulty, or that there is considerable resistance somewhere in the circuit.

3 If a fault in the circuit is suspected, disconnect the battery leads, the starter/solenoid wiring and the engine/transmission earth strap. Thoroughly clean the connections, and reconnect the leads and wiring, then use a voltmeter or test light to check that full battery voltage is available at the battery positive lead connection on the solenoid, and that the earth is sound.

4 If the battery and all connections are in good condition, check the circuit by disconnecting the wire from the solenoid terminal. Connect a voltmeter or test light between the wire end and a good earth (such as the battery negative terminal), and check that the wire is live when the ignition switch is turned to the start position. If it is, then the circuit is sound – if not, the circuit wiring can be checked as described in Chapter 12.

5 The solenoid contacts can be checked by connecting a voltmeter or test light between the terminal on the starter side of the solenoid,

and earth. When the ignition switch is turned to the start position, there should be a reading or lighted bulb, as applicable. If there is no reading or lighted bulb, the solenoid or contacts are faulty and the solenoid should be renewed.

6 If the circuit and solenoid are proved sound, the fault must lie in the starter motor. Begin checking the starter motor by removing it (see Section 10), and checking the brushes (see Section 11). If the fault does not lie in the brushes, the motor windings must be faulty. In this event, it may be possible to have the starter motor overhauled by a specialist, but check on the availability and cost of spares before proceeding, as it may prove more economical to obtain a new or exchange motor.

---

10 Starter motor – removal and refitting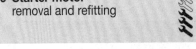

Removal

1 The starter motor is located on the left-hand rear side of the engine, and is bolted to the engine backplate and transmission. First remove the cover from the battery and disconnect the negative lead (refer to *Disconnecting the battery* in the *Reference* Chapter at the end of this manual).

2 Apply the handbrake, then jack up the front of the car and support on axle stands (see *Jacking and vehicle support*). Remove the engine undertray where fitted.

10.3 Withdraw the upper starter motor mounting bolt from the top of the transmission bellhousing

10.5 Remove the cable-tie to release the wiring loom

10.6 Unscrew the starter motor lower mounting nut

Petrol models

3 From inside the engine compartment, remove the starter motor upper mounting bolt **(see illustration)**.

4 Unscrew the nut(s) and disconnect the wiring terminal(s) from the starter/solenoid.

5 Cut and release the cable-tie from around the solenoid to release the wiring loom **(see illustration)**.

6 From under the vehicle, unscrew the lower starter motor mounting nut, then lower the starter motor from the engine compartment **(see illustration)**.

Diesel models

7 Unbolt the cover from the starter motor, then unscrew the rear bracket bolt which also retains the manifold support stay. Loosen the upper bolt and move the stay to one side.

8 Unscrew the nut(s) and disconnect the wiring terminal(s) from the starter/solenoid.

9 Unscrew the mounting bolts and lift the starter motor from the engine.

Refitting

10 Refitting is a reversal of removal, but tighten the mounting bolts to the specified torque.

11 Starter motor brushes – inspection and renewal

Note: *If the starter motor is thought to be defective, it should be taken to an auto-electrician for assessment. In the majority of cases, new starter motor brushes can be fitted at a reasonable cost, however, check the cost*

of repairs first as it may prove more economical to purchase a new or exchange motor. At the time of writing, it is only possible to obtain brushes from Saab for 1998 and 1999 petrol models, and, on later petrol models and all diesel models, no individual components are available.

1 Remove the starter motor as described in Section 10.

2 Unscrew the nut and disconnect the starter motor feed cable from the solenoid terminal **(see illustrations)**.

3 Unscrew and remove the two screws securing the cover to the end bracket. Lift off the cover and remove the seal **(see illustrations)**.

4 Extract the circlip, and remove the shim(s) and O-ring seal **(see illustration)**.

5 Unscrew the through-bolts securing the

11.2a Unscrew the nut . . .

11.2b . . . and disconnect the starter motor feed cable from the solenoid terminal

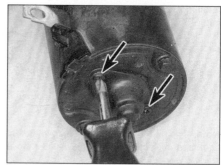

11.3a Unscrew and remove the two screws . . .

11.3b . . . lift off the cover . . .

11.3c . . . and remove the seal

11.4 Extracting the circlip shim(s)

11.5 Unscrew the through-bolts . . .

11.6 . . . and remove the commutator end bracket

11.7 Removing the brush holder assembly

commutator end bracket and yoke to the pinion end bracket **(see illustration)**. Mark the end bracket in relation to the yoke.

6 Remove the commutator end bracket **(see illustration)**.

7 Withdraw the brush holder assembly, at the same time releasing the feed cable grommet from the yoke. If the commutator/armature requires attention or cleaning, withdraw it from the yoke at this stage, then remove the brush holder assembly **(see illustration)**. As the holder assembly is removed, the brushes will be pushed out of their holders by the springs, but will be retained by the leads.

8 Check the brushes for wear, and renew as necessary. It may be possible to obtain individual brushes from a motor factor, otherwise the complete brush holder may have to be renewed. **Note:** *No minimum brush length is specified by the manufacturers, but it should be self-evident if the brushes are worn to the extent where renewal is required.* Clean all the components before reassembly. Clean

the commutator using fine glasspaper. If it is worn excessively, it may be possible to have it machined by an auto-electrician. Make sure that the brush holders are thoroughly cleaned, so that the new brushes will move freely in them.

9 Locate the brush plate without the brush holders part-way onto the commutator, then centralise the brushes, and fit the holders and springs over the brushes **(see illustration)**.

10 If removed, refit the armature inside the yoke.

11 Slide the complete bush holder assembly onto the armature commutator, while guiding the feed cable grommet in the yoke slot.

12 Locate the commutator end bracket on the armature, followed by the O-ring seal, shim(s) and circlip. Make sure that the O-ring seal is correctly fitted.

13 Refit the end bracket, making sure that the mark is aligned with the previously-made mark on the yoke. Insert and tighten the through-bolts to the specified torque.

14 Refit the shims and circlip, then refit the cover and seal to the end bracket, and tighten the two screws.

15 Reconnect the feed cable to the solenoid terminal, and tighten the nut.

16 Refit the starter motor with reference to Section 10.

11.9 Fitting the brush holders

Notes

Chapter 5 Part B:
Ignition system – petrol models

Contents

Degrees of difficulty

Easy, suitable for novice with little experience	**Fairly easy,** suitable for beginner with some experience	**Fairly difficult,** suitable for competent DIY mechanic	**Difficult,** suitable for experienced DIY mechanic	**Very difficult,** suitable for expert DIY or professional

Specifications

System type

System type:
Non-turbo models .... Hall-effect ignition, controlled by Bosch Motronic 2.10.3 engine management system
Turbo models .... Direct Ignition (DI) system incorporated in Saab Trionic engine management system

Hall-effect ignition system

Ignition HT coil winding resistances:
Primary .... 0.52 to 0.76 ohms
Secondary .... 7200 to 8200 ohms
HT lead resistances:
Coil to distributor .... 500 to 1500 ohms
Distributor to spark plug .... 2000 to 4000 ohms

Direct Ignition (DI) system

Ignition discharge module:
Capacitor voltage .... 400 volts
Ignition voltage (maximum) .... 40 000 volts
Ignition timing .... Preprogrammed in ECM

Firing order .... 1-3-4-2 (No 1 cylinder at timing chain end)

Torque wrench settings

	Nm	lbf ft
Ignition discharge module	11	8
Knock sensor	22	16
Spark plugs	27	20

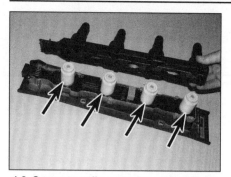

1.3 Separate coils – one for each cylinder

1 General information

Hall-effect ignition system

1 The system is a breakerless electronic ignition system, and comprises an impulse generator (Hall sensor in the distributor), the HT coil and spark plugs. The impulse generator uses the Hall-effect method to send signals to the Bosch Motronic engine management system electronic control unit (ECU), which then drives the low-tension circuit. The ECU monitors and regulates the ignition timing and dwell angle.

2 The distributor contains no centrifugal or vacuum advance mechanisms, as the speed and load related ignition advance is controlled solely by the engine management system.

Direct Ignition (DI) system

3 The Direct Ignition system is incorporated into the Saab Trionic engine management system. A single electronic control unit (ECU)

controls both the fuel injection and ignition functions. The system uses a separate HT coil for each spark plug **(see illustration)**, and an electronic control unit (ECU) monitors the engine by means of various sensors, in order to determine the most efficient ignition timing.

4 The components of the system are a crankshaft position/speed sensor, ignition discharge module with one coil per plug, diagnostic socket, ECU, pressure sensor in the inlet manifold (to determine engine load), and a solenoid valve (to regulate the turbocharger operation).

5 During starting at a crankshaft speed in excess of 150 rpm, HT sparks are triggered in the cylinder pair with the pistons at TDC. Under difficult conditions, multi-sparking occurs during this period, to aid starting. The ECU determines in which cylinder combustion is taking place by monitoring the flow of current across the spark plug electrodes, and then uses this information to determine the firing.

6 When the engine starts, the ignition timing is always set to 10° BTDC, and will remain at this setting until the engine speed exceeds 825 rpm. The ECU regulates the ignition timing at engine speeds above 825 rpm.

7 When the ignition is switched off and the engine stops, the main relay remains operational for a further 6 seconds. During this period, the Trionic control module earths all the trigger leads 210 times a second for 5 seconds, in order to burn off impurities from the spark plug electrodes.

8 Because the system does not use any HT leads, radio suppression must be incorporated in the spark plugs, so resistor-type plugs must always be used.

9 The Direct Ignition system uses the capacitive discharge method of producing an HT spark. Approximately 400 volts is stored

in a capacitor **(see illustrations)**, and at the time of ignition, this voltage is discharged through the primary circuit of the relevant coil. Approximately 40 000 volts is induced in the HT secondary coil, and this is discharged across the spark plug electrodes.

10 Should a fault occur in the system, a fault code is stored in the ECU. This code can only be accessed by a Saab dealer, using dedicated equipment.

11 Note that the starter motor must never be operated with the ignition module disconnected from the spark plugs but still connected to the wiring loom. This can cause irreversible damage to the module.

12 The engine management system controls engine precombustion via a knock sensor incorporated into the ignition system. Mounted onto the cylinder block, the sensor detects the high frequency vibrations caused when the engine starts to pre-ignite, or 'pink'. Under these conditions, the knock sensor sends an electrical signal to the ECU, which in turn retards the ignition advance setting in small steps until the 'pinking' ceases. With the Saab Trionic system, the spark plugs themselves are used as knock sensors, instead of employing a separate knock detector in the cylinder block. It achieves this by applying a small, direct current voltage across each spark plug. When two cylinders approach TDC, this voltage causes an ionisation current to flow across the terminals of the spark plug in the cylinder under combustion; a high current indicates that knock is occurring thus indicating which cylinder requires ignition retardation. Sequential control of the fuel injection is achieved in the same manner (see Chapter 4A).

2 Ignition system – testing

> ⚠ *Warning: Voltages produced by an electronic ignition system are considerably higher than those produced by conventional ignition systems. Extreme care must be taken when working on the system with the ignition switched on. Persons with surgically-implanted cardiac pacemaker devices should keep well clear*

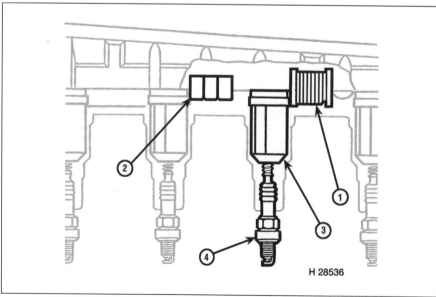

1.9a Direct Ignition module

1 Transformer (12 volts/400 volts)   2 Capacitor   3 Ignition coil   4 Spark plug

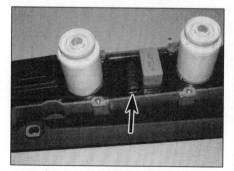

1.9b Direct Ignition capacitor located in the module

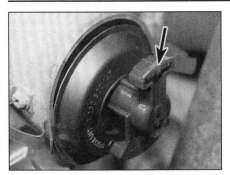

2.4 Rotor arm inside the distributor cap

of the ignition circuits, components and test equipment. Refer to the precautions in Chapter 5A, Section 1, before starting work. Always switch off the ignition before disconnecting or connecting any component, and when using a multimeter to check resistances.

Hall-effect ignition system

1 The components of the Hall-effect ignition system are normally very reliable; most faults are far more likely to be due to loose or dirty connections, or to 'tracking' of HT voltage due to dirt, dampness or damaged insulation, than to the failure of any of the system's components. **Always** check all wiring thoroughly before condemning an electrical component, and work methodically to eliminate all other possibilities before deciding that a particular component is faulty.

2 The old practice of checking for a spark by holding the live end of an HT lead a short distance away from the engine is **not** recommended; not only is there a high risk of a powerful electric shock, but the HT coil or amplifier unit may be damaged. Similarly, **never** try to 'diagnose' misfires by pulling off one HT lead at a time.

Engine will not start

3 If the engine either will not turn over at all, or only turns very slowly, check the battery and starter motor. Connect a voltmeter across the battery terminals (meter positive probe to battery positive terminal). Disconnect the ignition coil HT lead from the distributor cap, and earth it. Note the voltage reading obtained while turning over the engine on the starter for (no more than) ten seconds. If the reading obtained is less than approximately 9.5 volts, first check the battery, starter motor and charging system as described in Part A of this Chapter.

4 If the engine turns over at normal speed but will not start, check the HT circuit by connecting a timing light (following its manufacturer's instructions) and turning the engine over on the starter motor; if the light flashes, voltage is reaching the spark plugs, so these should be checked first. If the light does not flash, check the HT leads themselves, followed by the distributor cap, carbon brush and rotor arm **(see illustration)**.

5 If there is a spark, check the fuel system for faults, referring to Chapter 4A for further information.

6 If there is still no spark, check the voltage at the ignition HT coil '+' terminal; it should be the same as the battery voltage (ie, at least 11.7 volts). If the voltage at the coil is more than 1 volt less than that at the battery, check the feed from the battery until the fault is found.

7 If the feed to the HT coil is sound, check the coil's primary and secondary winding resistance as described later in this Chapter; renew the coil if faulty, but be careful to check carefully the condition of the LT connections themselves before doing so, to ensure that the fault is not due to dirty or poorly-fastened connectors.

8 If the HT coil is in good condition, the fault is probably within the amplifier unit or Hall generator circuit inside the distributor. Testing of these components should be entrusted to a Saab dealer.

Engine misfires

9 An irregular misfire suggests either a loose connection or intermittent fault on the primary circuit, or an HT lead fault.

10 With the ignition switched off, check carefully through the system, ensuring that all connections are clean and securely fastened.

11 Check that the HT coil, the distributor cap and the HT leads are clean and dry. Check the leads themselves and the spark plugs (by substitution, if necessary), then check the distributor cap, carbon brush and rotor arm.

12 Regular misfiring is almost certainly due to a fault in the distributor cap, HT leads or spark plugs. Use a timing light (paragraph 4 above) to check whether HT voltage is present at all leads.

13 If HT voltage is not present on any particular lead, the fault will be in that lead, or in the distributor cap. If HT is present on all leads, the fault will be in the spark plugs; check and renew them if there is any doubt about their condition.

14 If no HT is present, check the HT coil; its secondary windings may be breaking down under load.

Direct Ignition system

15 If a fault appears in the engine management system, first check that all wiring is secure and in good condition. If necessary, individual components of the Direct Ignition system may be removed for visual investigation as described later in this Chapter. Coils are best checked by substituting a suspect one with a known good coil, and checking if the misfire is cured.

16 Due to the location of the spark plugs beneath the ignition discharge module, it is not possible to easily check the HT circuit for faults. Further testing should be carried out by a Saab dealer, who will have equipment to access fault codes stored in the system ECU.

3 Ignition HT coil (Bosch Motronic) – removal, testing and refitting

Removal

1 The ignition HT coil is located at the front of the engine compartment, below the power steering fluid reservoir **(see illustration)**.

2 Remove the battery from its mounting tray as described in Chapter 5A.

3 Unplug the HT 'king' lead from the top of the distributor.

4 Identify the low tension leads for position, then disconnect them from the terminals on the coil **(see illustration)**.

5 Unscrew the mounting bracket clamp bolt, and remove the coil from the engine compartment.

Testing

6 Testing of the coil is carried out using a multimeter set to its resistance function, to check the primary (LT '+' to '-' terminals) and secondary (LT '+' to HT lead terminal) windings for continuity. Compare the results obtained to those given in the Specifications at the start of this Chapter. The resistance of the coil windings will vary slightly according to the coil temperature.

Refitting

7 Refitting is a reversal of removal, but make sure that the mounting clamp bolt is securely tightened, and that the wiring connectors are fitted correctly.

3.1 The ignition HT coil is located at the front of the engine compartment, below the power steering fluid reservoir

3.4 Disconnect the low tension leads from the terminals on the HT coil

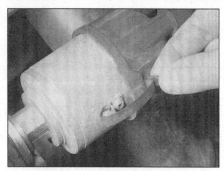

4.1 Releasing the distributor cap clips

4 Distributor (Bosch Motronic) – removal and refitting

Removal

1 Mark the spark plug HT leads to aid refitting, and pull them from the distributor cap. If it is required to remove them from the spark plugs, it will be necessary to remove the inspection cover from the centre of the cylinder head. Release the clips from each side of the distributor cap, and place the cap to one side **(see illustration)**. If the clips are tight, use a screwdriver to prise them off carefully.

2 Disconnect the wiring plug for the Hall-effect sensor.

3 Unscrew and remove the distributor flange bolt. **Note:** The distributor flange is not slotted and so the position of the distributor with respect to the cylinder head cannot be adjusted; the basic ignition timing is established by the engine management system.

4 Withdraw the distributor from the end of the cylinder head. Note that the distributor driveshaft incorporates an off-centre drive

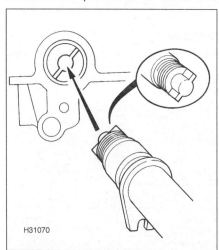

H31070

4.4b Note that the distributor driveshaft incorporates an off-centre drive dog, which engages a slot in the end of the exhaust camshaft

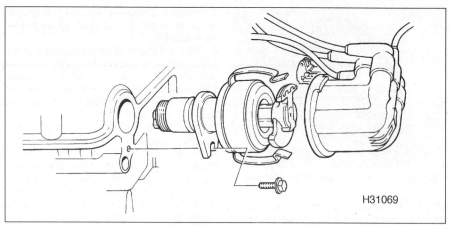

H31069

4.4a Withdraw the distributor from the end of the cylinder head

dog, which engages a slot in the end of the exhaust camshaft **(see illustrations)**.

Refitting

5 Turn the distributor so that the off centre drive dog lines up with the slot in the end of the camshaft.

6 Slide the distributor into the cylinder head, then insert the flange clamp bolt and tighten it securely.

7 Reconnect the wiring to the Hall-effect sensor.

8 Refit the distributor cap, then reconnect the HT leads.

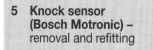

5 Knock sensor (Bosch Motronic) – removal and refitting

Removal

1 The knock sensor is located on the rear of the cylinder block, beneath the inlet manifold. First jack up the front of the car, and support on axle stands (see *Jacking and vehicle support*). Remove the engine upper cover.

2 Disconnect the wiring from the knock sensor.

3 Unscrew the knock sensor from the cylinder block.

6.2 Undo the four screws securing the ignition module

Refitting

4 Wipe clean the threads of the knock sensor, and the aperture in the cylinder block.

5 Insert the knock sensor, and tighten it to the specified torque. **Note:** *It is important to tighten the unit to the correct torque, otherwise it may send incorrect signals to the system ECU.*

6 Reconnect the wiring, and lower the car to the ground. Refit the engine upper cover, making sure that the O-rings are not deformed – if necessary, apply a little petroleum jelly to them to assist refitting.

6 Ignition discharge module (Saab Trionic) – removal and refitting

Removal

1 Open the bonnet, unclip the cover from the top of the battery and disconnect the battery negative lead (refer to *Disconnecting the battery* in the *Reference* Chapter at the end of this manual).

2 Undo the four screws securing the ignition module to the top of the cylinder head **(see illustration)**.

3 Disconnect the wiring plug, located on the left-hand end of the ignition discharge module **(see illustration)**.

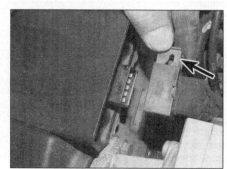

6.3 Release the retaining clip and disconnect the wiring connector

4 Lift the ignition module, at the same time releasing it from the tops of the spark plugs **(see illustration)**.

5 If necessary, the shroud may be removed from the bottom of the module, by inverting it and removing the retaining screws. Separate the black (lower) shroud from the module **(see illustrations)**.

6 The HT springs may be removed from the shroud by careful use of a screwdriver **(see illustration)**.

Refitting

7 Refitting is a reversal of removal, but tighten the retaining screws to the specified torque.

7 Ignition HT coils (Saab Trionic) – general information

The four ignition coils are an integral part of the ignition discharge module upper assembly and can only be purchased from Saab as a complete unit.

If required, the ignition discharge module can be removed from the vehicle as described in Section 6, then taken to your local Saab dealer or motor vehicle electrical specialist, where they can check the ignition coils.

6.4 Lift the module straight up to release it from the spark plugs

8 Slotted rotor for crankshaft sensor (Saab Trionic) – removal and refitting

Removal

1 The slotted rotor is located on the flywheel/driveplate end of the crankshaft. Remove the crankshaft as described in Chapter 2A.

2 Using a Torx key, unscrew the four screws securing the slotted rotor to the crankshaft, then remove the rotor over the end of the crankshaft.

Refitting

3 Refitting is a reversal of removal. Note that

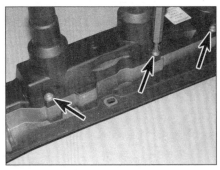

6.5a Undo the screws (three shown) . . .

the rotor can only be fitted in one position, since the bolt holes are unequally-spaced.

9 Ignition timing – general information

The ignition timing is preprogrammed into the system ECU, and cannot be adjusted or even checked with any accuracy. If the timing is thought to be incorrect, the car should be taken to a Saab dealer, who will have the necessary equipment to extract any fault codes stored in the ECU. For further information see Chapter 4A.

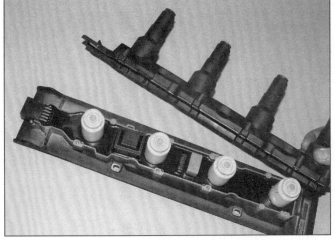

6.5b . . . and separate the black lower shroud from the module

6.6 Rubber sleeve and spring from inside lower shroud

Notes

Chapter 5 Part C:
Preheating system – diesel models

Contents

Degrees of difficulty

Easy, suitable for novice with little experience 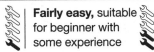	**Fairly easy,** suitable for beginner with some experience 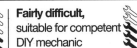	**Fairly difficult,** suitable for competent DIY mechanic	**Difficult,** suitable for experienced DIY mechanic	**Very difficult,** suitable for expert DIY or professional 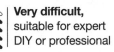

Specifications

Glow plugs

Electrical resistance (typical – no value quoted by Saab)	1.5 ohms
Current consumption (typical – no value quoted by Saab)	8 amps (per plug)

Torque wrench setting	Nm	lbf ft
Glow plugs	10	7

1 Preheating system – description and testing

Description

1 Each cylinder of the engine is fitted with a heater plug (commonly called a glow plug) screwed into it. The plugs are electrically-operated before and during start-up when the engine is cold. Electrical feed to the glow plugs is controlled via the injection system ECU.

2 A warning light in the instrument panel tells the driver that preheating is taking place. When the light goes out, the engine is ready to be started. The voltage supply to the glow plugs continues for several seconds after the light goes out. If no attempt is made to start, the timer then cuts off the supply, in order to avoid draining the battery and overheating the glow plugs.

3 The glow plugs also provide a 'post-heating' function, whereby the glow plugs remain switched on for a period after the engine has started when the engine speed is between 750 and 2500 rpm. The length of time 'post-heating' takes place for is also determined by the control unit but it can be anything up to 3 minutes, depending on engine temperature.

4 The fuel filter is fitted with a heating element to prevent the fuel 'waxing' in extreme conditions and to improve combustion. The heating element is fitted between the filter and its housing and is controlled by the preheating system control unit (ECU). The heating element is switched on if the temperature of the fuel passing through the filter is less than 0°C and switches off when the fuel temperature reaches 20°C.

Testing

5 If the system malfunctions, testing is ultimately by substitution of known good units, but some preliminary checks may be made as follows.

6 Connect a voltmeter or 12 volt test lamp in turn between each glow plug wiring connector and earth (engine or vehicle metal). Make sure that the live connection is kept clear of the engine and bodywork.

7 Have an assistant switch on the ignition, and check that voltage is applied to the glow plugs. Note the time for which the warning light is lit, and the total time for which voltage is applied before the system cuts out. Switch off the ignition.

8 At an under-bonnet temperature of 20°C, typical times noted should be approximately 3 seconds for warning light operation. Warning light time will increase with lower temperatures and decrease with higher temperatures.

9 If there is no supply at all, the control unit, relay or associated wiring is at fault.

10 To locate a defective glow plug, pull off the wiring connector from each plug, and use a continuity tester, or a 12 volt test lamp connected to the battery positive terminal, to check for continuity between each glow plug terminal and earth. The resistance of a glow plug in good condition is very low (less than 1 ohm), so if the test lamp does not light or the continuity tester shows a high resistance, the glow plug is certainly defective.

11 If an ammeter is available, the current draw of each glow plug can be checked. After an initial surge of 15 to 20 amps, each plug should draw 12 amps. Any plug which draws much more or less than this is probably defective.

12 As a final check, the glow plugs can be removed and inspected as described in the following Section.

2.2a On early models, unscrew the retaining nut from each glow plug . . .

2.2b . . . then disconnect the wiring . . .

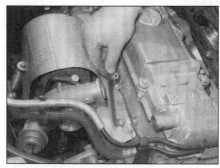

2.2c . . . and lift off the electrical connecting rails (where fitted)

2.2d On later models, pull the wiring connector from the top of each glow plug

2 Glow plugs – removal, inspection and refitting

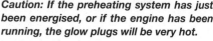

Caution: If the preheating system has just been energised, or if the engine has been running, the glow plugs will be very hot.

Removal

1 Remove the engine upper cover, then remove the inlet air duct leading to the turbocharger after loosening the retaining clips.

2 On early models, undo the retaining nuts and remove the washers from the top of each glow plug, then disconnect the wiring connectors and lift off the electrical connecting rails. On later models, simply pull the wiring connector from the top of each glow plug (**see illustrations**).

3 Unscrew the glow plugs and remove them from the cylinder head.

Inspection

4 Inspect each glow plug for physical damage. Burnt or eroded glow plug tips can be caused by a bad injector spray pattern. Have the injectors checked if this sort of damage is found.

5 If the glow plugs are in good physical condition, check them electrically using a 12 volt test lamp or continuity tester as described in the previous Section.

6 The glow plugs can be energised by applying 12 volts to them to verify that they heat up evenly and in the required time. Observe the following precautions.

a) Support the glow plug by clamping it carefully in a vice or self-locking pliers. Remember it will become red-hot.

b) Make sure that the power supply or test lead incorporates a fuse or overload trip to protect against damage from a short-circuit.

c) After testing, allow the glow plug to cool for several minutes before attempting to handle it.

7 A glow plug in good condition will start to glow red at the tip after drawing current for 5 seconds or so. Any plug which takes much longer to start glowing, or which starts glowing in the middle instead of at the tip, is defective.

Refitting

8 Refit the glow plugs and tighten to the specified torque. Do not overtighten, as this can damage the glow plug element.

9 Refit the wiring connector to the top of each glow plug, and tighten the nuts on early models.

10 Refit the inlet air duct and tighten the clips. Refit the engine upper cover.

3 Preheating system components – removal and refitting

Glow plug control module

Removal

1 The glow plug control module is located on the right-hand side of the engine compartment, to the rear of the air cleaner. First, loosen the mounting bolt and unhook the module from the bracket.

2 Disconnect the wiring and withdraw the module from the engine compartment.

Refitting

3 Refitting is a reversal of removal.

Coolant temperature sensor

4 The coolant temperature sensor is screwed into the thermostat housing. Refer to Chapter 4B for removal and refitting details.

Relays and fuses

5 The fuel heating element relays and fuses are located in the fusebox in the left-hand rear corner of the engine compartment. Refer to Chapter 12 for further details.

Chapter 6
Clutch

Contents

Degrees of difficulty

Easy, suitable for novice with little experience	**Fairly easy,** suitable for beginner with some experience	**Fairly difficult,** suitable for competent DIY mechanic	**Difficult,** suitable for experienced DIY mechanic	**Very difficult,** suitable for expert DIY or professional

Specifications

System type . . . . Single dry-plate clutch with diaphragm spring, operated by master/ slave cylinder hydraulic release system

Friction plate
Diameter . . . . 228 mm
Thickness:
   New . . . . 7.3 mm
   Minimum. . . . . 5.5 mm

Hydraulic release mechanism
Slave cylinder stroke . . . . 80.5 mm
Master cylinder piston diameter. . . . . 19.05 mm

Torque wrench settings

	Nm	lbf ft
Clutch pedal/master cylinder mounting bracket to bulkhead	24	18
Clutch pressure plate to flywheel:		
Petrol models	22	16
Diesel models.	15	11
Master cylinder securing screws	24	18
Slave cylinder.	10	7
Supply pipe to slave cylinder	22	16

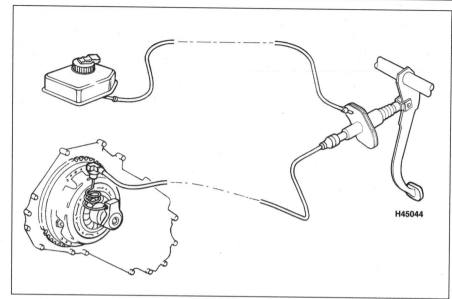

1.1 Hydraulic clutch release system

1 General description

1 The hydraulic clutch system is of single dry-plate type, and consists of the following main components: the clutch pedal, master cylinder, release bearing/slave cylinder, friction plate, and pressure plate with its integral diaphragm spring and cover (see illustration).

2 The friction plate is free to slide along the splines of the transmission input shaft. This is held in position between the flywheel and the pressure plate by the pressure exerted on the pressure plate by the diaphragm spring. Friction lining material is riveted to both sides of the friction plate. Spring cushioning between the friction linings and the hub absorbs transmission shocks, and helps to ensure a smooth take-up of power as the clutch is engaged.

3 The diaphragm spring is mounted on pins, and is held in place in the cover by annular fulcrum rings.

4 Effort is transmitted from the clutch pedal to the master cylinder, mounted on the rear of the engine compartment bulkhead, via a pushrod. The master cylinder piston forces hydraulic fluid through a supply pipe to the slave cylinder, which is located inside the transmission casing, mounted concentrically over the transmission input shaft. The fluid forces the piston out of the slave cylinder, thus actuating the release bearing.

5 When the clutch pedal is depressed, the release bearing is forced to slide along the input shaft sleeve, to bear against the centre of the diaphragm spring, thus pushing the centre of the diaphragm spring inwards. The diaphragm spring acts against a circular fulcrum ring in the cover. When the centre of the spring is pushed in, the outside of the

spring is pushed out, so allowing the pressure plate to move backwards away from the friction plate.

6 When the clutch pedal is released, the diaphragm spring forces the pressure plate into contact with the friction linings on the friction plate. This simultaneously pushes the friction plate forwards on its splines, forcing it against the flywheel. The friction plate is now firmly sandwiched between the pressure plate and the flywheel, and drive is taken up.

7 The fluid used in the hydraulic clutch system is the same as that used in the braking system, hence fluid is supplied to the master cylinder from a tapping on the brake fluid reservoir. The clutch hydraulic system must be sealed before work is carried out on any of its components and then, on completion, topped-up and bled to remove any air bubbles. Details of these procedures are given in Section 6 of this Chapter.

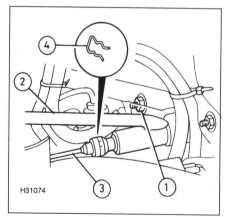

2.6 Disconnecting the hydraulic delivery pipe from the clutch master cylinder

1 Mounting nut   3 Delivery pipe
2 Supply hose   4 Retaining clip

2 Clutch pedal – removal and refitting

Removal

1 Disconnect the battery negative lead (refer to Disconnecting the battery in the Reference Chapter at the end of this manual). Move the driver's seat fully to the rear.

2 On left-hand drive models, unbolt the engine compartment fusebox from its mountings and position it to one side. Where applicable, also disconnect the wiring from the bonnet switch.

3 Apply a proprietary hose clamp to the hose between the fluid reservoir and the clutch master cylinder.

4 Remove all traces of dirt from the outside of the master cylinder and position some cloth beneath the cylinder to catch any spilt fluid.

5 Disconnect the supply hose from the top of the master cylinder. Mop-up the spilt hydraulic fluid using clean cloths and water.

6 Slide out the retaining clip and free the hydraulic delivery pipe from the front of the master cylinder (see illustration). Plug the pipe end and master cylinder port to minimise fluid loss and prevent the entry of dirt. Recover the sealing ring from the union and discard it; a new one must be used on refitting. Refit the retaining clip to the master cylinder groove, ensuring that it is correctly located.

7 Unscrew the two nuts securing the clutch pedal bracket to the bulkhead. Note that on left-hand drive models, the right-hand nut secures the right-hand section of the pedal bracket.

8 On right-hand drive models, carry out the following:

a) Refer to Chapter 10 and remove the steering wheel and column from inside the car.

b) Undo the screws and pivot the fusebox assembly (including the pedal switch) away from the right hand end of the facia.

c) Remove the bonnet release lever from the driver's footwell.

9 On left-hand drive models, carry out the following:

a) Remove the facia lower trim panel and knee shield.

b) Unbolt the diagnostic socket from the trim panel.

10 Remove the clutch pedal switch as described in Chapter 4A, Section 5.

11 Remove the side defroster and floor air ducts and release the wiring harness from the cable ties.

12 Loosen the upper mounting nut and withdraw the pedal bracket, together with master cylinder, from inside the car. Note that the upper mounting stud is located in a slotted bracket.

13 Release the spring clip and disconnect the master cylinder pushrod from the clutch pedal.

14 Remove the over-centre spring, then

3.5 Lift off the pressure plate, then recover the friction plate, noting its orientation

3.11 With the clutch removed, check the machined surface of the flywheel

3.14 Place the friction plate against the flywheel; the stamped lettering FLYWHEEL SIDE should face towards the flywheel

unscrew the nut and pull out the pedal pivot bolt. Remove the pedal from the bracket and recover the spacer and bush.

Refitting

15 Refitting is a reversal of removal, but tighten the clutch pedal bracket mounting nuts to the specified torque. On completion, bleed the clutch hydraulic system with reference to Section 6.

---

3 Clutch assembly – removal, inspection and refitting

> ⚠️ **Warning: Dust created by clutch wear and deposited on the clutch components may contain asbestos, which is a health hazard. DO NOT blow it out with compressed air, nor inhale any of it. DO NOT use petrol or petroleum-based solvents to clean off the dust. Brake system cleaner or methylated spirit should be used to flush the dust into a suitable receptacle. After the clutch components are wiped clean with clean rags, dispose of the contaminated rags and cleaner in a sealed, marked container.**
> **Note:** Although some friction materials may no longer contain asbestos, it is safest to assume that they DO, and to take precautions accordingly

Removal

1 Unless the complete engine/transmission is to be removed from the car and separated for major overhaul (see Chapter 2C), the clutch can be accessed by removing the transmission, as described in Chapter 7A.

2 Before disturbing any of the clutch components, mark the relationship between the pressure plate, friction plate and the flywheel.

3 To aid the removal of the pressure plate, the flywheel should ideally be locked in position by bolting a locking tool to one of the transmission mounting holes, and engaging it with the flywheel ring gear.

4 Working diagonally across the pressure plate, progressively unscrew the mounting bolts, half a turn at a time, until they can be removed by hand.

5 With all the bolts removed, lift off the clutch assembly. Be prepared to catch the friction plate as the cover assembly is lifted from the flywheel, and note which way round the friction plate is fitted **(see illustration)**.

Inspection

Note: *Due to the amount of work necessary to remove and refit clutch components, it is usually considered good practice to renew the clutch friction plate, pressure plate assembly and release bearing as a matched set, even if only one of these is actually worn enough to require renewal.*

6 When cleaning clutch components, observe the warning at the beginning of this Section regarding the hazards of handling the friction materials contained in clutch components; remove dust using a clean cloth, and working in a well-ventilated atmosphere.

7 Check the friction plate facings for signs of wear, damage or oil contamination. If the friction material is cracked, burnt, scored or damaged, or if it is contaminated with oil or grease (shown by shiny black patches), the friction plate must be renewed.

8 If the friction material is still serviceable, check that the centre boss splines are unworn, that the torsion springs are in good condition and securely fastened, and that all the rivets are tight. If any wear or damage is found, the friction plate must be renewed.

9 If the friction material is fouled with oil, this must be due to an oil leak from the crankshaft left-hand oil seal, from the sump-to-cylinder block joint, or from the transmission input shaft; renew the seal or repair the joint, as appropriate, as described in Chapter 2A, 2B or 7A before installing the new friction plate.

10 Check the pressure plate assembly for obvious signs of wear or damage; shake it to check for loose rivets or worn or damaged fulcrum rings, and check that the drive straps securing the pressure plate to the cover do not show signs of overheating (such as a deep yellow or blue discoloration). If the diaphragm spring is worn or damaged, or if its pressure is in any way suspect, the pressure plate assembly should be renewed.

11 Examine the machined bearing surfaces of the pressure plate and of the flywheel **(see illustration)**; they should be clean, completely flat and free from scratches or scoring. If either is discoloured from excessive heat or shows signs of cracks it should be renewed, although minor damage of this nature can sometimes be polished away using emery paper.

12 Check that the release bearing contact surface rotates smoothly and easily, with no sign of noise or roughness, and that the surface itself is smooth and unworn, with no signs of cracks, pitting or scoring. If there is any doubt about its condition, the bearing must be renewed; refer to Section 4 for guidance.

Refitting

13 On reassembly, ensure that the bearing surfaces of the flywheel and pressure plate are completely clean, smooth and free from oil or grease. Use solvent to remove any protective grease from new components.

14 Offer up the friction plate so that its spring hub assembly faces away from the flywheel; observe any manufacturer's markings which show which way around the plate should be fitted **(see illustration)**.

15 Refit the pressure plate assembly to the flywheel, engaging it with its locating dowels; align the marks made on dismantling if the original pressure plate is being re-used. Fit the pressure plate bolts, hand-tightening them only at this stage, so that the friction plate can be rotated to aid alignment, if necessary.

16 The friction plate must now be centralised inside the pressure plate assembly, so that when the transmission is refitted, the input shaft will pass through the splines at the centre of the friction plate. This can be achieved by passing a large screwdriver or wrench extension bar through the friction plate and into the hole in the crankshaft; the friction plate can then be moved around until it is centred over the crankshaft hole. Alternatively, a universal clutch alignment tool can be used; these can be obtained from most car accessory shops. Ensure that the friction plate alignment is correct before proceeding any further.

A clutch alignment device can be made up from a length of metal rod or wooden dowel which is either tapered at one end, or fits closely inside the crankshaft hole, and has insulating tape wound around it, to match the internal diameter of the friction plate splined hole.

17 When the friction plate is centralised, progressively tighten the pressure plate bolts in a diagonal sequence and to the specified torque setting.

18 Where applicable, remove the flywheel locking tool.

19 Apply a thin smear of high melting-point grease to the splines of the friction plate and the transmission input shaft.

20 Refit the transmission as described in Chapter 7A.

4 Clutch slave cylinder/release bearing – removal and refitting

Note: The clutch slave cylinder and thrust release bearing are integrated and can only be purchased as a complete assembly.

Removal

1 Unless the complete engine/transmission unit is to be removed from the car and separated for major overhaul (see Chapter 2C), the clutch release cylinder can only be reached by removing the transmission as described in Chapter 7A.

2 Wipe clean the outside of the slave cylinder then slacken the union nut and disconnect the hydraulic pipe. Wipe up any spilt fluid with a clean cloth.

3 Unscrew the three retaining bolts and slide the slave cylinder from the transmission input shaft **(see illustration)**. Where applicable, remove the sealing ring which is fitted between

the cylinder and transmission housing and discard it; a new one must be used on refitting. Whilst the cylinder is removed, take care not to allow any debris to enter the transmission unit.

4 The slave cylinder is a sealed unit and cannot be overhauled. If the cylinder seals have failed or the release bearing is noisy or rough in operation, then the complete unit must be renewed.

Refitting

5 Ensure the slave cylinder and transmission mating surfaces are clean and dry, then where applicable fit the new sealing ring to the transmission recess.

6 Lubricate the slave cylinder seal with a smear of transmission oil then carefully ease the cylinder along the input shaft and into position. Ensure the sealing ring is still correctly seated in its groove then refit the slave cylinder retaining bolts and tighten them to the specified torque.

7 Reconnect the hydraulic pipe to the slave cylinder, tightening its union nut to the specified torque.

8 Prime and bleed the slave cylinder with hydraulic fluid, as described in Section 6.

9 Refit the transmission unit as described in Chapter 7A.

5 Clutch master cylinder – removal and refitting

Removal

1 Remove the clutch pedal as described in Section 2.

2 Unscrew the mounting nuts and remove the clutch master cylinder from the bracket.

Refitting

3 Refitting is a reversal of removal, but tighten the mounting nuts to the specified torque. On completion, bleed the clutch hydraulic system with reference to Section 6.

6 Clutch hydraulic system – bleeding

⚠ **Warning:** Hydraulic fluid is poisonous; thoroughly wash off spills from bare skin without delay. Seek immediate medical advice if any fluid is swallowed or gets into the eyes. Certain types of hydraulic fluid are inflammable, and may ignite when brought into contact with hot components. When servicing any hydraulic system, it is safest to assume that the fluid IS inflammable, and to take precautions against the risk of fire as though it is petrol that is being handled. It is also hygroscopic (absorbs moisture from the air); excess moisture content lowers the fluid boiling point to an unacceptable level, resulting in a loss of hydraulic pressure. Old fluid may have suffered contamination, and should not be re-used. When topping-up or renewing the fluid, always use the recommended grade, and ensure that it comes from a freshly-opened sealed container.

HAYNES HINT Hydraulic fluid is an effective paint stripper, and will also attack many plastics. If spillage occurs onto painted bodywork or fittings, it should be washed off immediately, using copious quantities of fresh water.

General information

1 Whenever the clutch hydraulic lines are disconnected for service or repair, a certain amount of air will enter the system. The presence of air in any hydraulic system will cause a degree of elasticity; this will translate into poor pedal feel and reduced travel, leading to an inefficient clutch release action and difficult gearchanges. For this reason, the hydraulic system must be bled after repair or servicing, to remove any air bubbles.

2 The most effective way of bleeding the clutch hydraulic system is by pressurising it externally using a pressure brake bleeding kit.

3 These are readily available in motor accessory shops and are extremely effective; the following sub-section describes bleeding the clutch system using such a kit.

Bleeding the clutch

Note: If a new slave cylinder has been fitted, or if you suspect that the hydraulic fluid has been allowed to drain from the existing slave cylinder during servicing or repair, refer to the sub-section entitled 'Bleeding the slave cylinder' first.

4 Remove the dust cap from the bleed nipple **(see illustration)**.

5 Fit a ring spanner over the bleed nipple head, but do not slacken it at this point.

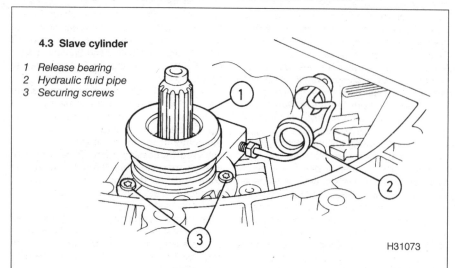

4.3 Slave cylinder

1 Release bearing
2 Hydraulic fluid pipe
3 Securing screws

H31073

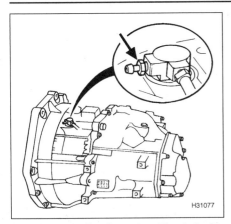

6.4 Clutch hydraulic system bleed nipple

Connect a length of clear plastic hose over the nipple, and insert the other end into a clean container. Pour hydraulic fluid into the container, such that the end of the hose is completely covered.

6 Following the kit manufacturer's instructions, pour hydraulic fluid into the bleeding kit vessel.

7 Unscrew the vehicle's fluid reservoir cap, then connect the bleeding kit fluid supply hose to the reservoir.

8 Connect the pressure hose to a supply of compressed air – a spare tyre is a convenient source.

Caution: Check that the pressure in the tyre does not exceed the maximum quoted by the kit manufacturer, let some air escape to reduce the pressure, if necessary. Gently open the air valve, and allow the air and fluid pressures to equalise. Check that there are no leaks before proceeding.

9 Using the spanner, slacken the bleed nipple until fluid and air bubbles can be seen to flow through the tube, into the container. Maintain a steady flow until the emerging fluid is free of air bubbles; keep a watchful eye on the level of fluid in the bleeding kit vessel and the vehicle's fluid reservoir – if it is allowed to drop too low, air may be forced into the system, defeating the object of the exercise. To refill the vessel, turn off the compressed air supply, remove the lid, and pour in an appropriate quantity of clean fluid from a new container – **do not** re-use the fluid collected in the receiving container. Repeat as necessary until the ejected fluid is bubble-free.

10 On completion, pump the clutch pedal several times to assess its feel and travel. If firm, constant pedal resistance is not felt throughout the pedal stroke, it is probable

that air is still present in the system – repeat the bleeding procedure until the pedal feel is restored.

11 Depressurise the bleeding kit, and remove it from the vehicle.

12 If a new slave cylinder has been fitted, or if you suspect that air has entered the existing slave cylinder, proceed as follows: with the receiving container still connected, open the bleed nipple, while an assistant fully depresses the clutch pedal and holds it there. Wait for the fluid to flow into the receiving container, then with the clutch pedal at the bottom of its stroke, tighten the bleed nipple, and allow the pedal to return to its rest position. Repeat this sequence until the fluid that flows from the bleed nipple into the receiving container is free from air bubbles. Keep a watchful eye on the level of fluid in the vehicle's fluid reservoir, topping-up if necessary.

13 On completion of the bleeding process, tighten the bleed nipple securely, disconnect the receiving container and then refit the nipple dust cap.

14 At this point, the fluid reservoir may well be 'over-full'; the excess should be removed using a *clean* pipette to reduce the level to the MAX mark.

15 Finally, road test the vehicle and check the operation of the clutch.

Bleeding the slave cylinder

16 Providing that the slave cylinder has not

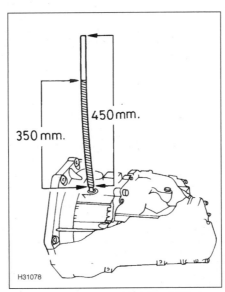

6.20 Fill the hose to a height of 350 mm (measured from the bleed nipple) with new brake fluid

been removed from the transmission during servicing or repair, the procedure described in the preceding sub-section should cause all air to be expelled from the clutch hydraulic system. If however, a large amount of fluid has drained from the slave cylinder, allowing air to enter, or if a new slave cylinder has been fitted, the procedure described above may not be sufficient to purge all the air from the slave cylinder. This is because the bleed nipple is positioned at the point where the hydraulic fluid enters the top of the slave cylinder – fluid is not forced through the slave cylinder during the bleeding process and the cylinder is not fully primed with hydraulic fluid. Consequently, some air may remain inside the slave cylinder housing.

17 To overcome this, the slave cylinder must be primed before the transmission is refitted to the transmission, as follows.

18 Take a 450 mm length of 8 mm diameter clear plastic hose and fit it to the slave cylinder bleed nipple.

19 Open the bleed nipple then press the release bearing along the input shaft sleeve towards the transmission, so that the piston is pushed fully into the slave cylinder. Catch any fluid ejected from the hose in a container.

20 Hold the hose vertically, then fill it to a height of 350 mm (measured from the bleed nipple) with new brake fluid **(see illustration)**.

21 Connect a foot pump or bicycle pump to the end of the hose, ensuring a good seal. Gradually apply pressure to the hose using the pump, until the brake fluid flows into the slave cylinder. Allow the piston to be pushed out of the slave cylinder to the end of its travel, *but no further* – the resistance felt at the pump should increase when the piston reaches the end of its travel.

22 Press the release bearing back along the input shaft sleeve towards the transmission, so that the piston is pushed back fully into the slave cylinder. Allow the air bubbles now flowing through the brake fluid to escape from the end of the plastic hose.

23 Repeat the steps described in paragraphs 21 and 22 until no more air escapes from the slave cylinder.

24 Leave the piston fully retracted inside the slave cylinder, then disconnect and drain the plastic hose. Refit the transmission as described in Chapter 7A, without disturbing the slave cylinder. On completion, bleed the entire hydraulic system as described in the previous sub-section, paying particular attention to paragraph 12.

Notes

Chapter 7 Part A:
Manual transmission

Contents

Degrees of difficulty

Easy, suitable for novice with little experience	Fairly easy, suitable for beginner with some experience	Fairly difficult, suitable for competent DIY mechanic	Difficult, suitable for experienced DIY mechanic	Very difficult, suitable for expert DIY or professional

Specifications

General

Type . . . .   Transversely-mounted, front-wheel-drive layout, with integral transaxle differential/final drive. Five forward speeds, one reverse, all with synchromesh

Torque wrench settings

	Nm	lbf ft
Bellhousing-to-engine block bolts............................	70	52
Gear lever housing-to-floorpan bolts..........................	8	6
Gear linkage-to-selector rod bolt............................	22	16
Gear linkage to transmission	22	16
Left-hand oil seal retaining housing	24	18
Oil level, filler and drain plugs	50	37
Reversing light switch	24	18
Selector rod pinch-bolt....................................	20	15
Selector rod to gear lever..................................	20	15

1 General information

The manual transmission is mounted transversely in the engine bay, bolted directly to the engine. This layout has the advantage of providing the shortest possible drive path to the front wheels, as well as locating the transmission in the airflow through the engine bay, optimising cooling.

Drive from the crankshaft is transmitted from the clutch to the gearbox input shaft, which is splined to accept the clutch friction plate. All six driving gears (pinions) are mounted on the input shaft; reverse, first and second speed pinions are journalled on sliding contact bearings, and the third, fourth and fifth speed pinions are carried on needle bearings.

The driven gears for all five forward speeds are mounted on the output shaft, again with third, fourth and fifth speed gears carried on needle bearings. Reverse gear is integral with the first/second speed synchromesh sleeve.

The pinions are in constant mesh with their corresponding driven gears, and are free to rotate independently of the gearbox shafts until a speed is selected. The difference in diameter and number of teeth between the pinions and gears provides the necessary shaft speed reduction and torque multiplication. Drive is then transmitted to the final drive gears/differential through the output shaft.

All gears are fitted with synchromesh, including reverse. When a speed is selected, the movement of the floor-mounted gear lever actuates a series of selector forks inside the gearbox, which are slotted onto the synchromesh sleeves. The sleeves, which slide axially over splined hubs, press

baulk rings into contact with the respective gear/pinion. The coned surfaces between the baulk rings and the pinion/gear act as a friction clutch, progressively matching the speed of the synchromesh sleeve (and hence the gearbox shaft) with that of the gear/pinion. The dog teeth on the baulk ring prevent the synchromesh sleeve ring from meshing with the gear/pinion until their speeds are exactly matched; this allows gearchanges to be carried out smoothly, and greatly reduces the noise and mechanical wear caused by rapid gearchanges.

When reverse gear is engaged, an idler gear is brought into mesh between the reverse pinion and the teeth on the outside of the first/second speed synchromesh sleeve. This arrangement introduces the necessary speed reduction, and also causes the output shaft to rotate in the opposite direction, allowing the vehicle to be driven in reverse.

2 Transmission –
draining and refilling

General information

1 The gearbox is filled with the correct quantity and grade of oil at manufacture. The level must be checked regularly, and if necessary topped-up in accordance with the maintenance schedule (see Chapter 1A or 1B). However, there is no requirement to drain and renew the oil during the normal lifetime of the gearbox, unless repair or overhaul is carried out.

Draining

2 Take the car on a road test of sufficient length to warm the engine/transmission up to normal operating temperature; this will speed up the draining process, and any sludge and debris will be more likely to be drained out.
3 Park the car on level ground, switch off the ignition, and apply the handbrake firmly. For improved access, jack up the front of the car and support it securely on axle stands. **Note:** *The car must be lowered to the ground and parked on a level surface, to ensure accuracy when refilling and checking the oil level.*
4 Wipe clean the area around the filler plug, which is situated on the top surface of the transmission. Unscrew the plug from the casing, and recover the sealing washer.
5 Position a container with a capacity of at least 2.5 litres (ideally with a large funnel) under the drain plug **(see illustrations)**. The drain plug is located at the rear of the transmission, under the left-hand driveshaft; use a wrench to unscrew the plug from the casing. Note that the drain plug contains an integral magnet, designed to catch the metal fragments produced as the transmission components wear. If the plug is clogged with a large amount of metal debris, this may be an early indication of component failure.
6 Allow all the oil to drain completely into the

2.5a Unscrew the drain plug from the transmission casing

container. If the oil is still hot, take precautions against scalding. Clean both the filler and drain plugs thoroughly, paying particular attention to the threads. Discard the original sealing washers; they should always be renewed whenever they are disturbed.

Refilling

7 When the oil has drained out completely, clean the plug hole threads in the transmission casing. Fit a new sealing washer to the drain plug. Coat the thread with thread-locking compound, and tighten it into the transmission casing. If the car was raised for the draining operation, lower it to the ground.
8 When refilling the transmission, allow plenty of time for the oil level to settle completely before attempting to check it. Note that the car must be parked on a flat, level surface when checking the oil level. Use a funnel if necessary to maintain a gradual, constant flow and avoid spillage.
9 Refill the transmission with the specified grade and quantity of oil, then check the oil level as described in Chapter 1A or 1B. If a large quantity flows out when the level checking plug is removed, refit both the filler and level plugs, then drive the car for a short distance so that the new oil is distributed fully around the transmission components. Recheck the level again upon your return.
10 On completion, fit the filler and level plugs with new sealing washers, and tighten them securely.

2.5b Note that the drain plug contains a removable magnetic insert

3 Gearchange linkage
– adjustment

1 If the action of the gearchange linkage is stiff, slack or vague, the alignment between the gearchange linkage and the gearbox selector rod may be incorrect (also check the oil level and type is correct). The operations in the following paragraphs describe how to check and, if necessary, adjust the alignment.
2 Park the vehicle, apply the handbrake and switch off the ignition.
3 Locate the alignment hole at the top of the gearbox casing, adjacent to the part number plate **(see illustrations)**. Prise out the plug to expose the alignment hole. Select 4th gear, then take the locking tool (a screwdriver with a shaft diameter of approximately 4 mm), and insert it into the alignment hole; this will lock the gearbox in 4th gear. **Note:** *Use a screwdriver; the handle will prevent the screwdriver from falling into the gearbox.*
4 Inside the car, remove the gear lever gaiter and mounting frame to expose the gearchange lever housing. Using a locking pin (screwdriver or drill bit) with a diameter of approximately 4 mm, insert it into the alignment hole in the side of the lever housing **(see illustration)**.
5 If the locking pin can be inserted without difficulty, then the gearchange linkage alignment is correct, and hence cannot be

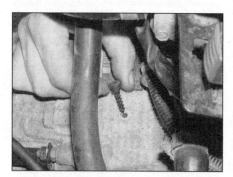

3.3a Prise the plug from the alignment hole at the top of the transmission casing . . .

3.3b . . . then select fourth gear, and insert a screwdriver into the alignment hole; this will lock the transmission in fourth gear

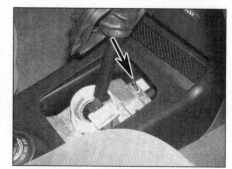

3.4 Inside the vehicle, insert a locking tool (drill bit) into the alignment hole in the side of the lever housing

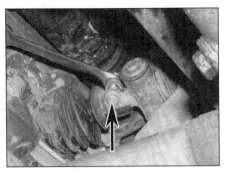

3.7 Slackening the selector rod pinch-bolt

blamed for the poor gearchange quality; the best course of action now is to remove the gearchange linkage and inspect it for wear or damage – refer to Section 4 for details.

6 If the locking pin (screwdriver or drill bit) cannot be inserted into the alignment hole, then the gearchange linkage is incorrectly adjusted.

7 From the engine bay, at the point where the selector rod passes through the bulkhead, slacken the pinch-bolt adjacent to the rubber coupling, to allow movement between the two halves of the selector rod **(see illustration)**.

8 Move the gearchange lever such that the locking pin (screwdriver shaft or drill bit) can be inserted into the alignment hole in the lever housing; ensure that the lever is still in the 4th gear position.

9 In the engine bay, tighten the pinch-bolt on the selector rod, observing the correct torque.

10 Remove the screwdriver from the gearbox alignment hole, and fit the plastic plug.

11 Remove the screwdriver from the gear lever housing alignment hole.

12 Refit the gear lever gaiter and mounting frame.

13 Before moving the vehicle, check that the gear lever can be moved from neutral to all six gear positions. **Note:** *Check the key can be removed while reverse is selected.*

14 Finally, road test the vehicle, and check that all gears can be obtained smoothly and precisely.

**4 Gearchange linkage
– removal, inspection and
refitting**

Gear lever housing

Removal

1 Park the vehicle, switch off the ignition, and apply the handbrake.

2 Referring to Chapter 11, remove the left hand front seat and the centre console. Unclip the rear passenger air duct from the side of the gear lever housing.

3 Lock the gearchange lever and transmission

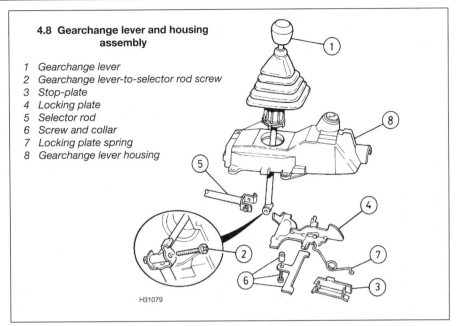

4.8 Gearchange lever and housing assembly

1 *Gearchange lever*
2 *Gearchange lever-to-selector rod screw*
3 *Stop-plate*
4 *Locking plate*
5 *Selector rod*
6 *Screw and collar*
7 *Locking plate spring*
8 *Gearchange lever housing*

selector shaft in the 4th gear position, as described in Section 3.

4 From the engine bay, at the point where the selector rod passes through the bulkhead, slacken the pinch-bolt adjacent to the rubber coupling (see Section 3).

5 Remove the gear lever locking tool, select 3rd gear, then reinsert the locking tool. This will cause the two halves of the selector rod to separate at the coupling in the engine bay.

6 Unscrew the four bolts that secure the gearchange lever housing to the floorpan.

7 Lift up the housing as far as possible and turn it over, then remove the two clamps securing the ignition switch wiring to the housing.

8 Disconnect the wiring from the ignition switch, then remove the housing by pulling it towards the rear of the vehicle, whilst withdrawing the selector rod through the floorpan aperture. Unbolt the gear lever from the selector shaft **(see illustration)**.

9 To remove the gear lever, undo the screws and detach the locking plate holder and retaining spring from the underside of the gear lever housing. Prise out the locking plate pivot using a screwdriver, then remove the stop-plate. Place the gear lever in the reverse gear position, then undo the screw and separate the selector rod from the base of the gearchange lever. At the top of the housing, depress the three clips around the edge of the gear lever's spherical plastic outer bearing and withdraw the lever and bearing assembly from its housing.

Inspection

10 It is most likely that any slack found in the mechanism will be caused by worn bushes between the gear lever and the selector rod. Extract the bushes from the gear lever linkage

(see illustration) and inspect them; if they appear worn or corroded, press them from the gear lever boss and renew them.

Refitting

11 Reassemble the gearchange lever to its housing, then reconnect the lever to the selector rod and tighten the bolt to the specified torque.

12 Press the stop-plate into position in the lever housing, then fit the locking plate into position, ensuring that the pivot pins snap into their respective recesses and that the bushings are correctly located.

13 Fit the locking plate holder, then coat the threads of the securing screws with locking fluid and fit them.

14 Fit the locking plate spring, then adjust the position of the locking plate by turning the locking plate holder securing screw, so that

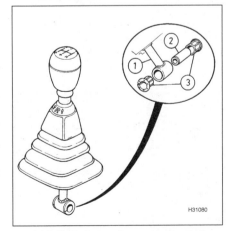

4.10 Gearchange lever selector rod bushes (inset)

1 *Gearchange lever*   2 *Sleeve*   3 *Bushes*

the edge of the locking plate is level with the heel in the lever housing. Ensure that the stop does not come into contact with the locking plate **(see illustration)**.

15 Refit the gear lever housing and selector rod assembly to the vehicle by reversing the removal sequence. Reconnect the selector rod to the transmission at the coupling in the engine bay as described in Section 3.

16 On completion, check that the gear lever can be moved from neutral to all six gear positions. Finally, road test the vehicle, and check that all gears can be obtained smoothly and precisely.

Selector rod

Removal

17 Refer to the previous sub-Section, and remove the gear lever housing. Ensure that 4th gear is selected before removal. Remove the plug from the alignment hole in the top of the gearbox casing, and lock the gearbox in 4th gear using a suitable screwdriver, as described in Section 3.

18 From within the engine bay, at the point where the selector rod passes through the bulkhead, loosen the pinch-bolt collar to detach the selector rod from the gearbox.

19 From inside the car, carefully withdraw the selector rod through the bulkhead, taking care to avoid damaging the rubber grommet in the bulkhead.

Refitting

20 Lubricate the selector rod with silicone grease, and push it through the grommet in the bulkhead; do not tighten the pinch-bolt collar at the gearbox at this stage.

21 Refit the gear lever housing as described in the previous sub-Section. Fit the bushes, and bolt the gear lever to the selector rod.

22 Lock the gear lever in 4th gear by inserting a screwdriver with a 4 mm shaft into the alignment hole on the gear lever housing, with reference to Section 3.

23 Tighten the pinch-bolt collar on the selector rod at the gearbox, observing the specified torque.

24 Remove the screwdriver from the housing, and refit the gear lever gaiter.

25 Before moving the vehicle, check that the gear lever can be moved from neutral to all six

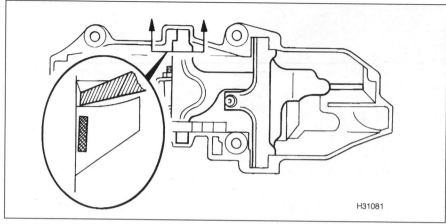

4.14 Adjust the position of the locking plate so that the edge of the locking plate is level with the heel in the lever housing

gear positions. Finally, road test the vehicle, and check that all gears can be obtained smoothly and precisely.

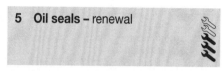

5   Oil seals – renewal

Right-hand driveshaft oil seal

1 Apply the handbrake, then jack up the front, right-hand side of the vehicle and support on an axle stand (see *Jacking and vehicle support*). Remove the right-hand front roadwheel. By raising just the right-hand side, there will be minimal loss of fluid from the transmission when the driveshaft is removed.

2 Refer to Section 2 and drain the transmission oil. Clean and refit the drain plug.

3 Refer to Chapter 8 and remove the intermediate driveshaft and bearing assembly **(see illustration)**.

4 Using a suitable lever, prise the driveshaft oil seal out from the transmission housing **(see illustration)**, taking care not to damage the sealing surface. Discard the old seal.

5 Thoroughly clean the mating surfaces of the bearing housing and differential casing; take precautions to prevent debris entering the bearings of either assembly.

6 Lubricate the new oil seal with clean oil, and carefully refit it into the transmission housing, ensuring that it is seated squarely **(see illustration)**.

7 Refer to Chapter 8 and refit the intermediate driveshaft and bearing assembly.

8 Refit the roadwheel, and lower the vehicle to the ground. Tighten the roadwheel bolts to the correct torque.

9 Refer to Section 2 and refill the transmission with oil of the correct grade.

Left-hand driveshaft oil seal and O-ring

10 Apply the handbrake, then jack up the front, left-hand side of the vehicle and support on an axle stand (see *Jacking and vehicle support*). Remove the left-hand front roadwheel. By raising just the left-hand side, there will be minimal loss of fluid from the transmission when the driveshaft is removed.

11 Refer to Section 2 and drain the transmission oil. Clean and refit the drain plug as described in Section 2.

12 Refer to Chapter 8 and disconnect the left-hand driveshaft from the transmission at the inboard universal joint.

13 Place a container beneath the driveshaft housing mating face, then unscrew and remove the five retaining bolts.

14 Withdraw the seal retaining housing from

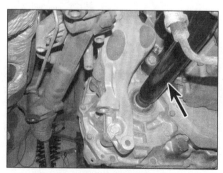

5.4 Driveshaft intermediate shaft

5.5 Levering out the oil seal, using a block of wood to allow better leverage

5.6 Using a large socket to refit the oil seal, making sure it seats squarely

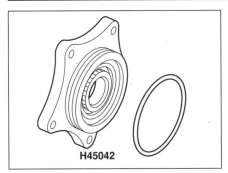

5.14 O-ring seal fitted to the driveshaft seal retaining housing

the transmission, then remove the O-ring seal from the housing **(see illustration)**.

15 Note the fitted depth of the oil seal in its housing and the correct fitted position. Using a suitable lever, carefully prise the oil seal out from the housing, taking care not to damage the sealing surface.

16 Thoroughly clean the mating surfaces of the bearing housing and differential casing; take precautions to prevent debris entering the bearings of either assembly.

17 Lubricate the new oil seal with clean oil, and carefully refit the it into the oil seal retaining housing, ensuring that it is seated squarely.

18 Refit the O-ring seal to the seal retaining housing, then refit the housing to the transmission. Tighten the five retaining screws to the specified torque setting.

19 Refer to Chapter 8 and reconnect the left-hand driveshaft at the universal joint.

20 Refit the roadwheel, and lower the vehicle to the ground. Tighten the roadwheel bolts to the correct torque.

21 Refer to Section 2 and refill the transmission with oil of the correct grade.

Input shaft oil seal

22 The oil seal is part of the clutch slave cylinder assembly and cannot be renewed separately, see Chapter 6 (*Clutch slave cylinder/release bearing – removal and refitting*) for further information.

Selector rod oil seal

23 Clean off the area around the selector rod seal in the transmission, to prevent dirt entering the transmission.

24 Ensure that 4th gear is selected, remove the plug from the alignment hole in the top of the gearbox casing, and lock the gearbox in 4th gear using a suitable 4 mm locking tool/screwdriver, as described in Section 3.

25 Slacken and remove the selector rod retaining bolt, then select 3rd gear to disengage the selector rod from the transmission.

26 Note the fitted position of the oil seal in its housing then, using a suitable lever, carefully prise the oil seal out from the transmission, taking care not to damage the sealing surface.

27 Thoroughly clean the sealing surface and

selector rod, check there are no burrs on the selector rod; take precautions to prevent debris entering the transmission.

28 Lubricate the new oil seal and selector rod with clean oil, and carefully refit the new seal into the transmission housing, ensuring that it is seated squarely.

29 Refit the selector rod and securely tighten the retaining bolt. Remove the locking tool/screwdriver from the housing, and check the gearchange linkage adjustment as described in Section 3.

30 Before moving the vehicle, check that the gear lever can be moved from neutral to all six gear positions. Check the transmission oil level. Finally, road test the vehicle, and check that all gears can be obtained smoothly and precisely.

6 Reversing light switch – testing, removal and refitting

Testing

1 Disconnect the battery negative lead (refer to *Disconnecting the battery* in the *Reference* Chapter at the end of this manual).

2 Unplug the wiring harness from the reversing light switch at the connector. The switch is located on the rear of the transmission casing **(see illustration)**.

3 Connect the probes of a continuity tester, or a multimeter set to the resistance function, across the terminals of the reversing light switch.

4 The switch contacts are normally open, so with any gear other than reverse selected, the tester/meter should indicate an open circuit. When reverse gear is then selected, the switch contacts should close, causing the tester/meter to indicate continuity.

5 If the switch does not function correctly, or is intermittent in its operation, it should be renewed.

Removal

6 Unplug the wiring harness from the reversing light switch at the connector.

7 Unscrew the switch, recovering any washers that may be fitted; these must be refitted, to ensure that the correct clearance exists between the switch shaft and the reverse gear shaft.

6.2 Reversing light switch location

Refitting

8 Refitting is a reversal of removal.

7 Speedometer drive – removal and refitting

General information

1 All models covered in this Manual are fitted with an electronic transducer in place of the drive gear fitted to earlier models. This device measures the rotational speed of the transmission final drive, and converts the information into an electronic signal, which is then sent to the speedometer module in the instrument panel. The signal is also used as an input by the engine management system ECU (and where fitted, by the cruise control ECU, the trip computer and the traction control system ECU).

Removal

2 Locate the speed transducer, which is on the differential housing, at the rear of the transmission case.

3 Unplug the wiring harness from the transducer, at the connector.

4 Undo the transducer retaining screw, and unscrew the unit from the transmission casing.

5 Where applicable, recover and discard the O-ring seal.

Refitting

6 Refit the transducer by following the removal procedure in reverse. **Note:** *Where applicable, a new O-ring seal must be used on refitting.*

8 Transmission – removal and refitting

Note: *Refer to Chapter 2C for details on removal of the engine and transmission as a complete assembly.*

Removal

1 Park the vehicle on a level surface, apply the handbrake and chock the rear wheels. Remove the wheel centre caps, and slacken the wheel bolts.

2 Apply the handbrake, then raise the front of the vehicle, support it securely on axle stands and remove the roadwheels; refer to *Jacking and vehicle support* for guidance. Remove the engine top cover, and, where applicable, also remove the intake resonator together with the air mass flow meter.

3 Refer to Section 2 of this Chapter and drain the oil from the transmission. Refit and tighten the drain plug.

4 Refer to Section 3, and set the gearchange linkage in a reference position, to ensure correct alignment of the linkage on refitting.

Undo the retaining bolt and disconnect the gear linkage from the transmission.

5 Referring to Chapter 5A, remove the battery cover, disconnect both battery cables and remove the battery.

6 Unbolt the battery tray from the side of the engine bay **(see illustration)**.

7 Refer to Chapter 6 and seal off the clutch hydraulic system by fitting a clamp to the flexible section of the slave cylinder supply hose.

8 Release the securing clip and disconnect the connection for the clutch slave cylinder hydraulic fluid delivery at the top of the transmission. Refit the securing clip to the connector after it has been disconnected for safe-keeping. Plug the aperture and fluid line to minimise leakage and to prevent the ingress of foreign material.

9 Unplug the wiring connector from the reversing light switch at the transmission (see Section 6 of this Chapter).

10 Unscrew and remove the three upper transmission retaining bolts.

11 Unplug the wiring connector from the oxygen sensor, and release the wiring from the support clamps.

12 Refer to Chapter 4A or 4B and remove the exhaust front pipe. This is necessary to prevent damage to the pipe flexible section.

13 Position a lifting beam across the engine bay, locating the support legs securely in the sills at either side, in line with the strut top mountings. Hook the jib onto the engine lifting eyelet and raise it, so that the weight of the engine is taken off the transmission mounting. Most people won't have access to an engine lifting beam, but it may be possible to hire one. Alternatively, an engine hoist may be used to support the engine, but when using this method, bear in mind that if the vehicle is lowered on its axle stands to adjust the working height, for example, then the hoist will have to be lowered accordingly, to avoid straining the engine mountings.

14 Remove the front subframe **(see illustration)** using the following procedure:

a) *Support the engine assembly using a suitable hoist or engine support bar which straddles the engine compartment. Slightly lift the engine assembly so that its weight is supported.*

b) *Remove the exhaust front pipe as described in Chapter 4A or 4B.*

c) *Disconnect the front suspension lower arms from the hub carriers, and remove the front anti-roll bar as described in Chapter 10.*

d) *Support the subframe using a trolley jack.*

e) *Unscrew and remove the subframe front and rear mounting bolts, and also the two mounting nuts, then lower the subframe to the ground.*

15 Unbolt the rear engine mounting bracket from the transmission.

16 With reference to Chapter 8, remove the left-hand driveshaft from the transmission.

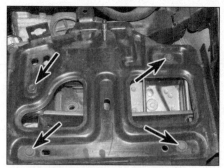

8.6 Undo the battery tray bolts

17 Undo the retaining bolts and remove the lower cover plate from the flywheel **(see illustration)**. **Note:** *On B234 and B235 models also remove the bolts between the transmission and the engine oil sump.*

18 Undo the retaining bolt(s) and disconnect the earth cable(s) from the transmission housing.

19 Unscrew the bolts securing the left-hand engine/transmission mounting to the bodywork, then lower the transmission approximately 5.0 cm taking care to avoid straining the other engine mountings as you do this. Make sure the engine/transmission is well supported by the lifting beam.

20 Position a jack underneath the transmission, and raise it to take the weight of the unit. Check that nothing remains connected to the transmission before attempting to separate it from the engine.

21 Work around the circumference of the bellhousing, and remove the retaining bolts from the bellhousing. Pull the transmission away from the engine, extracting the input shaft from the clutch friction plate – this task should only be attempted with the help of an assistant. When the input shaft is clear of the clutch friction plate, lower the transmission to the ground.

 Warning: Maintain firm support on the transmission, to ensure that it remains steady on the jack head.

22 Unbolt the left-hand mounting bracket from the transmission.

23 At this point with the transmission removed, it would be a good opportunity to check the clutch assembly, and renew it if necessary (see Chapter 6).

Refitting

24 Refit the transmission by reversing the removal procedure, noting the following points:

a) *Apply a smear of high melting-point grease to the transmission input shaft. Do not apply an excessive amount, as there is a possibility of the clutch friction plate being contaminated.*

b) *Refit the engine/transmission mountings with reference to Chapter 2A or 2B.*

c) *Observe the specified torque wrench*

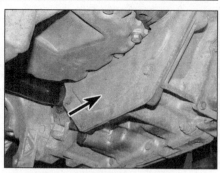

8.17 Remove the lower flywheel cover plate

settings (where applicable) when tightening all nuts and bolts.

d) *Bleed the clutch hydraulic system, referring to Chapter 6 for reference.*

e) *On completion, if the transmission was drained, refill with the specified type and quantity of oil as described in Section 2.*

9 Transmission overhaul – general information

The overhaul of a manual transmission is a complex (and often expensive) engineering task for the DIY home mechanic to undertake, which requires access to specialist equipment. It involves dismantling and reassembly of many small components, measuring clearances precisely, and if necessary adjusting them by the selection shims and spacers. Internal transmission components are also often difficult to obtain, and in many instances extremely expensive. Because of this, if the transmission develops a fault or becomes noisy, the best course of action is to have the unit overhauled by a specialist repairer, or to obtain an exchange reconditioned unit.

Nevertheless, it is not impossible for the more experienced mechanic to overhaul the transmission, if the special tools are available and the job is carried out in a deliberate step-by-step manner, to ensure that nothing is overlooked.

The tools necessary for an overhaul include internal and external circlip pliers, bearing pullers, a slide hammer, a set of pin punches, a dial test indicator (dial gauge), and possibly a hydraulic press. In addition, a large, sturdy workbench and a vice will be required.

During dismantling of the transmission, make careful notes of how each component is fitted, to make reassembly easier and accurate.

Before dismantling the transmission, it will help if you have some idea of where the problem lies. Certain problems can be closely related to specific areas in the transmission, which can make component examination and renewal easier. Refer to *Fault finding* at the end of this manual for more information.

Chapter 7 Part B:
Automatic transmission

Contents

Degrees of difficulty

Easy, suitable for novice with little experience	Fairly easy, suitable for beginner with some experience	Fairly difficult, suitable for competent DIY mechanic	Difficult, suitable for experienced DIY mechanic	Very difficult, suitable for expert DIY or professional

Specifications

General

Designation . . . .   AF20 or AF22 (automatic transmission front-wheel-drive)
Type*:
  FA44 . . . .   Four speed electronically-controlled automatic with three (Normal, Sport and Winter) driving modes

The type code is marked on a plate, attached to the top of the transmission casing

Torque wrench settings

	Nm	lbf ft
Drain plug.	40	30
Driveplate/lower bellhousing cover plate	8	6
Engine-to-transmission unit bolts	See Chapter 2A	
Fluid filler pipe retaining nut.	22	16
Fluid temperature sensor	25	18
Fluid temperature sensor cover plate bolt	25	18
Gear selector position sensor:		
Switch-to-transmission nut/screw	8	6
Lever-to-position sensor bolt	25	18
Input shaft speed sensor bolt.	6	4
Left-hand engine mounting	See Chapter 2A	
Oil cooler unions*	27	20
Output shaft speed sensor bolt	6	4
Speed sensor.	6	4
Torque converter-to-driveplate bolts*.	60	44

Use new fasteners

1 General information

1 Automatic transmission is available as an option on all petrol models except those fitted with the 2.3 litre turbo engine. The AF20/22 automatic transmission is an electronically-controlled four-speed unit, incorporating a lock-up function. It consists mainly of a planetary gear unit, a torque converter with lock-up clutch, a hydraulic control system and an electronic control system. The unit is controlled by the electronic control unit (ECU) via four electrically-operated solenoid valves. The transmission unit has three driving modes: Normal (economy), Sport and Winter modes.

2 The Normal (economy) mode is the standard mode for driving in which the transmission shifts up at relatively low engine speeds to combine reasonable performance with economy. If the transmission unit is switched into Sport mode, using the button on the selector lever, the transmission shifts up only at high engine speeds, giving improved acceleration and overtaking performance. When the transmission is in Sport mode, the indicator light in the instrument panel is illuminated. If the transmission is switched into Winter mode, using the button on the selector lever indicator panel, the transmission will select third gear as the vehicle pulls away from a standing start; this helps to maintain traction on very slippery surfaces.

3 The torque converter provides a fluid coupling between engine and transmission, which acts as an automatic clutch, and also

3.4 Remove the locking clip from the selector cable

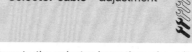

4.5a Remove the locking clip . . .

4.5b . . . and the anti-rattle clip . . .

provides a degree of torque multiplication when accelerating.

4 The epicyclic geartrain provides one of the forward or reverse gear ratios, according to which of its component parts are held stationary or allowed to turn. The components of the geartrain are held or released by brakes and clutches which are activated by the control unit. A fluid pump within the transmission provides the necessary hydraulic pressure to operate the brakes and clutches.

5 Driver control of the transmission is by a seven-position selector lever. The 'drive' D position, allows automatic changing throughout the range of all four gear ratios. An automatic kickdown facility shifts the transmission down a gear if the accelerator pedal is fully depressed. The transmission also has three 'hold' positions, 1 means only the first gear ratio can be selected, 2 allows both the first and second gear ratios position to be automatically selected and 3 allows automatic changing between the first three gear ratios. These 'hold' positions are useful for providing engine braking when travelling down steep gradients. Note, however, that the transmission should *never* be shifted down a position at high engine speeds.

6 Due to the complexity of the automatic transmission, any repair or overhaul work must be left to a Saab dealer with the necessary special equipment for fault diagnosis and repair. The contents of the following Sections are therefore confined to supplying general information, and any service information and instructions that can be used by the owner.

2 Transmission fluid – draining and refilling

Refer to the information given in Chapter 1A.

3 Selector cable – adjustment

1 Operate the selector lever throughout its entire range and check that the transmission engages the correct gear indicated on the selector lever position indicator.

2 Check the play in the selector lever while it is in position N and position D. If not the same, then adjustment is necessary as follows.

3 Inside the vehicle, position the selector lever in the P (Park) position.

4 Working in the engine compartment, lift the adjustment retaining clip on the transmission end of the selector cable **(see illustration)**.

5 Locate the lever on the transmission range switch, to which the selector cable is connected. Position the lever so that the transmission is set in the Park position.

6 With the handbrake in the off position, roll the car until the Park interlock engages.

7 With the aid of an assistant, hold the selector lever rearward in the Park position to take up the free play.

8 Working in the engine compartment, press down the adjustment clip at the transmission end to lock the cable.

9 Check the selector lever as described in

paragraphs 1 and 2 and, if necessary, repeat the adjustment procedure.

10 On completion, road test the vehicle to check the correct operation of the gearchange.

4 Selector cable – removal and refitting

Removal

1 Working in the engine compartment, remove the battery and battery tray (see Chapter 5A) in order to gain access to the transmission end of the selector cable.

2 Inside the car, carefully prise up the position indicator from the selector lever housing.

3 Remove the centre and floor consoles with reference to Chapter 11.

4 Disconnect the air duct to the rear air vent.

5 On the selector lever housing, remove the locking clip and anti-rattle clip, then drive out the pin while removing the end of the cable from the ball **(see illustrations)**.

6 Pull out the locking clip, then depress the catches and disengage the selector outer cable from the selector lever housing.

7 Unbolt the support bracket for the air conditioning and servo pipes.

8 On the transmission, unscrew the retaining nut and detach the lever from the range switch **(see illustration)**.

9 Pull out the locking clip and disengage the selector cable ferrule from the transmission bracket **(see illustrations)**.

10 At the bulkhead, press the rubber grommet

4.5c . . . then withdraw the pin from the selector

4.8 Remove the retaining nut and detach the selector lever from the range switch

4.9a Withdraw the locking clip . . .

4.9b ... and release the selector cable from the bracket

through the hole, then pull it out diagonally into the engine compartment. Withdraw the selector cable from the vehicle.

11 Examine the cable, looking for worn end fittings or a damaged outer casing, and for signs of fraying of the inner cable. Check the cable's operation; the inner cable should move smoothly and easily through the outer casing. Remember that a cable that appears serviceable when tested off the car may well be much heavier in operation when curved into its working position. Renew the cable if it shows any signs of excessive wear or any damage.

Refitting

12 Refitting is a reversal of removal, noting the following points:
 a) Ensure the cable is correctly routed and located securely in the bulkhead.
 b) Adjust the selector cable as described in Section 3.

5 Selector lever assembly – removal and refitting

Removal

1 Remove the centre and floor consoles, and the rear compartment air ducts, as described in Chapter 11.
2 Remove the locking clip and anti-rattle clip, then drive out the pin while removing the end of the cable from the ball.
3 Unscrew and remove the retaining bolts

then lift the gear selector lever housing away from the floorpan.
4 Disconnect any wiring block connectors from the gear selector housing, and release any cable ties from the wiring loom **(see illustrations)**.
5 Using a screwdriver, withdraw the securing clip and release the selector cable from the housing **(see illustrations)**. Remove the gear selector housing from the vehicle.
6 Inspect the selector lever mechanism for signs of wear or damage.

Refitting

7 Refitting is a reversal of removal, but adjust the selector cable as described in Section 3.

6 Oil seals – renewal

Driveshaft oil seals

Right-hand oil seal

1 Apply the handbrake, then jack up the front, right-hand side of the vehicle and support on an axle stand (see *Jacking and vehicle support*). Remove the right-hand front roadwheel. By raising just the right-hand side, there will be minimal loss of fluid from the automatic transmission when the driveshaft is removed.
2 Refer to Chapter 8 and remove the intermediate driveshaft and bearing assembly. Be prepared for some loss of fluid, by placing a container beneath the transmission.
3 Using a suitable lever, prise the driveshaft oil seal out from the transmission housing, taking care not to damage the sealing surface. Discard the old seal.
4 Thoroughly clean the mating surfaces of the bearing housing and differential casing; take precautions to prevent debris entering the bearings of either assembly.
5 Lubricate the new oil seal with clean fluid, and carefully refit it into the transmission housing, ensuring that it is seated squarely.
6 Refer to Chapter 8 and refit the intermediate driveshaft and bearing assembly.
7 Refit the roadwheel, and lower the vehicle to the ground. Tighten the roadwheel bolts to the correct torque.

8 Refer to Chapter 1A and check/top-up the transmission fluid level.

Left-hand oil seal

9 Apply the handbrake, then jack up the front, left-hand side of the vehicle and support on an axle stand (see *Jacking and vehicle support*). Remove the left-hand front roadwheel. By raising just the left-hand side, there will be minimal loss of fluid from the automatic transmission when the driveshaft is removed.
10 Refer to Chapter 10, and unscrew the clamp bolt securing the front suspension lower balljoint to the hub carrier, then lever down the lower arm and disconnect the balljoint. Secure the lower arm in this position using a block of wood positioned between the arm and anti-roll bar.
11 Carefully lever the driveshaft inner joint from the transmission, and support the driveshaft to one side. Be prepared for some loss of oil, and take care not to force the inner joint apart.
12 Using a suitable lever, prise the driveshaft oil seal out from the transmission housing, taking care not to damage the sealing surface. Discard the old seal.
13 Thoroughly clean the mating surfaces of the bearing housing and differential casing; take precautions to prevent debris entering the bearings of either assembly.
14 Lubricate the new oil seal with clean fluid, and carefully refit it into the transmission housing, ensuring that it is seated squarely.
15 Carefully insert the driveshaft into the transmission final drive, then refit the front suspension lower arm and balljoint with reference to Chapter 10.
16 Refit the roadwheel and lower the car to the ground. Tighten the roadwheel bolts to the correct torque.
17 Refer to Chapter 1A and check/top-up the transmission fluid level.

Torque converter oil seal

18 Remove the transmission as described in Section 9.
19 Carefully slide the torque converter off the transmission shaft whilst being prepared for fluid spillage.
20 Note the correct fitted position of the seal in the oil pump housing then carefully lever the seal out of position taking care not to mark the housing or input shaft.

5.4a Disconnect the wiring connector from the gear selector ...

5.4b ... and the ignition switch

5.5 Lever out the clip to remove the selector cable from the housing

21 Remove all traces of dirt from the area around the oil seal aperture then press the new seal into position, ensuring its sealing lip is facing inwards.

22 Lubricate the seal with clean transmission fluid then carefully ease the torque converter into position.

23 Refit the transmission (see Section 9).

7 Fluid cooler – general information

The transmission fluid cooler is an integral part of the radiator assembly. Refer to Chapter 3 for removal and refitting details. If the cooler is damaged the complete radiator assembly must be renewed.

8 Transmission control system electrical components – removal and refitting

Gear selector position sensor

General information

1 As well as informing the transmission ECU which gear is currently selected, the gear selector position sensor also contains contacts which control the operation of the reversing lights relay, and the starter motor inhibitor relay.

Removal

2 Remove the battery as described in Chapter 5A, then undo the retaining bolts and remove the battery tray.

3 Undo the securing nut and release the transmission fluid dipstick tube from the side of the transmission position sensor **(see illustration)**.

4 Select position 1, then undo the retaining nut and disconnect the selector lever from the transmission position sensor **(see illustration)**.

5 Unscrew and remove the nut/bolts that

8.3 Remove the securing nut to release the fluid dipstick tube

secure the gear selector position sensor to the transmission.

6 Unplug the wiring connector, then withdraw the position sensor from the transmission selector shaft and remove it from the engine compartment.

Refitting

7 Refitting is a reversal of removal. On completion, check the adjustment of the selector cable with reference to Section 3.

Kickdown switch

Removal

8 The kickdown switch is located beneath the accelerator pedal. Working in the driver's footwell, remove the trim panel at the base of the A-pillar (see Chapter 11, Section 26). On LHD models, remove the trim from the left-hand side of the centre console.

9 Lift the accelerator pedal, then peel up the carpet to expose the kickdown switch **(see illustration)**.

10 Unplug the wiring at the connector, then pull the kickdown switch from its mounting recess.

Refitting

11 Refitting is a reversal of removal, but adjust the accelerator cable as described in Chapter 4A. Ensure that the switch is pressed fully into its mounting recess and that the wiring is securely reconnected.

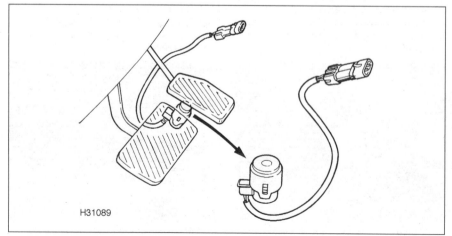

8.9 Lift the accelerator pedal, then peel up the carpet to expose the kickdown switch

8.4 Remove the retaining nut and detach the selector lever from the position sensor

Electronic control unit (ECU)

Removal

12 The ECU is located in the front passenger footwell. Prior to removal, disconnect the battery negative lead (refer to *Disconnecting the battery* in the *Reference* Chapter at the end of this manual).

13 Remove the glovebox as described in Chapter 11.

14 Release the retaining clip and disconnect the wiring connector from the ECU. Release the ECU from the mounting bracket and remove from the vehicle.

Refitting

15 Refitting is the reverse of removal, ensuring that the wiring is securely reconnected.

Input and output shaft speed sensors

Removal

16 The speed sensors are fitted to the top of the transmission unit. The input shaft speed sensor is the front of the two sensors and is nearest to the left-hand end of the transmission. The output shaft sensor is the rear of the two **(see illustration)**.

17 Access to the input shaft speed sensor is gained by temporarily unclipping the coolant expansion tank from its mountings and positioning it clear. Access to the output shaft speed sensor is from the rear of the engine compartment.

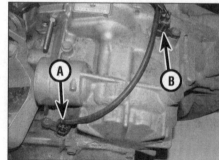

8.16 Automatic transmission input shaft speed sensor (A) and output shaft speed sensor (B) locations

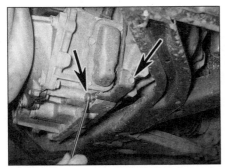

8.26 Undo the retaining bolts and remove the cover plate . . .

8.27 . . . to gain access to the fluid temperature sensor

Removal

1 Apply the handbrake, then jack up the front of the vehicle and support it on axle stands (see *Jacking and vehicle support*). Place the selector lever in the N (Neutral) position. Remove both front roadwheels and the engine undertray.

2 Remove the engine top cover/inlet manifold cover, and, where applicable, also remove the intake resonator together with the air mass flow meter.

3 Drain the transmission fluid as described in Chapter 1A, then refit the drain plug and tighten it to the specified torque.

4 Remove the battery as described in Chapter 5A.

5 Disconnect the battery earthing cable(s) from the transmission casing **(see illustrations)**. Release the cabling from the transmission fluid dipstick tube.

6 Unscrew the retaining bolt, then withdraw the dipstick and its tube from the transmission casing, and plug the open hole to prevent contamination.

7 Disconnect the breather hose (where fitted) from the top of the transmission unit.

8 Disconnect the selector cable from the transmission as described in Sections 3 and 4.

9 Unplug the transmission control system wiring at the two connectors located behind the battery position **(see illustration)**.

10 Trace the wiring back from the transmission switches and sensors and disconnect the various connectors by lifting their retaining clips. Release the main wiring harness from any clips or ties securing it to the transmission unit. Where necessary, disconnect the wiring to the oxygen sensors.

11 Position a lifting beam across the engine bay, locating the support legs securely in the sills at either side, in line with the strut top mountings. Hook the jib onto the engine lifting eye and raise it, so that the weight of the engine is taken off the transmission mounting. Most people won't have access to an engine lifting beam, but it may be possible to hire one. Alternatively, an engine hoist may be used to support the engine, but when using this method, bear in mind that if the vehicle is lowered on its axle stands to adjust the working height, for example, then the hoist

18 Disconnect the wiring, then wipe clean the area around the relevant sensor.

19 Undo the retaining bolt and remove the sensor from the transmission. Remove the sealing ring from the sensor and discard it, a new one should be used on refitting.

Refitting

20 Fit the new sealing ring to the sensor groove and lubricate it with a smear of transmission fluid.

21 Ease the sensor into position then refit the retaining bolt and tighten it to the specified torque setting. Reconnect the wiring connector.

22 Refit the battery and clip the expansion tank (where necessary) back into position.

Fluid temperature sensor

Removal

23 The fluid temperature sensor is screwed into the base of the transmission unit, at the front.

24 Apply the handbrake, then jack up the front of the vehicle and support it on axle stands (see *Jacking and vehicle support*). Remove the engine undertray, where fitted.

25 Trace the wiring back from the sensor, noting its correct routing. Disconnect the wiring connector and free the wiring from its retaining clips.

26 Undo the retaining bolts and remove the cover plate from the sensor **(see illustration)**.

27 Wipe clean the area around the sensor and have a suitable plug ready to minimise

fluid loss as the sensor is removed **(see illustration)**.

28 Unscrew the sensor and remove it from the transmission unit along with its sealing washer. Quickly plug the transmission aperture and wipe up any spilt fluid.

Refitting

29 Fit a new sealing washer to the sensor then remove the plug and quickly screw the sensor into the transmission unit. Tighten the sensor to the specified torque and wipe up any spilt fluid. Refit the cover plate and tighten its retaining bolts to the specified torque.

30 Ensure the wiring is correctly routed and retained by all the necessary clips then securely reconnect the wiring.

31 Refit the engine undertray where applicable, then lower the vehicle to the ground. Check and if necessary top-up the transmission fluid level as described in Chapter 1A.

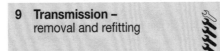

9 Transmission – removal and refitting

Note: *This section describes removal of the transmission, leaving the engine in the car – refer to Chapter 2C for details of engine and transmission removal as a complete assembly. New torque converter-to-driveplate bolts and fluid cooler union sealing rings will be required on refitting the transmission.*

9.5a Disconnect the earth cable from the front of the transmission . . .

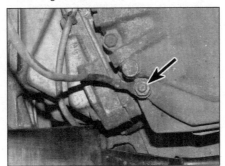

9.5b . . . and the earth cable from the end of the transmission

9.9 Release the securing clip and disconnect the wiring block connectors

will have to be lowered accordingly, to avoid straining the engine mountings.

12 Unbolt and remove the exhaust system front pipe (see Chapter 4A).

13 Position a container under the front of the transmission, then unscrew the unions and disconnect the transmission fluid cooler pipes. Recover the sealing washers, and plug the vacant holes to prevent entry of dust and dirt.

14 Unscrew and remove the three upper transmission retaining bolts.

15 Remove the rear engine mounting and bracket as described in Chapter 2A. **Note:** *Make sure the engine is adequately supported by the lifting beam, as the assembly will tend to tilt backwards, due to the position of the right-hand engine mounting on the front of the cylinder block.*

16 Remove the front subframe **(see illustration)** using the following procedure:

a) *Support the engine assembly using a suitable hoist or engine support bar which straddles the engine compartment. Slightly lift the engine assembly so that its weight is supported.*

b) *Remove the exhaust front pipe as described in Chapter 4A or 4B.*

c) *Disconnect the front suspension lower arms from the hub carriers, and remove the front anti-roll bar as described in Chapter 10*

d) *Support the subframe using a trolley jack.*

e) *Unscrew and remove the subframe front and rear mounting bolts, and also the two mounting nuts, then lower the subframe to the ground.*

17 With reference to Chapter 8, remove the both driveshafts from the transmission. If preferred, the driveshafts can remain attached to the hub carriers, and their inner ends supported or tied to the underbody.

18 Undo the retaining bolts and remove the lower cover plate from the driveplate. Turn the driveplate as necessary to position the torque converter retaining bolts at the bottom, then unscrew and remove the bolts **(see illustrations)**. Discard them as new ones must be used on refitting. **Note:** *As the transmission is removed, the torque converter must stay in the transmission bellhousing and not slide off the transmission shaft. A bracket can be made and bolted to the bellhousing to hold the torque converter in place.*

19 Position a jack under the transmission, and raise it to take the weight of the unit. Check that nothing remains connected to the transmission before attempting to separate it from the engine.

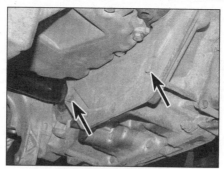

9.18a Undo the retaining bolts and remove the cover plate . . .

20 Unbolt the left-hand engine/transmission mounting and bracket from the body and transmission. Make sure the transmission is well-supported, and take care to avoid straining the right-hand engine mounting.

21 Unscrew and remove the remaining bolts holding the transmission to the engine.

 Warning: Maintain firm support on the transmission, to ensure that it remains steady on the jack head.

22 Make a final check that any components which would prevent the removal of the transmission from the car have been removed or disconnected. Ensure that components such as the gear selector cable are secured so that they cannot be damaged on removal.

23 Withdraw the transmission from the engine; keep the unit aligned with the engine until the bellhousing is clear of the driveplate and its mounting dowels. Make sure the torque converter does not slide off the transmission shaft.

24 Slowly lower the transmission assembly from the engine compartment, making sure that it clears the components on the surrounding panels. Lower the assembly to the ground and remove it from the engine compartment.

Refitting

25 The transmission is refitted by a reversal of the removal procedure, bearing in mind the following points.

a) *Remove all traces of old locking compound from the torque converter threads by running a tap of the correct thread diameter and pitch down the holes. In the absence of a suitable tap, use one of the old bolts with slots cut in its threads.*

b) *Ensure the engine/transmission locating dowels are correctly positioned and apply a smear of molybdenum disulphide*

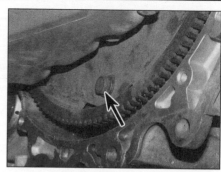

9.18b . . . then undo the torque converter bolts (one arrowed) – turn engine to access other bolts

grease to the torque converter locating pin and its centring bush in the end of the crankshaft.

c) *Once the transmission is fully in position on the engine, refit the securing bolts and tighten them to the specified torque.*

d) *Apply thread locking compound to the new torque converter-to-driveplate bolts, then insert them and tighten them progressively to the specified torque.*

e) *Tighten all nuts and bolts to the specified torque (where given).*

f) *Renew the driveshaft oil seals (see Section 6) and refit the driveshafts as described in Chapter 8.*

g) *Fit new sealing rings to the fluid cooler hose unions and ensure both unions are securely retained by their clips.*

h) *Ensure that all earthing cables are securely refitted.*

i) *On completion, refill the transmission with the specified type and quantity of fluid as described in Chapter 1A and adjust the selector cable as described in Section 3 of this Chapter.*

10 Transmission overhaul – general information

1 In the event of a fault occurring with the transmission, it is first necessary to determine whether it is of a mechanical or hydraulic nature, and to do this, special test equipment is required. It is therefore essential to have the work carried out by a Saab dealer if a transmission fault is suspected.

2 Do not remove the transmission from the car for possible repair before professional fault diagnosis has been carried out, since most tests require the transmission to be in the vehicle.

Chapter 8
Driveshafts

Contents

Degrees of difficulty

Easy, suitable for novice with little experience	**Fairly easy,** suitable for beginner with some experience	**Fairly difficult,** suitable for competent DIY mechanic	**Difficult,** suitable for experienced DIY mechanic	**Very difficult,** suitable for expert DIY or professional

Specifications

General

Driveshaft type	Steel shafts with outer constant velocity joints and inner tripod joints. Intermediate shaft from right-hand side of transmission to driveshaft
Lubrication (overhaul or repair only)	Use only special grease supplied in sachets with gaiter/overhaul kits; joints are otherwise prepacked with grease and sealed

Joint grease quantity

Outer joint	80 g
Inner joint	175 g

Torque wrench settings

	Nm	lbf ft
Driveshaft/hub nut (without groove)	290	214
Driveshaft/hub nut (with top groove):		
Stage 1	170	125
Stage 2	Angle-tighten a further 45°	
Intermediate driveshaft bracket-to-engine bolts	24	18
Wheel bolts	110	81

1 General information

Power is transmitted from the transmission final drive to the roadwheels by the driveshafts. The outer joints on all models are of 'constant velocity' (CV) type, consisting of six balls running in axial grooves. The driveshaft outer joints incorporate stub axles which are splined to the hubs located in the front suspension hub carriers. The inner 'universal' joints are designed to move in a smaller arc than the outer CV joints, and can also move axially to allow for movements of the front suspension. They are of tripod type consisting of a three-armed 'spider' with needle bearings and outer race, splined to the driveshaft, and an outer race, splined to the driveshaft, and an outer

housing with three corresponding cut-outs for the bearing races to slide in.

An intermediate shaft, with its own support bearing, is fitted between the transmission and right-hand driveshaft – a design which equalises driveshaft angles at all suspension positions, and reduces driveshaft flexing, improving directional stability under hard acceleration. On 2.3 litre turbo petrol engine models, the intermediate shaft has splines on its outer end, to engage the inner joint of the driveshaft, however, on all other models, the driveshaft inner joint housing and intermediate shaft are integral.

The universal and CV joints allow smooth transmission of drive to the wheels at all steering and suspension angles. The joints are protected by rubber gaiters, and are packed with grease to provide permanent lubrication. In the event of wear being detected, the joint

can be renewed separately from the driveshaft. The joints do not require additional lubrication, unless they have been renovated or the rubber gaiters have been damaged, allowing the grease to become contaminated. Refer to Chapter 1A or 1B for details of checking the condition of the driveshaft gaiters.

2 Driveshafts – removal and refitting

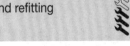

Removal

1 Park the vehicle on a level surface, apply the handbrake and chock the rear wheels.

2 Remove the wheel trim (or wheel centre cap for vehicles fitted with alloy wheels), then loosen the driveshaft nut, bearing in mind

2.4 Unscrewing the driveshaft nut

the high torque to which this nut is tightened – select a sturdy wrench and close-fitting socket to loosen it.

3 Apply the handbrake, then jack up the front of the vehicle and support it on axle stands (see *Jacking and vehicle support*). Remove the roadwheel.

4 Unscrew and remove the driveshaft nut **(see illustration)**. Discard the nut and obtain a new one which will have top grooves on it.

5 Unscrew the nut securing the anti-roll bar to the lower suspension arm support bar, and remove the washer and rubber bush.

6 Unscrew the nut, then disconnect the lower arm balljoint from the hub carrier/strut using a balljoint separator tool (see Chapter 10). Press the lower suspension arm down as far as possible, and move the hub carrier/strut to one side. Take care not to damage the balljoint rubber boot, and do not strain the brake hoses and brake pad wear warning wiring. **Note:** *Discard the balljoint nut as it must not be re-used. Obtain a new one.*

7 Using a mallet, carefully tap the driveshaft inwards from the splines in the hub while pulling out the bottom of the strut **(see illustration)**.

8 To remove the left-hand side driveshaft, position a container beneath the transmission to catch spilt oil, then pull out the driveshaft. The internal driveshaft circlip may be tight in the transmission side gear, in which case careful use of a lever against the transmission casing will be required. Lever against a block of wood to prevent damage to the casing, and take care not to damage the oil seal as the driveshaft is being removed **(see illustration)**. **Note:** *Pull only on the inner joint housing, not*

the driveshaft itself, otherwise the gaiter may be damaged.

9 To remove the right-hand side driveshaft on 2.3 litre turbo petrol engine models, pull the inner joint stub from the splines in the intermediate shaft. If necessary, use a lever to help release the internal circlip from the groove.

10 On all diesel models, and petrol models except the 2.3 litre turbo petrol engine, the right-hand driveshaft inner joint housing forms part of the intermediate shaft (see Section 5), and the driveshaft is removed by separating the outer section at the inner joint. Mark the inner joint housing and driveshaft in relation to each other, then loosen the clip, ease off the rubber gaiter, and pull the tripod out of the housing.

Refitting

11 Where applicable, check the condition of the circlip on the inner end of the driveshaft and, if necessary, renew it **(see illustration)**.

12 Clean the splines on each end of the driveshaft and in the hub, and where applicable wipe clean the oil seal in the transmission casing. Check the oil seal and if necessary renew it as described in Chapter 7A or 7B. Smear a little oil on the lips of the oil seal before fitting the driveshaft.

13 To refit the outer section of the right-hand driveshaft where removed separately, fill the inner joint with the specified quantity of grease, then locate the driveshaft tripod into the housing, aligning the previously-made marks. Ease the gaiter onto the housing, and refit the clip.

14 To refit the right-hand side driveshaft on 2.3 litre turbo petrol engine models, locate the inner joint stub into the splines in the intermediate shaft, and press in until the internal circlip engages the groove.

15 To refit the left-hand driveshaft, locate the inner end of the driveshaft into the transmission – turn the driveshaft as necessary to engage the splines. Press in the driveshaft until the internal circlip engages the groove. Check that the circlip is engaged by attempting to pull out the driveshaft with only moderate force.

16 Engage the outer end of the driveshaft with the splines in the hub, then press down the lower suspension arm and guide the bottom

of the hub carrier/strut onto the balljoint on the lower arm. Screw on the new nut and tighten to the specified torque (see Chapter 10).

17 Insert the anti-roll bar mounting in the lower arm support bar, then fit the rubber bush and washer and tighten the nut to the specified torque (see Chapter 10).

18 Screw on the new driveshaft nut and tighten just moderately at this stage.

19 Check and if necessary top-up the transmission oil/fluid level with reference to Chapter 1A or 1B.

20 Refit the roadwheel, then lower the vehicle to the ground and tighten the bolts to the specified torque.

21 Fully tighten the driveshaft nut to the specified torque and angle, and refit the wheel trim/cap.

---

3 Driveshafts – inspection, joint renewal and cleaning

Inspection

1 If any of the checks described in Chapter 1A or 1B reveal apparent excessive wear or play, first check that the hub nut (driveshaft outer nut) is tightened to the specified torque. Repeat this check on the hub nut on the other side.

2 To check for driveshaft wear, road test the vehicle, driving it slowly in a circle on full steering lock (carry out the test on both left and right lock), while listening for a metallic clicking or knocking sound coming from the front wheels. An assistant in the passenger seat can listen for the sound from the nearside joint. If such a sound is heard, this indicates wear in the outer joint.

3 If vibration proportional to roadspeed is felt through the car when accelerating or on over-run, there is a possibility of wear in the inner joints. For a more thorough check, remove and dismantle the driveshafts where possible as described in the following sub-Sections. Refer to a Saab dealer for information on the availability of driveshaft components.

4 Continual noise from the area of the right-hand driveshaft, increasing with roadspeed, may indicate wear in the support bearing.

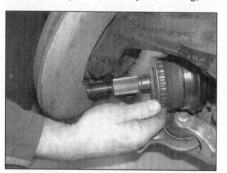

2.7 Removing the driveshaft from the splines in the hub

2.8 Withdrawing the driveshaft from the transmission

2.11 Checking the circlip on the inner end of the driveshaft

3.6 Remove the clip . . .

3.7 . . . release the rubber gaiter from the joint housing . . .

3.9a . . . then use circlip pliers to open the circlip . . .

Outer joint renewal

5 Remove the driveshaft as described in Section 2, then thoroughly clean it and mount it in a vice. It is important that foreign matter, such as dust and dirt, are prevented from entering the joint.

6 Release the large clip securing the rubber gaiter to the outer joint housing (see illustration), then similarly release the small clip securing the rubber gaiter to the driveshaft. Note the fitted position of the gaiter.

7 Slide the rubber gaiter along the driveshaft, away from the joint (see illustration). Scoop out as much of the grease as possible from the joint and gaiter.

8 Using a dab of paint, mark the outer joint and driveshaft in relation to each other to ensure correct refitting.

9 Using circlip pliers at the inner end of the joint, open the circlip then slide the joint from the end of the driveshaft (see illustrations). If it is tight, use a hammer and soft drift to tap the joint hub from the splines. Note that on later models, it may not be necessary to open the circlip, as it will release from the driveshaft as the joint is being tapped off.

10 With the joint removed, slide the rubber gaiter and small clip from the driveshaft (see illustration). Check the rubber gaiter for cracks or slits, and renew it if necessary.

3.9b . . . and slide the outer joint from the end of the driveshaft

11 Thoroughly clean the splines of the driveshaft and outer joint, and also the rubber gaiter contact surfaces. If the joint has been contaminated with road grit or water, it must be dismantled and cleaned as described later in this Section. Check the condition of the circlip which is captive in the outer joint, and renew it if necessary (see illustration).

12 Locate the gaiter, together with small clip, on the outer end of the driveshaft. Smear a little grease onto the driveshaft to facilitate this.

13 Pack the joint with the specified quantity of grease, working it well into the cavities of the housing (see illustration).

3.10 Removing the outer rubber gaiter

14 Locate the outer joint onto the driveshaft splines in its previously-noted position, and press it on until the internal circlip engages with the groove.

15 Reposition the rubber gaiter onto the joint outer housing in its previously-noted position, then refit the two clips. Tighten the clips securely.

16 Refit the driveshaft with reference to Section 2.

Inner joint renewal

17 Remove the driveshaft as described in Section 2 and, on all diesel models, and petrol models except the 2.3 litre turbo,

3.11 The circlip is captive in the outer joint

3.13 Pack the CV joint with grease from the service kit

3.20a Remove the circlip . . .

3.20b . . . then use a puller to remove the spider from the driveshaft splines

remove the inner joint housing/intermediate shaft as described in Section 5. On 2.3 litre turbo models, mark the inner joint housing and driveshaft in relation to each other, then loosen the clip, ease off the rubber gaiter, and pull the tripod out of the housing.

18 Release the small clip securing the rubber gaiter to the driveshaft. Note the fitted position of the gaiter. Where the original factory gaiter is fitted, it will be necessary to bend up the metal plate to release it from the joint housing, however, it is not necessary to bend the plate down for the refitting procedure.

19 Slide the rubber gaiter along the driveshaft, away from the joint. Scoop out as much of the grease as possible from the joint and gaiter.

20 Mark the driveshaft and tripod in relation to each other using a centre-punch or dab of paint. Using circlip pliers, expand and remove the circlip from the end of the driveshaft, then use a puller to remove the tripod together with the needle roller bearings **(see illustrations)**. Note that the chamfered edge of the tripod faces the centre of the driveshaft.

21 Slide the rubber gaiter and small clip from the driveshaft. Check the rubber gaiter for cracks or slits, and renew it if necessary.

22 Thoroughly clean the splines of the driveshaft and inner joint, and also the rubber gaiter contact surfaces. If the joint has been exposed to road grit or water, it should be thoroughly cleaned as described later in this Section. Check the condition of the circlip and renew it if necessary. Check that the three tripod bearings are free to rotate without

resistance, and that they are not excessively worn.

23 Locate the gaiter, together with small clip, on the inner end of the driveshaft in its previously-noted position. Smear a little grease onto the driveshaft to facilitate this. Tighten the small clip.

24 Locate the tripod on the driveshaft splines, chamfered edge first, making sure that the previously-made marks are aligned **(see illustration)**. Using a socket or metal tube, drive the tripod fully onto the driveshaft, then refit the circlip, making sure that it is correctly located in its groove.

25 Pack the tripod joint and inner joint housing with the specified quantity of grease, working it well into the bearings.

26 On all diesel models, and petrol models except the 2.3 litre turbo, refit the inner joint housing/intermediate shaft with reference to Section 5. On 2.3 litre turbo models, locate the inner joint housing onto the tripod in its previously-noted position. Reposition the rubber gaiter onto the inner joint housing in its previously-noted position, then refit and tighten the clip. If crimp-type clips are being fitted, use a crimping tool to tighten them **(see illustration)**.

27 Refit the driveshaft with reference to Section 2.

Joint cleaning

28 Where a joint has been contaminated with road grit or water through a damaged rubber gaiter, the joint should be completely dismantled and cleaned. Remove the joint as described previously in this Section.

29 To dismantle the outer joint, mount it vertically in a soft-jawed vice, then turn the splined hub and ball cage so that the balls can be removed individually. Remove the hub followed by the ball cage.

30 The inner joint is dismantled during removal, and, the tripod joint bearings should be washed in suitable solvent to remove all traces of grease.

31 Thoroughly clean the inner and outer joint housings, together with the ball-bearings, cages and hubs, removing all traces of grease and foreign matter.

32 To reassemble the outer joint, first insert the cage, followed by the splined hub. Manoeuvre the hub and carrier so that the balls can be inserted one at a time.

4 Driveshaft gaiters – renewal

1 Obtain a kit comprising new gaiters and retaining clips from a Saab dealer or motor factor.

2 Removal and refitting of the gaiters is described in Section 3.

5 Intermediate driveshaft and support bearing assembly – removal, overhaul and refitting

Removal

1 Apply the handbrake, then jack up the front of the vehicle and support it on axle stands (see *Jacking and vehicle support*). Remove the right-hand front roadwheel.

2 Working under the right-hand wheel arch, undo the fasteners and remove the splash cover for access to the right-hand side of the engine.

Petrol engine models

3 Disconnect the battery negative lead (refer to *Disconnecting the battery* in the *Reference* Chapter at the end of this manual).

4 In the engine compartment, remove the engine top cover.

5 On RHD models only, unbolt the engine compartment stay between the front suspension strut towers.

6 Note the fitted routing of the auxiliary drivebelt, and mark it with an arrow to indicate its normal running direction.

7 Using a square-drive extension bar, turn the tensioner clockwise to release its tension, then slip the auxiliary drivebelt off of the crankshaft, alternator, air conditioning compressor and idler pulleys. Release the tensioner.

8 Using an 8.0 mm Allen key, unbolt the tensioner from the engine. Also, unscrew and remove the alternator upper mounting bolt.

9 Unscrew the nut securing the anti-roll bar to the lower suspension arm support bar, and remove the washer and rubber bush.

10 Unscrew the nut, then disconnect the lower

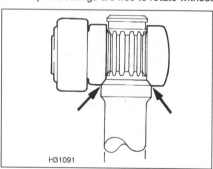

3.24 On the inner joint, make sure that the chamfer is located against the inner shoulder on the driveshaft

3.26 Using a crimping tool to tighten the gaiter clips

5.11 Intermediate driveshaft dust seal

5.19 Intermediate driveshaft support bearing bracket bolts

5.20 Removing the intermediate driveshaft from the transmission

arm balljoint from the hub carrier/strut using a balljoint separator tool (see Chapter 10). Press the lower suspension arm down as far as possible, and move the hub carrier/strut to one side; use a block of wood to hold the lower arm down. Take care not to damage the balljoint rubber boot, and do not strain the brake hoses and brake pad wear warning wiring.

11 On 2.3 litre turbo models, pull the inner joint stub from the splines in the intermediate shaft, and support the driveshaft to one side. If necessary, use a lever to help release the internal circlip from the groove. Note that the bearing dust seal may have come away with the driveshaft **(see illustration)**.

12 On models except the 2.3 litre turbo, mark the driveshaft inner joint housing and driveshaft in relation to each other, then loosen the clip, ease off the rubber gaiter, and pull the tripod out of the housing. Support the driveshaft to one side, and cover to prevent dust and dirt entry into the joint.

13 On the rear of the alternator, unscrew the nuts and disconnect the battery positive cable together with the warning light cable.

14 Unscrew the alternator lower mounting bolt and position the alternator to one side (refer to Chapter 5A if necessary).

Diesel engine models

15 Unscrew the nut securing the anti-roll bar to the lower suspension arm support bar, and remove the washer and rubber bush.

16 Unscrew the nut, then disconnect the lower arm balljoint from the hub carrier/strut using a balljoint separator tool (see Chapter 10). Press the lower suspension arm down as far as possible, and move the hub carrier/strut to one side; use a block of wood to hold the lower arm down. Take care not to damage the balljoint rubber boot, and do not strain the brake hoses and brake pad wear warning wiring.

17 Mark the driveshaft inner joint housing and driveshaft in relation to each other, then loosen the clip, ease off the rubber gaiter, and pull the tripod out of the housing. Support the

driveshaft to one side, and cover to prevent dust and dirt entry into the joint.

All models

18 Position a container beneath the transmission to catch spilled oil/fluid when the intermediate shaft is removed.

19 Unscrew the bolts securing the support bearing bracket to the rear of the cylinder block **(see illustration)**.

20 Using a screwdriver, lever the bracket away from the dowels on the cylinder block, then withdraw the intermediate driveshaft from the splined sun gear in the transmission **(see illustration)**.

Overhaul

21 The intermediate shaft must now be removed from the bearing. On 2.3 litre turbo petrol engine models, use circlip pliers to extract the outer small circlip from the end of the intermediate shaft, then support the bracket in a vice, and press or drive out the shaft. If the shaft is being renewed, extract the inner small circlip from the shaft as well **(see illustrations)**. On all other models, extract the small inner circlip from the shaft, support the bracket and drive out the shaft from the transmission end.

22 Using circlip pliers, extract the large circlip securing the bearing in the bracket. The bearing must now be pressed or driven out of the bracket. Support the bracket in a vice to do this.

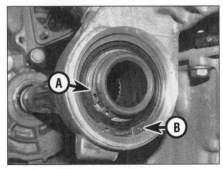

5.21a Intermediate shaft bearing small circlip (A) and large circlip (B)

23 Support the bracket with its open end upwards, then locate the new bearing and press or drive it fully in using a metal tube on the outer race. Fit the large circlip to secure the bearing in the bracket.

24 On 2.3 litre turbo petrol engine models, refit the small circlip to the driveshaft, mount the intermediate shaft in a vice, then refit the bearing with bracket onto the driveshaft and press or drive on the bearing inner race until it contacts the circlip. Make sure that the bracket is fitted the correct way round, and press only on the inner race. Refit the small circlip in the groove, making sure that the concave side faces the bearing, then fit a new dust seal over the outer end of the bearing.

25 On models except the 2.3 litre turbo, support the inner bearing race on a metal tube, then press or drive the intermediate shaft fully into the bearing. Make sure the shaft is fitted the correct way round. Refit the small inner circlip.

Refitting

26 Refitting is a reversal of removal, but note the following additional points:
  a) *Check the transmission oil seals and if necessary renew them with reference to Chapter 7A or 7B.*
  b) *Tighten all mounting nuts/bolts to the specified torque, where given.*
  c) *Top-up the transmission oil/fluid with reference to Chapter 1A or 1B.*

5.21b Inner small circlip on the driveshaft

Chapter 9
Braking system

Contents

Degrees of difficulty

Easy, suitable for novice with little experience

Fairly easy, suitable for beginner with some experience

Fairly difficult, suitable for competent DIY mechanic

Difficult, suitable for experienced DIY mechanic

Very difficult, suitable for expert DIY or professional

Specifications

General

Brake system type and layout:

Footbrake .... Diagonally-split dual hydraulic circuits; front left/rear right and front right/rear left. Discs fitted front and rear, ventilated at the front. Single-piston, sliding calipers on front, double-piston fixed calipers on rear. Anti-lock Braking System (ABS) fitted as standard on all models. Traction control (TCS) option on some models

Handbrake .... Lever and cable operation, acting on shoes in drums incorporated in rear discs

Front brakes

Discs:

Type .... Ventilated
Outside diameter .... 288.0 mm (308.0 mm on Viggen)
Thickness (new disc) .... 25.0 mm
Minimum thickness after grinding .... 23.5 mm
Minimum wear thickness .... 22.0 mm
Maximum run-out......... 0.08 mm
Maximum variation in disc thickness .... 0.015 mm

Calipers:

Type .... Single-piston, floating
Piston diameter .... 57.0 mm

Pads:

Minimum friction material thickness......... 5.0 mm
Thickness for acoustic warning device .... 3.0 mm

Rear brakes

Discs:

Type	Solid
Outside diameter	286.0 mm
Thickness (new disc)	10.0 mm
Minimum thickness after grinding	8.5 mm
Minimum wear thickness	8.0 mm
Maximum run-out................................	0.08 mm
Maximum variation in disc thickness	0.015 mm
Handbrake drum inner diameter................	160.0 mm
Handbrake drum maximum out-of-round	0.08 mm

Calipers:

Type	Fixed, double-piston
Piston diameter	35.0 mm

Pads:

Minimum friction material thickness...........	5.0 mm

Handbrake:

Shoe minimum friction material thickness	0.5 mm

ABS components

Front wheel sensors:

Resistance	1600 ± 160 ohms at 20°C
Clearance between sensor and tooth (not adjustable)............	0.3 to 1.3 mm

Rear wheel sensors:

Resistance	1130 ± 115 ohms at 20°C

Torque wrench settings

	Nm	lbf ft
ABS hydraulic union nuts.....................................	15	11
ABS hydraulic unit mounting nut	20	15
Brake caliper guide bolts	28	21
Front brake caliper bracket to hub carrier	110	81
Front brake hose to caliper	40	30
Rear brake caliper to backplate............................	80	59
Rear wheel hub to rear axle	50	37
Vacuum hose union nut	18	13
Vacuum pump lubrication banjo bolt (petrol models)...............	25	18
Vacuum pump (mechanical) mounting bolt:		
Petrol models	22	16
Diesel models...	8	6

1 General information

Braking is achieved by a dual-circuit hydraulic system, assisted by a vacuum servo unit. All models have discs fitted at the front and rear. The front discs are ventilated, to improve cooling and reduce brake fade.

The dual hydraulic circuits are diagonally-split; on LHD models, the primary circuit operates the front left and rear right brakes, and the secondary circuit operates the front right and rear left brakes. On RHD models, the circuits are opposite. This design ensures that at least 50% of the vehicle's braking capacity will be available, should pressure be lost in one of the hydraulic circuits. Under these circumstances, the diagonal layout should prevent the vehicle from becoming unstable if the brakes are applied when only one circuit is operational.

The front brake calipers are of floating single-piston type. Each caliper has two brake pads, one inboard and one outboard of the disc. During braking, hydraulic pressure forces the piston along its cylinder, and presses the inboard brake pad against the disc. The caliper body reacts to this effort by sliding along its guide pins, bringing the outboard pad into contact with the disc. In this manner, equal pressure is applied to each side of the disc by the brake pads. When the brake pedal is released, the hydraulic pressure drops and the piston seal retracts the piston from the brake pad.

The rear brake calipers are of fixed double-piston type with two brake pads, one inboard and one outboard of the disc. The pistons operate independently of each other.

The rear discs incorporate drums with internal brake shoes for operation of the handbrake. A single primary cable together with two secondary cables from the handbrake lever, operate the lever on each rear brake. The handbrake is not self-adjusting, and must be manually-adjusted regularly.

On petrol engine models, the brake vacuum servo unit uses engine inlet manifold vacuum to boost the effort applied to the master cylinder by the brake pedal. On automatic transmission turbo petrol models, the inlet manifold vacuum is supplemented by a voltage-variable-speed electric vacuum pump. The pump switches on when the inlet manifold vacuum is less than 0.35 bar, and switches off when the vacuum exceeds 0.4 bar. The pressure is monitored by a pressure sensor located on the inlet manifold. Non-return valves in the vacuum lines, isolate the inlet manifold and electric vacuum pump to maintain the required vacuum in the lines. The system is only operational with the ignition on and D selected. From 2000 MY-on (late 1999), the electric vacuum pump was superseded by a mechanical vacuum pump mounted on the left-hand end of the cylinder head and driven by the camshaft. From 2001 MY-on, manual transmission turbo models are fitted with a supplementary 'ejector' device to boost the vacuum to the vacuum servo. The device is fitted in the charge air pipe, and operates by speeding up the flow of air across a venturi, thus providing vacuum to the servo.

On diesel engine models, vacuum for the brake vacuum servo unit is supplied continuously by a pump driven directly from the exhaust camshaft.

The anti-lock braking system (ABS) fitted as

standard to all models prevents wheel lock-up under heavy braking, and not only optimises stopping distances, but also improves steering control. By electronically monitoring the speed of each roadwheel in relation to the other wheels, the system can detect when a wheel is about to lock-up, before control is actually lost. The brake fluid pressure applied to that wheel's brake caliper is then decreased and restored ('modulated') several times a second until control is regained. The system components comprise four wheel speed sensors, a hydraulic unit with integral Electronic Control Unit (ECU), brake lines and a dashboard-mounted warning light. The four wheel sensors are mounted on the wheel hub carriers. Each wheel has a rotating toothed hub mounted on the driveshaft (front) or on the hub (rear). The wheel speed sensors are mounted in close proximity to these hubs. The teeth produce a voltage waveform whose frequency varies with the speed of the hubs. These waveforms are transmitted to the ECU, and used to calculate the rotational speed of each wheel. The ECU has a self-diagnostic facility, to inhibit the operation of the ABS if a fault is detected, lighting the dashboard-mounted warning light. The braking system will then revert to conventional, non-ABS operation. If the nature of the fault is not immediately obvious upon inspection, the vehicle *must* be taken to a Saab dealer, who will have the diagnostic equipment required to interrogate the ABS ECU electronically and pin-point the problem.

The traction control system (TCS) is available as an option on some models, and uses the basic ABS system, with an additional pump and valves fitted to the hydraulic actuator. If wheelspin is detected at a speed below 30 mph, one of the valves opens, to allow the pump to pressurise the relevant brake, until the spinning wheel slows to a rotational speed corresponding to the speed of the vehicle. This has the effect of transferring torque to the wheel with most traction. At the same time, the throttle plate is closed slightly, to reduce the torque from the engine.

2 Hydraulic system – bleeding

Warning: Hydraulic fluid is poisonous; wash off immediately and thoroughly in the case of skin contact, and seek immediate medical advice if any fluid is swallowed or gets into the eyes. Certain types of hydraulic fluid are inflammable, and may ignite when brought into contact with hot components; when servicing any hydraulic system, it is safest to assume that the fluid is inflammable, and to take precautions against the risk of fire as though it is petrol that is being handled. Hydraulic fluid is also an effective paint stripper, and will attack plastics; if any is spilt, it should be washed off immediately, using copious quantities of fresh water. Finally, it is hygroscopic (it absorbs moisture from the air) – old fluid may be contaminated and unfit for further use. When topping-up or renewing the fluid, always use the recommended type, and ensure that it comes from a freshly-opened sealed container.

General

1 The correct operation of any hydraulic system is only possible after removing all air from the components and circuit; this is achieved by bleeding the system.

2 During the bleeding procedure, add only clean, unused hydraulic fluid of the recommended type; never re-use fluid that has already been bled from the system. Ensure that sufficient fluid is available before starting work.

3 If there is any possibility of incorrect fluid being already in the system, the brake components and circuit must be flushed completely with uncontaminated, correct fluid, and new seals should be fitted to the various components.

4 If hydraulic fluid has been lost from the system, or air has entered because of a leak, ensure that the fault is cured before proceeding further.

5 Park the vehicle over an inspection pit or on car ramps. Alternatively, apply the handbrake then jack up the front and rear of the vehicle and support it on axle stands (see *Jacking and vehicle support*). For improved access with the vehicle jacked up, remove the roadwheels.

6 Check that all pipes and hoses are secure, unions tight and bleed screws closed. Clean any dirt from around the bleed screws.

7 Unscrew the master cylinder reservoir cap, and top the master cylinder reservoir up to the MAX level line; refit the cap loosely, and remember to maintain the fluid level at least above the MIN level line throughout the procedure, otherwise there is a risk of further air entering the system.

8 There is a number of one-man, do-it-yourself brake bleeding kits currently available from motor accessory shops. It is recommended that one of these kits is used whenever possible, as they greatly simplify the bleeding operation, and also reduce the risk of expelled air and fluid being drawn back into the system. If such a kit is not available, the basic (two-man) method must be used, which is described in detail below.

9 If a kit is to be used, prepare the vehicle as described previously, and follow the kit manufacturer's instructions, as the procedure may vary slightly according to the type being used; generally, they are as outlined below in the relevant sub-section.

10 Whichever method is used, the same sequence must be followed (paragraphs 11 and 12) to ensure the removal of all air from the system.

Bleeding sequence

11 If the system has been only partially disconnected, and suitable precautions were taken to minimise fluid loss, it should only be necessary to bleed that part of the system (ie, the primary or secondary circuit).

12 If the complete system is to be bled, then it should be done working in the following sequence (**Note:** *On LHD models use opposite sides*):

   a) Right-hand front brake.
   b) Left-hand rear brake.
   c) Left-hand front brake.
   d) Right-hand rear brake.

Bleeding

Basic (two-man) method

13 Collect together a clean glass jar, a suitable length of plastic or rubber tubing which is a tight fit over the bleed screw, and a ring spanner to fit the screw. The help of an assistant will also be required.

14 Remove the dust cap from the first bleed screw in the sequence **(see illustration)**. Fit the spanner and tube to the screw, place the other end of the tube in the jar, and pour in sufficient fluid to cover the end of the tube.

15 Ensure that the master cylinder reservoir fluid level is maintained at least above the MIN level mark throughout the procedure.

16 Have the assistant fully depress and release the brake pedal several times to build-up initial pressure in the system.

17 Unscrew the bleed screw approximately half a turn then have the assistant slowly depress the brake pedal down to the floor and hold it there. Tighten the bleed screw and have the assistant slowly release the pedal to its rest position.

18 Repeat the procedure given in paragraph 17 until the fluid emerging from the bleed screw is free from air bubbles. After every two or three depressions of the pedal, check the level of fluid in the reservoir and top-up if necessary.

19 When no more air bubbles appear, securely tighten the bleed screw, remove the tube and spanner, and refit the dust cap. Do not overtighten the bleed screw.

20 Repeat the procedure on the remaining screws in the sequence, until all air is removed from the system and the brake pedal feels firm again.

2.14 Dust cap on the caliper bleed screw

2.22 Using a one-way valve kit to bleed the rear brake circuit

3.2 Rear brake flexible hose located between the underbody and trailing arm

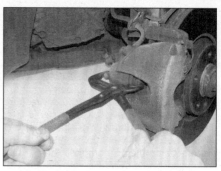

4.2 Using slip-joint pliers to press the piston into the caliper

Using a one-way valve kit

21 As the name implies, these kits consist of a length of tubing with a one-way valve fitted, to prevent expelled air and fluid being drawn back into the system; some kits include a translucent container, which can be positioned so that the air bubbles can be more easily seen flowing from the end of the tube.

22 The kit is connected to the bleed screw, which is then opened **(see illustration)**. The user returns to the driver's seat, depresses the brake pedal with a smooth, steady stroke, and slowly releases it; this is repeated until the expelled fluid is clear of air bubbles.

23 Note that these kits simplify work so much that it is easy to forget the master cylinder reservoir fluid level; ensure that this is maintained at least above the MIN level line at all times.

Using a pressure-bleeding kit

24 These kits are usually operated by a reservoir of pressurised air contained in the spare tyre. However, note that it will probably be necessary to reduce the pressure to a lower level than normal; refer to the instructions supplied with the kit.

25 By connecting a pressurised, fluid-filled container to the master cylinder reservoir, bleeding can be carried out simply by opening each screw in turn (in the specified sequence), and allowing the fluid to flow out until no more air bubbles can be seen in the expelled fluid.

26 This method has the advantage that the large reservoir of fluid provides an additional safeguard against air being drawn into the system during bleeding.

27 Pressure-bleeding is particularly effective when bleeding 'difficult' systems, or when bleeding the complete system at the time of routine fluid renewal.

All methods

28 When bleeding is complete, and firm pedal feel is restored, wipe off any spilt fluid, securely tighten the bleed screws, and refit the dust caps.

29 Check the hydraulic fluid level in the master cylinder reservoir, and top-up if necessary (see *Weekly checks*).

30 Discard any hydraulic fluid that has been bled from the system; it will not be fit for re-use.

31 Check the feel of the brake pedal. If it feels at all spongy, air must still be present in the system, and further bleeding is required. Failure to bleed satisfactorily after a reasonable repetition of the bleeding procedure may be due to worn master cylinder seals.

3 Hydraulic pipes and hoses – renewal

1 If any pipe or hose is to be renewed, minimise fluid loss by first removing the master cylinder reservoir cap, then tightening it down onto a piece of polythene to obtain an airtight seal. The cap incorporates a level warning float and, alternatively, hose clamps can be fitted to flexible hoses to isolate sections of the circuit; metal brake pipe unions can be plugged (if care is taken not to allow dirt into the system) or capped immediately they are disconnected. Place a wad of rag under any union that is to be disconnected, to catch any spilt fluid.

2 If a flexible hose is to be disconnected, unscrew the brake pipe union nut before removing the spring clip which secures the hose to its mounting bracket **(see illustration)**. Where applicable, unscrew the banjo union bolt securing the hose to the caliper and recover the copper washers. When removing the front flexible hose, pull out the spring clip and disconnect it from the strut.

3 To unscrew union nuts, it is preferable to obtain a 'split' brake pipe spanner of the correct size; these are available from most motor accessory shops. Failing this, a close-fitting open-ended spanner will be required, though if the nuts are tight or corroded, their flats may be rounded-off if the spanner slips. In such a case, a self-locking wrench is often the only way to unscrew a stubborn union, but it follows that the pipe and the damaged nuts must be renewed on reassembly. Always clean a union and surrounding area before disconnecting it. If disconnecting a component with more than one union, make a careful note of the connections before disturbing any of them.

4 If a brake pipe is to be renewed, it can be obtained, cut to length and with the union nuts and end flares in place, from a dealers parts shop. All that is then necessary is to bend it to shape, following the line of the original, before fitting it to the car. Alternatively, most motor accessory shops can make up brake pipes from kits, but this requires very careful measurement of the original, to ensure that the new one is of the correct length. The safest answer is usually to take the original to the shop as a pattern.

5 On refitting, do not overtighten the union nuts.

6 When refitting hoses to the calipers, always use new copper washers and tighten the banjo union bolts to the specified torque. Make sure that the hoses are positioned so that they will not touch surrounding bodywork or the roadwheels.

7 Ensure that the pipes and hoses are correctly routed, with no kinks, and that they are secured in the clips or brackets provided. After fitting, remove the polythene from the reservoir, and bleed the hydraulic system as described in Section 2. Wash off any spilt fluid, and check carefully for fluid leaks.

4 Front brake pads – renewal

⚠️ *Warning: Renew BOTH sets of front brake pads at the same time – NEVER renew the pads on only one wheel, as uneven braking may result. Note that the dust created by wear of the pads may contain asbestos, which is a health hazard. Never blow it out with compressed air, and do not inhale any of it. Use brake cleaner or methylated spirit to clean brake components.*

1 Apply the handbrake, then jack up the front of the vehicle and support it on axle stands (see *Jacking and vehicle support*). Remove both front roadwheels.

2 Using slip-joint pliers **(see illustration)**, press the piston fully into the caliper. **Note:** *Provided that the master cylinder reservoir has not been overfilled with hydraulic fluid, there should be no spillage, but keep a careful watch on the fluid level while retracting the piston. If the fluid level rises above the MAX level line at any time, the surplus should be syphoned off or ejected via a plastic tube connected to the bleed screw.*

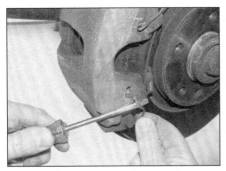

4.3a Lever out the retaining spring . . .

4.3b . . . and remove it from the caliper

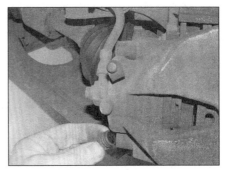

4.4 Remove the dust caps . . .

3 Carefully lever off the retaining spring from the holes on the outer surface of the caliper, noting how the spring is located on the caliper mounting bracket **(see illustrations)**

4 Remove the dust caps from the inner ends of the guide bolts **(see illustration)**.

5 Unscrew the guide bolts from the caliper, and lift the caliper and pads away from the mounting bracket **(see illustrations)**. Tie the caliper to the suspension strut using a suitable piece of wire. Do not allow the caliper to hang unsupported on the flexible brake hose.

6 Remove the inner and outer pads from the caliper, noting that the inner one is retained in the piston by a spring clip attached to the pad backing plate **(see illustrations)**. **Note:** *An acoustic wear warning device is fitted to the outer pad, consisting of a metal strip which contacts the brake disc when the thickness of* *the friction material is less than 3.0 mm. This device causes a scraping noise which warns the driver that the pads are worn excessively.*

7 Brush the dirt and dust from the caliper, but take care not to inhale it. Carefully remove any rust from the edge of the brake disc.

8 Measure the thickness of the friction material on each brake pad (excluding the backing plate). If either pad is worn at any point to the specified minimum thickness or less, all four pads must be renewed. The pads should also be renewed if any are contaminated with oil or grease; there is no satisfactory way of degreasing friction material. Trace and rectify the cause of contamination before reassembly.

9 If the brake pads are still serviceable, clean them using a clean, fine wire brush or similar, paying particular attention to the sides and back of the metal backing. Carefully clean the pad locations in the caliper body/mounting bracket.

10 Prior to fitting the pads, check that the guide bolts are a good fit in the caliper bushes. Brush the dust and dirt from the caliper and piston (see ***Warning*** at the beginning of this Section). Apply a little high melting-point copper brake grease to the areas on the pad backing plates which contact the caliper and piston. Inspect the dust seal around the piston for damage, and the piston for evidence of fluid leaks, corrosion or damage. If attention to any of these components is necessary, refer to Section 6.

11 Fit the inner pad to the caliper, ensuring that its clip is correctly located in the caliper piston. Make sure that the arrows on the pad point in the normal, forward direction of rotation of the brake disc **(see illustrations)**.

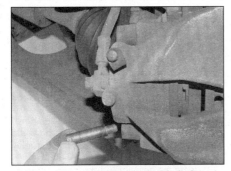

4.5a . . . then unscrew the guide bolts . . .

4.5b . . . and lift the caliper and pads away from the mounting bracket

4.6a Remove the outer pad from the caliper . . .

4.6b . . . then the inner pad, noting that it is retained in the piston by a spring clip

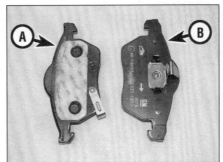

4.11a Outer (A) and inner (B) front brake pads

4.11b The pads must be fitted with the arrow pointing the normal, forward rotation of the brake disc

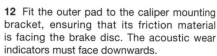

5.2 Using a punch to drive out the rear brake pad retaining pins

5.3 Removing the anti-squeal spring

5.5a Removing the inner rear brake pad

12 Fit the outer pad to the caliper mounting bracket, ensuring that its friction material is facing the brake disc. The acoustic wear indicators must face downwards.

13 Slide the caliper and inner pad into position over the outer pad, and locate it in the mounting bracket.

14 Insert the caliper guide bolts, and tighten them to the specified torque setting.

15 Refit the guide bolt dust caps.

16 Refit the retaining spring to the caliper, ensuring that its ends are correctly located in the caliper holes.

17 Depress the brake pedal repeatedly, until normal pedal pressure is restored.

18 Repeat the above procedure on the remaining front brake caliper.

19 Refit the roadwheels, then lower the vehicle to the ground and tighten the roadwheel bolts to the specified torque setting.

20 Check the hydraulic fluid level as described in *Weekly checks*.

5 Rear brake pads – renewal

> ⚠️ *Warning: Renew BOTH sets of rear brake pads at the same time – NEVER renew the pads on only one wheel, as uneven braking may result. Note that the dust created by wear of the pads may contain asbestos, which is a health hazard. Never blow it out with compressed air, and do not inhale any of it. Use brake cleaner or methylated spirit to clean brake components.*

1 Chock the front wheels, then jack up the rear of the vehicle and support on axle stands (see *Jacking and vehicle support*). Remove the rear roadwheels.

2 Note how the anti-squeal spring is located, then drive out the upper and lower pad retaining pins from the outside of the caliper using a punch **(see illustration)**.

3 Remove the anti-squeal spring **(see illustration)**.

4 Move the pads away from the disc slightly using a suitable lever or a pair of large adjustable pliers, then withdraw the outer pad from the caliper using pliers or a special removal tool.

5 Withdraw the inner pad from the caliper **(see illustrations)**.

6 Brush the dirt and dust from the caliper, but take care not to inhale it. Carefully remove any rust from the edge of the brake disc.

7 Measure the thickness of the friction material on each brake pad (excluding the backing plate). If either pad is worn at any point to the specified minimum thickness or less, all four pads must be renewed. The pads should also be renewed if any are contaminated with oil or grease; there is no satisfactory way of degreasing friction material. Trace and rectify the cause of contamination before reassembly.

8 If the brake pads are still serviceable, clean them using a clean, fine wire brush or similar, paying particular attention to the sides and back of the metal backing. Carefully clean the pad locations in the caliper body/mounting bracket.

9 Prior to fitting the pads, clean and check the pad retaining pins. Brush the dust and dirt from the caliper and piston (see **Warning** at the beginning of this Section). Apply a little high melting-point copper brake grease to the areas on the pad backing plates which contact the caliper and piston **(see illustration)**. Inspect the dust seal around the pistons for damage, and the pistons for evidence of fluid leaks, corrosion or damage. If attention to any of these components is necessary, refer to Section 7.

10 If new brake pads are to be fitted, the caliper pistons must be pushed back into the cylinder to make room for them. Either use a G-clamp or similar tool, or use suitable pieces of wood as levers. Provided that the master cylinder reservoir has not been overfilled with hydraulic fluid, there should be no spillage, but keep a careful watch on the fluid level while retracting the piston(s). If the fluid level rises above the MAX level line at any time, the surplus should be syphoned off or ejected via a plastic tube connected to the bleed screw.

> ⚠️ *Warning: Do not syphon the fluid by mouth, as it is poisonous; use a syringe or an old poultry baster.*

11 Using a steel rule, check that the cutaway recess in the pistons are positioned as shown **(see illustration)**. The recesses must be at the bottom of the caliper. If necessary, carefully turn the pistons to their correct positions.

12 Locate the new pads in the caliper. Ensure that the friction material faces the disc, and check that the pads are free to move.

13 Locate the anti-squeal spring on the pads,

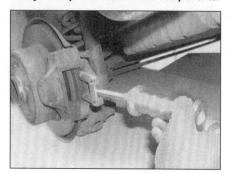

5.5b Using a removal tool to remove the inner rear brake pad

5.9 Apply a little high melting-point brake grease to the backs of the brake pads

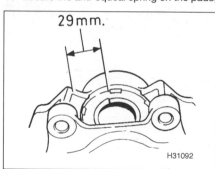

29mm.

H31092

5.11 Correct position of the piston in the rear brake caliper

then insert the pad retaining pins from the inside edge of the caliper, while depressing the spring. Tap the pins firmly into the caliper.

14 Depress the brake pedal repeatedly until normal pedal pressure is restored.

15 Repeat the above procedure on the remaining rear brake caliper.

16 Refit the roadwheels, then lower the vehicle to the ground and tighten the roadwheel bolts to the specified torque setting.

17 Check the hydraulic fluid level as described in *Weekly checks*.

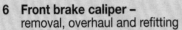

6 Front brake caliper – removal, overhaul and refitting

Removal

1 Apply the handbrake, then jack up the front of the vehicle and support it on axle stands (see *Jacking and vehicle support*). Remove the roadwheel.

2 Minimise fluid loss by first removing the master cylinder reservoir cap, then tightening it down onto a piece of polythene to obtain an airtight seal. Alternatively, use a brake hose clamp to clamp the flexible hose leading to the brake caliper.

3 Clean the area around the caliper brake hose union. Note the fitted angle of the hose (to ensure correct refitting), then unscrew and remove the union bolt and recover the copper sealing washer from each side of the hose union. Discard the washers; new ones must be used on refitting. Plug the hose end and caliper hole, to minimise fluid loss and prevent the ingress of dirt into the hydraulic system.

4 Remove the brake pads as described in Section 4, then remove the caliper from the vehicle.

5 If necessary, unbolt the caliper mounting bracket from the hub carrier **(see illustrations)**.

Overhaul

6 With the caliper on the bench, clean away all external dirt and debris.

7 Withdraw the piston from the caliper body, and remove the dust seal. The piston can be withdrawn by hand, or if necessary pushed out by applying compressed air to the brake hose union hole. Only low pressure should be required, such as from a foot pump.

8 Using a small screwdriver, carefully remove the piston seal from the caliper, taking care not to mark the bore.

9 Remove the guide bushes from the caliper body.

10 Thoroughly clean all components, using only methylated spirit or clean hydraulic fluid. Never use mineral-based solvents such as petrol or paraffin. Dry the components using compressed air or a clean, lint-free cloth. If available, use compressed air to blow clear the fluid passages.

11 Check all components, and renew any that are worn or damaged. If the piston and/or

6.5a Unscrew the bolts . . .

cylinder bore are scratched excessively, renew the complete caliper body. Similarly check the condition of the guide bushes and bolts; both bushes and bolts should be undamaged and a reasonably tight sliding fit. If there is any doubt about the condition of any component, renew it. Renew the caliper seals and dust covers as a matter of course; these are available as a repair kit, together with assembly grease.

12 On reassembly, ensure that all components are absolutely clean.

13 Lubricate the new seal with the grease supplied, or dip it in clean hydraulic fluid. Locate the seal in the cylinder bore groove, using only the fingers to manipulate it into position.

14 Fill the inner cavity of the dust seal with the grease supplied, or dip it in clean hydraulic fluid, then locate it on the piston.

15 Locate the piston on the caliper, then carefully press it fully into the bore, twisting it from side-to-side to ensure it enters the internal seal correctly. At the same time, make sure that the inner end of the dust seal enters the groove on the caliper body, and the outer end enters the groove in the piston.

16 Insert the guide bushes in the caliper body, using suitable grease to lubricate them.

Refitting

17 Locate the caliper mounting bracket on the hub carrier, then apply locking fluid to the threads of the mounting bolts, insert them, and tighten to the specified torque.

18 Refit the brake pads as described in Section 4, together with the caliper which at this stage will not have the hose attached.

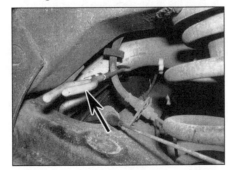

7.2 Brake hose clamp fitted to the flexible hose leading from the body to the brake line on the rear axle

6.5b . . . and remove the caliper mounting bracket from the hub carrier

19 Position a new copper sealing washer on each side of the hose union, and connect the brake hose to the caliper. Ensure that the hose is correctly positioned against the caliper body lug, then install the union bolt and tighten securely.

20 Remove the brake hose clamp or the polythene, where fitted, and bleed the hydraulic system as described in Section 2. Note that, providing the precautions described were taken to minimise brake fluid loss, it should only be necessary to bleed the relevant front brake.

21 Refit the roadwheel, then lower the vehicle to the ground and tighten the roadwheel bolts to the specified torque.

7 Rear brake caliper – removal, overhaul and refitting

Removal

1 Chock the front wheels, then jack up the rear of the vehicle and support on axle stands (see *Jacking and vehicle support*). Remove the roadwheel.

2 Minimise fluid loss by first removing the master cylinder reservoir cap, then tightening it down onto a piece of polythene to obtain an airtight seal. Alternatively, use a brake hose clamp on the flexible hose leading to the brake line on the rear axle **(see illustration)**.

3 Clean the area around the hydraulic line union nut, then loosen the nut **(see illustration)**. Do not fully unscrew the nut at this stage.

7.3 Unscrewing the hydraulic line union nut from the rear brake caliper

7.5 Removing the rear brake caliper mounting bolts

7.6 Removing the rear brake caliper

4 Remove the brake pads as described in Section 5.

5 Unscrew and remove the mounting bolts securing the caliper to the backplate **(see illustration)**. Recover the cover plate from under the bolt heads.

6 Fully unscrew the union nut and disconnect the hydraulic line from the caliper, then withdraw the caliper from the disc **(see illustration)**. Tape over or plug the hydraulic line to prevent entry of dust and dirt.

Overhaul

7 With the caliper on the bench, clean away all external dirt and debris.

8 Withdraw the piston(s) from the caliper body, and remove the dust seal(s). The piston(s) can be withdrawn by hand, or if necessary pushed out by applying compressed air to the brake hose union hole. Only low pressure should be required, such as from a foot pump.

Caution: Keep each piston identified for position to ensure correct refitting.

9 Using a small screwdriver, carefully remove the piston seals from the caliper, taking care not to mark the bores.

10 Thoroughly clean all components, using only methylated spirit or clean hydraulic fluid. Never use mineral-based solvents such as petrol or paraffin.

11 Dry the components using compressed air or a clean, lint-free cloth. If available, use compressed air to blow clear the fluid passages.

12 Check all components, and renew any that are worn or damaged. If the piston(s) and/ or cylinder bore(s) are scratched excessively, renew the complete caliper body. Renew the caliper seals and dust covers as a matter of course; these are available as a repair kit, together with assembly grease.

13 On reassembly, ensure that all components are absolutely clean.

14 Lubricate the new seal(s) with the grease supplied, or dip them in clean hydraulic fluid, then locate them in the cylinder bore groove(s),

using only the fingers to manipulate them into position.

15 Fill the inner cavities of the dust seals with the grease supplied, or dip them in clean hydraulic fluid, then locate them on the pistons.

16 Working on each piston at a time, locate the piston on the caliper so that the cutaway recesses are positioned as described in Section 5. Carefully press the piston fully into the caliper body, twisting it from side-to-side to ensure it enters the internal seal correctly. At the same time, make sure that the inner end of the dust seal enters the groove on the caliper body, and the outer end enters the groove in the piston. Make sure that the piston cutaway recesses are positioned as described in Section 5.

Refitting

17 With both pistons refitted, locate the caliper over the disc and onto the backplate, then insert the hydraulic line and screw in the union nut. Do not fully tighten the nut at this stage.

18 Apply a little locking fluid to the threads of the mounting bolts, then refit the cover plate and bolts, and tighten the bolts to the specified torque.

19 Refit the brake pads (see Section 5).

8.5 Checking the front brake disc with a dial gauge

20 Fully tighten the hydraulic union nut.

21 Remove the polythene, where fitted, and bleed the hydraulic system as described in Section 2. Note that, providing the precautions described were taken to minimise brake fluid loss, it should only be necessary to bleed the relevant rear brake.

22 Refit the roadwheel, then lower the vehicle to the ground and tighten the roadwheel bolts to the specified torque.

---

8 Front brake disc – inspection, removal and refitting

Inspection

1 Apply the handbrake, then jack up the front of the vehicle and support it on axle stands (see *Jacking and vehicle support*). Remove both front roadwheels.

2 For an accurate check and for access to each side of the disc, the brake caliper should be unbolted and suspended to one side as described in Section 4.

3 Check that the brake disc securing screw is tight, then fit spacers approximately 10.0 mm thick to each of the roadwheel bolts, and refit and tighten the bolts. This will hold the disc in its normal running position.

4 Rotate the brake disc, and examine it for deep scoring or grooving. Light scoring is normal, but if excessive, the disc should be removed and either renewed or machined (within the specified limits) by an engineering works. The minimum thickness is given in the Specifications at the beginning of this Chapter.

5 Using a dial gauge, or a flat metal block and feeler blades, check that the disc run-out does not exceed the figure given in the Specifications **(see illustration)**.

6 If the disc run-out is excessive, remove the disc as described later, and check that the

8.11a Front brake disc securing screw

8.11b Using an impact driver to loosen the brake disc securing screw

8.11c Removing the front brake disc

disc-to-hub surfaces are perfectly clean. Refit the disc and check the run-out again. If the run-out is still excessive, the disc should be renewed.

7 Using a micrometer check that the disc thickness is not less than that given in the Specifications. Take readings at several points around the disc.

8 Repeat the inspection on the other front brake disc.

Removal

9 Remove the roadwheel bolts and spacers used when checking the disc.

10 Remove the disc pads as described in Section 4, then tie the caliper to one side. Also remove the front brake caliper mounting bracket with reference to Section 6.

11 Remove the securing screw and withdraw the disc from the hub. If the screw is tight, use an impact driver to loosen it **(see illustrations)**.

Refitting

12 Refitting is a reversal of removal, but make sure that the mating faces of the disc and hub are perfectly clean, and apply a little locking fluid to the threads of the securing screw before tightening it. If a new disc is being fitted, remove the protective coating from the surface, using an appropriate solvent. Refit the disc pads as described in Section 4, then refit the roadwheel and lower the vehicle to the ground.

9 Rear brake disc – inspection, removal and refitting

Inspection

1 Chock the front wheels, then jack up the rear of the vehicle and support on axle stands (see *Jacking and vehicle support*). Remove both rear roadwheels.

2 For an accurate check and for access to each side of the disc, the brake caliper should be unbolted and suspended to one side as described later in Section 7.

3 Check that the brake disc securing screw is tight, then fit spacers approximately 10.0 mm thick to each of the roadwheel bolts, and refit and tighten the bolts. This will hold the disc in its normal running position.

4 Rotate the brake disc, and examine it for deep scoring or grooving. Light scoring is normal, but if excessive, the disc should be removed and either renewed or machined (within the specified limits) by an engineering works. The minimum thickness is given in the Specifications at the beginning of this Chapter.

5 Using a dial gauge, or a flat metal block and feeler blades, check that the disc run-out does not exceed the figure given in the Specifications.

6 If the disc run-out is excessive, remove the disc as described later, and check that the disc-to-hub surfaces are perfectly clean. Refit

the disc and check the run-out again. If the run-out is still excessive, the disc should be renewed.

7 Using a micrometer check that the disc thickness is not less than that given in the Specifications. Take readings at several points around the disc.

8 Repeat the inspection on the other rear brake disc.

Removal

9 Remove the roadwheel bolts and spacers used when checking the disc.

10 Remove the disc pads as described in Section 5.

11 Carefully release the rear brake hydraulic line from the clip on the rear axle, taking care not to bend the line excessively.

12 Unbolt and remove the rear brake caliper with reference to Section 7, and tie it to one side. A convenient place to secure the caliper on the left-hand side, is to the exhaust system, using a long plastic cable tie.

13 Using a screwdriver through the access hole, back off the handbrake shoe adjustment with reference to Section 16 **(see illustration)**.

14 Remove the securing screw and withdraw the disc from the hub **(see illustrations)**.

Refitting

15 Refitting is a reversal of removal, but make sure that the mating faces of the disc and hub are perfectly clean, and apply a little locking fluid to the threads of the securing screw

9.13 Back off the handbrake shoe adjustment using a screwdriver through the access hole in the disc

9.14a Remove the screw . . .

9.14b . . . and remove the rear brake disc

before tightening it. If a new disc is being fitted, remove the protective coating from the surface, using an appropriate solvent. Adjust the handbrake as described in Section 16, then refit the roadwheel and lower the vehicle to the ground.

10 Handbrake shoes
– inspection, removal and refitting

Warning: Renew BOTH sets of rear brake shoes at the same time. Note that the dust created by wear of the pads may contain asbestos, which is a health hazard. Never blow it out with compressed air, and do not inhale any of it. Use brake cleaner or methylated spirit to clean brake components.

Inspection

1 The handbrake operates independently of the footbrake, using brake shoes inside drums integral with the discs.

2 A quick check of the handbrake shoe wear may be made without removing the rear brake disc. Chock the front wheels, then jack up the rear of the vehicle and support it on axle stands (see *Jacking and vehicle support*). Turn the brake disc so that the automatic adjuster is visible through the hole in the disc (see Section 16). If the adjuster has more than 10 threads visible, the shoes are worn excessively and should be renewed.

10.6 Unhook and remove the cable return spring

3 For a thorough check, remove the rear brake disc as described in Section 9, then check the minimum thickness of the friction material on each handbrake shoe. If any one of the shoes has worn below the specified limit, all four handbrake shoes must be renewed as a set.

Removal

4 With the rear brake disc removed, clean the dust and dirt from the brake shoes and backplate.

5 It is possible to remove and refit the shoes without removing the rear hub, however, we found it much easier with the hub removed and the backplate on the bench, particularly for the reassembly procedure. Refer to Chapter 10 and remove the rear hub, and the backplate complete with handbrake shoes.

10.7 Disconnecting the handbrake cable end fitting from the lever on the backplate

6 Unhook the cable return spring from the hole in the backplate and from the cable end fitting **(see illustration)**.

7 Unhook the cable end fitting from the lever on the bottom of the backplate **(see illustration)**.

8 Note the fitted position of all components, and if necessary make a sketch of them **(see illustrations)**.

9 Remove the shoe hold-down cups, springs and pins by depressing the cups and turning them through 90° using a pair of pliers **(see illustration)**. If the hub is still fitted, insert a suitable tool through the hole in the hub flange.

10 Carefully lift the shoes directly from the backplate anchors and guide the expander lever through the rubber grommet **(see illustration)**.

10.8a Handbrake shoes fitted to the rear brake backplate

10.8b Handbrake shoe adjuster (left-hand rear brake) . . .

10.8c . . . expander . . .

10.8d . . . and hold-down springs

10.9 Removing the handbrake shoe hold-down cups, springs and pins

10.10 Lift the shoes directly from the backplate

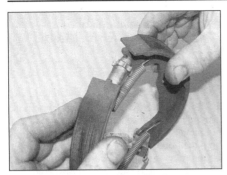

10.11a Remove the adjuster . . .

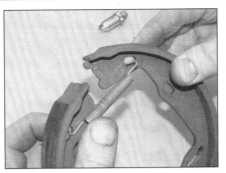

10.11b . . . followed by the upper return spring

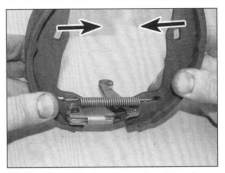

10.12a Swivel the upper ends of the shoes inwards . . .

11 Pull the shoes apart and remove the adjuster, followed by the upper return spring **(see illustrations)**.
12 Swivel the upper ends of the shoes inwards, and remove the expander from the bottom ends **(see illustrations)**.
13 Unhook the lower return spring from the shoes **(see illustration)**.
14 Dismantle the adjuster and expander components for cleaning **(see illustration)**.
15 If both handbrake assemblies are dismantled at the same time, take care not to mix them up.
16 Clean all components, then examine them for wear and damage. Renew worn or damaged components. Make sure that the expander and adjuster operate freely and are not seized – apply a spot of oil to the expander pivots, and apply a little high melting-point grease to the threads of the adjuster before

reassembling it. Set the adjuster to its minimum length.

Refitting

17 Clean the backplate thoroughly, and apply a little copper grease to the shoe contact points (see illustration).
18 Assemble the shoes onto the backplate using a reversal of the removal procedure.
19 Refit the backplate and rear hub with reference to Chapter 10.
20 Hook the cable end fitting on the expander lever and locate the cable holder in the bracket.
21 Hook the cable return spring in the backplate hole and on the end fitting.
22 Refit the rear brake disc and caliper as described in Section 9.
23 Adjust the handbrake shoes as described in Section 16, then refit the roadwheels and lower the vehicle to the ground.

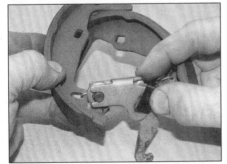

10.12b . . . and remove the expander

10.13 Unhook the lower return spring

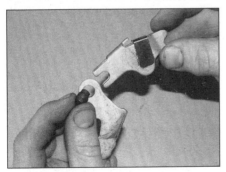

10.14 Dismantling the expander

10.17 Apply a little copper grease to the shoe contact points

11 Master cylinder – removal, overhaul and refitting

Removal

1 Exhaust the vacuum present in the brake servo unit by repeatedly depressing the brake pedal.
2 On left-hand drive models, remove the main fusebox and holder, then disconnect the wiring from the anti-theft alarm switch. To provide more working room, unbolt and remove the bracket.
3 Disconnect the wiring from the brake fluid warning switch in the reservoir filler cap.
4 Syphon out the fluid from the reservoir. Alternatively, open any convenient bleed screw in the system, and gently pump the brake pedal to expel the fluid through a plastic tube connected to the bleed screw (see Section 2).

⚠ **Warning: Do not syphon the fluid by mouth, as it is poisonous; use a syringe or an old poultry baster.**

5 Place cloth rags beneath the master cylinder to catch spilt fluid.
6 On manual transmission models, disconnect the clutch hydraulic hose from the brake fluid reservoir.
7 Refit the filler cap on the reservoir, then carefully lever the reservoir from the rubber grommets in the top of the master cylinder using a wide-bladed screwdriver.
8 Note the position of the brake lines, then unscrew the union nuts and move the lines to one side so that they are just clear of the master cylinder. Do not bend the brake lines excessively. If available, use a split spanner to unscrew the nuts, as they can be very tight. Tape over or plug the outlets of the brake lines and master cylinder.
9 Unscrew the mounting nuts and withdraw the master cylinder from the front of the vacuum servo. Recover the seal. Wrap the master cylinder in cloth rags and remove it from the engine compartment. Take care not to spill fluid on the vehicle paintwork.

Overhaul

10 Before dismantling the master cylinder check on the availability and cost of parts,

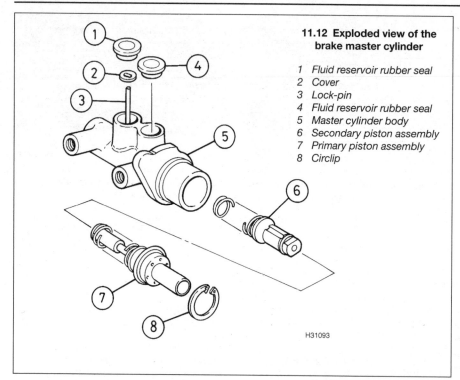

11.12 Exploded view of the brake master cylinder

1 Fluid reservoir rubber seal
2 Cover
3 Lock-pin
4 Fluid reservoir rubber seal
5 Master cylinder body
6 Secondary piston assembly
7 Primary piston assembly
8 Circlip

H31093

as it may be more economical to renew the complete unit.

11 Clean all dirt and debris from the exterior of the master cylinder.

12 Prise out the reservoir rubber seals from the top of the master cylinder (see illustration).

13 Remove the cover and the lock-pin from the fluid aperture to the secondary piston.

14 Using circlip pliers, extract the circlip from the mouth of the master cylinder while slightly depressing the piston against the spring tension.

15 Remove the primary and secondary pistons, together with their springs, from the master cylinder bore, noting their order of removal. If the pistons are tight, tap the cylinder on the work bench or on a block of wood to release them.

16 Thoroughly clean the master cylinder components with methylated spirit or clean brake fluid, and examine them for wear and damage. In particular, check the bore surfaces and rubber seals. The bore surface must not be pitted or scored, and the rubber seals must not be perished or worn. Clean the fluid entry ports of any rust or sediment.

17 If the cylinder bore is in good condition but the rubber seals are worn excessively, obtain new seals or complete new pistons and seals.

18 Lubricate the seals and bore surface with clean brake fluid. Insert the secondary piston assembly with the slot in line with the top of the cylinder, and then insert the lock-pin and cover to hold the piston in place. Make sure that the seal lip is not damaged as it enters the cylinder.

19 Insert the primary piston assembly, again making sure that the seal lip is not damaged as it enters the cylinder.

20 Depress the primary piston, then fit the circlip in the groove in the cylinder mouth. Release the piston.

21 Dip the rubber seals in clean fluid and locate them in the apertures on the top of the master cylinder.

Refitting

22 Ensure the mating surfaces are clean and dry then fit the new seal to the rear of the master cylinder.

23 Fit the master cylinder to the studs on the vacuum servo unit, ensuring that the servo unit pushrod enters the master cylinder piston centrally. Fit the retaining nuts and tighten them securely.

24 Remove the tape or plugs, and reconnect the brake lines to the master cylinder. Tighten the union nuts initially with the fingers to prevent cross-threading, then fully tighten them with a spanner.

25 Locate the fluid reservoir stubs in the rubber seals, and press firmly until it is fully entered.

26 On manual transmission models, reconnect the clutch hydraulic hose to the brake fluid reservoir.

27 Fill the fluid reservoir with fresh brake fluid up to the MAX level mark.

28 Reconnect the wiring to the brake fluid warning switch in the reservoir filler cap.

29 On left-hand drive models, reconnect the wiring to the anti-theft alarm switch. Refit the bracket, main fusebox and holder.

30 Bleed the hydraulic system as described in Section 2. Thoroughly check the operation of the braking system before using the vehicle on the road.

12 Vacuum servo unit non-return valve – removal, testing and refitting

Removal

1 The non-return valve is located in the hose leading from the vacuum servo unit to the inlet manifold. It cannot be obtained separately from the hose.

2 Carefully ease the hose adapter from the rubber grommet on the front of the servo unit.

3 Unscrew the union nut and disconnect the hose from the inlet manifold.

4 Release the hose from the support and remove from the engine compartment.

Testing

5 Examine the check valve and hose for signs of damage, and renew if necessary. The valve may be tested by blowing through the hose in both directions. Air should flow through the valve in one direction only – when blown through from the servo unit end. Renew the valve and hose complete if necessary.

6 Examine the sealing grommet in the vacuum servo unit for signs of damage or deterioration, and renew as necessary.

Refitting

7 Refitting is a reversal of removal, but tighten the union nut securely. On completion, start the engine and check the function of the brakes; also check that there are no air leaks.

13 Vacuum servo unit – testing, removal and refitting

Testing

1 To test the operation of the servo unit, with the engine off, depress the footbrake several times to dissipate the vacuum. Now start the engine, keeping the pedal firmly depressed. As the engine starts, there should be a noticeable 'give' in the brake pedal as the vacuum builds-up. Allow the engine to run for at least two minutes, then switch it off. The brake pedal should now feel normal, but further applications should result in the pedal feeling firmer, the pedal stroke decreasing with each application.

2 If the servo does not operate as described, first inspect the servo unit check valve as described in Section 12.

3 If the servo unit still fails to operate satisfactorily, the fault lies within the unit itself. Repairs to the unit are not possible; if faulty, the servo unit must be renewed.

Right-hand drive models

Removal

4 Remove both windscreen wiper arms as described in Chapter 12.

5 Remove the plastic cover from the engine

13.11a Unhook the brake pedal return spring . . .

13.11b . . . extract the spring clip . . .

13.11c . . . and remove the pushrod pivot pin

compartment rear bulkhead area for access to the wiper linkage. Disconnect the wiring then undo the mounting screws and lift out the wiper linkage assembly.

6 Remove the engine top cover, then unbolt the support bar from between the front suspension turrets.

7 Remove the brake master cylinder as described in Section 11.

8 Prise out the access plugs and unscrew the vacuum servo unit upper mounting bracket bolts.

9 Ease the vacuum hose adapter from the rubber grommet in the front of the vacuum servo unit.

10 Inside the vehicle, remove the lower trim panel from the right-hand side of the facia.

11 Unhook the brake pedal return spring, then extract the spring clip and pull out the pivot pin securing the pushrod clevis to the brake pedal **(see illustrations)**.

12 Remove the cruise control unit, and position it to one side (refer to Chapter 4A).

13 Withdraw the servo unit and upper mounting bracket from the bulkhead, and remove from the engine compartment.

14 Undo the nuts and remove the bracket from the rear of the servo unit.

Refitting

15 Fit the bracket to the rear of the servo unit, and tighten the nuts.

16 Locate the servo unit and mounting bracket on the bulkhead making sure that the upper bracket locates correctly on the lower bracket.

17 Apply locking fluid to the threads of the

13.18 Fitted position of the brake pedal return spring

upper mounting bracket bolts, then insert and tighten them. Refit the access plugs.

18 Inside the vehicle, connect the pushrod clevis on the pedal, then insert the pivot pin and secure with the spring clip. Reconnect the brake pedal return spring **(see illustration)**.

19 Adjust the brake stop-light switch with reference to Section 21.

20 Refit the lower trim panel.

21 Press the vacuum hose adapter in the rubber grommet in the front of the vacuum servo unit.

22 Refit the cruise control unit with reference to Chapter 4A.

23 Refit the brake master cylinder with reference to Section 11, and bleed the brake hydraulic system as described in Section 2.

24 Refit the support bar between the front suspension turrets and tighten the mounting bolt. Refit the engine top cover.

25 Refit the wiper linkage assembly and tighten the mounting screws. Reconnect the wiring and refit the plastic cover to the rear bulkhead area.

26 Refit the windscreen wiper arms with reference to Chapter 12.

27 On completion, start the engine and check for air leaks at the vacuum hose-to-servo unit connection. Check the operation of the braking system.

Left-hand drive models

Removal

28 Unbolt the support bar from between the front suspension turrets.

29 Where applicable, unclip and remove the air induction silencer from above the throttle body.

30 Remove the brake master cylinder as described in Section 11.

31 Carefully ease the hose adapter from the rubber grommet on the front of the servo unit.

32 For improved access, move the fusebox to one side.

33 Unscrew and remove the mounting nuts and washers securing the vacuum servo unit to the bracket.

34 Ease the rubber gaiter from the bulkhead behind the vacuum servo unit, and pull it towards the servo unit to expose the pedal pushrod.

35 Prise the spring clip from the sleeve, then withdraw the servo unit forwards from the

pedal pushrod and remove from the engine compartment.

Refitting

36 Locate the servo unit on the bracket and at the same time engage the sleeve with the pedal pushrod. With all the studs engaged, refit and tighten the mounting nuts and washers.

37 With the pedal pushrod fully engaged, press on the spring clip to secure. Check that the pushrod is engaged by attempting to pull it out of the sleeve.

38 Locate the rubber gaiter on the bulkhead.

39 Refit the fusebox.

40 Press the vacuum hose adapter into the rubber grommet on the front of the servo unit.

41 Refit the brake master cylinder with reference to Section 11, and bleed the brake hydraulic system as described in Section 2.

42 Where applicable, refit the air induction silencer over the throttle body.

43 Refit the support bar between the front suspension turrets and tighten the mounting bolts.

44 On completion, start the engine and check for air leaks at the vacuum hose-to-servo unit connection. Check the operation of the braking system.

14 Vacuum pump (electric) – removal and refitting

Note: *The electric vacuum pump is only fitted to pre-2001 MY petrol turbo models with automatic transmission.*

Removal

1 Apply the handbrake, then jack up the front of the vehicle and support it on axle stands (see *Jacking and vehicle support*). Remove the left-hand front wheel.

2 Remove the wheel arch liner and, where applicable, the engine undershield.

3 Disconnect the vacuum hose from the pump.

4 Disconnect the wiring.

5 Unscrew the mounting nuts and bolts and withdraw the vacuum pump.

Refitting

6 Refitting is a reversal of removal.

15.7 Depress the red locking ring to release the vacuum hose

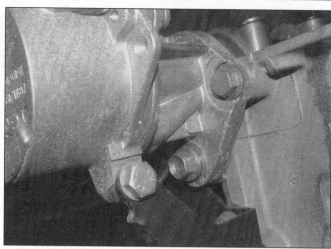

15.11 Mechanical brake vacuum pump mounting bolts (petrol models)

15 Vacuum pump (mechanical) – removal and refitting

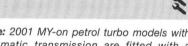

Note: *2001 MY-on petrol turbo models with automatic transmission are fitted with a mechanical vacuum pump, as are all diesel models.*

Removal

Petrol models

1 The vacuum pump is bolted directly to the left-hand end of the cylinder head. First, remove the engine top cover.

2 Disconnect the vacuum hose from the pressure sensor located on the side of the turbocharger.

3 Undo the screw, and detach the bypass pipe from the turbocharger inlet pipe.

4 Disconnect the bypass valve from the charge air pipe.

5 Disconnect the wiring from the temperature sensor on the charge air pipe.

6 Loosen the clips securing the charge air pipe to the throttle body and turbocharger, then unscrew the mounting bolt from the bracket on the cylinder head, and withdraw the pipe from the engine compartment. Temporarily tape over or cover the turbocharger and throttle body apertures.

7 Disconnect the vacuum hose from the vacuum pump on the left-hand end of the cylinder head. To do this, press in the red locking ring while pulling the hose out **(see illustration)**.

8 Disconnect the wiring from the ignition discharge module on the cylinder head.

9 Unscrew and remove the battery clamp mounting bolt, and move the battery as far forwards as possible on the battery tray.

10 Place some cloth rags below the vacuum pump lubrication banjo, then unscrew and remove the banjo bolt. Recover the outer seal.

11 Unscrew the pump mounting bolts, including the bracket bolt, then withdraw it from the cylinder head **(see illustration)**. Recover the inner lubrication seal and the main pump seal. Discard all seals as new ones must be used for refitting.

Diesel models

12 The vacuum pump is bolted directly to the left-hand end of the cylinder head **(see illustration)**. First, remove the engine top cover.

13 Disconnect the main brake servo vacuum line from the vacuum pump by counterholding the large union nut and unscrewing the small one **(see illustration)**.

14 Disconnect the small vacuum hose from the bottom of the vacuum pump.

15 Unscrew the mounting bolts, and withdraw the pump from the cylinder head.

16 Remove the O-ring from the groove in the pump. Discard the O-ring and obtain a new one.

15.12 Vacuum pump location on the left-hand end of the cylinder head (diesel models)

15.13 Unscrew the union nut and disconnect the pipe from the vacuum pump (diesel models)

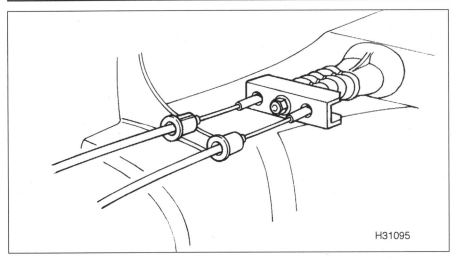

H31095

16.6 Handbrake cable adjustment nut and equaliser bar

Refitting

17 Refitting is a reversal of removal, but note the following additional points:
 a) *Clean the mating faces of the pump and cylinder head, and fit new O-ring(s).*
 b) *Position the pump drive dog so that it will engage with the slot in the end of the camshaft when refitted.*
 c) *On petrol models, fit a new O-ring seal to the lubrication banjo bolt.*
 d) *Tighten all nuts and bolts to the specified torque, where given.*

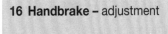

16 Handbrake – adjustment

1 It is normally only necessary to adjust the handbrake after dismantling or renewing the handbrake shoes or cables. First chock the front wheels, then jack up the rear of the vehicle and support on axle stands (see *Jacking and vehicle support*). Remove both rear wheels. Fully release the handbrake lever.
2 Check that the cables are not pulling the expander levers on the rear backplates. If they are, loosen the cable adjusting nut as necessary with reference to paragraph 6.
3 Working on each side at a time, adjust the shoe positions as follows. Turn the rear disc/drum until the access hole is positioned over the upper adjuster serrations. Using a screwdriver through the hole, turn the adjuster serrations until the disc/drum is locked. Now back off the serrations until the disc/drum is just free to turn. Repeat the adjustment on the remaining disc/drum.
4 Refit the rear wheels and tighten the bolts.
5 Set the handbrake lever on the 2nd notch.
6 The handbrake cable adjustment nut is located at the front of the equaliser bar, above a heat shield on the underbody. Unscrew the nuts and lower the heat shield **(see illustration)**.
7 Tighten the cable adjusting nut until slight

resistance is felt when turning the rear wheels. Fully release the handbrake lever and check that the rear wheels turn freely, then set the lever on the 3rd to 6th notch and check that the rear wheels are locked firmly. If necessary, make a final adjustment of the adjusting nut.
8 If only one rear wheel locks, one of the brake cables may be seized, and this must be attended to before finally adjusting the handbrake.
9 On completion, lower the vehicle to the ground.

17 Handbrake cables – removal and refitting

Note: This Section describes the removal and refitting of the secondary handbrake cables.

Removal

1 One primary and a double secondary cable are fitted. An equaliser is attached to the front of the secondary inner cables, and the primary cable is attached to the centre of the equaliser. The secondary cables and equaliser are supplied as one assembly, as are the primary cable and handbrake lever. First, chock the front wheels then jack up the rear of the vehicle and support on axle stands (see *Jacking and vehicle support*). Remove both rear roadwheels.
2 Unscrew the nuts from the underbody and move the centre and rear exhaust heatshields to one side.
3 At the equaliser bar at the front of the cables, measure the length of exposed thread protruding from the adjustment nut to the end of the handbrake lever pull-rod. This will act as a guide when refitting the cables.
4 Unscrew the adjusting nut and remove the equaliser from the rear of the pull-rod.
5 Support the fuel tank, then unscrew the nut from the left-hand tank strap and unhook the strap.

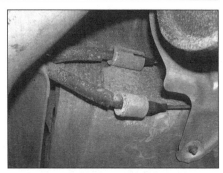

17.7 Handbrake rear cable guide sleeves and brackets

6 Disconnect the left- and right-hand return springs from the holes in the backplates and shoe operating levers.
7 Remove the rear cable guide sleeves from the brackets, and unhook the cable end fittings from the shoe operating levers on each side **(see illustration)**.
8 Pull the cables from the holes on the rear axle and from the brackets behind the rear heat shield.
9 Release the cables from the front bracket near the cable adjuster.
10 Remove the remaining plastic ties and withdraw the cable components from under the vehicle.

Refitting

11 Refitting is a reversal of removal, but finally adjust the handbrake as described in Section 16.

18 Handbrake lever – removal and refitting

Removal

1 Chock the front wheels, then jack up the rear of the vehicle and support on axle stands (see *Jacking and vehicle support*). Remove both rear wheels.
2 Working at each rear wheel brake, disconnect the left- and right-hand return springs from the holes in the backplates and shoe operating levers.
3 Press the rear cable guide sleeves from the brackets on the left- and right-hand side of the rear axle.
4 Press out the front cable guide sleeve, then unhook the rear cable end fittings from the shoe operating levers.
5 Unscrew the nuts and move the exhaust heat shield located in front of the fuel tank.
6 Disconnect the front of the handbrake cables from the lever pull-rod. To do this, it will be necessary to unscrew the adjustment nut and slide off the equaliser bar, however, make a note of the number of threads visible as an aid to refitting.
7 Slide the rubber gaiter from the rear of the pull-rod.
8 Working inside the vehicle, remove the

19.1 Handbrake ON warning light switch

21.3 Remove the stop-light switch from the bracket . . .

21.4 . . . and disconnect the wiring

driver's seat and the centre console as described in Chapter 11.

9 Unscrew and remove the handbrake lever side mounting bolts, and also remove the handbrake warning light switch. Lift the lever assembly from the floor and remove from inside the vehicle.

Refitting

10 Refitting is a reversal of removal, but finally adjust the handbrake as described in Section 16. Tighten the handbrake lever mounting bolts securely.

19 Handbrake ON warning light switch – removal, testing and refitting

Removal

1 The handbrake ON warning light switch is mounted on the front of the handbrake lever mounting bracket **(see illustration)**. Refer to Chapter 11 and remove the centre console.

2 Disconnect the wiring from the switch.

3 Undo the mounting screw and remove the switch.

Testing

4 Connect a multimeter or battery test probe to the wiring contact and switch body.

5 With the switch plunger at rest, there should be continuity and the multimeter should read no resistance, or the test light should light. With the plunger depressed, there should be infinity resistance or the test light should be extinguished.

6 Failure to operate correctly may indicate corroded contacts or ultimately a faulty switch. Check that there is a 12 volt supply to the wiring with the ignition switched on. Renew the switch if necessary.

Refitting

7 Refitting is a reversal of removal.

20 Brake pedal – removal and refitting

Note: *On automatic transmission models, ignore reference to the clutch pedal.*

Removal

1 Remove the clutch pedal and bracket as described in Chapter 6.

2 Extract the clip and remove the fulcrum pin holding the brake master cylinder pushrod to the brake pedal.

3 Disconnect the wiring from the pedal switch, then unscrew the nuts and withdraw the pedal bracket from inside the car.

4 Unscrew the nut and remove the pivot pin, then withdraw the pedal from the bracket.

Refitting

5 Refitting is a reversal of removal, but tighten all nuts and bolts to their correct specified torque where given.

21 Stop-light switch – removal, testing and refitting

Removal

1 The stop-light switch is mounted on top of the pedal bracket. An internal spring tensions the switch plunger so that the contacts are normally closed, however, when the brake pedal is released, the pedal return spring tension is greater than the switch spring, so the contacts are separated when the pedal is in its released position. When the brake pedal is depressed, the switch supplies a current of 12 volts to the central electronic control unit, which then supplies the stop-lights with power. The control unit checks the three stop-light bulbs and if necessary displays a warning on the instrument panel. Where a trailer is being towed, current to the trailer stop-lights is supplied direct from the stop-light switch.

2 To remove the switch, first remove the lower trim panel from the facia with reference to Chapter 11.

3 Twist the switch either clockwise or anti-clockwise 90° and withdraw it from the mounting bracket **(see illustration)**.

4 Disconnect the wiring from the switch **(see illustration)**.

Testing

5 The switch is a single-pole device, and has normally-closed contacts. The operation of the switch can be tested using either a multimeter (switched to the ohmmeter function), or a continuity tester made up of a flashlight bulb, dry cell battery and two pieces of wire. Connect the meter/tester to the switch connector terminals with the switch in its rest position, and check that the meter reads zero resistance or the tester lights up.

6 Press the switch plunger down, and check that the meter reads infinity resistance (open-circuit) or the tester is extinguished.

7 If the switch does not behave as described, or is intermittent in its operation, then a new switch must be fitted; the unit is not serviceable.

Refitting

8 Refit the brake stop-light switch by reversing the removal procedure.

22 Anti-lock Braking System (ABS) components – general information and fault finding

General information

1 The Anti-lock Braking System (ABS) is managed by an Electronic Control Unit (ECU), which has the capacity to monitor the status and condition of all the components in the system, including itself. If the ECU detects a fault, it responds by shutting down the ABS and illuminating the dashboard-mounted ABS warning light. Under these circumstances, conventional non-ABS braking is maintained. Note also that the warning light will be illuminated if the power supply to the ABS ECU is disconnected (eg, if the supply fuse blows). On models manufactured from late 1998, when the ABS warning light is illuminated, the standard brake warning light and central warning light are also illuminated.

2 If the ABS warning lights indicate a fault, it is very difficult to diagnose problems without the equipment and expertise to electronically 'interrogate' the ECU for fault codes. Therefore, this Section is limited firstly to a list of the basic checks that should be carried out, to establish the integrity of the system.

3 If the cause of the fault cannot be immediately identified using the check list described, the *only* course of action open is to take the vehicle to a Saab dealer for

examination. Dedicated test equipment is needed to interrogate the ABS ECU to determine the nature of the fault.

Basic fault finding checks

Brake fluid level

4 Check the brake fluid level (see *Weekly checks*). If the level is low, check the complete braking system for signs of leaks. Refer to Chapter 1A or 1B and carry out a check of the brake hoses and pipes throughout the vehicle. If no leaks are apparent, remove each roadwheel in turn, and check for leaks at the brake caliper pistons.

Fuses and relays

5 The fuse for the ABS is located beneath a cover on the end of the instrument panel. Remove the cover and pull out the fuse. Visually check the fuse filament; if it is difficult to see whether or not it has blown, use a multimeter to check the continuity of the fuse. If any of the fuses are blown, determine the cause before fitting a new one – if necessary, have the vehicle inspected by a Saab dealer.

6 The ABS system relay is located beneath a cover on the left-hand side of the engine compartment. In general, relays are difficult to test conclusively without any electrical specification. However, the metal contacts inside a relay can usually be felt (and often heard) to open or close as it operates – if the relay in question does not behave in this way when the ignition switch is turned on, it may be faulty. It should be noted that this is not a conclusive test, and substitution with a known good relay *of the same type* is the only way to verify the component operation. If any of the relays is suspected of being faulty, it can be renewed by pulling it out of its socket – noting its orientation – and pushing in a new unit.

Electrical connections and earthing points

7 The engine bay is a hostile environment for electrical connections, and even the best seals can sometimes be penetrated. Water, chemicals and air will induce corrosion on the connector's contacts and prevent good continuity, sometimes intermittently. Disconnect the battery negative cable, then check the security and condition of all connectors at the ABS hydraulic unit, situated on the left-hand side of the engine bay.

8 Unplug each connector, and examine the contacts inside. Clean any contacts that are found to be dirty or corroded. Avoid scraping the contacts clean with a blade, as this will accelerate corrosion later. Use a piece of lint-free cloth in conjunction with a proprietary cleaning solvent to produce a clean, shiny contact surface.

9 In addition, check the security and condition of the system electrical earthing point on the side of the hydraulic unit.

23 Anti-lock Braking System (ABS) components – removal and refitting

Note: *If the ABS system is faulty, have it checked by a Saab dealer before removing any component.*

Front wheel sensor

Removal

1 Apply the handbrake, then jack up the front of the vehicle and support it on axle stands (see *Jacking and vehicle support*). Remove the relevant roadwheel.

2 Disconnect the wiring plug in the engine compartment. For the front right-hand sensor it will be necessary to remove the air cleaner assembly. For the front left-hand sensor, it will be necessary to move the main fusebox to one side.

3 Clean the area around the wheel sensor on the front hub carrier, then unscrew the mounting bolt and remove the sensor.

4 Prise the rubber grommet from the inner wing panel, and pull out the wiring.

5 Release the wiring from the retaining clips on the inner wing panel and brake hose.

Refitting

6 Refitting is a reversal of removal, but tighten the mounting bolt securely.

Rear wheel sensor

Removal

7 The rear wheel sensors are integral with the rear wheel hubs, so this section essentially describes the removal of the hub. First, chock the front wheels then jack up the rear of the vehicle and support on axle stands (see *Jacking and vehicle support*). Remove the relevant roadwheel.

8 Remove the rear brake disc as described in Section 9.

9 Disconnect the wiring from the wheel sensor on the rear of the hub.

10 Unscrew the mounting nuts and withdraw the hub assembly from the rear axle. Leave the backplate, handbrake shoes and the spacer(s) hanging on the cable. **Note:** *Discard the hub nuts as new ones must be used on refitting.* Recover the shims where fitted.

Refitting

11 Clean the mounting faces of the rear axle, backplate, spacer(s) and hub then mount the components in the correct order. Fit and progressively tighten the new nuts to the torque wrench setting given in the Specifications.

12 Reconnect the wiring to the wheel sensor.

13 Refit the rear brake disc (see Section 9) and adjust the handbrake shoes (see Section 16).

14 Refit the roadwheel, then lower the vehicle to the ground.

15 Depress the footbrake pedal firmly to set the rear brake pads in their normal position.

ABS/TCS hydraulic unit

Note: *The ABS electronic control unit (ECU) is supplied as an integral part of the hydraulic unit and cannot be removed separately. After fitting a new unit, the ECU must be calibrated by a Saab dealer using the Saab Tech2 hand-held diagnostic instrument.*

Removal

16 Disconnect the battery negative lead (refer to *Disconnecting the battery* in the *Reference* Chapter).

17 Working in the left-hand rear corner of the engine compartment, release the fusebox holder.

18 Cut the plastic cable ties holding the battery positive cable to the main fusebox, then unscrew the nuts and position the fusebox to one side without disconnecting the wiring. If necessary, suspend the fusebox using a piece of string.

19 Minimise fluid loss by first removing the master cylinder reservoir cap, then tightening it down onto a piece of polythene to obtain an airtight seal. As the cap includes a fluid level warning switch, it may be preferable to fit a plain used cap if available. Also, place cloth rags beneath the unit to catch spilt fluid.

20 Disconnect the wiring plug from the electronic control unit and position the plug to one side.

21 Identify each hydraulic brake pipe for its location on the hydraulic unit, then unscrew the union nuts and disconnect the pipes. Tape over or plug the apertures and pipe ends to prevent entry of dust and dirt.

22 Unscrew the mounting nuts and remove the ABS hydraulic unit from the engine compartment. Take care not to spill hydraulic fluid on the vehicle paintwork.

Refitting

23 Refitting is a reversal of removal, but tighten the unit mounting nuts and the hydraulic brake pipe union nuts to the specified torque, and finally bleed the hydraulic system as described in Section 2.

Notes

Chapter 10
Suspension and steering

Contents

Degrees of difficulty

Easy, suitable for novice with little experience	**Fairly easy,** suitable for beginner with some experience	**Fairly difficult,** suitable for competent DIY mechanic	**Difficult,** suitable for experienced DIY mechanic	**Very difficult,** suitable for expert DIY or professional

Specifications

General

Front suspension type . . . . Independent with MacPherson struts and anti-roll bar. Struts incorporate gas-filled shock absorbers and coil springs. Lower arms and radius arms

Rear suspension type. . . . . Semi-rigid axle beam, consisting of spring links connected by intermediate section which acts as torsion bar. Two anti-roll bars, one internal and the other external, coil springs and gas-filled shock absorbers

Steering type . . . . Rack-and-pinion, hydraulic power assistance on all models

Wheel alignment (vehicle unladen with full tank)

Front:
  Toe-in:
    15" wheels . . . . 1.5 ± 0.5 mm
    16" wheels . . . . 1.6 ± 0.5 mm
    17" wheels . . . . 1.3 ± 0.3 mm
  Camber. . . . . -0.8° ± 0.8°
  Castor . . . . 1.85° ± 0.70°
  Kingpin inclination . . . . 13.3°
Rear:
  Toe . . . . 1.0 mm toe-out ± 2.0 mm
  Camber. . . . . -1.7° ± 0.3°
Steering angle toe-out on turns:
  Outer wheel . . . . 20.0°
  Inner wheel . . . . 20.9 ± 0.5°

Wheels

Size . . . . 6 x 15, 6.5 x 16, 6.5 x 16 or 7 x 17

Tyres

Size . . . . 185/65 R15, 195/60 R15, 205/50 R16 or 215/45 ZR17
Pressures . . . . See end of *Weekly checks*

Power steering

Steering wheel turns, lock-to-lock . . . . 3.0 turns

Torque wrench settings

	Nm	lbf ft
Front suspension		
Anti-roll bar clamp bolts....................................	26	19
Anti-roll bar link lower nut..................................	10	7
Anti-roll bar to subframe..................................	26	19
Lower arm to subframe.....................................	115	85
Radius arm to lower arm...................................	92	68
Radius arm to subframe:		
Stage 1..	100	74
Stage 2..............................	Angle-tighten a further 75°	
Shock absorber sleeve nut..................................	215	159
Shock absorber upper nut to strut mounting...................	75	55
Suspension lower balljoint to hub carrier/strut................	75	55
Strut top mounting bolts	24	18
Subframe centre mounting to underbody	190	140
Rear suspension		
Inner anti-roll bar mounting:		
Stage 1..	60	44
Stage 2..............................	Angle-tighten a further 65°	
Outer anti-roll bar mounting...............................	24	18
Rear axle to body mounting................................	75	55
Rear hub to rear axle:		
Stage 1..	50	37
Stage 2..............................	Angle-tighten a further 30°	
Shock absorber bottom mounting...........................	62	46
Shock absorber top mounting	20	15
Steering		
Hydraulic pipes to/from steering gear	28	21
Power steering pump delivery pipe:		
Petrol models...	28	21
Diesel models..	25	18
Power steering pump mounting bolts:		
Petrol models...	20	15
Diesel models..	28	21
Steering gear mounting bolts...............................	24	18
Steering wheel	38	28
Track rod end to steering arm	60	44
Track rod end/track rod clamp bolts	22	16
Track rod to steering gear	93	69
Wheels		
Roadwheel bolts..	110	81

1 General information

The front suspension is fully independent, utilising MacPherson struts and an anti-roll bar. The struts incorporate coil springs and gas-filled shock absorbers, and are integral with the hub carriers. The shock absorbers can be renewed separately from to the strut. The struts are located on the outer ends of the lower arms by balljoints. The lower arms are supported by radius arms attached to the rear of the subframe. The front lower suspension arms and radius arms are connected to the subframe by rubber bushes, and the balljoints are integral with the lower arms. The front hubs are located in double race bearings pressed into the hub carriers, and the driveshafts are splined to the hubs and retained by single hub nuts and thrustwashers.

The rear suspension is of semi-rigid type, incorporating trailing arms connected by a crossbar. Two anti-roll bars are fitted between the trailing arms, one internal and the other external. The trailing arms pivot at their front extensions in rubber bushes located on the underbody, and gas-filled shock absorbers are fitted between the rear ends of the arms and mountings on the underbody. The rear coil springs are located between the trailing arms and the underbody, and are supported at their upper ends in polyurethane seats and at their lower ends in rubber seats. The rear hubs and bearings are supplied as integral units which cannot be dismantled, and they are attached to the trailing arms by studs and nuts. Each rear hub incorporates an internal ABS sensor to monitor the wheel speed (see illustration).

A power-assisted, rack-and-pinion steering system is fitted to all models. The steering rack is essentially a hydraulic ram, which is actuated mechanically by a pinion gear, and hydraulically by pressurised hydraulic fluid, supplied by the power steering pump. The steering column transmits effort applied at the steering wheel to the pinion and a control

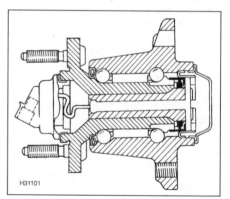

H31101

1.2 Cross-section of the rear hub and bearing

2.6 Removing the caliper bracket mounting bolts and locking plate

2.13a Unscrew the upper mounting nuts . . .

2.13b . . . and lower the strut from under the front wing

valve, which manages the supply of hydraulic fluid to the steering rack. When the steering wheel is turned, the valve directs fluid to the appropriate side of the ram, assisting the movement of the rack. The inner ends of the track rods are attached to the rack at the centre of the steering gear, unlike the more conventional method of attaching them to the ends of the rack. The outer ends of the track rods are attached to the steering arms on the struts/hub carriers by balljoints. The power steering pump is mounted externally on the engine, and is driven by the auxiliary drivebelt.

The design and mounting position of the steering column are such that, in the event of a head-on collision, it will absorb impact by crumpling longitudinally, and will also be deflected away from the driver.

2 Front suspension strut/hub carrier – removal, overhaul and refitting

Note: *Refer to the MOT Section at the rear of the Manual in order to check the shock absorbers before removing them. To ensure even handling, both front shock absorbers must be renewed at the same time.*

Removal

1 Before raising the front of the vehicle, prise off the wheel trim for access to the hub nut (driveshaft nut). Loosen the hub nut and the roadwheel bolts.

2 Apply the handbrake, then jack up the front of the vehicle and support it on axle stands (see *Jacking and vehicle support*). Remove the roadwheel.

3 Fully unscrew and remove the hub nut.

4 Undo the retaining screw and remove the ABS sensor from the strut/hub carrier.

5 Using a pair of grips, press the inner brake pad a little way into its cylinder so that the pads are clear of the disc.

6 Unscrew the caliper bracket mounting bolts and remove the locking plate, then withdraw the caliper and pads from the disc **(see illustration)**. Tie the caliper to one side taking care not to bend the hydraulic hose excessively.

7 Undo the screw and remove the brake disc.

8 Unbolt and remove the splash guard.

9 Unscrew the nut and disconnect the track rod end from the steering arm on the strut with reference to Section 19.

10 Unscrew the nut and remove the washer securing the anti-roll bar link to the lower arm. Pull out the anti-roll bar and recover the rubber bushes and upper washer.

11 Unscrew the nut from the lower balljoint and use a separator tool to separate the lower arm from the strut/hub carrier. Discard the nut as it is self-locking and must be renewed.

12 Pull out the bottom of the strut and at the same time push the driveshaft through the hub until clear of the splines.

13 Support the strut under the front wing, then unscrew the upper mounting nuts from inside the engine compartment. Lower the strut and remove it from under the front wing **(see illustrations)**.

Overhaul

⚠ *Warning: Before attempting to dismantle the front suspension strut, the coil spring must be first held in compression, using a suitable tool. Adjustable coil spring compressors are readily-available, and are essential for this operation. DO NOT attempt to dismantle the strut without such a tool, as damage and/or personal injury is likely.*

Note: *A new shock absorber top mounting nut must be used on reassembly.*

14 Support the strut by clamping it in a vice; avoid damaging the surface of the strut by lining the vice jaws with aluminium or wooden blocks.

15 Using the spring compressor, compress the coils of the spring just enough to relieve all pressure from the upper spring seat **(see illustration)**.

16 Unscrew the nut from the top of the shock absorber piston rod while holding the rod with a socket on the hexagon **(see illustrations)**. Discard the nut and obtain a new one.

⚠ *Warning: Ensure that the upper spring seat has been completely relieved of spring pressure before removing the retaining nut.*

17 Remove the cupped washer followed by the top mounting, thrust bearing,

2.15 Compress the front coil spring using a purpose-made coil spring compressor

2.16a Loosen the strut upper nut while holding the rod with a socket

2.16b Removing the strut upper nut

2.17a Remove the cupped washer . . .

2.17b . . . followed by the top mounting and thrust bearing . . .

2.17c . . . washer . . .

2.17d . . . buffer . . .

2.17e . . . and upper spring seat . . .

Refitting

28 Locate the strut/hub carrier under the front wing and lift it into position while guiding the mounting studs through the holes in the inner wing. Fit the nuts and progressively tighten to the specified torque.

29 Pull out the bottom of the strut, then engage the hub with the driveshaft splines and slide the hub on until it is possible to screw on the new hub nut a few threads.

30 Locate the bottom of the strut/hub carrier on the balljoint stud and fit the new nut. Tighten the nut to the specified torque.

31 Fit the anti-roll bar link to the lower arm together with the rubber bushes and washers. Fit and tighten the nut to the specified torque.

32 Reconnect the track rod end to the steering arm on the strut and tighten the nut to the specified torque with reference to Section 19.

33 Refit the splash guard and tighten the bolts securely.

34 Clean the contact faces then refit the brake disc and tighten the screw.

35 Refit the caliper together with the pads over the disc, and tighten the mounting bolts to the specified torque (refer to Chapter 9). Make sure the hydraulic hose is not twisted.

36 Refit the ABS sensor to the strut bracket and tighten the screw securely.

37 Tighten the hub nut moderately at this stage.

38 Refit the roadwheel and lower the vehicle to the ground.

39 Fully tighten the hub nut to the specified torque (see Chapter 8).

40 Tighten the roadwheel bolts to the specified torque.

41 Refit the wheel trim, then depress the footbrake pedal several times in order to move the brake pads to their normal working position.

washer, buffer, and upper spring seat **(see illustrations)**.

18 Remove the coil spring (making sure that the compressor remains firmly attached to it) and the bump stop **(see illustrations)**.

19 To remove the shock absorber, unscrew the sleeve nut. As this is quite large, it may prove better to clamp the nut in a vice and unscrew the strut/hub carrier from it. As a rough guide to tightening the nut to the correct torque on reassembly, mark the nut in relation to the strut before loosening it. With the nut removed, lift out the shock absorber.

20 Clean all the components and examine them for wear and damage. Renew the components as necessary. Check the upper mounting bearing for smooth operation by turning it by hand. Hub bearing renewal is described in Section 6.

21 Insert the shock absorber and secure

with the sleeve nut, tightened to the specified torque given in the Specifications.

22 Locate the bottom end of the coil spring in the strut, making sure its end abuts the location stop.

23 Locate the bump stop onto the piston rod.

24 Fit the upper spring seat on top of the spring, making sure the end stop abuts the end of the spring.

25 Fit the buffer, washer (with its part number facing downwards), thrust bearing, top mounting, and cupped washer.

26 Fit the new nut to the top of the shock absorber piston rod, and tighten it to the specified torque while holding the rod stationary with a spanner on the hexagon.

27 Carefully loosen the spring compressor while at the same time making sure the spring ends located correctly in the upper and lower spring seats. Remove the compressor.

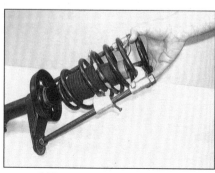

2.18a . . . front coil spring . . .

2.18b . . . and bump stop

3 Front suspension lower arm – removal, overhaul and refitting

Removal

1 Apply the handbrake, then jack up the front of the vehicle and support it on axle stands (see *Jacking and vehicle support*). Remove the roadwheel.

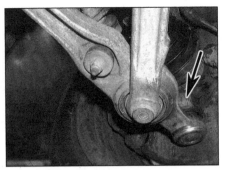

3.3a Front suspension lower arm and balljoint nut

3.3b Separate the lower arm from the strut/hub carrier

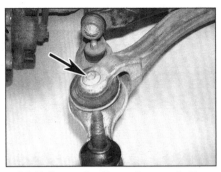

3.4 Bolt securing the radius arm to the lower arm

2 Unscrew the nut and remove the washer securing the anti-roll bar link to the lower arm. Pull out the anti-roll bar and recover the rubber bushes and upper washer.

3 Unscrew the nut from the lower balljoint and use a separator tool to separate the lower arm from the strut/hub carrier **(see illustrations)**. Discard the nut as it is self-locking and must be renewed.

4 Using a Torx key, unscrew and remove the bolt securing the radius arm to the lower arm, then lever the radius arm away from the lower arm **(see illustration)**.

5 Unscrew and remove the inner pivot bolt from the front of the subframe, then ease out the lower arm and withdraw from under the vehicle **(see illustration)**. On the right-hand side, a cover must be removed for access to the bolt.

Overhaul

6 It is not possible to renew the lower balljoint separate to the lower arm, although the balljoint rubber boot may be obtained separately. If the lower balljoint is worn excessively, the lower arm must be renewed complete.

7 Similarly, the inner pivot bush cannot be renewed separate to the arm.

8 If the radius arm location bush in the lower arm is worn, it can be removed using a press and a new one fitted.

9 Check the lower arm for damage and if necessary renew it.

Refitting

10 Locate the lower arm in the subframe

3.5 Front suspension lower arm inner pivot bolt

and insert the pivot bolt from the front. Hand-tighten the bolt at this stage, as it must be fully tightened with the weight of the vehicle on the front suspension.

11 Press the radius arm onto the lower arm, align the holes, and insert the bolt. Fully tighten the bolt to the specified torque.

12 Locate the lower balljoint stud in the bottom of the strut/hub carrier, then fit the new nut and tighten to the specified torque.

13 Fit the anti-roll bar link to the lower arm together with the rubber bushes and washers. Fit and tighten the nut to the specified torque.

14 Refit the roadwheel and lower the vehicle to the ground.

15 Tighten the lower arm-to-subframe bolt.

---

4 Front suspension radius arm – removal, overhaul and refitting

Removal

1 Apply the handbrake, then jack up the front of the vehicle and support it on axle stands (see *Jacking and vehicle support*). Remove the roadwheel.

2 Using a trolley jack, raise the lower arm to its normal running position.

3 Unscrew and remove the bolt securing the radius arm to the lower arm, then lever the radius arm away from the lower arm.

4 Unscrew and remove the bolt securing the radius arm to the subframe, then ease out the radius arm and withdraw from under the vehicle **(see illustration)**.

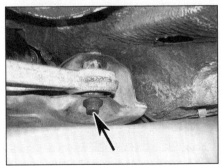

4.4 Bolt securing the radius arm to the subframe

Overhaul

5 Check the inner rubber bush for wear and damage, and if necessary renew it using a press to force out the old bush and insert the new one.

6 Check the radius arm location bush in the lower arm and if necessary renew it by removing the lower arm as described in Section 3.

7 Check the radius arm for damage and if necessary renew it.

Refitting

8 Locate the radius arm inner end in the subframe making sure that the concave side is facing outwards. Insert the bolt, hand-tight at this stage.

9 Locate the outer end of the arm on the lower arm and insert the bolt and nut. Fully tighten both the inner and outer bolts to their specified torque.

10 Refit the roadwheel and lower the vehicle to the ground.

---

5 Front anti-roll bar – removal, overhaul and refitting

Removal

1 Apply the handbrake, then jack up the front of the vehicle and support it on axle stands (see *Jacking and vehicle support*). Remove both roadwheels.

2 The engine assembly must be supported while the subframe is removed. To do this, use a suitable hoist or engine support bar which straddles the engine compartment. Slightly lift the engine assembly so that its weight is supported.

3 Unscrew the clamp bolts connecting the exhaust downpipe to the intermediate section, then separate and lower the front section and suspend it with wire or string from the underbody.

4 Support the subframe using a trolley jack.

5 Loosen the subframe front mounting bolts but do not remove them.

6 At the rear of the subframe, unscrew and remove the four mounting bolts and the two mounting nuts. Lower the subframe as far as possible.

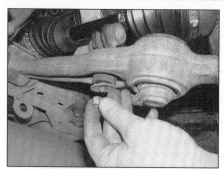

5.7a Unscrew the front anti-roll bar nuts . . .

5.7b . . . and recover the lower washer and rubber mounting

5.11 Front anti-roll bar link nuts

7 Unscrew the nuts securing the anti-roll bar links to the lower arm, and recover the lower washer and rubber mounting **(see illustrations)**.

8 Unscrew the bolts and unhook the mounting clamps.

9 Lift the anti-roll bar and withdraw it from one side. Recover the link upper washers and rubber mountings.

10 Remove the split clamp mounting rubbers from the anti-roll bar.

Overhaul

11 Check the anti-roll bar and mountings for signs of wear and damage. If necessary, unscrew the nuts and remove the side links, then fit new ones and tighten the nuts **(see illustration)**.

12 Check the split clamp mounting rubbers and renew them if necessary.

Refitting

13 Dip the split clamp mounting rubbers in soapy water and locate them on the anti-roll bar.

14 Locate the upper washers and rubber mountings on the links.

15 Check that the mounting rubbers and washers are in place on the links, then insert the anti-roll bar onto the subframe and locate the links in the lower arm.

16 Position the split clamp mounting rubbers and fit the clamps. Insert the clamp mounting bolts hand-tight at this stage.

17 Fit the lower rubber mountings and washers to the anti-roll bar links, then tighten the nuts to the specified torque.

6.3 Inner circlip securing the front hub bearing in the front suspension strut/hub

18 Fully tighten the clamp mounting bolts to the specified torque.

19 Raise the subframe and insert the four rear mounting bolts and two nuts. Note that the washers on the rear bolts must contact the underbody. Fully tighten all the subframe mounting bolts and nuts to the specified torque.

20 Reconnect the exhaust downpipe to the intermediate section and fit the clamp. Tighten the clamp bolts securely.

21 Remove the hoist or support bar.

22 Refit the roadwheels and lower the vehicle to the ground.

6 Front hub bearing – renewal

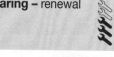

Note: *The action of pressing out the hub may damage the bearing, therefore it is not recommended that a removed bearing is re-used.*

1 Remove the front suspension strut/hub carrier as described in Section 2, but do not dismantle the coil spring, etc.

2 Support the hub carrier on its outer point behind the hub flange. This is best achieved on a hydraulic press. Press or drive the hub from the bearings using a metal tube or large socket in contact with the inner end of the hub.

3 Using circlip pliers, extract the circlips from each side of the hub bearing **(see illustration)**.

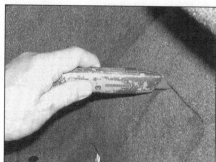

7.2 Access to the shock absorber upper mounting nut is gained by cutting open a flap in the rear luggage compartment trim

4 Support the hub carrier again on its outer point and press or drive out the bearing using a metal tube or large socket in contact with the bearing outer race.

5 Clean the hub and the inside of the hub carrier.

6 Using the circlip pliers, fit the outer circlip to its groove in the hub carrier, positioning the circlip opening at the bottom.

7 Smear some multi-purpose grease on the outer periphery of the bearing and in the hub carrier.

8 Support the outer point of the hub carrier and press or drive in the bearing until it contacts the outer circlip, using a metal tube or large socket on the bearing outer race.

9 Using the circlip pliers, fit the inner circlip to its groove in the hub carrier, positioning the circlip opening at the bottom.

10 Support the inner end of the bearing with a metal tube or large socket on the inner race, then press or drive in the hub from the outside.

11 Refit the front suspension strut/hub carrier as described in Section 2.

7 Rear shock absorber – removal and refitting

Note: *To ensure even handling, both rear shock absorbers must be renewed at the same time.*

Removal

1 Position the rear of the vehicle over an inspection pit or on car ramps. Alternatively, raise and support the rear of the vehicle (see *Jacking and vehicle support*), then remove the roadwheel and support the rear axle with an axle stand or trolley jack on the appropriate side.

2 Open the tailgate for access to the rear shock absorber turret. Using a sharp knife, cut open a flap in the trim as shown **(see illustration)**.

3 Unscrew the rear shock absorber upper mounting nut and recover the washer and rubber bush.

4 Working beneath the vehicle, unscrew

7.4 Rear shock absorber lower mounting bolt

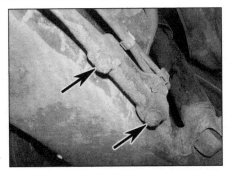

8.2 Mounting bolts for the rear outer anti-roll bar

9.5 Rear coil spring

and remove the lower mounting bolt **(see illustration)**.

5 Withdraw the rear shock absorber, then remove the remaining rubber bush from the top of the shock absorber.

6 Examine the rubber bushes for wear and damage, and renew them if necessary. Note that the lower bush may be pressed out of the shock absorber and a new one fitted. Dip the new bush in soapy water before pressing it into position.

Refitting

7 Refitting is a reversal of removal, but tighten the mounting bolt and nut to the specified torque.

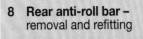

8 Rear anti-roll bar – removal and refitting

Outer anti-roll bar

Removal

1 Chock the front wheels, then jack up the rear of the vehicle and support on axle stands positioned clear of the rear anti-roll bar (see *Jacking and vehicle support*). Remove both rear roadwheels.

2 Unscrew the mounting bolts and lower the anti-roll bar from the rear axle **(see illustration)**.

3 Remove the nut lockplate from the rear axle flange.

4 Examine the anti-roll bar for damage or distortion and renew it as necessary.

Refitting

5 Refitting is a reversal of removal, but tighten the mounting bolts to the specified torque.

Inner anti-roll bar

Removal

6 Chock the front wheels, then jack up the rear of the vehicle and support on axle stands (see *Jacking and vehicle support*). Remove both rear roadwheels.

7 Unscrew and remove the anti-roll bar mounting nuts and bolts located on the outer flanges of the rear axle.

8 Withdraw the anti-roll bar from one side

of the rear axle, pulling it through one of the mounting apertures. Release it from the central rubber block at the same time.

Refitting

9 Before refitting the anti-roll bar, smear it with a little grease before sliding it into the rear axle. Check that it is located correctly in the rubber block.

10 Tighten the mounting nuts and bolts to the specified torque and angle.

11 Refit the roadwheels, and lower the vehicle to the ground.

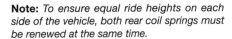

9 Rear coil spring – removal and refitting

Note: *To ensure equal ride heights on each side of the vehicle, both rear coil springs must be renewed at the same time.*

Removal

1 Chock the front wheels, then jack up the rear of the vehicle and support on axle stands (see *Jacking and vehicle support*). Remove the roadwheel.

2 Position a trolley jack beneath the trailing arm and slightly raise it.

3 Unscrew and remove the rear shock absorber lower mounting bolt.

4 Lower the trailing arm as far as possible and remove the trolley jack.

5 Check for any markings on the rear face of the coil spring – if there are no markings, use a dab of paint to ensure that the spring is refitted the same way around **(see illustration)**.

6 Insert a suitable lever in the shock absorber lower mounting, and lever down the trailing arm far enough to remove the coil spring.

7 Recover the upper spring seat and bump stop, and the lower spring seat.

8 Clean the spring seat locations on the rear axle and underbody.

Refitting

9 Locate the lower spring seat on the rear axle.

10 Position the upper spring seat in the coil spring.

11 Lever down the trailing arm, then refit the

coil spring and upper seat making sure that the marking faces rearwards.

12 Raise the trailing arm with the trolley jack until the shock absorber can be located in its lower mounting. Insert the bolt and tighten to the specified torque.

13 Remove the trolley jack, then refit the roadwheel and lower the vehicle to the ground.

10 Rear axle assembly – removal, overhaul and refitting

Removal

1 Chock the front wheels, then jack up the rear of the vehicle and support on axle stands (see *Jacking and vehicle support*). Remove both rear roadwheels.

2 Disconnect the wiring from the ABS sensors on both sides, and release the wiring from the trailing arms.

3 Unhook the handbrake cable return springs from the holes in the backplates and from the cable end fittings.

4 Working on each side, press the handbrake cable guide sleeves from the brackets on the rear axle, and release the cables from the handbrake levers on the rear backplates.

5 Remove the exhaust system rear silencer and tailpipe as described in Chapter 4A or 4B.

6 Remove the outer anti-roll bar as described in Section 8.

7 Before disconnecting the hydraulic line, minimise fluid loss by removing the master cylinder reservoir cap then tightening it down onto a piece of polythene to obtain an airtight seal. Alternatively, use a brake hose clamp to clamp the flexible hose leading from the body to the brake line on the rear axle.

8 Clean the area around the hydraulic line union nuts, then unscrew the nuts from each rear caliper and flexible hose and remove the hydraulic lines. Tape over or plug the hoses and caliper apertures to prevent the entry of dust and dirt.

9 Pull out the retaining clips and remove the hydraulic hoses from the supports.

10 Using a trolley jack, raise the trailing arm on one side of the rear axle then unscrew

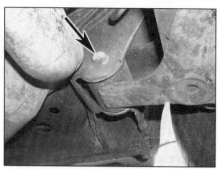

10.14 Rear axle assembly side mounting bolt

11.2 Disconnecting the wiring from the ABS sensor

and remove the rear shock absorber lower mounting bolt and press the shock absorber out of the mounting.

11 Using a lever, press down the trailing arm and remove the coil spring and seat.

12 Support the rear brake caliper, disc and hub assembly, then unscrew and remove the hub mounting nuts from the inside of the trailing arm and lift off the assembly together with the spacer. Place the assembly to one side. Discard the nuts as new ones must be fitted on reassembly.

13 Repeat the procedure described in paragraphs 10 to 12 inclusive, and remove the hub assembly on the remaining side.

14 Support the middle of the rear axle with the trolley jack, then unscrew and remove the side mounting bolts **(see illustration)**.

15 Withdraw the rear axle from the underbody and remove from under the vehicle.

16 Remove the inner anti-roll bar and centre block as described in Section 8.

17 Unbolt the brake hose and handbrake cable support brackets. Also if necessary unbolt the tie-down bracket.

Overhaul

18 Check the rear axle bushes for wear and damage. If necessary, press out the old bushes using suitable metal tubes, a long bolt, nuts and washers.

19 Press in the new bushes using the same method, however note that they must be fitted with their compression holes in the horizontal plane.

Refitting

20 Refit the brake hose and handbrake cable support brackets and the tie-down bracket, and tighten the bolts securely.

21 Refit the rear inner anti-roll bar and centre block with reference to Section 8.

22 Position the rear axle on a trolley jack beneath the rear of the vehicle, and raise it onto the mountings. Insert the mounting bolts hand-tight at this stage.

23 Using the trolley jack, raise one of the trailing arms until the distance between the edge of the wheel arch and the upper edge of the hub centre is 37 cm. Tighten the rear axle mounting bolt on this side of the rear axle to the specified torque.

24 Locate the lower spring seat on the rear axle.

25 Position the upper spring seat in the coil spring.

26 Lever down the trailing arm, then refit the coil spring and upper seat making sure that the marking faces rearwards (refer to Section 9 if necessary).

27 Raise the trailing arm with the trolley jack until the shock absorber can be located in its lower mounting. Insert the bolt and tighten to the specified torque.

28 Repeat the procedure given in paragraphs 23 to 27 on the remaining side.

29 Locate the rear hub assemblies together with calipers and discs on the trailing arms, and secure with new nuts tightened to the specified torque. Make sure the spacers are positioned between the hubs and trailing arms.

30 Refit the hydraulic hoses to the supports and secure with the retaining clips.

31 Refit the hydraulic lines to each side and tighten the union nuts securely. Remove the hose clamps or polythene.

32 Refit the rear outer anti-roll bar with reference to Section 8 and tighten the mounting bolts to the specified torque.

33 Refit the exhaust system rear silencer and tailpipe with reference to Chapter 4A or 4B.

34 Working on each side, locate the handbrake cables in the brackets and connect the end fittings on the levers on the rear backplates. Also refit the equaliser on the single handbrake cable.

35 Reconnect the return springs to the holes in the backplates and cable end fittings.

36 Reconnect the ABS sensor wiring and support it with the clips.

37 Bleed the brake hydraulic system as described in Chapter 9.

38 Refit the rear roadwheels and lower the vehicle to the ground.

11 Rear hub assembly – removal and refitting

Removal

1 Remove the rear brake disc as described in Chapter 9. Take care not to bend the brake line excessively, however, if preferred the line can be disconnected as described in Chapter 9 for the removal of the brake caliper.

2 Disconnect the wiring from the ABS sensor **(see illustration)**.

3 Unhook the handbrake cable return spring from the hole in the backplates and from the cable end fitting.

4 Release the handbrake cable from the lever on the rear backplate, then unhook the cable end fitting.

5 Support the hub and backplate assembly, then unscrew and remove the hub mounting nuts from the inside of the trailing arm and lift off the assembly together with the spacer. Place the assembly to one side. Discard the nuts as new ones must be fitted on reassembly.

6 Separate the hub from the backplate.

Refitting

7 Clean the contact surfaces of the hub, backplate, spacer and trailing arm.

8 Locate the backplate on the hub studs, followed by the spacer, then locate the assembly on the trailing arm and tighten the new nuts securely. Make sure the spacer is positioned between the hub and trailing arm.

9 Reconnect the handbrake cable end fitting on the backplate lever, then reconnect the return spring.

10 Reconnect the wiring to the ABS sensor.

11 Refit the rear brake disc with reference to Chapter 9. If removed, refit the brake caliper making sure that locking fluid is applied to the threads of the mounting bolts before tightening them.

12 If the brake caliper was removed, bleed the hydraulic system as described in Chapter 9.

12 Steering wheel – removal and refitting

Removal

1 Disconnect the battery negative (earth) lead (see *Disconnecting the battery*).

2 Turn the front wheels to the 'straight-ahead' position.

3 Remove the driver's airbag module from the steering wheel as described in Chapter 11.
Caution: Observe the safety instructions meticulously.

4 Disconnect the horn wiring from the steering wheel **(see illustration)**.

12.4 Disconnecting the horn wiring

12.5a Use a long breaker bar to loosen the steering wheel retaining nut

12.5b Removing the steering wheel retaining nut and washer

12.6 Removing the steering wheel while feeding the horn and airbag wiring through the hole

5 Unscrew and remove the steering wheel retaining nut and washer **(see illustrations)**. Mark the steering wheel and column in relation to each other with a dab of paint.

6 Carefully ease the steering wheel from the column splines while feeding the horn and airbag wiring through the hole **(see illustration)**.

Caution: Do not use a hammer or mallet to tap the steering wheel from the splines, as this may damage the collapsible inner column. Also take care not to damage the contact roller located over the top of the column.

7 Using adhesive tape, secure the contact spring unit in its central position.

Refitting

8 Remove the adhesive tape from the contact spring unit. If its central position has been lost, first check that the front wheels are pointing straight-ahead, then turn the unit fully clockwise. Now turn the unit back 2.5 turns exactly.

9 Locate the steering wheel on the column splines, with the previously-made marks aligned, while feeding the airbag and horn wiring through the hole.

10 Refit the washer and retaining nut and tighten the nut to the specified torque.

11 Reconnect the horn wiring.

12 Refit the driver's airbag module with reference to Chapter 11.

13 Reconnect the battery negative (earth) lead.

14 Have the vehicle electronic control system checked for fault codes by a Saab dealer.

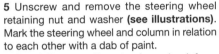

13 Steering column – removal and refitting

Removal

1 Remove the steering wheel as described in Section 12.

2 Undo the crosshead screws and remove the upper and lower shrouds from the steering column.

3 Undo the screws and disconnect the wiring, then remove the contact spring unit. Keep it in its central position using adhesive tape.

4 Remove the combination switch from the steering column with reference to Chapter 12, Section 4. Remove the stalk switches and cable from the bearing housing.

5 Remove the facia lower trim panel and the air duct **(see illustration)**.

6 Unscrew the bolts and remove the knee protection panel from under the steering column.

7 At the bottom of the steering column, unscrew and remove the clamp bolt and slide the universal joint from the steering gear pinion shaft **(see illustration)**. Mark the shaft and column if necessary to ensure correct refitting.

8 Unscrew and remove the column lower mounting bolt located above the ventilation duct **(see illustration)**.

9 Unscrew and remove the upper mounting nuts located beneath the instrument panel, then withdraw the steering column from the bulkhead bracket.

Refitting

10 Locate the steering column on the bulkhead bracket studs, and screw on the nuts loosely at this stage.

11 Engage the universal joint on the bottom of the column with the steering gear pinion shaft, making sure that the bolt hole is aligned with the cut-out in the shaft and the alignment marks are adjacent as previously noted. Tighten the clamp bolt securely.

12 Insert and tighten the column lower mounting bolt, then fully tighten the upper mounting nuts.

13 Refit the knee protection panel beneath the steering column.

14 Refit the facia lower trim panel.

15 Refit the combination switch to the steering column with reference to Chapter 12. Also refit the stalk switches and cable to the bearing housing.

16 Remove the adhesive tape from the contact spring unit. If its central position has been lost, first check that the front wheels are pointing straight-ahead, then turn the unit fully clockwise. Now turn the unit back 2.5 turns exactly. Tighten the mounting screws, then reconnect the wiring.

17 Refit the upper and lower shrouds, then refit the steering wheel as described in Section 12.

13.5 Removing the air duct from under the right-hand side of the facia

13.7 Steering column lower clamp bolt

13.8 Steering column upper and lower mounting bolts

14 Steering column upper bearing – renewal

1 Remove the steering wheel as described in Section 12.
2 Undo the crosshead screws and remove the upper and lower shrouds from the steering column.
3 Undo the screws and disconnect the wiring, then remove the contact spring unit. Keep it in its central position using adhesive tape.
4 Remove the locking ring from the top of the column. Discard the ring as a new one must be fitted on reassembly.
5 Unbolt and remove the bearing housing, and remove the plastic ring, where fitted.
6 Fit the new plastic ring, where fitted, then locate the new bearing housing over the top of the column and secure with the mounting bolt.
7 Fit the new locking ring.
8 Remove the adhesive tape from the contact spring unit. If its central position has been lost, first check that the front wheels are pointing straight-ahead, then turn the unit fully clockwise. Now turn the unit back 2.5 turns exactly. Tighten the mounting screws, then reconnect the wiring.
9 Refit the upper and lower shrouds and tighten the screws.
10 Refit the steering wheel as described in Section 12.

15 Power steering hydraulic system – draining, refilling and bleeding

Note: *The power steering hydraulic system must be bled if any part of the system has been disconnected.*

Draining

1 To drain the complete hydraulic system of fluid, position a container (having a capacity of at least one litre) beneath the power steering pump on the right-hand front of the engine. Loosen the clip and disconnect the return hose from the pump. Allow the fluid to drain into the container from the return hose.
2 Secure the container in the engine bay, away from any moving components and direct sources of heat. Start the engine, and allow the hydraulic fluid to be pumped into the container. Turn the steering lock-to-lock several times, to purge the fluid from the steering rack. When the flow of fluid ceases, turn off the engine immediately; **do not** allow the power steering pump to run dry for any length of time.
3 Reconnect the return hose and tighten the clip.

Refilling

4 Remove the fluid reservoir filler cap, and top-up to the maximum level mark with fluid of the specified type and grade; refer to Chapter 1A or 1B for guidance.

Bleeding

5 Park the vehicle on a level surface and apply the handbrake.
6 With the engine stopped, slowly move the steering from lock-to-lock several times to purge any trapped air, then top-up the level in the fluid reservoir. Repeat this procedure until the fluid level in the reservoir does not drop any further.
7 Start the engine, then slowly move the steering from lock-to-lock several times to purge out any remaining air in the system. Repeat this procedure until bubbles cease to appear in the fluid reservoir.
8 If an abnormal noise is heard from the pump or fluid pipes when the steering is operated, this is an indication that there is still air in the system. Confirm this by turning the wheels to the straight-ahead position and switching off the engine. If the fluid level in the reservoir rises, then air is present in the system, and further bleeding will be necessary. Repeat the above procedure as necessary.
9 Once all traces of air have been purged from the power steering hydraulic system, stop the engine and allow the system to cool. Finally, check that the fluid level is up to the maximum mark on the reservoir, and top-up if necessary.

16 Steering gear assembly – removal and refitting

Removal

1 Apply the handbrake, then jack up the front of the vehicle and support it on axle stands (see *Jacking and vehicle support*). Remove both front roadwheels.
2 Drain the hydraulic fluid from the power steering system as described in Section 15, then return the steering to the straight-ahead position.
3 Disconnect the battery negative (earth) lead (see *Disconnecting the battery*).
4 Remove the air inlet resonator (see Chapter 4A or 4B).
5 Unbolt and remove the brace between the front suspension struts in the engine compartment.
6 On RHD models carry out the following:
 a) *On diesel models, remove the air cleaner cover complete with mass airflow meter and hoses.*
 b) *Also, where fitted on diesel models, unbolt the auxiliary heater exhaust pipe and position to one side, then disconnect the wiring and remove the control valve from the bulkhead. Suspend the heater to one side of the bulkhead.*
 c) *On all models, remove the wiper linkage as described in Chapter 12, then prise out the rubber plugs and unscrew the brake servo bolts.*

7 On LHD models, carry out the following:
 a) *Remove the main fusebox from the left-hand rear corner of the engine compartment for access to the power steering fluid pipes.*
 b) *On diesel models, remove the air cleaner cover complete with mass airflow meter and hoses. Unbolt the pedal position sensor and heater, and position to one side.*
8 Remove the facia lower trim panel.
9 At the bottom of the steering column, unscrew and remove the clamp bolt and slide the universal joint from the steering gear pinion shaft. Mark the shaft and column if necessary to ensure correct refitting.
Caution: Prevent the steering wheel from turning using adhesive tape attached to the facia, otherwise there is a danger of breaking the spring in the contact spring unit.
10 Where fitted, prise the lockplate from the bolts securing the inner ends of the track rods to the steering gear **(see illustration)**.
11 Unscrew the bolts and remove the track rods from the steering gear. Position them to one side, and recover the mounting plate and washers.
12 Unscrew the nut from the track rod end on the right-hand side (RHD models) or left-hand side (LHD models), then separate the track rod end from the steering arm on the hub carrier using a separator tool. Remove the track rod from the vehicle.
13 Position a container beneath the steering gear to catch spilt fluid. Identify the supply and return hydraulic pipes for location, then unscrew the union nuts and carefully position the pipes to one side. Recover the O-ring seals. Tape over or plug the ends of the pipes and the steering gear apertures to prevent entry of dust and dirt.
14 Unscrew the union nuts and disconnect the internal pipes from the valve body. Recover the O-ring seals. Tape over or plug the pipes and apertures to prevent entry of dust and dirt.
15 Support the steering gear, then unscrew the mounting nuts and bolts and remove the clamps. Note the location of the cable support. Withdraw the steering gear upwards from the engine compartment.

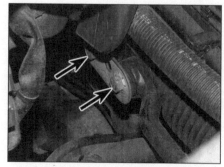

16.10 Bolts securing the inner ends of the track rods to the steering gear

16 Examine the mounting rubbers for wear and damage and renew them if necessary. If a new steering gear is to be fitted, transfer the internal pipes from the old unit and fit new O-ring seals. Tighten the union nuts securely. Check the bulkhead rubber gaiter and renew if necessary.

Refitting

17 Refitting is a reversal of removal, but note the following additional points.

a) Lubricate the bulkhead rubber with a little petroleum jelly.

b) Fit new O-ring seals where necessary.

c) Tighten all nuts and bolts to the specified torque where given.

d) Refit the inner ends of the track rods to the steering gear together with the mounting plate and washers. The mounting plate must be positioned next to the bolt heads, and the washers must be positioned between the track rods and the rack.

e) Engage the universal joint on the bottom of the column with the steering gear pinion shaft, making sure that the bolt hole is aligned with the cut-out in the shaft and the alignment marks are adjacent as previously noted.

f) Fill the power steering system with the specified hydraulic fluid and bleed the system with reference to Section 15.

g) Have the front wheel alignment checked at the earliest opportunity (see Section 20).

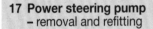

17 Power steering pump
– removal and refitting

Removal

1 Drain the hydraulic fluid from the power steering system as described in Section 15, then return the steering to the straight-ahead position. If preferred, fit a hose clamp to the fluid supply hose instead of completely draining the system.

Petrol models

2 Remove the air cleaner from the right-hand

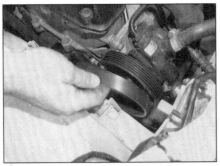

17.4 Removing the auxiliary drivebelt from the power steering pump pulley

front corner of the engine compartment (see Chapter 4A).

3 On RHD Viggen models, unbolt the brace from between the front suspension strut towers.

4 Remove the auxiliary drivebelt from the power steering pump pulley as described in Chapter 1A. To do this, lever the automatic tensioner clockwise until a peg or drill bit can be inserted through the special holes to hold the tensioner **(see illustration)**.

5 Unscrew the union nut securing the feed pipe to the pump.

6 Loosen the clip and disconnect the return hose from the pump.

7 Unscrew the mounting bolts, noting that one of them secures the feed pipe support bracket. Access to the bolt at the pulley end is gained through the hole in the pulley **(see illustrations)**. Note that Viggen models have a through-bolt and nut.

8 Withdraw the pump from the engine **(see illustration)**. Wrap it in cloth rag to prevent fluid dropping onto the vehicle paintwork.

Diesel models

9 Apply the handbrake, then jack up the front of the vehicle and support it on axle stands (see *Jacking and vehicle support*). Remove the front right-hand roadwheel, the engine undertray and top cover, the right-hand spoiler and the wheel arch liner.

10 Remove the auxiliary drivebelt from the power steering pump pulley as described in Chapter 1B. To do this, turn the tensioner anti-clockwise to release the tension on the belt.

11 Unbolt the pulley from the pump, then lever the engine slightly to the left and withdraw the pulley.

12 Remove the air filter assembly (see Chapter 4B).

13 Unscrew the pressure line support bolt, noting that it also supports the dipstick tube.

14 Unscrew the union bolt and disconnect the pressure line from the pump.

15 Unscrew the mounting bolts and withdraw the pump from the bracket on the engine, taking care to keep the sections of the pump together. Wrap it in cloth rag to prevent fluid dropping onto the vehicle paintwork. Remove the sealing rings and discard them; new ones must be obtained for refitting. To remove the bracket from the engine, remove the right-hand engine mounting (see Chapter 2B), then unbolt the air conditioning compressor and suspend it to one side; the bracket can then be unbolted.

Refitting

16 Refitting is a reversal of removal, but note the following additional points.

a) Tighten all nuts and bolts to the specified torque where given.

b) If a new pump is being fitted, unbolt the transit kit and remove the transit sealing rings.

c) On diesel models, apply silicone grease to the sealing rings and locate them on the pump. Make sure that the pump rear cover is located correctly in the guide pin and held with the retaining ring. Fit the pump to the bracket and progressively tighten the bolts initially by hand, then to the specified torque.

d) Fill the hydraulic system with fluid and bleed it as described in Section 15.

18 Steering rack rubber gaiter
– renewal

1 Remove the steering gear as described in Section 16.

2 Unscrew the union nuts and remove the internal hydraulic pipes from the steering gear. Recover the O-ring seals.

17.7a Unscrew the mounting bolts from the power steering pump

17.7b One of the mounting bolts is accessed through the power steering pump pulley

17.8 Removing the power steering pump from the engine

19.3 Unscrew the track rod end securing nut . . .

19.4a . . . then use a separator tool to release the track rod end . . .

19.4b . . . and remove the track rod end from the steering arm

3 Remove the outer rubber mounting from the end of the steering gear housing opposite to the pinion.
4 Loosen the clips, and slide the rubber gaiter from the end of the housing.
5 Wipe clean the housing, then fit the new gaiter and locate in the grooves. Fit and tighten the retaining clips.
6 Locate the outer rubber mounting on the steering gear housing.
7 Fit the internal hydraulic pipes on the steering gear together with new O-ring seals. With the pipes aligned correctly, tighten the union nuts. Note that the ends which locate in the valve housing are not fitted at this stage.
8 Refit the steering gear with reference to Section 16.

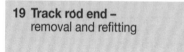

19 Track rod end –
  removal and refitting

Removal

1 Apply the handbrake, then jack up the front of the vehicle and support it on axle stands (see *Jacking and vehicle support*). Remove the roadwheel.
2 Slightly loosen (two or three turns) the clamp bolt securing the track rod end to the adjustment screw. Do not loosen the clamp bolt on the track rod.
3 Unscrew the nut securing the track rod end to the steering arm on the hub carrier **(see illustration)**.
4 Using a separator tool, disconnect the track rod end from the steering arm **(see illustrations)**.
5 Using a steel rule or vernier calipers, measure the length of thread visible on the outer end of the adjustment screw. This is necessary to ensure that the track rod end is refitted in exactly the same position.
6 While holding the adjustment screw with a spanner on the flats provided, unscrew and remove the track rod end while counting the number of turns necessary to do so.

Refitting

7 Screw on the track rod end the exact number of turns noted on removal. Check that

the length of thread visible is as previously noted.
8 Locate the track rod end stub in the steering arm, then tighten the nut to the specified torque.
9 With the track rod end balljoint housing parallel to the steering arm, tighten the clamp bolt to the specified torque.
10 Refit the roadwheel and lower the vehicle to the ground.
11 Have the front wheel alignment checked at the earliest opportunity (see Section 20).

20 Wheel alignment and
  steering angles – general
  information

Front wheel alignment

1 Accurate front wheel alignment is essential to good steering and for even tyre wear. Before considering the steering angles, check that the tyres are correctly inflated, that the front wheels are not buckled, the hub bearings are not worn and that the steering linkage is in good order without slackness or wear at the joints. The fuel tank must be full and the vehicle must be without any passengers.
2 Wheel alignment consists of four factors **(see illustration):**
 Camber is the angle at which the roadwheels are set from the vertical when viewed from the front or rear of the vehicle. Positive camber is the angle (in degrees) that the wheels are tilted outwards at the top from the vertical. Negative camber is the angle that the wheels are tilted inwards at the top from the vertical. This angle is not adjustable.
 Castor is the angle between the steering axis and a vertical line when viewed from each side of the vehicle. Positive castor is indicated when the steering axis is inclined towards the rear of the vehicle at its upper end. This angle is not adjustable.
 Steering axis inclination (kingpin inclination, or swivel pin inclination) is the angle, when viewed from the front or rear of the vehicle, between the vertical and an imaginary line drawn between the upper and lower front suspension strut mountings. This angle is not adjustable.

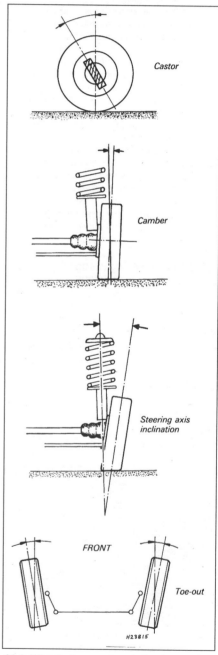

20.2 Wheel alignment and steering angles

Toe is the amount by which the distance between the front inside edges of the roadwheel rim differs from that between the rear inside edges. If the distance between the front edges is less than that at the rear, the wheels are said to toe-in. If the distance between the front inside edges is greater than that at the rear, the wheels toe-out.

3 Owing to the need for precision gauges to measure the small angles of the steering and suspension settings, the checking of camber, castor and steering axis inclination must be carried out by a service station having the necessary equipment. Any deviation from the specified angle will be due to accident damage or gross wear in the suspension mountings.

4 To check the front wheel alignment, first make sure that the lengths of both track-rods are equal when the steering is in the straight-ahead position. To do this, measure the distance between the track rod end and the track rod on each side. The dimension must not be in excess of 52.0 mm, and the dimension must be the same on each side. The flats of the adjustment screws must be positioned centrally between the track rod and track rod end, or within a maximum of 3.0 mm of each other **(see illustration)**. The clamp bolts must be loosened before turning the adjustment screws.

5 Obtain a tracking gauge. These are available in various forms from accessory stores, or one can be fabricated from a length of steel tubing suitably cranked to clear the sump and transmission, and having a setscrew and locknut at one end.

6 With the gauge, measure the distances between the two wheel inner rims (at hub height) at the rear of the wheel. Push the vehicle forward to rotate the wheel through 180° (half a turn) and measure the distance between the wheel inner rims, again at hub height, at the front of the wheel. This last measurement should differ from the first by the appropriate toe-in which is given in the Specifications. The vehicle must be on level ground.

7 If the toe-in is found to be incorrect, release the clamp bolts and turn the adjustment screws equally and in the same direction. Only turn them a quarter-of-a-turn at a time before rechecking the alignment. Turn the adjustment screws with a spanner on the flats, and after making an adjustment, make sure that the track rod end balljoint housing is parallel to the steering arm. It is important not to allow the track rods to become unequal in length during adjustment, otherwise the alignment of the steering wheel will become incorrect and tyre scrubbing will occur on turns.

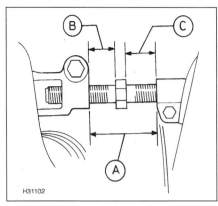

H31102

20.4 Track adjustment screw dimensions

A Must not exceed 52.0 mm on each side
Difference between dimension B and C must not exceed 3.0 mm

8 On completion tighten the clamp bolts without disturbing the setting. Check that the balljoints are at the centre of their arcs of travel.

Rear wheel alignment

9 The rear wheel toe and camber settings are given for reference only since no adjustment is possible.

Chapter 11
Bodywork and fittings

Contents

Degrees of difficulty

Easy, suitable for novice with little experience	**Fairly easy,** suitable for beginner with some experience	**Fairly difficult,** suitable for competent DIY mechanic	**Difficult,** suitable for experienced DIY mechanic	**Very difficult,** suitable for expert DIY or professional

Specifications

Torque wrench settings	Nm	lbf ft
Fixed side window (3-door models)	3	2
Front and rear doors	47	35
Front bumper	39	29
Front seat	24	18
Front seat belt:		
Reel	45	33
Height adjuster	24	18
Buckle	45	33
Slide rail (3-door)	45	33
Passenger airbag	9	7
Passenger airbag safety band bolt	9	7
Rear bumper	39	29
Rear quarter light (5-door models)	3	2
Rear seat belt:		
Reel	38	28
Floor anchorage	45	33
Soft top cover inner cover	14	10
Soft top mounting nuts	28	21

1 General information

The vehicle's body is constructed from pressed-steel sections that are either spot-welded or seam-welded together. The overall rigidity of the body is increased by the use of stiffening beams built into the body panels, steel flanges in the window and door openings, and the application of adhesive in fixed glass joints.

The front subframe assembly provides mounting points for the engine/transmission unit and front suspension, and the steering gear is bolted to the bulkhead. The front wings are also bolted on, rather than welded on, allowing accident damage to be repaired easily.

The vehicle's underside is coated with polyester underseal and an anti-corrosion compound. This treatment provides protection against the elements, and also serves as an effective sound insulation layer. The cabin, luggage area and engine compartment are also lined with bituminous felt and other sound-insulating materials, to provide further noise damping.

All models are fitted with electric windows at the front and rear. The window glass is raised and lowered by an electric motor, directly operating a scissor-action regulator.

Central locking is fitted to all models, and is actuated from the driver's or passenger's door lock. It operates the locks on all four doors, the tailgate, and the fuel filler cap. The lock mechanisms are actuated by servo motor units, and the system is controlled by an Electronic Control Unit (ECU).

All models are fitted with a driver's airbag, located in the centre of the steering wheel. Passenger airbags are an optional extra. The front seat belts incorporate automatic tensioners which operate in the event of a front-end collision. The airbags form part of the Supplementary Restraint System (SRS) which is controlled by an Electronic Control Unit (ECU). Sensors, built into the ECU casing and the front of the engine bay, are triggered in the event of a front-end collision, and prompt the ECU to activate the airbag(s) and the seat belt tensioners.

⚠️ *Warning: Section 30 details the special precautions that need to be observed when working on vehicles with an airbag.*

2 Maintenance – bodywork and underframe

The general condition of a vehicle's bodywork is the one thing that significantly affects its value. Maintenance is easy, but needs to be regular. Neglect, particularly after minor damage, can lead quickly to further deterioration and costly repair bills. It is important also to keep watch on those parts of the vehicle not immediately visible, for instance the underside, inside all the wheel arches, and the lower part of the engine compartment.

The basic maintenance routine for the bodywork is washing – preferably with a lot of water, from a hose. This will remove all the loose solids which may have stuck to the vehicle. It is important to flush these off in such a way as to prevent grit from scratching the finish. The wheel arches and underframe need washing in the same way, to remove any accumulated mud which will retain moisture and tend to encourage rust. Paradoxically enough, the best time to clean the underframe and wheel arches is in wet weather, when the mud is thoroughly wet and soft. In very wet weather, the underframe is usually cleaned of large accumulations automatically, and this is a good time for inspection.

Periodically, except on vehicles with a wax-based underbody protective coating, it is a good idea to have the whole of the underframe of the vehicle steam-cleaned, engine compartment included, so that a thorough inspection can be carried out to see what minor repairs and renovations are necessary. Steam-cleaning is available at many garages, and is necessary for the removal of the accumulation of oily grime, which sometimes is allowed to become thick in certain areas. If steam-cleaning facilities are not available, there are one or two excellent grease solvents available, which can be brush-applied; the dirt can then be simply hosed off. Note that these methods should not be used on vehicles with wax-based underbody protective coating, or the coating will be removed. Such vehicles should be inspected annually, preferably just prior to Winter, when the underbody should be washed down, and any damage to the wax coating repaired. Ideally, a completely fresh coat should be applied. It would also be worth considering the use of such wax-based protection for injection into door panels, sills, box sections, etc, as an additional safeguard against rust damage, where such protection is not provided by the vehicle manufacturer.

After washing paintwork, wipe off with a chamois leather to give an unspotted clear finish. A coat of clear protective wax polish will give added protection against chemical pollutants in the air. If the paintwork sheen has dulled or oxidised, use a cleaner/polisher combination to restore the brilliance of the shine. This requires a little effort, but such dulling is usually caused because regular washing has been neglected. Care needs to be taken with metallic paintwork, as special non-abrasive cleaner/polisher is required to avoid damage to the finish. Always check that the door and ventilator opening drain holes and pipes are completely clear, so that water can be drained out. Brightwork should be treated in the same way as paintwork. Windscreens and windows can be kept clear of the smeary film which often appears, by the use of proprietary glass cleaner. Never use any form of wax or other body or chromium polish on glass.

3 Maintenance – upholstery and carpets

Mats and carpets should be brushed or vacuum-cleaned regularly, to keep them free of grit. If they are badly stained, remove them from the vehicle for scrubbing or sponging, and make quite sure they are dry before refitting. Seats and interior trim panels can be kept clean by wiping with a damp cloth. If they do become stained (which can be more apparent on light-coloured upholstery), use a little liquid detergent and a soft nail brush to scour the grime out of the grain of the material. Do not forget to keep the headlining clean in the same way as the upholstery. When using liquid cleaners inside the vehicle, do not over-wet the surfaces being cleaned. Excessive damp could get into the seams and padded interior, causing stains, offensive odours or even rot. If the inside of the vehicle gets wet accidentally, it is worthwhile taking some trouble to dry it out properly, particularly where carpets are involved. *Do not leave oil or electric heaters inside the vehicle for this purpose.*

4 Minor body damage – repair

Minor scratches

If the scratch is very superficial, and does not penetrate to the metal of the bodywork, repair is very simple. Lightly rub the area of the scratch with a paintwork renovator, or a very fine cutting paste, to remove loose paint from the scratch, and to clear the surrounding bodywork of wax polish. Rinse the area with clean water.

Apply touch-up paint to the scratch using a fine paint brush; continue to apply fine layers of paint until the surface of the paint in the scratch is level with the surrounding paintwork. Allow the new paint at least two weeks to harden, then blend it into the surrounding paintwork by rubbing the scratch area with a paintwork renovator or a very fine cutting paste. Finally, apply wax polish.

Where the scratch has penetrated right through to the metal of the bodywork, causing the metal to rust, a different repair technique is required. Remove any loose rust from the bottom of the scratch with a penknife, then apply rust-inhibiting paint, to prevent the formation of rust in the future. Using a rubber or nylon applicator, fill the scratch with bodystopper paste. If required, this paste can be mixed with cellulose thinners, to provide a very thin paste which is ideal for filling narrow scratches. Before the stopper-paste in the scratch hardens, wrap a piece of smooth cotton rag around the top of a finger. Dip the finger in cellulose thinners, and quickly sweep it across the surface of the stopper-paste in the scratch; this will ensure that the surface of the stopper-paste is slightly hollowed. The scratch can now be painted over as described earlier in this Section.

Dents

When deep denting of the vehicle's bodywork has taken place, the first task is to pull the dent out, until the affected bodywork almost attains its original shape. There is little point in trying to restore the original shape completely, as the metal in the damaged area will have stretched on impact, and cannot be reshaped fully to its original contour. It is better to bring the level of the dent up to a point which is about 3 mm below the level of the surrounding bodywork. In cases where the dent is very shallow anyway, it is not worth trying to pull it out at all. If the underside of the dent is accessible, it can be hammered out gently from behind, using a mallet with a wooden or plastic head. Whilst doing this, hold a suitable block of wood firmly against the outside of the panel, to absorb the impact from the hammer blows and thus prevent a large area of the bodywork from being 'belled-out'.

Should the dent be in a section of the bodywork which has a double skin, or some other factor making it inaccessible from behind, a different technique is called for. Drill several small holes through the metal inside the area – particularly in the deeper section. Then screw long self-tapping screws into the holes, just sufficiently for them to gain a good purchase in the metal. Now the dent can be pulled out by pulling on the protruding heads of the screws with a pair of pliers.

The next stage of the repair is the removal of the paint from the damaged area, and from an inch or so of the surrounding 'sound' bodywork. This is accomplished most easily by using a wire brush or abrasive pad on a power drill, although it can be done just as effectively by hand, using sheets of abrasive paper. To complete the preparation for filling, score the surface of the bare metal with a screwdriver or the tang of a file, or alternatively, drill small holes in the affected area. This will provide a really good 'key' for the filler paste.

To complete the repair, see the Section on filling and respraying.

Rust holes or gashes

Remove all paint from the affected area, and from an inch or so of the surrounding 'sound' bodywork, using an abrasive pad or a wire brush on a power drill. If these are not available, a few sheets of abrasive paper will do the job most effectively. With the paint removed, you will be able to judge the severity of the corrosion, and therefore decide whether to renew the whole panel (if this is possible) or to repair the affected area. New body panels are not as expensive as most people think, and it is often quicker and more satisfactory to fit a new panel than to attempt to repair large areas of corrosion.

Remove all fittings from the affected area, except those which will act as a guide to the original shape of the damaged bodywork (eg headlamp shells etc). Then, using tin snips or a hacksaw blade, remove all loose metal and any other metal badly affected by corrosion. Hammer the edges of the hole inwards, in order to create a slight depression for the filler paste.

Wire-brush the affected area to remove the powdery rust from the surface of the remaining metal. Paint the affected area with rust-inhibiting paint; if the back of the rusted area is accessible, treat this also.

Before filling can take place, it will be necessary to block the hole in some way. This can be achieved by the use of aluminium or plastic mesh, or aluminium tape.

Aluminium or plastic mesh, or glass-fibre matting is probably the best material to use for a large hole. Cut a piece to the approximate size and shape of the hole to be filled, then position it in the hole so that its edges are below the level of the surrounding bodywork. It can be retained in position by several blobs of filler paste around its periphery.

Aluminium tape should be used for small or very narrow holes. Pull a piece off the roll, trim it to the approximate size and shape required, then pull off the backing paper (if used) and stick the tape over the hole; it can be overlapped if the thickness of one piece is insufficient. Burnish down the edges of the tape with the handle of a screwdriver or similar, to ensure that the tape is securely attached to the metal underneath.

Filling and respraying

Before using this Section, see the Sections on dent, deep scratch, rust holes and gash repairs.

Many types of bodyfiller are available, but generally speaking, those proprietary kits which contain a tin of filler paste and a tube of resin hardener are best for this type of repair. A wide, flexible plastic or nylon applicator will be found invaluable for imparting a smooth and well-contoured finish to the surface of the filler.

Mix up a little filler on a clean piece of card or board – measure the hardener carefully (follow the maker's instructions on the pack), otherwise the filler will set too rapidly or too slowly. Using the applicator, apply the filler paste to the prepared area; draw the applicator across the surface of the filler to achieve the correct contour and to level the surface. As soon as a contour that approximates to the correct one is achieved, stop working the paste – if you carry on too long, the paste will become sticky and begin to 'pick-up' on the applicator. Continue to add thin layers of filler paste at 20-minute intervals, until the level of the filler is just proud of the surrounding bodywork.

Once the filler has hardened, the excess can be removed using a metal plane or file. From then on, progressively-finer grades of abrasive paper should be used, starting with a 40-grade production paper, and finishing with a 400-grade wet-and-dry paper. Always wrap the abrasive paper around a flat rubber, cork, or wooden block – otherwise the surface of the filler will not be completely flat. During the smoothing of the filler surface, the wet-and-dry paper should be periodically rinsed in water. This will ensure that a very smooth finish is imparted to the filler at the final stage.

At this stage, the 'dent' should be surrounded by a ring of bare metal, which in turn should be encircled by the finely 'feathered' edge of the good paintwork. Rinse the repair area with clean water, until all of the dust produced by the rubbing-down operation has gone.

Spray the whole area with a light coat of primer – this will show up any imperfections in the surface of the filler. Repair these imperfections with fresh filler paste or bodystopper, and once more smooth the surface with abrasive paper. If bodystopper is used, it can be mixed with cellulose thinners, to form a really thin paste which is ideal for filling small holes. Repeat this spray-and-repair procedure until you are satisfied that the surface of the filler, and the feathered edge of the paintwork, are perfect. Clean the repair area with clean water, and allow to dry fully.

The repair area is now ready for final spraying. Paint spraying must be carried out in a warm, dry, windless and dust-free atmosphere. This condition can be created artificially if you have access to a large indoor working area, but if you are forced to work in the open, you will have to pick your day very carefully. If you are working indoors, dousing the floor in the work area with water will help to settle the dust which would otherwise be in the atmosphere. If the repair area is confined to one body panel, mask off the surrounding panels; this will help to minimise the effects of a slight mis-match in paint colours. Bodywork fittings (eg chrome strips, door handles etc) will also need to be masked off. Use genuine masking tape, and several thicknesses of newspaper, for the masking operations.

Before commencing to spray, agitate the aerosol can thoroughly, then spray a test area (an old tin, or similar) until the technique is mastered. Cover the repair area with a thick coat of primer; the thickness should be built up using several thin layers of paint, rather than one thick one. Using 400 grade wet-and-dry paper, rub down the surface of the primer until it is really smooth. While doing this, the work area should be thoroughly doused with water, and the wet-and-dry paper periodically rinsed in water. Allow to dry before spraying on more paint.

Spray on the top coat, again building up the thickness by using several thin layers of paint. Start spraying at the top of the repair area, and then, using a side-to-side motion, work downwards until the whole repair area and about 2 inches of the surrounding original paintwork is covered. Remove all masking

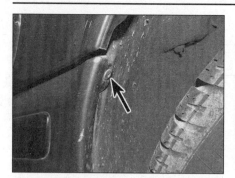

6.3 Detach the wheel arch liners from the rear ends of the front bumper

6.5 Lift the wiper arms from the headlamps and unclip the washer tubing

6.9 Disconnect the wiring from the ambient temperature sensor

material 10 to 15 minutes after spraying on the final coat of paint.

Allow the new paint at least two weeks to harden, then, using a paintwork renovator or a very fine cutting paste, blend the edges of the paint into the existing paintwork. Finally, apply wax polish.

Plastic components

With the use of more and more plastic body components by the vehicle manufacturers (eg bumpers. spoilers, and in some cases major body panels), rectification of more serious damage to such items has become a matter of either entrusting repair work to a specialist in this field, or renewing complete components. Repair of such damage by the DIY owner is not really feasible, owing to the cost of the equipment and materials required for effecting such repairs. The basic technique involves making a groove along the line of the crack in the plastic, using a rotary burr in a power drill. The damaged part is then welded back together, using a hot air gun to heat up and fuse a plastic filler rod into the groove. Any excess plastic is then removed, and the area rubbed down to a smooth finish. It is important that a filler rod of the correct plastic is used, as body components can be made of a variety of different types (eg polycarbonate, ABS, polypropylene).

Damage of a less serious nature (abrasions, minor cracks etc) can be repaired by the DIY owner using a two-part epoxy filler repair. Once mixed in equal, this is used in similar fashion to the bodywork filler used on metal panels. The filler is usually cured in twenty to thirty minutes, ready for sanding and painting.

If the owner is renewing a complete component himself, or if he has repaired it with epoxy filler, he will be left with the problem of finding a suitable paint for finishing which is compatible with the type of plastic used. At one time, the use of a universal paint was not possible, owing to the complex range of plastics encountered in body component applications. Standard paints, generally speaking, will not bond to plastic or rubber satisfactorily, but suitable paints to match any plastic or rubber finish, can be obtained from dealers. However, it is now possible to obtain a plastic body parts finishing kit which consists of a pre-primer treatment, a primer

and coloured top coat. Full instructions are normally supplied with a kit, but basically, the method of use is to first apply the pre-primer to the component concerned, and allow it to dry for up to 30 minutes. Then the primer is applied, and left to dry for about an hour before finally applying the special-coloured top coat. The result is a correctly-coloured component, where the paint will flex with the plastic or rubber, a property that standard paint does not normally possess.

5 Major body damage – repair

Where serious damage has occurred, or large areas need renewal due to neglect, it means that complete new panels will need welding-in, and this is best left to professionals. If the damage is due to impact, it will also be necessary to check completely the alignment of the bodyshell, and this can only be carried out accurately by a dealer using special jigs. If the body is left misaligned, it is primarily dangerous, as the car will not handle properly, and secondly, uneven stresses will be imposed on the steering, suspension and possibly transmission, causing abnormal wear, or complete failure, particularly to such items as the tyres.

6 Front bumper – removal and refitting

Removal

1 Apply the handbrake, then jack up the front of the vehicle and support it on axle stands (see *Jacking and vehicle support*).
2 Unbolt and remove the splash shields from under each end of the front bumper.
3 Undo the screws and detach the wheel arch liners from the rear ends of the bumper **(see illustration)**.
4 With the bonnet open, remove the radiator grille as described in Section 8.
5 Lift the wiper arms from the headlamps and unclip the washer tubing from the rear edge of the bumper **(see illustration)**. Where fitted, remove the wiper motors.

6 Remove the headlights and indicator lamps from both sides of the vehicle with reference to Chapter 12, Section 6.
7 Unscrew and remove the bolts securing the bumper to the body. The bolts are located in the headlight apertures.
8 Disconnect the wiring from the foglights and release the cable ties.
9 Working beneath the middle of the bumper, disconnect the wiring from the ambient temperature sensor **(see illustration)**. Remove the adhesive tape holding the wiring in position.
10 With the aid of an assistant, lift the front bumper and pull it forwards from the brackets in the front wings.
11 If fitting a new bumper, transfer the number plate, trim insert, spoiler and splash shields to the new unit.

Refitting

12 Lift the bumper into position and locate it in the brackets. Insert the mounting bolts and tighten to the specified torque.
13 Reconnect the wiring to the temperature sensor and attach the wiring to the underside of the bumper with adhesive tape.
14 Reconnect the wiring to the foglights and secure the wiring with new cable ties.
15 Refit the headlights and indicator lamps with reference to Chapter 12.
16 Clip the washer tubing to the rear edge of the bumper. Lower the wiper arms onto the headlights. Where fitted, refit the wiper motors.
17 Refit the radiator grille with reference to Section 8.
18 Refit the wheel arch liners inside the rear edge of the bumper and secure with the screws.
19 Refit the splash shields under each end of the bumper.
20 Lower the vehicle to the ground. If necessary, adjust the headlight alignment (see Chapter 12).

7 Rear bumper – removal and refitting

Removal

1 With the tailgate open, release the rubber weatherstrip from the rear valance and inner trim. Do not completely remove it.
2 Unbolt and remove the two load securing

7.2 Load securing eyelets in the luggage compartment

7.3 Removing the rear valance trim panel

7.4 Rear bumper mounting nuts

eyelets from each side of the luggage compartment **(see illustration)**.

3 Fold the luggage compartment carpet forwards, then undo the plastic nuts and unclip the rear valance trim panel from over the tailgate striker **(see illustration)**.

4 Unscrew and remove the rear bumper mounting nuts **(see illustration)**.

5 At the front ends of the bumper, release the mouldings from the wheel arches **(see illustration)**. On some models two screws secure the mouldings, however, where rivets are used it is possible to pull the mouldings forwards and disconnect them from the wheel arches. If necessary, drill out the rivets.

6 With the help of an assistant, pull the bumper rearwards while releasing it from the side brackets. Take care not to damage the vehicle paintwork.

Refitting

7 Lift the bumper into position and slide it forwards. Make sure the bumper engages correctly with the side brackets by having the assistant press the sides of the bumper inwards while the bumper is pushed forwards. Check for correct positioning by looking beneath the bumper.

8 Refit and tighten the mounting nuts to the specified torque.

9 Refit the mouldings to the wheel arches, using new rivets where necessary.

10 Refit the trim panel and tighten the nuts, then fold the carpet back.

11 Refit the two load securing eyelets and tighten the bolts.

12 Refit the rubber weatherstrip and close the tailgate.

8 Bonnet, struts and front grille – removal and refitting

Bonnet

> ⚠ **Warning: It is essential to enlist the help of an assistant for this operation.**

Removal

1 With the bonnet open, place some cloth rags or card between the rear edge of the bonnet and the windscreen valance.

2 Disconnect the washer tube from the adapter on the bulkhead cover.

3 Have the assistant support the bonnet open.

4 Disconnect the struts from the bonnet by prising out the retaining clips with a screwdriver, then pulling off the struts **(see illustration)**. Lower the struts onto the front wings.

5 Using a pencil, mark the position of the hinges on the bonnet.

6 While the assistant supports the bonnet, unscrew and remove the hinge bolts using a Torx key **(see illustration)**. Carefully lift the bonnet from the vehicle and place in a safe position, taking care not to damage the paintwork.

7 If necessary, remove the wiper arms and bulkhead cover, then unbolt and remove the hinges from the body. If a new bonnet is being fitted, transfer the sound insulation and weatherseal to the new unit.

Refitting

8 Refitting is a reversal of removal. When first closing the bonnet, lower it slowly and check that the striker is aligned with the lock. Also check that the bonnet is positioned central between the front wings. If necessary, loosen the bolts and reposition the bonnet on the hinges before fully closing the bonnet. Tighten the bolts on completion. Check that the front of the bonnet is level with the front wings, and if necessary screw in or out the rubber stops located in the front corners of the engine compartment.

Struts

Removal

9 Open the bonnet. If removing just one strut, the remaining strut will hold the bonnet up, however if removing both struts an assistant will be required to hold the bonnet open. Alternatively, use a length of wood to prop the bonnet open.

10 Using a screwdriver, prise the spring clip from the top of the strut and disconnect the strut.

11 Disconnect the bottom of the strut by prising out the spring clip.

Refitting

12 Refitting is a reversal of removal.

Front grille

Removal

13 With the bonnet open, depress the

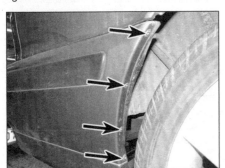

7.5 Rear bumper front mounting

8.4 Strut attachment to the bonnet

8.6 Bolts securing the bonnet to the hinges

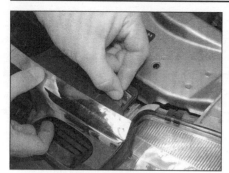

8.13 Release the retaining clips . . .

8.14 . . . and lift the grille upwards from the two locating holes

9.5 The bonnet release lever located beneath the right-hand side of the facia

retaining clips and release the grille from the engine compartment front crossmember **(see illustration)**.

14 Lift the grille upwards from the two locating holes **(see illustration)**.

Refitting

15 Refitting is a reversal of removal.

9 Bonnet release cable and lever – removal and refitting

Removal

1 With the bonnet open, undo the screw and remove the clamp securing the release cable to the engine compartment front crossmember.

2 Prise out the small rubber plug, then release the bonnet lock spring from the crossmember using a pair of grips to unhook it. With the

10.1a Remove the rubber plug . . .

10.1b . . . and disconnect the bonnet lock spring

spring loose, disconnect the cable from it.

3 Withdraw the cable from the clips in the engine compartment.

4 Working inside the vehicle on the driver's side, remove the fusebox cover, lower trim panel, and heater duct then remove the electronic module and relays. Unbolt the fusebox and position it to one side.

5 Fold back the carpet then remove the bonnet release lever using two screwdrivers to prise free the locking tabs at the top and bottom **(see illustration)**.

6 Tie a length of string to the inner end of the cable as an aid to refitting the cable correctly. Withdraw the lever and cable assembly through the bulkhead and remove from the passenger compartment. Untie the string and leave it through the bulkhead.

Refitting

7 Tie the string to the cable and wrap adhesive tape around the end of the cable to assist it through the bulkhead. Pull the cable through into the engine compartment and untie the string.

8 Press the release lever firmly into place inside the vehicle, and reposition the carpet.

9 Insert and tighten the fusebox screws.

10 Refit the electronic module and relays, the heater duct, lower trim panel and fusebox cover.

11 Inside the engine compartment, locate the cable in the clips.

12 Attach the cable to the bonnet lock spring, then refit the spring and hook it into the hole. Refit the rubber plug.

13 Position the outer cable so that there is no

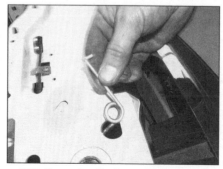

10.3 Removing the bonnet lock spring from the crossmember

free play, then refit the clamp and tighten the screw.

14 Close the bonnet and check that the cable operates the release spring correctly.

10 Bonnet lock spring – removal and refitting

Removal

1 With the bonnet open, prise out the small rubber plug then release the bonnet lock spring from the engine compartment crossmember using pliers to unhook it **(see illustrations)**.

2 With the spring loose, disconnect the cable from it beneath the crossmember.

3 Withdraw the spring from the crossmember **(see illustration)**.

Refitting

4 Refitting is a reversal of removal, but apply a little grease to the part of the spring which contacts the bonnet striker.

11 Doors – removal, refitting and adjustment

Front
Removal

1 Open the door and disconnect the wiring by depressing and turning the plug and socket located between the door and A-pillar **(see illustration)**.

11.1 Disconnecting the front door wiring

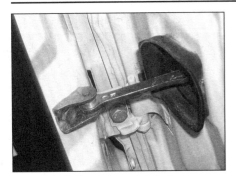

11.2 Front door check strap

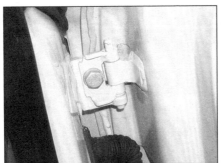

11.3 Front door upper hinge

11.8 Rear door lower hinge and check strap

2 Unbolt the check strap from the A-pillar **(see illustration)**.
3 Mark the position of the hinge plates on the A-pillar brackets in relation to each other **(see illustration)**.
4 With the help of an assistant, unscrew the mounting bolts and withdraw the door from the vehicle. Take care not to damage the paintwork.

Refitting and adjustment

5 Refitting is a reversal of removal, but tighten the mounting bolts to the specified torque. Check that the door lock aligns correctly with the striker on the B-pillar, and that the gap between the door and surrounding bodywork is equal when the door is shut. If necessary, the striker may be adjusted slightly by loosening it. Tighten it on completion. To adjust the vertical position of the door, loosen the hinge bolts; if there is insufficient downward adjustment, grind off the lower hinge lug to a maximum of 4.0 mm. Rearward adjustment is made with shims fitted between the hinge and pillar.

Rear

Removal

6 Open the front and rear doors on the relevant side.
7 Pull back the sheathing for access to the plug and socket, then disconnect the wiring.
8 Using a suitable drift, drive out the door check bush from below **(see illustration)**.

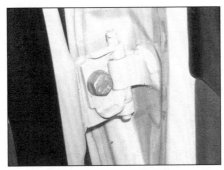

11.9 Rear door upper hinge

9 Mark the position of the hinge plates on the B-pillar brackets in relation to each other **(see illustration)**.
10 With the help of an assistant, unscrew the mounting bolts and withdraw the door from the vehicle. Take care not to damage the paintwork.

Refitting and adjustment

11 Refitting is a reversal of removal, but tighten the mounting bolts to the specified torque. Check that the door lock aligns correctly with the striker on the C-pillar, and that the gap between the door and surrounding bodywork is equal when the door is shut. If necessary, the striker may be adjusted slightly by loosening it **(see illustration)**. Tighten it on completion. To adjust the vertical position

11.11 Rear door striker

of the door, loosen the hinge bolts; if there is insufficient downward adjustment, grind off the lower hinge lug to a maximum of 4.0 mm. Rearward adjustment is made with shims fitted between the hinge and pillar.

12 Door inner trim panel
– removal and refitting

Front

Removal

1 Carefully prise the tailgate/boot lid opening button from the door inner trim panel using a small screwdriver, and disconnect the wiring **(see illustrations)**.

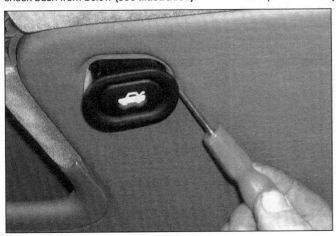

12.1a Prise out the tailgate opening button . . .

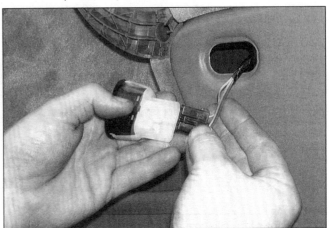

12.1b . . . and disconnect the wiring

12.2a Prise off the plastic cover . . .

12.2b . . . then undo the screw . . .

12.2c . . . and disconnect the handle from the operating rod

12.2d Operating rod at 'rest' position

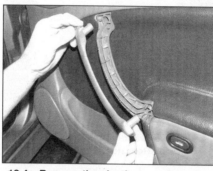

12.4a Remove the plastic cover from the door pull . . .

2 Prise the plastic cover from the inner door handle, then undo the screw and unclip the handle from the operating rod **(see illustrations)**.

3 Using a screwdriver inserted at the front of the exterior mirror inner trim panel, carefully prise out the panel and disconnect the wiring from the control switch.

4 Prise the plastic cover from the door pull and undo the screws **(see illustrations)**.

5 Undo the screws securing the bottom of the trim to the door panel **(see illustration)**.

6 Remove the clip from the rear edge of the trim panel by depressing the centre pin **(see illustration)**. On Convertible models, release the clip from the front of the trim by depressing the centre pin.

7 Using a wide-bladed screwdriver, carefully prise out the clips securing the trim panel to the door. Take care not to damage the trim panel or break the clips by prising as near to the clip positions as possible.

8 With the clips released, lift the trim panel upwards over the locking button.

9 If necessary carefully remove the membranes from the door inner panel **(see illustration)**.

Refitting

10 Refitting is a reversal of removal. Note when fitting a new trim panel on Convertible models, it is necessary to cut off the front upper corner using a hacksaw, as the trim also fits Coupe models. Determine how much to cut off by comparing to the original panel.

12.4b . . . and undo the screws

12.5 Removing the front door trim panel lower screws

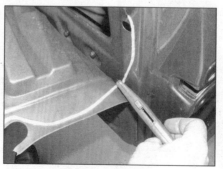

12.6 Removing the clip from the rear edge of the door trim

12.9a Removing the front door main membrane . . .

12.9b . . . and lower membrane

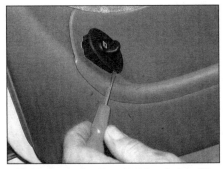

12.11 Removing the electric window lift switch from the rear door trim

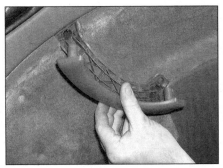

12.12a Prise the plastic cover from the door pull . . .

12.12b . . . then undo the retaining screws

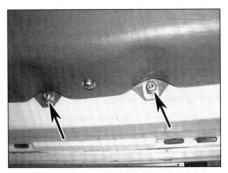

12.13 Undo the two retaining screws arrowed

12.14a Prise off the cover . . .

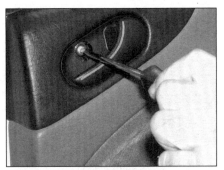

12.14b . . . then undo the screw . . .

Rear

Removal

11 Carefully prise the electric window lift switch from the door inner trim panel using a small screwdriver, and disconnect the wiring **(see illustration)**.

12 Prise the plastic cover from the door pull, then unscrew the trim panel retaining screws now visible **(see illustrations)**.

13 On the lower edge of the trim panel, undo the two retaining screws. Do not unscrew the centre screw as this secures the storage compartment to the trim panel **(see illustration)**.

14 Prise the plastic cover from the inner door handle, then undo the screw and unclip the handle from the operating rod **(see illustrations)**.

15 Using a wide-bladed screwdriver, carefully prise out the clips securing the trim panel to the door. Take care not to damage the trim panel or break the clips by prising as near to the clip positions as possible.

16 With the clips released, lift the trim panel upwards over the locking button.

17 If necessary carefully pull the membranes from the door inner panel **(see illustrations)**.

Refitting

18 Refitting is a reversal of removal.

13 Door handle and lock components – removal and refitting

Interior door handle

Removal

1 Prise the plastic cover from the inner door handle, then undo the screw and unclip the handle from the operating rod.

Refitting

2 Refitting is a reversal of removal.

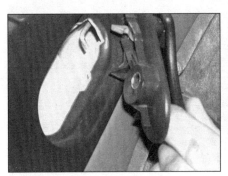

12.14c . . . and unclip the handle from the operating rod

12.17a Removing the rear door main membrane . . .

12.17b . . . and lower membrane

13.7 Disconnecting the central locking wiring

13.8 Door lock retaining screws

13.9a Withdraw the door lock and central locking motor . . .

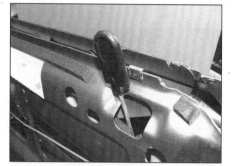

13.9b . . . while guiding the locking knob through the hole

Front door lock

Removal

3 With the window closed, remove the door trim and membranes (see Section 12).

4 Reach inside the door and disconnect the inner handle operating rod from the lock. To do this, push up the plastic retainer then release the rod.

5 Unscrew and remove the window rear guide channel lower bolt.

6 Disconnect the lock cylinder operating rod from the lock by pushing up the plastic retainer.

7 Disconnect the central locking wiring from the lock **(see illustration)**.

8 Undo the screws securing the lock to the rear edge of the door, and remove the plate where fitted **(see illustration)**.

9 Withdraw the door lock complete with central locking motor through the aperture in the door. As the lock assembly is being removed, feed the locking knob down through the hole in the door **(see illustrations)**.

10 If necessary, undo the screws and remove the central locking motor from the lock.

Refitting

11 Refitting is a reversal of removal, however before refitting the door trim, make sure that the lock operates correctly.

Rear door lock

Removal

12 With the window closed, remove the door trim and membranes (see Section 12). Also remove the packing from inside the door.

13 Reach inside the door and disconnect the inner handle operating rod from the lock. To do this, push up the plastic retainer then release the rod.

14 Disconnect the locking knob rod from the lock by pushing up the plastic retainer. If necessary, the complete rod can be removed by removing the crank.

15 Unscrew and remove the window rear guide channel lower bolt.

16 Disconnect the central locking wiring from the lock.

17 Undo the screws securing the lock to the rear edge of the door.

18 Withdraw the door lock complete with central locking motor through the aperture in the door.

19 If necessary, undo the screws and remove the central locking motor from the lock.

Refitting

20 Refitting is a reversal of removal.

Front door exterior handle

Removal

21 With the window closed, remove the door trim and membranes (see Section 12).

22 Reach inside the door and disconnect the inner handle operating rod from the lock. To do this, push up the plastic retainer then release the rod.

23 Unscrew and remove the window rear guide channel lower bolt **(see illustration)**. On 5-door models, move the channel slightly out but do not disconnect the top of the channel. On 3-door models, pull the channel down slightly then pull it out of the top slot and remove it.

24 Reach inside the door and release the clip securing the microswitch to the rear of the exterior door handle. Position the switch to one side.

25 If working on the driver's door, disconnect the lock cylinder operating rod from the lock.

26 Support the exterior door handle from

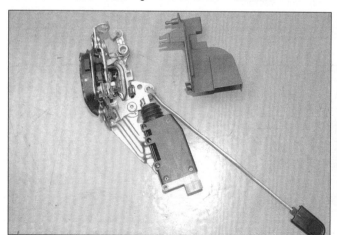

13.9c Door lock and central locking motor removed from the door

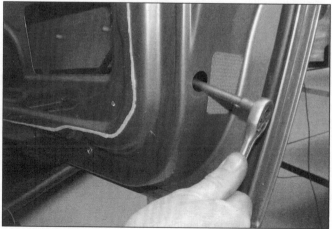

13.23 Unscrew the window rear guide channel lower bolt

outside, then unscrew the nut from inside and remove the mounting plate **(see illustrations)**.

27 Disconnect the exterior door handle operating rod from the lock.

28 If necessary for improved access, remove the lock completely as described earlier in this Section.

29 Carefully remove the exterior door handle from outside taking care not to damage the paintwork **(see illustrations)**.

Refitting

30 Refitting is a reversal of removal.

Rear door exterior handle
Removal

31 With the window fully open, remove the door trim and membranes (see Section 12).

32 Reach inside the door and disconnect the inner handle operating rod from the lock. To do this, push up the plastic retainer then release the rod.

33 Remove the rear triangular trim panel, releasing it from the rear edge first.

34 Remove the inner door glass moulding.

35 Unscrew and remove the window rear guide channel lower bolt, then angle the channel up out of the window frame.

36 Raise the window, then unscrew the nut and remove the retainer plate from the rear of the door handle. If necessary for improved access, remove the lock completely as described earlier in this Section.

37 Disconnect the exterior door handle operating rod from the lock.

38 Carefully remove the exterior door handle from outside taking care not to damage the paintwork.

Lock cylinder (driver's door)
Removal

39 Remove the front door exterior door handle as described earlier in this Section.

40 With the handle on the bench, remove the microswitch by prising out the clip and lifting it from the groove.

41 Extract the circlip securing the lever to the lock cylinder.

42 Withdraw the lock mounting making sure that the roller remains in the mounting. With the mounting removed, recover the roller and keep in a safe place.

43 Remove the door handle gasket.

13.26a Unscrew the nut . . .

13.29a Removing the front door exterior handle

13.26b . . . and remove the mounting plate

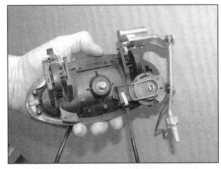
13.29b Door handle removed from the door

44 Using a screwdriver, slowly prise out the circlip holding the lock cylinder in the handle. When the end of the circlip is visible in the drain hole, bend it out and pull it out with pliers, taking care not to scratch the handle. Note which groove the circlip is fitted in.

45 Press out the lock cylinder and recover the two rollers. Keep the rollers in a safe place.

Refitting

46 Fit a new circlip in the groove on the lock cylinder.

47 Smear some grease onto the lock cylinder, then fit the two rollers in their slots.

48 Insert the lock cylinder into the handle, making sure that the circlip end gap is located over the drain hole.

49 Refit the door handle gasket.

50 Fit the remaining roller in the lock lever, then refit the lever to the lock cylinder and secure with the circlip.

51 Refit the microswitch and secure with the

clip. The flat part of the clip should be facing upwards.

52 Refit the handle as described earlier in this Section.

14 Door/side window glass – removal and refitting

Front door
Removal

1 Fully lower the window, then remove the inner door trim panel and membranes as described in Section 12, noting the location of the wiring.

2 At the rear edge of the door, press out the outer weatherseal then lift it from the outside of the door.

3 Prise out the fasteners, then remove the cover and inner weatherseal from the door **(see illustrations)**.

14.3a Prise out the fasteners . . .

14.3b . . . then remove the cover . . .

14.3c . . . and inner weatherseal from the door

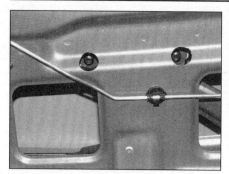

14.5 Window glass lower mounting screws

14.6a Extract the clips . . .

14.6b . . . then prise the regulator pins from the rollers

4 Unscrew and remove the window rear guide channel lower bolt.

5 Temporarily reconnect the switch to the electric window lifting motor and raise the window slightly until the bottom of the window is visible through the openings in the door panel. On Convertible models, position the window so that the lower mounting screws of the window are visible through the openings in the door panel **(see illustration)**.

6 Extract the retaining clips from the channel rollers, then carefully prise the regulator pins from the rollers while supporting the window **(see illustrations)**. The pins are a tight fit in the rollers so take care not to apply excessive pressure to the glass.

7 Carefully lift the rear of the window and withdraw it from the outside of the door **(see illustration)**. On Convertible models, if it is found that the guide channels restrict removal

of the glass, unbolt the rear channel from the glass first.

8 Remove the channel rollers from the glass.

Refitting

9 Lubricate the window glass bottom channel with grease, then locate the rollers in it.

10 Lower the glass into position and locate it in the front and rear guide channels.

11 Press the regulator pins into the rollers then refit the clips.

12 Insert and tighten the window rear guide channel lower bolt.

13 Temporarily reconnect the switch to the electric window lifting motor, then loosen the regulator rearmost adjustment nut and fully raise the window. Now lower the window until it is 3.0 cm from its closed position, and press the window fully to the rear. The top edge of the window should be parallel with the door panel. Tighten the rearmost adjustment nut.

14 Press the inner weatherseal into the door.

15 Refit the outer weatherseal and press the location peg into the hole.

16 Refit the inner door trim panel and membranes (see Section 12).

Rear door

Removal

17 Fully lower the window, then remove the inner door trim panel and membranes as described in Section 12.

18 Using a screwdriver, carefully prise out the triangular trim cover from the door and remove the packing **(see illustration)**.

19 Prise up the inner weatherseal from the door, starting from the rear **(see illustration)**.

20 Prise up the outer weatherseal from the door **(see illustration)**.

21 Remove the rubber seal from the rear guide channel **(see illustration)**.

14.7a Removing the window glass from the front door – Hatchback and Coupe models

14.7b Removing the window glass from the front door – Convertible models

14.18 Removing the triangular trim cover

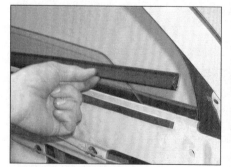

14.19 Removing the inner weatherseal from the rear door

14.20 Removing the outer weatherseal

14.21 Removing the rubber seal from the rear guide channel

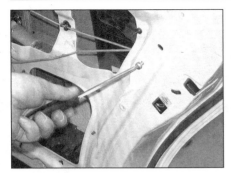

14.23a Remove the guide channel lower screw . . .

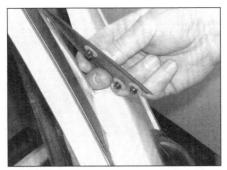

14.23b . . . then remove the triangular trim . . .

14.23c . . . and withdraw the window rear guide channel

22 Disconnect the inner door handle operating rod from the lock by pushing up the plastic retainer.

23 Unscrew and remove the window rear guide channel lower screw. Remove the outer triangular trim, then disconnect the channel upper end and turn as necessary to remove it (see illustrations).

24 Carefully raise the rear of the glass and release the bottom channel from the regulator. Reposition the glass horizontally, then lift it upwards and remove it from the inside of the door (see illustrations).

Refitting

25 Lubricate the window glass bottom channel with grease.

26 Lower the glass into position and engage the bottom channel with the regulator.

27 Locate the glass in the front guide channel, then refit the rear guide channel and secure with the lower bolt. Make sure the upper end of the channel is correctly located.

28 Reconnect the inner door handle operating rod to the lock and secure with the plastic retainer.

29 Smear some petroleum jelly on the rubber seal, then locate it in the rear guide channel.

30 Refit the inner and outer weatherseals, making sure that they are pressed down firmly.

31 Refit the quarter trim cover and packing, pressing them firmly into place.

32 Refit the inner door trim panel and membranes as described in Section 12.

33 Raise the window and check its operation.

Side window (Convertible)

Removal

34 Remove the rear side trim as described in Section 26.

35 Mark the position of the side window inner weatherseal panel bolts, then unscrew the bolts and remove the panel (see illustrations).

36 Remove the side window outer weatherseal by prising up carefully (see illustration).

37 Remove the loudspeaker (see Chapter 12).

38 Fully raise the side window.

14.24a Release the bottom channel from the regulator . . .

14.24b . . . then withdraw the window from the rear door

14.35a Mark the position of the bolts . . .

14.35b . . . then remove them . . .

14.35c . . . and remove the weatherseal inner panel

14.36 Removing the side window outer weatherseal

14.39 Removing the side window on Convertible models

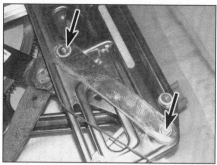

14.40 Bolts securing the window glass to the regulator on Convertible models

14.41 The plastic screws are used to adjust the height setting of the side window

39 Loosen only the nuts retaining the side window mechanism to the body, then lift the side window and disconnect the wiring **(see illustration)**.
40 Mark the position of the bolts, then unscrew them and remove the window glass from the mechanism **(see illustration)**.

Refitting

41 Refitting is a reversal of removal. Check that the upper edge of the window is approximately 1.0 to 2.0 mm lower than the upper edge of the front window, when closed. The clearance between the front and side window glasses should be approximately 8.0 mm. The plastic screws **(see illustration)** are used to adjust the height setting, and the in/out studs are used to adjust the inclination.

15 Door/side window regulator – removal and refitting

Front door

Removal

1 Remove the inner door trim panel and membranes as described in Section 12.
2 Temporarily reconnect the window operating switch, then lower the window approximately 10 cm and retain in this position using adhesive tape. The window bottom channel and regulator arm ends should now be visible through the apertures in the door inner panel.
3 Prise out the retaining clips from the channel

rollers, then carefully prise the regulator pins from the rollers while supporting the window. The pins are a tight fit in the rollers so take care not to apply excessive pressure to the glass.
4 Temporarily reconnect the window operating switch, then operate the motor until the regulator arms are horizontal. This will enable the regulator to be removed more easily through the door aperture.
5 Support the regulator, then drill off the heads of the rivets securing the regulator to the door panel **(see illustration)**. Tap out the rivets with a small punch.
6 Disconnect the wiring from the electric motor **(see illustration)**.
7 Mark the position of the adjustment channel, then unscrew the retaining nuts.
8 Withdraw the regulator and motor from inside the door **(see illustration)**.

15.5 Drill out the rivets securing the regulator to the front door

9 If necessary, unbolt the motor from the regulator **(see illustration)**. Where one of the retaining bolts is concealed by the regulator, it will be necessary to remove the stator for access to the armature, then turn the armature while pressing down on the segment for access to the bolt.

Refitting

10 If necessary, refit the motor to the regulator and tighten the bolts.
11 Locate the regulator and motor inside the door, then refit the adjustment channel in its previously noted position and tighten the nuts.
12 Reconnect the wiring to the electric motor.
13 Temporarily reconnect the switch then raise the regulator arms slightly.
14 Position the regulator on the door and secure with new rivets **(see illustration)**.

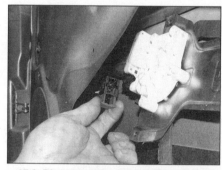

15.6 Disconnecting the wiring from the front door window regulator

15.8 Removing the front door window regulator

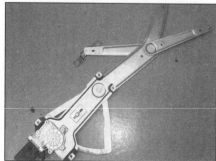

15.9 Front door and window regulator removed from the door on Convertible models

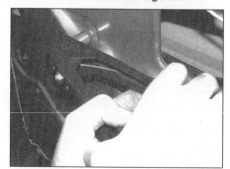

15.14 Secure the window regulator with new rivets

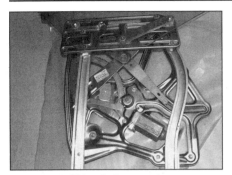

15.31 Side window regulator on Convertible models

16.4 Removing the grab handle

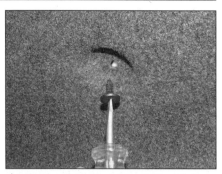

16.5 Removing the trim panel retaining screws

15 Engage the regulator pins with the window channel rollers and refit the clips.

16 With the adjustment nuts loose, fully raise the window. Now lower the window until it is 3.0 cm from its closed position, and press the window fully to the rear. The top edge of the window should be parallel with the door panel. Tighten the adjustment nuts.

17 Refit the inner door trim panel and membranes with reference to Section 12.

Rear door

Removal

18 Remove the inner door trim panel and membranes as described in Section 12.

19 Prise up the outer weatherseal from the door, starting at the rear.

20 Unscrew and remove the window rear guide channel lower bolt.

21 Temporarily reconnect the window operating switch, then lower the window approximately 10 cm and retain in this position using adhesive tape. The window bottom channel and regulator arm ends should now be visible through the apertures in the door inner panel.

22 Disconnect the wiring from the electric motor.

23 Support the regulator, then drill off the heads of the rivets securing the regulator to the door panel. Tap out the rivets with a small punch.

24 Release the regulator arms from the window bottom channel, then carefully withdraw the regulator and motor through the

aperture in the door panel. **Note:** *The motor and regulator cannot be separated.*

Refitting

25 Locate the regulator inside the door panel, and engage the arms with the window bottom channel.

26 Position the regulator and secure with new rivets.

27 Reconnect the electric motor wiring.

28 Insert and tighten the window rear guide channel lower bolt.

29 Refit the outer weatherseal to the door.

30 Refit the inner door trim panel and membranes with reference to Section 12.

Side window

31 Removal of the side window regulator is part of the window glass removal described in Section 14 **(see illustration)**.

---

16 Tailgate/boot lid and support struts – removal and refitting

---

Tailgate

Removal

1 Disconnect the battery negative (earth) lead (see *Disconnecting the battery*).

2 With the tailgate open, place some cloth rags between the tailgate and the bodywork to prevent any damage.

3 Remove the rear parcel shelf.

4 Using a Torx key, undo the screws and remove the grab handle from the tailgate **(see illustration)**.

5 Using a screwdriver, undo the screws and remove the main trim panel from the inside of the tailgate **(see illustration)**. Also carefully prise the plastic trim panels from the sides of the tailgate using a screwdriver.

6 Unscrew the central locking motor mounting bolts, then disconnect the lever and wiring and remove the motor.

7 Note the location of the remaining wiring in the tailgate, then disconnect it and release it from the cable ties **(see illustration)**.

8 At the top of the tailgate, prise out the wiring protector from the inner hole **(see illustration)**, then use a screwdriver through the hole to release the one upper and two lower catches securing the wiring grommet.

9 Carefully withdraw the wiring through the top of the tailgate.

10 Turn the washer nozzle through 90° and pull it out of the tailgate, then disconnect the tubing.

11 Remove the rubber stop and remove the washer tubing.

12 While an assistant supports the weight of the tailgate, disconnect the struts by prising out the spring clips **(see illustration)**. Position the struts on the rear body.

13 Extract the circlip from the hinge pins, then use a suitable drift to drive them out.

14 Lift the tailgate from the rear body and place it in a safe position on cloth rags or card to protect the paintwork.

16.7 Disconnect the wiring

16.8 Prise out the wiring protector

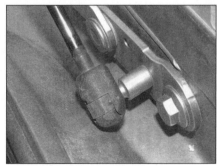

16.12 Disconnect the struts

Refitting

15 With the help of an assistant, lift the tailgate into position. Lightly grease the hinge pins then refit them and secure with the circlips.

16 Reconnect the struts and refit the spring clips.

17 Insert the washer tubing and rubber stop, then reconnect the tubing to the nozzle. Insert the nozzle and turn through 90° to secure.

18 Feed the wiring into the tailgate and refit the grommet making sure that the catches are correctly engaged. Refit the wiring protector.

19 Locate the wiring as previously noted and secure with the cable ties.

20 Refit the central locking motor and reconnect the lever and wiring. Insert the bolts and tighten.

21 Refit the trim panels and tighten the screws.

22 Refit the grab handle and tighten the screws.

23 Refit the parcel shelf.

24 Reconnect the battery negative lead.

25 Check that the tailgate closes properly and is located centrally within the body aperture. Adjustment is possible by lowering the headlining and loosening the hinge bolts. Check that the tailgate rests in the rubber buffers located on each side, and if necessary adjust the buffers by removing the trim and loosening the nuts. Check that the striker enters the lock centrally, and if necessary loosen the striker screws to adjust its position.

Boot lid

Removal

26 Carry out the procedure described in paragraphs 1 to 9, but ignore the reference to the rear parcel shelf.

27 While an assistant supports the weight of the boot lid, disconnect the struts by prising out the spring clips. Position the struts on the rear body.

28 In the rear luggage compartment, fold down the trim near the left-hand rear light, and unplug the boot lid wiring harness.

29 Remove the wiring harness grommet from the side panel **(see illustration)**. Also, remove the strut balljoint near the side panel.

30 Mark the position of the boot lid on the hinges, then, with the help of an assistant,

17.5 Boot lid lock and mounting bolts

16.29 Wiring harness grommet in the side panel

unscrew the nuts and remove the boot lid **(see illustration)**.

Refitting

31 Refitting is a reversal of removal.

---

17 Tailgate/boot lid lock components – removal and refitting

Tailgate/boot lid lock

Removal

1 Remove the rear parcel shelf on Hatchback/Coupe models.

2 Using a Torx key, undo the screws and remove the grab handle from the tailgate/boot lid.

3 Using a screwdriver, undo the screws and remove the main trim panel from the inside of the tailgate/boot lid.

4 Disconnect the operating rod from the crank located near the central locking motor. To do this, press off the plastic clip.

5 Unscrew the mounting bolts and withdraw the lock together with the operating rod from the hole in the tailgate/boot lid **(see illustration)**.

6 Disconnect the operating rod.

Refitting

7 Refitting is a reversal of removal.

Tailgate/boot lid lock cylinder

Removal

8 Remove the rear parcel shelf on Hatchback/Coupe models.

9 Using a Torx key, undo the screws and

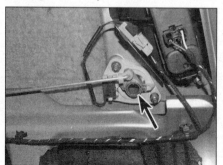

17.11 Boot lid lock cylinder

16.30 Boot lid hinge

remove the grab handle from the tailgate/boot lid.

10 Using a screwdriver, undo the screws and remove the main trim panel from the inside of the tailgate/boot lid.

11 Press off the plastic clip and disconnect the operating rod from the lock cylinder **(see illustration)**.

12 If necessary, prise off the clip and remove the microswitch. Alternatively, just disconnect the wiring.

13 Unscrew the mounting nuts and withdraw the lock cylinder from the tailgate/boot lid.

14 Insert the ignition key into the lock cylinder, then extract the circlip and remove the lever and spring.

15 Press out the cylinder.

16 Check the rubber O-ring and if necessary renew it.

Refitting

17 Refitting is a reversal of removal. Make sure that the lock cylinder is fitted with the drain hole facing downwards.

Tailgate/boot lid handle

Removal

18 Remove the rear parcel shelf on Hatchback/Coupe models.

19 Using a Torx key, undo the screws and remove the grab handle from the tailgate/boot lid.

20 Using a screwdriver, undo the screws and remove the main trim panel from the inside of the tailgate/boot lid.

21 Unscrew the two handle retaining nuts located next to the central locking unit **(see illustration)**.

17.21 Boot lid handle/cover and central locking unit

22 Unbolt the rear number plate light panel.
23 Unscrew the nuts and remove the left-hand rear light. Disconnect the wiring.
24 Remove the left-hand clip and pull the tailgate/boot lid handle assembly to the left until it slides out of the right-hand clip. Withdraw the assembly from the tailgate.

Refitting
25 Refitting is a reversal of removal.

Spoiler
Removal
26 Remove the rear parcel shelf.
27 Using a Torx key, undo the screws and remove the grab handle from the tailgate.
28 Using a screwdriver, undo the screws and remove the main trim panel from the inside of the tailgate.
29 Remove the tailgate wiper motor as described in Chapter 12.
30 Unscrew the mounting nuts and remove the spoiler from the tailgate.

Refitting
31 Refitting is a reversal of removal.

18 Central locking servo motors – removal and refitting

Tailgate/boot lid motors
Removal
1 Remove the rear parcel shelf on Hatchback/Coupe models.

20.1a Removing the triangular trim (Hatchback and Coupe models)

20.2b . . . and from the mirror

2 Using a Torx key, undo the screws and remove the grab handle from the tailgate/boot lid.
3 Using a screwdriver, undo the screws and remove the main trim panel from the inside of the tailgate/boot lid. Also carefully prise the plastic trim panels from the sides of the tailgate/boot lid using a screwdriver.
4 Unscrew the central locking motor mounting bolts, then remove the expander rivet holding the plastic pivots to the tailgate.
5 Withdraw the motor and turn it to release it from the plastic hinge **(see illustration)**. Disconnect the wiring.

Refitting
6 Refitting is a reversal of removal.

Door motors
Removal and refitting
7 Removal and refitting of the door servo motors is included in the lock procedure described in Section 13.

19 Electric window motor – removal and refitting

The procedure for removing and refitting the front door electric window motor is described in Section 15. It is not possible to separate the rear door electric window motor from the regulator.

20.1b Removing the triangular trim (Convertible models)

20.3a Undo the mounting screws . . .

18.5 Tailgate central locking motor

20 Exterior door mirror and glass – removal and refitting

Mirror
Removal
1 With the front door open, on Hatchback and Coupe models, prise off the triangular trim cover by inserting a screwdriver beneath the front edge, then remove the packing **(see illustration)**. On Convertible models, press the centres of the fasteners through, and remove the triangular trim cover at the front upper corner of the front door **(see illustration)**.
2 Disconnect the wiring from the mirror control switch and from the mirror **(see illustrations)**.
3 Undo the mounting screws and withdraw the mirror from the outside of the door **(see illustrations)**.

20.2a Disconnect the wiring from the control switch . . .

20.3b . . . and withdraw the mirror from the door

20.5 Prising out the exterior door mirror glass

Refitting

4 Refitting is a reversal of removal.

Glass

Removal

5 Using a wide-bladed screwdriver, prise out the top of the glass until it is released from the clip **(see illustration)**.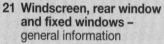

6 Disconnect the heater wires **(see illustration)**.

Refitting

7 Reconnect the wiring.

8 Using a wad of cloth rag, press the mirror into position until the clip engages.

21 Windscreen, rear window and fixed windows – general information

Windscreen and rear window

1 The windscreen and rear window glass are bonded in position with a special adhesive. Renewal of such fixed glass is a complex, messy and time-consuming task, which is beyond the scope of the home mechanic; without the benefit of extensive practice, it is difficult to attain a secure, waterproof fit. Furthermore, the task carries a high risk of accidental breakage – this applies especially to the laminated glass windscreen. In view of this, owners are strongly advised to entrust work of this nature to a Saab dealer, or one of the many specialist windscreen fitters.

Fixed side window (3-door models)

Note: *The fixed side window is sealed to the body with butyl tape and is not therefore considered to be a suitable job for the average home mechanic. However, the following information is given for those who may wish to carry out the work themselves.*

Removal

2 With the door open, pull the rubber weatherstrip from the door opening in the vicinity of the fixed side window.

3 Using a wide-bladed screwdriver, carefully prise the trim panel from the top inside of the

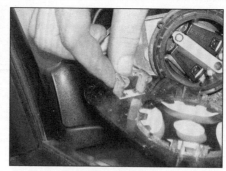

20.6 Disconnecting the heater wires from the exterior door mirror

B-pillar. Lower the panel over the seat belt to the floor.

4 Carefully prise off the kickplate from the bottom of the door opening.

5 Fold the rear seat cushion forwards then fold the rear seat backrest forwards. Unscrew and remove the fastener from the rear of the side trim.

6 Fold the backrest rearwards, then remove the remaining fasteners and withdraw the side trim.

7 With the tailgate open, pull the rubber weatherstrip from the opening in the vicinity of the fixed side window.

8 Carefully prise off the trim panel from the C-pillar.

9 Pull down the headlining and unscrew the upper nuts securing the side window to the body.

10 Unscrew the remaining nuts then have an assistant support the window while the butyl tape is cut with a suitable knife. Withdraw the window.

Refitting

11 Remove all traces of old tape, then fit new butyl tape around the inside of the fixed window making sure that it is located around the outside of the studs.

12 Locate the window in the body and tighten the mounting nuts to the specified torque.

13 Refit the headlining, trim panels and rubber weatherstrips.

Rear quarter light (5-door models)

Note: *The rear quarter light is sealed to the body with butyl tape and is not therefore considered to be a suitable job for the average home mechanic. However, the following information is given for those who may still wish to carry out the work themselves.*

Removal

14 With the door and tailgate open, pull the rubber weatherstrips from the body openings in the vicinity of the fixed side window.

15 Using a wide-bladed screwdriver, carefully prise the trim panel from the C-pillar.

16 Unscrew the nuts securing the quarter light to the body.

17 Have an assistant support the window while the butyl tape is cut with a suitable knife. Withdraw the quarter light.

Refitting

18 Remove all traces of old tape, then fit new butyl tape around the inside of the quarter light making sure that it is located around the outside of the studs.

19 Locate the quarter light in the body and tighten the mounting nuts to the specified torque.

20 Refit the trim panels and rubber weather-strips.

22 Sunroof assembly – removal and refitting

1 Due to the complexity of the tilt/slide sunroof mechanism, considerable expertise is required to repair, renew or adjust the sunroof components successfully. Removal of the sunroof first requires that the headlining be removed, which is a tedious operation, not to be undertaken lightly (see Section 26). Therefore, this Section is limited to a description of the drive motor assembly removal/refitting, and it is recommended that any other problems related to the sunroof are referred to a Saab dealer.

Drive motor assembly

Note: *If the drive motor is faulty, it is possible to operate the sunroof using a screwdriver. Slide off the cover from the overhead switch panel, and turn the motor shaft with the screwdriver.*

Removal

2 Remove the interior light with reference to Chapter 12, Section 5.

3 Undo the screws and lower the switch panel from the headlining.

4 Disconnect the motor earth wire.

5 Undo the mounting screws and lower the drive motor from the roof.

Refitting

6 Refitting is a reversal of removal.

23 Body exterior fittings – removal and refitting

Badges and trim mouldings

Removal

1 Side trim panels, rubbing strips, bonnet, boot lid and tailgate emblems are all secured in place by adhesive tape or nuts.

2 To remove the fittings from the bodywork, select an implement to use as a lever that will not damage the paintwork, such as a plastic spatula, or a filling knife wrapped in PVC tape. On items secured with adhesive tape, it will help if heat is applied from a heat gun.

3 Insert the lever between the top edge of the fitting and the bodywork, and carefully prise it away.

4 Progressively pull the lower edge of the fitting away from the bodywork, allowing the adhesive tape to peel off.

5 Clean the bodywork surface, removing all traces of dirt and the remains of any adhesive tape.

Refitting

6 Peel the backing strip from the new fitting. Offer it up to its mounting position, top edge first, and press the stud fixings into their holes. Smooth the lower edge of the fitting into place, then press down on it firmly to ensure that the tape adheres along its whole length.

Wheel arch trims

Removal

7 To remove, unscrew the flange nuts from the studs that protrude inside the wheel arch. Pull the trim away from the wheel arch, guiding the stud threads through their mounting holes.

Refitting

8 Clean the surface of the wheel arch before refitting the trim, and brush out any dirt from around the mounting holes, inside the wheel arch.

Front wheel arch liners

Removal

9 The front wheel arch liners are secured by means of screws, nuts, and clips. First apply the handbrake, then jack up the front of the vehicle and support it on axle stands (see *Jacking and vehicle support*). Remove the front wheel.

10 Undo the screws and nut and remove the mudflap from the rear of the liner.

11 Undo the remaining screws and remove the clips by pressing out their centre pins. Note the screws which are located on the spoiler and bumper.

12 Remove the wheel arch liner from under the wing.

Refitting

13 Refitting is a reversal of removal.

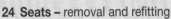

24 Seats – removal and refitting

Front seat

Note: *If the height adjustment motor is inoperative, or if seat removal is required in order to remove the TCS electronic units, the seat must be removed together with the floor brackets.*

Removal

1 Raise the seat to its highest position.

2 On 5-door models, disconnect the seat belt from the seat with reference to Section 25.

3 Slide the seat fully forwards, then unscrew and remove the rear mounting bolts **(see illustration)**.

24.3 Unscrewing the front seat rear mounting bolts

4 Slide the seat fully to the rear, then unscrew and remove the front mounting bolts.

5 Where applicable, cut free the plastic cable ties securing the wiring beneath the seat then disconnect the wiring at the plug.

6 Lift the seat from inside the vehicle.

Refitting

7 Refitting is a reversal of removal, but tighten the mounting bolts to the specified torque. The inner bolt should be tightened first both at the front and rear.

Rear seat cushion

Removal

8 Fold the rear seat cushion forwards.

9 Extract the circlips from the hinge pins, then use a suitable drift to drive them out **(see illustration)**.

10 Lift the cushion from inside the vehicle.

Refitting

11 Refitting is a reversal of removal. All hinge pins must be fitted from right to left.

Rear seat backrest (40% section)

Removal

12 Move the seat belt to one side and fold the backrest forwards (leave the crossbar in position).

13 Unscrew the nuts from the brackets at the centre of the backrest **(see illustration)**.

14 Withdraw the pivot from the outer bracket and lift out the backrest from inside the vehicle.

24.9 Extracting the circlips from the rear seat cushion

Refitting

15 Refitting is a reversal of removal.

Rear seat backrest (60% section)

Removal

16 Remove the 40% section rear seat backrest as described earlier.

17 Move the seat belt to one side and fold the backrest forwards (leave the crossbar in position).

18 Unscrew the nuts and remove the centre seat belt anchorage.

19 Unscrew the nuts and remove the right-hand bracket.

20 Withdraw the pivot from the outer bracket, then release the fabric tensioner and lift out the backrest from inside the vehicle.

Refitting

21 Refitting is a reversal of removal.

25 Seat belts – removal and refitting

⚠ **Warning: If the vehicle has been involved in an accident which caused the seat belt pretensioners to be activated, the complete seat belt must be renewed.**

Front seat belt (3-door)

Removal

1 Undo the front bolt securing the slide rail to the inner sill panel and slide off the belt.

2 Using a wide-bladed screwdriver, prise the kickplate from the door opening.

3 Pull out the vent, then undo the screw securing the inner trim to the outer trim. Carefully prise off the upper and lower trim panels.

4 Fold the rear seat cushion forwards then fold the rear seat backrest forwards. Unscrew and remove the fastener from the rear of the side trim.

5 Fold the backrest rearwards, then remove the remaining fasteners and withdraw the side trim.

6 Lock the pretensioner on the seat belt reel by engaging the red plastic lever with the safety catch.

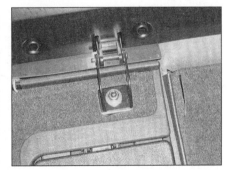

24.13 Rear seat backrest central mounting bracket

25.14 Front seat belt guide on the B-pillar

25.15 Front seat belt height adjuster on the B-pillar

25.16 Front seat belt reel and pretensioner

7 Drill out the rivet securing the clamp to the pretensioner tube.

8 Unbolt the seat belt guide from the B-pillar, then unscrew the top bolt securing the seat belt height adjuster to the B-pillar and remove the adjuster.

9 Undo the slide rail rear bolt and remove the rail followed by the reel.

10 To remove the buckle, the front seat must be removed as described in Section 24, then the mounting bolt unscrewed.

Refitting

11 Refitting is a reversal of removal, but tighten the mounting bolts to the specified torque. Make sure that the red plastic lever is released so that the pretensioner is free to operate in the event of an accident.

Front seat belt (5-door)

Removal

12 Carefully remove the trim panels from the B-pillar using a wide-bladed screwdriver.

13 Lock the pretensioner on the seat belt reel by engaging the red plastic lever with the safety catch. Drill out the rivet securing the clamp to the pretensioner tube.

14 Unbolt the seat belt guide from the B-pillar **(see illustration)**.

15 Unscrew the top bolt securing the seat belt height adjuster to the B-pillar, then remove the adjuster **(see illustration)**.

16 Unscrew the bolt and remove the seat belt reel and pretensioner from the B-pillar **(see illustration)**.

17 Release the front end of the seat belt from the seat by inserting a screwdriver between the trim and depressing the spring tensioned catch. If preferred, the tilt knob and trim can be removed first **(see illustrations)**.

18 To remove the buckle, the front seat must be removed as described in Section 24, then the mounting bolt unscrewed.

Refitting

19 Refitting is a reversal of removal, but tighten the mounting bolts to the specified torque. Make sure that the red plastic lever is released so that the pretensioner is free to operate in the event of an accident.

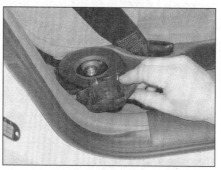

25.17a Remove the tilt knob and trim . . .

Front seat belt (Convertible)

Removal

20 The front seat belt reels are located in the B-pillar. First remove the rear seat cushion.

21 Working in the rear passenger compartment, carry out the following:

a) *Unscrew the bolt securing the front seat belt to the floor, and position the belt to one side.*

b) *Carefully prise off the door entry scuff plate.*

c) *Prise off the cover from the B-pillar, then prise out the cover and undo the screw securing the side trim to the B-pillar.*

d) *Prise out the fasteners from the bottom of the side trim, then fold the backrest forwards and unscrew the bolt and prise*

25.17b . . . then depress the catch and disconnect the seat belt from the front seat

out the fastener from the rear edge of the side trim.

e) *Pull up the side trim at its upper rear corner and release it from the clip. To ensure the clip does not separate from the trim, lever on the bottom of the clip.*

f) *Withdraw the side trim while feeding the rear seat belt through the guide. Also, disconnect the wiring from the rear interior light. If necessary, remove the light completely from the side trim.*

22 Disconnect the wiring from the reel at the bottom of the B-pillar.

23 Unbolt the belt upper guide from the top of the B-pillar **(see illustration)**.

24 Unscrew the bolt and remove the seat belt reel from the B-pillar, while feeding it through the guide **(see illustrations)**.

25.23 Front seat belt upper guide bolt

25.24a Front seat belt reel and mounting bolt

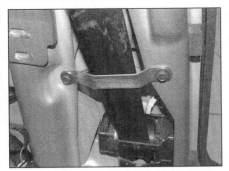

25.24b Front seat belt guide on the B-pillar

25.25 Front seat belt buckle

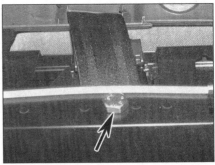

25.28 Remove the rear door kickplate

25 To remove the buckle, the front seat must be removed as described in Section 24, then the mounting bolt unscrewed **(see illustration)**.

Refitting

26 Refitting is a reversal of removal, but tighten the mounting bolts to the specified torque.

Rear seat belt (Hatchback and Coupe)

Removal

27 The rear seat belt reels are located in the crossbar. First fold the rear seat cushions forwards.

28 On 5-door models, carefully prise up the kickplates from the rear door openings **(see illustration)**.

29 Unscrew the seat belt lower anchorage bolt, noting the location of the bracket **(see illustration)**.

30 Using a Torx key, unscrew the centre belt anchorage bolt **(see illustration)**.

31 Lift out the rear head restraints, then remove the head restraint inserts from the crossbar. To do this, depress the plastic tags with a screwdriver, then use a hammer to tap the inserts up from the crossbar **(see illustrations)**.

32 Prise out the centre plastic cover.

33 Pull out the locking handle from the right-hand (40%) side, then remove the cover and disconnect the cable end fitting from the lever **(see illustrations)**.

25.29 Rear seat belt lower anchorage bolt

25.30 Rear seat belt centre anchorage and bolt

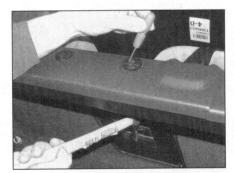

25.31a Depress the plastic tags and tap up the head restraint insert . . .

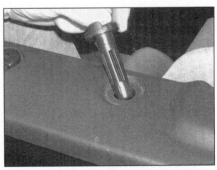

25.31b . . . then remove the insert from the crossbar

25.33a Pull out the locking handle . . .

25.33b . . . remove the cover . . .

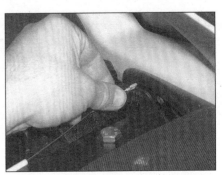

25.33c . . . then disconnect the cable end fitting from the lever

25.34a Undo the screws . . .

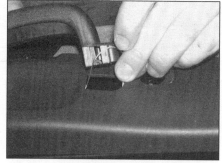

25.34b . . . and disconnect the cable from the locking handle . . .

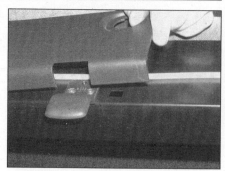

25.34c . . . then lift off the cover . . .

34 On the left-hand side of the crossbar, undo the screws securing the locking handle, then lift it slightly and disconnect the inner cable, noting how it is fitted to the two levers. Remove the cover and unhook the cable end fitting **(see illustrations)**.

35 Remove the seat belt cover then unscrew the reel mounting bolts and withdraw the reel **(see illustration)**.

Refitting

36 Refitting is a reversal of removal, but tighten the mounting bolts to the specified torque. When refitting the locking handle, make sure that the inner cable is not trapped between the handle and crossbar.

Rear seat belt (Convertible)

Removal

37 The rear seat belt reels are located in the rear seat backrests. First remove the rear seat cushion.

38 Working in the rear passenger compartment, carry out the following:

a) *Unscrew the bolt securing the front seat belt to the floor, and position the belt to one side.*

b) *Carefully prise off the door entry scuff plate.*

c) *Prise off the cover from the B-pillar, then prise out the cover and undo the screw securing the side trim to the B-pillar.*

d) *Prise out the fasteners from the bottom of the side trim, then fold the backrest*

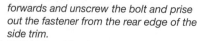

25.34d . . . and disconnect the cable end fitting from the lever

forwards and unscrew the bolt and prise out the fastener from the rear edge of the side trim.

e) *Pull up the side trim at its upper rear corner and release it from the clip. To ensure the clip does not separate from the trim, lever on the bottom of the clip.*

f) *Withdraw the side trim while feeding the rear seat belt through the guide. Also, disconnect the wiring from the rear interior light. If necessary, remove the light completely from the side trim.*

39 Unscrew the bolt securing the seat belt to the floor **(see illustration)**.

40 Unscrew the bolt securing the seat belt guide to the top of the backrest **(see illustration)**.

41 Unclip the trim from the rear crossbar.

42 At the top of the backrest, move the trim

25.35 Rear seat belt reel mounting bolt

to one side and unscrew the reel mounting bolt. Remove the seat belt.

43 To remove the buckles, unbolt them from the centre tunnel **(see illustration)**.

Refitting

44 Refitting is a reversal of removal, but tighten the mounting bolts to the specified torque.

26 Interior trim panels – removal and refitting

A-pillar trim panels

1 Open the relevant front door, and pull the rubber weatherstrip from the door aperture at the A-pillar.

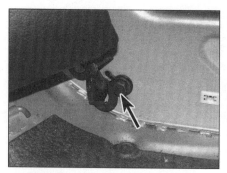

25.39 Rear seat belt floor mounting

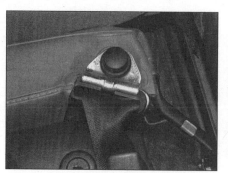

25.40 Rear seat belt guide on the top of the backrest

25.43 Rear seat belt buckles

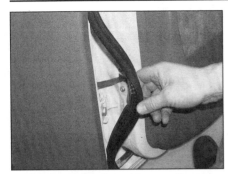

26.10 Removing the rubber weatherstrip from the B-pillar

26.12a Remove the air vent . . .

26.12b . . . then use a screwdriver to prise off . . .

2 Working from the headlining down, grasp the panel firmly and progressively ease it away from the pillar, allowing the press-studs beneath to disengage one at a time.

3 To refit, offer the panel up to its mounted position, and apply firm pressure over each press-stud until it engages. Press the door aperture weatherstrip back into place.

B-pillar trim panels

3-door models

4 Move the front seat fully forwards, then unscrew the slide rail front bolt and slide off the belt.

5 Pull out the air vent, then undo the screw securing the inner trim panel to the outer panel.

6 Carefully prise off the trim panel. Undo the bolt and remove the height adjuster.

7 Unclip the outer trim panel.

8 Refitting is a reversal of removal.

5-door models

9 Move the front seat fully forwards, then use a wide-bladed screwdriver to prise the kickplates from the front and rear door openings.

10 Pull the rubber weatherstrip from each side of the B-pillar **(see illustration)**.

11 Release the front end of the seat belt from the seat by inserting a screwdriver between the trim and depressing the spring-tensioned catch.

12 Prise out the air vent from the upper trim panel, then carefully prise off the upper and lower trim panels. Feed the front seat belt through the hole in the inner trim **(see illustrations)**.

13 Using a screwdriver, prise off the lower trim panel from the B-pillar **(see illustration)**.

14 Unscrew the upper bolt then unhook the height adjuster from the B-pillar.

15 Refitting is a reversal of removal.

C-pillar trim panels

16 Remove the parcel shelf and fold the rear seats forwards, together with the crossbar.

17 On 3-door models, carefully prise out the speaker grille using a screwdriver, then undo the screws and remove the speaker frame.

18 Pull the weatherstrip away from the tailgate opening in the vicinity of the C-pillar.

19 On 5-door models, pull the rear door weatherstrip away from the door opening in the vicinity of the C-pillar.

20 Using a wide-bladed screwdriver, carefully prise the trim panel away from the C-pillar.

21 Withdraw the panel from inside the vehicle.

22 Refitting is a reversal of removal.

Convertible rear side trim panel

23 Operate the soft top so that it is fully open and in the storage compartment, then raise the cover so that it is vertical.

24 Remove the rear seat cushion.

25 Unscrew the bolt securing the rear seat belt to the floor, and position the belt to one side.

26 Carefully prise off the door entry scuff plate.

27 Prise off the cover from the B-pillar, then prise out the cover and undo the screw securing the side trim to the B-pillar.

28 Prise out the fasteners from the bottom of the side trim, then fold the backrest forwards and unscrew the bolt and prise out the fastener from the rear edge of the side trim.

29 Pull up the side trim at its upper rear corner and release it from the clip. To ensure the clip does not separate from the trim, lever on the bottom of the clip.

30 Withdraw the side trim while feeding the rear seat belt through the guide. Also, disconnect the wiring from the rear interior light. If necessary, remove the light completely from the side trim.

Luggage area side trim panel

31 With the tailgate open, remove the parcel shelf and fold the rear seats forwards.

32 Release the front clips and remove the carpet from the luggage compartment.

33 Where necessary, unbolt the lashing eyes on each side of the luggage compartment.

34 Remove the clips from the centre of the rear valance trim by pressing in the centre pins.

35 Pull the rear valance trim away and remove.

36 Remove the clips securing the luggage compartment side trim panel to the rear body.

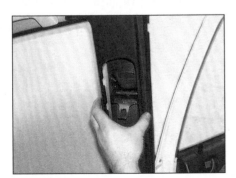

26.12c . . . the upper trim panel . . .

26.12d . . . remove the inner trim panel . . .

26.13 . . . and prise off the lower trim panel

26.37a Prise out the speaker grille . . .

26.37b . . . then unscrew the bolts . . .

26.37c . . . and remove the speaker frame

26.43a Remove the cover . . .

26.43b . . . then undo the screws and remove the rear view mirror

26.46 Removing the A-pillar trim panels

37 Using a screwdriver carefully prise out the speaker grille, then unbolt the speaker frame **(see illustrations)**.

38 Remove the relevant rear seat cushion and backrest as described in Section 24.

39 Bend up the backrest trim tensioner bracket, then remove the side trim panel from inside the vehicle.

40 Refitting is a reversal of removal.

Headlining

Note: *This sub-Section does not include the headlining removal for Convertible models, as this is considered beyond the scope of the home mechanic.*

41 Open the tailgate and remove the parcel shelf.

42 Undo the screws and remove the sun visors from the front of the headlining.

43 Prise off the cover from the rear view mirror, then undo the screws and remove the mirror **(see illustrations)**.

44 Remove the interior courtesy lights with reference to Chapter 12, Section 5, then undo the screws and remove the light surrounds.

45 On models with a sunroof, carefully prise out the surround from the sunroof, and disconnect the wiring from the sunroof motor.

46 Pull the rubber weatherstrip from the A-pillars in the vicinity of the windscreen, then prise off the A-pillar trim panels **(see illustration)**.

47 Prise up the covers from the grab handles then undo the screws and remove the handles **(see illustration)**.

48 Remove the trim panels from the B-pillars and C-pillars as described earlier in this Section.

49 Release the clips from the rear edge of the headlining by turning them through 90°.

50 Pull the rubber weatherstrip from the tailgate upper opening and carefully pull down the headlining.

51 Release the tape securing the wiring to the headlining.

52 Withdraw the headlining through the tailgate opening.

53 Refitting is a reversal of removal.

27 Centre console – removal and refitting

Removal

1 Disconnect the battery negative (earth) lead (see *Disconnecting the battery*). With the handbrake lever applied, engage reverse gear or P (as applicable) and remove the ignition key.

2 Remove the ignition switch antenna/ immobiliser unit by turning it slightly clockwise, then lifting it while turning anti-clockwise to release the inner tags from the bayonet fitting **(see illustrations)**. **Do not** attempt to turn the

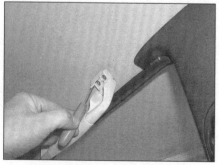

26.47 Removing the grab handles

27.2a Turn the ignition switch antenna/ immobiliser slightly clockwise . . .

27.2b . . . then anti-clockwise to remove it

27.3 Remove the ignition switch cover plate

27.4a Remove the rear ashtray . . .

27.4b . . . undo the screw . . .

unit anti-clockwise first, as the inner tags will be broken.

3 Using a screwdriver, carefully prise off the ignition switch cover. Insert the screwdriver first at the rear edge, then disconnect the front edge **(see illustration)**.

4 Remove the rear ashtray or cover and undo the screw now visible, then undo the upper screws from inside the oddments box, and remove the housing from the rear section **(see illustrations)**.

5 Prise out the electric window switch module and disconnect the wiring **(see illustrations)**. Also, where fitted, disconnect the wiring from the rear seat heater.

6 On Convertible models, prise out the interior lighting switch and disconnect the wiring **(see illustrations)**.

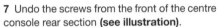

27.4c . . . and remove the housing from the rear of the console

7 Undo the screws from the front of the centre console rear section **(see illustration)**.

8 Remove the remote control (TRW) receiver,

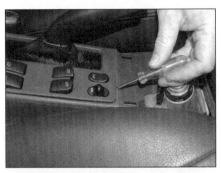

27.5a Prise up the front edge of the electric window switch module . . .

then undo the rear nuts and pull the rear section back a little **(see illustration)**.

9 Lift out the rear section of the centre

27.5b . . . move it forwards to remove it . . .

27.5c . . . then disconnect the wiring

27.6a Prise out the interior lighting switch . . .

27.6b . . . and disconnect the wiring

27.7 Centre console rear section retaining screws

27.8 Remove the remote control (TRW) receiver

27.9 Removing the rear section of the centre console

27.10a Remove the sound-deadening material . . .

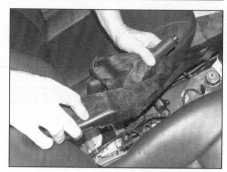

27.10b . . . and remove the rear compartment air duct

console over the handbrake lever, and remove from inside the car **(see illustration)**.
10 Remove the sound-deadening material and disconnect the rear compartment air duct from the front duct **(see illustrations)**.

27.11 Removing the front trim panels

27.13 Remove the selector lever surround

27.19 Disconnect the wiring from the rear of the centre console

11 Undo the screws and remove the front trim panels from each side of the centre console **(see illustration)**.

Manual transmission models

12 Prise out the gear lever gaiter.

Automatic transmission models

13 Prise out the selector lever indicator panel, then remove the surround from the top of the lever **(see illustration)**. Leave the indicator panel in position.

Air conditioned models

14 Press out the A/C module and disconnect the wiring **(see illustrations)**.

Models without air conditioning

15 Press out the heating control panel from behind, then remove the air distribution shaft.
16 Disconnect the wiring for the air distribution control lighting, fan speed, heated rear window and air recirculation.

27.14a Press out the air conditioning/ climate control module . . .

27.20 Centre console retaining clips

17 Release the retainer and remove the heating control cable from the control module.
18 Withdraw the heating control panel from inside the car.

All models

19 Disconnect all the wiring from the centre console, noting their locations **(see illustration)**.
20 Release the clips securing the centre console to the facia panel by pressing in the centre pins **(see illustration)**.
21 Withdraw the centre console over the gear/selector lever, and from inside the car **(see illustration)**.

Refitting

22 Refitting is a reversal of removal. When refitting the antenna/immobiliser unit, press it directly downwards in its normal position, until the inner tags 'click' onto the bayonet fitting.

27.14b . . . and disconnect the wiring

27.21 Removing the centre console

28.7a Undo the upper screws . . .

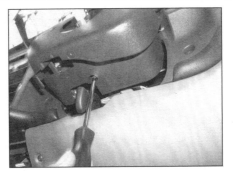

28.7b . . . and lower screw . . .

28.7c . . . and remove the steering column shrouds

28 Facia assembly – removal and refitting

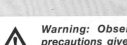

Warning: Observe the safety precautions given in Section 30 when working on or near the airbags.

Removal

1 Disconnect the battery negative (earth) lead (see *Disconnecting the battery*).
2 Adjust the steering wheel to its fully extended position.
3 Undo the screws located either side of the steering wheel, and withdraw the airbag module until the wiring connector can be disconnected. Place the module with its upper face pointing upwards in a safe position, making sure that it cannot be tampered with or damaged.
4 Disconnect the wiring from the horn.
5 With the front wheels pointing straight-ahead, unscrew and remove the steering wheel retaining nut. Mark the steering wheel hub in relation to the steering column, then rock the steering wheel firmly from side-to-side until it is released from the splines.
6 Withdraw the steering wheel while feeding the wiring connectors through the hole.
7 Undo the screws and remove the steering column shrouds **(see illustrations)**.

8 Disconnect the wiring from the combination switches on each side of the steering column, then remove the switches by depressing the plastic tabs located on the top and bottom of the switches.
9 Undo the screws and remove the diagnostic socket from under the facia on the driver's side **(see illustration)**.
10 Undo the screws and release the clips then remove the lower trim panel **(see illustrations)**.
11 Remove the radio as described in Chapter 12.
12 Bend back the tabs, and remove the radio mounting box.
13 Where applicable, release the upper clips and pull out the storage compartment **(see illustration)**.
14 Using two M3 screws inserted in the

special holes, pull out the auxiliary instrument display panel (SID).
15 Prise out the light switch and headlight beam switch.
16 Remove the instrument panel as described in Chapter 12.
17 With the glovebox open, prise up the covers and undo the mounting screws and bolt **(see illustration)**. Where necessary, release the clips on the front edge and remove the catch.
18 Prise out the glovebox illumination light and disconnect the wiring.
19 Withdraw the glovebox from the facia (see Section 29).
20 Pull the rubber weatherstrip away from the A-pillars on each side of the facia.
21 Carefully prise away the trim panels from the A-pillars.

28.9 Removing the diagnostic socket from under the facia

28.10a Undo the screws . . .

28.10b . . . and remove the lower trim panel

28.13 Removing the storage compartment

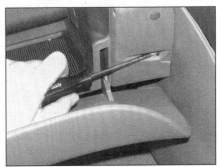

28.17 Undo the mounting screws and remove the glovebox

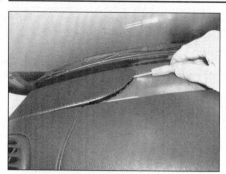

28.22 Prising out the speaker grilles

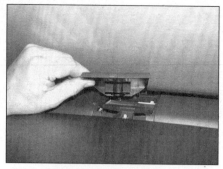

28.23 Removing the sun sensor from the top of the facia

28.25 Removing the defroster panel

28.26 Wiring loom location on the underside of the facia

28.27 Removing the air duct on the left-hand side

28.28 Undo the fusebox screws from the right-hand side of the facia

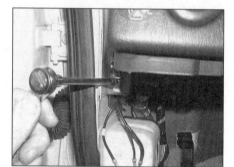

28.29 Unscrewing the facia bolts from the A-pillars

22 Using a screwdriver, prise off the speaker grilles on each side of the facia (see illustration).

23 Slide the sun sensor surround slightly to the rear and lift it off (see illustration).
24 On models with air conditioning and/or an alarm, disconnect the wiring from the sun sensor or alarm.
25 Unscrew the nuts from the top centre of the facia, then lift the rear edge of the defroster panel, move it sideways, and withdraw (see illustration).
26 Observe the location of the wiring loom on the underside of the facia, and if necessary make notes to ensure correct refitting. Release the cable ties (see illustration).
27 Detach the floor air duct on the left-hand side (see illustration).
28 Undo the screws and remove the fusebox from the right-hand side of the facia (see illustration). Position it to one side, but do not disconnect the wiring.

29 Unscrew and remove the facia mounting bolts located on the A-pillars (see illustration).
30 Remove the centre console as described in Section 27.
31 On models fitted with a passenger airbag, disconnect the wiring from the airbag and unscrew the nut from the stay.
32 Disconnect and remove the air vent ducting from each side.
33 Disconnect the wiring from the speakers on each side of the facia, and release the cable ties.
34 Unscrew the facia mounting bolts located near the top speakers (see illustration).
35 With the help of an assistant, carefully withdraw the facia from the bulkhead and withdraw from the car (see illustration).

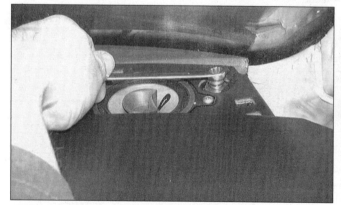

28.34 Unscrewing the facia bolts located near the top speakers

28.35 Withdrawing the facia from the bulkhead

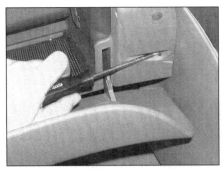

29.1a Unscrewing the glovebox lower right . . .

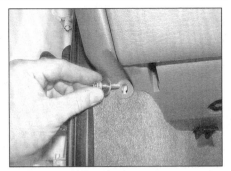

29.1b . . . and lower left mounting screws

29.2 Removing the glovebox retaining clips

Refitting

36 Refitting is a reversal of removal, but refer to Section 30 for details of refitting the airbags. In particular, observe the precautions.

29 Glovebox –
removal and refitting

Removal

1 With the glovebox open, undo the mounting screws **(see illustrations)**.
2 Release the clips from the front edge of the glovebox by depressing the centre pins **(see illustration)**.
3 Remove the glovebox illumination lamp or alternatively disconnect the wiring **(see illustration)**.
4 Withdraw the glovebox from the facia **(see illustration)**.
5 If necessary, the lid can be removed by undoing the damper screw, and pressing out the pivot pins.
6 To remove the lock, drill a circle of 2.0 mm holes inside the circle embossed on the rear of the lid and carefully cut out the circle. Take care not to drill more than the thickness of the plastic. Bend back the tabs and remove

the lock from the glovebox. Prise off the lock holder.

Refitting

7 Refitting is a reversal of removal. If fitting a new lock, stick the plug supplied with the new lock over the cut circle.

30 Supplementary Restraint System (SRS) components
– removal and refitting

General information

The operation of the SRS is managed by an Electronic Control Unit (ECU). When the vehicle's ignition switch is turned on, the ECU performs self-test checks of the system's components; if a fault is detected, the ECU records it in memory as a fault 'flag'. Following this, the ECU illuminates the instrument panel-mounted SRS warning light. If this should occur, the vehicle should be taken to a Saab dealer for examination. Dedicated test equipment is needed to interrogate the SRS ECU, firstly to determine the nature and incidence of the fault, and secondly to clear the stored fault 'flag', thus preventing the fault from being displayed by the warning light once the fault has been rectified.

For safety reasons, owners are strongly advised against attempting to diagnose problems with the SRS using standard workshop equipment. The information in this Section is therefore limited to those components in the SRS which must occasionally be removed to gain access to other components on the vehicle.

⚠ *Warning: A number of additional precautions must be observed when working on vehicles with airbags/SRS:*

• *Always make sure that the ignition switch is in the OFF position before removing SRS components.*
• *Do not attempt to splice into any of the electric cables in the SRS wiring harness.*
• *Avoid hammering or causing any harsh vibration at the front of the vehicle, particularly in the engine bay, as this may trigger the crash sensors and activate the SRS.*
• *Do not use ohmmeters or any other device capable of supplying current on any of the SRS components, as this may cause accidental detonation.*
• *Airbags (and seat belt tensioners) are classed as pyrotechnical (explosive) devices, and must be stored and handled according to the relevant laws in the*

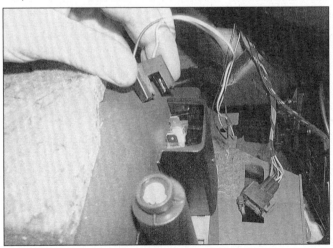

29.3 Disconnecting the wiring from the glovebox illumination lamp

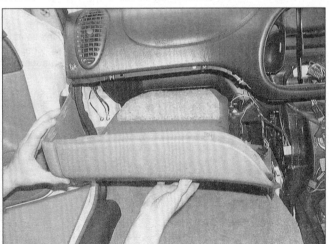

29.4 Withdrawing the glovebox from the facia

30.2a Prise out the plugs . . .

30.2b . . . then undo the screws located on either side of the steering wheel

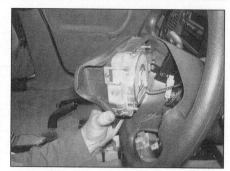

30.3a Carefully lift the airbag from the steering wheel . . .

country concerned. In general, do not leave these components disconnected from their electrical wiring any longer than is absolutely necessary; in this state they are unstable, and the risk of accidental detonation is introduced. Rest a disconnected airbag with the metal bracket facing downwards, away from flammable materials – never leave it unattended.

Driver's airbag

Removal

1 Make sure the ignition switch is in the OFF position.

2 Prise out the plugs then undo the screws securing the airbag to the steering wheel. The screws are located on either side of the steering wheel **(see illustrations)**.

3 Carefully lift the airbag from the steering wheel far enough to disconnect the wiring **(see illustrations)**.

4 Rest the airbag in a safe place with the metal bracket facing downwards.

Refitting

5 Locate the airbag over the steering wheel and reconnect the wiring, making sure that it is firmly pressed onto the terminal.

6 Lower the airbag into the steering wheel, then insert and tighten the retaining screws. Refit the rubber plugs.

7 Switch on the ignition, wait at least 10 seconds, and check that the SRS warning light goes out. If not, the control unit probably has a fault code stored in it and it will be necessary to have a Saab dealer check the system.

Passenger's airbag

Removal

8 Make sure the ignition switch is in the OFF position.

9 Remove the glovebox as described in Section 29.

10 Undo the screw and remove the heater side panel.

11 Remove the knee shield, floor air duct, and side air duct.

12 Reach up under the facia and disconnect the wiring from the passenger airbag **(see illustration)**.

13 Unscrew the bolt securing the safety band to the steering column bracket.

14 Unscrew the airbag mounting nuts and lift it from the facia **(see illustration)**.

15 Rest the airbag in a safe place with the metal bracket facing downwards.

Refitting

16 Position the airbag in the facia and tighten the nuts to the specified torque. Make sure that there are no loose objects between the facia and airbag.

17 Refit the bolt securing the safety band and tighten it to the specified torque, making sure that it engages its original threads. Failure to do this will impair its grip.

18 The remaining refitting procedure is a reversal of removal.

19 Switch on the ignition and check that the SRS warning light goes out. If not, the control unit probably has a fault code stored in it and it will be necessary to have a Saab dealer check the system.

Steering wheel contact roller

Removal

20 Make sure the ignition switch is in the OFF position.

21 Remove the steering wheel as described in Chapter 10.

22 To prevent damage to the contact roller, use adhesive tape to hold it in its central position.

23 Undo the screws and remove the steering column shrouds.

24 Disconnect the wiring to the contact roller at the two plugs located beneath the steering column.

25 Undo the screws and carefully lift the contact roller over the top of the steering column.

Refitting

26 To prevent damage to the contact roller whilst it is being refitted, use adhesive tape to hold it in its central position.

27 Offer the contact roller over the top of the steering column and reconnect the two wiring plugs.

28 Insert the mounting screws and tighten.

29 Refit the steering column shrouds and tighten the screws.

30 Check that the contact roller is set at its central position as follows. With the front wheels pointing straight-ahead, rotate the contact roller fully clockwise. Now turn the contact roller back 2 1/2 turns.

31 Refit the steering wheel as described in Chapter 10.

32 Switch on the ignition and check that the

30.3b . . . and disconnect the wiring

30.12 Disconnecting the wiring from the passenger airbag

30.14 Passenger's airbag viewed from under the facia

30.36 SRS ECU located under the centre console rear section

SRS warning light goes out. If not, the control unit probably has a fault code stored in it and it will be necessary to have a Saab dealer check the system.

Electronic control unit (ECU)

Note: *If a new electronic control unit is fitted, it must be reprogrammed by a Saab dealer.*

Removal

33 Make sure the ignition switch is in the OFF position.
34 Remove the rear section of the centre console as described in Section 27.
35 Disconnect the wiring from the ECU.
36 Unscrew the nuts and remove the ECU from inside the car **(see illustration)**. Note which way round the ECU is fitted, as it will not work if fitted incorrectly.

Refitting

37 Refitting is a reversal of removal.

31 Soft top – general

The Convertible soft top is raised and lowered by an electrically-operated hydraulic unit together with five hydraulic cylinders. The system is controlled by a module which monitors the action progress in stages by means of microswitches, and sanctions subsequent actions in the hydraulic unit. The soft top is secured at its rear by latches which lock the 5th bow to the cover, and the cover is locked in position by latches in the side mechanism, which are operated by cable from the hydraulic cylinders. Any malfunction of the soft top will generate a trouble code and a corresponding message will appear on the Saab Information Display on the instrument panel.

The module also operates the side windows in the doors and rear panel. Before opening the soft top, the windows are opened a small distance, then after the top has been closed, the windows assume their normal closed position. This is to ensure the upper edges of the windows are positioned on the inside of the soft top to prevent rain entry.

In the event of failure of the soft top, the car should be taken to a Saab dealer who will use a special diagnostic tool to pinpoint the problem area. If the soft top operates normally to a particular stage, then stops, it is likely that one of the microswitches is at fault. Failure of the hydraulic system may be due to lack of fluid or a faulty hydraulic unit motor.

32 Soft top – removal and refitting

Removal

1 Lower the soft top into its storage space and position the cover vertical.
2 Remove the rear seat cushion **(see illustration)**.
3 Working on each side of the car in turn, carry out the following:
 a) *Unscrew the bolt securing the front seat belt to the floor, and position the belt to one side (see illustration).*
 b) *Undo the screws and carefully prise off the door entry scuff plate (see illustration).*
 c) *Prise off the weatherstrip from the B-pillar, then prise out the cover and undo the screw securing the side trim to the B-pillar (see illustration).*
 d) *Prise out the fasteners from the bottom of the side trim (see illustration), then fold the backrest forwards and unscrew the bolt and prise out the fastener from the rear edge of the side trim.*
 e) *Pull up the side trim at its upper rear corner and release it from the clip. To ensure the clip does not separate from the trim, lever on the bottom of the clip.*
 f) *Withdraw the side trim while feeding the rear seat belt through the guide (see illustration). Also, disconnect the wiring from the rear interior light. If necessary, remove the light completely from the side trim.*

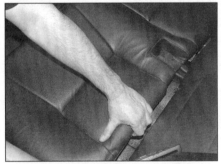

32.2 Remove the rear seat cushion

32.3a Unscrew the rear seat belt anchorage . . .

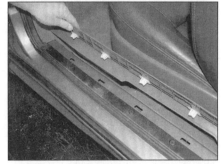

32.3b . . . remove the door entry scuff plate . . .

32.3c . . . remove the weatherstrip . . .

32.3d . . . remove the side trim bottom fasteners . . .

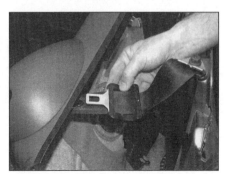

32.3f . . . remove the side trim and feed the rear seat belt through the guide

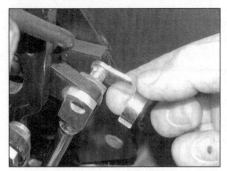

32.6 Removing the cylinder top clips

32.7a Extract the circlips . . .

32.7b . . . and remove the pins

4 Undo the screws and release the relay holders from the body on each side. Do not disconnect the wiring, but place the holders to one side.

5 Close the soft top so that the soft top cover and 5th bow are vertical.

6 Working on each side in turn, remove the clips securing the top of the vertical cylinder pushrods to the levers **(see illustration)**.

7 Working on each side in turn, extract the circlips securing the pins to the horizontal levers, then remove the pins from the levers **(see illustrations)**. Lay the cylinders in the soft top storage area.

8 With the help of an assistant, cover the cylinders with cloth rag **(see illustration)**, then manually lower the complete soft top into the storage area, taking care not to turn the pushrods.

9 Disconnect the wiring for the soft top cover on each side **(see illustration)**.

10 Before removing the soft top, place some protection around the storage area as the vinyl is easily punctured. Stiff card is ideal for this **(see illustration)**.

11 While an assistant takes the weight of the soft top, unscrew the soft top mounting nuts on each side. There is one single top nut and two lower nuts. Note that shims are fitted between the mechanism and the body, and it is important to record the number shims in order to retain the correct positioning of the soft top on refitting **(see illustration)**.

12 Ideally three people are required to lift the soft top from the car, as the wiring must be fed through the holes in the body on each side, and the assembly is very heavy. Carefully note the number and position of the shims as

they are removed **(see illustrations)**. With the soft top removed, place it in a clean area.

Refitting

13 Refitting is a reversal of removal, but note the following additional points:
a) *Do not turn the pushrods within their cylinders, as the end position microswitches may be damaged.*
b) *Tighten the mounting nuts to the specified torque.*
c) *If adjustment of the soft top is required, the vehicle must be taken to a Saab dealer who will have the jigs necessary to carry out the work.*
d) *If the system display unit indicates any soft top fault codes, a Saab dealer must erase them using a diagnostic tool.*

32.8 Cover the cylinders with cloth before lowering the soft top into the storage area

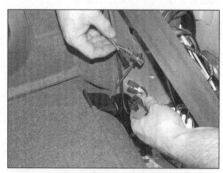

32.9 Disconnecting the soft top wiring

32.10 Place stiff card around the storage area before removing the soft top

32.11 Unscrew the mounting nuts . . .

32.12a . . . lift the soft top from the storage area . . .

32.12b . . . and recover the shims

33 Soft top covering – removal and refitting

Note: *Extra care must be taken during the following procedure to prevent damage to the covering while it is being fitted. Removal and refitting of the heated rear window is a skilled job best left to a Saab dealer or upholsterer.*

Removal

1 Operate the soft top to its half open position so that its rear edge is at the highest point, then switch off the ignition. The rear edge must now be supported with a suitable metal bar or length of wood, so that the soft top does not fall when the hydraulic pressure is subsequently released. Saab technicians use a special metal bar, although a suitable alternative can easily be fabricated.

2 From the lower front section of the soft top, undo the screws and remove the rear seals and their retainers.

3 From the front edge of the 1st bow, undo the screws and remove the retainer strip.

4 Remove the locking handle using a small screwdriver to lift the upholstery section next to the handle, then pulling the pins from their grooves.

5 Remove the front covers from the front rail by prising out the two plastic clips. Make sure that the supporting bar still remains in position.

6 Undo the single screw each side, then unhook the headlining from the 1st bow. Also, release the side elastic bands.

7 Fold up the soft top covering from the 1st bow.

8 Drill out the three pop rivets each side securing the side cables, and clean away the debris.

9 Remove the soft top support bar and balance the assembly.

10 Prise out the clips and remove the plastic retainer from the 2nd bow.

11 Remove the screws and clips and remove the plastic retainer from the 3rd bow.

12 Drill out the rivets securing the elastic bands to the side rails and clean away the debris.

13 Undo the screws and remove the clips securing the headlining to the rear rail.

14 Remove the seal from the rear rail, then remove the cable.

15 Remove the soft top covering from the 2nd and 3rd bows.

16 Drill out the rivets securing the elastic bands to the 4th bow, and clean away the debris.

17 Lift up the front of the soft top, then pull out the cables.

18 Lift up the 5th bow, and remove the elastic bands from the lock lugs.

19 From the rear edge of the 5th bow, undo the three screws securing the headlining, then remove the headlining rod.

20 Remove the cable retainer and the rear window electric heating connector, then remove the window guide and elastic band.

21 Using a pencil, mark the middle position of the 5th bow on the seal, then undo the screws and remove the seal. Take care not to damage the seal.

22 On models with a VIN up to and including X7020925, drill out the pop rivets from the 5th bow corners, and release the soft top covering from the 5th bow and rear rail.

23 Remove the rear window mounting from the locking lugs, then lift the soft top covering and headlining, complete with heated rear window, away from the framework.

Refitting

24 Refitting is a reversal of removal, using new rivets and clips, however, **do not** fit new rivets to the 5th bow corners on models with a VIN up to and including X7020925. Adjustment of the cable brackets can be made using a spring balance – apply 6 kg to the cable then tighten the cable bracket. Note that screws or rivets may be used to secure the plastic retainer to the 3rd bow.

34 Soft top cover – removal and refitting

Removal

1 Operate the soft top so that the cover is open and vertical.

2 Undo the screws and remove the clips then remove the inner cover **(see illustrations)**.

3 Undo the screws and remove the safety cables **(see illustration)**.

4 Mark the position of the latch strikers on the cover, then undo the screws and remove them **(see illustration)**.

5 From the front extensions of the cover, undo the screws securing the access flaps **(see illustration)**.

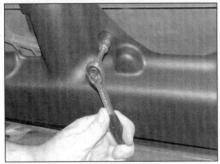

34.2a Undo the screws . . .

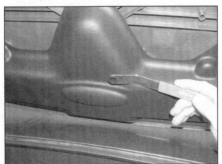

34.2b . . . remove the clips . . .

34.2c . . . then remove the cover

34.3 Safety cable and securing screws

34.4 Soft top cover latch striker

34.5 Access flap securing screws

34.6 Soft top cover hinges and mounting nuts

34.7 Soft top cover locking motor and rods

34.8a Soft top cover lift spring and bracket

34.8b Soft top cover driveshaft connection to the main mechanism

35.2 Use the ignition key to unlock the rear seat backrest, and fold it forwards

35.5 Soft top cover latch

6 Mark the position of the soft top cover mounting nuts on the hinges, then undo them and lift away the cover **(see illustration)**.

7 If necessary, remove the locking motor and rods **(see illustration)**.

8 To gain access to the cover lift spring and mechanism, remove the trim from the luggage compartment **(see illustrations)**.

Refitting

9 Refitting is a reversal of removal.

35 Soft top cover latch
– removal and refitting

Removal

1 Follow paragraphs 1 to 3 of Section 32, and remove the rear side trim from the relevant side.

2 Fold the rear seat backrest forwards **(see illustration)**, then note the position of the control cable adjustment before unscrewing the adjustment nut.

3 Release the cable end fitting from the lever and withdraw the cable from the latch.

4 Undo the screws and remove the microswitch.

5 Mark the position of the latch on the body, then unscrew the nuts and remove it **(see illustration)**.

Refitting

6 Refitting is a reversal of removal.

7 If adjustment of the soft top is required, the vehicle must be taken to a Saab dealer who will have the jigs necessary to carry out the work.

36 Soft top hydraulic system
– checking oil level

Caution: Only use Saab part number (16) 30 32 356. Do not use the oil specified for the Saab 900.

1 Fully open the soft top into the storage area.

2 Open the boot lid and remove the clips

securing the carpet to the front lower crossmember of the luggage compartment.

3 With the carpet raised, use a flashlight to check the hydraulic fluid level, looking through the two access holes. The fluid level should be between the MIN and MAX marks. **Note:** *The fluid level can be checked with the soft top closed, however, in this case it is acceptable for the level to be a few millimetres below the MIN mark.*

4 To top-up the fluid level, first close the soft top.

5 Fold the rear seat backrest forwards, then remove the fasteners, and withdraw the cover from the hydraulic unit **(see illustrations)**.

6 Unscrew the mounting bolts and lift the

36.5a Remove the fasteners . . .

36.5b . . . and withdraw the cover

hydraulic unit and mounting plate from the crossmember **(see illustrations)**.

7 Unscrew the filler plug and add fluid using a funnel. The complete system holds 0.55 litres, and the volume between the MIN and MAX marks is 65 ml.

8 After topping-up the level, refit and tighten the filler plug, then refit the hydraulic unit and tighten the mounting bolts securely.

9 Recheck the fluid level, then refit the cover and secure the carpet in the luggage compartment.

37 Soft top hydraulic system – bleeding

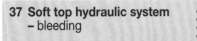

1 Check and if necessary top-up the hydraulic fluid level as described in Section 36.

2 Operate the soft top so that the *cover* and the 5th bow are both raised. If it is not possible to operate the soft top due to an electrical or hydraulic fault, carry out the following procedure, however, ideally this requires the use of the Saab diagnostic tool not normally available to the home mechanic; the alternative is to take the car to a Saab dealer:

a) *Fold the rear seat backrest forwards.*

b) *Prise out the cover and open the emergency valve approximately half a turn* **(see illustration)**.

c) *Unlock the front of the soft top, then use the diagnostic tool to unlock the 5th bow from its catches, and fully raise the 5th bow. If the tool is unavailable, remove the trim from the luggage compartment and release the catches manually.*

d) *On the right-hand side of the luggage compartment, insert the wheelbrace (from the tool kit) through the hole in the trim and into the drive mechanism link arm* **(see illustration)**. *Pull the wheelbrace rearwards until the soft top lifts far enough for an assistant to support it, then remove the wheelbrace, and lift the 5th bow vertical.*

e) *Close the boot lid and fully open the soft top cover.*

3 On the left-hand side, place some cloth rag around the top of the 5th bow cylinder,

36.6a Unscrew the mounting bolts . . .

then unscrew the hose and check if hydraulic fluid, free of air bubbles, runs out. If this is so, reconnect and tighten the hose and continue to paragraph 8. If not, leave the hose disconnected for about 5 minutes to allow air into the system, then reconnect and tighten the hose.

4 With the help of an assistant, manually fully open the soft top, then close it again.

5 Check the hose for leaks and wait one minute to allow air to separate in the fluid reservoir.

6 With the help of an assistant, again manually fully open the soft top, then close it again.

7 The soft top must now be left for at least 2 hours, although it is permitted to drive the car, if required. **Do not** operate the soft top during this period. After the 2 hours, continue to paragraph 8.

8 Operate the soft top through 2 complete cycles while listening for unusual noises or any hesitation indicating air still in the system.

9 If still not operating correctly, manually raise the 5th bow, and close the soft top *cover* without locking it.

10 With the boot lid open, remove the rear scuff plate cover, right-hand luggage compartment trim **(see illustration)**, and the right-hand rear light unit (see Chapter 12, Section 6).

11 Remove the soft top *cover* cylinder from the mechanism by extracting the clips and pins, but do not disconnect the hydraulic hose. Two persons are now required to bleed the soft top *cover* cylinder. First insert a hand lamp through the light unit aperture, then close

36.6b . . . and withdraw the hydraulic unit and mounting plate from the crossmember

the boot lid. One person must now operate the soft top so that the soft top cover cylinder piston rod moves in and out. The other person must hold the cylinder through the light unit aperture, making sure that the piston rod end is uppermost when the piston presses out, and down when the piston retracts. This procedure should be repeated for at least 10 cycles.

12 Refit the cylinder and recheck the fluid level, then manually operate the soft top through 5 complete cycles, using the wheelbrace.

13 Check the fluid level again, and refit the luggage compartment trim.

38 Soft top hydraulic unit – removal and refitting

Removal

1 Operate the soft top so that the cover is raised and the 5th bow horizontal.

2 Fold the rear seat backrest forwards, then remove the cover from the hydraulic unit.

3 Unscrew the mounting bolts and lift the hydraulic unit from its well. Note the fluid level as a guide to refilling the reservoir.

4 Place cloth rags beneath the hydraulic unit, then disconnect the wiring.

5 Identify the hose positions, unscrew the retaining bolts and disconnect them. Considering there are ten hoses, it is recommended that a drawing be made to ensure correct refitting.

37.2a The hydraulic unit emergency valve is located beneath a cover

37.2b Use the wheelbrace inserted into the soft top mechanism to operate the soft top manually

37.10 Removing the trim from the luggage compartment

39.4 Soft top control module located beneath the rear left-hand side trim

40.1 The soft top relays are located behind the rear seat side trim panel

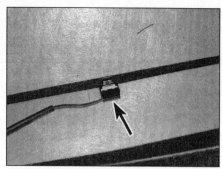

42.1 Soft top storage bag microswitch

6 Release the hose cable ties and withdraw the hydraulic unit from the car.

Refitting

7 Refitting is a reversal of removal, but note the following additional points:
   a) Note that the hoses must not be bent to less than a 40 mm radius.
   b) Fill the fluid reservoir to the level noted on removal.
   c) Operate the soft top through 5 cycles and check for correct function. If necessary, bleed the system as described in Section 37.
   d) If the system display unit indicates any soft top fault codes, a Saab dealer must erase them using a diagnostic tool.

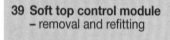

39 Soft top control module – removal and refitting

Removal

1 Lower the soft top into its storage space and position the cover vertical.
2 Remove the rear seat cushion.
3 Working on the left-hand side of the car, carry out the following:
   a) Unscrew the bolt securing the front seat belt to the floor, and position the belt to one side.
   b) Carefully prise off the door entry scuff plate.
   c) Prise off the cover from the B-pillar, then prise out the cover and undo the screw securing the side trim to the B-pillar.
   d) Prise out the fasteners from the bottom of the side trim, then fold the backrest forwards and unscrew the bolt and prise out the fastener from the rear edge of the side trim.
   e) Pull up the side trim at its upper rear corner and release it from the clip. To ensure the clip does not separate from the trim, lever on the bottom of the clip.
   f) Withdraw the side trim while feeding the rear seat belt through the guide. Also, disconnect the wiring from the rear interior light. If necessary, remove the light completely from the side trim.
4 Unscrew the mounting nuts and withdraw the control module **(see illustration)**, then disconnect the wiring, however, just prior

to disconnecting the wiring, earth yourself by touching a metal part of the body. This is because the module is sensitive to static electricity which could damage internal circuits and components.

Refitting

5 Refitting is a reversal of removal. If the system display unit indicates any soft top fault codes, a Saab dealer must erase them using a diagnostic tool.

40 Soft top relay – removal and refitting

Removal

1 The soft top relays are located behind the rear seat side trim panel **(see illustration)**. First, lower the soft top into its storage space and position the cover vertical.
2 Remove the rear seat cushion.
3 Working on the relevant side of the car, carry out the following:
   a) Unscrew the bolt securing the front seat belt to the floor, and position the belt to one side.
   b) Carefully prise off the door entry scuff plate.
   c) Prise off the cover from the B-pillar, then prise out the cover and undo the screw securing the side trim to the B-pillar.
   d) Prise out the fasteners from the bottom of the side trim, then fold the backrest forwards and unscrew the bolt and prise out the fastener from the rear edge of the side trim.
   e) Pull up the side trim at its upper rear corner and release it from the clip. To ensure the clip does not separate from the trim, lever on the bottom of the clip.
   f) Withdraw the side trim while feeding the rear seat belt through the guide. Also, disconnect the wiring from the rear interior light. If necessary, remove the light completely from the side trim.
4 Remove the relay holder, then pull out the relay. There are 3 relays on each side. On the left-hand side, the rear relay operates the front left window lift, the centre relay operates the pump relay, and the front relay operates the

rear left window lift. On the right-hand side, the front relay operates the rear right window lift, the centre relay operates the 5th bow, and the rear relay operates the front right window lift.

Refitting

5 Refitting is a reversal of removal. If the system display unit indicates any soft top fault codes, a Saab dealer must erase them using a diagnostic tool.

41 Soft top hydraulic unit relay – removal and refitting

Removal

1 The soft top hydraulic relay is located on the top of the hydraulic unit. First, operate the soft top so that the cover is raised and the 5th bow horizontal.
2 Fold the rear seat backrest forwards, then remove the cover from the hydraulic unit.
3 Unscrew the mounting bolts and lift the hydraulic unit from its well.
4 Disconnect the wiring.
5 Remove the fasteners by pressing out the centre pins, then remove the relay holder and pull out the relay.

Refitting

6 Refitting is a reversal of removal. If the system display unit indicates any soft top fault codes, a Saab dealer must erase them using a diagnostic tool.

42 Soft top storage bag microswitch – removal and refitting

Removal

1 There are two microswitches in the soft top storage bag. In the luggage compartment, release the clips and lower the trim for access to the switches **(see illustration)**.
2 Release the clip, detach the switch from the trim, and disconnect the wiring.

Refitting

3 Refitting is a reversal of removal.

Chapter 12
Body electrical system

Contents

Degrees of difficulty

Easy, suitable for novice with little experience	Fairly easy, suitable for beginner with some experience	Fairly difficult, suitable for competent DIY mechanic	Difficult, suitable for experienced DIY mechanic	Very difficult, suitable for expert DIY or professional

Specifications

System type . . . . 12 volt negative earth

Bulb ratings   Watts

Front and rear direction indicators 21
Front foglights 55
Headlights 60/55
Illumination for ashtray, cigarette lighter and seat belt warning 1.2
Interior dome light, luggage compartment light and glove
   compartment light 10
Rear foglight and reversing light 21
Rear reading lights 5
Side repeater light, number plate lights, front reading lights and
   sidelights 5
Stop/tail lights 21/5

1 General information and precautions

General information

The electrical system is of the 12 volt negative earth type and comprises a 12 volt battery, an alternator with integral voltage regulator, a starter motor and related electrical accessories, components and wiring.

Electronic control modules/units are provided for the following systems (see Section 20):

a) Engine management.
b) Diesel fuel pump.
c) Automatic transmission.
d) Dashboard Integrated Central Electronics (DICE).
e) Instrument panel.
f) Saab Information Display (SID).
g) Theft Warning and Integrated Central Electronics (TWICE).
h) Cruise control.
i) Anti-lock Braking System (ABS).
j) Airbag SRS system.
k) Convertible Soft top Control (STC).
l) Automatic Climate Control (ACC).
m) Electrically adjustable door mirrors with memory (PMM).
n) Electrically adjustable driver's seat with memory (PSM).

Most models are fitted with an anti-theft alarm system consisting of sensors on the doors, tailgate and bonnet. A glass breakage sensor is also fitted in the interior light on the front of the headlining. The system is controlled by a central electronic control module which operates the warning horn.

While some repair procedures are given, the usual course of action is to renew a defective component. The owner whose interest extends beyond mere component renewal should obtain a copy of the *Automotive Electrical & Electronic Systems Manual*, available from the publishers of this Manual.

Precautions

It is necessary to take extra care when working on the electrical system to avoid damage to semi-conductor devices (diodes and transistors) and to avoid the risk of personal injury. Certain procedures must be followed when removing the SRS components; refer to Chapter 11 for more information. In addition to the precautions given in *Safety first!* at the beginning of this Manual, observe the following when working on the system:

a) *Always remove rings, watches, etc, before working on the electrical system. Even with the battery disconnected, capacitive discharge could occur if a component's live terminal is earthed through a metal object. This could cause a shock or nasty burn.*
b) *Do not reverse the battery connections. Components such as the alternator, fuel injection/ignition system ECU, or any other having semi-conductor circuitry could be irreparably damaged.*
c) *Do not allow the engine to turn the alternator when the alternator is not connected.*
d) *Always ensure that the battery negative lead is disconnected when working on the electrical system.*
e) *Before using electric-arc welding equipment on the vehicle, disconnect the battery, alternator and components such as the fuel injection/ignition system ECU to protect them.*

2 Electrical fault finding – general information

Note: *Refer to the precautions given in 'Safety first!' and in Section 1 of this Chapter before starting work. The following tests relate to testing of the main electrical circuits, and should not be used to test delicate electronic circuits (such as anti-lock braking systems), particularly where an electronic control unit (ECU) is involved.*

General

1 A typical electrical circuit consists of an electrical component, any switches, relays, motors, fuses, fusible links or circuit breakers related to that component, and the wiring and connectors which link the component to both the battery and the chassis. To help to pinpoint a problem in an electrical circuit, wiring diagrams are included at the end of this Chapter.

2 Before attempting to diagnose an electrical fault, first study the appropriate wiring diagram, to obtain a more complete understanding of the components included in the particular circuit concerned. The possible sources of a fault can be narrowed down by noting whether other components related to the circuit are operating properly. If several components or circuits fail at one time, the problem is likely to be related to a shared fuse or earth connection.

3 Electrical problems usually stem from simple causes, such as loose or corroded connections, a faulty earth connection, a blown fuse, a melted fusible link, or a faulty relay (refer to Section 3 for details of testing relays). Visually inspect the condition of all fuses, wires and connections in a problem circuit before testing the components. Use the wiring diagrams to determine which terminal connections will need to be checked, in order to pinpoint the trouble-spot.

4 The basic tools required for electrical fault finding include: a circuit tester or voltmeter (a 12 volt bulb with a set of test leads can also be used for certain tests), a self-powered test light (sometimes known as a continuity tester), an ohmmeter (to measure resistance), a battery and set of test leads, and a jumper wire, preferably with a circuit breaker or fuse incorporated, which can be used to bypass suspect wires or electrical components. Before attempting to locate a problem with test instruments, use the wiring diagram to determine where to make the connections.

5 To find the source of an intermittent wiring fault (usually due to a poor or dirty connection, or damaged wiring insulation), an integrity test can be performed on the wiring, which involves moving the wiring by hand, to see if the fault occurs as the wiring is moved. It should be possible to narrow down the source of the fault to a particular section of wiring. This method of testing can be used in conjunction with any of the tests described in the following sub-Sections.

6 Apart from problems due to poor connections, two basic types of fault can occur in an electrical circuit – open-circuit, or short-circuit.

7 Open-circuit faults are caused by a break somewhere in the circuit, which prevents current from flowing. An open-circuit fault will prevent a component from working, but will not cause the relevant circuit fuse to blow.

8 Short-circuit faults are caused by a 'short' somewhere in the circuit, which allows the current flowing in the circuit to 'escape' along an alternative route, usually to earth. Short-circuit faults are normally caused by a breakdown in wiring insulation, which allows a feed wire to touch either another wire, or an earthed component such as the bodyshell. A short-circuit fault will normally cause the relevant circuit fuse to blow. **Note:** *A short-circuit that occurs in the wiring between a circuit's battery supply and its fuse will not cause the fuse in that particular circuit to blow. This part of the circuit is unprotected – bear this in mind when fault finding on the vehicle's electrical system.*

Finding an open-circuit

9 To check for an open-circuit, connect one lead of a circuit tester or voltmeter to either the negative battery terminal or a known good earth.

10 Connect the other lead to a connector in the circuit being tested, preferably nearest to the battery or fuse.

11 Switch on the circuit, bearing in mind that some circuits are live only when the ignition switch is moved to a particular position.

12 If voltage is present (indicated either by the tester bulb lighting or a voltmeter reading, as applicable), this means that the section of the circuit between the relevant connector and the battery is problem-free.

13 Continue to check the remainder of the circuit in the same fashion.

14 When a point is reached at which no voltage is present, the problem must lie between that point and the previous test point with voltage. Most problems can be traced to a broken, corroded or loose connection.

3.3a The facia fusebox

3.3b The fusebox located in the left-hand rear of the engine compartment

Finding a short-circuit

15 To check for a short-circuit, first disconnect the load(s) from the circuit (loads are the components which draw current from a circuit, such as bulbs, motors, heating elements, etc).

16 Remove the relevant fuse from the circuit, and connect a circuit tester or voltmeter to the fuse connections.

17 Switch on the circuit, bearing in mind that some circuits are live only when the ignition switch is moved to a particular position.

18 If voltage is present (indicated either by the tester bulb lighting or a voltmeter reading, as applicable), this means that there is a short-circuit.

19 If no voltage is present, but the fuse still blows with the load(s) connected, this indicates an internal fault in the load(s).

Finding an earth fault

20 The battery negative terminal is connected to 'earth' – the metal of the engine/transmission and the car body – and most systems are wired so that they only receive a positive feed, the current returning via the metal of the car body. This means that the component mounting and the body form part of that circuit. Loose or corroded mountings can therefore cause a range of electrical faults, ranging from total failure of a circuit, to a puzzling partial fault. In particular, lights may shine dimly (especially when another circuit sharing the same earth point is in operation), motors (eg, wiper motors or the radiator cooling fan motor) may run slowly, and the operation of one circuit may have an apparently-unrelated effect on another. Note that on many vehicles, earth straps are used between certain components, such as the engine/transmission and the body, usually where there is no metal-to-metal contact between components, due to flexible rubber mountings, etc.

21 To check whether a component is properly earthed, disconnect the battery, and connect one lead of an ohmmeter to a known good earth point. Connect the other lead to the wire or earth connection being tested. The resistance reading should be zero; if not, check the connection as follows.

22 If an earth connection is thought to be faulty, dismantle the connection, and clean back to bare metal both the bodyshell and the wire terminal, or the component's earth connection mating surface. Be careful to remove all traces of dirt and corrosion, then use a knife to trim away any paint, so that a clean metal-to-metal joint is made. On reassembly, tighten the joint fasteners securely; if a wire terminal is being refitted, use serrated washers between the terminal and the bodyshell, to ensure a clean and secure connection. When the connection is remade, prevent the onset of corrosion in the future by applying a coat of petroleum jelly or silicone-based grease, or by spraying on (at regular intervals) a proprietary ignition sealer or a water-dispersant lubricant.

3 Fuses and relays – general information

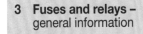

Fuses

1 Fuses are designed to break an electrical circuit when a predetermined current limit is reached, in order to protect the components and wiring which could be damaged by excessive current flow. Any excessive current flow will be due to a fault in the circuit, usually a short-circuit (see Section 2).

2 The fuses are located either in the fusebox located on the right-hand end of the facia, or in the fusebox located in the left-hand rear of the engine compartment. The engine compartment fusebox also includes the main relays.

3.4 Removing a fuse with the plastic tool provided

3 Access to the facia fusebox is gained by opening the right-hand front door and releasing the plastic cover. The engine compartment fusebox is opened by opening the bonnet and lifting the plastic cover **(see illustrations)**.

4 To remove a fuse, use the plastic tool provided in the fusebox to pull the fuse from its socket **(see illustration)**.

5 Inspect the fuse from the side, through the transparent plastic body – a blown fuse can be recognised by its melted or broken wire.

6 Spare fuses are provided in the blank terminal positions in the fusebox. **Note:** *As from model year 2000, fuse 15 activates the daytime headlights (parking and dipped main beam); if daytime headlights are not required, simply remove fuse 15.*

7 Before renewing a blown fuse, trace and rectify the cause, and always use a fuse of the correct rating.

Caution: Never substitute a fuse of a higher rating, or make temporary repairs using wire or metal foil; more serious damage, or even a fire, could result.

8 Note that the fuses are colour-coded, as described below – refer to the wiring diagrams for details of the fuse ratings and the circuits protected.

Colour	Rating
Brown	5A
Red	10A
Blue	15A
Yellow	20A
Clear	25A
Green	30A

9 In addition to the system fuses, fusible links are also located next to the battery **(see illustration)** and also in the fusebox at the rear of the engine compartment. There are four fusible links in each location, and their purpose is to protect certain areas of the car's electrical wiring, each including more than one electrical component. They will not blow as the result of a fault in a single component. Their ratings are as follows:

Colour	Rating
Orange	40A (maximum)
Blue	60A (maximum)

Relays

10 A relay is an electrically-operated

3.9 The fusible links are located next to the battery

3.11 Additional relays located beneath the right-hand side of the facia

3.13 Removing a relay

mechanical switch, which is used for the following reasons:

a) *A relay can switch a heavy current remotely from the circuit in which the current is flowing, therefore allowing the use of lighter-gauge wiring and switch contacts.*

b) *A relay can receive more than one control input, unlike a mechanically-operated switch.*

c) *A relay can have a timer function, although on the Saab models in this Manual this function is carried out by the ICE Control module.*

11 The main relays are located in the fusebox at the left-hand rear corner of the engine compartment. Lift off the cover for access to the relays. Additional relays are located

beneath the right-hand side of the facia **(see illustration)**.

12 If a circuit or system that is controlled by a relay develops a fault and the performance of the relay is in doubt, switch on the system in question. *In general*, if the relay is functioning, it should be possible to hear it 'click' as it is energised. If this is found to be the case, then it is probable that the fault lies with the system's components or wiring. If the relay cannot be heard to energise, then either the relay is not receiving a main supply or switching voltage, or the relay itself is faulty. Verification can be carried out by the substitution of a known good unit, but be careful – while some relays are identical in appearance and operation, others look similar but perform different

functions – ensure that the substitute relay is of exactly the same type.

13 To remove a relay, first ensure that the relevant circuit is switched off. The relay can then simply be pulled out from the socket, and pushed back into position **(see illustration)**.

4 Switches and controls – removal and refitting

Ignition switch and lock

Removal

1 On models with manual transmission, refer to Chapter 7A, Section 4, and unbolt the gearchange lever housing from the floorpan. Undo the screws and detach the locking plate holder and retaining spring from the underside of the gear lever housing. Prise out the locking plate pivot using a screwdriver, then remove the stop plate.

2 On models with automatic transmission, remove the selector lever assembly from the floorpan as described in Chapter 7B.

3 Unplug the wiring from the base of the ignition switch, then remove the switch retaining screws (5) and withdraw the assembly from the base of the ignition lock **(see illustration)**. If required, remove the securing screw (4) and withdraw the lock from the lever housing.

Refitting

4 Locate the ignition lock in the housing, then fit and tighten the securing screw. Fit the ignition switch, then fit and tighten the ignition securing screws. Reconnect the wiring to the rear of the ignition switch.

5 On models with manual transmission, press the stop plate into position in the lever housing, then fit the locking plate into position, ensuring that the pivot pins snap into their respective recesses and that the bushings are correctly located. Fit the locking plate holder, then coat the threads of the securing screws with locking fluid and fit them. Fit the locking plate spring, then adjust the position of the locking plate by turning the locking plate holder securing screw, so that the edge of the locking plate is level with the heel in the lever housing. Ensure that the stop does not come into contact with the locking plate (see Chapter 7A).

6 On models with automatic transmission, check the adjustment of the parking lock mechanism, as described in Chapter 7B, Section 5.

7 Refer to Chapter 7A or 7B as applicable for details of refitting the gearchange/selector lever assembly.

Steering column switches

Removal

8 Remove the steering wheel contact roller as described in Chapter 11, Section 30.

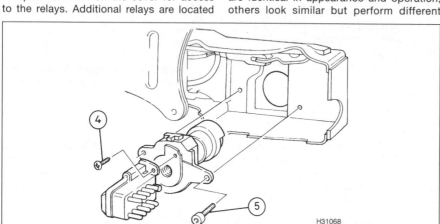

4.3 Remove the switch retaining screws and withdraw the assembly from the base of the ignition lock (see text for 4 and 5)

4.9a Depress the tabs to remove the combination switch . . .

4.9b . . . then disconnect the wiring

4.11 Prise out the electric window control switch with a screwdriver . . .

4.12 . . . then disconnect the wiring

4.14 Press out the headlight height adjustment switch . . .

9 Remove the relevant switch by depressing the top and bottom plastic tabs, then disconnect the wiring **(see illustrations)**.

Refitting

10 Refitting is a reversal of removal.

Electric window control

Removal

11 Using a screwdriver, carefully prise up the front of the switch from the centre console **(see illustration)**.
12 Disconnect the wiring **(see illustration)**.

Refitting

13 Refitting is a reversal of removal.

Headlight height adjustment

Removal

14 Using a screwdriver, carefully prise the switch from the facia panel. If it is tight, remove

the lower trim panel and press the switch out from behind **(see illustration)**.
15 Disconnect the wiring **(see illustration)**.

Refitting

16 Refitting is a reversal of removal.

Interior lighting control

Removal

17 Using a screwdriver, carefully prise the switch from the centre console rear section. If it is tight, temporarily slide the rear section slightly to the rear and press out the switch from below **(see illustration)**.
18 Disconnect the wiring **(see illustration)**.

Refitting

19 Refitting is a reversal of removal.

Instrument illumination rheostat

Removal

20 Using a screwdriver, carefully prise the switch from the facia panel. If it is tight, remove

the lower trim panel and press the switch out from behind **(see illustration)**.
21 Disconnect the wiring.

Refitting

22 Refitting is a reversal of removal.

Rear foglight switch

Removal

23 Using a screwdriver, carefully prise the switch from the facia panel. If it is tight, remove the lower trim panel and press the switch out from behind **(see illustration)**.
24 Disconnect the wiring.

Refitting

25 Refitting is a reversal of removal.

Lighting switch

Removal

26 Carefully prise the switch from the facia using a screwdriver **(see illustration)**.

4.15 . . . and disconnect the wiring

4.17 Remove the interior lighting control switch . . .

4.18 . . . and disconnect the wiring

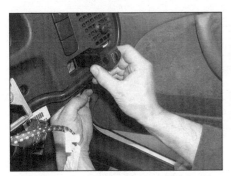

4.20 Removing the instrument illumination rheostat

4.23 Removing the rear foglight switch

4.26 Remove the lighting switch . . .

4.27 . . . and disconnect the wiring

4.29 Brake stop-light switch

4.36a Undo the screw . . .

27 Disconnect the wiring **(see illustration)**.

Refitting
28 Refitting is a reversal of removal.

4.36b . . . and withdraw the door courtesy light switch

Stop-light switch
Removal and refitting
29 Refer to Chapter 9 **(see illustration)**.

Hazard warning light switch
Removal
30 Carefully prise the switch from the facia using a screwdriver.
31 Disconnect the wiring.
Refitting
32 Refitting is a reversal of removal.

Electric door mirror switch
Removal
33 Carefully prise the switch from the triangular cover on the front door.
34 Disconnect the wiring.
Refitting
35 Refitting is a reversal of removal.

Door courtesy light switch
Removal
36 With the door open, undo the screw and withdraw the switch from the door pillar **(see illustrations)**.
37 Disconnect the wiring, making sure that it does not drop back into the bodywork.

> **HAYNES HINT** *Tape the wiring to the door, to prevent it falling back into the door pillar. Alternatively, tie a length of string to the wiring to retrieve it.*

Refitting
38 Refitting is a reversal of removal.

5 Interior light bulbs – renewal

Instrument panel
1 Remove the instrument panel as described in Section 9.
2 Undo the screws (noting the locations of the short and long ones) and unclip the back panel and module from the instrument panel. Carefully disconnect the wiring plugs **(see illustrations)**.
3 Using a screwdriver undo the relevant bulbholder from the instrument panel **(see illustrations)**.

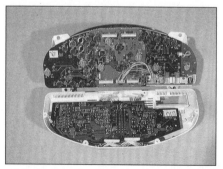

5.2a Undo the screws and lift the back panel . . .

5.2b . . . then disconnect the wiring plugs

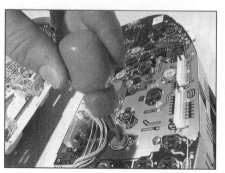

5.3a Unscrew the bulbholder . . .

5.3b . . . and remove it from the instrument panel

5.2c Instrument panel main console and back panel

5.6a Unscrew the bulbholder . . .

5.6b . . . and remove it from the clock/SID module

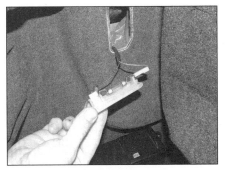

5.8 Removing the interior light from the luggage compartment side trim

4 Fit the new bulb using a reversal of the removal procedure.

Clock/SID module

5 Remove the clock/SID module as described in Section 10.
6 Using a screwdriver or curved pair of pliers, twist the relevant bulbholder and remove the bulb **(see illustrations)**.
7 Fit the new bulb using a reversal of the removal procedure.

Interior lights

8 Using a screwdriver carefully prise the interior light from the headlining or side trim, as applicable **(see illustration)**.
9 Remove the festoon type bulb from the terminals. On Convertible models, the interior light for the rear passengers is located in the side trim panel, and the bulb is a wedge-type – remove the bulbholder from the light, then pull out the bulb **(see illustration)**.
10 Fit the new bulb using a reversal of the removal procedure.

Electric window switch illumination

11 Remove the electric window control switch as described in Section 4.
12 Using a screwdriver, twist the bulbholder anticlockwise to remove it **(see illustration)**.

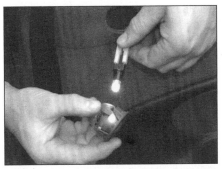

5.9 Removing the interior light bulb holder on Convertible models

13 Fit the new bulb using a reversal of the removal procedure.

Air conditioning/ climate control illumination

14 Undo the screws and remove the front trim panels from each side of the centre console.
15 Press out the air conditioning/climate control module and disconnect the wiring.
16 Unscrew the relevant bulbholder from the rear of the module, then pull out the wedge-type bulb **(see illustrations)**.
17 Fit the new bulb using a reversal of the removal procedure.

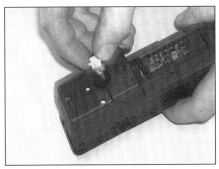

5.12 Removing the illumination bulbholder from the electric window control switch

6 Exterior light units – removal and refitting

Headlight

Removal

1 With the bonnet open, remove the radiator grille as described in Chapter 11.
2 Lift the wiper arms from the headlamps, where fitted.
3 Through the aperture at the rear of the headlight, loosen only the bolt securing the

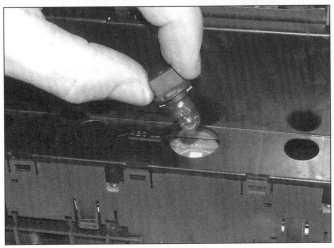

5.16a Unscrew the bulbholder . . .

5.16b . . . and pull out the wedge-type bulb

6.3 Loosen the direction indicator unit retaining screw . . .

6.4a . . . then withdraw the unit . . .

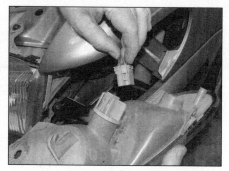

6.4b . . . and disconnect the wiring

direction indicator unit to the headlight **(see illustration)**. The bolt does not have to be completely removed.

4 Withdraw the direction indicator light unit and disconnect the wiring plug **(see illustrations)**.

5 Undo the headlight mounting screws **(see illustrations)**.

6 Carefully lift the headlight unit from the front of the car and disconnect the wiring from the main beam and parking light bulbs **(see illustrations)**.

Refitting

7 Refitting is a reversal of removal.

Front direction indicator light

Removal

8 With the bonnet open, use a socket through the aperture at the rear of the headlight to loosen only the bolt securing the direction

indicator unit to the headlight. The bolt does not have to be completely removed.

9 Withdraw the direction indicator light unit.

10 Disconnect the bulb wiring plug.

11 If necessary, remove the bulbholder and bulb.

Refitting

12 Refitting is a reversal of removal.

Side repeater light

Removal

13 Carefully press the light forwards against the tension of the plastic clip, then release the rear of the light from the front wing.

14 Twist the bulbholder and remove the light unit.

Refitting

15 Refitting is a reversal of removal.

Rear light cluster

Removal

16 Remove the rear valance and luggage compartment trim with reference to Chapter 11, Section 26, for access to the relevant rear light cluster.

17 Disconnect the wiring from the bulbholder.

18 Unscrew the nuts and withdraw the cluster **(see illustration)**.

Refitting

19 Refitting is a reversal of removal.

Front foglight

Removal

20 Reach up behind the front bumper and disconnect the wiring for the front foglight.

21 Unscrew the two lower mounting bolts and single upper nut, and withdraw the foglight from the front bumper.

Refitting

22 Refitting is a reversal of removal.

Number plate light

Removal

23 Undo the screws and withdraw the lens from the number plate light, then prise the light unit from the tailgate.

24 Disconnect the wiring.

Refitting

25 Refitting is a reversal of removal.

6.5a Unscrew the upper mounting screws . . .

6.5b . . . and lower mounting screw

6.6a Withdraw the headlight from the car . . .

6.6b . . . and disconnect the wiring

6.18 Rear light cluster mounting nuts

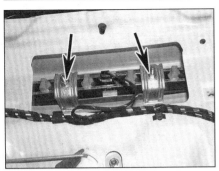

6.27 High-level stop-light mounting nuts and clamps

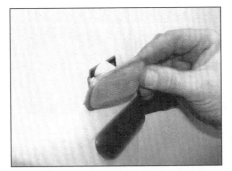

7.14 Remove the side repeater light . . .

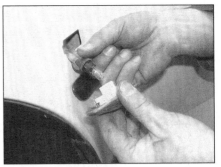

7.15a . . . twist the bulbholder to remove it from the lens unit

High-level stop-light

Removal

26 With the tailgate/boot lid open, remove the trim for access to the high-level stop-light mounting nuts.

27 Prise out the rubber plugs where fitted, then unscrew the light mounting nuts, and recover the clamps **(see illustration)**.

28 Reach up into the tailgate, and disconnect the wiring.

29 Press the cover away, then use a wide-bladed screwdriver or similar tool to prise out the light from the side clips. Prise first on the right-hand side of the rear window washer nozzle, then prise out the left-hand side. Take care not to damage the paintwork.

Refitting

30 Refitting is a reversal of removal.

7 Exterior light bulbs – renewal

1 Whenever a bulb is renewed, note the following points:

a) *Remember that, if the light has just been in use, the bulb may be extremely hot.*

b) *Do not touch the bulb glass with the fingers, as this can result in early failure or a dull reflector.*

c) *Always check the bulb contacts and holder, ensuring that there is clean metal-*

to-metal contact between the bulb and its live and earth. Clean off any corrosion or dirt before fitting a new bulb.

d) *Ensure that the new bulb is of the correct rating.*

Headlight main beam

2 With the bonnet open, unscrew the plastic cover from the rear of the headlight.

3 Disconnect the wiring from the main beam bulb.

4 Release the spring clip and remove the bulb. Use a tissue or clean cloth to prevent touching the bulb.

5 Fit the new bulb using a reversal of the removal procedure, but make sure that the bulb location lugs engage correctly in the rear of the headlight.

Front sidelight

6 The front sidelight bulb is located on the main beam headlight assembly. First unscrew the plastic cover from the rear of the headlight.

7 Disconnect the wiring from the front sidelight bulbholder.

8 Pull the bulbholder from the headlight, then pull the bulb from the bulbholder.

9 Fit the new bulb using a reversal of the removal procedure.

Front direction indicator

10 With the bonnet open, use a socket

through the aperture at the rear of the headlight to loosen only the bolt securing the direction indicator unit to the headlight. The bolt does not have to be completely removed.

11 Withdraw the direction indicator light unit.

12 Twist the bulbholder anti-clockwise and remove it, then depress and twist the bulb to remove it from the bulbholder.

13 Fit the new bulb using a reversal of the removal procedure.

Side repeater lights

14 Carefully press the light forwards against the tension of the plastic clip, then release the rear of the light from the front wing **(see illustration)**.

15 Twist the bulbholder and remove the lens unit, then pull out the wedge-type bulb **(see illustrations)**. Do not allow the wiring to drop into the space behind the wing.

16 Fit the new bulb using a reversal of removal procedure.

Rear light cluster

17 With the tailgate open, unscrew the nut and open the carpet flap behind the rear light cluster.

18 Squeeze together the locking tabs and remove the bulbholder from the cluster **(see illustrations)**.

19 Depress and twist the relevant bulb

7.15b . . . and pull out the wedge-type bulb

7.18a Squeeze together the locking tabs . . .

7.18b . . . and remove the bulbholder

7.19 Depress and twist the relevant bulb to remove it

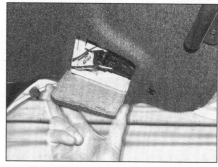

7.21 Prise open the carpet flap . . .

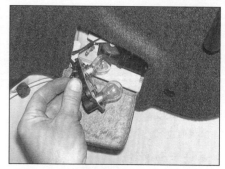

7.22 . . . and withdraw the reversing and rear foglight bulbholder . . .

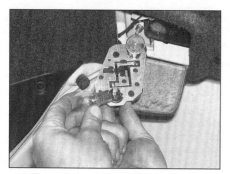

7.23 . . . then remove the relevant bulb

7.29a Undo the screws . . .

7.29b . . . withdraw the lens . . .

and remove it from the bulbholder **(see illustration)**.

20 Fit the new bulb using a reversal of the removal procedure.

Reversing and rear foglights

21 With the tailgate/boot lid open, prise open the carpet flap from over the reversing and rear foglights **(see illustration)**.

22 Release the clip and pull the bulbholder from the light **(see illustration)**.

23 Depress and twist the relevant bulb and remove it from the bulbholder **(see illustration)**.

24 Fit the new bulb using a reversal of the removal procedure.

Front foglight

25 Where necessary, undo the screws and remove the cover from the bottom of the front foglight. Recover the seal.

26 To remove the foglight bulb, twist the bulbholder 45° anti-clockwise, then pull out the bulb. If it is to be refitted, do not touch the glass with your fingers.

27 On some models, an additional standard bulb is fitted to the foglight. To remove this bulb, twist the bulbholder anti-clockwise from the foglight, then depress and twist the bulb to remove it.

28 Fit the new bulb using a reversal of the removal procedure.

Number plate light

29 Undo the screws and withdraw the lens from the number plate light **(see illustrations)**.

30 Pull out the wedge-type bulb **(see illustration)**.

31 Fit the new bulb using a reversal of the removal procedure.

High-level stop-light

32 Remove the trim by first removing the hand grip, then carefully prising out the clips.

33 Twist the relevant bulbholder anti-clockwise, then pull out the wedge-type bulb **(see illustrations)**.

34 Fit the new bulb using a reversal of the removal procedure.

8 Headlight beam adjustment – general information

1 Accurate adjustment of the headlight beam is only possible using optical beam-setting equipment, and this work should therefore be carried out by a Saab dealer or suitably-equipped workshop. In an emergency, it is possible to adjust the headlights by turning

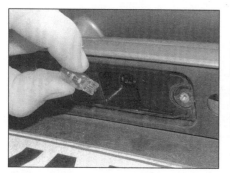

7.30 . . . and pull out the wedge-type bulb

7.33a Twist out the bulbholder . . .

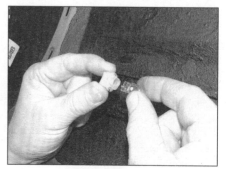

7.33b . . . then pull out the wedge-type bulb

8.1 Headlight beam adjustment knobs on the rear of the headlight

the knobs located on the rear of the headlight **(see illustration)**.

2 Most models have a headlight beam adjustment control, which allows the aim of the headlights to be adjusted to compensate for variation in the vehicle's payload. The aim is altered by means of facia-mounted switch, which controls electric adjuster motors located in the rear of the headlight assemblies. The switch should be positioned as follows, according to the load being carried in the vehicle:

Switch position	Vehicle load
0	*Up to 3 occupants (no more than one in the rear seat), no luggage.*
1	*Up to 3 occupants in rear seats, up to 30 kg in luggage.*
2	*Up to 3 occupants in rear seats, up to 80 kg in luggage.*
3	*Up to 5 occupants, luggage area full – or up to 5 occupants, luggage area full, towing caravan/trailer.*

9 Instrument panel – removal and refitting

Note: *If a new instrument panel is fitted, it must be reprogrammed by a Saab dealer.*

Removal

1 Undo the screws and remove the steering column shrouds.

9.7 Undo the screws . . .

9.5a Undo the screws . . .

2 Remove the steering column combination switches as described in Section 4, however, there is no need to remove the steering wheel.

3 Remove the radio/cassette player and SID module as described in Sections 16 and 10.

4 Refer to Section 4 and remove all of the switches from the instrument panel surround.

5 Undo the screws and remove the surround – there are 9 screws in all **(see illustrations)**.

6 Where applicable, disconnect the wiring from the small display panel at the top of the surround **(see illustration)**.

7 Undo the instrument panel mounting screws **(see illustration)**.

8 Withdraw the instrument panel far enough to disconnect the wiring **(see illustrations)**.

Refitting

9 Refitting is a reversal of removal.

10 Clock/SID module – removal and refitting

Note: *If a new module is fitted, it must be reprogrammed by a Saab dealer.*

Removal

1 The Saab Information Display (SID) module and clock is located in the centre of the facia above the radio. First disconnect the battery negative (earth) lead (see *Disconnecting the battery*).

9.8a . . . then withdraw the instrument panel . . .

9.5b . . . and remove the instrument panel surround

9.6 Disconnecting the wiring from the small display panel

2 Remove the radio/cassette player as described in Section 16.

3 Reaching through the radio aperture, push out the module from behind.

4 Disconnect the wiring and remove the module.

Refitting

5 Refitting is a reversal of removal.

11 Cigarette lighter – removal and refitting

Removal

1 Remove the centre console as described in Chapter 11.

2 Undo the screws and remove the front trim panel from the side of the centre console.

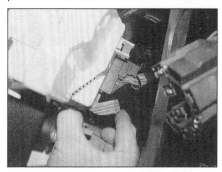

9.8b . . . and disconnect the wiring

11.3 Disconnecting the wiring from the cigarette lighter

12.2 Horn and wiring connector

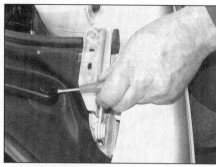

13.2a Insert a screwdriver . . .

3 Disconnect the wiring from the rear of the cigarette lighter **(see illustration)**.
4 Remove the illumination ring, then remove the cigarette lighter from the centre console.

Refitting

5 Refitting is a reversal of removal.

12 Horn – removal and refitting

Removal

1 Remove the radiator grille as described in Chapter 11.
2 Disconnect the wiring from the horn **(see illustration)**.

3 Unscrew the bracket mounting bolt and lift the horn assembly from the front crossmember.

Refitting

4 Refitting is a reversal of removal.

13 Windscreen, tailgate and headlight wiper arms – removal and refitting

Windscreen wiper arm

Removal

1 Make sure that the windscreen wipers are at their rest positions. Use a piece of tape to

mark the position on the windscreen.
2 Using a screwdriver, prise up the cover from the windscreen wiper arm **(see illustrations)**.
3 Unscrew the nut securing the wiper arm to the shaft **(see illustration)**.
4 Ease the arm from the shaft by carefully rocking it side-to-side **(see illustration)**.

Refitting

5 Refitting is a reversal of removal.

Tailgate wiper arm

Removal

6 Make sure that the wiper is at its rest position. Use a piece of tape to mark the position on the screen.
7 Lift up the cover at the base of the tailgate wiper arm.
8 Unscrew the nut securing the wiper arm to the shaft **(see illustration)**.
9 Ease the arm from the shaft by carefully rocking it side-to-side **(see illustration)**.

Refitting

10 Refitting is a reversal of removal.

Headlight wiper arm

Removal

11 Note the rest position of the headlight wiper arms. Use a piece of tape to mark the position on the headlight.
12 Using a screwdriver, prise up the cover from the arm.

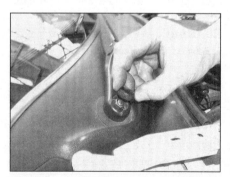

13.2b . . . and lift the cover from the windscreen wiper arm

13.3 Unscrew the nut . . .

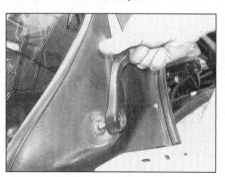

13.4 . . . and ease the wiper arm from the shaft

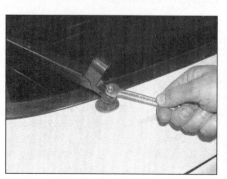

13.8 Unscrew the nut . . .

13.9 . . . and ease the wiper arm from the shaft

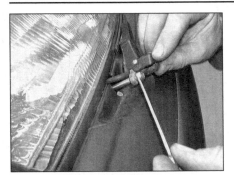

13.13 Unscrew the nut . . .

13.14a . . . then ease the arm from the shaft . . .

13.14b . . . and disconnect the washer tubing

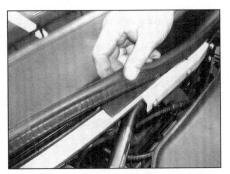

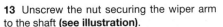

14.5 Pull up the weatherstrip from the bulkhead . . .

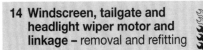

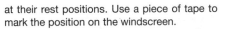

14.6 . . . then lift the cover and disconnect the washer tube . . .

14.7 . . . disconnect the wiring . . .

13 Unscrew the nut securing the wiper arm to the shaft **(see illustration)**.

14 Ease the arm from the shaft by rocking it side-to-side, then disconnect the washer tubing. Remove the arm **(see illustrations)**.

Refitting

15 Refitting is a reversal of removal.

---

14 Windscreen, tailgate and headlight wiper motor and linkage – removal and refitting

Windscreen wiper motor

Removal

1 Make sure that the windscreen wipers are at their rest positions. Use a piece of tape to mark the position on the windscreen.

2 Using a screwdriver, prise the cover from the windscreen wiper arm.

3 Unscrew the nut securing the wiper arm to the shaft.

4 Ease the arm from the shaft by carefully rocking it side-to-side.

5 Pull the weatherstrip from the bulkhead **(see illustration)**.

6 Lift up the bulkhead cover and disconnect the washer tube from the adapter **(see illustration)**.

7 Disconnect the wiring from the wiper motor **(see illustration)**.

8 Unscrew the mounting bolts and lift the wiper motor and linkage from the bulkhead **(see illustration)**.

Refitting

9 Refitting is a reversal of removal.

Tailgate wiper motor

Removal

10 With the tailgate open, using a Torx key, undo the screws and remove the grab handle from the tailgate.

11 Using a screwdriver, undo the screws and remove the main trim panel from the inside of the tailgate

12 Remove the wiper arm (see Section 13).

13 Disconnect the wiring from the wiper motor **(see illustration)**.

14 Unscrew the mounting bolts and lower the wiper motor from the tailgate, while guiding

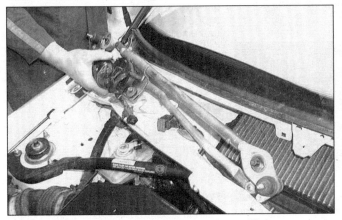

14.8 . . . and unbolt the wiper motor and linkage

14.13 Disconnect the wiring from the tailgate wiper motor . . .

14.14a ... then unscrew the bolts and lower the wiper motor from the tailgate

14.14b Wiper motor assembly removed from the tailgate

14.19 Disconnect the wiring from the headlight wiper motor assembly

the shaft through the rubber grommet (see illustrations).

15 If necessary, remove the grommet.

Refitting

16 Refitting is a reversal of removal.

Headlight wiper motor

Removal

17 Remove the headlight unit as described in Section 6.

18 Remove the wiper arm as described in Section 13.

19 Disconnect the wiring from the motor (see illustration).

20 Unscrew the mounting nuts and withdraw the wiper motor assembly from the front valance.

Refitting

21 Refitting is a reversal of removal.

15 Windscreen, tailgate and headlight washer system – removal and refitting

Removal

1 The washer fluid reservoir and pump are located beneath the front left-hand wing. For access to them, remove the wheel arch liner and, where necessary, the front bumper.

2 To remove the pump, position a container beneath the reservoir, then disconnect the pump wiring and washer tubes and allow the fluid to drain. Pull the pump out of the reservoir then remove the bush.

3 To remove the reservoir, first remove the pump. Unscrew the nut and disconnect the upper filler neck from the reservoir, then unscrew the mounting bolts and remove the reservoir.

Refitting

4 Refitting is a reversal of removal.

16 Radio/cassette player – removal and refitting

Note: *The radio/cassette player is security-coded; once the battery has been disconnected, the unit cannot be re-activated until the appropriate security code has been entered. Do not remove the unit unless the appropriate code is known.*

Removal

1 The standard radio is retained by DIN fixings, and two DIN removal tools will be required to release the retaining clips. The tools are available from car accessory shops, and are inserted into the holes on each side of the radio until they are felt to engage with the retaining strips. Non-standard radios may be retained by other means, but the method of removal is similar. On the project car, two lengths of plastic cable tie were inserted through holes at the top of the radio in order to release the retaining clips (see illustration).

2 With the clips released, carefully withdraw the radio from the facia.

3 Disconnect the wiring and aerial cable from the rear of the radio (see illustrations).

4 If necessary, the radio mounting box can be removed from the facia by bending up the retaining tabs (see illustration).

Refitting

5 Refitting is a reversal of removal.

17 Loudspeakers – removal and refitting

Facia-mounted speaker

1 Using a screwdriver carefully prise out the grille from the relevant speaker.

16.1 On this type of radio, insert two lengths of plastic cable tie to release it

16.3a Disconnecting the wiring ...

16.3b ... and aerial cable

16.4 Removing the radio mounting box

17.2 Facia-mounted speaker

17.21 Rear loudspeaker on Convertible models

17.22 Disconnecting the wiring

2 Using a Torx key, undo the screws securing the speaker in the facia, and carefully lift it out **(see illustration)**.
3 Disconnect the wiring and tape it to the facia to prevent it dropping down inside.
4 Refitting is a reversal of removal.

Front door-mounted speaker

5 Remove the door inner trim panel as described in Chapter 11.
6 Undo the mounting screws, then withdraw the speaker and disconnect the wiring.
7 Refitting is a reversal of removal.

Rear speaker

Hatchback and Coupe

8 With the tailgate open, remove the parcel shelf.
9 Using a screwdriver carefully prise out the speaker grille.
10 Undo the screws and remove the speaker frame.
11 Undo the screws and lift out the speaker, then disconnect the wiring.
12 Refitting is a reversal of removal.

Convertible

13 Operate the soft top so that it is fully open and in the storage compartment, then raise the cover so that it is vertical.
14 Remove the rear seat cushion.
15 Unscrew the bolt securing the rear seat belt to the floor, and position the belt to one side.
16 Carefully prise off the door entry scuff plate.
17 Prise off the cover from the B-pillar, then prise out the cover and undo the screw securing the side trim to the B-pillar.
18 Prise out the fasteners from the bottom of the side trim, then fold the backrest forwards and unscrew the bolt and prise out the fastener from the rear edge of the side trim.
19 Pull up the side trim at its upper rear corner and release it from the clip. To ensure the clip does not separate from the trim, lever on the bottom of the clip.
20 Withdraw the side trim while feeding the rear seat belt through the guide. Also, disconnect the wiring from the rear interior light. If necessary, remove the light completely from the side trim.

21 Undo the mounting screws, and unclip the loudspeaker from the body (see illustration).
22 Disconnect the wiring and remove the loudspeaker (see illustration).
23 Refitting is a reversal of removal.

18 Aerial – removal and refitting

Removal

1 With the tailgate open, unclip the left-hand side luggage compartment interior trim and bend it to one side. Note that it will also be necessary to unscrew the rear speaker grille support screws.
2 To remove the fixed aerial, disconnect the aerial cable then unscrew the bottom mounting bolt. At the top of the aerial, unscrew the collar and remove the adapter, then withdraw the aerial downwards from inside the luggage compartment.
3 To remove the electric aerial, unscrew the bottom mounting nut and also the two bracket screws. At the top of the aerial, unscrew the collar and remove the adapter, then lower the aerial and bracket into the luggage compartment and disconnect the cable. If necessary, the motor can be removed from the bracket.

Refitting

4 Refitting is a reversal of removal.

19 Heated front seat components – general information

Certain models are fitted with thermostatically-regulated heated front seats. Individual control switches are provided for each seat, which allow the heating element temperature to be set to one of three levels, or switched off completely.

Two heating elements are fitted to each seat – one in the backrest, and one in the seat cushion. Access to the heating elements can only be gained by removing the upholstery from the seat – this is an operation which should be entrusted to a Saab dealer.

20 Electronic Control Modules/ Units – general information

1 The control modules for the various electronic systems are located as follows:

Engine management
- Right-hand side of the front right-hand footwell, below the A-pillar.

Diesel fuel pump
- On the diesel fuel pump (right-hand front of the engine).

Automatic transmission
- Behind the glovebox.

Dashboard Integrated Central Electronics (DICE)
- Behind (RHD) or above (LHD) the facia relay holder.

Instrument panel
- On rear of instrument panel.

Saab Information Display (SID)
- Middle of the centre console, next to the hazard flasher switch.

Theft Warning and Integrated Central Electronics (TWICE)
- Beneath the left-hand seat.

Cruise control
- Right-hand rear corner of the engine compartment.

Anti-lock Braking System (ABS)
- Left-hand rear of the engine compartment.

Airbag SRS system
- Between the front seats, under the centre console.

Convertible Soft top Control (STC)
- By the left-hand rear seat loudspeaker.

Automatic Climate Control (ACC)
- Beneath the radio on the facia.

Electrically adjustable door mirrors with memory (PMM)
- In the driver's door.

Electrically adjustable driver's seat with memory (PSM)
- Beneath the driver's seat.

21 Anti-theft alarm system components – removal and refitting

Electronic control module

Removal

1 Remove the left-hand front seat as described in Chapter 11.
2 Lift up the carpet just in front of the B-pillar for access to the electronic control module. On 3-door models, unscrew and remove the seat belt anchor bolt from the floor first.
3 Disconnect the wiring from the control module.
4 Unscrew the nut and remove the module from inside the car.

Refitting

5 Refitting is a reversal of removal.

Glass breakage sensor

Removal

6 Remove the interior light from the front of the headlining as described in Section 5.
7 On the rear of the light unit, disconnect the wiring.

Refitting

8 Refitting is a reversal of removal.

Warning LED on top of the facia

Removal

9 Slide the LED panel to the rear and lift it up from the facia.
10 Disconnect the wiring and remove the LED.

Refitting

11 Refitting is a reversal of removal.

Bonnet switch

Removal

12 With the bonnet open, slide the bonnet switch up from its location on the fusebox in the left-hand rear of the engine compartment.
13 Disconnect the wiring.

Refitting

14 Refitting is a reversal of removal.

Horn

Removal

15 Disconnect the battery negative (earth) lead (see *Disconnecting the battery*).
16 Working beneath the front left-hand wheel arch, remove the rear section of the wheel arch liner.
17 Unscrew the mounting nut, then disconnect the wiring.

Refitting

18 Refitting is a reversal of removal.

Saab 9-3 wiring diagrams

Diagram 1

Key to symbols

 Fusible link,
link number and rating
L1 150A

 Fuse, fuse number and rating
F15 10A

 Bulb

 Heating element with indicated current rating
1 Amp

 Electric motor

 Dotted outline indicates the item (bulb) is part of a larger assembly

 Solid outline and drop shadow indicates the item (bulb) is an individual part and not part of a larger assembly

 Interface connector pins

4 Number indicates pin number

11 Shape indicates the pin is grouped to one particular connector on the item

 Ganged switch with multiple contacts

 Single switch with multiple contacts

 Momentary switch

 Relay

Micro Processor Graphical representation of a component for which no additional detail is provided

 Link to another circuit; where appropriate the interfacing pin numbers are shown

6c Item reference; refering to key at top of diagram page

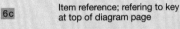 Connecting wires

 Wire splice or soldered joint

Alternative layout depending on model / year

— G/U — Wire colour (Green with blue tracer)

 Continuation point (follow arrow) used to improve diagram readability

 Wire enclosed in a screen (bonded both ends)

Diode

 Chain dashed box indicates item specific to a paricular variant
Petrol models only via fusebox

Earth point

 Earth point with reference (see earth locations on this page)

Key to circuits

Diagram 1   Information on wiring diagrams.

Diagram 2   Power supply distribution.

Diagram 3   Starting and charging systems, brake vacuum pump, radiator fan.

Diagram 4   Driving lights & headlights, sidelights.

Diagram 5   Front and rear fog lights, brake lights, reversing lights.

Diagram 6   Directional indicators, headlight levelling, switch illumination, horn.

Diagram 7   Windscreen wipers, rear screen wiper, headlight wiper, washers.

Diagram 8   Central locking, motorised door mirrors, window lifts.

Diagram 9   Sunroof, cigar lighter, phone connector, trailer connector, bus schematic and diagnostic connector.

Diagram 10   Anti-lock brakes, heating and ventilation controls.

Diagram 11   Interior and luggage compartment lighting, audio system.

Diagram 12   Instruments.

Diagram 13   Engine and passenger fusebox details.

Earth locations

E5   Structural member forward of left wheel housing

E1   Battery ground, left structural member

E8   Connector bracket below left hand A post

E9   Side wall behind connector bracket below A post

E10   On floor to rear of passenger seat member

E11   On console for motorised antenna

E7   Floor of luggage compartment below light cluster

E6   Structural member forward of right wheel housing

E3   Side of intake manifold to cylinder No.4

E2   Below right hand A post

E4   Under driver seat on floor to rear of seat member

H33450

Wire colours

B	Black	P	Purple
G	Green	R	Red
K	Pink	S	Grey
Lg	Light green	U	Blue
N	Brown	W	White
O	Orange	Y	Yellow

Key to items

1 Battery
2 Engine bay fuse box (501)
3 Engine bay fuse box (342a)
4 Dashboard fuse box (22a)
5 Ignition switch
6 Ignition switch relay (22b-E)
8 Fuel pump relay [petrol models] (22b-I)

10 Main relay [Engine management] (22b-L)

Diagram 2

H33451

Power supply distribution, ignition switch and primary circuit relays

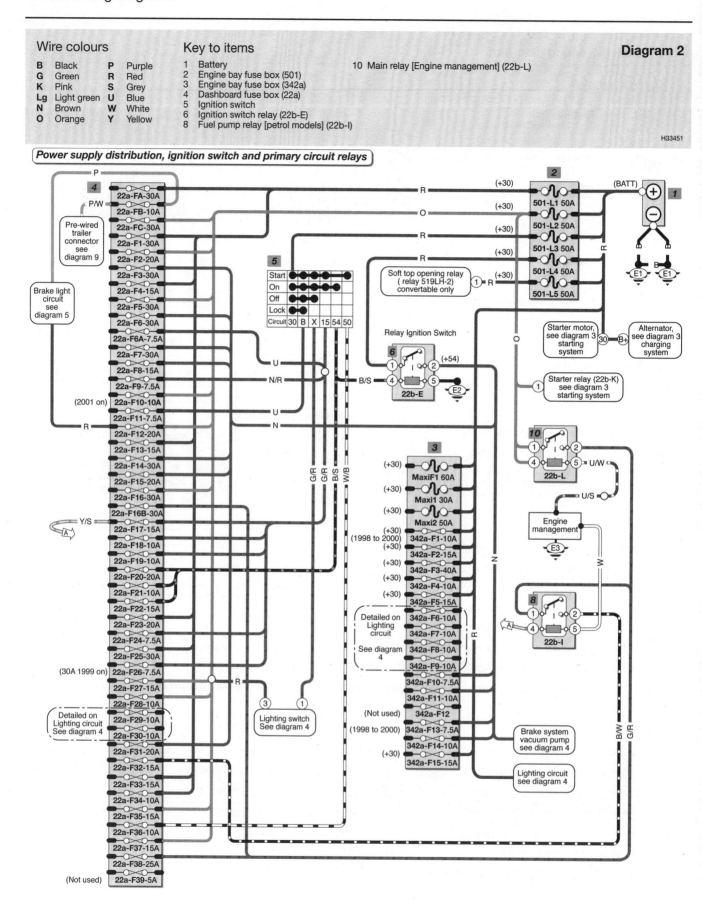

Wire colours

B	Black	**P**	Purple
G	Green	**R**	Red
K	Pink	**S**	Grey
Lg	Light green	**U**	Blue
N	Brown	**W**	White
O	Orange	**Y**	Yellow

Key to items

11 Starter motor
12 Transmission range switch (Auto transmission only)
13 Starter relay (22b-K)
14 Main instruments
15 Alternator
16 Radiator fan motor
17 Resistor - 2 speed fan

18 Fan relay - low speed (342b-D)
19 Fan relay - High speed (342b-I)
20 Vacuum pump relay (342b-C2)
21 Diode pack
22 Vacuum pump
23 Dashboard Integrated Central Electronics (DICE)
24 Theft Warning & Integrated Central Electronics (TWICE)

Diagram 3

H33452

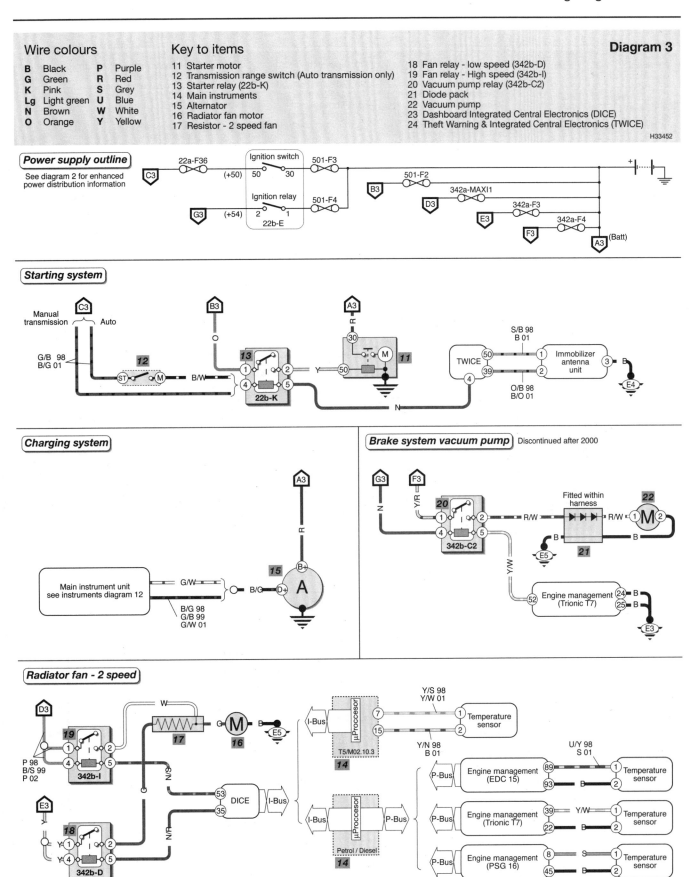

Power supply outline
See diagram 2 for enhanced power distribution information

Starting system

Charging system

Brake system vacuum pump Discontinued after 2000

Radiator fan - 2 speed

Wire colours

B	Black	P	Purple
G	Green	R	Red
K	Pink	S	Grey
Lg	Light green	U	Blue
N	Brown	W	White
O	Orange	Y	Yellow

Key to items

3   Engine bay fuse box (342a)
4   Dashboard fuse box (22a)
7   Lighting switch - 3 position
23 Dashboard Integrated Central
    Electronics (DICE)
24 Theft Warning & Integrated
    Central Electronics (TWICE)
25 Saab Information Display (SID)

26 Dip switch
27 Headlamp relay (342b-A)
28 Dip switch relay (342b-B)
29 Filament monitor
30 RH Head lamp
    a = dip filament
    b = main beam filament
    c = side light

31 RH Head lamp
    a = dip filament
    b = main beam filament
    c = side light
32 Tail light cluster RH
    a = side light
33 Tail light cluster LH
    a = side light

Diagram 4

H33453

Power supply outline

See diagram 2 for enhanced power distribution information

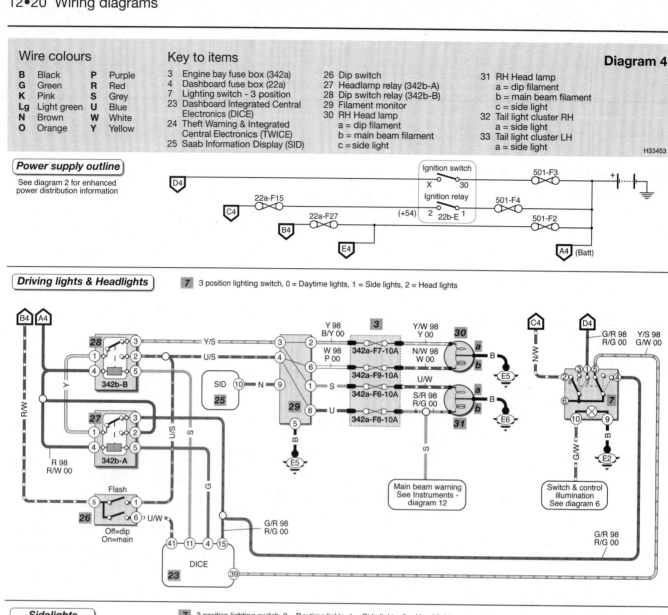

Driving lights & Headlights

7 3 position lighting switch, 0 = Daytime lights, 1 = Side lights, 2 = Head lights

Sidelights

7 3 position lighting switch, 0 = Daytime lights, 1 = Side lights, 2 = Head lights

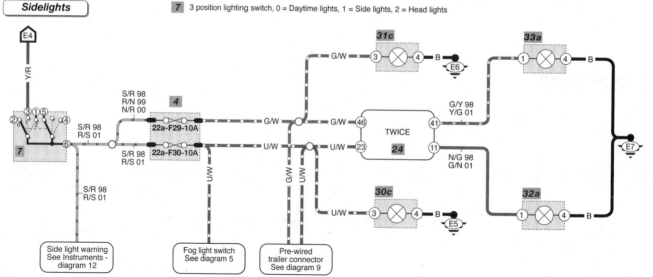

Wire colours

B	Black	P	Purple
G	Green	R	Red
K	Pink	S	Grey
Lg	Light green	U	Blue
N	Brown	W	White
O	Orange	Y	Yellow

Key to items

9   Brake light switch
12 Transmission range switch
23 Dashboard Integrated Central
    Electronics (DICE)
24 Theft Warning & Integrated
    Central Electronics (TWICE)
32 Tail light cluster RH
    b = brake light

33 Tail light cluster LH
    b = brake light
34 High level brake light
35 Front fog light switch
36 Rear fog light switch
37 Front fog light relay (342b-G2)
38 Front fog light RH
39 Front fog light LH

40 Rear fog light RH
41 Rear fog light LH
44 Reversing light switch (manual transmission)
45 Reversing light RH
46 Reversing light LH

Diagram 5

H33454

Power supply outline

See diagram 2 for enhanced
power distribution information

Front fog lights

Rear fog lights

Brake lights

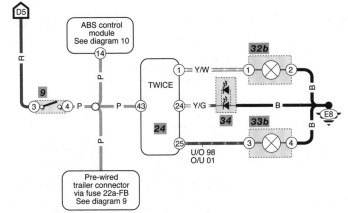

Reversing lights

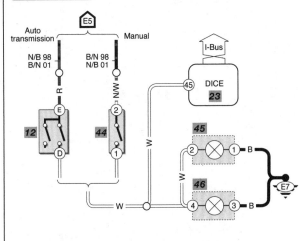

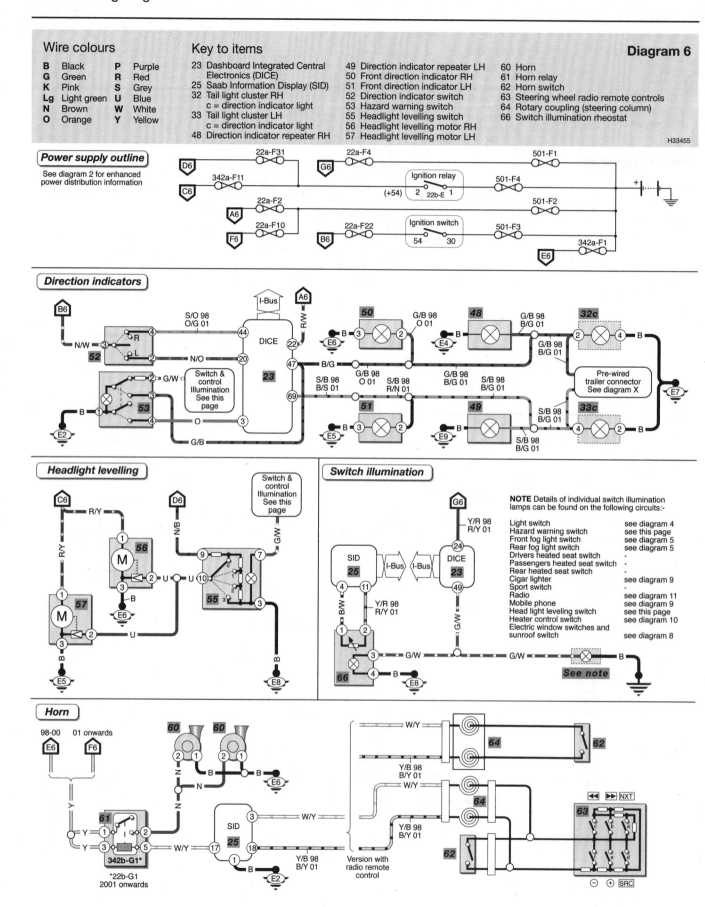

Wire colours

B	Black	**P**	Purple
G	Green	**R**	Red
K	Pink	**S**	Grey
Lg	Light green	**U**	Blue
N	Brown	**W**	White
O	Orange	**Y**	Yellow

Key to items

23 Dashboard Integrated Central Electronics (DICE)
25 Saab Information Display (SID)
32 Tail light cluster RH
   c = direction indicator light
33 Tail light cluster LH
   c = direction indicator light
48 Direction indicator repeater RH

49 Direction indicator repeater LH
50 Front direction indicator RH
51 Front direction indicator LH
52 Direction indicator switch
53 Hazard warning switch
55 Headlight levelling switch
56 Headlight levelling motor RH
57 Headlight levelling motor LH

60 Horn
61 Horn relay
62 Horn switch
63 Steering wheel radio remote controls
64 Rotary coupling (steering column)
66 Switch illumination rheostat

Diagram 6

H33455

Power supply outline
See diagram 2 for enhanced power distribution information

Direction indicators

Headlight levelling

Switch illumination

NOTE Details of individual switch illumination lamps can be found on the following circuits:-

Light switch	see diagram 4
Hazard warning switch	see this page
Front fog light switch	see diagram 5
Rear fog light switch	see diagram 5
Drivers heated seat switch	-
Passengers heated seat switch	-
Rear heated seat switch	-
Cigar lighter	see diagram 9
Sport switch	-
Radio	see diagram 11
Mobile phone	see diagram 9
Head light leveling switch	see this page
Heater control switch	see diagram 10
Electric window switches and sunroof switch	see diagram 8

Horn

Wire colours

B	Black	P	Purple
G	Green	R	Red
K	Pink	S	Grey
Lg	Light green	U	Blue
N	Brown	W	White
O	Orange	Y	Yellow

Key to items

23 Dashboard Integrated Central
   Electronics (DICE)
68 Windscreen wiper switch, 4 position
69 Intermittent wiper relay (22b-G)
70 Wiper motor
71 Rear screen wiper switch
72 Intermittent rear wiper
   relay (22b-D1)

73 Rear wiper motor
74 Washer fluid pump relay (22b-D2)
75 Washer fluid pump motor
76 Headlight wiper relay (342b-G1)
77 Headlight wiper motor RH
78 Headlight wiper motor LH

Diagram 7

H33456

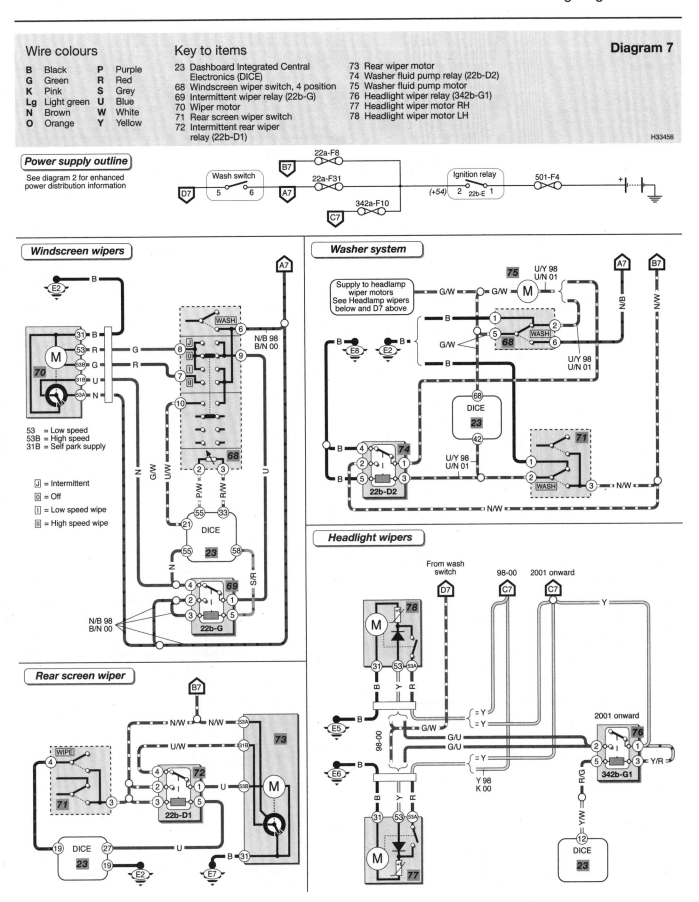

Power supply outline

See diagram 2 for enhanced
power distribution information

Windscreen wipers

53 = Low speed
53B = High speed
31B = Self park supply

[J] = Intermittent
[0] = Off
[I] = Low speed wipe
[III] = High speed wipe

Rear screen wiper

Washer system

Headlight wipers

Wire colours

B	Black	**P**	Purple
G	Green	**R**	Red
K	Pink	**S**	Grey
Lg	Light green	**U**	Blue
N	Brown	**W**	White
O	Orange	**Y**	Yellow

Key to items

Diagram 8

24 Theft Warning & Integrated Central Electronics (TWICE)
77 Drivers door central locking motor
78 Drivers door micro switch
79 Passenger door motor
80 Rear door motor RH
81 Rear door motor LH
82 Locking filler cap solenoid
83 Passenger door micro switch
84 Remote control antenna
85 Window / door switch console
a = drivers door window switch
b = passenger door window switch
c = RH rear door window
d = LH rear door window
e = rear window enable switch
f = central locking switch (all doors)
86 Electric door mirror switch (1998-2000)
87 Electric door mirror switch (2000 on)
88 Drivers door mirror
89 Passenger door mirror
90 Drivers door window motor
91 Passenger door window motor
92 RH rear window motor
93 LH rear window motor
94 RH rear window switch
95 LH rear window switch

H33457

Power supply outline

See diagram 2 for enhanced power distribution information

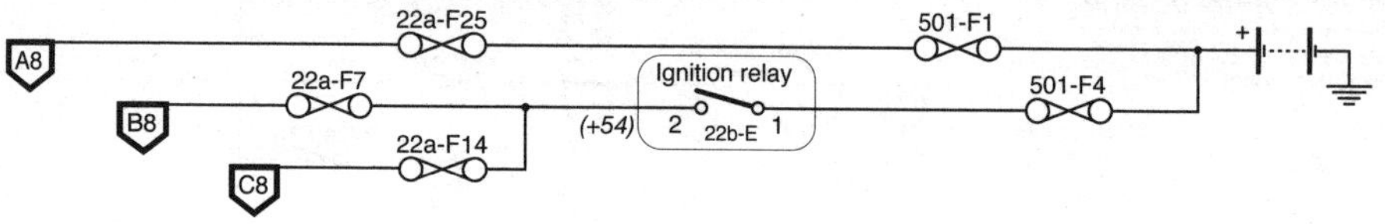

A8
B8
C8
22a-F25
22a-F7
22a-F14
Ignition relay
(+54)
2
22b-E
1
501-F1
501-F4

Typical central locking

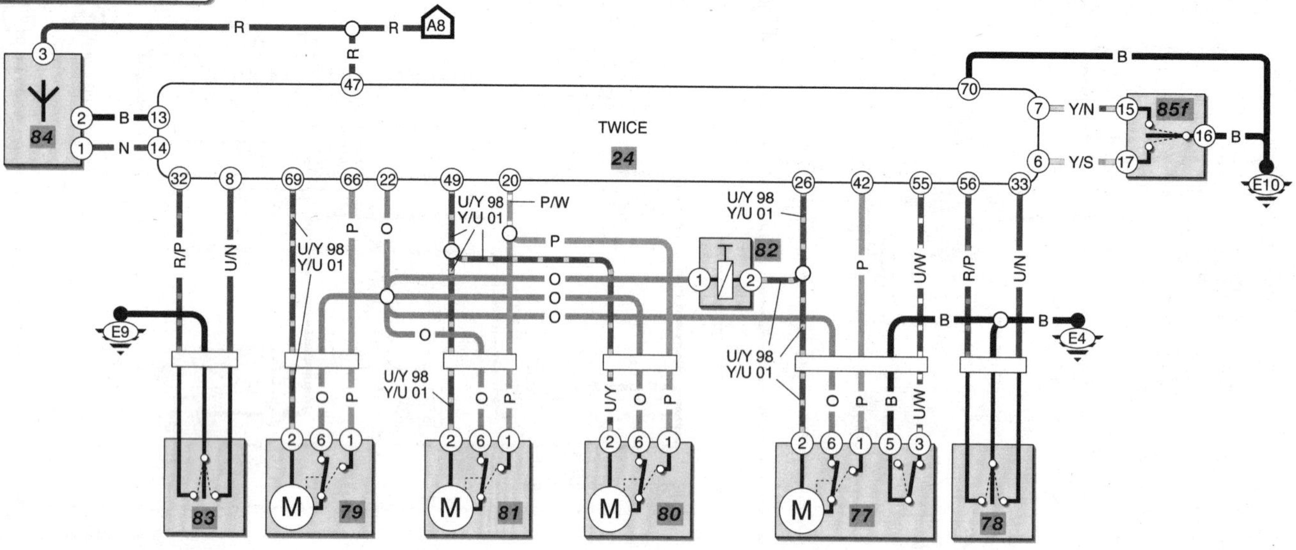

R
A8
TWICE
24
84
E9
E4
E10
85f
82
83
79
81
80
77
78
M
U/Y 98
Y/U 01
P/W
R/P
U/N
U/W
Y/N
Y/S

Motorised door mirrors

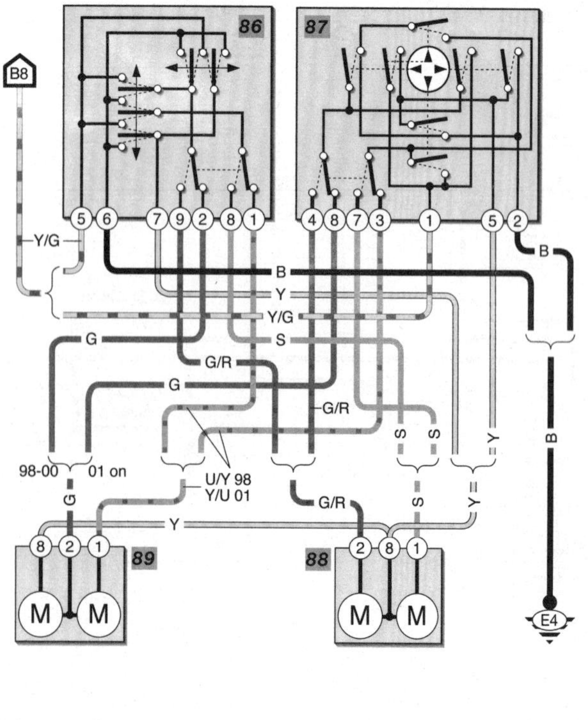

86
87
B8
Y/G
B
Y
S
G
G/R
98-00
01 on
U/Y 98
Y/U 01
89
88
E4
M

Motorised window lifts

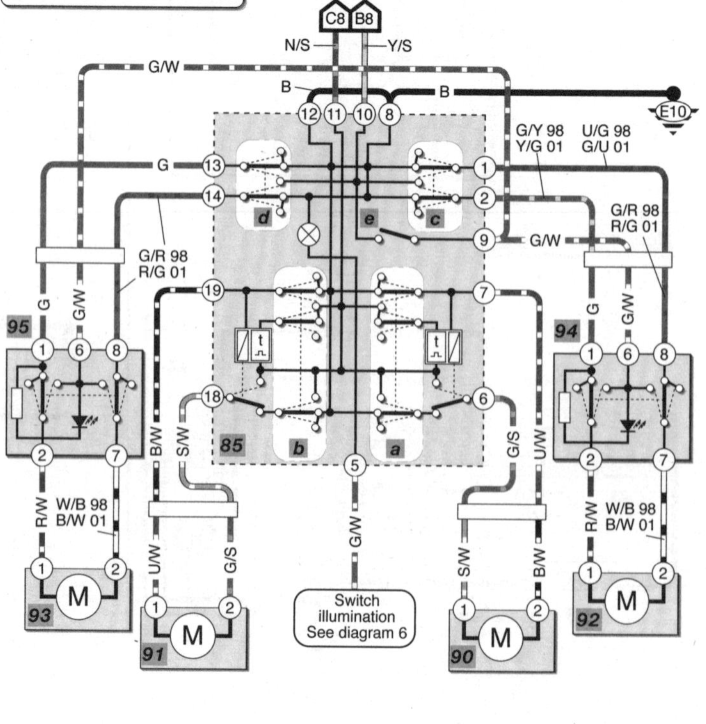

C8
B8
N/S
Y/S
G/W
E10
G/Y 98
Y/G 01
U/G 98
G/U 01
G/R 98
R/G 01
95
94
85
a
b
c
d
e
R/W
W/B 98
B/W 01
U/W
G/S
S/W
93
91
90
92
Switch illumination
See diagram 6
M

Wire colours

B	Black	P	Purple
G	Green	R	Red
K	Pink	S	Grey
Lg	Light green	U	Blue
N	Brown	W	White
O	Orange	Y	Yellow

Key to items

8 Fuel pump relay (22b-L)
14 Main instrument unit
23 Dashboard Integrated Central
    Electronics (DICE)
24 Theft Warning & Integrated
    Central Electronics (TWICE)
25 Saab Information Display (SID)

85 Window / door switch console
    g = sunroof switch
96 Sunroof motor
97 Cigar lighter
98 Instrument bus (I-Bus) (CAN)
99 Power train bus (P-Bus) (CAN)
100 EDC15 engine management ECU
101 Trionic engine management ECU

102 Motronic engine management ECU
103 Supplimentary restraint system
104 Diagnostics data link connector

Diagram 9

H33458

Power supply outline

See diagram 2 for enhanced
power distribution information

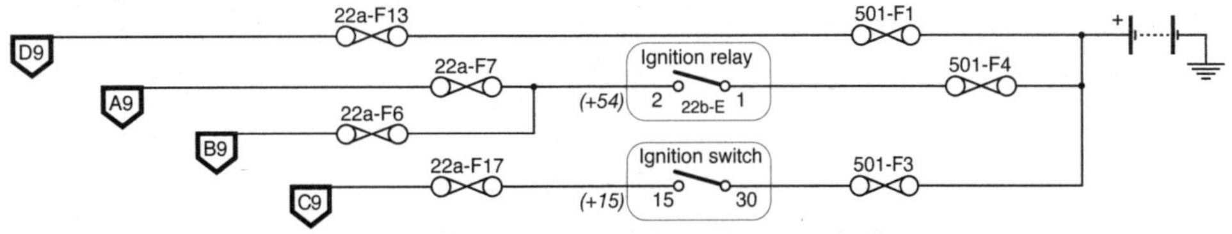

22a-F13 501-F1
22a-F7 Ignition relay 501-F4
(+54) 2 22b-E 1
22a-F6
22a-F17 Ignition switch 501-F3
(+15) 15 30

D9 A9 B9 C9

Electric sunroof

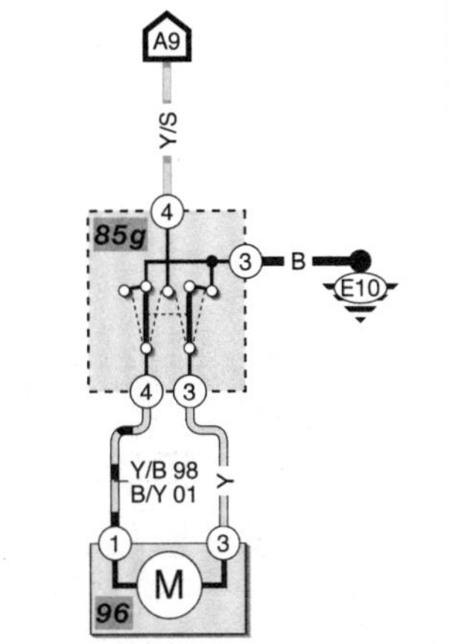

A9
Y/S
85g
B
E10
Y/B 98
B/Y 01
Y
96 M

Cigar lighter

B9
N/R
G/W Switch & control
illumination
See diagram 6
97
B
E2

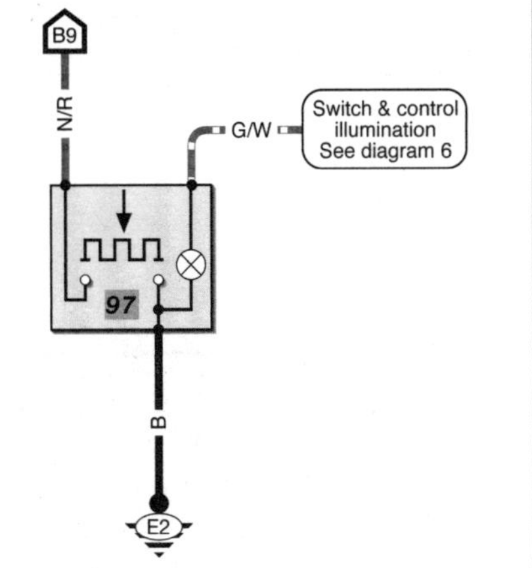

Pre-wired telephone connector

Type TEL1 (handsfree phone) connector, located behind side panel of centre console.
Antenna connector behind radio compartment.

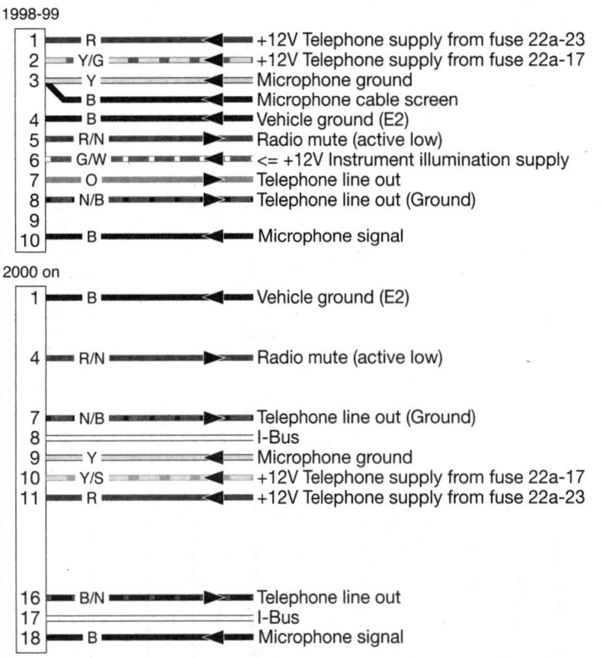

1998-99

1	R	+12V Telephone supply from fuse 22a-23
2	Y/G	+12V Telephone supply from fuse 22a-17
3	Y	Microphone ground
	B	Microphone cable screen
4	B	Vehicle ground (E2)
5	R/N	Radio mute (active low)
6	G/W	<= +12V Instrument illumination supply
7	O	Telephone line out
8	N/B	Telephone line out (Ground)
9		
10	B	Microphone signal

2000 on

1	B	Vehicle ground (E2)
4	R/N	Radio mute (active low)
7	N/B	Telephone line out (Ground)
8		I-Bus
9	Y	Microphone ground
10	Y/S	+12V Telephone supply from fuse 22a-17
11	R	+12V Telephone supply from fuse 22a-23
16	B/N	Telephone line out
17		I-Bus
18	B	Microphone signal

Pre-wired trailer connector

Located beneath left rear light cluster
in luggage compartment

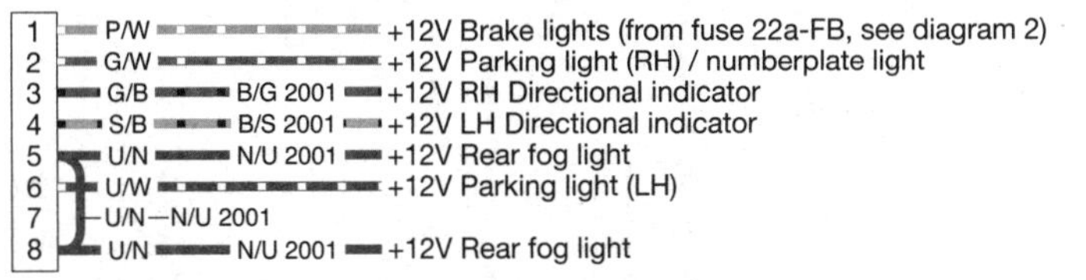

1	P/W		+12V Brake lights (from fuse 22a-FB, see diagram 2)
2	G/W		+12V Parking light (RH) / numberplate light
3	G/B	B/G 2001	+12V RH Directional indicator
4	S/B	B/S 2001	+12V LH Directional indicator
5	U/N	N/U 2001	+12V Rear fog light
6	U/W		+12V Parking light (LH)
7	U/N—N/U 2001		
8	U/N	N/U 2001	+12V Rear fog light

Bus schematic and diagnostic connector

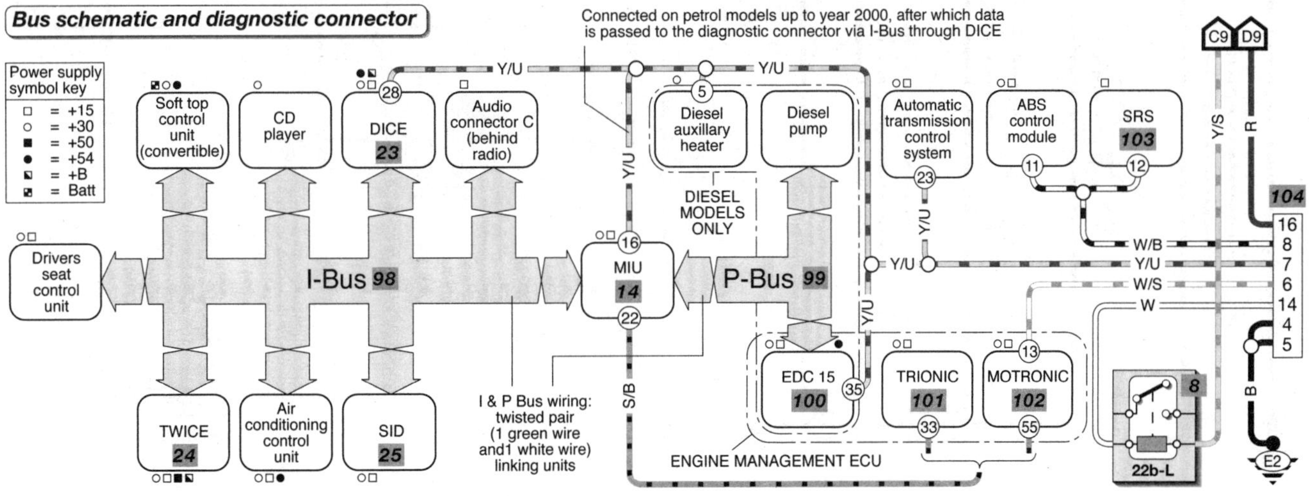

Connected on petrol models up to year 2000, after which data
is passed to the diagnostic connector via I-Bus through DICE

Power supply symbol key
☐ = +15
○ = +30
■ = +50
● = +54
▣ = +B
▨ = Batt

Soft top control unit (convertible)
CD player
DICE 23
Audio connector C (behind radio)
Diesel auxillary heater
Diesel pump
Automatic transmission control system
ABS control module
SRS 103

DIESEL MODELS ONLY

Drivers seat control unit
I-Bus 98
MIU 14
P-Bus 99

Y/U

C9 D9
Y/S R

104
16
8
7
6
14
4
5

W/B
Y/U
W/S
W

TWICE 24
Air conditioning control unit
SID 25

I & P Bus wiring:
twisted pair
(1 green wire
and 1 white wire)
linking units

EDC 15 100
TRIONIC 101
MOTRONIC 102

ENGINE MANAGEMENT ECU

8
22b-L

B
E2

Wire colours

B	Black	P	Purple
G	Green	R	Red
K	Pink	S	Grey
Lg	Light green	U	Blue
N	Brown	W	White
O	Orange	Y	Yellow

Key to items

23 Dashboard Integrated Central Electronics (DICE)
88 Drivers door mirror
   b = heating element
89 Passengers door mirror
   b = heating element
105 Anti-lock brake system
106 Wheel sensor, front right

107 Wheel sensor, front left
108 Wheel sensor, rear right
109 Wheel sensor, rear, left
110 Heater and ventilation controls
   a = recirculation switch
   b = heated rear window switch
   c = air conditioning switch
   d = fan speed selector

111 Recirculation flap motor
112 Ventilation fan
113 Rear window heater & heated mirrors (22b-H)
114 Rear window heating element

Diagram 10

H33459

Power supply outline

See diagram 2 for enhanced power distribution information

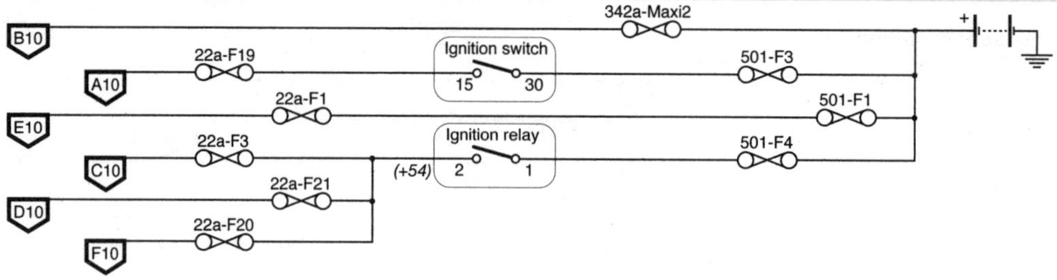

Anti-lock brake system

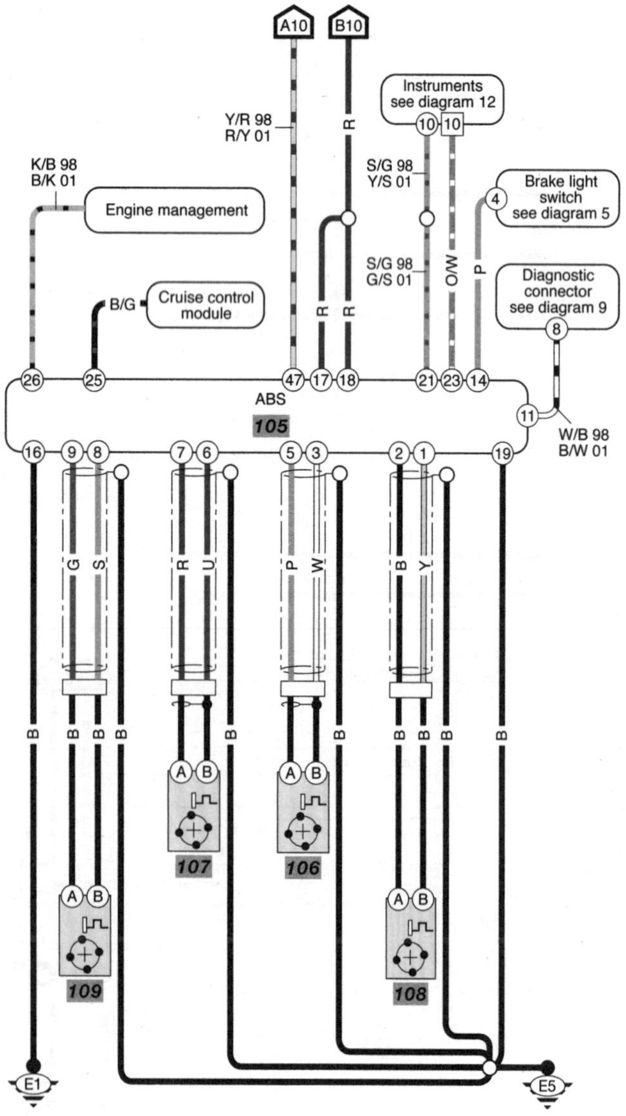

Heating and ventilation controls

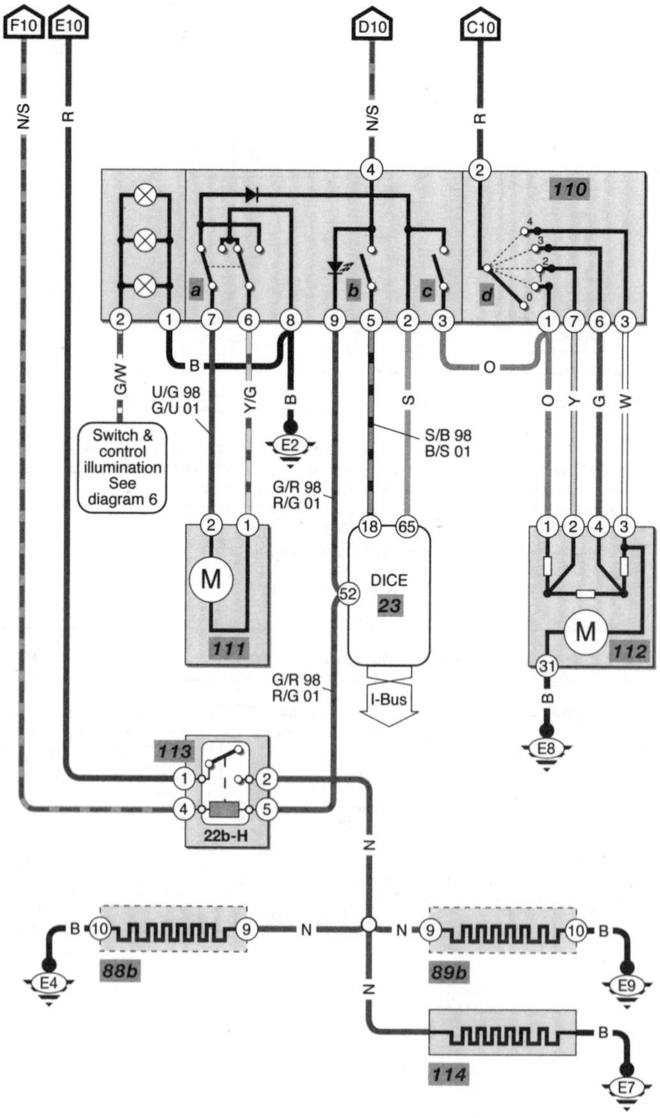

Wire colours

B	Black	P	Purple
G	Green	R	Red
K	Pink	S	Grey
Lg	Light green	U	Blue
N	Brown	W	White
O	Orange	Y	Yellow

Key to items

23 Dashboard Integrated Central Electronics (DICE)
24 Theft Warning and Integrated Central Electronics (TWICE)
116 Luggage compartment light/switch
117 Luggage compartment illumination switch
118 Interior light switch
119 Light (front, roof)
120 Light (centre, roof)
121 Make-up mirror light RH
122 Make-up mirror light LH
123 Glove box light/switch
125 Main audio unit (dashboard)
126 Amplifier (behind centre console) (Saab audio system III only)
127 CD auto changer
128 Motorised radio antenna
129 Front speakers (dashboard) a = right, b = left
130 Rear speakers (parcel shelf) a = right, b = left
131 Door speakers a = right, b = left

Diagram 11

H33460

Power supply outline

See diagram 2 for enhanced power distribution information

Interior and luggage compartment lighting

Typical audio system

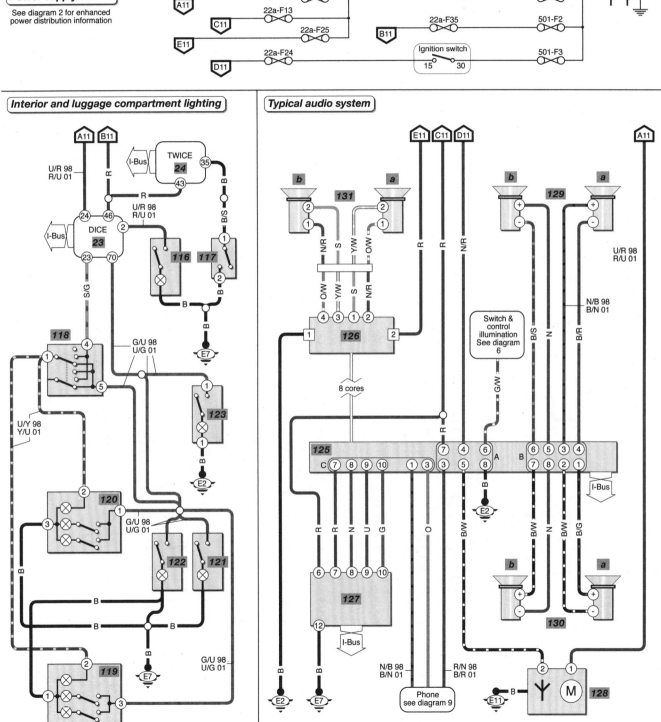

Wire colours

B	Black	**P**	Purple
G	Green	**R**	Red
K	Pink	**S**	Grey
Lg	Light green	**U**	Blue
N	Brown	**W**	White
O	Orange	**Y**	Yellow

Key to items

14 Main instrument unit
132 Handbrake switch
133 Brake fluid level switch

Diagram 12

H33461

Power supply outline

See diagram 2 for enhanced power distribution information

Instruments

Notes:

1. P-Bus interface not fitted to 98-99 petrol models.
2. BD indicates bus derived signals, in which case the signals are taken from the P-Bus and not the connectorised interface quoted.
3. N/C indicates interface not connected to vehicle wiring loom.
4. Interfaces marked with a cross indicate that the interface is not fitted to the main instrument unit of that vehicle type / year.

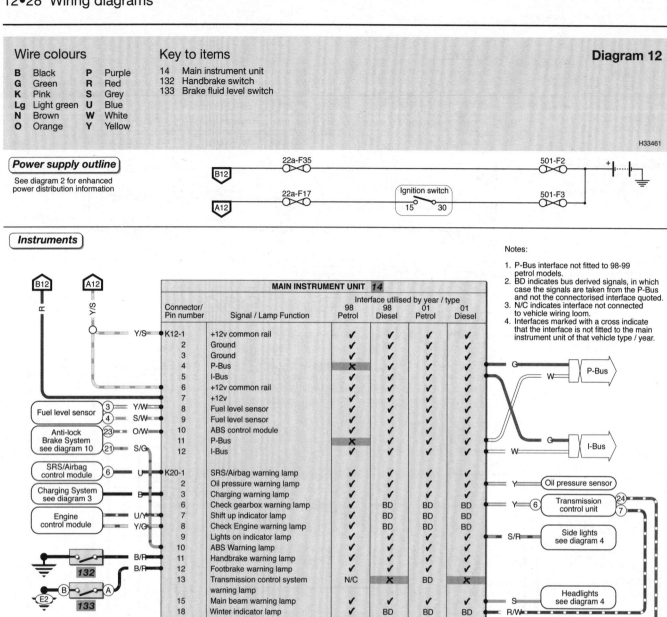

Diagram 13

Passenger compartment fuse box (22a) 4

Fuse	Rating	Function
FA	30A	Trailer hitch connector
FB	10A	Brake light, trailer connector
FC	30A	Ventilation fan automatic climate control
F1	30A	Heated rear window and door mirrors
F2	20A	DICE, Direction indicators
F3	30A	Ventilation fan (manual control)
F4	15A	Interior lighting, Motorised antenna
F5	30A	Electrically adjustable seat RH
F6	30A	Cigar lighter
F6A	7.5A	Automatic transmission control system
F7	30A	Electric window lifts, Rear sunroof, Door mirrors
F8	15A	Rear window wiper
F9	7.5A	Automatic climate control
F10	10A	1998 - Not used
		2001 - Horn
F11	7.5A	DICE/TWICE
F12	20A	Brake lights, DICE, Fog lights
F13	15A	Radio, Data link connector
F14	30A	Electric window lifts, Front solenoid valves, Soft top
F15	20A	Daylight driving lights
F16	30A	Electrically adjustable seat LH
F16B	30A	1998 - Engine management system
		2001 - As 98 + (Petrol) Injectors, Mass air flow sensor
		(Diesel) Glow plugs, Mass air flow sensor
F17	15A	1998 - Engine management system, Main instruments,
		DICE/TWICE, Powered seat memory
		2001 - As 98 + SID, Pedal switches, Cruise control
F18	10A	Airbag, Secondary restraint system
F19	10A	ABS, Rear fog lights, Air conditioning
F20	10A	Electrically heated seats
F21	10A	Manual air conditioning, Soft top
F22	15A	1998 - Cruise control system, DICE, Direction indicators
		2001 - As 98 + Cruise control
F23	20A	Soft top, Telephone connector
F24	7.5A	Radio
F25	30A	Central locking system, Tank hatch solenoid
F26	7.5A	1998 - Heated rear seat
	30A	1999 - Trionic T7
F27	15A	Main beam flash, Automatic climate control system
F28	10A	1998 - Engine management system
		2001 - Trionic T7
F29	10A	Parking light, Rear number plate light
F30	10A	LH parking light
F31	20A	Windscren wipers, Reversing light, Headlight levelling
F32	15A	Fuel pump (petrol)
F33	15A	Electrically heated seat
F34	10A	SID, Automatic transmission control system
F35	15A	Main instruments, Make-up lights, DICE/TWICE
F36	10A	Starter motor relay
F37	15A	1998 - Diesel fuel filter heater
		1999 - As 98 + Limp home solenoid
F38	25A	1998 - Oxygen sensor
	15A	1999 - As 98 + Diesel fuel pump
		2001 - As 99 + Mass air flow sensor, Control valve unit, EGR

Engine compartment fuse box (342a) 3

Fuse	Rating	Function
F1	10A	1998 - Horn
		2001 - Not used
F2	15A	Fog lights
F3	40A	Radiator fan, low speed
F4	10A	1998 - Vacuum pump
		2001 - Not used
F5	15A	Air conditioning compressor
F6	10A	LH Dip headlight
F7	10A	RH Dip headlight
F8	10A	LH Main beam headlight
F9	10A	RH Main beam headlight
F10	7.5A	Headlight wipers
F11	10A	Headlight levelling
F12	-	(Spot lights)
F13	7.5A	1998 - APC
		2001 - Not used
F14	10A	Diesel parking heater connection
F15	15A	Diesel auxillary heater
Maxi1	30A	Radiator fan, high speed
Maxi2	50A	Anti lock braking system
MaxiF1	60A	Diesel glow plugs
MaxiF2	-	Not used

Engine compartment fuse box (501) 2

Fuse	Rating	Function
F1	60A	+30 circuit fuse, supply to fuse box 22a
F1	60A	+30 circuit fuse, supply to fuse box 22a
F1	60A	+50/+54/+15/+X/+B circuit fuse, supply to ignition switch
F1	60A	+54 circuit fuse, supply via ignition relay
F1	60A	Soft top hydraulic opening system

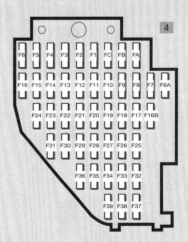

Location: Dashboard RHS by drivers door

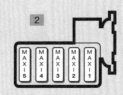

Location: Engine bay by battery

Location: Inside dashboard next to steering column

H33462

Dimensions and weights

Note: *All figures are approximate, and vary according to model. Refer to manufacturer's data for exact figures.*

Dimensions

Overall length (including bumpers	4629 to 4639 mm
Overall width (including wing mirrors)	1936 mm
Overall height:	
Hatchback and Coupe	1428 mm
Cabriolet*	2200 mm
Maximum clearance required when soft top is operated.	
Wheelbase	2605 mm
Track width:	
Front	1452 to 1466 mm
Rear	1442 to 1456 mm
Ground clearance (at max weight)	100 mm
Turning circle diameter:	
Wall-to-wall.	11.1 m
Kerb-to-kerb.	10.5 m

Weights

Kerb weight	1325 to 1510 kg
Maximum axle load, front.	1045 kg
Maximum axle load, rear	875 kg
Maximum roof rack load	100 kg
Maximum towing weight:	
Unbraked trailer	750 kg
Braked trailer	1600 kg

Length (distance)

Inches (in)	x 25.4	= Millimetres (mm)	x 0.0394	= Inches (in)
Feet (ft)	x 0.305	= Metres (m)	x 3.281	= Feet (ft)
Miles	x 1.609	= Kilometres (km)	x 0.621	= Miles

Volume (capacity)

Cubic inches (cu in; in³)	x 16.387	= Cubic centimetres (cc; cm³)	x 0.061	= Cubic inches (cu in; in³)
Imperial pints (Imp pt)	x 0.568	= Litres (l)	x 1.76	= Imperial pints (Imp pt)
Imperial quarts (Imp qt)	x 1.137	= Litres (l)	x 0.88	= Imperial quarts (Imp qt)
Imperial quarts (Imp qt)	x 1.201	= US quarts (US qt)	x 0.833	= Imperial quarts (Imp qt)
US quarts (US qt)	x 0.946	= Litres (l)	x 1.057	= US quarts (US qt)
Imperial gallons (Imp gal)	x 4.546	= Litres (l)	x 0.22	= Imperial gallons (Imp gal)
Imperial gallons (Imp gal)	x 1.201	= US gallons (US gal)	x 0.833	= Imperial gallons (Imp gal)
US gallons (US gal)	x 3.785	= Litres (l)	x 0.264	= US gallons (US gal)

Mass (weight)

Ounces (oz)	x 28.35	= Grams (g)	x 0.035	= Ounces (oz)
Pounds (lb)	x 0.454	= Kilograms (kg)	x 2.205	= Pounds (lb)

Force

Ounces-force (ozf; oz)	x 0.278	= Newtons (N)	x 3.6	= Ounces-force (ozf; oz)
Pounds-force (lbf; lb)	x 4.448	= Newtons (N)	x 0.225	= Pounds-force (lbf; lb)
Newtons (N)	x 0.1	= Kilograms-force (kgf; kg)	x 9.81	= Newtons (N)

Pressure

Pounds-force per square inch (psi; lbf/in²; lb/in²)	x 0.070	= Kilograms-force per square centimetre (kgf/cm²; kg/cm²)	x 14.223	= Pounds-force per square inch (psi; lbf/in²; lb/in²)
Pounds-force per square inch (psi; lbf/in²; lb/in²)	x 0.068	= Atmospheres (atm)	x 14.696	= Pounds-force per square inch (psi; lbf/in²; lb/in²)
Pounds-force per square inch (psi; lbf/in²; lb/in²)	x 0.069	= Bars	x 14.5	= Pounds-force per square inch (psi; lbf/in²; lb/in²)
Pounds-force per square inch (psi; lbf/in²; lb/in²)	x 6.895	= Kilopascals (kPa)	x 0.145	= Pounds-force per square inch (psi; lbf/in²; lb/in²)
Kilopascals (kPa)	x 0.01	= Kilograms-force per square centimetre (kgf/cm²; kg/cm²)	x 98.1	= Kilopascals (kPa)
Millibar (mbar)	x 100	= Pascals (Pa)	x 0.01	= Millibar (mbar)
Millibar (mbar)	x 0.0145	= Pounds-force per square inch (psi; lbf/in²; lb/in²)	x 68.947	= Millibar (mbar)
Millibar (mbar)	x 0.75	= Millimetres of mercury (mmHg)	x 1.333	= Millibar (mbar)
Millibar (mbar)	x 0.401	= Inches of water (inH₂O)	x 2.491	= Millibar (mbar)
Millimetres of mercury (mmHg)	x 0.535	= Inches of water (inH₂O)	x 1.868	= Millimetres of mercury (mmHg)
Inches of water (inH₂O)	x 0.036	= Pounds-force per square inch (psi; lbf/in²; lb/in²)	x 27.68	= Inches of water (inH₂O)

Torque (moment of force)

Pounds-force inches (lbf in; lb in)	x 1.152	= Kilograms-force centimetre (kgf cm; kg cm)	x 0.868	= Pounds-force inches (lbf in; lb in)
Pounds-force inches (lbf in; lb in)	x 0.113	= Newton metres (Nm)	x 8.85	= Pounds-force inches (lbf in; lb in)
Pounds-force inches (lbf in; lb in)	x 0.083	= Pounds-force feet (lbf ft; lb ft)	x 12	= Pounds-force inches (lbf in; lb in)
Pounds-force feet (lbf ft; lb ft)	x 0.138	= Kilograms-force metres (kgf m; kg m)	x 7.233	= Pounds-force feet (lbf ft; lb ft)
Pounds-force feet (lbf ft; lb ft)	x 1.356	= Newton metres (Nm)	x 0.738	= Pounds-force feet (lbf ft; lb ft)
Newton metres (Nm)	x 0.102	= Kilograms-force metres (kgf m; kg m)	x 9.804	= Newton metres (Nm)

Power

Horsepower (hp)	x 745.7	= Watts (W)	x 0.0013	= Horsepower (hp)

Velocity (speed)

Miles per hour (miles/hr; mph)	x 1.609	= Kilometres per hour (km/hr; kph)	x 0.621	= Miles per hour (miles/hr; mph)

Fuel consumption*

Miles per gallon, Imperial (mpg)	x 0.354	= Kilometres per litre (km/l)	x 2.825	= Miles per gallon, Imperial (mpg)
Miles per gallon, US (mpg)	x 0.425	= Kilometres per litre (km/l)	x 2.352	= Miles per gallon, US (mpg)

Temperature

Degrees Fahrenheit = (°C x 1.8) + 32   Degrees Celsius (Degrees Centigrade; °C) = (°F - 32) x 0.56

It is common practice to convert from miles per gallon (mpg) to litres/100 kilometres (l/100km), where mpg x l/100 km = 282

Spare parts are available from many sources, including maker's appointed garages, accessory shops, and motor factors. To be sure of obtaining the correct parts, it will sometimes be necessary to quote the vehicle identification number. If possible, it can also be useful to take the old parts along for positive identification. Items such as starter motors and alternators may be available under a service exchange scheme – any parts returned should be clean.

Our advice regarding spare parts is as follows.

Officially appointed garages

This is the best source of parts which are peculiar to your car, and which are not otherwise generally available (eg, badges, interior trim, certain body panels, etc). It is also the only place at which you should buy parts if the vehicle is still under warranty.

Accessory shops

These are very good places to buy materials and components needed for the maintenance of your car (oil, air and fuel filters, light bulbs, drivebelts, greases, brake pads, tough-up paint, etc). Components of this nature sold by a reputable shop are of the same standard as those used by the car manufacturer.

Besides components, these shops also sell tools and general accessories, usually have convenient opening hours, charge lower prices, and can often be found close to home. Some accessory shops have parts counters where components needed for almost any repair job can be purchased or ordered.

Motor factors

Good factors will stock all the more important components which wear out comparatively quickly, and can sometimes supply individual components needed for the overhaul of a larger assembly (eg, brake seals and hydraulic parts, bearing shells, pistons, valves). They may also handle work such as cylinder block reboring, crankshaft regrinding, etc.

Tyre and exhaust specialists

These outlets may be independent, or members of a local or national chain. They frequently offer competitive prices when compared with a main dealer or local garage, but it will pay to obtain several quotes before making a decision. When researching prices, also ask what 'extras' may be added – for instance fitting a new valve and balancing the wheel are both commonly charged on top of the price of a new tyre.

Other sources

Beware of parts or materials obtained from market stalls, car boot sales or similar outlets. Such items are not invariably sub-standard, but there is little chance of compensation if they do prove unsatisfactory. In the case of safety-critical components such as brake pads, there is the risk not only of financial loss, but also of an accident causing injury or death.

Second-hand components or assemblies obtained from a car breaker can be a good buy in some circumstances, but his sort of purchase is best made by the experienced DIY mechanic..

Vehicle identification

Modifications are a continuing and unpublicised process in vehicle manufacture, quite apart from major model changes. Spare parts manuals and lists are compiled upon a numerical basis, the individual vehicle identification numbers being essential to correct identification of the component concerned.

When ordering spare parts, always give as much information as possible. Quote the car model, year of manufacture, body and engine numbers as appropriate.

The *Vehicle Identification Number (VIN)* or *chassis number* appears in several places on the vehicle:
a) On a metal plate riveted to the crossmember at the front right hand side of the engine compartment **(see illustration)**
b) Stamped on the bulkhead at the rear of the engine compartment
c) Printed on a plate, attached to the top of the facia, behind the windscreen

The *Engine number* is stamped on the front left-hand side of the cylinder block.

The *Transmission number* is printed on a plate, attached to the front/top of the transmission casing.

The *Body number* is stamped on a metal plate riveted to the crossmember at the front left hand side of the engine compartment.

The *Paint codes* are printed on a label attached to the trailing edge of the passenger door, next to the tyre pressure chart.

Character 1
B   Petrol engine
D   Diesel engine
Characters 2 & 3
20   1985 cc
22   2171 cc
23   2290 cc
Character 4
3   4 cylinders, in-line block with 2 balancer shafts, single overhead camshaft with 4 valves per cylinder
4   4 cylinders, in-line block with 2 balancer shafts, double overhead camshafts with 4 valves per cylinder
5   4 cylinders, in-line block with 2 balancer shafts, double overhead camshafts with 4 valves per cylinder, low-friction engine
Character 5
i   Fuel injection engine, non-turbo
E   Low-pressure turbocharged engine with intercooler
L   Turbocharged engine with intercooler – Stage 1
R   Turbocharged engine with intercooler – Stage 2

Character 6
D   Saab 9-3
1   Saab 9-3 with exhaust emission control ECE-R15/04
3, 5 and 7
      Saab 9-3 with exhaust emission control to European, Swedish and US standards
Character 7
A   Automatic transmission
M   Manual transmission
Characters 8 & 9
00   Basic engine
18   Engine adapted for automatic
19   Engine with oil cooler
20   Engine with OBD II
Character 10
W   1998
X   1999
Y   2000
1   2001
2   2002
Characters 11 to 16
Serial numbers

Vehicle Identification Number (VIN) stamped on a plate riveted to the engine compartment front crossmember

Whenever servicing, repair or overhaul work is carried out on the car or its components, observe the following procedures and instructions. This will assist in carrying out the operation efficiently and to a professional standard of workmanship.

Joint mating faces and gaskets

When separating components at their mating faces, never insert screwdrivers or similar implements into the joint between the faces in order to prise them apart. This can cause severe damage which results in oil leaks, coolant leaks, etc upon reassembly. Separation is usually achieved by tapping along the joint with a soft-faced hammer in order to break the seal. However, note that this method may not be suitable where dowels are used for component location.

Where a gasket is used between the mating faces of two components, a new one must be fitted on reassembly; fit it dry unless otherwise stated in the repair procedure. Make sure that the mating faces are clean and dry, with all traces of old gasket removed. When cleaning a joint face, use a tool which is unlikely to score or damage the face, and remove any burrs or nicks with an oilstone or fine file.

Make sure that tapped holes are cleaned with a pipe cleaner, and keep them free of jointing compound, if this is being used, unless specifically instructed otherwise.

Ensure that all orifices, channels or pipes are clear, and blow through them, preferably using compressed air.

Oil seals

Oil seals can be removed by levering them out with a wide flat-bladed screwdriver or similar implement. Alternatively, a number of self-tapping screws may be screwed into the seal, and these used as a purchase for pliers or some similar device in order to pull the seal free.

Whenever an oil seal is removed from its working location, either individually or as part of an assembly, it should be renewed.

The very fine sealing lip of the seal is easily damaged, and will not seal if the surface it contacts is not completely clean and free from scratches, nicks or grooves. If the original sealing surface of the component cannot be restored, and the manufacturer has not made provision for slight relocation of the seal relative to the sealing surface, the component should be renewed.

Protect the lips of the seal from any surface which may damage them in the course of fitting. Use tape or a conical sleeve where possible. Lubricate the seal lips with oil before fitting and, on dual-lipped seals, fill the space between the lips with grease.

Unless otherwise stated, oil seals must be fitted with their sealing lips toward the lubricant to be sealed.

Use a tubular drift or block of wood of the appropriate size to install the seal and, if the seal housing is shouldered, drive the seal down to the shoulder. If the seal housing is unshouldered, the seal should be fitted with its face flush with the housing top face (unless otherwise instructed).

Screw threads and fastenings

Seized nuts, bolts and screws are quite a common occurrence where corrosion has set in, and the use of penetrating oil or releasing fluid will often overcome this problem if the offending item is soaked for a while before attempting to release it. The use of an impact driver may also provide a means of releasing such stubborn fastening devices, when used in conjunction with the appropriate screwdriver bit or socket. If none of these methods works, it may be necessary to resort to the careful application of heat, or the use of a hacksaw or nut splitter device.

Studs are usually removed by locking two nuts together on the threaded part, and then using a spanner on the lower nut to unscrew the stud. Studs or bolts which have broken off below the surface of the component in which they are mounted can sometimes be removed using a stud extractor. Always ensure that a blind tapped hole is completely free from oil, grease, water or other fluid before installing the bolt or stud. Failure to do this could cause the housing to crack due to the hydraulic action of the bolt or stud as it is screwed in.

When tightening a castellated nut to accept a split pin, tighten the nut to the specified torque, where applicable, and then tighten further to the next split pin hole. Never slacken the nut to align the split pin hole, unless stated in the repair procedure.

When checking or retightening a nut or bolt to a specified torque setting, slacken the nut or bolt by a quarter of a turn, and then retighten to the specified setting. However, this should not be attempted where angular tightening has been used.

For some screw fastenings, notably cylinder head bolts or nuts, torque wrench settings are no longer specified for the latter stages of tightening, "angle-tightening" being called up instead. Typically, a fairly low torque wrench setting will be applied to the bolts/nuts in the correct sequence, followed by one or more stages of tightening through specified angles.

Locknuts, locktabs and washers

Any fastening which will rotate against a component or housing during tightening should always have a washer between it and the relevant component or housing.

Spring or split washers should always be renewed when they are used to lock a critical component such as a big-end bearing retaining bolt or nut. Locktabs which are folded over to retain a nut or bolt should always be renewed.

Self-locking nuts can be re-used in non-critical areas, providing resistance can be felt when the locking portion passes over the bolt or stud thread. However, it should be noted that self-locking stiffnuts tend to lose their effectiveness after long periods of use, and should then be renewed as a matter of course.

Split pins must always be replaced with new ones of the correct size for the hole.

When thread-locking compound is found on the threads of a fastener which is to be re-used, it should be cleaned off with a wire brush and solvent, and fresh compound applied on reassembly.

Special tools

Some repair procedures in this manual entail the use of special tools such as a press, two or three-legged pullers, spring compressors, etc. Wherever possible, suitable readily-available alternatives to the manufacturer's special tools are described, and are shown in use. In some instances, where no alternative is possible, it has been necessary to resort to the use of a manufacturer's tool, and this has been done for reasons of safety as well as the efficient completion of the repair operation. Unless you are highly-skilled and have a thorough understanding of the procedures described, never attempt to bypass the use of any special tool when the procedure described specifies its use. Not only is there a very great risk of personal injury, but expensive damage could be caused to the components involved.

Environmental considerations

When disposing of used engine oil, brake fluid, antifreeze, etc, give due consideration to any detrimental environmental effects. Do not, for instance, pour any of the above liquids down drains into the general sewage system, or onto the ground to soak away. Many local council refuse tips provide a facility for waste oil disposal, as do some garages. If none of these facilities are available, consult your local Environmental Health Department, or the National Rivers Authority, for further advice.

With the universal tightening-up of legislation regarding the emission of environmentally-harmful substances from motor vehicles, most vehicles have tamperproof devices fitted to the main adjustment points of the fuel system. These devices are primarily designed to prevent unqualified persons from adjusting the fuel/air mixture, with the chance of a consequent increase in toxic emissions. If such devices are found during servicing or overhaul, they should, wherever possible, be renewed or refitted in accordance with the manufacturer's requirements or current legislation.

Note: It is antisocial and illegal to dump oil down the drain. To find the location of your local oil recycling bank, call this number free.

OIL BANK LINE
0800 66 33 66
www.oilbankline.org.uk

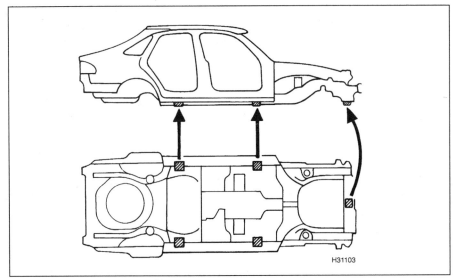

Jacking points for hydraulic jack (arrowed)

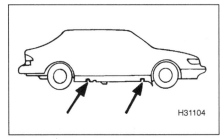

Wheel changing jacking points (arrowed)

The jack supplied with the vehicle tool kit should only be used for changing the roadwheels – see *Wheel changing* at the front of this manual. When carrying out any other kind of work, raise the vehicle using a hydraulic trolley jack, and always supplement the jack with axle stands positioned under the vehicle jacking points.

When using a trolley jack or axle stands, always position the jack head or axle stand head under, or adjacent to one of the relevant wheel changing jacking points under the sills.

Use a block of wood between the jack or axle stand and the sill – the block of wood should have a groove cut into it, in which the welded flange of the sill will locate **(see illustrations)**.

Do **not** attempt to jack the vehicle under the rear axle, floorpan, engine sump, automatic transmission sump, or any of the suspension components.

The jack supplied with the vehicle locates in the jacking points on the underside of the sills – see *Wheel changing* at the front of this manual. Ensure that the jack head is correctly engaged before attempting to raise the vehicle.

Never work under, around, or near a raised vehicle, unless it is adequately supported in at least two places.

Disconnecting the battery

Note: *If a non-standard radio/cassette unit is installed, note the security code before disconnecting the battery.*

 Warning: Never disconnect the battery while the engine is running.

1 The battery is located on the front left-hand side of the engine compartment.
2 Lift off the battery heat protection cover/box, then slacken the battery negative (-) terminal and lift it from the battery post. Always disconnect the negative terminal first.

3 Similarly slacken the battery positive (+) terminal and lift it from the battery post.
4 When re-connecting the battery terminals, always connect the negative terminal last.

Radio/cassette unit anti-theft system – precautions

The radio/cassette unit fitted may be equipped with a built-in security code, to deter thieves. If the power source to the unit is cut, the anti-theft system will activate. Even if the power source is immediately reconnected, the radio/cassette unit will not function until the correct security code has been entered. Therefore if you do not know the correct security code for the unit, **do not** disconnect the battery negative lead, or remove the radio/cassette unit from the vehicle.

If the security code is lost or forgotten, seek the advice of your Saab dealer. On presentation of proof of ownership, a Saab dealer will be able to provide you with a new security code.

Introduction

A selection of good tools is a fundamental requirement for anyone contemplating the maintenance and repair of a motor vehicle. For the owner who does not possess any, their purchase will prove a considerable expense, offsetting some of the savings made by doing-it-yourself. However, provided that the tools purchased meet the relevant national safety standards and are of good quality, they will last for many years and prove an extremely worthwhile investment.

To help the average owner to decide which tools are needed to carry out the various tasks detailed in this manual, we have compiled three lists of tools under the following headings: *Maintenance and minor repair, Repair and overhaul*, and *Special*. Newcomers to practical mechanics should start off with the *Maintenance and minor repair* tool kit, and confine themselves to the simpler jobs around the vehicle. Then, as confidence and experience grow, more difficult tasks can be undertaken, with extra tools being purchased as, and when, they are needed. In this way, a *Maintenance and minor repair* tool kit can be built up into a *Repair and overhaul* tool kit over a considerable period of time, without any major cash outlays. The experienced do-it-yourselfer will have a tool kit good enough for most repair and overhaul procedures, and will add tools from the *Special* category when it is felt that the expense is justified by the amount of use to which these tools will be put.

Maintenance and minor repair tool kit

The tools given in this list should be considered as a minimum requirement if routine maintenance, servicing and minor repair operations are to be undertaken. We recommend the purchase of combination spanners (ring one end, open-ended the other); although more expensive than open-ended ones, they do give the advantages of both types of spanner.

☐ *Combination spanners:*
Metric - 8 to 19 mm inclusive
☐ *Adjustable spanner - 35 mm jaw (approx.)*
☐ *Spark plug spanner (with rubber insert) - petrol models*
☐ *Spark plug gap adjustment tool - petrol models*
☐ *Set of feeler gauges*
☐ *Brake bleed nipple spanner*
☐ *Screwdrivers:*
Flat blade - 100 mm long x 6 mm dia
Cross blade - 100 mm long x 6 mm dia
Torx - various sizes (not all vehicles)
☐ *Combination pliers*
☐ *Hacksaw (junior)*
☐ *Tyre pump*
☐ *Tyre pressure gauge*
☐ *Oil can*
☐ *Oil filter removal tool*
☐ *Fine emery cloth*
☐ *Wire brush (small)*
☐ *Funnel (medium size)*
☐ *Sump drain plug key (not all vehicles)*

Repair and overhaul tool kit

These tools are virtually essential for anyone undertaking any major repairs to a motor vehicle, and are additional to those given in the *Maintenance and minor repair* list. Included in this list is a comprehensive set of sockets. Although these are expensive, they will be found invaluable as they are so versatile - particularly if various drives are included in the set. We recommend the half-inch square-drive type, as this can be used with most proprietary torque wrenches.

The tools in this list will sometimes need to be supplemented by tools from the *Special* list:

☐ *Sockets (or box spanners) to cover range in previous list (including Torx sockets)*
☐ *Reversible ratchet drive (for use with sockets)*
☐ *Extension piece, 250 mm (for use with sockets)*
☐ *Universal joint (for use with sockets)*
☐ *Flexible handle or sliding T "breaker bar" (for use with sockets)*
☐ *Torque wrench (for use with sockets)*
☐ *Self-locking grips*
☐ *Ball pein hammer*
☐ *Soft-faced mallet (plastic or rubber)*
☐ *Screwdrivers:*
Flat blade - long & sturdy, short (chubby), and narrow (electrician's) types
Cross blade - long & sturdy, and short (chubby) types
☐ *Pliers:*
Long-nosed
Side cutters (electrician's)
Circlip (internal and external)
☐ *Cold chisel - 25 mm*
☐ *Scriber*
☐ *Scraper*
☐ *Centre-punch*
☐ *Pin punch*
☐ *Hacksaw*
☐ *Brake hose clamp*
☐ *Brake/clutch bleeding kit*
☐ *Selection of twist drills*
☐ *Steel rule/straight-edge*
☐ *Allen keys (inc. splined/Torx type)*
☐ *Selection of files*
☐ *Wire brush*
☐ *Axle stands*
☐ *Jack (strong trolley or hydraulic type)*
☐ *Light with extension lead*
☐ *Universal electrical multi-meter*

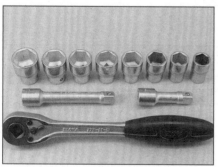

Sockets and reversible ratchet drive

Brake bleeding kit

Torx key, socket and bit

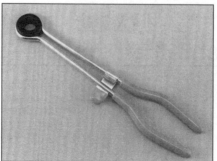

Hose clamp

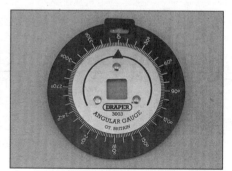

Angular-tightening gauge

Special tools

The tools in this list are those which are not used regularly, are expensive to buy, or which need to be used in accordance with their manufacturers' instructions. Unless relatively difficult mechanical jobs are undertaken frequently, it will not be economic to buy many of these tools. Where this is the case, you could consider clubbing together with friends (or joining a motorists' club) to make a joint purchase, or borrowing the tools against a deposit from a local garage or tool hire specialist. It is worth noting that many of the larger DIY superstores now carry a large range of special tools for hire at modest rates.

The following list contains only those tools and instruments freely available to the public, and not those special tools produced by the vehicle manufacturer specifically for its dealer network. You will find occasional references to these manufacturers' special tools in the text of this manual. Generally, an alternative method of doing the job without the vehicle manufacturers' special tool is given. However, sometimes there is no alternative to using them. Where this is the case and the relevant tool cannot be bought or borrowed, you will have to entrust the work to a dealer.

- [ ] Angular-tightening gauge
- [ ] Valve spring compressor
- [ ] Valve grinding tool
- [ ] Piston ring compressor
- [ ] Piston ring removal/installation tool
- [ ] Cylinder bore hone
- [ ] Balljoint separator
- [ ] Coil spring compressors (where applicable)
- [ ] Two/three-legged hub and bearing puller
- [ ] Impact screwdriver
- [ ] Micrometer and/or vernier calipers
- [ ] Dial gauge
- [ ] Stroboscopic timing light
- [ ] Dwell angle meter/tachometer
- [ ] Fault code reader
- [ ] Cylinder compression gauge
- [ ] Hand-operated vacuum pump and gauge
- [ ] Clutch plate alignment set
- [ ] Brake shoe steady spring cup removal tool
- [ ] Bush and bearing removal/installation set
- [ ] Stud extractors
- [ ] Tap and die set
- [ ] Lifting tackle
- [ ] Trolley jack

Buying tools

Reputable motor accessory shops and superstores often offer excellent quality tools at discount prices, so it pays to shop around.

Remember, you don't have to buy the most expensive items on the shelf, but it is always advisable to steer clear of the very cheap tools. Beware of 'bargains' offered on market stalls or at car boot sales. There are plenty of good tools around at reasonable prices, but always aim to purchase items which meet the relevant national safety standards. If in doubt, ask the proprietor or manager of the shop for advice before making a purchase.

Care and maintenance of tools

Having purchased a reasonable tool kit, it is necessary to keep the tools in a clean and serviceable condition. After use, always wipe off any dirt, grease and metal particles using a clean, dry cloth, before putting the tools away. Never leave them lying around after they have been used. A simple tool rack on the garage or workshop wall for items such as screwdrivers and pliers is a good idea. Store all normal spanners and sockets in a metal box. Any measuring instruments, gauges, meters, etc, must be carefully stored where they cannot be damaged or become rusty.

Take a little care when tools are used. Hammer heads inevitably become marked, and screwdrivers lose the keen edge on their blades from time to time. A little timely attention with emery cloth or a file will soon restore items like this to a good finish.

Working facilities

Not to be forgotten when discussing tools is the workshop itself. If anything more than routine maintenance is to be carried out, a suitable working area becomes essential.

It is appreciated that many an owner-mechanic is forced by circumstances to remove an engine or similar item without the benefit of a garage or workshop. Having done this, any repairs should always be done under the cover of a roof.

Wherever possible, any dismantling should be done on a clean, flat workbench or table at a suitable working height.

Any workbench needs a vice; one with a jaw opening of 100 mm is suitable for most jobs. As mentioned previously, some clean dry storage space is also required for tools, as well as for any lubricants, cleaning fluids, touch-up paints etc, which become necessary.

Another item which may be required, and which has a much more general usage, is an electric drill with a chuck capacity of at least 8 mm. This, together with a good range of twist drills, is virtually essential for fitting accessories.

Last, but not least, always keep a supply of old newspapers and clean, lint-free rags available, and try to keep any working area as clean as possible.

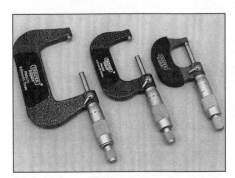

Micrometers

Dial test indicator ("dial gauge")

Strap wrench

Compression tester

Fault code reader

This is a guide to getting your vehicle through the MOT test. Obviously it will not be possible to examine the vehicle to the same standard as the professional MOT tester. However, working through the following checks will enable you to identify any problem areas before submitting the vehicle for the test.

Where a testable component is in borderline condition, the tester has discretion in deciding whether to pass or fail it. The basis of such discretion is whether the tester would be happy for a close relative or friend to use the vehicle with the component in that condition. If the vehicle presented is clean and evidently well cared for, the tester may be more inclined to pass a borderline component than if the vehicle is scruffy and apparently neglected.

It has only been possible to summarise the test requirements here, based on the regulations in force at the time of printing. Test standards are becoming increasingly stringent, although there are some exemptions for older vehicles.

An assistant will be needed to help carry out some of these checks.

The checks have been sub-divided into four categories, as follows:

1 Checks carried out **FROM THE DRIVER'S SEAT**

2 Checks carried out **WITH THE VEHICLE ON THE GROUND**

3 Checks carried out **WITH THE VEHICLE RAISED AND THE WHEELS FREE TO TURN**

4 Checks carried out on **YOUR VEHICLE'S EXHAUST EMISSION SYSTEM**

---

1 Checks carried out **FROM THE DRIVER'S SEAT**

Handbrake

☐ Test the operation of the handbrake. Excessive travel (too many clicks) indicates incorrect brake or cable adjustment.

☐ Check that the handbrake cannot be released by tapping the lever sideways. Check the security of the lever mountings.

Footbrake

☐ Depress the brake pedal and check that it does not creep down to the floor, indicating a master cylinder fault. Release the pedal, wait a few seconds, then depress it again. If the pedal travels nearly to the floor before firm resistance is felt, brake adjustment or repair is necessary. If the pedal feels spongy, there is air in the hydraulic system which must be removed by bleeding.

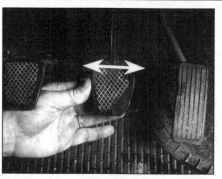

☐ Check that the brake pedal is secure and in good condition. Check also for signs of fluid leaks on the pedal, floor or carpets, which would indicate failed seals in the brake master cylinder.

☐ Check the servo unit (when applicable) by operating the brake pedal several times, then keeping the pedal depressed and starting the engine. As the engine starts, the pedal will move down slightly. If not, the vacuum hose or the servo itself may be faulty.

Steering wheel and column

☐ Examine the steering wheel for fractures or looseness of the hub, spokes or rim.

☐ Move the steering wheel from side to side and then up and down. Check that the steering wheel is not loose on the column, indicating wear or a loose retaining nut. Continue moving the steering wheel as before, but also turn it slightly from left to right.

☐ Check that the steering wheel is not loose on the column, and that there is no abnormal

movement of the steering wheel, indicating wear in the column support bearings or couplings.

Windscreen, mirrors and sunvisor

☐ The windscreen must be free of cracks or other significant damage within the driver's field of view. (Small stone chips are acceptable.) Rear view mirrors must be secure, intact, and capable of being adjusted.

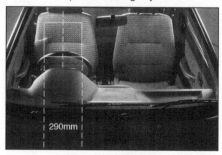

☐ The driver's sunvisor must be capable of being stored in the "up" position.

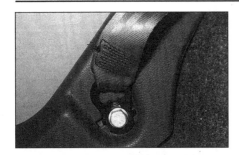

Seat belts and seats

Note: *The following checks are applicable to all seat belts, front and rear.*

☐ Examine the webbing of all the belts (including rear belts if fitted) for cuts, serious fraying or deterioration. Fasten and unfasten each belt to check the buckles. If applicable, check the retracting mechanism. Check the security of all seat belt mountings accessible from inside the vehicle.

☐ Seat belts with pre-tensioners, once activated, have a "flag" or similar showing on the seat belt stalk. This, in itself, is not a reason for test failure.

☐ The front seats themselves must be securely attached and the backrests must lock in the upright position.

Doors

☐ Both front doors must be able to be opened and closed from outside and inside, and must latch securely when closed.

2 Checks carried out WITH THE VEHICLE ON THE GROUND

Vehicle identification

☐ Number plates must be in good condition, secure and legible, with letters and numbers correctly spaced – spacing at (A) should be at least twice that at (B).

☐ The VIN plate and/or homologation plate must be legible.

Electrical equipment

☐ Switch on the ignition and check the operation of the horn.

☐ Check the windscreen washers and wipers, examining the wiper blades; renew damaged or perished blades. Also check the operation of the stop-lights.

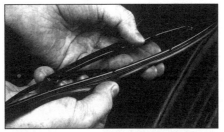

☐ Check the operation of the sidelights and number plate lights. The lenses and reflectors must be secure, clean and undamaged.

☐ Check the operation and alignment of the headlights. The headlight reflectors must not be tarnished and the lenses must be undamaged.

☐ Switch on the ignition and check the operation of the direction indicators (including the instrument panel tell-tale) and the hazard warning lights. Operation of the sidelights and stop-lights must not affect the indicators - if it does, the cause is usually a bad earth at the rear light cluster.

☐ Check the operation of the rear foglight(s), including the warning light on the instrument panel or in the switch.

☐ The ABS warning light must illuminate in accordance with the manufacturers' design. For most vehicles, the ABS warning light should illuminate when the ignition is switched on, and (if the system is operating properly) extinguish after a few seconds. Refer to the owner's handbook.

Footbrake

☐ Examine the master cylinder, brake pipes and servo unit for leaks, loose mountings, corrosion or other damage.

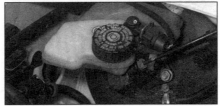

☐ The fluid reservoir must be secure and the fluid level must be between the upper (A) and lower (B) markings.

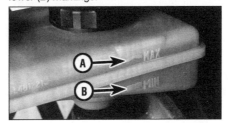

☐ Inspect both front brake flexible hoses for cracks or deterioration of the rubber. Turn the steering from lock to lock, and ensure that the hoses do not contact the wheel, tyre, or any part of the steering or suspension mechanism. With the brake pedal firmly depressed, check the hoses for bulges or leaks under pressure.

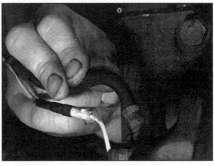

Steering and suspension

☐ Have your assistant turn the steering wheel from side to side slightly, up to the point where the steering gear just begins to transmit this movement to the roadwheels. Check for excessive free play between the steering wheel and the steering gear, indicating wear or insecurity of the steering column joints, the column-to-steering gear coupling, or the steering gear itself.

☐ Have your assistant turn the steering wheel more vigorously in each direction, so that the roadwheels just begin to turn. As this is done, examine all the steering joints, linkages, fittings and attachments. Renew any component that shows signs of wear or damage. On vehicles with power steering, check the security and condition of the steering pump, drivebelt and hoses.

☐ Check that the vehicle is standing level, and at approximately the correct ride height.

Shock absorbers

☐ Depress each corner of the vehicle in turn, then release it. The vehicle should rise and then settle in its normal position. If the vehicle continues to rise and fall, the shock absorber is defective. A shock absorber which has seized will also cause the vehicle to fail.

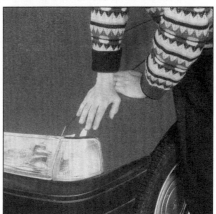

Exhaust system

☐ Start the engine. With your assistant holding a rag over the tailpipe, check the entire system for leaks. Repair or renew leaking sections.

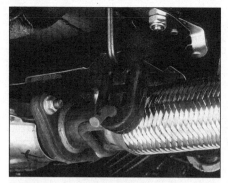

3 Checks carried out **WITH THE VEHICLE RAISED AND THE WHEELS FREE TO TURN**

Jack up the front and rear of the vehicle, and securely support it on axle stands. Position the stands clear of the suspension assemblies. Ensure that the wheels are clear of the ground and that the steering can be turned from lock to lock.

Steering mechanism

☐ Have your assistant turn the steering from lock to lock. Check that the steering turns smoothly, and that no part of the steering mechanism, including a wheel or tyre, fouls any brake hose or pipe or any part of the body structure.

☐ Examine the steering rack rubber gaiters for damage or insecurity of the retaining clips. If power steering is fitted, check for signs of damage or leakage of the fluid hoses, pipes or connections. Also check for excessive stiffness or binding of the steering, a missing split pin or locking device, or severe corrosion of the body structure within 30 cm of any steering component attachment point.

Front and rear suspension and wheel bearings

☐ Starting at the front right-hand side, grasp the roadwheel at the 3 o'clock and 9 o'clock positions and rock gently but firmly. Check for free play or insecurity at the wheel bearings, suspension balljoints, or suspension mountings, pivots and attachments.

☐ Now grasp the wheel at the 12 o'clock and 6 o'clock positions and repeat the previous inspection. Spin the wheel, and check for roughness or tightness of the front wheel bearing.

☐ If excess free play is suspected at a component pivot point, this can be confirmed by using a large screwdriver or similar tool and levering between the mounting and the component attachment. This will confirm whether the wear is in the pivot bush, its retaining bolt, or in the mounting itself (the bolt holes can often become elongated).

☐ Carry out all the above checks at the other front wheel, and then at both rear wheels.

Springs and shock absorbers

☐ Examine the suspension struts (when applicable) for serious fluid leakage, corrosion, or damage to the casing. Also check the security of the mounting points.

☐ If coil springs are fitted, check that the spring ends locate in their seats, and that the spring is not corroded, cracked or broken.

☐ If leaf springs are fitted, check that all leaves are intact, that the axle is securely attached to each spring, and that there is no deterioration of the spring eye mountings, bushes, and shackles.

☐ The same general checks apply to vehicles fitted with other suspension types, such as torsion bars, hydraulic displacer units, etc. Ensure that all mountings and attachments are secure, that there are no signs of excessive wear, corrosion or damage, and (on hydraulic types) that there are no fluid leaks or damaged pipes.

☐ Inspect the shock absorbers for signs of serious fluid leakage. Check for wear of the mounting bushes or attachments, or damage to the body of the unit.

Driveshafts (fwd vehicles only)

☐ Rotate each front wheel in turn and inspect the constant velocity joint gaiters for splits or damage. Also check that each driveshaft is straight and undamaged.

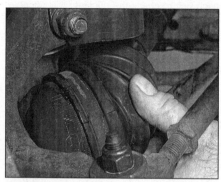

Braking system

☐ If possible without dismantling, check brake pad wear and disc condition. Ensure that the friction lining material has not worn excessively, (A) and that the discs are not fractured, pitted, scored or badly worn (B).

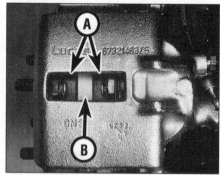

☐ Examine all the rigid brake pipes underneath the vehicle, and the flexible hose(s) at the rear. Look for corrosion, chafing or insecurity of the pipes, and for signs of bulging under pressure, chafing, splits or deterioration of the flexible hoses.

☐ Look for signs of fluid leaks at the brake calipers or on the brake backplates. Repair or renew leaking components.

☐ Slowly spin each wheel, while your assistant depresses and releases the footbrake. Ensure that each brake is operating and does not bind when the pedal is released.

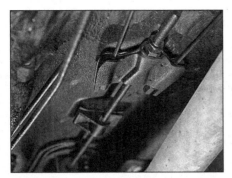

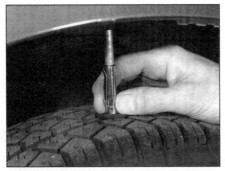

☐ Examine the handbrake mechanism, checking for frayed or broken cables, excessive corrosion, or wear or insecurity of the linkage. Check that the mechanism works on each relevant wheel, and releases fully, without binding.

☐ It is not possible to test brake efficiency without special equipment, but a road test can be carried out later to check that the vehicle pulls up in a straight line.

Fuel and exhaust systems

☐ Inspect the fuel tank (including the filler cap), fuel pipes, hoses and unions. All components must be secure and free from leaks.

☐ Examine the exhaust system over its entire length, checking for any damaged, broken or missing mountings, security of the retaining clamps and rust or corrosion.

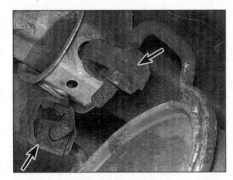

Wheels and tyres

☐ Examine the sidewalls and tread area of each tyre in turn. Check for cuts, tears, lumps, bulges, separation of the tread, and exposure of the ply or cord due to wear or damage. Check that the tyre bead is correctly seated on the wheel rim, that the valve is sound and properly seated, and that the wheel is not distorted or damaged.

☐ Check that the tyres are of the correct size for the vehicle, that they are of the same size

and type on each axle, and that the pressures are correct.

☐ Check the tyre tread depth. The legal minimum at the time of writing is 1.6 mm over at least three-quarters of the tread width. Abnormal tread wear may indicate incorrect front wheel alignment.

Body corrosion

☐ Check the condition of the entire vehicle structure for signs of corrosion in load-bearing areas. (These include chassis box sections, side sills, cross-members, pillars, and all suspension, steering, braking system and seat belt mountings and anchorages.) Any corrosion which has seriously reduced the thickness of a load-bearing area is likely to cause the vehicle to fail. In this case professional repairs are likely to be needed.

☐ Damage or corrosion which causes sharp or otherwise dangerous edges to be exposed will also cause the vehicle to fail.

4 Checks carried out on YOUR VEHICLE'S EXHAUST EMISSION SYSTEM

Petrol models

☐ The engine should be warmed up, and running well (ignition system in good order, air filter element clean, etc).

☐ Before testing, run the engine at around 2500 rpm for 20 seconds. Let the engine drop to idle, and watch for smoke from the exhaust. If the idle speed is too high, or if dense blue or black smoke emerges for more than 5 seconds, the vehicle will fail. Typically, blue smoke signifies oil burning (engine wear); black smoke means unburnt fuel (dirty air cleaner element, or other fuel system fault).

☐ An exhaust gas analyser for measuring carbon monoxide (CO) and hydrocarbons (HC) is now needed. If one cannot be hired or borrowed, have a local garage perform the check.

CO emissions (mixture)

☐ The MOT tester has access to the CO limits for all vehicles. The CO level is measured at idle speed, and at 'fast idle' (2500 to 3000 rpm). The following limits are given as a general guide:

At idle speed – Less than 0.5% CO
At 'fast idle' – Less than 0.3% CO
Lambda reading – 0.97 to 1.03

☐ If the CO level is too high, this may point to poor maintenance, a fuel injection system problem, faulty lambda (oxygen) sensor or catalytic converter. Try an injector cleaning treatment, and check the vehicle's ECU for fault codes.

HC emissions

☐ The MOT tester has access to HC limits for all vehicles. The HC level is measured at 'fast idle' (2500 to 3000 rpm). The following limits are given as a general guide:

At 'fast idle' – Less then 200 ppm

☐ Excessive HC emissions are typically caused by oil being burnt (worn engine), or by a blocked crankcase ventilation system ('breather'). If the engine oil is old and thin, an oil change may help. If the engine is running badly, check the vehicle's ECU for fault codes.

Diesel models

☐ The only emission test for diesel engines is measuring exhaust smoke density, using a calibrated smoke meter. The test involves accelerating the engine at least 3 times to its maximum unloaded speed.

Note: *On engines with a timing belt, it is VITAL that the belt is in good condition before the test is carried out.*

☐ With the engine warmed up, it is first purged by running at around 2500 rpm for 20 seconds. A governor check is then carried out, by slowly accelerating the engine to its maximum speed. After this, the smoke meter is connected, and the engine is accelerated quickly to maximum speed three times. If the smoke density is less than the limits given below, the vehicle will pass:

Non-turbo vehicles: 2.5m-1
Turbocharged vehicles: 3.0m-1

☐ If excess smoke is produced, try fitting a new air cleaner element, or using an injector cleaning treatment. If the engine is running badly, where applicable, check the vehicle's ECU for fault codes. Also check the vehicle's EGR system, where applicable. At high mileages, the injectors may require professional attention.

Engine

- ☐ Engine fails to rotate when attempting to start
- ☐ Engine rotates, but will not start
- ☐ Engine difficult to start when cold
- ☐ Engine difficult to start when hot
- ☐ Starter motor noisy or excessively-rough in engagement
- ☐ Engine starts, but stops immediately
- ☐ Engine idles erratically
- ☐ Engine misfires at idle speed
- ☐ Engine misfires throughout the driving speed range
- ☐ Engine hesitates on acceleration
- ☐ Engine stalls
- ☐ Engine lacks power
- ☐ Engine backfires
- ☐ Oil pressure warning light illuminated with engine running
- ☐ Engine runs-on after switching off
- ☐ Engine noises

Cooling system

- ☐ Overheating
- ☐ Overcooling
- ☐ External coolant leakage
- ☐ Internal coolant leakage
- ☐ Corrosion

Fuel and exhaust systems

- ☐ Excessive fuel consumption
- ☐ Fuel leakage and/or fuel odour
- ☐ Excessive noise or fumes from the exhaust system

Clutch

- ☐ Pedal travels to floor – no pressure or very little resistance
- ☐ Clutch fails to disengage (unable to select gears)
- ☐ Clutch slips (engine speed increases, with no increase in vehicle speed)
- ☐ Judder as clutch is engaged
- ☐ Noise when depressing or releasing clutch pedal

Manual transmission

- ☐ Noisy in neutral with engine running
- ☐ Noisy in one particular gear
- ☐ Difficulty engaging gears
- ☐ Jumps out of gear
- ☐ Vibration
- ☐ Lubricant leaks

Automatic transmission

- ☐ Fluid leakage
- ☐ Transmission fluid brown, or has burned smell
- ☐ Engine will not start in any gear, or starts in gears other than Park or Neutral
- ☐ General gear selection problems
- ☐ Transmission will not downshift (kickdown) with accelerator pedal fully depressed
- ☐ Transmission slips, shifts roughly, is noisy, or has no drive in forward or reverse gears

Driveshafts

- ☐ Vibration when accelerating or decelerating
- ☐ Clicking or knocking noise on turns (at slow speed on full-lock)

Braking system

- ☐ Vehicle pulls to one side under braking
- ☐ Noise (grinding or high-pitched squeal) when brakes applied
- ☐ Excessive brake pedal travel
- ☐ Brake pedal feels spongy when depressed
- ☐ Excessive brake pedal effort required to stop vehicle
- ☐ Judder felt through brake pedal or steering wheel when braking
- ☐ Pedal pulsates when braking hard
- ☐ Brakes binding
- ☐ Rear wheels locking under normal braking

Steering and suspension

- ☐ Vehicle pulls to one side
- ☐ Wheel wobble and vibration
- ☐ Excessive pitching and/or rolling around corners, or during braking
- ☐ Wandering or general instability
- ☐ Excessively-stiff steering
- ☐ Excessive play in steering
- ☐ Lack of power assistance
- ☐ Tyre wear excessive

Electrical system

- ☐ Battery will not hold a charge for more than a few days
- ☐ Ignition/no-charge warning light remains illuminated with engine running
- ☐ Ignition/no-charge warning light fails to come on
- ☐ Lights inoperative
- ☐ Instrument readings inaccurate or erratic
- ☐ Horn inoperative, or unsatisfactory in operation
- ☐ Windscreen/tailgate wipers inoperative, or unsatisfactory in operation
- ☐ Windscreen/tailgate washers inoperative, or unsatisfactory in operation
- ☐ Electric windows inoperative, or unsatisfactory in operation
- ☐ Central locking system inoperative, or unsatisfactory in operation

Introduction

The vehicle owner who does his or her own maintenance according to the recommended service schedules should not have to use this section of the manual very often. Modern component reliability is such that, provided those items subject to wear or deterioration are inspected or renewed at the specified intervals, sudden failure is comparatively rare. Faults do not usually just happen as a result of sudden failure, but develop over a period of time. Major mechanical failures in particular are usually preceded by characteristic symptoms over hundreds or even thousands of miles. Those components which do occasionally fail without warning are often small and easily carried in the vehicle.

With any fault-finding, the first step is to decide where to begin investigations. Sometimes this is obvious, but on other occasions, a little detective work will be necessary. The owner who makes half a dozen haphazard adjustments or replacements may be successful in curing a fault (or its symptoms), but will be none the wiser if the fault recurs, and ultimately may have spent more time and money than was necessary. A calm and logical approach will be found to be more satisfactory in the long run. Always take into account any warning signs or abnormalities that may have been noticed in the period preceding the fault – power loss, high or low gauge readings, unusual smells, etc – and remember that failure of components such as fuses or spark plugs may only be pointers to some underlying fault.

The pages which follow provide an easy-reference guide to the more common problems which may occur during the operation of the vehicle. These problems and their possible causes are grouped under headings denoting various components or systems, such as Engine, Cooling system, etc. The general

Chapter which deals with the problem is also shown in brackets; refer to the relevant part of that Chapter for system-specific information. Whatever the fault, certain basic principles apply. These are as follows:

Verify the fault. This is simply a matter of being sure that you know what the symptoms are before starting work. This is particularly important if you are investigating a fault for someone else, who may not have described it very accurately.

Don't overlook the obvious. For example, if the vehicle won't start, is there fuel in the tank? (Don't take anyone else's word on this particular point, and don't trust the fuel gauge either!) If an electrical fault is indicated, look for loose or broken wires before digging out the test gear.

Cure the disease, not the symptom. Substituting a flat battery with a fully-charged one will get you off the hard shoulder, but if the underlying cause is not attended to, the new battery will go the same way. Similarly, changing oil-fouled spark plugs for a new set will get you moving again, but remember that the reason for the fouling (if it wasn't simply an incorrect grade of plug) will have to be established and corrected.

Don't take anything for granted. Particularly, don't forget that a 'new' component may itself be defective (especially if it's been rattling around in the boot for months), and don't leave components out of a fault diagnosis sequence just because they are new or recently-fitted. When you do finally diagnose a difficult fault, you'll probably realise that all the evidence was there from the start.

Engine

Engine fails to rotate when attempting to start

- ☐ Battery terminal connections loose or corroded (see *Weekly checks*).
- ☐ Battery discharged or faulty (Chapter 5A).
- ☐ Broken, loose or disconnected wiring in the starting circuit (Chapter 5A).
- ☐ Defective starter solenoid or switch (Chapter 5A).
- ☐ Defective starter motor (Chapter 5A).
- ☐ Starter pinion or flywheel ring gear teeth loose or broken (Chapters 2A, 2B and 5A).
- ☐ Engine earth strap broken or disconnected (Chapter 5A).

Engine rotates, but will not start

- ☐ Fuel tank empty.
- ☐ Battery discharged (engine rotates slowly) (Chapter 5A).
- ☐ Battery terminal connections loose or corroded (see *Weekly checks*).
- ☐ Ignition components damp or damaged – petrol models (Chapters 1A and 5B).
- ☐ Broken, loose or disconnected wiring in the ignition circuit – petrol models (Chapters 1A and 5B).
- ☐ Worn, faulty or incorrectly-gapped spark plugs – petrol models (Chapter 1A).
- ☐ Preheating system faulty – diesel models (Chapter 5C).
- ☐ Fuel injection system faulty – petrol models (Chapter 4A).
- ☐ Stop solenoid faulty – diesel models (Chapter 4B).
- ☐ Air in fuel system – diesel models (Chapter 4B).
- ☐ Major mechanical failure (eg camshaft drive) (Chapter 2).

Engine difficult to start when cold

- ☐ Battery discharged (Chapter 5A).
- ☐ Battery terminal connections loose or corroded (see *Weekly checks*).
- ☐ Worn, faulty or incorrectly-gapped spark plugs – petrol models (Chapter 1A).
- ☐ Preheating system faulty – diesel models (Chapter 5C).
- ☐ Fuel injection system faulty – petrol models (Chapter 4A).
- ☐ Other ignition system fault – petrol models (Chapters 1A and 5B).
- ☐ Low cylinder compressions (Chapter 2A or 2B).

Engine difficult to start when hot

- ☐ Air filter element dirty or clogged (Chapter 1A or 1B).
- ☐ Fuel injection system faulty – petrol models (Chapter 4A).
- ☐ Low cylinder compressions (Chapter 2).

Starter motor noisy or excessively-rough in engagement

- ☐ Starter pinion or flywheel ring gear teeth loose or broken (Chapters 2A, 2B and 5A).
- ☐ Starter motor mounting bolts loose (Chapter 5A).
- ☐ Starter motor internal components worn or damaged (Chapter 5A).

Engine starts, but stops immediately

- ☐ Loose or faulty electrical connections in the ignition circuit – petrol models (Chapters 1A and 5B).
- ☐ Vacuum leak at the throttle body or inlet manifold – petrol models (Chapter 4A).
- ☐ Blocked injector/fuel injection system fault – petrol models (Chapter 4A).

Engine idles erratically

- ☐ Air filter element clogged (Chapter 1A or 1B).
- ☐ Vacuum leak at the throttle body, inlet manifold or associated hoses – petrol models (Chapter 4A).
- ☐ Worn, faulty or incorrectly-gapped spark plugs – petrol models (Chapter 1A).
- ☐ Uneven or low cylinder compressions (Chapter 2).
- ☐ Camshaft lobes worn (Chapter 2A or 2B).
- ☐ Timing chain incorrectly fitted (Chapter 2A or 2B).
- ☐ Blocked injector/fuel injection system fault – petrol models (Chapter 4A).
- ☐ Faulty injector(s) – diesel models (Chapter 4B).

Engine misfires at idle speed

- ☐ Worn, faulty or incorrectly-gapped spark plugs – petrol models (Chapter 1A).
- ☐ Faulty spark plug HT leads – petrol models (Chapter 1A).
- ☐ Vacuum leak at the throttle body, inlet manifold or associated hoses – petrol models (Chapter 4A).
- ☐ Blocked injector/fuel injection system fault – petrol models (Chapter 4A).
- ☐ Faulty injector(s) – diesel models (Chapter 4B).
- ☐ Uneven or low cylinder compressions (Chapter 2A or 2B).
- ☐ Disconnected, leaking, or perished crankcase ventilation hoses (Chapter 4C).

Engine misfires throughout the driving speed range

- ☐ Fuel filter choked (Chapter 1A or 1B).
- ☐ Fuel pump faulty, or delivery pressure low – petrol models (Chapter 4A).
- ☐ Fuel tank vent blocked, or fuel pipes restricted (Chapter 4A or 4B).
- ☐ Vacuum leak at the throttle body, inlet manifold or associated hoses – petrol models (Chapter 4A).
- ☐ Worn, faulty or incorrectly-gapped spark plugs – petrol models (Chapter 1A).
- ☐ Faulty spark plug HT leads – petrol models (Chapter 1A).
- ☐ Faulty injector(s) – diesel models (Chapter 4B).
- ☐ Faulty ignition coil – petrol models (Chapter 5B).
- ☐ Uneven or low cylinder compressions (Chapter 2A or 2B).
- ☐ Blocked injector/fuel injection system fault – petrol models (Chapter 4A).

Engine (continued)

Engine hesitates on acceleration

- [ ] Worn, faulty or incorrectly-gapped spark plugs – petrol models (Chapter 1A).
- [ ] Vacuum leak at the throttle body, inlet manifold or associated hoses – petrol models (Chapter 4A).
- [ ] Blocked injector/fuel injection system fault – petrol models (Chapter 4A).
- [ ] Faulty injector(s) – diesel models (Chapter 4B).

Engine stalls

- [ ] Vacuum leak at the throttle body, inlet manifold or associated hoses – petrol models (Chapter 4A).
- [ ] Fuel filter choked (Chapter 1A or 1B).
- [ ] Fuel pump faulty, or delivery pressure low – petrol models (Chapter 4A).
- [ ] Fuel tank vent blocked, or fuel pipes restricted (Chapter 4A or 4B).
- [ ] Blocked injector/fuel injection system fault – petrol models (Chapter 4A).
- [ ] Faulty injector(s) – diesel models (Chapter 4B).

Engine lacks power

- [ ] Timing chain incorrectly fitted or tensioned (Chapter 2A or 2B).
- [ ] Fuel filter choked (Chapter 1A or 1B).
- [ ] Fuel pump faulty, or delivery pressure low – petrol models (Chapter 4A).
- [ ] Uneven or low cylinder compressions (Chapter 2A or 2B).
- [ ] Worn, faulty or incorrectly-gapped spark plugs – petrol models (Chapter 1A).
- [ ] Vacuum leak at the throttle body, inlet manifold or associated hoses – petrol models (Chapter 4A).
- [ ] Blocked injector/fuel injection system fault – petrol models (Chapter 4A).
- [ ] Faulty injector(s) – diesel models (Chapter 4B).
- [ ] Injection pump timing incorrect – diesel models (Chapter 4B).
- [ ] Brakes binding (Chapters 1A, 1B and 9).
- [ ] Clutch slipping (Chapter 6).

Engine backfires

- [ ] Timing chain incorrectly fitted or tensioned (Chapter 2A or 2B).
- [ ] Vacuum leak at the throttle body, inlet manifold or associated hoses – petrol models (Chapter 4A).
- [ ] Blocked injector/fuel injection system fault – petrol models (Chapter 4A).

Oil pressure warning light illuminated with engine running

- [ ] Low oil level, or incorrect oil grade (*Weekly checks*).
- [ ] Faulty oil pressure sensor (Chapter 5A).
- [ ] Worn engine bearings and/or oil pump (Chapter 2C).
- [ ] High engine operating temperature (Chapter 3).
- [ ] Oil pressure relief valve defective (Chapter 2C).
- [ ] Oil pick-up strainer clogged (Chapter 2A or 2B).

Engine runs-on after switching off

- [ ] Excessive carbon build-up in engine (Chapter 2C).
- [ ] High engine operating temperature (Chapter 3).
- [ ] Fuel injection system faulty – petrol models (Chapter 4A).
- [ ] Faulty stop solenoid – diesel models (Chapter 4B).

Engine noises

Pre-ignition (pinking) or knocking during acceleration or under load

- [ ] Ignition timing incorrect/ignition system fault – petrol models (Chapters 1A and 5B).
- [ ] Incorrect grade of spark plug – petrol models (Chapter 1A).
- [ ] Incorrect grade of fuel (Chapter 4A or 4B).
- [ ] Vacuum leak at the throttle body, inlet manifold or associated hoses – petrol models (Chapter 4A).
- [ ] Excessive carbon build-up in engine (Chapter 2C).
- [ ] Blocked injector/fuel injection system fault – petrol models (Chapter 4A).

Whistling or wheezing noises

- [ ] Leaking inlet manifold or throttle body gasket – petrol models (Chapter 4A).
- [ ] Leaking exhaust manifold gasket or pipe-to-manifold joint (Chapter 4A or 4B).
- [ ] Leaking vacuum hose (Chapters 4A, 4B, 5 and 9).
- [ ] Blowing cylinder head gasket (Chapter 2A or 2B).

Tapping or rattling noises

- [ ] Worn valve gear or camshaft (Chapter 2C).
- [ ] Ancillary component fault (coolant pump, alternator, etc) (Chapters 3, 5, etc).

Knocking or thumping noises

- [ ] Worn big-end bearings (regular heavy knocking, perhaps less under load) (Chapter 2C).
- [ ] Worn main bearings (rumbling and knocking, perhaps worsening under load) (Chapter 2C).
- [ ] Piston slap (most noticeable when cold) (Chapter 2C).
- [ ] Ancillary component fault (coolant pump, alternator, etc) (Chapters 3, 5, etc).

Cooling system

Overheating

- [ ] Insufficient coolant in system (*Weekly Checks*).
- [ ] Thermostat faulty (Chapter 3).
- [ ] Radiator core blocked, or grille restricted (Chapter 3).
- [ ] Electric cooling fan or thermostatic switch faulty (Chapter 3).
- [ ] Inaccurate temperature gauge sender unit (Chapter 3).
- [ ] Airlock in cooling system (Chapter 3).
- [ ] Expansion tank pressure cap faulty (Chapter 3).

Overcooling

- [ ] Thermostat faulty (Chapter 3).
- [ ] Inaccurate temperature gauge sender unit (Chapter 3).

External coolant leakage

- [ ] Deteriorated or damaged hoses or hose clips (Chapter 1A or 1B).
- [ ] Radiator core or heater matrix leaking (Chapter 3).
- [ ] Pressure cap faulty (Chapter 3).
- [ ] Coolant pump internal seal leaking (Chapter 3).
- [ ] Coolant pump-to-block seal leaking (Chapter 3).
- [ ] Boiling due to overheating (Chapter 3).
- [ ] Core plug leaking (Chapter 2C).

Internal coolant leakage

- [ ] Leaking cylinder head gasket (Chapter 2A or 2B).
- [ ] Cracked cylinder head or cylinder block (Chapter 2A, 2B or 2C).

Corrosion

- [ ] Infrequent draining and flushing (Chapter 1A or 1B).
- [ ] Incorrect coolant mixture or inappropriate coolant type (see *Weekly checks*).

Fuel and exhaust systems

Excessive fuel consumption

- ☐ Air filter element dirty or clogged (Chapter 1A or 1B).
- ☐ Fuel injection system faulty – petrol models (Chapter 4A).
- ☐ Faulty injector(s) – diesel models (Chapter 4B).
- ☐ Ignition timing incorrect/ignition system faulty – petrol models (Chapters 1A and 5B).
- ☐ Tyres under-inflated (see *Weekly checks*).

Fuel leakage and/or fuel odour

- ☐ Damaged or corroded fuel tank, pipes or connections (Chapter 4A or 4B).

Excessive noise or fumes from the exhaust system

- ☐ Leaking exhaust system or manifold joints (Chapters 1A, 1B and 4).
- ☐ Leaking, corroded or damaged silencers or pipe (Chapters 1A, 1B and 4).
- ☐ Broken mountings causing body or suspension contact (Chapter 4A or 4B).

Clutch

Pedal travels to floor – no pressure or very little resistance

- ☐ Air in hydraulic system/faulty master or slave cylinder (Chapter 6).
- ☐ Faulty hydraulic release system (Chapter 6).
- ☐ Broken clutch release bearing or arm (Chapter 6).
- ☐ Broken diaphragm spring in clutch pressure plate (Chapter 6).

Clutch fails to disengage (unable to select gears)

- ☐ Air in hydraulic system/faulty master or slave cylinder (Chapter 6).
- ☐ Faulty hydraulic release system (Chapter 6).
- ☐ Clutch disc sticking on gearbox input shaft splines (Chapter 6).
- ☐ Clutch disc sticking to flywheel or pressure plate (Chapter 6).
- ☐ Faulty pressure plate assembly (Chapter 6).
- ☐ Clutch release mechanism worn or incorrectly assembled (Chapter 6).

Clutch slips (engine speed increases, with no increase in vehicle speed)

- ☐ Faulty hydraulic release system (Chapter 6).

- ☐ Clutch disc linings excessively worn (Chapter 6).
- ☐ Clutch disc linings contaminated with oil or grease (Chapter 6).
- ☐ Faulty pressure plate or weak diaphragm spring (Chapter 6).

Judder as clutch is engaged

- ☐ Clutch disc linings contaminated with oil or grease (Chapter 6).
- ☐ Clutch disc linings excessively worn (Chapter 6).
- ☐ Faulty or distorted pressure plate or diaphragm spring (Chapter 6).
- ☐ Worn or loose engine or gearbox mountings (Chapter 2A or 2B).
- ☐ Clutch disc hub or gearbox input shaft splines worn (Chapter 6).

Noise when depressing or releasing clutch pedal

- ☐ Worn clutch release bearing (Chapter 6).
- ☐ Worn or dry clutch pedal pivot (Chapter 6).
- ☐ Faulty pressure plate assembly (Chapter 6).
- ☐ Pressure plate diaphragm spring broken (Chapter 6).
- ☐ Broken clutch friction plate cushioning springs (Chapter 6).

Manual transmission

Noisy in neutral with engine running

- ☐ Input shaft bearings worn (noise apparent with clutch pedal released, but not when depressed) (Chapter 7A).*
- ☐ Clutch release bearing worn (noise apparent with clutch pedal depressed, possibly less when released) (Chapter 6).

Noisy in one particular gear

- ☐ Worn, damaged or chipped gear teeth (Chapter 7A).*

Difficulty engaging gears

- ☐ Clutch faulty (Chapter 6).
- ☐ Worn or damaged gear linkage (Chapter 7A).
- ☐ Worn synchroniser units (Chapter 7A).*

Jumps out of gear

- ☐ Worn or damaged gear linkage (Chapter 7A).

- ☐ Worn synchroniser units (Chapter 7A).*
- ☐ Worn selector forks (Chapter 7A).*

Vibration

- ☐ Lack of oil (Chapter 1A or 1B).
- ☐ Worn bearings (Chapter 7A).*

Lubricant leaks

- ☐ Leaking oil seal (Chapter 7A).
- ☐ Leaking housing joint (Chapter 7A).*
- ☐ Leaking input shaft oil seal (Chapter 7A).*

Although the corrective action necessary to remedy the symptoms described is beyond the scope of the home mechanic, the above information should be helpful in isolating the cause of the condition, so that the owner can communicate clearly with a professional mechanic.

Automatic transmission

Note: *Due to the complexity of the automatic transmission, it is difficult for the home mechanic to properly diagnose and service this unit. For problems other than the following, the vehicle should be taken to a dealer service department or automatic transmission specialist. Do not be too hasty in removing the transmission if a fault is suspected, as most of the testing is carried out with the unit still fitted.*

Fluid leakage

☐ Automatic transmission fluid is usually dark in colour. Fluid leaks should not be confused with engine oil, which can easily be blown onto the transmission by airflow.

☐ To determine the source of a leak, first remove all built-up dirt and grime from the transmission housing and surrounding areas using a degreasing agent, or by steam-cleaning. Drive the vehicle at low speed, so airflow will not blow the leak far from its source. Raise and support the vehicle, and determine where the leak is coming from. The following are common areas of leakage:

a) Oil pan (Chapter 1A, 1B and 7B).
b) Dipstick tube (Chapter 1A, 1B and 7B).
c) Transmission-to-fluid cooler pipes/unions (Chapter 7B).

Transmission fluid brown, or has burned smell

☐ Transmission fluid level low, or fluid in need of renewal (Chapter 1A, 1B and 7B).

Engine will not start in any gear, or starts in gears other than Park or Neutral

☐ Incorrect starter/inhibitor switch adjustment (Chapter 7B).
☐ Incorrect selector cable adjustment (Chapter 7B).

General gear selection problems

☐ Chapter 7B deals with checking and adjusting the selector cable on automatic transmissions. The following are common problems which may be caused by a poorly-adjusted cable:
a) Engine starting in gears other than Park or Neutral.
b) Indicator panel indicating a gear other than the one actually being used.
c) Vehicle moves when in Park or Neutral.
d) Poor gear shift quality or erratic gear changes.
☐ Refer to Chapter 7B for the selector cable adjustment procedure.

Transmission will not downshift (kickdown) with accelerator pedal fully depressed

☐ Low transmission fluid level (Chapter 1A or 1B).
☐ Incorrect selector cable adjustment (Chapter 7B).

Transmission slips, shifts roughly, is noisy, or has no drive in forward or reverse gears

☐ There are many probable causes for the above problems, but the home mechanic should be concerned with only one possibility – fluid level. Before taking the vehicle to a dealer or transmission specialist, check the fluid level and condition of the fluid as described in Chapter 1A, 1B or 7B, as applicable. Correct the fluid level as necessary, or change the fluid and filter if needed. If the problem persists, professional help will be necessary.

Driveshafts

Vibration when accelerating or decelerating

☐ Worn inner constant velocity joint (Chapter 8).
☐ Bent or distorted driveshaft (Chapter 8).
☐ Worn intermediate bearing – where applicable (Chapter 8).

Clicking or knocking noise on turns (at slow speed on full-lock)

☐ Worn outer constant velocity joint (Chapter 8).
☐ Lack of constant velocity joint lubricant, possibly due to damaged gaiter (Chapter 8).

Braking system

Note: *Before assuming that a brake problem exists, make sure that the tyres are in good condition and correctly inflated, that the front wheel alignment is correct, and that the vehicle is not loaded with weight in an unequal manner. Apart from checking the condition of all pipe and hose connections, any faults occurring on the anti-lock braking system should be referred to a Saab dealer for diagnosis.*

Vehicle pulls to one side under braking

☐ Worn, defective, damaged or contaminated front or rear brake pads/shoes on one side (Chapters 1A, 1B and 9).
☐ Seized or partially-seized front or rear brake caliper/wheel cylinder piston (Chapter 9).
☐ A mixture of brake pad/shoe lining materials fitted between sides (Chapter 9).
☐ Brake caliper or rear brake backplate mounting bolts loose (Chapter 9).
☐ Worn or damaged steering or suspension components (Chapters 1A, 1B and 10).

Noise (grinding or high-pitched squeal) when brakes applied

☐ Brake pad/shoe friction lining material worn down to metal backing (Chapters 1A, 1B and 9).
☐ Excessive corrosion of brake disc or drum – may be apparent after the vehicle has been standing for some time (Chapters 1A, 1B and 9).
☐ Foreign object (stone chipping, etc) trapped between brake disc and shield (Chapters 1A, 1B and 9).

Excessive brake pedal travel

☐ Faulty rear drum brake self-adjust mechanism (Chapter 9).
☐ Faulty master cylinder (Chapter 9).
☐ Air in hydraulic system (Chapter 9).
☐ Faulty vacuum servo unit (Chapter 9).
☐ Faulty vacuum pump – diesel models (Chapter 9).

Brake pedal feels spongy when depressed

☐ Air in hydraulic system (Chapter 9).

☐ Deteriorated flexible rubber brake hoses (Chapters 1A, 1B and 9).
☐ Master cylinder mountings loose (Chapter 9).
☐ Faulty master cylinder (Chapter 9).

Excessive brake pedal effort required to stop vehicle

☐ Faulty vacuum servo unit (Chapter 9).
☐ Disconnected, damaged or insecure brake servo vacuum hose (Chapters 1A, 1B and 9).
☐ Faulty vacuum pump – diesel models (Chapter 9).
☐ Primary or secondary hydraulic circuit failure (Chapter 9).
☐ Seized brake caliper or wheel cylinder piston(s) (Chapter 9).
☐ Brake pads/shoes incorrectly fitted (Chapter 9).
☐ Incorrect grade of brake pads/shoes fitted (Chapter 9).
☐ Brake pads/shoe linings contaminated (Chapter 9).

Judder felt through brake pedal or steering wheel when braking

☐ Excessive run-out or distortion of brake disc(s) or drum(s) (Chapter 9).
☐ Brake pad/shoe linings worn (Chapters 1A, 1B and 9).
☐ Brake caliper or rear brake backplate mounting bolts loose (Chapter 9).
☐ Wear in suspension or steering components or mountings (Chapters 1A, 1B and 10).

Pedal pulsates when braking hard

☐ Normal feature of ABS – no fault

Brakes binding

☐ Seized brake caliper/wheel cylinder piston(s) (Chapter 9).
☐ Incorrectly-adjusted handbrake mechanism (Chapter 9).
☐ Faulty master cylinder (Chapter 9).

Rear wheels locking under normal braking

☐ Rear brake pad/shoe linings contaminated (Chapters 1A, 1B and 9).
☐ Rear brake discs/drums warped (Chapters 1A, 1B and 9).

Steering and suspension

Note: *Before diagnosing suspension or steering faults, be sure that the trouble is not due to incorrect tyre pressures, mixtures of tyre types, or binding brakes.*

Vehicle pulls to one side

- [ ] Defective tyre (see *Weekly checks*).
- [ ] Excessive wear in suspension or steering components (Chapters 1A, 1B and 10).
- [ ] Incorrect front wheel alignment (Chapter 10).
- [ ] Accident damage to steering or suspension components (Chapters 1A, 1B and 10).

Wheel wobble and vibration

- [ ] Front roadwheels out of balance (vibration felt mainly through the steering wheel) (Chapter 10).
- [ ] Rear roadwheels out of balance (vibration felt throughout the vehicle) (Chapter 10).
- [ ] Roadwheels damaged or distorted (Chapter 10).
- [ ] Faulty or damaged tyre (*Weekly Checks*).
- [ ] Worn steering or suspension joints, bushes or components (Chapters 1A, 1B and 10).
- [ ] Wheel bolts loose (Chapter 1A, 1B and 10).

Excessive pitching and/or rolling around corners, or during braking

- [ ] Defective shock absorbers (Chapters 1A, 1B and 10).
- [ ] Broken or weak coil spring and/or suspension component (Chapters 1A, 1B and 10).
- [ ] Worn or damaged anti-roll bar or mountings (Chapter 10).

Wandering or general instability

- [ ] Incorrect front wheel alignment (Chapter 10).
- [ ] Worn steering or suspension joints, bushes or components (Chapters 1A, 1B and 10).
- [ ] Roadwheels out of balance (Chapter 10).
- [ ] Faulty or damaged tyre (*Weekly Checks*).
- [ ] Wheel bolts loose (Chapter 10).
- [ ] Defective shock absorbers (Chapters 1A, 1B and 10).

Excessively-stiff steering

- [ ] Seized track rod end balljoint or suspension balljoint (Chapters 1A, 1B and 10).
- [ ] Broken or incorrectly adjusted auxiliary drivebelt (Chapter 1A or 1B).

- [ ] Incorrect front wheel alignment (Chapter 10).
- [ ] Steering gear damaged (Chapter 10).

Excessive play in steering

- [ ] Worn steering column universal joint(s) (Chapter 10).
- [ ] Worn steering track rod end balljoints (Chapters 1A, 1B and 10).
- [ ] Worn steering gear (Chapter 10).
- [ ] Worn steering or suspension joints, bushes or components (Chapters 1A, 1B and 10).

Lack of power assistance

- [ ] Broken or incorrectly-adjusted auxiliary drivebelt (Chapter 1A or 1B).
- [ ] Incorrect power steering fluid level (*Weekly Checks*).
- [ ] Restriction in power steering fluid hoses (Chapter 10).
- [ ] Faulty power steering pump (Chapter 10).
- [ ] Faulty steering gear (Chapter 10).

Tyre wear excessive

Tyres worn on inside or outside edges

- [ ] Tyres under-inflated (wear on both edges) (*Weekly Checks*).
- [ ] Incorrect camber or castor angles (wear on one edge only) (Chapter 10).
- [ ] Worn steering or suspension joints, bushes or components (Chapters 1A, 1B and 10).
- [ ] Excessively-hard cornering.
- [ ] Accident damage.

Tyre treads exhibit feathered edges

- [ ] Incorrect toe setting (Chapter 10).

Tyres worn in centre of tread

- [ ] Tyres over-inflated (*Weekly Checks*).

Tyres worn on inside and outside edges

- [ ] Tyres under-inflated (*Weekly Checks*).
- [ ] Worn shock absorbers (Chapter 10).

Tyres worn unevenly

- [ ] Tyres/wheels out of balance (*Weekly Checks*).
- [ ] Excessive wheel or tyre run-out (Chapter 10).
- [ ] Worn shock absorbers (Chapters 1A, 1B and 10).
- [ ] Faulty tyre (*Weekly Checks*).

Electrical system

Note: *For problems associated with the starting system, refer to the faults listed under 'Engine' earlier in this Section.*

Battery will not hold a charge for more than a few days

- [ ] Battery defective internally (Chapter 5A).
- [ ] Battery electrolyte level low – where applicable (*Weekly Checks*).
- [ ] Battery terminal connections loose or corroded (*Weekly Checks*).
- [ ] Auxiliary drivebelt worn – or incorrectly adjusted, where applicable (Chapter 1A or 1B).
- [ ] Alternator not charging at correct output (Chapter 5A).
- [ ] Alternator or voltage regulator faulty (Chapter 5A).
- [ ] Short-circuit causing continual battery drain (Chapters 5 and 12).

Ignition/no-charge warning light remains illuminated with engine running

- [ ] Auxiliary drivebelt broken, worn, or incorrectly adjusted (Chapter 1A or 1B).
- [ ] Internal fault in alternator or voltage regulator (Chapter 5A).
- [ ] Broken, disconnected, or loose wiring in charging circuit (Chapter 5A).

Ignition/no-charge warning light fails to come on

- [ ] Warning light bulb blown (Chapter 12).
- [ ] Broken, disconnected, or loose wiring in warning light circuit (Chapter 12).
- [ ] Alternator faulty (Chapter 5A).

Electrical system (continued)

Lights inoperative

- [ ] Bulb blown (Chapter 12).
- [ ] Corrosion of bulb or bulbholder contacts (Chapter 12).
- [ ] Blown fuse (Chapter 12).
- [ ] Faulty relay (Chapter 12).
- [ ] Broken, loose, or disconnected wiring (Chapter 12).
- [ ] Faulty switch (Chapter 12).

Instrument readings inaccurate or erratic

Instrument readings increase with engine speed

- [ ] Faulty voltage regulator (Chapter 12).

Fuel or temperature gauges give no reading

- [ ] Faulty gauge sender unit (Chapters 3 and 4A or 4B).
- [ ] Wiring open-circuit (Chapter 12).
- [ ] Faulty gauge (Chapter 12).

Fuel or temperature gauges give continuous maximum reading

- [ ] Faulty gauge sender unit (Chapters 3 and 4A or 4B).
- [ ] Wiring short-circuit (Chapter 12).
- [ ] Faulty gauge (Chapter 12).

Horn inoperative, or unsatisfactory in operation

Horn operates all the time

- [ ] Horn contacts permanently bridged or horn push stuck down (Chapter 12).

Horn fails to operate

- [ ] Blown fuse (Chapter 12).
- [ ] Cable or cable connections loose, broken or disconnected (Chapter 12).
- [ ] Faulty horn (Chapter 12).

Horn emits intermittent or unsatisfactory sound

- [ ] Cable connections loose (Chapter 12).
- [ ] Horn mountings loose (Chapter 12).
- [ ] Faulty horn (Chapter 12).

Windscreen/tailgate wipers inoperative, or unsatisfactory in operation

Wipers fail to operate, or operate very slowly

- [ ] Wiper blades stuck to screen, or linkage seized or binding (*Weekly Checks* and Chapter 12).
- [ ] Blown fuse (Chapter 12).
- [ ] Cable or cable connections loose, broken or disconnected (Chapter 12).
- [ ] Faulty relay (Chapter 12).
- [ ] Faulty wiper motor (Chapter 12).

Wiper blades sweep over too large or too small an area of the glass

- [ ] Wiper arms incorrectly positioned on spindles (Chapter 12).
- [ ] Excessive wear of wiper linkage (Chapter 12).
- [ ] Wiper motor or linkage mountings loose or insecure (Chapter 12).

Wiper blades fail to clean the glass effectively

- [ ] Wiper blade rubbers worn or perished (*Weekly Checks*).
- [ ] Wiper arm tension springs broken, or arm pivots seized (Chapter 12).
- [ ] Insufficient windscreen washer additive to adequately remove road film (*Weekly Checks*).

Windscreen/tailgate washers inoperative, or unsatisfactory in operation

One or more washer jets inoperative

- [ ] Blocked washer jet (Chapter 12).
- [ ] Disconnected, kinked or restricted fluid hose (Chapter 12).
- [ ] Insufficient fluid in washer reservoir (*Weekly Checks*).

Washer pump fails to operate

- [ ] Broken or disconnected wiring or connections (Chapter 12).
- [ ] Blown fuse (Chapter 12).
- [ ] Faulty washer switch (Chapter 12).
- [ ] Faulty washer pump (Chapter 12).

Washer pump runs for some time before fluid is emitted from jets

- [ ] Faulty one-way valve in fluid supply hose (Chapter 12).

Electric windows inoperative, or unsatisfactory in operation

Window glass will only move in one direction

- [ ] Faulty switch (Chapter 12).

Window glass slow to move

- [ ] Regulator seized or damaged, or in need of lubrication (Chapter 11).
- [ ] Door internal components or trim fouling regulator (Chapter 11).
- [ ] Faulty motor (Chapter 11).

Window glass fails to move

- [ ] Blown fuse (Chapter 12).
- [ ] Faulty relay (Chapter 12).
- [ ] Broken or disconnected wiring or connections (Chapter 12).
- [ ] Faulty motor (Chapter 12).

Central locking system inoperative, or unsatisfactory in operation

Complete system failure

- [ ] Blown fuse (Chapter 12).
- [ ] Faulty relay (Chapter 12).
- [ ] Broken or disconnected wiring or connections (Chapter 12).
- [ ] Faulty motor (Chapter 11).

Latch locks but will not unlock, or unlocks but will not lock

- [ ] Faulty switch (Chapter 12).
- [ ] Broken or disconnected latch operating rods or levers (Chapter 11).
- [ ] Faulty relay (Chapter 12).
- [ ] Faulty motor (Chapter 11).

One solenoid/motor fails to operate

- [ ] Broken or disconnected wiring or connections (Chapter 12).
- [ ] Faulty motor (Chapter 11).
- [ ] Broken, binding or disconnected lock operating rods or levers (Chapter 11).
- [ ] Fault in door lock (Chapter 11).

A

ABS (Anti-lock brake system) A system, usually electronically controlled, that senses incipient wheel lockup during braking and relieves hydraulic pressure at wheels that are about to skid.

Air bag An inflatable bag hidden in the steering wheel (driver's side) or the dash or glovebox (passenger side). In a head-on collision, the bags inflate, preventing the driver and front passenger from being thrown forward into the steering wheel or windscreen.

Air cleaner A metal or plastic housing, containing a filter element, which removes dust and dirt from the air being drawn into the engine.

Air filter element The actual filter in an air cleaner system, usually manufactured from pleated paper and requiring renewal at regular intervals.

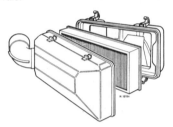
Air filter

Allen key A hexagonal wrench which fits into a recessed hexagonal hole.

Alligator clip A long-nosed spring-loaded metal clip with meshing teeth. Used to make temporary electrical connections.

Alternator A component in the electrical system which converts mechanical energy from a drivebelt into electrical energy to charge the battery and to operate the starting system, ignition system and electrical accessories.

Ampere (amp) A unit of measurement for the flow of electric current. One amp is the amount of current produced by one volt acting through a resistance of one ohm.

Anaerobic sealer A substance used to prevent bolts and screws from loosening. Anaerobic means that it does not require oxygen for activation. The Loctite brand is widely used.

Antifreeze A substance (usually ethylene glycol) mixed with water, and added to a vehicle's cooling system, to prevent freezing of the coolant in winter. Antifreeze also contains chemicals to inhibit corrosion and the formation of rust and other deposits that would tend to clog the radiator and coolant passages and reduce cooling efficiency.

Anti-seize compound A coating that reduces the risk of seizing on fasteners that are subjected to high temperatures, such as exhaust manifold bolts and nuts.

Asbestos A natural fibrous mineral with great heat resistance, commonly used in the composition of brake friction materials. Asbestos is a health hazard and the dust created by brake systems should never be inhaled or ingested.

Axle A shaft on which a wheel revolves, or which revolves with a wheel. Also, a solid beam that connects the two wheels at one end of the vehicle. An axle which also transmits power to the wheels is known as a live axle.

Axleshaft A single rotating shaft, on either side of the differential, which delivers power from the final drive assembly to the drive wheels. Also called a driveshaft or a halfshaft.

B

Ball bearing An anti-friction bearing consisting of a hardened inner and outer race with hardened steel balls between two races.

Bearing The curved surface on a shaft or in a bore, or the part assembled into either, that permits relative motion between them with minimum wear and friction.

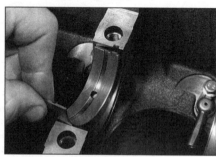
Bearing

Big-end bearing The bearing in the end of the connecting rod that's attached to the crankshaft.

Bleed nipple A valve on a brake wheel cylinder, caliper or other hydraulic component that is opened to purge the hydraulic system of air. Also called a bleed screw.

Brake bleeding Procedure for removing air from lines of a hydraulic brake system.

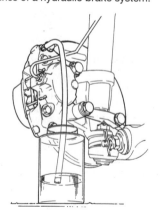
Brake bleeding

Brake disc The component of a disc brake that rotates with the wheels.

Brake drum The component of a drum brake that rotates with the wheels.

Brake linings The friction material which contacts the brake disc or drum to retard the vehicle's speed. The linings are bonded or riveted to the brake pads or shoes.

Brake pads The replaceable friction pads that pinch the brake disc when the brakes are applied. Brake pads consist of a friction material bonded or riveted to a rigid backing plate.

Brake shoe The crescent-shaped carrier to which the brake linings are mounted and which forces the lining against the rotating drum during braking.

Braking systems For more information on braking systems, consult the *Haynes Automotive Brake Manual*.

Breaker bar A long socket wrench handle providing greater leverage.

Bulkhead The insulated partition between the engine and the passenger compartment.

C

Caliper The non-rotating part of a disc-brake assembly that straddles the disc and carries the brake pads. The caliper also contains the hydraulic components that cause the pads to pinch the disc when the brakes are applied. A caliper is also a measuring tool that can be set to measure inside or outside dimensions of an object.

Camshaft A rotating shaft on which a series of cam lobes operate the valve mechanisms. The camshaft may be driven by gears, by sprockets and chain or by sprockets and a belt.

Canister A container in an evaporative emission control system; contains activated charcoal granules to trap vapours from the fuel system.

Canister

Carburettor A device which mixes fuel with air in the proper proportions to provide a desired power output from a spark ignition internal combustion engine.

Castellated Resembling the parapets along the top of a castle wall. For example, a castellated balljoint stud nut.

Castor In wheel alignment, the backward or forward tilt of the steering axis. Castor is positive when the steering axis is inclined rearward at the top.

Catalytic converter A silencer-like device in the exhaust system which converts certain pollutants in the exhaust gases into less harmful substances.

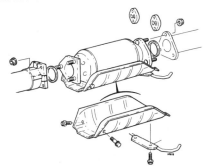

Catalytic converter

Circlip A ring-shaped clip used to prevent endwise movement of cylindrical parts and shafts. An internal circlip is installed in a groove in a housing; an external circlip fits into a groove on the outside of a cylindrical piece such as a shaft.

Clearance The amount of space between two parts. For example, between a piston and a cylinder, between a bearing and a journal, etc.

Coil spring A spiral of elastic steel found in various sizes throughout a vehicle, for example as a springing medium in the suspension and in the valve train.

Compression Reduction in volume, and increase in pressure and temperature, of a gas, caused by squeezing it into a smaller space.

Compression ratio The relationship between cylinder volume when the piston is at top dead centre and cylinder volume when the piston is at bottom dead centre.

Constant velocity (CV) joint A type of universal joint that cancels out vibrations caused by driving power being transmitted through an angle.

Core plug A disc or cup-shaped metal device inserted in a hole in a casting through which core was removed when the casting was formed. Also known as a freeze plug or expansion plug.

Crankcase The lower part of the engine block in which the crankshaft rotates.

Crankshaft The main rotating member, or shaft, running the length of the crankcase, with offset "throws" to which the connecting rods are attached.

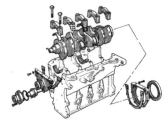

Crankshaft assembly

Crocodile clip See Alligator clip

D

Diagnostic code Code numbers obtained by accessing the diagnostic mode of an engine management computer. This code can be used to determine the area in the system where a malfunction may be located.

Disc brake A brake design incorporating a rotating disc onto which brake pads are squeezed. The resulting friction converts the energy of a moving vehicle into heat.

Double-overhead cam (DOHC) An engine that uses two overhead camshafts, usually one for the intake valves and one for the exhaust valves.

Drivebelt(s) The belt(s) used to drive accessories such as the alternator, water pump, power steering pump, air conditioning compressor, etc. off the crankshaft pulley.

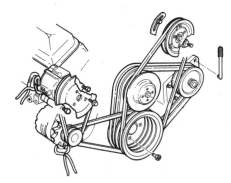

Accessory drivebelts

Driveshaft Any shaft used to transmit motion. Commonly used when referring to the axleshafts on a front wheel drive vehicle.

Drum brake A type of brake using a drum-shaped metal cylinder attached to the inner surface of the wheel. When the brake pedal is pressed, curved brake shoes with friction linings press against the inside of the drum to slow or stop the vehicle.

E

EGR valve A valve used to introduce exhaust gases into the intake air stream.

Electronic control unit (ECU) A computer which controls (for instance) ignition and fuel injection systems, or an anti-lock braking system. For more information refer to the *Haynes Automotive Electrical and Electronic Systems Manual*.

Electronic Fuel Injection (EFI) A computer controlled fuel system that distributes fuel through an injector located in each intake port of the engine.

Emergency brake A braking system, independent of the main hydraulic system, that can be used to slow or stop the vehicle if the primary brakes fail, or to hold the vehicle stationary even though the brake pedal isn't depressed. It usually consists of a hand lever that actuates either front or rear brakes mechanically through a series of cables and linkages. Also known as a handbrake or parking brake.

Endfloat The amount of lengthwise movement between two parts. As applied to a crankshaft, the distance that the crankshaft can move forward and back in the cylinder block.

Engine management system (EMS) A computer controlled system which manages the fuel injection and the ignition systems in an integrated fashion.

Exhaust manifold A part with several passages through which exhaust gases leave the engine combustion chambers and enter the exhaust pipe.

F

Fan clutch A viscous (fluid) drive coupling device which permits variable engine fan speeds in relation to engine speeds.

Feeler blade A thin strip or blade of hardened steel, ground to an exact thickness, used to check or measure clearances between parts.

Feeler blade

Firing order The order in which the engine cylinders fire, or deliver their power strokes, beginning with the number one cylinder.

Flywheel A heavy spinning wheel in which energy is absorbed and stored by means of momentum. On cars, the flywheel is attached to the crankshaft to smooth out firing impulses.

Free play The amount of travel before any action takes place. The "looseness" in a linkage, or an assembly of parts, between the initial application of force and actual movement. For example, the distance the brake pedal moves before the pistons in the master cylinder are actuated.

Fuse An electrical device which protects a circuit against accidental overload. The typical fuse contains a soft piece of metal which is calibrated to melt at a predetermined current flow (expressed as amps) and break the circuit.

Fusible link A circuit protection device consisting of a conductor surrounded by heat-resistant insulation. The conductor is smaller than the wire it protects, so it acts as the weakest link in the circuit. Unlike a blown fuse, a failed fusible link must frequently be cut from the wire for replacement.

G

Gap The distance the spark must travel in jumping from the centre electrode to the side electrode in a spark plug. Also refers to the spacing between the points in a contact breaker assembly in a conventional points-type ignition, or to the distance between the reluctor or rotor and the pickup coil in an electronic ignition.

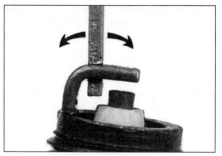

Adjusting spark plug gap

Gasket Any thin, soft material - usually cork, cardboard, asbestos or soft metal - installed between two metal surfaces to ensure a good seal. For instance, the cylinder head gasket seals the joint between the block and the cylinder head.

Gasket

Gauge An instrument panel display used to monitor engine conditions. A gauge with a movable pointer on a dial or a fixed scale is an analogue gauge. A gauge with a numerical readout is called a digital gauge.

H

Halfshaft A rotating shaft that transmits power from the final drive unit to a drive wheel, usually when referring to a live rear axle.

Harmonic balancer A device designed to reduce torsion or twisting vibration in the crankshaft. May be incorporated in the crankshaft pulley. Also known as a vibration damper.

Hone An abrasive tool for correcting small irregularities or differences in diameter in an engine cylinder, brake cylinder, etc.

Hydraulic tappet A tappet that utilises hydraulic pressure from the engine's lubrication system to maintain zero clearance (constant contact with both camshaft and valve stem). Automatically adjusts to variation in valve stem length. Hydraulic tappets also reduce valve noise.

I

Ignition timing The moment at which the spark plug fires, usually expressed in the number of crankshaft degrees before the piston reaches the top of its stroke.

Inlet manifold A tube or housing with passages through which flows the air-fuel mixture (carburettor vehicles and vehicles with throttle body injection) or air only (port fuel-injected vehicles) to the port openings in the cylinder head.

J

Jump start Starting the engine of a vehicle with a discharged or weak battery by attaching jump leads from the weak battery to a charged or helper battery.

L

Load Sensing Proportioning Valve (LSPV) A brake hydraulic system control valve that works like a proportioning valve, but also takes into consideration the amount of weight carried by the rear axle.

Locknut A nut used to lock an adjustment nut, or other threaded component, in place. For example, a locknut is employed to keep the adjusting nut on the rocker arm in position.

Lockwasher A form of washer designed to prevent an attaching nut from working loose.

M

MacPherson strut A type of front suspension system devised by Earle MacPherson at Ford of England. In its original form, a simple lateral link with the anti-roll bar creates the lower control arm. A long strut - an integral coil spring and shock absorber - is mounted between the body and the steering knuckle. Many modern so-called MacPherson strut systems use a conventional lower A-arm and don't rely on the anti-roll bar for location.

Multimeter An electrical test instrument with the capability to measure voltage, current and resistance.

N

NOx Oxides of Nitrogen. A common toxic pollutant emitted by petrol and diesel engines at higher temperatures.

O

Ohm The unit of electrical resistance. One volt applied to a resistance of one ohm will produce a current of one amp.

Ohmmeter An instrument for measuring electrical resistance.

O-ring A type of sealing ring made of a special rubber-like material; in use, the O-ring is compressed into a groove to provide the sealing action.

Overhead cam (ohc) engine An engine with the camshaft(s) located on top of the cylinder head(s).

Overhead valve (ohv) engine An engine with the valves located in the cylinder head, but with the camshaft located in the engine block.

Oxygen sensor A device installed in the engine exhaust manifold, which senses the oxygen content in the exhaust and converts this information into an electric current. Also called a Lambda sensor.

P

Phillips screw A type of screw head having a cross instead of a slot for a corresponding type of screwdriver.

Plastigage A thin strip of plastic thread, available in different sizes, used for measuring clearances. For example, a strip of Plastigage is laid across a bearing journal. The parts are assembled and dismantled; the width of the crushed strip indicates the clearance between journal and bearing.

Plastigage

Propeller shaft The long hollow tube with universal joints at both ends that carries power from the transmission to the differential on front-engined rear wheel drive vehicles.

Proportioning valve A hydraulic control valve which limits the amount of pressure to the rear brakes during panic stops to prevent wheel lock-up.

R

Rack-and-pinion steering A steering system with a pinion gear on the end of the steering shaft that mates with a rack (think of a geared wheel opened up and laid flat). When the steering wheel is turned, the pinion turns, moving the rack to the left or right. This movement is transmitted through the track rods to the steering arms at the wheels.

Radiator A liquid-to-air heat transfer device designed to reduce the temperature of the coolant in an internal combustion engine cooling system.

Refrigerant Any substance used as a heat transfer agent in an air-conditioning system. R-12 has been the principle refrigerant for many years; recently, however, manufacturers have begun using R-134a, a non-CFC substance that is considered less harmful to the ozone in the upper atmosphere.

Rocker arm A lever arm that rocks on a shaft or pivots on a stud. In an overhead valve engine, the rocker arm converts the upward movement of the pushrod into a downward movement to open a valve.

Rotor In a distributor, the rotating device inside the cap that connects the centre electrode and the outer terminals as it turns, distributing the high voltage from the coil secondary winding to the proper spark plug. Also, that part of an alternator which rotates inside the stator. Also, the rotating assembly of a turbocharger, including the compressor wheel, shaft and turbine wheel.

Runout The amount of wobble (in-and-out movement) of a gear or wheel as it's rotated. The amount a shaft rotates "out-of-true." The out-of-round condition of a rotating part.

S

Sealant A liquid or paste used to prevent leakage at a joint. Sometimes used in conjunction with a gasket.

Sealed beam lamp An older headlight design which integrates the reflector, lens and filaments into a hermetically-sealed one-piece unit. When a filament burns out or the lens cracks, the entire unit is simply replaced.

Serpentine drivebelt A single, long, wide accessory drivebelt that's used on some newer vehicles to drive all the accessories, instead of a series of smaller, shorter belts. Serpentine drivebelts are usually tensioned by an automatic tensioner.

Serpentine drivebelt

Shim Thin spacer, commonly used to adjust the clearance or relative positions between two parts. For example, shims inserted into or under bucket tappets control valve clearances. Clearance is adjusted by changing the thickness of the shim.

Slide hammer A special puller that screws into or hooks onto a component such as a shaft or bearing; a heavy sliding handle on the shaft bottoms against the end of the shaft to knock the component free.

Sprocket A tooth or projection on the periphery of a wheel, shaped to engage with a chain or drivebelt. Commonly used to refer to the sprocket wheel itself.

Starter inhibitor switch On vehicles with an automatic transmission, a switch that prevents starting if the vehicle is not in Neutral or Park.

Strut See MacPherson strut.

T

Tappet A cylindrical component which transmits motion from the cam to the valve stem, either directly or via a pushrod and rocker arm. Also called a cam follower.

Thermostat A heat-controlled valve that regulates the flow of coolant between the cylinder block and the radiator, so maintaining optimum engine operating temperature. A thermostat is also used in some air cleaners in which the temperature is regulated.

Thrust bearing The bearing in the clutch assembly that is moved in to the release levers by clutch pedal action to disengage the clutch. Also referred to as a release bearing.

Timing belt A toothed belt which drives the camshaft. Serious engine damage may result if it breaks in service.

Timing chain A chain which drives the camshaft.

Toe-in The amount the front wheels are closer together at the front than at the rear. On rear wheel drive vehicles, a slight amount of toe-in is usually specified to keep the front wheels running parallel on the road by offsetting other forces that tend to spread the wheels apart.

Toe-out The amount the front wheels are closer together at the rear than at the front. On front wheel drive vehicles, a slight amount of toe-out is usually specified.

Tools For full information on choosing and using tools, refer to the *Haynes Automotive Tools Manual*.

Tracer A stripe of a second colour applied to a wire insulator to distinguish that wire from another one with the same colour insulator.

Tune-up A process of accurate and careful adjustments and parts replacement to obtain the best possible engine performance.

Turbocharger A centrifugal device, driven by exhaust gases, that pressurises the intake air. Normally used to increase the power output from a given engine displacement, but can also be used primarily to reduce exhaust emissions (as on VW's "Umwelt" Diesel engine).

U

Universal joint or U-joint A double-pivoted connection for transmitting power from a driving to a driven shaft through an angle. A U-joint consists of two Y-shaped yokes and a cross-shaped member called the spider.

V

Valve A device through which the flow of liquid, gas, vacuum, or loose material in bulk may be started, stopped, or regulated by a movable part that opens, shuts, or partially obstructs one or more ports or passageways. A valve is also the movable part of such a device.

Valve clearance The clearance between the valve tip (the end of the valve stem) and the rocker arm or tappet. The valve clearance is measured when the valve is closed.

Vernier caliper A precision measuring instrument that measures inside and outside dimensions. Not quite as accurate as a micrometer, but more convenient.

Viscosity The thickness of a liquid or its resistance to flow.

Volt A unit for expressing electrical "pressure" in a circuit. One volt that will produce a current of one ampere through a resistance of one ohm.

W

Welding Various processes used to join metal items by heating the areas to be joined to a molten state and fusing them together. For more information refer to the *Haynes Automotive Welding Manual*.

Wiring diagram A drawing portraying the components and wires in a vehicle's electrical system, using standardised symbols. For more information refer to the *Haynes Automotive Electrical and Electronic Systems Manual*.

Note: *References throughout this index are in the form* **"Chapter number"** • **"Page number"**. *So, for example, 2A•15 refers to page 15 of Chapter 2A.*

Note: *References throughout this index are in the form* "**Chapter number**" • "**Page number**". *So, for example, 2A•15 refers to page 15 of Chapter 2A.*

Note: *References throughout this index are in the form "Chapter number" • "Page number". So, for example, 2A•15 refers to page 15 of Chapter 2A.*

Note: *References throughout this index are in the form "**Chapter number**" • "**Page number**". So, for example, 2A•15 refers to page 15 of Chapter 2A.*

Preserving Our Motoring Heritage

< *The Model J Duesenberg Derham Tourster. Only eight of these magnificent cars were ever built – this is the only example to be found outside the United States of America*

Almost every car you've ever loved, loathed or desired is gathered under one roof at the Haynes Motor Museum. Over 300 immaculately presented cars and motorbikes represent every aspect of our motoring heritage, from elegant reminders of bygone days, such as the superb Model J Duesenberg to curiosities like the bug-eyed BMW Isetta. There are also many old friends and flames. Perhaps you remember the 1959 Ford Popular that you did your courting in? The magnificent 'Red Collection' is a spectacle of classic sports cars including AC, Alfa Romeo, Austin Healey, Ferrari, Lamborghini, Maserati, MG, Riley, Porsche and Triumph.

A Perfect Day Out

Each and every vehicle at the Haynes Motor Museum has played its part in the history and culture of Motoring. Today, they make a wonderful spectacle and a great day out for all the family. Bring the kids, bring Mum and Dad, but above all bring your camera to capture those golden memories for ever. You will also find an impressive array of motoring memorabilia, a comfortable 70 seat video cinema and one of the most extensive transport book shops in Britain. The Pit Stop Cafe serves everything from a cup of tea to wholesome, home-made meals or, if you prefer, you can enjoy the large picnic area nestled in the beautiful rural surroundings of Somerset.

> *John Haynes O.B.E., Founder and Chairman of the museum at the wheel of a Haynes Light 12.*

< *Graham Hill's Lola Cosworth Formula 1 car next to a 1934 Riley Sports.*

The Museum is situated on the A359 Yeovil to Frome road at Sparkford, just off the A303 in Somerset. It is about 40 miles south of Bristol, and 25 minutes drive from the M5 intersection at Taunton.

Open 9.30am - 5.30pm (10.00am - 4.00pm Winter) 7 days a week, *except Christmas Day, Boxing Day and New Years Day*
Special rates available for schools, coach parties and outings Charitable Trust No. 292048